Lecture Notes in Computer Science 7583

Commenced Publication in 1973
Founding and Former Series Editors:
Gerhard Goos, Juris Hartmanis, and Jan van Leeuwen

Andrea Fusiello   Vittorio Murino
Rita Cucchiara (Eds.)

Computer Vision – ECCV 2012

Workshops and Demonstrations

Florence, Italy, October 7-13, 2012
Proceedings, Part I

 Springer

Volume Editors

Andrea Fusiello
Università degli Studi di Udine
Dipartimento di Ingegneria Elettrica,
Gestionale e Meccanica (DIEGM)
Via delle Scienze, 208, 33100 Udine, Italy
E-mail: andrea.fusiello@uniud.it

Vittorio Murino
IIT Istituto Italiano di Tecnologia
Via Morego 30, 16163 Genoa, Italy
E-mail: vittorio.murino@iit.it

Rita Cucchiara
Università degli Studi di Modena e Reggio Emilia
Strada Vignolege, 905, 41125 Modena, Italy
E-mail: rita.cucchiara@unimore.it

ISSN 0302-9743   e-ISSN 1611-3349
ISBN 978-3-642-33862-5   e-ISBN 978-3-642-33863-2
DOI 10.1007/978-3-642-33863-2
Springer Heidelberg Dordrecht London New York

Library of Congress Control Number: 2012948004

CR Subject Classification (1998): I.4, I.5, I.2.10, I.2, H.5, H.3

LNCS Sublibrary: SL 6 – Image Processing, Computer Vision, Pattern Recognition,
and Graphics

Typesetting: Camera-ready by author, data conversion by Scientific Publishing Services, Chennai, India

Printed on acid-free paper

Springer is part of Springer Science+Business Media (www.springer.com)

Foreword

The European Conference on Computer Vision is one of the top conferences for researchers in this field and is held biennially in alternation with the International Conference on Computer Vision. It was first held in 1990 in Antibes (France) with subsequent conferences in Santa Margherita Ligure (Italy) in 1992, Stockholm (Sweden) in 1994, Cambridge (UK) in 1996, Freiburg (Germany) in 1998, Dublin (Ireland) in 2000, Copenhagen (Denmark) in 2002, Prague (Czech Republic) in 2004, Graz (Austria) in 2006, Marseille (France) in 2008, and Heraklion (Greece) in 2010. To our great delight, the 12th conference was held in Florence, Italy.

ECCV has an established tradition of very high scientific quality and an overall duration of one week. ECCV 2012 began with a keynote lecture from the honorary chair, Tomaso Poggio. The main conference followed over four days with 40 orals, 368 posters, 22 demos, and 12 industrial exhibits. There were also 9 tutorials and 21 workshops held before and after the main event. For this event we introduced some novelties. These included innovations in the review policy, the publication of a conference booklet with all paper abstracts and the full video recording of oral presentations.

This conference is the result of a great deal of hard work by many people, who have been working enthusiastically since our first meetings in 2008. We are particularly grateful to the Program Chairs, who handled the review of about 1500 submissions and co-ordinated the efforts of over 50 area chairs and about 1000 reviewers (see details of the process in their preface to the proceedings). We are also indebted to all the other chairs who, with the support of our research teams (names listed below), diligently helped us manage all aspects of the main conference, tutorials, workshops, exhibits, demos, proceedings, and web presence. Finally we thank our generous sponsors and Consulta Umbria for handling the registration of delegates and all financial aspects associated with the conference.

We hope you enjoyed ECCV 2012. Benvenuti a Firenze!

October 2012

Roberto Cipolla
Carlo Colombo
Alberto Del Bimbo

Preface

Welcome to the Workshops and Demonstrations proceedings of the 12th European Conference on Computer Vision, held during October 7–13, 2012 in Florence, Italy. We are delighted that the main ECCV 2012 was accompanied by 21 workshops and 22 demonstrations.

We received 38 workshop proposals on diverse computer vision topics. The evaluation process was not easy because of the high quality of the submissions, and the final 21 selected workshops complemented the main conference program. They were mostly one-day workshops, with a few limited to half day, and one workshop lasting one day and a half. In the end, the addressed workshop topics constituted a good mix between novel current trends and traditional issues, without forgetting to address the fundamentals of the computational vision area.

On Sunday, October 7, three workshops took place: the 5th Workshop on Non-Rigid Shape Analysis and Deformable Image Alignment (NORDIA), the First Workshop on Visual Analysis and Geo-Localization of Large-Scale Imagery, and the Workshop on Web-scale Vision and Social Media.

The majority of the workshops were held on Friday 12 and Saturday 13. On October 12 we had nine workshops: WebVision, the Workshop on Computer Vision for the Web, with only invited speakers, the traditional PASCAL Visual Object Classes Challenge 2012 (VOC2012) Workshop, the 4th International Workshop on Video Event Categorization, Tagging and Retrieval (VECTaR 2012), the First International Workshop on Re-Identification (Re-Id 2012), the Workshop on Biological and Computer Vision Interfaces, also with only invited speakers, VISART, "Where Computer Vision Meets Art" Workshop, the Second Workshop on Consumer Depth Cameras for Computer Vision (CDC4CV), the Workshop on Unsolved Problems in Optical Flow and Stereo Estimation, and the "What's in a Face?" Workshop.

On October 13, ten workshops were held: The remaining half day of the WebVision Workshop, the 4th Color and Photometry in Computer Vision Workshop, the Third Workshop on Computer Vision in Vehicle Technology: From Earth to Mars, the Second Workshop on Parts and Attributes, the Third IEEE International Workshop on Analysis and Retrieval of Tracked Events and Motion in Imagery Streams (ARTEMIS 2012), the First Workshop on Action Recognition and Pose Estimation in Still Images, the Workshop on Higher-Order Models and Global Constraints in Computer Vision, the Workshop on Information Fusion in Computer Vision for Concept Recognition, the QU3ST Workshop "2.5D Sensing Technologies in Motion: The Quest for 3D", and the Second International Workshop on Benchmarking Facial Image Analysis Technologies (BeFIT 2012).

We hope that participants enjoyed the workshops, together with the associated 179 papers included in these volumes.

Following the tradition of the major conferences in the field, ECCV 2012 was also proud to host live demonstrations given by companies and academic research groups. These were presented during the days of the main conference and are described in detail in the papers of the last volume.

Presenting a demo is one of the most concrete and exciting ways of demonstrating results of research and providing strong interaction between researchers, practitioners, and scholars in many topics, both theoretical and practical, of computer vision.

Among the proposed demos, submitted with a four-page summary together with slides, videos and rich supplementary material, after peer-review, we selected 22 demos on different subjects spanning topics such as biometry, content-based retrieval, classification and categorization, vision for computer graphics, 3D vision for interfaces, tracking and pose estimation, gesture analysis for human–computer interaction, text recognition, augmented reality, surveillance, and assisted driving.

Demos were presented by authors coming from different nations of Europe (Czech Republic, France, Germany, Italy, The Netherlands, Spain, Switzerland, and UK) and of the rest of the world (Australia, China, Japan, Taiwan, and USA).

The best demo was selected based on the scientific value and the technical presentation as well as the success in researcher interaction during the Demo Sessions.

We believe the scientific prototypes and the technical demonstrations presented at ECCV 2012 will contribute to strengthen the great success of computer vision technologies in industrial, entertainment, social, and everyday applications.

Finally, we would like to thank the individual chairs of each workshop (listed in the respective workshop programs) for soliciting and reviewing submissions, and the demo proposers, who made it possible to build such a rich supplementary program beside the main ECCV 2012 scientific plan.

October 2012   Andrea Fusiello
                                                               Vittorio Murino
                                                               Rita Cucchiara

Organization

General Chairs

Roberto Cipolla   University of Cambridge, UK
Carlo Colombo   University of Florence, Italy
Alberto Del Bimbo   University of Florence, Italy

Program Coordinator

Pietro Perona   California Institute of Technology, USA

Program Chairs

Andrew Fitzgibbon   Microsoft Research, Cambridge, UK
Svetlana Lazebnik   University of Illinois at Urbana-Champaign, USA
Yoichi Sato   The University of Tokyo, Japan
Cordelia Schmid   INRIA, Grenoble, France

Honorary Chair

Tomaso Poggio   Massachusetts Institute of Technology, USA

Tutorial Chairs

Emanuele Trucco   University of Dundee, UK
Alessandro Verri   University of Genoa, Italy

Workshop Chairs

Andrea Fusiello   University of Udine, Italy
Vittorio Murino   Istituto Italiano di Tecnologia, Genoa, Italy

Demonstration Chair

Rita Cucchiara   University of Modena and Reggio Emilia, Italy

Industrial Liaison Chair

Björn Stenger   Toshiba Research Europe, Cambridge, UK

Web Chair

Marco Bertini   University of Florence, Italy

Publicity Chairs

Terrance E. Boult   University of Colorado at Colorado Springs, USA
Tat Jen Cham   Nanyang Technological University, Singapore
Marcello Pelillo   University Ca' Foscari of Venice, Italy

Publication Chair

Massimo Tistarelli   University of Sassari, Italy

Video Processing Chairs

Sebastiano Battiato   University of Catania, Italy
Giovanni M. Farinella   University of Catania, Italy

Travel Grants Chair

Luigi Di Stefano   University of Bologna, Italy

Travel Visa Chair

Stefano Berretti   University of Florence, Italy

Local Committee Chair

Andrew Bagdanov   MICC, Florence, Italy

Local Committee

Lamberto Ballan   Giuseppe Lisanti
Laura Benassi   Iacopo Masi
Marco Fanfani   Fabio Pazzaglia
Andrea Ferracani   Federico Pernici
Claudio Guida   Lorenzo Seidenari
Lea Landucci   Giuseppe Serra

Workshops Organizers

5th Workshop on Non-Rigid Shape Analysis and Deformable Image Alignment (NORDIA)

Stefano Berretti	University of Florence, Italy
Alexander Bronstein	Tel Aviv University, Israel
Michael Bronstein	University of Lugano, Switzerland
Umberto Castellani	University of Verona, Italy

First Workshop on Visual Analysis and Geo-Localization of Large-Scale Imagery

Mubarak Shah	University of Central Florida, USA
Luc Van Gool	ETH Zurich, Switzerland
Asaad Hakeem	ObjectVideo, USA
Alexei Efros	Carnegie Mellon University, USA
Niels Haering	ObjectVideo, USA
James Hays	Brown University, USA
Hui Cheng	SRI International Sarnoff, USA

Workshop on Web-Scale Vision and Social Media

Lamberto Ballan	University of Florence, Italy
Alex C. Berg	Stony Brook University, USA
Marco Bertini	University of Florence, Italy
Cees G.M. Snoek	University of Amsterdam, The Netherlands

WebVision: The Workshop on Computer Vision for the Web

Manik Varma	Microsoft Research India
Samy Bengio	Google, USA

The PASCAL Visual Object Classes Challenge 2012 (VOC2012) Workshop

Chris Williams	University of Edinburgh, UK
John Winn	MSR Cambridge, UK
Luc Van Gool	ETH Zurich, Switzerland
Andrew Zisserman	University of Oxford, UK
Alex Berg	Stony Brook University, USA
Fei-Fei Li	University of Stanford, USA

4th International Workshop on Video Event Categorization, Tagging and Retrieval (VECTaR 2012)

Tieniu Tan	Chinese Academy of Sciences, China
Thomas S. Huang	University of Illinois at Urbana-Champaign, USA
Ling Shao	University of Sheffield, UK
Jianguo Zhang	University of Dundee, UK
Liang Wang	Chinese Academy of Sciences, China

First International Workshop on Re-Identification (Re-Id 2012)

Marco Cristani	University of Verona, Italy
Shaogang Gong	Queen Mary University London, UK
Yan Shuicheng	NUS, Singapore

Workshop on Biological and Computer Vision Interfaces

Olivier Faugeras	INRIA, France
Pierre Kornprobst	INRIA, France

VISART: "Where Computer Vision Meets Art" Workshop

João Paulo Costeira	IST Lisbon, Portugal
Gustavo Carneiro	University of Adelaide, Australia
Nuno Pinho da Silva	IST Lisbon, Portugal
Alessio Del Bue	Istituto Italiano di Tecnologia, Italy

Second Workshop on Consumer Depth Cameras for Computer Vision (CDC4CV)

Andrea Fossati	ETH Zurich, Switzerland
Jürgen Gall	Max-Planck-Institut für Informatik, Germany
Helmut Grabner	ETH Zurich, Switzerland
Xiaofeng Ren	Intel Labs, USA
Kurt Konolige	Industrial Perception, USA
Seungkyu Lee	Samsung, South Korea
Miles Hansard	Queen Mary University London, UK

Workshop on Unsolved Problems in Optical Flow and Stereo Estimation

Daniel Kondermann	University of Heidelberg, Germany
Bernd Jähne	University of Heidelberg, Germany
Daniel Scharstein	Middlebury College, USA

"What's in a Face?" Workshop

Arun Ross	West Virginia University, USA
Alice O'Toole	University of Texas, USA
Maja Pantic	Imperial College London, UK
Antitza Dantcheva	West Virginia University, USA
Stefanos Zafeiriou	Imperial College London, UK

4th Color and Photometry in Computer Vision Workshop

Theo Gevers	University of Amsterdam, The Netherlands
Raimondo Schettini	University of Milano Bicocca, Italy
Joost van de Weijer	Universitat Autònoma de Barcelona, Spain
Todd Zickler	Harvard University, USA
Javier Vazquez-Corral	Universitat Autònoma de Barcelona, Spain

Third Workshop on Computer Vision in Vehicle Technology: From Earth to Mars

Atsushi Imiya   IMIT, Japan
Antonio M. López   UAB/CVC, Spain

Second Workshop on Parts and Attributes

Christoph H. Lampert   IST, Austria
Rogerio S. Feris   IBM Research, USA

Third IEEE International Workshop on Analysis and Retrieval of Tracked Events and Motion in Imagery Streams (ARTEMIS 2012)

Anastasios Doulamis   TUC, Greece
Nikolaos D. Doulamis   NTUA, Greece
Jordi Gonzàlez   UAB/CVC, Spain
Thomas B. Moeslund   University of Aalborg, Denmark
Marco Bertini   University of Florence, Italy

First Workshop on Action Recognition and Pose Estimation in Still Images

Vittorio Ferrari   University of Edinburgh, UK
Ivan Laptev   INRIA/Ecole Normale Superieure, France
Josef Sivic   INRIA/Ecole Normale Superieure, France
Bangpeng Yao   Stanford University, USA

Workshop on Higher-Order Models and Global Constraints in Computer Vision

Karteek Alahari   INRIA-WILLOW/Ecole Normale Superieure, France
Dhruv Batra   TTI-Chicago, USA
Srikumar Ramalingam   MERL, USA
Nikos Paragios   Paristech, France
Rich Zemel   University of Toronto, Canada

Workshop on Information Fusion in Computer Vision for Concept Recognition

Jenny Benois-Pineau   LABRI, University of Bordeaux, France
Georges Quenot   LIG INPG, Grenoble, France
Tomas Piatrik   Queen Mary University London, UK
Bogdan Ionescu   LAPI, University Politehnica of Bucharest, Romania

QU3ST Workshop - 2.5D Sensing Technologies in Motion: The Quest for 3D

David Fofi   Université de Bourgogne, France
Adrien Bartoli   Université d'Auvergne, France

Second International Workshop on Benchmarking Facial Image Analysis Technologies (BeFIT 2012)

Hazim Kemal Ekenel   KIT, Germany/Istanbul Technical University, Turkey
Gang Hua   Stevens Institute of Technology/IBM Research, USA
Shiguang Shan   Chinese Academy of Sciences, China

Sponsoring Companies and Institutions

Gold Sponsors

Silver Sponsors

Bronze Sponsors

Institutional Sponsors

Table of Contents

First Workshop on Visual Analysis and Geo-localization of Large-Scale Imagery

Web-Scale Vision and Social Media

4th International Workshop on Video Event Categorization, Tagging and Retrieval (VECTaR 2012)

First International Workshop on Re-identification (Re-Id 2012)

Biological and Computer Vision Interfaces (BCVI)

Where Computer Vision Meets Art (VISART)

Second Workshop on Consumer Depth Cameras for Computer Vision (CDC4CV)

Putting the Pieces Together: Regularized Multi-part Shape Matching

Or Litany[1], Alexander M. Bronstein[1], and Michael M. Bronstein[2]

[1] School of Electrical Engineering, Tel Aviv University, Israel
[2] Institute of Computational Science, Faculty of Informatics
Universita della Svizzera Italiana, Lugano, Switzerland
Paper ID 314

Abstract. Multi-part shape matching is an important class of problems, arising in many fields such as computational archaeology, biology, geometry processing, computer graphics and vision. In this paper, we address the problem of simultaneous matching and segmentation of multiple shapes. We assume to be given a reference shape and multiple parts partially matching the reference. Each of these parts can have additional clutter, have overlap with other parts, or there might be missing parts. We show experimental results of efficient and accurate assembly of fractured synthetic and real objects.

1 Introduction

Multi-part shape matching is an important class of problems, arising in computational archaeology (assembly of fractured objects [9,19,18,10]), computational biology (protein docking [12]), and computer vision (merging of partial 3D scans [17,21] and assembling 2D and 3D puzzles [13,7]). Traditionally, the matching of rigid 3D shapes has been performed using variants of the classical *iterative closest point* (ICP) algorithm [2,6,15,8], trying to optimally align the shapes by means of

Fig. 1. Assembling the Stanford bunny: 3D-printed bunny fractured into multiple parts (left); each part is scanned individually with clutter (center); the parts are matched to the reference shape (right) using the proposed approach

A. Fusiello et al. (Eds.): ECCV 2012 Ws/Demos, Part I, LNCS 7583, pp. 1–11, 2012.

a rigid transformation minimizing a surface-to-surface distance between them. Matching of multiple shapes has been done using graph-based methods [11], iterative pairwise part registration [21], as well as "multi-part ICP" where optimization is performed over rigid transformation parameters of all parts [14]. In [20], a correspondence-less partial matching was proposed using optimization over parts that maximize the similarity of local descriptors.

In the partial matching setting when parts are missing (e.g. due to occlusions in the scan process) or conversely, clutter is present (e.g. if each part is scanned individually), the ICP algorithms can be modified by introducing weights that reject points with a "bad" correspondence. The shortcoming of such weighting is that it does not allow direct control of the size and regularity of the matching parts. A remedy to this problem was proposed in [5], where the authors used the partial matching framework of [3], optimizing simultaneously for part similarity, size, and regularity.

Here, we extend this approach to multiple parts, performing matching and segmentation of multiple shapes at the same time. In the setting we address, we are given a reference shape and multiple parts partially matching the reference. Each of these parts can have additional clutter, have overlap with other parts (like in the 3D view merging); furthermore, there might be uncovered parts of the reference shape. Some of the applications of the presented method arise, for example, in assisting orthopedic surgeons in putting fragmented bones back together using a healthy bone 3D model (taken pre-trauma or from a symmetric bone). Another uses are in automated car parts assembly.

2   Background

Given two rigid shapes X and Y, a standard way to match them is to look for a rigid transformation $\mathbf{T}$ (rotation+translation) of one of them (w.l.o.g. Y) such that some distance between $\mathbf{T}Y$ and X is minimized,

$$\min_{\mathbf{T}\in SE(3)} D(X, \mathbf{T}Y). \tag{1}$$

The shape-to-shape distance D can be e.g. the *Hausdorff distance*,

$$D_{\mathrm{H}}(X, Y) = \max\left\{\max_{x\in X}\min_{y\in Y}\|x - y\|, \max_{y\in Y}\min_{x\in X}\|x - y\|\right\}.$$

Denoting by $y^*(x) = \operatorname{argmin}_{y\in Y}\|x - y\|^2$ and $x^*(y) = \operatorname{argmin}_{x\in X}\|x - y\|^2$ the closest point from x on Y and from y on X, respectively, D_{H} can be written as

$$D_{\mathrm{H}}(X, Y) = \max\left\{\max_{x\in X}\|x - y^*(x)\|, \max_{y\in Y}\|x^*(y) - y\|\right\}.$$

This formulation allows solving (2) by means of alternating optimization: first, for a fixed transformation $\mathbf{T}$, find the closest correspondences x^*, y^*. Second, fixing the correspondences x^*, y^* find the transformation $\mathbf{T}$ minimizing $D_{\mathrm{H}}(X, \mathbf{T}Y)$.

Such methods are known as *iterative closest point* (ICP). In practice, it is preferable to use a more robust L_2-version of a shape-to-shape distance,

$$D(X,Y) = \int_X \|x - y^*(x)\|^2 dx + \int_Y \|y - x^*(y)\|^2 dy,$$

or a non-symmetric version thereof.

When the shapes X and Y are only partially matching (i.e., there exist unknown in advance parts $X' \subset X, Y' \subset Y$ and a transformation $\mathbf{T}$ such that $D(X', \mathbf{T}Y') \approx 0$), the above method can be adapted by introducing weighting into the shape-to-shape distance,

$$D(X,Y) = \int_X \|x - y^*(x)\|^2 w(x) dx.$$

The weight is set to reject "bad" correspondences, e.g.,

$$w(x) = \begin{cases} 1 \ \|x - y^*(x)\| < \epsilon \\ 0 \ \text{else} \end{cases}$$

thus effectively excluding the non-overlapping parts of X and Y (rejection can also be made using additional criteria such as angle between normals). Modifying the threshold ϵ implicitly changes the area of the matched parts; however, there is no explicit control of their regularity and area. To overcome this problem, in [5] it was proposed to simultaneously optimize the part dissimilarity, area, and regularity over the parts and the transformation,

$$\min_{\mathbf{T} \in SE(3), X', Y'} D(X', \mathbf{T}Y') - (A(X') + A(Y')) + (R(X') + R(Y')) \qquad (2)$$

where $A(X')$ denotes the area and $R(X')$ the irregularity (e.g. boundary length) of part X'. The purpose of this paper is to extend this idea to multiple part matching, as described in the following.

3   Regularized Multi-part Shape Matching

In the simplest multi-part setting, we have the reference shape X and its unaligned non-overlapping parts $Y_1, \ldots, Y_n$. we assume an initial coarse alignment (e.g. using some global registration); devising a dedicated initialization scheme is deferred to future work. The goal is to match the parts to the references by means of rigid transformations $\mathbf{T}_1, \ldots, \mathbf{T}_n$ such that the matching regions $X_1, \ldots, X_n$ on X are non-overlapping, cover the whole X, regular, and match the area of Y_i (in Sections 3.1 and 3.2, we consider the extension when not all X is covered, and when the parts are cluttered).

The above problem of simultaneous multi-part registration and segmentation can be formulated as

$$\min_{\substack{\{\mathbf{T}_i \in SE(3)\} \\ \{X_i \subseteq X\}}} \sum_{i=1}^{n} D(X_i, \mathbf{T}_i Y_i) + \lambda \sum_{i=1}^{n} R(X_i) \quad \text{s.t.} \quad \begin{cases} X_i \cap X_j = \emptyset, \ i \neq j \\ X_1 \cup \cdots \cup X_n = X \\ A(X_i) = A(Y_i), \end{cases} \qquad (3)$$

where the first aggregate constitutes the data term measuring the proximity of the transformed parts $\mathbf{T}_i Y_i$ to the corresponding segments X_i on the model, while the second aggregate is the regularization term measuring the irregularity of each segment. The first two constraint guarantee that $\{X_i\}$ is a valid partitioning of X, that is, a covering of the latter by disjoint sets. The area constraints ensure that the areas of the segments X_i selected on the model match those of the correspoding parts Y_i.

In order to prevent the segmentation from producing fragmented and irregular segments, we penalize for their boundary length, setting $R(X_i) = L(\partial X_i)$. The discretization of the above problem results in a combinatorial complexity. To circumvent this difficulty, the problem can be relaxed by replacing the crisp parts X_i by fuzzy membership functions u_i on X, and the functional (3) by a generalization of the Mumford-Shah functional [16] to surfaces [4,5]. Here, we adopt this relaxation as well as the Ambrosio-Tortorelli [1] approximation of the Mumford-Shah functional,

$$R(u; \rho) = \frac{\lambda_{\mathrm{s}}}{2} \int_X \rho^2 \|\nabla u\|^2 da + \lambda_{\mathrm{b}} \epsilon \int_X \|\nabla \rho\|^2 da + \frac{\lambda_{\mathrm{b}}}{4\epsilon} \int_X (1 - \rho)^2 da, \quad (4)$$

where ρ is the *phase field* indicating the discontinuities of u, and $\epsilon > 0$ is a parameter. The first term of R above imposes piece-wise smoothness of the fuzzy part u. By setting a sufficiently large λ_{s}, the parts become approximately piece-wise constant as desired in the original crisp formulation (3). The second term of R is analogous to the segment boundary length and converges to the latter as $\epsilon \to 0$.

Using this fuzzy formulation, the data term for each u is expressed as

$$D(u, \mathbf{T}Y) = \int_X \|\mathbf{T}\mathbf{y}^*(\mathbf{x}) - \mathbf{x}\|^2 u(\mathbf{x}) da, \quad (5)$$

where Y denotes the corresponding part, one of the Y_i's, and $\mathbf{T}$ its transformation, one of the $\mathbf{T}_i$'s. Combining the data and the regularization terms, we rewrite problem (3) as

$$\min_{\substack{\{\mathbf{T}_i \in \mathrm{SE}(3)\} \\ \{u_i \geq 0, \rho_i \geq 0\}}} \sum_{i=1}^n D(u_i, \mathbf{T}_i Y_i) + \sum_{i=1}^n R(u_i, \rho_i) \quad \text{s.t.} \quad \begin{cases} \sum_{i=1}^n u_i = 1 \\ \int_X u_i da = \int_{Y_i} da. \end{cases} \quad (6)$$

The optimization is performed over n Euclidean transformations $\mathbf{T}_i$, n indicator functions u_i, and corresponding n phase fields ρ_i. The first constraint ensures that the segments u_i constitute a fuzzy partitioning of X and are defined for each point x on X. The rest of the constraints are the fuzzy counterparts of the crisp area constraints in (3).

Missing Parts. In many practical settings, the observed parts Y_i might not cover X entirely e.g. due to occlusions during the acquiring of the objects. In order to handle this scenario, an indicator function u_0 of a "null segment" is added to problem (6). Not corresponding to any of the Y_i's, the null segment is not subject to area constraints and has no data term; however, it does have a regularity term $R(u_0, \rho_0)$ which is added to the objective. Finally, since the null segment complements the true segments, $u_1, \ldots, u_n$, the point-wise constraint is modified to $\sum_{i=0}^{n} u_i = 1$.

Cluttered Parts. Other practical scenarios may involve the parts Y_i contaminated by clutter, that is, containing foreign objects unrelated to X. We can therefore formulate a partial matching problem by looking for sub-parts $Z_i \subseteq Y_i$ and corresponding segments $X_i \subseteq X$ covering a part of X. In order to address this setting, the previous optimization problem is further extended by adding another set of variables, the indicator functions v_i and the corresponding phase fields σ_i on the Y_i's,

$$
\min_{\substack{\{\mathbf{T}_i \in SE(3)\} \\ \{u_i \geq 0, \rho_i \geq 0\} \\ \{v_i \geq 0, \sigma_i \geq 0\}}} \sum_{i=1}^{n} D(u_i, v_i, \mathbf{T}_i Y_i) + \sum_{i=0}^{n} R(u_i, \rho_i) + \sum_{i=1}^{n} R(v_i, \sigma_i)
$$

$$
\text{s.t.} \quad
\begin{cases}
\displaystyle\sum_{i=0}^{n} u_i = 1; \quad v_i \leq 1 \\[2mm]
\displaystyle\int_X u_i \, da = \int_{Y_i} v_i \, da \geq \alpha_i.
\end{cases}
\tag{7}
$$

Note that we still enforce the area constraint, demanding that the area of at least A_i is selected from each Y_i. The latter is a parameter, which may be selected to be either absolute or relative, $\alpha_i = \alpha A(Y_i)$. The data term becomes

$$
D(u, v, \mathbf{T}Y) = \frac{1}{2} \int_X \|\mathbf{T}\mathbf{y}^*(\mathbf{x}) - \mathbf{x}\|^2 u(\mathbf{x}) v(\mathbf{y}^*(\mathbf{x})) da(\mathbf{x}) +
$$
$$
\frac{1}{2} \int_Y \|\mathbf{T}\mathbf{y} - \mathbf{x}^*(\mathbf{y})\|^2 u(\mathbf{y}) v(\mathbf{x}^*(\mathbf{y})) da(\mathbf{y}).
\tag{8}
$$

While in some applications one can assume reasonable knowledge of α_i, these parameters are often difficult to decide upon *a priori*. As an alternative, we propose reformulate the matching problem with the data term in the constraint, aiming at finding the largest area of the segments (or, equivalently, the smallest area of the null segment) producing a bounded alignment error:

$$
\min_{\substack{\{\mathbf{T}_i \in SE(3)\} \\ \{u_i \geq 0, \rho_i \geq 0\} \\ \{v_i \geq 0, \sigma_i \geq 0\}}} \int_X u_0 \, da + \sum_{i=0}^{n} R(u_i, \rho_i) + \sum_{i=1}^{n} R(v_i, \sigma_i)
$$

$$
\text{s.t.} \quad
\begin{cases}
\displaystyle\sum_{i=0}^{n} u_i = 1; \quad v_i \leq 1 \\[2mm]
\displaystyle\frac{1}{\beta^2} D(u_i, v_i, \mathbf{T}_i Y_i) \leq \int_X u_i \, da = \int_{Y_i} v_i \, da
\end{cases}
\tag{9}
$$

The parameter β^2 controls the maximum allowed mean squared error.

Both problems (7) and (9) are non-convex, yet can be viewed as iteratively reweighted ICP. Indeed, by fixing the u_i's and v_i's, the optimization boils down to solving n weighted rigid matching problems

$$\min_{\{\mathbf{T}_i \in \mathrm{SE}(3)\}} D(u_i, v_i, \mathbf{T}_i Y_i). \tag{10}$$

Next, $\mathbf{T}_i$ are fixed and u_i and v_i and the corresponding ρ_i and σ_i are updated. The process is repeated until convergence. Further details of this alternating minimization algorithm are developed in the sequel.

4 Discretization and Numerical Aspects

We represent the surface X as triangular mesh constructed upon the samples $\{\mathbf{x}_1, \ldots, \mathbf{x}_m\}$ and denote by $\mathbf{a} = (a_1, \ldots, a_m)^{\mathrm{T}}$ the corresponding area elements at each vertex (the computation of the a_i's is described later). $\mathbf{A} = \mathrm{diag}\{\mathbf{a}\}$ denote the diagonal $m \times m$ matrix created out of $\mathbf{a}$. Each membership function u_i is sampled at each vertex and represented as the vector $\mathbf{u}_i = (u_1^i, \ldots, u_m^i)^{\mathrm{T}}$. Similarly, the phase field is represented as the vector $\boldsymbol{\rho}_i = (\rho_1^i, \ldots, \rho_m^i)^{\mathrm{T}}$. Whenever possible, we will omit the index i to simplify notation. Each of the parts Y_i is represented in the same way as a mesh constructed upon the samples $\{\mathbf{y}_1^i, \ldots, \mathbf{y}_{n_i}^i\}$. The area elements are denoted by $\mathbf{b}_i = (b_1^i, \ldots, b_{n_i}^i)^{\mathrm{T}}$; the membership and the phase field vectors are denoted by $\mathbf{v}_i$ and $\boldsymbol{\sigma}_i$, respectively.

Data Term. For a given part Y (one of the Y_i's), let $\mathbf{y}_i^*$ denote the point corresponding to $\mathbf{x}_i$. The alignment error can be written as $\mathbf{e} = (\|\mathbf{x}_1 - \mathbf{y}_1^*\|^2, \ldots, \|\mathbf{x}_m - \mathbf{y}_m^*\|^2)^{\mathrm{T}}$, and the data term for one part as $D(\mathbf{u}, Y) = \mathbf{u}^{\mathrm{T}} \mathbf{e}$.

Regularization Term. We start by deriving the discretization of a single term $\rho^2 \|\nabla u\|^2 da$ at some point $\mathbf{x}_i$ on the shape. Let us denote by $\mathcal{N}(\mathbf{x}_i)$ the 1-ring of $\mathbf{x}_i$ formed by t vertices $\mathbf{x}_1, \ldots, \mathbf{x}_t$ ordered e.g. in clock-wise order (to simplify notation, we assume without loss of generality consecutive indices). We pick some j-th triangle in $\mathcal{N}(\mathbf{x}_i)$ formed by the central vertex $\mathbf{x}_i$ and the vertices $\mathbf{x}_j$ and $\mathbf{x}_k$ for $k = j \bmod t + 1$. Let us denote by $\mathbf{X}_j = (\mathbf{x}_j - \mathbf{x}_i, \mathbf{x}_k - \mathbf{x}_i)$ the 3×2 matrix whose columns are the vectors forming the triangle, and by $\alpha_j = \frac{1}{2}\sqrt{\det(\mathbf{X}_j^{\mathrm{T}} \mathbf{X}_j)}$ its area. Let also $\mathbf{D}_j$ be the sparse $2 \times m$ matrix with $+1$ at indices $(1, j)$ and $(2, k)$, and -1 at $(1, i)$ and $(2, i)$. $\mathbf{D}_j$ is constructed in such a way to give the differences of values of u on the vertices of the triangle with respect to the values at the central vertex, $\mathbf{D}_j \mathbf{u} = (u_j - u_i, u_k - u_i)^{\mathrm{T}}$. Here, $\mathbf{u}$ denotes one of the membership vectors, $\mathbf{u}_i$. The gradient of the function u is constant on the triangle and can be expressed in these terms by $\mathbf{g}_j = (\mathbf{X}_j^{\mathrm{T}} \mathbf{X}_j)^{-1/2} \mathbf{D}_j \mathbf{u} = \mathbf{E}_j \mathbf{u}$. The area element corresponding to $\mathbf{x}_i$ is given by $a_i = \frac{1}{3}(\alpha_1 + \cdots + \alpha_t)$, and the gradient at that vertex can be expressed by averaging the $\mathbf{g}_j$'s with the weights α_j. This yields

$$\nabla u \, da \approx \frac{1}{3}\sum_{j=1}^{t} \alpha_j \mathbf{g}_j = \frac{1}{3}\sum_{j=1}^{t} \alpha_j \mathbf{E}_j \mathbf{u} = \frac{1}{3}((\alpha_1, \ldots, \alpha_t) \otimes \mathbf{I})\mathbf{E}\mathbf{u}, \tag{11}$$

where $\mathbf{1}$ is a $2t \times 1$ vector of ones, $\mathbf{E}$ is the $2t \times m$ matrix stacking $\mathbf{E}_j$'s, $\mathbf{I}$ is the 2×2 identity matrix, and $\otimes$ denotes the Kroenecker product $(\alpha_1, \dots, \alpha_t) \otimes \mathbf{I} = (\alpha_1 \mathbf{I}, \dots, \alpha_t \mathbf{I})$. Denoting by $\mathbf{G}_i$ the $2 \times m$ matrix $\frac{1}{3}((\alpha_1, \dots, \alpha_t) \otimes \mathbf{I})\mathbf{E}$ corresponding to the vertex $\mathbf{x}_i$, we can write $\nabla u \, da \approx \mathbf{G}_i \mathbf{u}$.

Let us now consider all the points of the shape. We have

$$\int_X \rho^2 \|\nabla u\|^2 da \approx \sum_{i=1}^m \frac{\rho_i^2}{a_i} \mathbf{u}^T \mathbf{G}_i^T \mathbf{G}_i \mathbf{u}. \tag{12}$$

Introducing a $2m \times m$ matrix

$$\mathbf{G} = \left(\operatorname{diag} \left\{ \frac{1}{\sqrt{a_1}}, \dots, \frac{1}{\sqrt{a_m}} \right\} \otimes \mathbf{I} \right) \begin{pmatrix} \mathbf{G}_1 \\ \vdots \\ \mathbf{G}_m \end{pmatrix} \tag{13}$$

allows to rewrite the former integral as

$$\int_X \rho^2 \|\nabla u\|^2 da \approx \|(\operatorname{diag}\{\boldsymbol{\rho}\} \otimes \mathbf{I})\mathbf{G}\mathbf{u}\|^2 = \mathbf{u}^T \mathbf{G}^T (\operatorname{diag}\{\boldsymbol{\rho}^2\} \otimes \mathbf{I})\mathbf{G}\mathbf{u}. \tag{14}$$

Similarly,

$$\int_X \|\nabla \rho\|^2 da \approx \|\mathbf{G}\boldsymbol{\rho}\|^2 = \boldsymbol{\rho}^T \mathbf{G}^T \mathbf{G}\boldsymbol{\rho} \tag{15}$$

$$\int_X (1 - \rho)^2 da \approx \boldsymbol{\rho}^T \mathbf{A}\boldsymbol{\rho} - 2\mathbf{a}^T \boldsymbol{\rho} + \mathbf{1}^T \mathbf{a}. \tag{16}$$

The discretized regularization term

$$R(\mathbf{u}, \boldsymbol{\rho}) = \frac{\lambda_s}{2} \mathbf{u}^T \mathbf{G}^T (\operatorname{diag}\{\boldsymbol{\rho}^2\} \otimes \mathbf{I})\mathbf{G}\mathbf{u} +$$
$$\lambda_b \boldsymbol{\rho}^T \left(\epsilon \mathbf{G}^T \mathbf{G} + \frac{1}{4\epsilon} \mathbf{A} \right) \boldsymbol{\rho} - \frac{\lambda_b}{4\epsilon} (2\mathbf{a}^T \boldsymbol{\rho} + \mathbf{1}^T \mathbf{a}) \tag{17}$$

is, therefore, quadratic in $\mathbf{u}$ and $\boldsymbol{\rho}$ independently (but not in both simultaneously!). Regularization terms for $\mathbf{v}_i$ and $\boldsymbol{\sigma}_i$ are obtained in the same manner.

Alternating Minimization. The problem (6) is solved by means of alternating minimization, in the following steps:

1. Fix $\{\mathbf{u}_i, \boldsymbol{\rho}_i\}$ and compute the transformation $\{\mathbf{T}_i\}$ minimizing the data term $\sum_{i=1}^n D(\mathbf{u}_i, \mathbf{T}_i Y_i)$. This step is akin to a step of multiple individual weighted ICP problems.
2. Update $Y_i = \mathbf{T}_i Y_i$, compute the correspondence and the alignment errors $\mathbf{e}_i$.
3. Fix $\{\mathbf{T}_i, \mathbf{e}_i, \boldsymbol{\rho}_i\}$ and compute the weights $\{\mathbf{u}_i\}$ solving the *quadratic programming* (QP) problem

$$\min_{\{\mathbf{u}_i\}} \sum_{i=1}^n \mathbf{u}_i^T \mathbf{e}_i + \frac{\lambda_s}{2} \mathbf{u}_i^T \mathbf{B}_i \mathbf{u}_i \quad \text{s.t.} \quad \sum_{i=1}^n \mathbf{u}_i = 1; \quad \mathbf{a}^T \mathbf{u}_i = A(Y_i); \quad \mathbf{u}_i \ge 0$$

where $\mathbf{B} = \mathbf{G}^T (\operatorname{diag}\{\boldsymbol{\rho}^2\} \otimes \mathbf{I})\mathbf{G}$ as defined in (17).
4. Fix $\{\mathbf{T}_i, \mathbf{e}_i, \mathbf{u}_i\}$ and compute the phase fields $\{\boldsymbol{\rho}_i\}$ by solving the unconstrained optimization problem

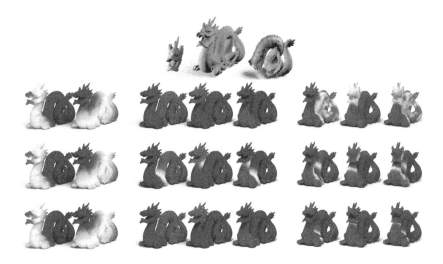

Fig. 2. Multi-part marching with missing parts. First row: two parts and the reference shape; Second row: initialization with ICP; Third row: first iteration of alternate minimization; Fourth row: final result. Columns 1-2: data term; columns 3-5: u_i, columns 6-8: ρ_i.

$$\min_{\{\rho_i\}} \sum_{i=1}^{n} \boldsymbol{\rho}_i^{\mathrm{T}} \mathbf{C}_i \boldsymbol{\rho}_i - \frac{\lambda_{\mathrm{b}}}{2\epsilon} \mathbf{a}^{\mathrm{T}} \boldsymbol{\rho}_i$$

where $\mathbf{C} = \left(\frac{\lambda_{\mathrm{s}}}{2} \mathbf{S}(\mathbf{u}) + \lambda_{\mathrm{b}} \epsilon \mathbf{G}^{\mathrm{T}} \mathbf{G} + \frac{\lambda_{\mathrm{b}}}{4\epsilon} \mathbf{A} \right)$, $\mathbf{S}(\mathbf{u}) = \mathrm{diag}\{s_1, \ldots, s_m\}$ and $s_i = \frac{1}{a_i} \mathbf{u}^{\mathrm{T}} \mathbf{G}_i^{\mathrm{T}} \mathbf{G}_i \mathbf{u} \approx \|\nabla u\|^2 da$ at vertex $\mathbf{x}_i$. The solution for each $\boldsymbol{\rho}_i$ is given by

$$\boldsymbol{\rho} = \left(2 \frac{\lambda_{\mathrm{s}} \epsilon}{\lambda_{\mathrm{b}}} \mathbf{S}(\mathbf{u}) + 4\epsilon^2 \mathbf{G}^{\mathrm{T}} \mathbf{G} + \mathbf{A} \right)^{-1} \mathbf{a}.$$

Problems (7)–(9)) are solved in a similar way: we fix all the parameters above, compute the correspondence and follow steps 3 and 4 for $\{\mathbf{v}_i\}$ and $\{\boldsymbol{\sigma}_i\}$, respectively.

5   Experimental Results

In this section, we show the performance of our algorithm under different settings on three shapes from the Stanford repository (bunny, armadillo, and dragon). The algorithm was implemented in MATLAB. Execution time depended on the number of vertices and parts; typical execution time for a reference shape with 10^3 points and 5 parts was 3.5 sec. Figure 2 illustrates the different stages of our algorithm on the problem of matching two parts (head and tail) of the dragon shape with a missing part (chest).

Effect of Regularization. is shown in Figure 3. In this experiment, we use the armadillo model fragmented into 4 parts, contaminated by Gaussian noise. The resulting segmentation of the reference model varies with the modification of

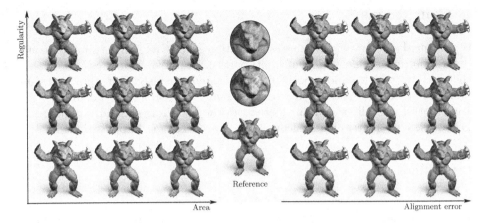

Fig. 3. The effect of different terms and constraints in the problem. Note the effect of over-regularization which causes shortening of the segment boundaries (top close-up), and under-regularization causing fragmented segments (bottom close-up).

Fig. 4. Noisy parts of the dragon shape (left) and the matching result (right) using the area constraint setting. The reference shape is shown in gray.

the area (Figure 3, left) and alignment error (Figure 3, right) constraints. Small area constraint results in large portions of the shape marked as "missing part". A similar result is obtained when allowing small alignment error. Increasing the regularity penalty encourages segmentation into parts with smoother boundaries.

Handling Noise. is shown in Figure 4, where we fragmented the dragon shape into four parts contaminated by gaussian noise and matched them to the clean reference shape using our approach (the area constraint was computed on the clean parts).

Handling Clutter. is shown in Figure 1. In this experiment, we printed the bunny shape fragmented into ten parts using a 3D printer. Leaving one part (the right ear) out, we scanned the remaining parts using a 3D scanner. The scan imperfections are clearly seen as noise, clutter, and holes. Solving our problem with the error in the constraint for indicators on the model and on each of the parts, we get the segmentation shown in Figure 1 (center). Having removed the clutter in this way, the segmented fragments fit together correction (Figure 1, right).

6   Conclusions

We presented an efficient alternate optimization scheme for solving simultaneous registration and segmentation of multi-part shapes. We are not aware of any other method which handle both problems simultaneously. Our approach can handle noise, clutter, and missing part, as shown on real 3D data examples. In future works, we will extend our method to the matching of solid (volumetric) 3D shapes, such as fragments encountered in archaeological applications.

References

1. Ambrosio, L., Tortorelli, V.M.: Approximation of functional depending on jumps by elliptic functional via t-convergence. Communications on Pure and Applied Mathematics 43(8), 999–1036 (1990)
2. Besl, P.J., McKay, N.D.: A method for registration of 3D shapes. Trans. PAMI 14(2), 239–256 (1992)
3. Bronstein, A., Bronstein, M., Bruckstein, A., Kimmel, R.: Partial similarity of objects, or how to compare a centaur to a horse. IJCV 84(2), 163–183 (2009)
4. Bronstein, A.M., Bronstein, M.M.: Not only size matters: regularized partial matching of nonrigid shapes. In: Proc. NORDIA (2008)
5. Bronstein, A.M., Bronstein, M.M.: Regularized Partial Matching of Rigid Shapes. In: Forsyth, D., Torr, P., Zisserman, A. (eds.) ECCV 2008, Part II. LNCS, vol. 5303, pp. 143–154. Springer, Heidelberg (2008)
6. Chen, Y., Medioni, G.: Object modeling by registration of multiple range images. In: Proc. Conf. Robotics and Automation (1991)
7. Domokos, C., Kato, Z.: Affine Puzzle: Realigning Deformed Object Fragments without Correspondences. In: Daniilidis, K., Maragos, P., Paragios, N. (eds.) ECCV 2010, Part II. LNCS, vol. 6312, pp. 777–790. Springer, Heidelberg (2010)
8. Gelfand, N., Mitra, N.J., Guibas, L.J., Pottmann, H.: Robust global registration. In: Proc. SGP (2005)
9. Hori, K., Imai, M., Ogasawara, T.: Joint detection for potsherds of broken earthenware. In: Proc. CVPR (1999)
10. Huang, Q.X., Flöry, S., Gelfand, N., Hofer, M., Pottmann, H.: Reassembling fractured objects by geometric matching. In: TOG, vol. 25, pp. 569–578 (2006)
11. Huber, D.F.: Automatic three-dimensional modeling from reality. PhD thesis, Carnegy Mellon University (2002)
12. Inbar, Y., Wolfson, H.J., Nussinov, R.: Multiple docking for protein structure prediction. International Journal of Robotics Research 24(2-3), 131–150 (2005)
13. Kong, W., Kimia, B.B.: On solving 2d and 3d puzzles using curve matching. In: Proc. CVPR (2001)
14. Krishnan, S., Lee, P.Y., Moore, J.B., Venkatasubramanian, S.: Global registration of multiple 3d point sets via optimization-on-a-manifold. In: Proc. SGP (2005)
15. Mitra, N.J., Gelfand, N., Pottmann, H., Guibas, L.J.: Registration of point cloud data from a geometric optimization perspective. In: Proc. Eurographics Symposium on Geometry Processing, pp. 23–32 (2004)
16. Mumford, D., Shah, J.: Optimal approximations by piecewise smooth functions and associated variational problems. Communications on Pure and Applied Mathematics 42(5), 577–685 (1989)

17. Neugebauer, P.J.: Reconstruction of real-world objects via simultaneous registration and robust combination of multiple range images. International Journal of Shape Modeling 3, 71–90 (1997)
18. Papaioannou, G., Karabassi, E.A.: On the automatic assemblage of arbitrary broken solid artefacts. Image and Vision Computing 21(5), 401–412 (2003)
19. Papaioannou, G., Karabassi, E.A., Theoharis, T.: Virtual archaeologist: Assembling the past. Computer Graphics and Applications 21(2), 53–59 (2001)
20. Pokrass, J., Bronstein, A.M., Bronstein, M.M.: A correspondence-less approach to matching of deformable shapes. In: Proc. SSVM (2012)
21. Pulli, K.: Multiview registration for large data sets. In: Prof. Conf. 3D Digital Imaging and Modeling (1999)

Combined Motion Estimation and Reconstruction in Tomography

Geert Van Eyndhoven[1], Jan Sijbers[1], and Joost Batenburg[2]

[1] IBBT-Vision Lab, University of Antwerp
Universiteitsplein 1, B-2610, Wilrijk, Belgium
geert.vaneyndhoven@ua.ac.be
[2] Centrum Wiskunde en Informatica, Science Park 123,
NL-1098XG, Amsterdam, The Netherlands

Abstract. If objects or patients move during a CT scan, reconstructions suffer from severe motion artifacts. Time dependent computed tomography (4DCT) tries to minimize these artifacts by estimating motion and/or reconstruction simultaneously. Most current methods assume a known deformation or a reconstruction without artifacts at a certain time point. This work explores the possibilities of estimating the motion model and reconstruction simultaneously. It does so by modifying the simultaneous iterative reconstruction technique (SIRT) to incorporate motion (trans-SIRT) and uses this method in an optimization routine that computes motion and reconstruction at the same time. Results show that the optimization routine is able to estimate motion accurately, assuming only the type of parametrization for the motion model. Our approach can potentially be extended to more complex motion models.

Keywords: Computed tomography, motion correction.

1 Introduction

Time-dependent computed tomography (4DCT) is a highly active research area which involves the estimation of object and/or motion from tomographic projections acquired from an object subjected to some form of motion. Among its most obvious applications is the reconstruction of patient anatomy when scanning under free breathing conditions. Without compensation for motion, reconstructions suffer from serious motion artifacts. A standard technique to counter these motion artifacts is to minimize the motion itself by fixing the object or asking patients to hold their breath. There are, however, numerous situations where such precautions cannot be taken and hence other methods for 4DCT are being developed, which are roughly subdividable into two categories: gated CT and methods that explicitly incorporate a motion model.

Gated CT sorts projections into several phase bins and generates a reconstruction for every separate phase bin. The sorting can depend on an external breathing signal, which is currently acquired in most medical applications using external markers and a detection system [1], spirometry [2], or other data correlated to the breathing signal. Promising research has been reported where phase

A. Fusiello et al. (Eds.): ECCV 2012 Ws/Demos, Part I, LNCS 7583, pp. 12–21, 2012.

bins are extracted from the tomographic data itself [3]. Since each phase bin reconstruction is created from only a fraction of all available projections, it lacks accuracy. In order to improve reconstruction quality, the correlation of reconstructions at adjacent phases can be exploited for temporal regularization [4,5]. Another class of methods explicitly incorporates a motion model in the reconstruction algorithm, either in projection or object space. In projection space, the class of possible motion models for straight ray geometry is limited to affine transformations [6] and a slightly more general class, where the spacing and angles between rays can also be adapted [7]. If the condition of a straight ray geometry is relaxed, one can model any kind of deformation by properly adapting the projection matrix [8].

If the modeling is performed in object space, any transformation can be directly applied to the object. Usually, either the deformation or a motionless reconstruction is assumed to be known in advance. If the deformation is known, a modified Feldkamp or FBP algorithm can directly calculate a motionless reconstruction at a reference phase [9]. If a motionless reconstruction is assumed, the deformation can be estimated by a parameterized B-spline or PCA model that minimizes the projection distance [10,11]. Several efforts have been made to generate general motion models. A popular modeling approach, which was already mentioned before, is the use of B-splines for parameterizing the motion field [10]. For modeling lung motion, Erthardt et al. created an 4D mean motion model using patient data, which can be adapted to a specific patient by performing a diffeomorphic image registration of a 3D volume at a reference phase to an average lung atlas [12]. By generating a patient specific lung motion model using PCA, a surrogate signal obtained from one marker could be sufficient to obtain the entire lung motion at a specific time point [13].

The above mentioned methods assume some kind of prior information. Gated CT assumes a motionless object for the duration of the scan in each phase bin, projection space modeling includes only a limited class of transformations, and object space modeling assumes a reference scan or a known deformation.

This paper describes a proof-of-concept study where as little prior information as possible is assumed. In Section 2, we start by introducing some notations and concepts and work our way forward to an iterative algorithm that reconstructs an object with given motion (trans-SIRT), which is thereafter used in an iterative optimization routine for estimating motion and object simultaneously. Simulation experiments and their corresponding results are discussed in Section 3 and 4. Finally, conclusions are drawn in Section 5.

2   Methods

2.1   Notations and Concepts

A 2D object can be described as a function $f : \mathbb{R} \times \mathbb{R} \to \mathbb{R}$. The projection process in tomography consists of straight rays traversing the object f at a certain angle θ and a signed distance s from the center of the detector to the ray (see Fig. 1). In a parallel beam geometry setup, the object is scanned at n_θ

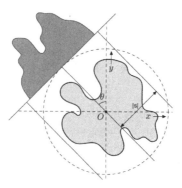

Fig. 1. Schematic overview of the projection process

angles, with all rays parallel per projection angle. In this paper, we use a parallel beam geometry with equidistant spacing between adjacent rays. To model the projection process, we introduce the 2D Radon transform

$$\mathcal{R}f(\theta, s) = \int_{-\infty}^{\infty} f\big((t \sin \theta + s \cos \theta), (-t \cos \theta + s \sin \theta)\big)\, dt \qquad (1)$$

in which $\theta \in [0, \pi)$. The function $\mathcal{R}f(\theta, s)$ yields the integral of f along the line described by $x \cos \theta + y \sin \theta = s$ (Fig. 1). In a real tomographic scanner, there are only a finite number of detector pixels at a finite number of angles, denoted by d and n_θ, respectively. The (log-corrected) measured projection data $p_{\theta,s}$ at angle $\theta \in \{\theta_1, \ldots, \theta_{n_\theta}\}$ and offset $s \in \{s_1, \ldots, s_d\}$ can be ordered in a vector

$$\boldsymbol{p} = (p_{\theta_1,s_1}, \ldots, p_{\theta_1,s_d}, p_{\theta_2,s_1}, \ldots, p_{\theta_{n_\theta},s_d})^T \quad . \qquad (2)$$

We refer to $\boldsymbol{p}$ as the *projection data* or the *sinogram*. The 2D object f can be approximated on a rectangular grid of N pixels, represented by a vector $\boldsymbol{x} = (x_1, \ldots, x_N) \in \mathbb{R}^N$, where we assume that f is constant over the domain of every pixel i. The line integral (1) can then be computed by the summation $\sum_{j=1}^{N} a_{ij} x_j$ where a_{ij} represents the contribution of pixel j to detector pixel i. Combining these discrete summations for all detector positions and all angles yields the system of linear equations $\boldsymbol{Ax} = \boldsymbol{p}$. Since this system is typically inconsistent, due to noise and discretization effects, one typically tries to minimize the projection distance $\|\boldsymbol{Ax} - \boldsymbol{p}\|$.

Now consider a time varying object $\{f_1, f_2, \ldots\}$, where f_i represents the object at time t_i. Throughout the paper, it will be assumed that motion during the acquisition of a single projection can be neglected and that the object can be represented on a pixel grid as $\{\boldsymbol{x}_1, \boldsymbol{x}_2, \ldots, \boldsymbol{x}_{n_\theta}\}$. Finally, we assume that at every time point t_i, the object is a transformation of the original object at time t_1: $\boldsymbol{x}_i = \boldsymbol{T}_{\theta_i}(\boldsymbol{x}_1)$ $(i = 1, \ldots, n_\theta)$. Evidently, this implies that $\boldsymbol{T}_{\theta_1}$ is the identity transformation. In practice, we calculate $\boldsymbol{T}_{\theta_i}(\boldsymbol{x}_1)$ by applying a deformation vector field (DVF) to the pixel coordinates of $\boldsymbol{x}_1$, followed by an interpolation step to obtain the pixel values of x_i. Since we use bilinear interpolation, we are able to represent T_{θ_i} as an $N \times N$ matrix. Notice that this assumption does not restricts the object's motion to be linear, as this can be given by *any* DVF.

2.2   Trans-SIRT

In this section, the simultaneous iterative reconstruction technique (SIRT) [14] is modified to incorporate a known transformation. For every iteration k, the standard SIRT algorithm updates every jth pixel $(j = 1, \ldots, N)$ as

$$x_j^{(k+1)} = x_j^{(k)} + \frac{\sum_i a_{ij}\left(p_i - \sum_h a_{ih} x_h^{(k)}\right) / \sum_h a_{ih}}{\sum_i a_{ij}} \quad . \tag{3}$$

Usually, $x^{(0)}$ is taken to be a zero image. SIRT can also be represented in matrix notation as

$$x^{(k+1)} = x^{(k)} + C A^T R(p - A x^{(k)}) \quad , \tag{4}$$

where C and R are the diagonal matrices with inverse column and row sums, respectively. As is noted in [14], SIRT computes the solution of the weighted least square problem $x^* = \operatorname{argmin}_x \left(\|Ax - p\|_R^2\right)$. To be able to introduce a known transformation in Eq. (4), we start by introducing some notations. Let A_{θ_l} be the part of the projection matrix A that represents the projection in direction θ_l. Define

$$\tilde{A} := \begin{bmatrix} A_{\theta_1} & 0 & \cdots & 0 \\ 0 & A_{\theta_2} & & 0 \\ \vdots & & \ddots & \vdots \\ 0 & 0 & \cdots & A_{\theta_{n_\theta}} \end{bmatrix} \in \mathbb{R}^{d n_\theta \times n_\theta N}, \quad \tilde{C} := \begin{bmatrix} C & 0 & \cdots & 0 \\ 0 & C & & 0 \\ \vdots & & \ddots & \vdots \\ 0 & 0 & \cdots & C \end{bmatrix} \in \mathbb{R}^{n_\theta N \times n_\theta N} \tag{5}$$

and

$$T := \begin{bmatrix} T_{\theta_1} \\ \vdots \\ T_{\theta_{n_\theta}} \end{bmatrix} \in \mathbb{R}^{n_\theta N \times N}, \quad T^{*-1} := \begin{bmatrix} T_{\theta_1}^{-1} \cdots T_{\theta_{n_\theta}}^{-1} \end{bmatrix} \in \mathbb{R}^{N \times n_\theta N} \quad . \tag{6}$$

The introduced notation allows us to describe the trans-SIRT algorithm as follows:

$$x^{(k+1)} = x^{(k)} + T^{*-1} \tilde{C} \tilde{A}^T R(p - \tilde{A} T x^{(k)}) \quad . \tag{7}$$

By an analogous argument as in [14], we will show the connection between trans-SIRT and the weighted least squares minimization problem

$$\operatorname*{argmin}_{y} \left(\|\tilde{A} y - p\|_R^2\right) \quad \text{subjected to} \quad y = T x \quad . \tag{8}$$

Multiplying the normal equations of Eq. (8) with $T^{*-1} \tilde{C}$ and replacing y with $T x$ gives

$$T^{*-1} \tilde{C} \tilde{A}^T R \tilde{A} T x = T^{*-1} \tilde{C} \tilde{A}^T R p \quad . \tag{9}$$

This can be rewritten as

$$(I - (I - T^{*-1}\tilde{C}\tilde{A}^T R\tilde{A}T))x = T^{*-1}\tilde{C}\tilde{A}^T Rp \qquad (10)$$

$$\Leftrightarrow x = x + T^{*-1}\tilde{C}\tilde{A}^T R(p - \tilde{A}Tx) \quad . \qquad (11)$$

Applying a fixed point iteration to Eq. (11) results in the iterative algorithm described by Eq. (7).

Note that we introduced Eq. (7) rather for the mathematical derivation and to have a compact description of trans-SIRT. In the implementation of trans-SIRT we calculate the transformation using bilinear interpolation and instead of multiplying with $\tilde{A}$, the projections are calculated using A_θ per projection angle θ. In Eq. (7), it was assumed that the inverse $T_{\theta_i}^{-1}$ exists. This assumption is, however, not too restrictive, since realistic physical motion is invertible. Preferably an analytic inverse should be used. For more complex models this inverse will, however, no longer be available and must be calculated with a numerical method.

2.3   Simultaneous Estimation of Motion and Reconstruction

To simultaneously estimate object and motion, we use a motion model $\mathcal{T}$ depending on some parameters α^1, where we assume that the transformation T_θ can be parameterized as $\mathcal{T}(\alpha, \theta)$ for each angle θ. Discrete approximations of these transformations can be collected in a large matrix $T(\alpha)$ analogous to Eq. (6). If we define $x_1(\alpha)$ to be the trans-SIRT solution for motion model $\mathcal{T}(\alpha, \theta)$, the optimal parameters α (and hence also the optimal trans-SIRT solution $x_1(\alpha)$) can be found by solving the following optimization problem:

$$\alpha^* = \underset{\alpha}{\operatorname{argmin}} \left(||\tilde{A}T(\alpha)x_1(\alpha) - p||_2^2 \right) \quad . \qquad (12)$$

Essentially, the solution of Eq. (12) minimizes the projection distance and hence optimizes the projections consistency. It does so by varying the motion model parameters α, computing an optimal trans-SIRT solution for these parameters and finally comparing the projections of this solution to the original projections. The function is minimized using the Levenberg-Marquardt algorithm (see for example [15]). Since the landscape of the objective function in Eq. (12) is rather coarse, the Jacobian needed by the Levenberg-Marquardt algorithm is computed using a finite difference scheme, starting from an initial stepsize which is halved every time the solver has found a minimum for the current stepsize.

3   Experiments

3.1   Trans-SIRT

To validate the trans-SIRT algorithm, a standard Shepp-Logan phantom of size 500×500 pixels was used, whereas the reconstruction was computed on a coarser

---

[1] Here, any motion model which transforms the pixel coordinates followed by an interpolation step can be used. A specific model will be tested in Section 3.

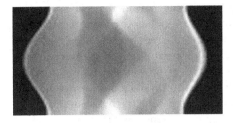

(a) Sinogram of Shepp-Logan without motion

(b) Sinogram of Shepp-Logan when B-spline based DVF is applied

Fig. 2. Sinogram of Shepp-Logan phantom

Table 1. aRMSE for each experiment and reconstruction

Experiment	True transformation	Gold standard	Optimized transformation
Regular signal	0.090319	0.1001	0.10156
Irregular signal	0.089871	0.10093	0.10302

grid of 100×100 pixels. Projections are calculated from the phantom (500×500) using a strip kernel (see for example Section 7.4.1 of [16]). To compare trans-SIRT to regular SIRT, the following experiment was performed. A SIRT reconstruction was calculated using 51 projection angles uniformly sampled from the interval $[0, \pi]$ and a detector consisting of 100 pixels. A trans-SIRT reconstruction was computed using the same projection data, but regarding it as coming from a stationary detector and a moving Shepp-Logan phantom that turns in the opposite direction. In both cases, a circular reconstruction domain was used. The two cases are illustrated in Fig. 3(a). As a measure for accuracy, the root mean square error (RMSE) between reconstruction and phantom was calculated.

In another test, we used the same phantom but a rather complicated transformation represented by a DVF and based on quadratic B-splines using 6 knots in every dimension. The inverse DVF was calculated using Chen's method [17]. Again 51 equiangular projections (with 100 detectors each) were taken. The sinogram is displayed in Fig. 2.

3.2 Motion Parameter Estimation

For our experiments, we used a simple motion model that scales the object differently at every time point. If s_i is the scaling parameter at time t_i, then $f_i(x, y) = f_1(s_i x, s_i y)$. Instead of modeling every s_i individually, we approximate the time varying scaling coefficient series $\{s_i\}_{i=1,\ldots,n_\theta}$ by a cubic spline model with 12 or 16 parameters. The first scaling coefficient s_1 is forced to be 1 such that $\boldsymbol{T}_{\theta_1} = \boldsymbol{I}$. If this model would be regarded as a simplification of a breathing motion, then it would not be confined to regular breathing, since the spline approximation can model a large class of continuous function over a certain time interval. In a first test, the time varying scaling parameter series was the one displayed in Fig. 4(d). A spline model was used based on 12 parameters and uniform knot spacing. As a second test a more irregular scaling signal was employed, see Fig. 5(a). In this test, a spline approximation of 16 parameters and uniform knot spacing was used. The RMSE error was calculated for the reconstruction at every time point t_i and averaged to produce an average RMSE (aRMSE). The series $\{s_i\}_{i=1,\dots,n_\theta}$ was approximated directly by a cubic spline, which we then regarded as the gold standard. The same phantom was used as in the trans-SIRT validation. To make the experiment more realistic, Poisson distributed projections with incident beam intensity $I_0 = 50000$ (photon count) were generated from the simulated projection data. We used 50 SIRT iterations and 50 trans-SIRT iterations in every experiment. This number of iterations was determined experimentally to have the lowest RMSE in terms of reconstruction

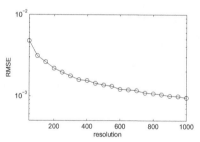

(a) Set up for experiment for case 1 and 2

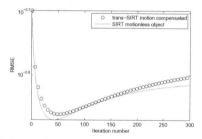

(b) RMSE of SIRT and trans-SIRT (case 1 and 2) as a function of iteration number

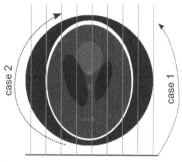

(c) RMSE between reconstruction in case 1 and reconstruction in case 2 as a function of resolution. Resolution grows from 50×50 with steps of 50 until 1000×1000

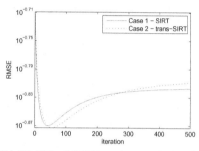

(d) RMSE as a function of iteration number for deformed Shepp-Logan phantom using spline based DVF

Fig. 3. A validation of trans-SIRT is performed in a first test (Fig. (a)-(c)), where a SIRT reconstruction is calculated using a rotating detector and a stationary object (case 1) and trans-SIRT is used to calculate a reconstruction for a stationary detector and rotating object (case 2). Figure (d) is the result of the experiment with the spline based DVF

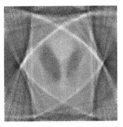
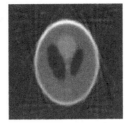
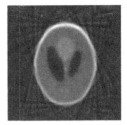

(a)   Reconstruction without motion correction

(b) Gold standard reconstruction

(c) Reconstruction after optimization

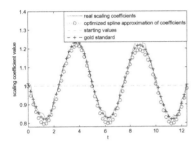
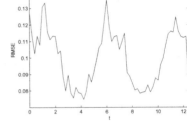

(d) Approximation of scaling parameters

(e) RMSE of optimized reconstruction

Fig. 4. Optimization results (regular scaling parameter signal)

quality, when estimating motion parameters any number of iterations ranging from 20-500 gave equally good results.

4 Results

4.1 Trans-SIRT

In Fig. 3(b), the RMSE for SIRT and trans-SIRT is displayed as a function of the iteration number. We can see that the curves are almost identical. The fact that there is a difference can be explained by the discrete nature of our algorithm and the different types of interpolation for the two cases. That being said, the two solutions should approach one another in terms of RMSE (calculated between the reconstruction of case 1 and the reconstruction of case 2) if the resolution in the reconstruction domain increases. This was tested and the result is displayed in Fig. 3(c). The results for the spline based DVF are displayed in Fig. 3(d).

4.2 Motion Parameter Estimation

The results for the test with the regular scaling coefficient signal are displayed in Fig. 4. In Fig. 4(a)-(c), the reconstruction at time $t = 0$ is shown for regular SIRT

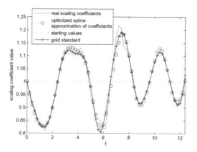
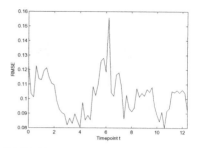

(a) Approximation of scaling parameters   (b) RMSE of optimized reconstruction

Fig. 5. Optimization results (irregular scaling parameter signal)

(no motion correction), the gold standard (i.e. based on prior knowledge of the transformation) and the optimization problem in Eq. (12), respectively. Fig. 4(d) shows the starting values, the true scaling parameters, the gold standard, and the solution of the optimization problem with regards to time. The RMSE for every time point of the optimized reconstruction is shown in Fig. 4(e). The same figure was generated for the test with the irregular scaling parameter signal (Fig. 5). The aRMSE for each of the reconstructions is summarized in Table 1. It can be noticed that the optimization method does not require the signal to be regular to produce good results. Visually there is hardly any difference between the gold standard solution and the optimized solution, which is confirmed numerically in Table 1.

5   Conclusion

We conducted a proof-of-concept in which motion and reconstruction is estimated simultaneously from tomographic data created with an object subjected to some form of motion. Simulation experiments confirmed the feasibility of this technique. For a known motion, trans-SIRT is able to produce results that are as accurate as regular SIRT for the same object without motion. We have also developed an optimization routine which simultaneously estimates motion and reconstruction, without the need for extra data. A major advantage of our approach is that any parameterized motion model can be incorporated and that only few assumptions were made, in contrast to many other current methods. A run of the optimization algorithm required about 5 minutes of computation time when using an unoptimized GPU-based implementation of trans-SIRT. In future work we aim to extend our methodology to more complex motion models that have several parameters.

References

1. Vedam, S.S., Keall, P.J., Kini, V.R., Mostafavi, H., Shukla, H.P., Mohan, R.: Acquiring a four-dimensional computed tomography dataset using an external respiratory signal. Physics in Medicine and Biology 48, 45–62 (2003)
2. Low, D.a., Nystrom, M., Kalinin, E., Parikh, P., Dempsey, J.F., Bradley, J.D., Mutic, S., Wahab, S.H., Islam, T., Christensen, G., Politte, D.G., Whiting, B.R.: A method for the reconstruction of four-dimensional synchronized CT scans acquired during free breathing. Medical Physics 30, 1254 (2003)
3. Vergalasova, I., Cai, J., Yin, F.F.: A novel technique for markerless, self-sorted 4D-CBCT: Feasibility study. Medical Physics 39, 1442 (2012)
4. Jia, X., Lou, Y., Dong, B., Tian, Z., Jiang, S.: 4D computed tomography reconstruction from few-projection data via temporal non-local regularization. In: Medical Image Computing and Computer Assisted Intervention (MICCAI), vol. 13, pp. 143–150 (2010)
5. Gao, H., Cai, J.F., Shen, Z., Zhao, H.: Robust principal component analysis-based four-dimensional computed tomography. Physics in Medicine and Biology 56, 3181–3198 (2011)
6. Mooser, R., Forsberg, F., Hack, E., Székely, G., Sennhauser, U.: Estimation of affine transformations directly from tomographic projections in two and three dimensions. Machine Vision and Applications, 1–16 (October 2011)
7. Desbat, L., Roux, S.: Compensation of some time dependent deformations in tomography. IEEE Transactions on Medical Imaging 2, 1–20 (2007)
8. Rit, S., Sarrut, D., Desbat, L.: Comparison of analytic and algebraic methods for motion-compensated cone-beam CT reconstruction of the thorax. IEEE Transactions on Medical Imaging 28, 1513–1525 (2009)
9. Li, T., Schreibmann, E., Yang, Y., Xing, L.: Motion correction for improved target localization with on-board cone-beam computed tomography. Physics in Medicine and Biology 51, 253–267 (2006)
10. Docef, A., Murphy, M.J.: Reconstruction of 4D deformed CT for moving anatomy. International Journal of Computer Assisted Radiology and Surgery 3, 591–598 (2008)
11. Staub, D., Docef, A., Brock, R.S., Vaman, C., Murphy, M.J.: 4D Cone-beam CT reconstruction using a motion model based on principal component analysis. Medical Physics 38, 6697–6709 (2011)
12. Ehrhardt, J., Werner, R., Schmidt-Richberg, A., Handels, H.: Statistical modeling of 4D respiratory lung motion using diffeomorphic image registration. IEEE Transactions on Medical Imaging 30, 251–265 (2011)
13. Li, R., Lewis, J.H., Jia, X., Zhao, T., Liu, W., Wuenschel, S., Lamb, J., Yang, D., Low, D.a., Jiang, S.B.: On a PCA-based lung motion model. Physics in Medicine and Biology 56, 6009–6030 (2011)
14. Gregor, J., Benson, T.: Computational analysis and improvement of SIRT. IEEE Transactions on Medical Imaging 27, 918–924 (2008)
15. Madsen, K., Nielsen, H.: Methods for non-linear least squares problems. Informatics and Mathematical Modelling - Technical University of Denmark (2004)
16. Kak, A.C., Slaney, M.: Principles of Computerized Tomographic Imaging. Society of Industrial and Applied Mathematics (2001)
17. Chen, M., Lu, W., Chen, Q., Ruchala, K.J., Olivera, G.H.: A simple fixed-point approach to invert a deformation field. Medical Physics 35, 81 (2008)

3D Object Classification Using Scale Invariant Heat Kernels with Collaborative Classification

Mostafa Abdelrahman[1], Moumen El-Melegy[1,2], and Aly Farag[1]

[1] Computer Vision and Image Processing Laboratory,
University of Louisville, Louisville, KY 40292, USA
[2] Electrical Engineering Department, Assiut University, Assiut 71516, Egypt
{mostafa.abdelrahman,moumen.elmelegy,aly.farag}@louisville.edu
http://www.cvip.uofl.edu/

Abstract. One of the major goals of computer vision is the development of flexible and efficient methods for shape representation. This paper proposes an approach for shape matching and retrieval based on scale-invariant heat kernel (HK). The approach uses a novel descriptor based on the histograms of the scale-invariant HK for a number of critical points on the shape at different time scales. We propose an improved method to introduce scale-invariance of HK to avoid noise-sensitive operations in the original method. A collaborative classification (CC) scheme is then employed for object classification. For comparison we compare our approach to well-known approaches on a standard benchmark dataset: the SHREC 2011. The results have indeed confirmed the high performance of the proposed approach on the shape retrieval problem.

Keywords: Heat kernels, shape retrieval, collaborative classification, 3D shape descriptors.

1 Introduction

Recently, using 3D objects data has become more important in the area of computer vision, as recognition based on 3D models is less sensitive, or may be invariant, to lighting conditions and pose variations as compared to 2D models. The emergence of laser/lidar sensors, reliable multi-view stereo techniques and more recently consumer depth cameras have made the acquisition of 3D models easier than before. The domain of the presented work is the classification of these 3D objects into a set of pre-defined classes. One of the main challenges in that regard is the development of flexible and efficient methods for shape representation or the creation of a shape descriptor or signature for shape matching. The descriptor captures the properties of the shape that distinguish it from shapes belonging to other classes.

Shape descriptor should have as many of the following properties as possible: 1) Isometry invariant: isometric shapes should have the same descriptor independently of the objects given representation and location. 2) Scale invariant: For some applications, it is necessary that the descriptor is independent of the

A. Fusiello et al. (Eds.): ECCV 2012 Ws/Demos, Part I, LNCS 7583, pp. 22–31, 2012.

objects size, therefore the descriptor should optionally be scale invariant. 3) Similarity: Similarly shaped objects should have similar descriptors. 4) Efficiency: The time and space needed to compute those descriptor should be reasonable. 5) Completeness or shape-awareness: descriptor should give a complete characterization of the shape, thus representing the shape uniquely.

1.1   Review of Related Work

Although global shape descriptors (e.g., [2]) have shown good performance on many data sets, they have an underlying assumption that shapes are rigidly transformed. Other approaches have used local feature detection and local descriptor to describe 3D shapes, such as spin images [10], local patches [11], and conformal factor [12]. But these methods cannot deal with the non-rigid shape deformation, and cannot cover the properties of the desired shape descriptor.

The problem of non-rigid shape deformation needs more work to compensate for the degrees of freedom resulting from local deformations. Early work by Elad and Kimmel [3] proposed modeling shapes as metric spaces with the geodesic distances as an intrinsic metric, which are invariant to inelastic deformations. Bronstein et al [4] used this framework with a metric defined by internal distances in 2D shapes. Reuter et al. [5] used the Laplacian spectra as intrinsic shape descriptors, and they employed the Laplace-Beltrami spectra as 'shape-DNA' or a numerical fingerprint of any 2D or 3D manifold (surface or solid). They proved that 'shape-DNA' is an isometry-invariant shape descriptor.

Recently Sun et al. [8] proposed heat kernel signatures (HKS) as a deformation-invariant descriptors based on diffusion of multi-scale heat kernels. HKS is a point based signature satisfying all of the good descriptor properties except for scale invariance. It characterizes each vertex on the meshed surface using a vector. However, the authors did not demonstrate how to retrieve shapes using HKS, although they pointed out the future potentials in shape retrieval applications. Fang et al [9] defined the temperature distribution (TD) of the heat mean signature (HMS) as a shape descriptor for shape matching. Their TD is a global shape descriptor and they used $L2$ norm which is a very basic matching method to compute the distance between two TD descriptors. Bronstein et al [7] solved the HKS scale problem through a series of transformations. The same research group has recently introduced the Shape Google approach [17] based on the scaled-invariant HKS. The idea is to use HKS at all points of a shape, or alternatively at some shape feature points, to represent the shape by a Bag of Features (BoF) vector. Sparsity in the time domain is enforced by preselecting some values of the time.

1.2   Paper Contribution

In this paper, we present an approach for shape matching and retrieval based on scale-invariant heat kernel (HK). Several aspects are novel in our approach. We use the first non-trivial Laplace-Beltrami eigenfunction to detect a small number of sparse critical points on the shape surface. These points are robust to the shape class, and their number can in itself be used as one of the discriminatory features among the various classes. Then we calculate the HK for the detected critical points at different time scales. Then scale invariance is achieved using an improved method to Bronstein et al's approach [17]. A concatenation of the histograms of the significant components of the scale-invariant HK for all the points is used as a feature vector for classification. The resulting descriptor captures the local as well as global shape information since it uses the temperature distribution at the critical points at several time samples. For the sake of comparison we compare our approach to the Shape Google approach [17], the shape-DNA [6] and the TD approach of [9] on the SHREC 2011-Shape Retrieval Contest of Non-rigid 3D Watertight Meshes [13]. In particular, we demonstrate that our approach can perform partial matching, when there are missing data, and more robust performance against noise. In [18] similar approach to this work but the scale invariance achieved by different way, also the classification is done by different technique.

2   Heat Kernel Basics

In this section we start with the basics of diffusion on Riemannian manifolds that are necessary to define the proposed heat kernel signature. We will model the shape as a Riemannian manifold, possibly with boundary. The heat kernel quantitatively encodes the heat flow across a manifold $\mathbf{M}$ and is uniquely defined for any two vertices i, j on the manifold. The heat diffusion propagation over $\mathbf{M}$ is governed by the heat equation

$$\triangle_{\mathbf{M}} u(x, t) = -\frac{\partial}{\partial t} u(x, t), \tag{1}$$

where $\triangle_{\mathbf{M}}$ denotes the positive semi-definite Laplace- Beltrami operator of $\mathbf{M}$, which is Riemannian equivalent of the Laplacian. The solution $u(x, t)$ of the heat equation with initial condition $u(x, 0) = u_0(x)$ describes the amount of heat on the surface at point x in time t. $u(x, t)$ is required to satisfy the Dirichlet boundary condition $u(x, t) = 0$ for all $x \in \partial M$ and all t. Given an initial heat distribution $f : M \to \mathbb{R}$, let $H_t(f)$ denote the heat distribution at time t, namely $H_t(f)$ satisfies the heat equation for all t, and $\lim_{t \to 0} H_t(f) = f$. H_t is called the heat operator. Both $\triangle_{\mathbf{M}}$ and H_t are operators that map one real valued function defined on $\mathbf{M}$ to another such function. It is easy to verify that they satisfy the following relation $H_t = e^{-t\triangle_{\mathbf{M}}}$. Thus both operators share the same eigenfunctions and if λ is an eigenvalue of $\triangle_{\mathbf{M}}$, then $e^{-\lambda t}$ is an eigenvalue of H_t corresponding to the same eigenfunction. The solution of (1) is called heat kernel and can be thought of as the amount of heat that is transferred from x to y in time t given a unit heat source at x. In other words, $H_t(x, .) = H_t(\delta_x)$, where δ_x is the Dirac delta function at $x : \delta_x(z) = 0$ for any $z \neq x$, and $\int_{\mathbf{M}} \delta_x(z) dz = 1$.

If $\mathbf{M}$ is compact then the heat kernel has the following eigen decomposition

$$H_t(x, y) = \sum_{k=1}^{\infty} e^{-\lambda_i t} \phi_i(x) \phi_i(y), \tag{2}$$

where λ_i and ϕ_i are the ith eigenvalue and the ith eigenfunction of the Laplace-Beltrami operator respectively, and x and y denote two vertices. The $H_t(x,y)$ is defined as the heat affinity $H_{af}(x,y)$ between a pair of vertices which is a measure of heat transfered between node x and y after time t.

Properties of the Heat Kernel: The heat kernel $H_t(x,y)$ has many good properties [8]. It is symmetric: or $H_t(x,y) = H_t(y,x)$. It is invariant under isometric deformations: which is a direct consequence of the invariance of the Laplace-Beltrami operator. It is informative: by only considering its restriction to the temporal domain we can obtain a concise and informative signature. It is multi-scale: for different values of t the heat kernel reflects local properties of the shape around x at small t and the global structure of M from the point of view of x at large values of t. And it is stable under perturbations of the underlying manifold.

3 Proposed Approach

In this paper, we propose to construct the shape descriptor as follows: HKs are calculated at some critical points detected on the surface (see below) at various time samples (about 150). Then scale-invariance is introduced in the computed HK as explained in the following subsection. Since the complexity of using the heat kernel as a signature is extremely high, and it would be difficult to compare descriptors of two different points, we use histograms to overcome the descriptor alignment problem and to reduce the descriptor size. At each time sample, (as described in the Scale Invariance sec. 3.1) after taking the logarithmic transformation, and the amplitude of the Fourier transform, a histogram of 100 pins is calculated for the low-frequency components. Then all the histograms from all detected critical points are concatenated to build a long feature vector. Then the normalized eigenvalues of the Laplace-Beltrami operator are appended to this vector. This vector, dubbed Critical Points-based Heat Kernel (CP-HK), can be used for classification using some well-known classifiers. However, for the latter part, we use collaborative classification [21]. In order to construct the HK at a given vertex x based on formula (2), we use a finite number eigenfunctions and eigenvalues of the Laplace-Beltrami operator which is replaced by its cotangent formula for triangular meshes [14]:

$$(\triangle_\mathbf{M} u)_i = -\frac{1}{A_i} \sum_{j \in N_{ei(i)}} (\cot \alpha_{ij} + \cot \beta_{ij})(u_i - u_j), \qquad (3)$$

where $(\triangle_\mathbf{M} u)_i$ for a mesh function u denotes its discrete Laplacian evaluated at vertex i (for $i = 1; 2; ....; N$, N number of vertices); A_i is the Voronoi area at the ith mesh vertex [14]; ans α_{ij}, β_{ij} are the two angles supporting the edge connecting vertices i and j. This discretization preserves many important properties of the continuous Laplace-Beltrami operator, such as positive semi-definiteness, symmetry, and locality, and it is numerically consistent [15]. In a matrix form we can write

$$(\triangle_\mathbf{M} u)_i = A^{-1} L u, \qquad (4)$$

where $A = diag(A_i)$, $L = diag(\sum_{l \neq i} w_{il}) - w_{ij}$, and $w_{ij} = (\cot \alpha_{ij} + \cot \beta_{ij})$. The first k smallest eigenvalues and eigenfunctions of the Laplace-Beltrami operator discretized according to (4) are computed by solving the generalized eigende-composition problem $W\phi = \lambda A\phi$, where $L = \phi \Lambda \phi^T$, Λ is a diagonal matrix of eigenvalues, and ϕ is a $N X(k+1)$ matrix whose columns correspond to the right eigenvectors of L.

3.1   Scale Invariance

Scale invariance can be achieved by four different methods: (1) trying to detect scale, as done in most feature descriptors in image analysis (e.g. SIFT). However, 3D shapes are usually poorer in features and scale detection can be done reliably only at a sparse set of feature points. (2) through the normalization of Laplace-Beltrami eigenvalues, but this method may suffer if the object has missing parts [7]. In such case, the scale invariance must be introduced locally rather than globally. (3) Using a series of transformations applied to the HKS [7] in order to avoid scale detection. This allows creating a dense descriptor. This method is considered local, thus can work with objects with missing parts. (4) the local equi-affine invariant Laplace-Beltrami operator proposed by Raviv et al [1].

In this paper, we propose an improved variant of the third method to achieve scale invariance. It was shown [7] that scaling a shape by a factor β results in changing $H_t(x, y)$ to $\beta^2 H_{\beta^2 t}(x, y)$. Thus a series of transformations are applied to HK as follows. Starting from each critical point x, the HK is sampled at every surface point y logarithmically in time $(t = \alpha^\tau)$ and the function $h_\tau = H_{\alpha^\tau}(x, y)$ is formed. Scaling the shape by β results in a time shift $s = 2 \log_\alpha \beta$ and amplitude scaling by β^2. That is, $h'_\tau = \beta^2 h_{\tau+s}$. The logarithmic transformation $\log h'_\tau$ decouples the multiplicative constant from $h_{\tau+s}$. Bronstein et al [7] proposed to take the derivative afterwards to remove the effect of the resulting additive β^2 term and then taking the amplitude of the Fourier transform (FT) of the derivative to remove the effect of the time shift s. Since the derivative operator is sensitive to noise, in a departure from [7], we propose to apply the Fourier transform directly to $\log h'_\tau$. The effect of the multiplicative constant β^2 is eliminated by dropping the DC (zero frequency) component of the FT, and then the amplitude of the remaining significant FT components (we normally use 6) are attained. This eliminates the scale effect without having to use the noise-sensitive derivative operation.

3.2   Critical Points

For a piecewise linear real-valued function ϕ given by the values at the vertices (ϕ_i) of a triangle mesh, we define a critical point as a vertex i whose function ϕ_i is a maximum or minimum over its neighborhood (in two rings). These points are detected using the local maxima/minima of the first non-trivial Laplace-Beltrami eigenfunction [19]. Critical point detected near the boundary are discarded. Figure 1 shows the critical points detected from the first non-trivial eigenfunction for sample shapes. The figure gives the total number of critical points for each shape.

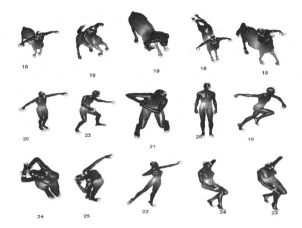

Fig. 1. Critical points detected for several shapes. Number below each shape represents the total number of shape critical points. Colors visualize the average temperature induced from these critical points throughout all shape vertices.

It is interesting to observe that shapes belonging to the same class consistently have almost the same number of critical points, whereas these numbers differ from one class to another. As such, this number can be used as one of the discriminatory features between the different classes, in addition to the HK descriptor.

3.3   Collaborative Classification

Recently, collaborative representation has also been used in pattern classification. Zhang [20] proposed a new classification scheme, namely collaborative representation (CR) based classification with regularized least square (CRC-RLS), which has significantly less complexity than the sparse representation based classification (SRC) but leads to very competitive classification results. Then [21] propose a relaxed collaborative representation (RCR) model, which considers both the similarity and distinctiveness of different features in coding and classification stages. Zhang [21] showed that RCR is simple, and very competitive with state-of-the-art image classification methods. We use the RCR approach for the coding and classification of our proposed descriptors. More details about the algorithm in [21].

4   Experimental Results

To test the performance of the proposed approach we use the SHREC 2011 - Shape Retrieval data set [13]. This is a large-scale database which consists of 600 non-rigid 3D objects that are derived from 30 original models. For the sake of comparison, we show the results of the Shape-DNA approach [6], describing shapes by the vector of the first eigenvalues of the Laplace-Beltrami operator. We used first 15 eigenvalues to construct the Shape-DNA descriptors. Eigenvalues were computed using the same cotangent weight discretization. We also compare our results to the method in [9] that uses the (TD) as a shape descriptor and the Shape Google approach [17]. Figure 2 shows sample shape retrieval results of the CP-HK descriptor on the SHREC 2011 dataset. The figure shows the first 15 matches for each query ranked according to the distance measure of the RCR classifier. Afterwards, the objects ranked from 30-35 for each query are shown on the right. Several of these objects are also similar in shape to the query object.

Fig. 2. Shape retrieval results of SHERC 2011 dataset. Left: queries. Middle: First 15 matches using the HK descriptor. Right: matches from 30 to 35. The color represents the first component HK at each point. The detected critical points shown in yellow.

Table 1. Results on SHERC11 dataset. Note the results for the Shape Google method is from our implementation as described [17]

Feature	SI	Classifier	NN	1-Tier	2-Tier	e-Measure	DCG
TD	–	NN	0.6483	0.3704	0.4768	0.3369	0.6684
Shape-DNA	–	NN	0.9900	0.8588	0.9295	0.6797	0.9649
SI-HKS	[17]	BOF	0.9567	0.6225	0.7288	0.5245	0.8718
CP-HK	Our method	RCR	**0.9733**	**0.7798**	**0.8823**	**0.6443**	**0.9364**

For the sake of quantitative assessment of the approach performance with all the tested classifiers, we record the following standard five evaluation measures (see [16] for detailed definitions): Nearest Neighbor (NN) where N = 1, First Tier (FT), Second Tier (ST), E-measure (E), and Discounted Cumulative Gain (DCG). Table 1 shows the performance on the SHERC 2011 dataset. The table compares the proposed descriptor against TD, Shape-DNA and Shape Google. The proposed approach significantly outperforms the TD approach and performs higher than the Shape Google. Although the Shape-DNA shows the

Table 2. Performance versus noise, shot-noise, and scale in three severity levels of the CP-HK descriptor using the RCR classifier compaerd to the results of Shape Google [17]. (1.00 mean 100%)

Noise L.	NN our	NN [17]	Shot N. L.	NN our	NN [17]	Sclae L.	NN our	NN [17]
1	1.0000	1.0000	1	0.9333	0.9333	1	1.0000	0.8000
2	1.0000	0.9000	2	0.8666	0.8666	2	1.0000	0.4666
3	0.9333	0.1333	3	0.8000	0.5333	3	1.0000	0.2333

Fig. 3. Some shape retrieval results for different shapes with different noise levels

best performance in this experiment, it severely suffers when there are missing parts in the objects (i.e., on partial shape matching, different scale and noise). This was clearly demonstrated in [17] compared with the Shape Google approached.

Another experiment is carried out to assess the approach performance under several distorted data scenarios. Here we compare the performance of the proposed approach with that of the Shape Google approaches. We have formed a query set consisting of 30 shapes taken from the SHERC11 data set, after applying several distortions: a Gaussian white noise, shot-noise, scaling, and missing parts. The performance versus white noise in three different levels of severity is shown in Table 2. Figure 3,and 4 illustrates sample shapes corrupted with these three different noise, and shot noise levels. Clearly the proposed approach shows a more robust noise performance.

The average performance of the two approaches in the case of shot noise is summarized, and lists the overall performance versus query objects with several scales are also shown in Table 2. The proposed approach has retrieved the shapes with different scales with 100% accuracy. The Shape Google presented considerably lower performance. The performance against missing parts is demonstrated in Figure 5. The results show that the proposed approach is better to handle partial data. Note that we used data set consists of 30 class and we don't ignore similar-class positive shapes (males and females, centaur, horse, and human shapes) as in Shape Google experiment [17]. This justifies why the results of Shape Google in Table 2 are lower compared to the results reported in [17].

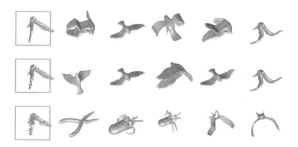

Fig. 4. Some shape retrieval results for different shapes with different shot noise levels

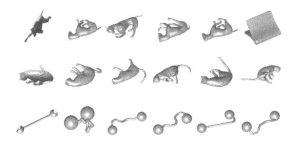

Fig. 5. Some shape retrieval results for different shapes with different missing parts. Left: queries. Right: the first 5 matched shapes.

5   Conclusion and Future Work

In this paper, we have presented an approach for shape matching and retrieval based on scale-invariant heat kernel (HK). An improved method to introduce scale-invariance has been also proposed to avoid noise-sensitive operations in the original transformation method. We have also proposed to use the first non-trivial Laplace-Beltrami eigenfunction to detect a small number of sparse critical points on the surface of the shape. These points were shown to be robust to the shape class, and their number can in itself be used as one of the discriminatory features among the various classes. We have utilized a collaborative classification scheme for object matching and retrieval. Our experimental results have shown that the proposed descriptor can achieve high performance on a public, well-known benchmark dataset. An important observation from our experiments is that the proposed approach is more able to handle data under several distortion scenarios (noise, shot-noise, scale, under missing parts) than the well-known Shape Google approach. Therefore, the proposed approach is more suitable for partial shape matching and retrieval from databases. Our current research is directed towards using the proposed approach to address dense correspondence between non-rigid shapes.

References

1. Raviv, D., et al.: Affine-invariant diffusion geometry for the analysis of deformable 3D shapes. In: Proc. Computer Vision and Pattern Recognition, CVPR (2011)
2. Kazhdan, M., et al.: Rotation invariant spherical harmonic representation of 3D shape descriptors. In: Proc. SGP, pp. 156–164 (2003)
3. Elad, A., Kimmel, R.: Bending invariant representations for surfaces. In: Proc. CVPR, pp. 168–174 (2001)
4. Bronstein, A.M., Bronstein, M.M., Bruckstein, A.M., Kimmel, R.: Analysis of two-dimensional non-rigid shapes. IJCV (2008)
5. Reuter, M., et al.: Discrete Laplace-Beltrami operators for shape analysis and segmentation. Computers and Graphics 33(3), 381–390 (2009)
6. Reuter, M., Wolter, F.E., Peinecke, N.: Laplace-Beltrami spectra as Shape-DNA of surfaces and solids. Computer-Aided Design 38(4), 342–366 (2006)
7. Bronstein, M., Kokkinos, I.: Scale-invariant heat kernel signatures for non-rigid shape recognition. In: IEEE Computer vision and pattern recognition (CVPR), pp. 1704–1711 (2010)
8. Sun, J., Ovsjanikov, M., Guibas, L.: A concise and provably informative multi-scale signature based on heat diffusion. In: SGP 2009: Proceedings of the Symposium on Geometry Processing, pp. 1383–1392 (2009)
9. Fang, Y., Sun, M., Ramani, K.: Temperature Distribution Descriptor for Robust 3D Shape Retrieval. In, NORDIA 2011 (2011) (CVPRW)
10. Johnson, A., Hebert, M.: Using spin images for efficient object recognition in cluttered 3 d scenes. Trans. PAMI 21(5), 433–449 (1999)
11. Toldo, R., Castellani, U., Fusiello, A.: Visual vocabulary signature for 3D object retrieval and partial matching. In: Proc. Eurographics Workshop on 3D Object Retrieval (2009)
12. Ben-Chen, M., Weber, O., Gotsman, C.: Characterizing shape using conformal factors. In: Proc. Eurographics Workshop on Shape Retrieval (2008)
13. Lian, Z., et al.: SHREC 2011 Track: Shape Retrieval on Non-rigid 3D Watertight Meshes. In: Proceedings of the Eurographics/ACM SIGGRAPH Symposium on 3D Object Retrieval (2011)
14. Grinspun, E., Gingold, Y., Reisman, J., Zorin, D.: Computing discrete shape operators on general meshes. [Eurographics (2006) Best Paper, 3rd Place]. Eurographics (Computer Graphics Forum) 25(3), 547–556 (2006)
15. Wardetzky, M., Mathur, S., Kalberer, F., Grinspun, E.: Discrete Laplace operators: no free lunch. In: Conf. Comp. Grap. and Interactive Techniques (2008)
16. Shilane, P., Min, P., Kazhdan, M., Funkhouser, T.: The princeton shape benchmark. In: Proc. SMI 2004, pp. 167–178 (2004)
17. Bronstein, A.M., Bronstein, M.M., Ovsjanikov, M., Guibas, L.J.: Shape Google: geometric words and expressions for invariant shape retrieval. ACM Trans. Graphics (TOG) 30(1), 1–20 (2011)
18. Abdelrahman, M., El-Melegy, M.T., Farag, A.A.: Heat Kernels for Non-Rigid Shape Retrieval: Sparse Representation and Efficient Classification. In: CRV, pp. 153–160 (2012)
19. Reuter, M.: Hierarchical shape segmentation and registration via topological features of laplace-beltrami eigenfunctions. Proc. IJCV 89(2), 287–308 (2010)
20. Zhang, L., Yang, M., Feng, X.: Sparse Representation or Collaborative Representation: Which Helps Face Recognition? In: ICCV (2011)
21. Yang, M., Zhang, L., Zhang, D., Wang, S.: Relaxed Collaborative Representation for Pattern Classification. In: CVPR (2012)

3D Facial Landmark Localization Using Combinatorial Search and Shape Regression

Federico M. Sukno[1,2], John L. Waddington[2], and Paul F. Whelan[1]

[1] Centre for Image Processing & Analysis, Dublin City University, Dublin 9, Ireland
[2] Molecular & Cellular Therapeutics, Royal College of Surgeons in Ireland, Dublin 2, Ireland

Abstract. This paper presents a method for the automatic detection of facial landmarks. The algorithm receives a set of 3D candidate points for each landmark (e.g. from a feature detector) and performs combinatorial search constrained by a deformable shape model. A key assumption of our approach is that for some landmarks there might not be an accurate candidate in the input set. This is tackled by detecting partial subsets of landmarks and inferring those that are missing so that the probability of the deformable model is maximized. The ability of the model to work with incomplete information makes it possible to limit the number of candidates that need to be retained, substantially reducing the number of possible combinations to be tested with respect to the alternative of trying to always detect the complete set of landmarks. We demonstrate the accuracy of the proposed method in a set of 144 facial scans acquired by means of a hand-held laser scanner in the context of clinical craniofacial dysmorphology research. Using spin images to describe the geometry and targeting 11 facial landmarks, we obtain an average error below 3 mm, which compares favorably with other state of the art approaches based on geometric descriptors.

1 Introduction

Accurate and automated detection of facial landmarks in 3D is an important problem in computer vision, with applications to biometric identification and medicine. Biometric applications [1,2] are typically concerned with the robustness of the algorithm (e.g. to occlusions, expressions, non-collaborative subjects) to achieve systems that can be deployed in a wide variety of scenarios. In this context, state of the art algorithms target the most prominent facial landmarks on large databases with diverse acquisition artifacts (e.g. holes, spikes) that help in assessing performance in challenging scenarios.

In medical applications such as craniofacial dysmorphology [3], which is the focus of our research, there is greater interest in the highly accurate localization of landmarks, as they constitute the basis for analysis, often aimed at detecting quite small shape differences. Acquisition conditions are therefore carefully controlled to minimize holes and other artifacts. For example, using a hand held laser scanner it is possible to obtain a high quality ear-to-ear facial scan.

A. Fusiello et al. (Eds.): ECCV 2012 Ws/Demos, Part I, LNCS 7583, pp. 32–41, 2012.

The availability of high quality surfaces poses an important challenge to land-mark localization algorithms, namely what accuracy can we obtain for facial landmarks in the presence of high quality data?

1.1   Related Work

To take full advantage of three dimensional data, there is a particular interest in methods that localize facial landmarks based purely on geometric information (i.e. without including texture information). The most widely used feature to encode the facial geometry for landmark detection has been surface curvature [1,4,5]. Other geometric features include relief curves [6], the response of range data when convolved with a set of primitive filters [7] or Gabor wavelets [8].

Regardless of the features that are used, it is unlikely that unique and highly accurate detection can be achieved for a given landmark. Even the nose tip, so far the most successfully detected facial landmark, suffers from both false positives and negatives. Thus, responses from feature detectors are usually combined with prior knowledge to improve performance. Methods targeting a small subset of landmarks typically encode prior knowledge by a set of carefully designed rules about the human face, sometimes with the help of anthropometric statistics [1]. A weakness of these methods is that they usually follow a chain of rules that depend on one another. Therefore, missing or incorrectly detecting one landmark hampers the detection of all subsequent landmarks in the chain.

Statistical methods can derive prior knowledge from an annotated training set. At the expense of requiring that such a set is available, they are more flexible than their training-free counterparts in the landmarks that can be targeted, as there is no need to derive specific rules for each point. Examples of this strategy include the use of graph matching [9] and statistical shape models [5,10,11]. However, these methods still rely on the detection of all targeted points, which can prove difficult for most feature detectors.

To alleviate this problem, Creusot et al. [12] use partial graph matching and determine the final alignment by clustering transformations from triplets of points while Amberg & Vetter [13] use Branch and Bound to optimize the search of extended sets of landmarks (so that the missing ones are less important). However, in both cases a rigid shape is used, which is an important limitation for facial modeling. In contrast, Passalis et al. [14] present an algorithm that allows non-rigid deformations by using a deformable shape model. They exploit facial symmetry to account for possible occlusions, but still require the full visibility (and detection) of the landmarks of the left or right side. As a consequence, they need to retain a large number of candidates for each landmark and test nearly billions of combinations even though they target only 5 to 8 landmarks.

1.2   Contribution

In this paper we present a method for the detection of landmarks for craniofacial research that can handle missing points, allowing non-rigid deformations. It is assumed that for each targeted landmark there will be a set of *candidates* that may or may not contain a suitable solution (i.e. one that is close enough to the *correct* position of the landmark). This is analogous to the point-matching problem found in algorithms that search for correspondences [15,2]. However, the human face is a non-rigid object and these point-matching algorithms are typically restricted to rigid transformations[1].

Our matching algorithm, based on RANSAC [16], consists of analyzing subsets of candidates and completing the missing information by inferring the coordinates that maximize the probability of a deformable shape model. Thus, despite the resulting subset possibly containing only part of the targeted landmarks, estimates for the remaining coordinates are inferred by regression from the priors encoded in the model. Subsets of candidates that fulfill the statistical constraints of the model are retained and additional landmarks are incorporated iteratively as long as the set remains a plausible instance of the shape model.

The ability of the model to work with incomplete information makes it possible to limit the number of candidates to be retained for each landmark, which substantively reduces the number of combinations to test with respect to the alternative of trying to always detect the complete set of landmarks. We experimentally demonstrate the accuracy of our approach, comparing it with two recent methods: one [4] based on heuristics on curvature and profile projections and another [14], closer to ours, which uses a statistical model.

2   Shape Regression with Incomplete Local Features

Our algorithm has three components: *i*) selection of candidates through local feature detection; *ii*) partial set matching to infer missing landmarks by regression; *iii*) combinatorial search, that integrates the other two components.

2.1   Local Feature Detection

Let $\mathcal{M}$ represent a 3D surface, whose vertices we denote by $\mathbf{v} \in \mathcal{M}$. Also, let $d(\mathbf{v})$ be the (Euclidean) distance from $\mathbf{v}$ to the ground truth (i.e. manual location of the considered landmark) and $s(\mathbf{v})$ the descriptor score (i.e. the value resulting from the evaluation of the descriptor *template* at vertex $\mathbf{v}$). For example, spin images [17] are a descriptor and the average per landmark over a training set can be used as a template.

Ideally, vertices with high $s(\mathbf{v})$ should be close to the target and have small $d(\mathbf{v})$. However, very often there are false positives with high $s(\mathbf{v})$ and $d(\mathbf{v})$ at the same time. We wish to retain enough candidates (the top-N_c) so that at least one of them is close enough to the target, i.e. there is some $\mathbf{v}$ so that $d(\mathbf{v}) \leq r_A$, where r_A is the acceptance radius. Unfortunately, this derives a very large N_c. Given a training set $\{\mathcal{M}_i\}_{i=1}^{N}$, if we compute the candidates required for each mesh, $N_c^{(i)}$, we find a very skewed distribution, where the maxima are typically outliers.

---

[1] While some robustness to deformations has been demonstrated experimentally in the literature, the formulation of these algorithms is constrained to rigid transformations.

Thus, we set N_c as an outlier threshold for the distribution of $N_c^{(i)}$; specifically, we used 1.5 times the inter-quartile distance from the upper quartile, which is accepted as a standard setting. We found that, for some landmarks, this choice can reduce the number of retained candidates by up to an order of magnitude.

Choosing N_c based on an outlier threshold for the distribution implies that, in the vast majority of cases, we will detect a candidate that is close enough to the target (e.g. within r_A) but we will miss a small proportion (the outliers).

2.2   Partial Set Matching with Statistical Shape Models

Let $\mathbf{x} = (x_1, y_1, z_1, x_2, y_2, z_2, \ldots, x_L, y_L, z_L)^T$ be a shape vector, constructed by concatenating the coordinates of L landmarks[2]. By applying Principal Component Analysis (PCA) over a representative training set [18], we get the mean shape $\overline{\mathbf{x}}$ and the eigenvector and eigenvalue matrices $\mathbf{\Phi}$ and $\mathbf{\Lambda}$, respectively, sorted in descending order ($\Lambda_{ii} \geq \Lambda_{jj}, \forall i < j$). Given any set of L points $\mathbf{x}$, we can obtain its PCA representation as $\mathbf{b} = \mathbf{\Phi}^T(\mathbf{x} - \overline{\mathbf{x}})$, which will be considered to comply with the PCA model (i.e. to be a valid object within such model) if

$$\sum_{m=1}^{M} \left(\frac{b_m^2}{\Lambda_{mm}} \right) < \beta_e^2 \tag{1}$$

where M is the number of retained principal components and β_e is a constant that determines the flexibility of the model.

However, if the point set is incomplete, we may want to use the available points and the model statistics to infer those that are missing. Let $\mathbf{x}^f$ be the *fixed* (or available) landmarks, and $\mathbf{x}^g$ the unknown landmarks (the ones to *guess*). Without loss of generality we group the missing landmarks from 1 to $3g$:

$$\mathbf{x}^g = (x_1, y_1, z_1, \ldots, x_g, y_g, z_g)^T$$
$$\mathbf{x}^f = (x_{g+1}, y_{g+1}, z_{g+1}, \ldots, x_L, y_L, z_L)^T$$
$$\mathbf{x} = \begin{pmatrix} \mathbf{x}^g \\ \mathbf{x}^f \end{pmatrix}, \qquad \mathbf{\Phi} = \begin{pmatrix} \mathbf{\Phi}^g \\ \mathbf{\Phi}^f \end{pmatrix} \tag{2}$$

The objective is to infer the coordinates of landmarks $\mathbf{x}^g$ so that the probability of the resulting shape complying with the PCA model is maximized, ideally without modifying the coordinates in $\mathbf{x}^f$. Assuming that the model follows a multi-variate Gaussian distribution $\mathcal{N}(\mathbf{0}, \mathbf{\Lambda})$ in PCA-space, it can be shown that (see Appendix A in supplementary material):

$$\mathbf{x}^g = \overline{\mathbf{x}}^g - \left(\mathbf{\Phi}^g \mathbf{\Lambda}^{-1} (\mathbf{\Phi}^g)^T \right)^{-1} \left(\mathbf{\Phi}^g \mathbf{\Lambda}^{-1} (\mathbf{\Phi}^f)^T \right) (\mathbf{x}^f - \overline{\mathbf{x}}^f) \tag{3}$$

The idea of using statistical constraints to complete missing landmarks has been explored previously by other authors [19,20]. While Blanc et al. [19] use an

---

[2] We assume that the shape has been aligned (e.g. by Procrustes analysis) so that Similarity is removed.

iterative approach to solve the resulting system of equations, de Bruijne et al. [20] obtain a closed form solution by applying linear regression. They use the maximum likelihood estimate of $\mathbf{x}^g|\mathbf{x}^f$ from the covariance matrix of the training set, which produces results very similar to ours. The difference is that we maximize the probability of the shape after the projection into model space, which results in higher probability of compliance with the model at the expense of having also a higher reconstruction error.

2.3   Combinatorial Feature Matching

We use RANSAC as the basis for our feature matching procedure, as described in Algorithm 1. We start from L sets of candidate points, one set for each landmark. All combinations of 4 landmarks are then evaluated[3]. In principle, we could also start from subsets of 3 points as we use Similarity alignment (7 degrees of freedom), but 4 points were found to provide more robustness to estimate the initial alignment.

We use equation (3) to complete the shape by inferring the missing landmarks. As long as the generated shape fulfills the model constraints, we successively add candidates from the remaining landmarks in a sequential forward selection strategy [21]. The cost of including a new candidate $\mathbf{c}_k$ into $\mathbf{x}^f$ is computed as the median of squared distances to $\mathbf{x}^f_{test}$, taking the closest candidates to the current estimate for the missing landmarks:

$$\gamma(\mathbf{c}_k) = median(\Delta\hat{\mathbf{x}}_{test}) \tag{4}$$

$$\Delta\hat{\mathbf{x}}_{test} = \begin{cases} \|\hat{\mathbf{x}}_{test}(\ell_j) - \mathbf{x}^f_{test}(\ell_j)\|^2, & \forall \ell_j \in \mathbf{x}^f_{test} \\ \min_{\mathbf{c}_j} \|\hat{\mathbf{x}}_{test}(\ell_j) - \mathbf{c}_j\|^2, & \forall \ell_j \notin \mathbf{x}^f_{test} \end{cases}$$

where ℓ_j is the j-th landmark, and $\mathbf{c}_j$ are each of the candidates for landmark j. We use $\mathbf{x}(\ell_j)$ to indicate the j-th landmark of the shape, and $\hat{\mathbf{x}}$ is the best PCA reconstruction of shape $\mathbf{x}$ in a least squares sense.

The inclusion cost in (4) is a key aspect of the algorithm and is divided in two parts, from the definition of $\Delta\hat{\mathbf{x}}_{test}$. The first part is the reconstruction error for the *fixed* landmarks, while the second part considers the distance from the inferred landmarks to their closest candidates. Note that a possible alternative would be using $\|\mathbf{\Phi}^T(\hat{\mathbf{x}} - \bar{\mathbf{x}})\|$ as the inclusion cost. However, this option neglects the effect of the coordinates inferred from $\hat{\mathbf{x}}^g$. We have found that it is important to constrain the solution to be within the mesh surface and using the landmark candidates is a convenient alternative to achieve this. The definition of $\gamma(\mathbf{c}_k)$ based on the median implies that the landmark cost $\gamma(k)$, in line 12, is the least median of squares [22], which provides robustness to potential outliers (e.g. landmarks for which no nearby candidates have been found).

Finally, for each set that is checked a score is computed. The candidates successfully included in $\mathbf{x}^f$ (i.e. those which allow completion of a shape fulfilling

---

[3] Note that, as we are interested in accuracy, we do an exhaustive search instead of random sampling but we do retain the idea of consensus as the figure of merit.

Algorithm 1. SRILF: Shape Regression with Incomplete Local Features

---

1: Start from a set of candidates for each landmark
2: **for** (all 4-tuple combinations of landmarks and candidates $\mathbf{x}_4$) **do**
3:     Initialize $\mathbf{x}^f = \mathbf{x}_4$
4:     Infer $\hat{\mathbf{x}}^g$ using (3), obtaining $\hat{\mathbf{x}}$
5:     **while** ($\hat{\mathbf{x}}$ fulfills the constraints in (1)) **do**
6:         **for** (all other landmarks, $\ell_k \notin \mathbf{x}^f$) **do**
7:             **for** (all candidates $\mathbf{c}_k$ for landmark ℓ_k) **do**
8:                 Add the candidate $\mathbf{c}_k$ to $\mathbf{x}^f$ to obtain $\mathbf{x}^f_{test}$
9:                 Infer $\hat{\mathbf{x}}^g_{test}$ from $\mathbf{x}^f_{test}$ to obtain $\hat{\mathbf{x}}_{test}$
10:                 Compute the resulting cost $\gamma(\mathbf{c}_k)$ as in (4)
11:             **end for**
12:             Compute the landmark cost $\gamma(k) = \min_k \gamma(\mathbf{c}_k)$
13:         **end for**
14:         Update $\mathbf{x}^f$ adding the landmark with minimum $\gamma(k)$
15:         Infer $\hat{\mathbf{x}}^g$ from the updated $\mathbf{x}^f$ to obtain $\hat{\mathbf{x}}$
16:     **end while**
17:     Compute the score for $\mathbf{x}_4$ as $\#(\mathbf{x}^f) + e^{-\gamma(k)}$
18: **end for**
19: Keep the subset that achieved the highest score

---

the PCA constraints) are considered inliers. Thus, the cardinality of $\mathbf{x}^f$ is used as the main component of the score. Upon equality of inliers, the subset with smallest $\gamma(k)$ is preferred.

3   Experimental Evaluation

Our test dataset consisted of 144 facial scans acquired by means of a hand-held laser scanner (FastSCAN^{TM}, Colchester, VT, USA). Special care was taken to avoid occlusions due to facial hair. There is some heterogeneity regarding the extent to which neck and shoulders were included. The extracted surfaces were subsampled by a factor of 4 : 1, to facilitate comparison to [14]. As a result, there were, on average, approximately 21.3 thousand vertices per mesh.

The dataset contains exclusively healthy volunteers who acted as controls in the context of craniofacial dysmorphology research. Each scan was annotated with a number of anatomical landmarks [3], among which we target the following 11: the nose root or *nasion* (n); the nose tip or *pronasale* (prn); the chin tip or *pogonion* (pg); the inner-eye corners or *endocanthion* (en, left & right); the outer-eye corners or *exocanthion* (ex, left & right) the nose corners or *alare crest* (ac, left & right) and the mouth corners or *cheilion* (ch, left & right).

All experiments were performed using 6-fold cross-validation. For each fold, the 120 surfaces composing the training set were used to build the PCA model and to determine the feature candidates to be retained. For the PCA model, we kept 99% of the total variance, with the flexibility parameter set to $\beta_e = 4$. We chose spin images [17] as our local geometry descriptor, adopting the parameters indicated in [14] (16 bins of 2 mm each). For each targeted landmark we compute

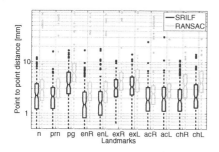 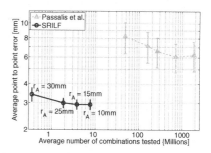

Fig. 1. Left: accuracy of SRILF and RANSAC with respect to ground truth annotations. For symmetric landmarks, L̲eft or R̲ight are additionally indicated. Right: Accuracy and number of combinations tested for SRILF and the method by Passalis et al. [14] when varying the parameters that control the number of candidates retained. Error bars indicate a 95% confidence interval of the mean.

a descriptor template as the median over the training set and determine the number of candidates N_c as described in Section 2.1. Unless otherwise stated, reported results correspond to $r_A = 20$ mm.

3.1   Localization Accuracy

We measured the accuracy of our method by comparing the automatic results with manual annotations from [3] that were used as independent ground truth.

To assess the necessity of a deformable model, the same experiment was repeated with a rigid template (the mean-shape of the PCA model). The resulting algorithm is much like RANSAC. The *fixed* landmarks are now simply those in the 4-tuple being tested, which are used to align the mean-shape to the test shape. Since deformation is not allowed, the shape is automatically completed and we have a rigid guess[4] for the remaining landmarks. Then we can use the same cost as in SRILF, defined in (4). Such a choice is equivalent to defining a minimum support of 50% in the RANSAC algorithm.

The localization results are shown in Fig. 1 (left). As expected, the deformable model is superior to the rigid one and this is verified for all tested landmarks. Since variations in our dataset are mainly due to identity with only residual expression changes, this is a remarkable result in favor of non-rigid modeling *vis-à-vis* the rigid registration used, for example, by Creusot et al. [12] and Ambert & Vetter [13]. The median errors of SRILF were below 3 mm for all landmarks except the chin tip and outer eye corners. Less than 2% of landmarks had errors above 10 mm and only in two cases did errors exceed 20 mm.

As suggested by the example in Fig. 2, our method does not actually locate a suitable candidate for every landmark. Therefore, only some of the targeted

---

[4] The alignment is performed using a Similarity transformation and hence uniform re-scaling is possible, but the model shape is not allowed to deform.

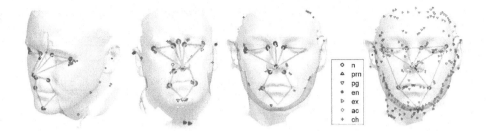

Fig. 2. Three examples of SRILF results (left) and one of the method by Passalis et al. (right). Solid lines show the obtained shape and red circles indicate successfully detected candidates. In SRILF the shape is completed by inference. All retained candidates for each landmark are also indicated according to the markers in the key.

landmarks are detected with the remainder inferred using statistics from the shape model. In our experiments, an average of 8.67 landmarks were found for each shape ($\sim$ 78.8%). The most frequently detected point was the nose tip (found in more than 93% of faces) and the least frequent was the chin tip (only found in 48% of faces). Note that all errors reported for our method are averages over all 144 shapes including both detected and inferred landmarks.

3.2 Comparison to Other Methods

In this section we provide a quantitative comparison with two recently published methods. The first method, from Segundo et al. [4], has reported state of the art accuracy (among methods purely based on geometry) using a training-free approach, completely different from ours. In contrast, the second method, from Passalis et al. [14], is based on statistical shape models and is closer to the approach proposed here. Indeed, some of the settings used in our experiments were chosen following [14] to facilitate comparison. The key difference is that their approach is based on *fixed* models of 5 landmarks that need to be detected in all cases (i.e. a *suitable* candidate for every landmark is always required). This leads them to define heuristics to keep large sets of candidates which, in addition to a potential increase of mismatches, considerably raises the computational load, as illustrated by the examples in Figure 2.

Table 1 summarizes the comparison results. Statistically significant differences with respect to SRILF are indicated by an asterisk[5]. It can be observed that our method performs consistently best for all compared landmarks except the nose tip, where [4] obtained similar accuracy. The average run time for our algorithm was 4.1 seconds[6].

Fig. 1 (right) provides further comparison to [14]: we found its performance very dependent on the number of candidates retained. While Passalis et al. specify an upper limit, the actual number kept depends on a threshold on the

---

[5] $p < 0.05$ both in a paired t-test and a paired Wilcoxon signed rank test.

[6] Non-optimized C++ implementation on an Intel Xeon E5320 @1.86 GHz.

Table 1. Localization accuracy [mm] per landmark (mean ± standard error) for the different methods

Landmark	n	prn	pg	en	ex	ac	ch
Passalis et al. [14]	n/a	2.89(*) ±0.15	9.19(*) ±0.97	3.42 ±0.66	6.98(*) ±1.35	n/a	5.88(*) ±0.96
Segundo et al. [4]	n/a	2.63 ±0.13	n/a	5.64(*) ±0.61	n/a	4.93(*) ±0.21	n/a
SRILF	3.08 ±0.22	2.43 ±0.15	4.52 ±0.25	2.26 ±0.20	3.67 ±0.18	2.45 ±0.22	2.69 ±0.19

spin-image scores below which candidates are discarded. The much larger number of candidates retained in [14] not only increases computational load but also impairs accuracy, as it is more likely to find combinations of points that, while being off-target, still comply with the statistical constraints. The need of a suitable candidate for every targeted landmark makes it necessary to retain those large sets, which might even be insufficient in some cases. For example, in order to always detect both mouth corners in our dataset, we would need to retain more than 1000 candidates, while the heuristics defined in [14] limit this value to 256. A similar situation was observed for the eye corners and the chin tip.

4 Conclusions

We present a method for the localization of facial landmarks that uses regression from a deformable shape model to tackle the potential false negatives in the detection of some landmarks. This allows an important reduction in the number of candidates to test, hence reducing the space of possible solutions.

We compared our method with two state of the art approaches targeting 11 landmarks on a dataset of 144 facial surfaces acquired with a hand-held laser scanner, in the context of craniofacial dysmorphology research. Despite the moderate size of the database, there were statistically significant differences in favor of the proposed approach for the majority of targeted points. We also showed that the capability to tackle non-rigid deformations through the deformable shape model clearly outperforms the alternative of using a rigid template.

The method is general and not constrained in any way to the landmarks selected for our experiments. The only requirement, as a learning-based method, is the availability of an annotated training set. Furthermore, the reduction in computational complexity with respect to similar approaches suggests that a larger number of landmarks might be targeted. Nonetheless, this would be linked to the accuracy of the utilized descriptor, so that the number of candidates that must be retained is kept within acceptable bounds.

Acknowledgments. The authors would like to thank their colleagues in the Face3D Consortium (www.face3d.ac.uk), and the financial support provided for it from the Wellcome Trust (grant 086901/Z/08/Z).

References

1. Gupta, S., Markey, M., Bovik, A.: Antopometric 3D face recognition. Int. J. Comput. Vis. 90, 331–349 (2010)
2. Zhang, G., Wang, Y.: Robust 3D face recognition based on resolution invariant features. Pattern Recogn. Lett. 32, 1009–1019 (2011)
3. Hennessy, R., Kinsella, A., Waddington, J.: 3D laser surface scanning and geometric morphometric analysis of craniofacial shape as an index of cerebro-craniofacial morphogenesis: initial application to sexual dimorphism. Biol. Psychiatry. 51, 507–514 (2002)
4. Segundo, M., Silva, L., Bellon, O.P., et al.: Automatic face segmentation and facial landmark detection in range images. IEEE Trans. Syst., Man, Cybern. B 40, 1319–1330 (2010)
5. Szeptycki, P., Ardabilian, M., Chen, L.: A coarse-to-fine curvature analysis-based rotation invariant 3D face landmarking. In: BTAS, pp. 1–6 (2009)
6. Faltemier, T., Bowyer, K., Flynn, P.: Rotated profile signatures for robust 3D feature detection. In: FG, pp. 1–7 (2008)
7. Yu, T., Moon, Y.: A novel genetic algorithm for 3D facial landmark localization. In: BTAS, pp. 1–6 (2008)
8. D' Hose, J., Colineau, J.: Bichon, et al.: Precise localization of landmarks on 3D faces using Gabor wavelets. In: BTAS, pp. 1–6 (2007)
9. Romero-Huertas, M., Pears, N.: Landmark localisation in 3D face data. In: Int. Conf. on Adv. Video and Signal Based Surveillance, pp. 73–78 (2009)
10. Zhao, X., Szeptycki, P.: Dellandrea, et al.: Precise 2.5D facial landmarking via an analysis by synthesis approach. In: Workshop on Appl. of Comput. Vis., pp. 1–7 (2009)
11. Nair, P., Cavallaro, A.: 3-D face detection, landmark localization and registration using a point distribution model. IEEE Trans. Multimedia 11, 611–623 (2009)
12. Creusot, C., Pears, N., Austin, J.: 3D face landmark labelling. In: ACM Workshop on 3D Object Retrieval, pp. 23–32 (2010)
13. Amberg, B., Vetter, T.: Optimal landmark detection using shape models and branch and bound. In: ICCV, pp. 455–462 (2011)
14. Passalis, G., Perakis, N., Theoharis, T., et al.: Using facial symmetry to handle pose variations in real-world 3D face recognition. IEEE Trans. Pattern Anal. Mach. Intell. 33, 1938–1951 (2011)
15. Jiang, H., Yu, S., Martin, D.: Linear scale and rotation invariant matching. IEEE Trans. Pattern Anal. Mach. Intell. 33, 1339–1355 (2011)
16. Fischler, M., Bolles, R.: Random sample consensus: A paradigm for model fitting with applications to image analysis and automated cartography. Comm. of the ACM 24, 381–395 (1981)
17. Johnson, A., Hebert, M.: Using spin images for efficient object recognition in cluttered 3D scenes. IEEE Trans. Pattern Anal. Mach. Intell. 21, 433–449 (1999)
18. Cootes, T., Taylor, C.: Statistical models of appearance for computer vision. Technical report, Wolfson Image Analysis Unit, University of Manchester, UK (2001)
19. Blanc, R., Syrkina, E., Székely, G.: Estimating the Confidence of Statistical Model Based Shape Prediction. In: Prince, J.L., Pham, D.L., Myers, K.J. (eds.) IPMI 2009. LNCS, vol. 5636, pp. 602–613. Springer, Heidelberg (2009)
20. de Bruijne, M., Lund, M., Tanko, et al.: Quantitative vertebral morphometry using neighbor-conditional shape models. Med. Image Anal. 11, 503–512 (2007)
21. Kudo, M., Sklansky, J.: Comparison of algorithms that select features for pattern classifiers. Pattern Recogn. 33, 25–41 (2000)
22. Rousseeuw, P.: Least median of squares regression. J. Am. Stat. Assoc. 79, 871–880 (1984)

Statistical Shape Analysis for Population Studies via Level-Set Based Shape Morphing[*]

Tammy Riklin Raviv, Yi Gao, James J. Levitt, and Sylvain Bouix

Psychiatry and Neuroimaging Laboratory, Brigram and Women Hospital,
Harvard Medical School

Abstract. We present a method that allows the detection, localization and quantification of statistically significant morphological differences in complex brain structures between populations. This is accomplished by a novel level-set framework for shape morphing and a *multi-shape* dissimilarity-measure derived by a modified version of the Hausdorff distance. The proposed method does not require explicit one-to-one point correspondences and is fast, robust and easy to implement regardless of the topological complexity of the anatomical surface under study.

The proposed model has been applied to different populations using a variety of brain structures including left and right striatum, caudate, amygdala-hippocampal complex and superior- temporal gyrus (STG) in normal controls and patients. The synthetic databases allow quantitative evaluations of the proposed algorithm while the results obtained for the real clinical data are in line with published findings on gray matter reduction in the tested cortical and sub-cortical structures in schizophrenia patients.

1 Introduction

The objective of the proposed study is the detection of morphometric differences in anatomical structures between different populations. We address this challenge via a novel and robust mathematical shape model equipped with a new parametrization-free shape metric. A variational framework, based on level-sets is the key concept in the proposed methodology avoiding some of the bottlenecks that are typical of numerous shape analysis applications – i.e. re-parametrization or calculation of one-to-one point correspondences. The suggested model allows to extract statistics that are sensitive enough to detect subtle changes between populations, yet robust enough to avoid common statistical errors.

Detection of shape changes in neurodevelopmental and or neurodegenerative diseases may shed new light on how illness impacts brain morphology. This hypothesis, and the recent advent of sophisticated computer algorithms, have led to many morphometric studies of brain anatomy in normal neurodevelopment.

There exist several general approaches to shape analysis. Perhaps the most common one is based on a surface representation of the objects, which are then

---

[*] This work was supported by the NIH grant R01 MH82918.

A. Fusiello et al. (Eds.): ECCV 2012 Ws/Demos, Part I, LNCS 7583, pp. 42–51, 2012.
© Springer-Verlag Berlin Heidelberg 2012

registered to each other to establish one-to-one correspondences [1–6]. This approach however involves difficult computational challenges, most notably establishing local correspondences within the population of objects and computing robust statistics. Medial representations (e.g. [7, 8]) while more compact, face similar challenges. Other methods represent a shape by a relatively small feature vector (e.g. [9, 10]). Such methods are usually numerically stable and allow for the computation of robust statistics. However, the resulting feature vectors are rarely intuitive making the interpretation of the results difficult.

In this paper we define a shape dissimilarity-measure, which is a generalization of the symmetrical Hausdorff distance between two objects (represented as binary maps). Let S_1 and S_2 be two distinctive point sets which may have a different cardinality, i.e. $|S_1| \neq |S_2|$. The classical definition of the Hausdorff distance $D_H(S_1, S_2)$ is as follows:

$$\max\{ \sup_{\mathbf{x}_1 \in S_1} \inf_{\mathbf{x}_2 \in S_2} d(\mathbf{x}_1, \mathbf{x}_2), \sup_{\mathbf{x}_2 \in S_2} \inf_{\mathbf{x}_1 \in S_1} d(\mathbf{x}_1, \mathbf{x}_2)\}, \tag{1}$$

where $d(x_1, x_2)$ is the Euclidean distance between points $x_1 \in S_1$ and $x_2 \in S_2$. When the maximum of the left and the right terms in Eq. (1) is replaced by their sum, this measure becomes symmetrical. In the proposed framework, we use a modified version of the symmetrical dissimilarity measure defined as follows:

$$D_m H(S_1, S_2) = \sum_{\mathbf{x}_1 \in S_1} \inf_{\mathbf{x}_2 \in S_2} d(\mathbf{x}_1, \mathbf{x}_2) + \sum_{\mathbf{x}_2 \in S_2} \inf_{\mathbf{x}_1 \in S_1} d(\mathbf{x}_1, \mathbf{x}_2), \tag{2}$$

which is more robust in the presence of noise and irregularities [11]. The minimum distance between a boundary voxel $\mathbf{x}$ in S_1 (or S_2) and the boundary voxels of the other shape S_2 (or S_1) is simply the value of the signed distance function (SDF) of S_2 (or S_1) in voxel $\mathbf{x}$. This connection allows us to represent shapes by signed distance functions (SDFs) or equivalently with level-sets [12]. The Hausdorff distance and the related Gromov-Hausdorff distance have been used before by e.g. [13–15] to define distances between point sets. For example in [13] the Gromov-Hausdorff distance was used for calculating the diffusion distance, rather than the geodesic path between points on a surface, allowing the comparison of pairs of non-rigid shapes with different topology. Here, the modified Hausdorff distance is used to define a level-set functional for the construction of the mean of a shape ensemble.

Our algorithm jointly constructs the mean of the given shape ensemble via a non-parametric shape deformation process derived by minimizing the proposed level-set functional and searches for the affine transformations that minimize the distances of the shapes to the evolved mean.

Spatial statistical analysis is obtained by calculating the minimal distance of each point on the mean shape surface to each of the affine registered input shapes. We then compute two-sample t-tests at every location on the mean shape surface to look for statistically significant differences between populations. The resulting raw p-values are adjusted for multiple comparison using the False Discovery Rate [16].

We test the proposed method on well-defined regions of interest using both synthetic and real data sets. The structures were selected for their importance with respect to brain regions implicated in schizophrenia and other neurological disorders. This includes synthetic sets of the striatum and the amygdala-hippocampal complex (AHC) and real data of the superior-temporal gyrus (STG) in first-episode schizophrenia patients and the caudate nucleus in women with schizotypal personality disorder (SPD) . We show that our algorithm can accurately detect, locate and quantify known morphological changes. Note that very few shape algorithms have been both qualitatively and quantitatively evaluated on ground truth data. Our results obtained for the clinical data are in line with previous findings of volumetric differences of the tested brain structures between schizophrenia patients and normal controls.

2   Methods

2.1   Shape Representation and Metric

A shape S_i is defined by the image region $\omega_i \subset \Omega$ that corresponds to the structure of interest, where $\Omega \in \mathbb{R}^3$ is the image domain. The boundary of ω_i is denoted by $\partial \omega_i$. Our representation of S_i is the signed distance function of its boundary: $\phi_{S_i} : \Omega \to \mathbb{R}$ such that the Eikonal equation $\|\nabla \phi_{S_i}\| = 1$ holds. We define the distance between S_i and S_j as the modified symmetrical Hausdorff distance between their boundaries using the continuous form of Eq. (2):

$$\mathbf{dist}(S_i, S_j) = \int_{\partial \omega_i} |\phi_{S_j}| d\mathbf{x} + \int_{\partial \omega_j} |\phi_{S_i}| d\mathbf{x} \qquad (3)$$

As ϕ_{S_j} is a signed distance function, its absolute value in $\mathbf{x}$ represents the minimal Euclidean distance from $\mathbf{x}$ to the boundary of ω_j ($\partial \omega_j$). The same applies for ϕ_{S_i} and $\partial \omega_i$. Formally, the signed distance of voxel $\mathbf{x} \in \partial \omega_i$ from ω_j is:

$$\mathbf{dist}(\mathbf{x} \in \partial \omega_i, S_j) = \phi_{S_j}(\mathbf{x}). \qquad (4)$$

We define the mean S^M of a shape ensemble $\{S_1 \ldots S_N\}$, as the shape that minimizes the sum of the distances from all the shapes in the set:

$$\hat{S}^M = \arg \min_{S^M} \sum_{i=1}^{N} \mathbf{dist}(S_i \circ \hat{T}_{i,M}, S^M), \qquad (5)$$

where $\hat{T}_{i,M}$ is the estimated affine trasformation that aligns a shape S_i to the mean shape as will be described next.

2.2   Alignment of Shapes

As in [17], we define 'shape' as a set of geometric features of an object that is invariant to 12-parameter affine transformation. It is thus necessary to remove the affine components differentiating the input objects before computing statistics over populations. We use a group-wise registration framework in which each shape S_i is registered by an affine transform to the estimated mean shape $\hat{S}^M$ such that the modified Hausdorff distance, defined in Eq. 3 is minimized:

$$\hat{T}_{i,M} = \arg\min_{T_{i,M}} \mathbf{dist}(S_i \circ T_{i,M}, \hat{S}^M). \tag{6}$$

2.3   Joint Group-Wise Registration and Mean Shape Evolution

As neither the mean shape S^M nor the affine parameters $T_{i,M}$ that aligns each shape S_i to the mean are known, we use an alternating minimization technique in which Eq. (6) (for each shape S_i in the ensemble) and Eq. (5) are jointly solved. While the affine transformation parameters are inferred by using a global optimization method [18] the mean shape is generated via gradient descent optimization of a level-set functional. The signed distance functions $\{\phi_{S_i}\}$ can be viewed as level-set functions, where their zero levels define the boundaries of the respective shapes. In the spirit of [19] we use the sigmoidal "logistic" function of ϕ as a regularized form of the Heaviside function :

$$H_\epsilon(\phi) = \frac{1}{2}\left(1 + \tanh\left(\frac{\phi}{2\epsilon}\right)\right) = \frac{1}{1 + e^{-\phi/\epsilon}}, \tag{7}$$

The boundary of a shape S_i can be therefore approximated by $\partial\omega_{S_i} = |\nabla H_\epsilon(\phi_{S_i})|$ defining the distance between S^M and the shape set $\{S_i\}$ as follows [1]:

$$D(S^M, \{S_i\}) = \sum_i \int_\Omega [\|\phi_{S^M}\|\nabla H_\epsilon(\phi_{S_i})| + \|\phi_{S_i}\|\nabla H_\epsilon(\phi_{S^M})|] \, d\mathbf{x}. \tag{8}$$

We estimate ϕ_{SM} iteratively:

$$\hat{\phi}_{SM} = \arg\min_{\phi_{S_M}} D(S^M, \{S_i\}). \tag{9}$$

The gradient descent equation that determines the evolution of ϕ_{SM} is derived from the first variation of the functional in equation (8):

$$\phi_t^M = \sum_i \left[\text{sign}(\phi_{SM})|\nabla H_\epsilon(\phi_{S_i})| + \delta_\epsilon(\phi_{SM})\text{div}\left(\frac{\nabla\phi_{SM}}{|\nabla\phi_{SM}|}|\phi_{S_i}|\right)\right], \tag{10}$$

where $\text{sign}(\cdot)$ is the sign function; **div** is the divergence operator and $\delta_\epsilon(\phi)$ is the derivative of $H_\epsilon(\phi)$ with respect to ϕ.

2.4   Implementation

The ensemble shapes are first aligned by translation such that the center of mass of each shape coincides with the mean of the centers of mass of all the shapes. We then average the shape, defining an 'approximate' mean and calculate the

---

[1] Hereafter, $S_i \circ T_{M,i}$ is represented as S_i to simplify the notation.

affine transformations of each shape to that mean. Then a better approximation to the mean shape is calculated by averaging the affine-transformed shapes. We use the approximated mean shape to initialize the level-set-based gradient descent process.

Averaging over the set of SDFs, i.e. $\phi_1, \ldots, \phi_N$, will not result in a valid SDF representation as the mean of SDFs is not an SDF. We instead use the logistic functions of the SDFs as in Eq. (7) folowing [20]. In practice, we average the regularized Heaviside functions of the SDFs, i.e. $H(\phi_i)$. The boundary of the mean shape, $\partial\omega_{\mathrm{Mean}}$, is the 0.5 level set of the mean probability map. The underlying assumption here is that the morphological variability of an anatomical structure within different subjects, even across populations, is sufficiently small such that the high-dimensional points that represent the shape ensemble lie in close proximity to each other upon the shape manifold. Therefore their mean (used for initialization) is approximately on the manifold, as well.

2.5 Localization of Shape Differences between Populations

We now present how our model can effectively detect local shape deformations within a population. Given a point on the mean shape boundary, $\mathbf{x} \in \partial\omega_{\mathrm{Mean}}$, we can directly obtain its signed distance to each of the affine aligned shapes, by looking up the distance in the corresponding SDF $\phi_n(\mathbf{x})$. For each of those voxels, statistics on the $\phi_n(\mathbf{x})$ can capture local thickening or thinning of structure as well as more complex boundary displacements not removed by the affine transformation.

Let $\phi_1^*, \ldots, \phi_N^*$ and $\phi_1^{**}, \ldots, \phi_M^{**}$ be the signed distance functions representing shapes of a particular anatomical structure in two populations. Let $d^*(\mathbf{x})$ and $d^{**}(\mathbf{x})$ be two vectors of lengths N and M respectively of the (signed) distances of the corresponding shape ensembles to $\mathbf{x}$. We can now apply two-sample t-tests (or another statistic) at each location on the boundary to look for statistically significant differences between the two populations. In the following experiments, we also use False Discovery Rate (FDR) to correct for multiple comparisons [16].

3 Experiments

We evaluated the proposed algorithm using synthetic and real data sets: synthetic sets of the amygdala-hippocampal complex (AHC) and of the striatum, and real data of the superior-temporal gyrus (STG) in first episode schizophrenics and the caudate nucleus in women with schizotypal personality disorder (SPD) . All results were corrected for multiple comparisons using the FDR approach in [16]. We applied a false discovery rate of 5%.

3.1 Synthetic Amygdala-Hippocampal Complex

Manual segmentations of the left amygdala-hippocampus complexes (AHC) in 40 normal controls were taken from the laboratory database. An unbiased atlas of the AHC was created from the 40 samples [21]. The resulting atlas was then warped back to subject space using 20 randomly selected inverse warps obtained in the previous step. The resulting samples compose the normal control group (NC). The remaining 20 were manipulated by adding (or removing) a specific number of voxels using a hemisphere such that either a bump (or dimple) would be created and labeled "abnormal" (AB). Eight pairs of NC/AB data sets were generated. Each AB set had a bump (or a dimple) located in the head of the AHC and with a radius of $3, 4, 5$ and 6 voxels respectively.

For each AB/NC data set, we generated the mean AHC and performed a t-test comparing the NC and AB distances to the mean at each point on the mean shape's surface. Successful results of these eight experiments ({bump,dimple} $\times \{3, 4, 5, 6\}$) are shown in Fig. 1. We also evaluated the method by looking at the ratio of the statistically significant voxels over the total number of surface voxels for the bump (dimple) as the size of the deformation increases (Fig. 2).

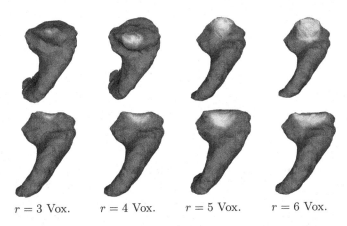

| $r = 3$ Vox. | $r = 4$ Vox. | $r = 5$ Vox. | $r = 6$ Vox. |

Fig. 1. AHC data set. p-value maps displayed on the mean shapes of NC/AB data sets with a bump (top row) or dimple (bottom row) of radius (from left to right) $3, 4, 5$ and 6. Red indicates non-significant p-values while the yellow colors present a scale of FDR corrected p-values (below the threshold).

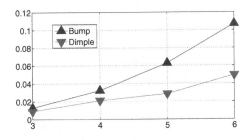

Fig. 2. Method evaluation for the synthetic AHC datasets. The ratio of the statistically significant mean shape surface voxels over the total number of surface voxels increases as the size of the synthetic distortion (bump or dimple) increases.

3.2   Synthetic Striatum

Synthetic striatum shapes were generated through manifold learning based on a training set of 27 real samples [22]. Abnormal examples were generated via random processes of either thinning or thickening of specific, well define regions of the striatum (see Fig. 3a-c,e-g). Two sets of examples for the right and the left striatum, each containing 50 normal and 50 abnormal examples, were tested. Results are shown in Fig. 3. Note that the distorted regions (highlighted in red) - corresponding to voxels with significant (FDR corrected) p-values (Fig. 3 d,h) were precisely detected.

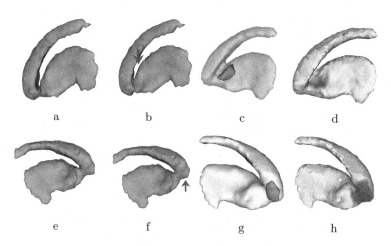

Fig. 3. Left (top) and Right (bottom) Striatum data sets. (a,e) Randomly selected examples of the left (a) and the right (e) striatum. (b,f) Left (b) and right (f) striatum shapes after applying shape deformations to the respective shapes shown in (a,e). (c,g) Mean (left and right) striatum shapes along with the averaged artificial deformation (red) (d,h) Mean (left and right) striatum shapes along with the respective p-value maps comparing distorted and undistorted data sets. Yellow indicates non-significant p-values. Red colors present a scale of FDR corrected p-values (below the threshold). Note that although the deformations and the extent of the deformed regions (pointed by arrows) are subtle, they were successfully detected by our algorithm.

3.3   STG in First Episode Schizophrenic Patients

We used manual segmentation of the left and right STGs in 19 patients diagnosed with first episode schizophrenia and 14 matched normal controls originally acquired for a brain volumetric study [23]. Examples of the left STG of some of the subjects are shown in Fig. 4.

We generated the mean shapes of the patients and NC data sets for the left and right STG. We computed a t-test comparing the two populations at each point on the mean shape's surface. The resulting p-values were thresholded at an

FDR of 0.05. Qualitative results are shown in Figs. 5. We were able to detect and locate morphological differences between populations in the left STG. Moreover, most of the shape differences in the STG were detected in the planum temporale (Fig. 5a, in red) and the heschl gyrus (Fig. 5a, in green). These findings are in line with the recent literature on volumetric studies in schizophrenia [24].

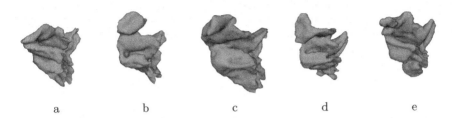

a   b   c   d   e

Fig. 4. Left STG of first episode schizophrenics. A few examples demonstrating the complexity of this structure and its variability among patients.

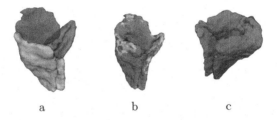

a   b   c

Fig. 5. STG in first episode schizophrenia. (a) Left STG composed of its substructures: planum temporale (red), heschl's gyrus (green), rest of the STG (yellow); (b) p-value map of the left STG comparing schizophrenics and NCs; (c) p-value map of the right STG Left for the same populations. Red indicates non-significant p-values, green-to-purple colors present a scale of p-vales below the 0.05 FDR threshold. Note that the right STG shows no differences.

3.4   Caudate Nucleus in Schizotypal Personality Disorder (SPD) Patients

MR brain scans of 61 women, 32 SPD patients and 29 NC, were manually segmented to extract the caudate nucleus in the left and right hemispheres [25] . Statistically significant morphological differences have been detected in the right caudate using the proposed algorithm (Fig. 6). Our results in these subjects are comparable to the manual volumetric measures as well as to the shape statistics obtained from using spherical harmonic-point distribution model (SPHARM-PDM) methodology [25].

Fig. 6. Caudate nucleus in SPD patients. (a,c) Lateral and medial views of the mean right caudate along with the respective p-value maps. Red indicates non-significant p-values. Yellow-to-blue indicate p-value below a 0.05 FDR. (b,d) Signed differences between the SPD patients and the NC. Negative values (deflation) are in red, positive values (inflation) in dark blue.

4   Discussion

We presented a robust and simple framework to perform shape analysis for population studies. The core of the method is a novel-level set algorithm based on the modified Hausdorff distance for shape morphing.

Our experiments on synthetic data show the ability of the method to detect small deformations of complex shapes such as the striatum. Very few boundary based methods are able to address such convoluted shapes and, as far as we know, have not been tested thoroughly on synthetic data. In addition, we were able to find shape differences between patients and their controls in the left STG and the right caudate which are consistent with the prior finding based on manual segmentation. Finally, while we acknowledge that the geodesics upon the shape ensemble manifolds are only roughly approximated by the modified Hausdorff distances our experiments show that in practice they can be used as accurate and reliable measures to perform population studies.

References

1. Cates, J.E., Fletcher, P.T., Styner, M.A., Hazlett, H.C., Whitaker, R.T.: Particle-Based Shape Analysis of Multi-object Complexes. In: Metaxas, D., Axel, L., Fichtinger, G., Székely, G. (eds.) MICCAI 2008, Part I. LNCS, vol. 5241, pp. 477–485. Springer, Heidelberg (2008)
2. Chen, T., Vemuri, B., Rangarajan, A., Eisenschenk, S.: Group-wise point-set registration using a novel cdf-based havrda-charvt divergence. International Journal of Computer Vision 86, 111–124 (2010)
3. Kurtek, S., Klassen, E., Ding, Z., Jacobson, S., Jacobson, J., Avison, M., Srivastava, A.: Parameterization-invariant shape comparisons of anatomical surfaces. IEEE Trans. Med. Imaging 30, 849–858 (2011)
4. Shen, L., Farid, H., McPeek, M.A.: Modeling 3-dimensional morphological structures using spherical harmonics. Evolution 63, 1003–1016 (2009)
5. Styner, M., Lieberman, J., Pantazis, D., Gerig, G.: Boundary and medial shape analysis of the hippocampus in schizophrenia. Medical Image Analysis, 197–203 (2004)
6. Thompson, P., et al.: Mapping hippocampal and ventricular change in alzheimer disease. NeuroImage 22, 1754–1766 (2004)

7. Styner, M., et al.: Statistical shape analysis of neuroanatomical structures based on medial models. Medical Image Analysis 7, 207–220 (2003)

8. Yushkevich, P.A., Zhang, H., Gee, J.C.: Continuous medial representation for anatomical structures. Medical Image Analysis 25, 1547–1564 (2006)

9. Mangin, J., et al.: Brain morphometry using 3D moment invariants. Medical Image Analysis 8, 187–196 (2004)

10. Niethammer, M., Reuter, M., Wolter, F.-E., Bouix, S., Peinecke, N., Koo, M.-S., Shenton, M.E.: Global Medical Shape Analysis Using the Laplace-Beltrami Spectrum. In: Ayache, N., Ourselin, S., Maeder, A. (eds.) MICCAI 2007, Part I. LNCS, vol. 4791, pp. 850–857. Springer, Heidelberg (2007)

11. Dubuisson, M., Jain, A.: A modified hausdorff distance for object matching. In: ICPR, vol. 1, pp. 566–568 (1994)

12. Osher, S., Sethian, J.A.: Fronts propagating with curvature-dependent speed: Algorithms based on Hamilton-Jacobi formulations. Journal of Computational Physics 79, 12–49 (1988)

13. Bronstein, A.M., Bronstein, M.M., Kimmel, R., Mahmoudi, M., Sapiro, G.: A gromov-hausdorff framework with diffusion geometry for topologically-robust non-rigid shape matching. International Journal of Computer Vision 89, 266–286 (2010)

14. Charpiat, G., Faugeras, O., Keriven, R., Maurel, P.: Statistics and Analysis of Shapes: Approximations of Shape Metrics and Application to Shape Warping and Empirical Shape Statistics. Krim, H., Yezzi Jr., A. (eds.) (2006)

15. Memoli, F., Sapiro, G.: A theoretical and computational framework for isometry invariant recognition of point cloud data. Foundations of Computational Mathematics 5, 313–347 (2005)

16. Nichols, T., Hayasaka, S.: Controlling the familywise error rate in functional neuroimaging: A comparative review. Stat. Meth. Med. Research 12, 419–446 (2003)

17. Ashburner, J., Friston, K.J.: Voxel-based morphometry – the methods. NeuroImage 11, 805–821 (2000)

18. Jenkinson, M., Smith, S.: A global optimisation method for robust affine registration of brain images. Medical Image Analysis 5, 143–156 (2001)

19. Chan, T., Vese, L.: Active contours without edges. IEEE Transactions on Image Processing 10, 266–277 (2001)

20. Pohl, K., et al.: Using the logarithm of odds to define a vector space on probabilistic atlases. Medical Image Analysis 11, 465–477 (2007)

21. Sabuncu, M.R., Yeo, B.T.T., Van Leemput, K., Vercauteren, T., Golland, P.: Asymmetric Image-Template Registration. In: Yang, G.-Z., Hawkes, D., Rueckert, D., Noble, A., Taylor, C. (eds.) MICCAI 2009, Part I. LNCS, vol. 5761, pp. 565–573. Springer, Heidelberg (2009)

22. Gao, Y., Bouix, S.: Synthesis of realistic subcortical anatomy with known surface deformations. In: MICCAI Workshop on Mesh Processing in Medical Image Analysis (October 2012)

23. Hirayasu, Y., et al.: Lower left temporal lobe MRI volumes in patients with first-episode schizophrenia compared with psychotic patients with first-episode affective disorder and normal subjects. Amer. J. Psychiatry 155, 1384–1391 (1998)

24. Shenton, et al.: A review of MRI findings in schizophrenia. Schizophrenia Research 49, 1–52 (2001)

25. Levitt, et al.: Shape abnormalities of caudate nucleus in schizotypal personality disorder. Schizophr Res. 110, 127–139 (2009)

Group-Valued Regularization
for Analysis of Articulated Motion

Guy Rosman[1,*], Alex M. Bronstein[2], Michael M. Bronstein[3],
Xue-Cheng Tai[4], and Ron Kimmel[5]

[1] Dept. of Computer Science
Technion - IIT
Haifa 32000 Israel
{rosman,ron}@cs.technion.ac.il
[2] School of Electrical Engineering
Faculty of Engineering
Tel Aviv University
Ramat Aviv 69978, Israel
bron@eng.tau.ac.il
[3] Institute of Computational Science, Faculty of Informatics
Universitá della Svizzera Italiana
CH - 6904 Lugano, Switzerland
michael.bronstein@usi.ch
[4] Dept. of Mathematics
University of Bergen
Johaness Brunsgate 12
Bergen 5007 Norway
tai@mi.uib.no

Abstract. We present a novel method for estimation of articulated motion in depth scans. The method is based on a framework for regularization of vector- and matrix- valued functions on parametric surfaces.

We extend augmented-Lagrangian total variation regularization to smooth rigid motion cues on the scanned $3D$ surface obtained from a range scanner. We demonstrate the resulting smoothed motion maps to be a powerful tool in articulated scene understanding, providing a basis for rigid parts segmentation, with little prior assumptions on the scene, despite the noisy depth measurements that often appear in commodity depth scanners.

Keywords: Parameteric Surfaces, Motion Segmentation, Articulated Motion.

1 Introduction

Depth scanners are becoming an ever-more prevalent data source for computer vision applications. Interpretation of such data is still a challenge, especially

---

* This research was supported by the European Community's FP7- ERC program, grant agreement no. 267414.

A. Fusiello et al. (Eds.): ECCV 2012 Ws/Demos, Part I, LNCS 7583, pp. 52–62, 2012.

given the wide range of environments and applications in which depth sensors are expected to be used. While many algorithms classify objects in range data (see [8,23,33,17] and references therein), obtaining meaningful cues for the general settings in an efficient way is still a topic of intense research.

Motion cues are important for scene understanding [6,14]. Obtaining a meaningful dense motion descriptor for $3D$ data is an important preprocessing step for the understanding of arbitrary scenes. Articulated motion is one specific type of motion, common in many natural and man-made scenes. Detection and understanding of articulated motion have therefore attracted the attention of numerous research efforts, see [1,41,2,29,26] for a few examples.

When treating rigid and articulated motion, Lie-group theory provides us with a well-motivated representation of motion. Lie-groups have been used extensively for motion interpretation [27,38,22,29], tracking [37,35], and modeling [7,18], among other uses. It is only natural to use them as a dense motion descriptor to be used in the understanding process of $3D$ motions. While motion vectors alone can also be used to represent the *scene flow* [42], the *overparameterized* [25,30] representation we favor leads naturally to interpretation of the scene in terms of piecewise rigid motions, as we demonstrate in this paper.

In this paper, we present a novel approach for characterizing articulated motion obtained from depth sensors, without assuming an explicit skeletal model. Instead, we favor an implicit approach, aggregating motion cues in local neighborhoods in a bottom-up manner. While a similar approach, could have been to perform diffusion of the Lie-group elements using the Lie-algebra, as suggested, for example in [29], this is done by an explicit approach to the evolution of the smoothing process, which is inherently slow. In this paper we try to alleviate the limitations associated with such approaches.

We do so using a regularization method that is based on an augmented-Lagrangian scheme for group-valued regularization on parameteric surfaces such as depth scans. This algorithm extends our recent work on fast total variation regularization of group-valued images [31], modifying it algorithm to handle smoothness on parameteric surfaces.

Using this regularization, we are able to create a scale-space re-interpreting the scene-flow in terms of local rigid transformations. Experiments shown in this paper demonstrate the usefulness of the resulting images for motion segmentation from noisy depth data.

The smoothing process we describe and associated preprocessing steps are highly parallelizable, lending themselves to real-time implementation on parallel hardware such as *graphics processing units* (GPUs), as shown for example, in [31]. The results obtained demonstrate the method's usefulness in identifying components of piecewise-rigid motion in real-life, noisy, range data.

Contribution. The contribution of the paper is two-fold: a. We extend the framework of fast TV regularization to parametric surfaces, both for the scalar and the group-valued case. b. Based on this framework, we describe a fast method to obtain and segment rigid motion cues from depth-image videos, demonstrating its effectiveness on real depth videos.

In Section 2 we describe the model and functional behind our method. The algorithm and relevant numerical schemes are given in Section 3. Finally, we demonstrate the results of our method in Section 4, and discuss the results and potential uses in Section 5.

2   Model Description

We now describe our setting and model, and the resulting functional. We are given a depth video of an object undergoing articulated motion so that most of the object's visible surface is composed of rigidly moving parts. These parts are connected by joints, for which the motion is merely assumed to be smooth. At each frame in the sequence, we have a depth image of the object, with subsequent frames differing by small, piecewise-rigid motion. For an arbitrary depth video, a predetermined articulated skeleton cannot be assumed at this low-level vision phase. Instead, we propose to obtain a strong cue for detecting rigidly moving parts by spatially regularizing the observed motion in a piecewise-rigid manner. Rigid motions can be described by the elements of the *Lie-group* $SE(3)$, the Lie-group of rigid transformations in $\mathbb{R}^3$. We expect each point to be loosely associated with a local rigid motion, and wish to smooth the field of *motion particles* in the $3D$ scene. We therefore define our motion description by a group-valued function $u(x) \in SE(3)$, where x denotes a point on the surface of the object at one frame. The resulting piecewise-smooth $SE(3)$ image is highly informative, and in many cases allows straightforward segmentation of the motion, without using data-driven classifiers [3] or growing the parts in a bottom-up manner and letting motion models compete [2,12].

2.1   The Special-Euclidean Group $SE(3)$

Lie-groups are algebraic groups endowed with a manifold structure. Their structure allows us to discuss smoothness of motion parameters in a well-defined manner. We refer the reader to standard literature on the topic for an in-depth discussion [15]. Because of the group nature of $SE(3)$, the tangent plane at each point on the Lie-group can be mapped onto the identity element's tangent plane, allowing us to define a linear space uniformly throughout the group. This space, the *Lie-algebra* associated with a Lie-group, allows us to define differentiation on the Lie-group.

Specifically, we look at the group of rigid $3D$ motions, the *special-Euclidean* group $SE(3)$,

$$SE(3) = \left\{ (\mathbf{Rt}) \,|\, \mathbf{R} \in \mathbb{R}_{3\times3}, \mathbf{R}^T\mathbf{R} = \mathbf{I}, \mathbf{t} \in \mathbb{R}^3 \right\}, \tag{1}$$

and a map u from points on the object surface onto an embedding of $SE(3)$ in $\mathbb{R}^{12}$. This map will be regularized by minimizing the functional we now describe.

2.2   Group-Valued Regularization on Parametric Surfaces

The functional we wish to minimize should describe the irregularity of the motion field in terms of the scanned $3D$ surface with two or more poses. Since our input is a range image, it makes sense to use the $2D$ image domain as the integration domain. Our notion of smoothness, however, should be defined in terms of the $3D$ surface tangent plane. Thus, the regularization term we seek is intimately linked to the problem of image processing for images defined on parametric surfaces [34,19,40]. The measure of smoothness of the associated locally-rigid motion should take into account the geometry of the $3D$ surface. We therefore take the *total variation* (TV, [32])

$$E_S(u) = \int_{\Omega \in \mathbb{R}^2} \|\nabla_\mathcal{M} u\| d\Omega, \tag{2}$$

to be our measure of regularity, defined in terms of $\nabla_\mathcal{M}$, the gradient of the function u on the surface itself. For vector-valued functions, we denote by $\|\nabla u\|$ the Frobenius norm of the Jacobian matrix $\left(\frac{\partial u_i}{\partial x_j}\right)_{ij}$. In the case where u is a Lie-group matrix whose elements are isometries, there is justification to use the embedding space gradient norm $\|\nabla u\|$ and not the group's intrinsic regularity measure $\|u^{-1}\nabla u\|$.

We note that expressing the gradient on the surface in terms of the parameter-ization plane is relatively simple given the *first fundamental form* of the surface (see for example, [13], page 102, or the supplementary notes).

In addition, we also require a data term. The simplest data term in use is the least squares fitting term,

$$E_D = \int_{\Omega \in \mathbb{R}^2} \|u - u_0\|^2 d\Omega = \int_{\Omega \in \mathbb{R}^2} \|u_0^{-1} u - Id\|^2 d\Omega, \tag{3}$$

where $\|\cdot\|$ is the Frobenius norm, and u_0 is the given input function, for example a local motion estimate given by local *iterative closest point* search [4,9], or by least-square fitting a rigid motion model to a deformation result based on other algorithms [5,24]. We note that by inverting u_0, this distance is the same as the distance often used between $SE(3)$ elements [20]. We suggest an efficient non-rigid registration method in Subsection 3.3, which can be easily extended to include robust data terms.

The overall cost function we intend to minimize will be of the form

$$\min_{u \,\in\, SE(3)} E_S(u) + \lambda E_D(u), \tag{4}$$

where λ describes the relative strength of the data term. We describe in Section 3 a fast minimization algorithm for this cost function.

3   Numerical Methods

We now try to minimize the overall cost function (4). In order to enforce the constraint $u \in SE(3)$ we use an auxiliary variable v such that $v = u, v \in$

$SE(3)$. We obtain $v = u$ using an augmented Lagrangian term added to the cost function. The resulting constraint causes the optimization with respect to v to become a projection operation per-pixel, using *singular value decomposition* (SVD). This transforms the minimization problem into a saddle-point problem

$$\max_{\mu} \min_{v \,\in\, SE(3),\, u} \int_{\Omega} \|\nabla_{\mathcal{M}} u\| + \frac{r}{2}\|v - u\|^2 + \mu^T (v - u) + \|u - u_0\|^2 d\Omega \quad (5)$$

Unlike previous approaches for augmented Lagrangian TV regularization [36], our approach differs in the measure of smoothness we use. We note that while the update step for v comes from minimizing the cost function, it is highly linked to the intuitive choice of updating u and then projecting it, as well as to optimization by proximal operators [11], and can be made provably convergent with minor modifications, as shown in [31]. We now modify the augmented Lagrangian TV framework for the smoothness term described in (2).

3.1   Augmented Lagrangian TV Optimization of Vector Valued Functions on Parametric Surfaces

Let us start with the simpler case of a general vectorial function u, and formulate an efficient iterative scheme for smoothing (in the TV sense) functions on a parametric surface. In our case, this surface will be obtained from a range scanner, and the parametrization domain will be the image plane with its coordinates system. In order to efficiently regularize images on parametric surfaces, we sample the parametrization domain on a Cartesian grid.

The scheme we present is based on the augmented Lagrangian TV optimization scheme [36]. We use an auxiliary variable p to describe the surface-domain gradient, rather than the image-domain gradient. That is, we add an auxiliary variable $p = J_{\mathcal{M}} \nabla u$, and optimize with respect to it using a shrinkage operator, similar to the image-domain TV case [36]. $J_{\mathcal{M}}$ denotes the Jacobian relating image coordinates and surface coordinates. We enforce the gradient constraint by adding an augmented Lagrangian term with Lagrange multipliers. We update u, p, and the Lagrange multiplier iteratively. For the vector-valued TV case, minimizing the functional now becomes a solution of the saddle-point problem

$$\max_{\mu_2} \min_{u, p} \int_{\Omega} \|p\| + \frac{r_2}{2}\|J_{\mathcal{M}} \nabla u - p\|^2 + \mu_2^T (J_{\mathcal{M}} \nabla u - p) + \lambda \|u - u_0\|^2 d\Omega, \quad (6)$$

where μ_2 is our Lagrange multiplier for the gradient constraint. The optimization of (6) with respect to u is given by a diffusion equation

$$-r_2 \operatorname{div} \left(J_{\mathcal{M}}^T (J_{\mathcal{M}} \nabla u - p) \right) + \operatorname{div} J_{\mathcal{M}}^T \mu_2 + 2\lambda (u - u_0) = 0. \quad (7)$$

Optimization with respect to p can be expressed in closed form [39,36] by a shrinkage operator,

$$p = \max \left(0, 1 - \frac{1}{r_2} \frac{1}{\|w\|} \right) w, w = J_{\mathcal{M}} \nabla u - \frac{\mu_2}{r_2}, \quad (8)$$

Finally, updating μ_2 is given according to the augmented Lagrangian method [28,16].

3.2   Augmented Lagrangian Regularization of Group-Valued Maps on Parametric Surfaces

Using an augmented Lagrangian term in order to enforce the constraint of $u = v \in SE(3)$, the overall functional reads

$$\max_{\mu,\mu_2} \min_{\substack{v \in SE(3) \\ u}} \int_\Omega \left[\begin{array}{c} \|p\| + \frac{r}{2}\|u - v\|^2 + \mu^T(u - v)+ \\ \frac{r_2}{2}\|J_\mathcal{M}\nabla u - p\|^2 + \mu_2^T(J_\mathcal{M}\nabla u - p) + \lambda\|u - u_0\|^2 \end{array} \right] d\Omega. \quad (9)$$

Minimization with respect to u is done as in the same as in subsection 3.1. Minimization with respect to p is given by equation 8. We update μ according to the augmented Lagrangian method [28,16].

Optimization with respect to v is using the same projection operator per-pixel as in [31]. Looking at optimization with respect to v, we obtain

$$\underset{v \in SE(3)}{\operatorname{argmin}} \frac{r}{2}\|v - u\|^2 + \langle \mu, u - v \rangle = \underset{v \in SE(3)}{\operatorname{argmin}} \frac{r}{2}\left\|v - \left(\frac{\mu}{r} + u\right)\right\|^2 = \operatorname*{Proj}_{SE(3)}\left(\frac{\mu}{r} + u\right), \quad (10)$$

where $\operatorname{Proj}_{SE(3)}(\cdot)$ denotes the orthogonal projection operator onto $SE(3)$, given by an SVD operation, setting the singular values of v to all-ones.

An algorithmic description of the resulting scheme is given as Algorithm 1. For further numerical details, the reader is referred to the supplementary material.

Algorithm 1. Fast TV regularization of group-valued images on parametric surfaces

---

1: **for** $k = 1, 2, \ldots$, until convergence **do**
2:    Update $u^k(x)$, according to (7).
3:    Update $p^k(x)$, according to (8).
4:    Update $v^k(x)$, by projection onto the matrix group, using SVD.
5:    Update $\mu^k(x), \mu_2^k(x)$, according to the augmented Lagrangian scheme.
6: **end for**

3.3   Estimating Non-rigid Motion in Depth Videos

In order to estimate the non-rigid motion occuring between two subsequent time-frames of a depth video, we first apply a simple non-rigid registration process, similar to the approach suggested by Li et al. [21], followed by the estimation of a locally-rigid motion model, as described in the supplementary material. In general, any motion estimation method can be used.

Since the overall motion field can involve both piecewise rigid and non-rigid motion components, and because of the noisy scan results often obtained from commodity depth scanners, the estimated instantaneous motion is quite noisy, as can be seen in Figure 2. The motion field should be post-processed so as to obtain locally-rigid interpretation. This can be obtained by the regularization process described in Section 3.2. The overall algorithm is summarized as Algorithm 2.

During the third step of the algorithm different λ values can be used so as to obtain a scale-space of motion interpretation, for detecting salient candidates for rigid parts, or as features for learning-based motion segmentation.

Algorithm 2. Regularized estimation of rigid motion from depth video

---

1: **for** $k = 1, 2, \ldots$, until convergence **do**
2:      Estimate motion field between depth frames according to a non-rigid ICP.
3:      Estimate $u_0(x)$ at each point using least median squares fitting.
4:      Regularize $u_0(x)$ using Algorithm (1).
5: **end for**

---

4   Results

We now demonstrate the results of our algorithm on both synthetic and real data. In Figure 1, we demonstrate results based on a synthetic hand model undergoing motion. We used the non-rigid registration model to track the surface over several frames so as to obtain a sufficiently large motion. While the detected motion is not completely piecewise-rigid due to skinning artifacts, occlusions, etc, the fingers are detected quite well. Using a standard mean-shift algorithm on the log-coordinates of the rotation matrices, we obtain segmentation of the fingers and the phalanges that undergo motion.

In Figure 2, we demonstrate TV regularization of $SE(3)$ for several frame pairs in a depth sequence by a Kinect sensor. Visualization is done using log-coordinates of the rotation matrix. The resulting estimated rigid motion allows segmentation of body parts and finger phalanges. In Figure 3 we use the mean-shift clustering algorithm [10] on the $SE(3)$ images' projection onto the small rotations standard linearization basis in order to segment the main moving parts. Despite the simple choice of the segmentation algorithm, that does not take into account the geometry of the surface and linearizes the Lie-group in the simplest possible manner, the segmentation of the moving parts is clear. It is expected that utilizing geometric prior on the regions size will prevent artifacts such as

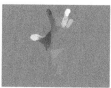

Fig. 1. TV regularization based on Equation (9) of an $SE3$-valued image placed on a rendered depth surface. Left-To-Right, Top-To-Bottom: An overlay of the two consecutive time-frames used to obtain motion estimation, the estimated and regularized $SE(3)$ images, and a resulting segmentation using mean-shift.

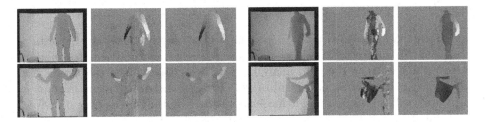

Fig. 2. TV regularization based on Equation (9) of an $SE3$-valued image given on a scanned depth surface. . Each row represents results on two different frames from a depth sequence. Left-To-Right, for each frame: An overlay of the two consecutive time-frames used to obtain motion estimation, the estimated $SE(3)$ measurement, and regularized image. Raw depth data is used to estimate the motion. The regularized $SE(3)$ image hints at joint locations for parts that were moving at the time the depth frames were taken. Note in the last example, using a slightly stronger regularization, a nonrigid object (a shirt) is still separated clearly from the arms.

Fig. 3. Segmentation based on mean-shift clustering of the $SE(3)$ image. Left-to-right: The motion between the two frames, the segmentation obtained using the raw estimated $SE(3)$, and the segmentation obtained using the regularized result, showing a segmentation of the moving limb parts.

Fig. 4. A scale-space obtained by changing the fidelity coefficient through the values $\lambda = 5, 2.5, 1.5, 0.8$

oversegmentation. In the examples shown here, QVGA resolution (320×240) was used. The estimation of motion coefficients takes in Matlab about 5 seconds on an Intel i3 CPU. The regularization is similar algorithmically to [31], which took about a tenth of a second to compute on GPU. Preliminary results support this efficiency claim.

5 Conclusions

In this paper we extended the notion of fast $SE(3)$-valued image regularization to parametric surfaces. This allowed us to selectively smooth articulated motion based on noisy depth data. In many cases this regularized representation can provide a partition of an object into rigid parts, as shown in several examples. In future work, we intend to further explore the resulting scale-space of $SE(3)$ images and their use for scene understanding and $3D$ object segmentation as well as investigate several priors and data terms.

References

1. Adiv, G.: Determining three-dimensional motion structure from optic flow generated by several moving object. IEEE Trans. PAMI 7(4), 384–401 (1985)
2. Anguelov, D., Koller, D., Pang, H.-C., Srinivasan, P., Thrun, S.: Recovering articulated object models from 3D range data. In: Proc. Conf. on Uncertainty in Artificial Intelligence, pp. 18–26. AUAI Press (2004)
3. Benhabiles, H., Lavoué, G., Vandeborre, J.-P., Daoudi, M.: Learning boundary edges for 3D-mesh segmentation. Comp. Graphics Forum (2011)
4. Besl, P.J., McKay, N.D.: A method for registration of 3D shapes. IEEE Trans. PAMI 14(2), 239–256 (1992)
5. Bronstein, A.M., Bronstein, M.M., Kimmel, R.: Generalized multidimensional scaling: a framework for isometry-invariant partial surface matching. Proc. Natl. Acad. Sci. USA 103(5), 1168–1172 (2006)
6. Brox, T., Rousson, M., Deriche Dr., R., Weickert, J.: Colour, texture, and motion in level set based segmentation and tracking. Image and Vision Computing 28(3), 376–390 (2010)
7. Celledoni, E., Owren, B.: Lie group methods for rigid body dynamics and time integration on manifolds. Computer Methods in Applied Mechanics and Engineering 19, 421–438 (1999)
8. Chen, H., Bhanu, B.: 3D free form object recognition in range images using local surface patches. Pattern Recognition Letters 28, 1252–1262 (2007)
9. Chen, Y., Medioni, G.: Object modelling by registration of multiple range images. Image Vision Comput. 10, 145–155 (1992)
10. Comaniciu, D., Meer, P.: Mean shift: A robust approach toward feature space analysis. IEEE Trans. PAMI 24, 603–619 (2002)
11. Combettes, P.L., Pesquet, J.-C.: Proximal splitting methods in signal processing (May 2010)
12. Cremers, D., Soatto, S.: Motion competition: A variational framework for piecewise parametric motion segmentation. IJCV 62(3), 249–265 (2005)
13. do Carmo, M.P.: Differential Geometry of Curves and Surfaces. Prentice-Hall (1976)
14. Fayad, J., Russell, C., de Agapito, L.: Automated articulated structure and 3D shape recovery from point correspondences. In: ICCV, pp. 431–438 (2011)
15. Hall, B.C.: Lie Groups, Lie Algebras,and Representations, An Elementary Introduction. Springer (2004)

16. Hesteness, M.R.: Multipliers and gradient methods. J. of Optimization Theory and Applications 4, 303–320 (1969)
17. Kim, E., Medioni, G.G.: 3D object recognition in range images using visibility context. In: IROS, pp. 3800–3807 (2011)
18. Kobilarov, M., Crane, K., Desbrun, M.: Lie group integrators for animation and control of vehicles. ACM Trans. Graph. 28(2), 1–14 (2009)
19. Lai, R., Chan, T.F.: A framework for intrinsic image processing on surfaces. Comput. Vis. Image Underst. 115, 1647–1661 (2011)
20. Larochelle, P.M., Murray, A.P., Angeles, J.: A Distance Metric for Finite Sets of Rigid-Body Displacements via the Polar Decomposition. Journal of Mechanical Design 129 (2007)
21. Li, H., Sumner, R.W., Pauly, M.: Global correspondence optimization for non-rigid registration of depth scans. Computer Graphics Forum 27(5) (July 2008)
22. Lin, D., Grimson, W., Fisher, J.: Learning visual flows: A Lie algebraic approach. In: CVPR, pp. 747–754 (2009)
23. Lo, T.-W.R., Siebert, J.P.: Local feature extraction and matching on range images: 2.5D SIFT. Comput. Vis. Image Underst. 113, 1235–1250 (2009)
24. Myronenko, A., Song, X.B.: Point-set registration: Coherent point drift. CoRR, abs/0905.2635 (2009)
25. Nir, T., Bruckstein, A.M., Kimmel, R.: Over-parameterized variational optical flow. IJCV 76(2), 205–216 (2008)
26. Paladini, M., Del Bue, A., Xavier, J.a., Agapito, L., Stošić, M., Dodig, M.: Optimal metric projections for deformable and articulated Structure-from-Motion. IJCV, 1–25 (July 2011)
27. Park, F.C., Bobrow, J.E., Ploen, S.R.: A Lie group formulation of robot dynamics. Int. J. Rob. Res. 14, 609–618 (1995)
28. Powell, M.J.: A method for nonlinear constraints in minimization problems. In: Optimization. Academic Press (1969)
29. Rosman, G., Bronstein, M.M., Bronstein, A.M., Kimmel, R.: Articulated motion segmentation of point clouds by group-valued regularization. In: Eurographics Workshop on 3D Object Retrieval (2012)
30. Rosman, G., Shem-Tov, S., Bitton, D., Nir, T., Adiv, G., Kimmel, R., Feuer, A., Bruckstein, A.M.: Over-Parameterized Optical Flow Using a Stereoscopic Constraint. In: Bruckstein, A.M., ter Haar Romeny, B.M., Bronstein, A.M., Bronstein, M.M. (eds.) SSVM 2011. LNCS, vol. 6667, pp. 761–772. Springer, Heidelberg (2012)
31. Rosman, G., Wang, Y., Tai, X.-C., Kimmel, R., Bruckstein, A.M.: Fast Regularization of Matrix-Valued Images. In: Fitzgibbon, A., Lazebnik, S., Perona, P., Sato, Y., Schmid, C. (eds.) ECCV 2012, Part III. LNCS, vol. 7574, pp. 173–186. Springer, Heidelberg (2012)
32. Rudin, L.I., Osher, S., Fatemi, E.: Nonlinear total variation based noise removal algorithms. Physica D Letters 60, 259–268 (1992)
33. Shotton, J., Fitzgibbon, A., Cook, M., Sharp, T., Finocchio, M., Moore, R., Kipman, A., Blake, A.: Real-Time human pose recognition in parts from single depth images (June 2011)
34. Spira, A., Kimmel, R.: Geometric curve flows on parametric manifolds. J. Comput. Phys. 223, 235–249 (2007)
35. Subbarao, R., Meer, P.: Nonlinear mean shift over Riemannian manifolds. IJCV 84(1), 1–20 (2009)
36. Tai, X.-C., Wu, C.: Augmented Lagrangian method, dual methods and split Bregman iteration for ROF model. In: SSVM, pp. 502–513 (2009)

37. Tuzel, O., Porikli, F., Meer, P.: Learning on Lie groups for invariant detection and tracking. In: CVPR (2008)
38. Žefran, M., Kumar, V., Croke, C.: On the generation of smooth three-dimensional rigid body motions. IEEE Transactions on Robotics and Automation 14(4), 576–589 (1998)
39. Wang, Y., Yang, J., Yin, W., Zhang, Y.: A new alternating minimization algorithm for total variation image reconstruction. SIAM J. Imag. Sci. 1(3), 248–272 (2008)
40. Wu, C., Zhang, J., Duan, Y., Tai, X.-C.: Augmented lagrangian method for total variation based image restoration and segmentation over triangulated surfaces. J. Sci. Comput. 50(1), 145–166 (2012)
41. Yacoob, Y., Davis, L.S.: Learned models for estimation of rigid and articulated human motion from stationary or moving camera. IJCV 36, 5–30 (2000)
42. Zhang, Y., Kambhamettu, C.: Integrated 3D scene flow and structure recovery from multiview image sequences. In: CVPR, vol. 2, p. 2674 (2000)

Drawing an Automatic Sketch of Deformable Objects Using Only a Few Images

Smit Marvaniya, Sreyasee Bhattacharjee,
Venkatesh Manickavasagam, and Anurag Mittal

Indian Institute of Technology Madras, India
{smit,amittal}@cse.iitm.ac.in,
{sreya.iit,venky9111}@gmail.com

Abstract. We propose a method to automatically extract a sketch of a common object structure present in a small set of real world weakly-labeled images. Applying a part-based deformable contour matching technique gives the location of repeatable contours. An initial deformable search strategy selects a set of salient, repeatable contours robust to a large range of non-rigid deformations. A contour completion technique based on a locally greedy bi-directional search strategy is adopted to merge the repeatable contour fragments for obtaining a complete shape. The output of our algorithm is used as an input to a sketch-based object-recognizer with results that are either better, or on par with those obtained with the ground truth sketches provided with the dataset.

Keywords: Salient Contours, Part-based Deformable Contour Matching, Contour Completion.

1 Introduction

Building a contour model using edge information is an important problem in computer vision that has received considerable attention from many researchers. In this paper, we propose a technique to extract a compact sketch of an object from a few training images. The object shape is allowed to vary under conditions such as non-rigid deformations, affine transformations and a cluttered background. However, we believe that the common object shares a similar geometrical structure across the training images. We intend to capture this common shape in terms of a rough sketch through a completely automated process. While most established methods [1, 2] obtain the training images from carefully chosen dataset elements, or are captured against a uniform background, we allow the system to automatically extract a set of training images from any resource including web-engines.

Popular methods rely on either part-based [3], region based [4] or a combination of both shape and region based cues [5]. Contour-based methods are attractive since it is well-known that humans are able to identify an object simply from its contour or shape. Furthermore, while the region-based approaches [6] perform well only on good quality images, learning-based approaches [1–3, 7] are becoming increasingly popular due to their ability to handle a wide range of deformations for object recognition. However, in most cases, the basic prerequisite of these approaches is a huge set of positive training

A. Fusiello et al. (Eds.): ECCV 2012 Ws/Demos, Part I, LNCS 7583, pp. 63–72, 2012.

images with annotated bounding boxes, except an appearance-based model proposed by Bagon et.al. [8]. This requirement may be expensive and hard to obtain. The weakly supervised learning based techniques [5, 9] typically perform well in terms of learning an object model from the data by indicating the presence of an instance from a category without specifying its exact location in the training images.

Our contour based deformable matching technique helps in extracting a common shape from a handful of weakly labeled images and can therefore be treated as a cost-effective alternative. Our multi-stage automatic sketching process first attempts to identify a non-trivial commonality from training images using FDCM [10], with a localization up to rough bounding boxes. The next step involves extracting a group of repeatable, salient contours which combined together represent almost the whole structure of the common object shape. The resultant rough sketch can be used as an input to any sketch-based object-recognizer [11–13] for object recognition. The entire process is described in Figure 1.

The main contributions of this paper are: 1) Proposing a completely automatic process for drawing a sketch of the common object from a set of weakly labeled data using only contour based cues. 2) Proposing an efficient contour matching technique, which can handle a cluttered environment, scale, orientation and view point variations to a certain extent. 3) Shortlisting some repeatable contours in a deformation invariant fashion based on a novel deformable matching technique proposed by Ravishankar et.al. [11].

The rest of the paper is organized as follows: Section 2 describes the process of extracting a set of salient contours and the process of localization up to rough bounding boxes is explained in Section 3. Section 4 illustrates the process of obtaining a set of repeatable contours and Section 5 elaborates on the mechanism for completing the repeatable salient contours using a bi-directional search strategy to obtain an initial model. Finally, the experimental results are shown in Section 6.

2   Extracting a Set of Salient Contours

Given a set of training images $\{I_1, ..., I_k\}$, we first resize them to a predefined standard width in order to reduce the effect of large scale variance. We use the Berkeley edge detector [14] to get the edge map of the images in the training set and then use hysteresis thresholding followed by an efficient contour grouping proposed by Zhu et. al. [15] for extracting a set of potential contour groups from the output edge map. The saliency of a contour is defined using the following three components:

1. **Length of a contour**: A contour should be sufficiently long to represent some meaningful feature. Small spurious contours are eliminated as noise. The threshold on the contour length is calculated based on the size of the image.
2. **Salient points on a contour**: The number of high curvature points on a contour is an important cue to represent the descriptive power of a contour. However, too many high curvature points close to each other indicate that the contour probably originated from a cluttered background or some other kind of noise.
3. **Complexity Measure**: Complexity of a salient contour gives information about its smoothness. It is defined as the sum of the supplementary inner angles between line segments constituting the salient contour. A less complex salient contour doesn't

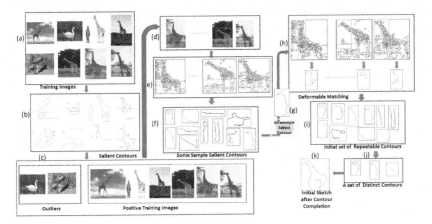

Fig. 1. (a) Training Images, (b) Salient Contours of the Training Images, (c) Classifying the training images, (d) Some example images with annotated bounding boxes obtained using method described in Section 3.1, (e) Binarized edge response of Berkeley edge detector on those images, (f) Examples of some salient contours extracted, (h) Explains the deformable matching technique adopted for getting the deformation component of the repeatability score of a salient contour using the 'neck' of a giraffe in (g), (i) Some examples of repeatable contours, a small set of distinct contours shown in (j) is obtained and used to draw an initial sketch shown in (k).

possess unique shape information while a highly complex one ends up making the system rigid.

Initially, a bunch of salient contours are identified using the first two saliency criteria. In order to reduce the effect of noise and partial matching, the salient contours are broken at every branch point into smaller fragments. We then calculate the Elastica measure [16, 17] at each branch point of the contour. Given two consecutive tangent directions, ϕ_1 and ϕ_2, the quantity $El(c_1, c_2) = 4(\varphi_1^2 \times \varphi_2^2 - \varphi_1 \times \varphi_2)$ provides a good approximation of the Elastica energy for curvature consistency at the junction of contours c_1 and c_2(see figure 3(b)). The pair of fragments having the minimum curvature inconsistency (min. Elastica cost) are then combined to resolve the branch point. The process is repeated till all the branch points in the shape have been resolved.

3   Identifying Repeated Contours Following a Deformable Matching Strategy across Images

Given a set of images represented by a collection of initial salient contours, the system attempts to extract a recurring shape structure (if any) across many of these image instances. The proposed system needs to be flexible enough to deal with the problem of occlusion, intra-class deformation and cluttered background. Our proposed matching strategy is based on the observation that, in some images at least some of the object parts are clearly visible. Clearly visible parts help the system to get the repeated salient contour set (wherever available). The salient contours of a particular image are represented at various levels of granularity - *Child Contours* and *Parent Contours*.

1. **Child contour**: The salient contours are represented in terms of a set of child contours. Child contours are constructed by first decomposing all the salient contours according to the first two saliency criteria mentioned in Section 2. Of those contours that do not satisfy both criteria, those which satisfy the length criterion alone are also considered as child contours.

2. **Parent contour**: Parent contours are formed by merging consecutive child contours, where the extent of merging is governed by the complexity measure. This process ends when the complexity measure reaches a predefined threshold Cp_{th}.

The similarity values between all pairs of images computed using the proposed matching strategy, explained in Section 3.1, are finally stored in our repository.

3.1   Matching Strategy

In order to retrieve a mutual commonality among images, the basic matching algorithm using edges as features should be tolerant to small deformations of shapes and fragmentations of edges. In this work, we use Fast Directional Chamfer Matching (FDCM) [18] which works much better in such a scenario. The local maxima for a given matched contour in an image are determined by non-maximal suppression and represented on a map overlaid on the image by the location of their mid and the two end-points. The FDCM score M_{dc}, evaluating the goodness of a match found in the image, is also retained for each subsegment. From such information, a rough scale and rotation angle of the match are also precomputed for later use.

Given a *Parent contour* P_k originating from an underlying image I, FDCM is used to extract a few smaller windows (if any) as a set of potential matched locations. We add Parent contour P_k into the Matched Contour Set MC by adding its constituent child contours. We then identify its nearest neighboring child contour c_j from MC_{P_k} in I. The relative location of c_j with respect to MC_{P_k} can extract a roughly similar region in I' (Figure 2), which is searched for a potential match for c_j using FDCM. A match is declared as reasonably good, if c_j satisfies the goodness measure $G(c_j)$. We again add the constituting child contours c_j of P_k into MC_{P_k} in I. The above steps are repeated until no nearest neighbor is found and the region in I' with respect to c_j is marked using dynamic programming to prevent it from being matched multiple times to the contour in the model image. The Matched Contour Set MC_{P_k} grows with each match.

$$G(c_{i,j}^{N_c}) = w_a \times M_{dc}(c_{i,j}^{N_c}) + w_b \times A(c_{i,j}^{N_c}) + w_c \times T(c_{i,j}^{N_c}) \tag{1}$$

$$A(c_{i,j}^{N_c}) = [1 - e^{-\frac{\triangle \theta_{i,j}}{180} * \pi}] \tag{2}$$

$$T(c_{i,j}^{N_c}) = \frac{\sqrt{((\triangle x_l)^2 + (\triangle y_l)^2)}}{D_l} \tag{3}$$

where N_c is the total number of child contours in I_i, $\triangle \theta_{i,j} = \theta'_{i,j} - \theta_{i,j}$ accounts for local angular inconsistency where $\theta_{i,j}$, $\theta'_{i,j}$ represents the relative spatial information in between two neighboring Child contours in I and I' respectively. $T(c_{i,j}^{N_c})$ represents a quantitative measure for translational inconsistency to evaluate the amount of deviation

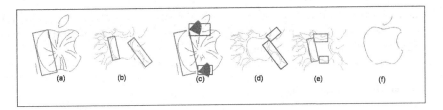

Fig. 2. (a) Model image highlighted with Parent Contour. (b) Target image shown with multiple matches with respect to parent contour. (c) Identifying the nearest child contour using bidirectional search technique. In (d) and (e), with respect to the already estimated locations for Parent contour, similar regions are explored in the target image to obtain a suitable match for the Child contour. The System failed to obtain a suitable match for Child contour in (d). The final Repeated Contours are shown in (f).

of the present position of $c_{i,j}^{N_c}$ from its estimated position with respect to its parent segment $c_{i,j+1}^{N_c}$ where D_l is the l_2-diagonal length of the image I.

$$SC(\mathcal{S}_{i,j}^{c_0}, P_k) = \frac{1}{n} \sum_n G(c_{i,j}^n) + \sum_m S_{const} \times w_m + M_{dc}(P_k) \times w_p \qquad (4)$$

where n and m are the number of matched and skipped child contours respectively, w_m is the defined as $\frac{1}{N_c}$, w_p is defined as $\frac{1}{N_{p_c}}$ where N_{p_c} is the number of Child contours constituting the parent contour P_k and S_{const} is the penalty for those child contours that do not find a match in the target image. We take $w_a=1$, $w_b=0.5$, w_c is set based on the image size. We repeat the above process for each parent contour and the Matched Contour Set MC of those with the minimum dissimilarity score is considered a Repeated Contour Set. Finally, the pairwise image score $PS(i,j)$ is defined as follows:

$$PS(i,j) = min\left\{SC(\mathcal{S}_{i,j}^{c_0}, P_k)\right\}_k \qquad (5)$$

3.2   Bounding Box for the Positive Images

For getting the bounding box for image I_i, we calculate the repeatable contours $RC(I_i)$ across the remaining training images in the training set which satisfy the repeatability threshold R_{th}.

$$RC(I_i) = \left\{Rep(c_{i,j}^{N_c}) > R_{th}\right\}_k \qquad (6)$$

where $Rep(c_{I_i,j}^n)$ is the repeatability of jth child contour in i^{th} image and $1 \leq i \leq k$. The bounding box for I_i is the tight bounding box for $RC(I_i)$.

4   Extracting a Set of Candidate Foreground Contours from Images

Due to the influence of noise and other external clutter, the prediction of the bounding box described above is rough. In order to reduce the effect of scale, images are cropped along their annotated bounding boxes and resized in a standardized frame for further consideration. Given an image, only salient contours lying within its cropped sub window are retained for describing it.

4.1 Repeatability of a Contour

The repeatability measure of a salient contour is defined using its Deformable Matching Score, a Shape Context [19] based similarity score and its length. In the following subsections we will discuss each of these components in detail.

Deformable Matching Score: In order to be repeatable, a salient contour c_j, originating from I_j should have a potential match at a similar location in another training image I_i. Unlike most existing methods that rely on rigid matching, we attempt to handle shapes that may undergo an amount of non-rigid deformation. In order to do so, we use the deformable *Fine Matching* strategy proposed by Ravishankar et.al. [11] to deal with a large set of non-rigid deformations and assign a deformable matching score to every salient contour from an image. The algorithm had shown to achieve among the best results on the standard ETHZ dataset, if only a sketch was available.

The tight bounding box around c_j extracts a patch P_j from I_j. Patch P_i from a similar location in the edge map of one of the remaining training images is found. While treating P_j as a model sketch of the contour, the deformable fine-matching strategy was adopted to find its good match in P_i. Each model contour is broken at high curvature points to be represented in terms of k-segments and a dynamic programming based matching strategy finds a suitable match in the target image. The resulting comprehensive matching cost(Q) takes into account inter-segment scale and orientation variations as well as edge strength and intra-segment bending deformations of the matched contour segment in P_i. Finally, the repeatability score R_j (e^{-Q}) is computed as a function of Q, ensuring a goodness measure for c_j. By its very definition, the value of Q always lies within a tractable range, ensuring an effective repeatability score for c_j.

Accumulated Weighted Repeatability Score (AWR Score): Any true object contour should have reasonably good matches in many training images which in turn would increase its repeatability score (defined above in Section 4.1). The accumulated weighted repeatability (AWR) score of a contour c_j is thus computed as follows:

$$R(c_j) = \sum_i ((\underbrace{1 - we^{-L(C_i')}}_{LC(i)}) \times SC_j(i) \times R_j(i)) \tag{7}$$

where $LC(i)$ works as a weighing term providing a positive bias to longer matched contours. $SC_j(i)$ computes a Shape Context [19] based similarity score obtained from matching c_j in i^{th} image. While R_j computes a goodness measure from a deformable point of view, the shape context based matching score aims to extract the amount of overall similarity between c_j and its match in each training image. These measures prove to be an effective combination for achieving a robust AWR score. A smaller group of salient contours having nonzero repeatability scores are shortlisted as C_{rep}.

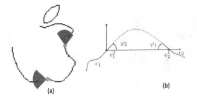

Fig. 3. (a) An example of the neighborhood search for contour completion using oriented sectors, (b) Contour continuity at the adjoining end points e_1^2 and e_2^1 of two contours c_1 and c_2 is measured using Elastica completion cost

However, a contour completion strategy is required to verify and merge the potential candidate contours to extract a fully (or mostly) complete sketch for an object category.

5   Contour Completion Using Neighborhood Search

In order to evaluate the relative structural configurations of a set of salient contours $\mathcal{C}_I (\in \mathcal{C}_{rep})$ originating from I, we propose a deformable contour completion that results in a sub-sequence of contours from $\mathcal{C}_I$. Given a repeatable primary contour c originating from an image I, a bi-directional search process (redrawn from Ravishankar et.al [11] as shown in Figure 3(a)) explores neighborhoods at both end points of a contour in parallel. In a one-Vs-many matching strategy, if there is a similar spatial contour layout observed in many training images, we declare that contour extension to be valid. The entire contour chain is built in steps. The comprehensive compatibility score corresponding to the goodness of an extended contour is dependent on its length, curvature continuity at the connections computed using Elastica Completion cost [16, 17] and an average repeatability score computed as follows:

$$CC(c_1, c_2) = El(c_1, c_2) \times \frac{L(c_1)}{(L(c_1) + L(c_2))} \times R_{mean}(c_1, c_2) \qquad (8)$$

where, $CC(c_1, c_2)$ evaluates the goodness score at the connection point of c_1 and c_2. In the case that there are multiple candidates for extension, we follow a locally greedy approach to choose the locally best neighbor for merging (Figure 3(b)). The search process at both its end points is continued until we reach a stage where there is no reasonably compatible neighbor to extend it further. A similar iterative process is repeated until $\mathcal{C}_I$ is empty. However at this stage it would be unrealistic to assume that only one complete contour would be able to cover the entire object shape. In contrast, we may land up achieving a set (S) of contour chains. Initiated with the highest repeatable contour chain, contours are iteratively merged with all the other elements of S if their relative spatial configuration is mostly similar in many images.

6   Experimental Results

Given a user-specified object category, we performed experiments using different number (n) of training images. We conducted tests on automatically downloaded images

Fig. 4. Some results using a small training set of five images, taken from ETHZ dataset

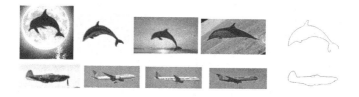

Fig. 5. Some results using a small training set of four images, taken from Caltech101 dataset

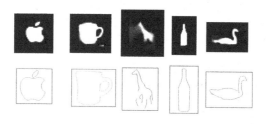

Fig. 6. Our results are shown in the second row

from a search engine and also on images from the ETHZ [20]/Caltech101 dataset. The comparative study is reported on the ETHZ dataset which has different classes of objects: Apple logo (40), Bottle (48), Giraffe (87), Mug (48) and Swan (32). The objects in the images are at various scales, orientations, illumination changes and a substantial amount of intra-class variations which make it a difficult dataset to work on. For each value of n in the range 4-10, results of some experiments on five training images of each category chosen from the ETHZ dataset and on four training images from Caltech101 dataset are shown in Figures 4 and 5 respectively. As seen in Figure 6, the sketch obtained by Bagon et.al [8] loses important information in the deformable parts of the object, such as giraffe's legs and swan's beak, while we are able to obtain such details due to a *deformable* approach.

The best extracted sketch is treated as the output of our system. The parameters used to obtain such a sketch are set independent of the image category. A sketch obtained from a particular iteration was used for object recognition using the algorithm of Ravishankar et.al [11] on the ETHZ dataset and the corresponding detection rate was used to evaluate the quality of the sketch. Table 1 shows the detection rates at 0.4 and 0.3 FPPI averaged over 100 iterations. We have also referred to other state of the art results for completeness. However, the important observation is that the same algorithm proposed by Ravishankar et.al [11] sometimes performs better than the original sketches due to some additional information extracted by our system. In other cases, the performance achieved by Ravishankar et.al using some hand-drawn sketches remains the same. Our system's improved performance on the giraffe category is due to the more complete sketch obtained by it. It was partly successful in obtaining 'legs' that enabled it to achieve a better result, rather than by using the ground truth model provided along with the dataset. We have achieved a detection rate of 93.4% at a FPPI as low as 0.1 on giraffe images. The results on swan category were again marginally better due to the better sketches obtained by our system. We allowed it to include some outliers at random so that its robustness to outliers would systematically evolve(ref. Table 1).

Table 1. Comparison of detection rates of objects at 0.4 FPPI / 0.3 FPPI

Ref	Applelogo	Bottle	Giraffe	Mug	Swan
Ravishankar et al. [11]	97.7/95.5	92.7/90.9	93.4/91.2	95.3/93.7	96.9/93.9
Lu et al. [13]	92.5/92	95.8/95.8	92.0/86.2	85.4/83.3	93.8/93.8
Zhu et al. [21]	80.0/80.0	92.9/92.9	68.1/68.1	74.2/64.5	82.4/82.4
Riemenschneider et al. [22]	93.3/93.3	97.0/97.0	81.9/79.2	86.3/84.6	92.6/92.6
Our System	97.7/97.7	92.7/90.9	93.4/93.4	95.8/95.8	96.87/96.87

7 Conclusion

We have demonstrated a method for drawing an automatic sketch from a very small set of training images that may have outliers. Such a sketch was found to be effective for object recognition. Apart from a visually appealing output, our work can form a part of a complete object recognition system that can automatically find objects in images obtained using a text query from a search engine.

References

1. Ferrari, V., Jurie, F., Schmid, C.: From images to shape models for object detection. International Journal of Computer Vision 87(3), 284–303 (2010)
2. Srinivasan, P., Zhu, Q., Shi, J.: Many-to-one contour matching for describing and discriminating object shape. In: CVPR (2010)
3. Felzenszwalb, P., Girshick, R., McAllester, D., Ramanan, D.: Object detection with discriminatively trained part-based models. IEEE Transactions on Pattern Analysis and Machine Intelligence 32(9), 1627–1645 (2010)
4. Todorovic, S., Ahuja, N.: Extracting subimages of an unknown category from a set of images. In: CVPR, pp. 927–934 (2006)
5. Lee, Y.J., Grauman, K.: Shape Discovery from Unlabeled Image Collections. In: CVPR (2009)
6. Felzenszwalb, P.F., Huttenlocher, D.P.: Pictorial structures for object recognition. International Journal of Computer Vision 61(1), 55–79 (2005)
7. Wu, B., Nevatia, R.: Simultaneous object detection and segmentation by boosting local shape feature based classifier. In: ICCV, pp. 1–8 (2007)
8. Bagon, S., Brostovski, O., Galun, M., Irani, M.: Detecting and sketching the common. In: 2010 IEEE Conference on Computer Vision and Pattern Recognition (CVPR), pp. 33–40 (2010)
9. Prest, A., Schmid, C., Ferrari, V.: Weakly supervised learning of interactions between humans and objects. IEEE Trans. Pattern Anal. Mach. Intell. 34(3), 601–614 (2012)
10. Liu, M.Y., Tuzel, O., Veeraraghavan, A., Chellappa, R.: Fast directional chamfer matching. In: CVPR, pp. 1696–1703 (2010)
11. Ravishankar, S., Jain, A., Mittal, A.: Multi-stage Contour Based Detection of Deformable Objects. In: Forsyth, D., Torr, P., Zisserman, A. (eds.) ECCV 2008, Part I. LNCS, vol. 5302, pp. 483–496. Springer, Heidelberg (2008)
12. Bai, X., Latecki, L.J., Li, Q., Liu, W., Tu, Z.: Shape band: A deformable object detection approach. In: CVPR (2009)
13. Lu, C., Latecki, L.J., Adluru, N., Yang, X., Ling, H.: Shape guided contour grouping with particle filters. In: ICCV, pp. 1–8 (2009)
14. Martin, D., Fowlkes, C., Malik, J.: Learning to detect natural boundaries using local brightness, color and texture cues. IEEE Transactions on Pattern Analysis and Machine Intelligence 26(5), 530–549 (2004)
15. Zhu, Q., Song, G., Shi, J.: Untangling cycles for contour grouping. In: CVPR (2007)
16. Kokkinos, I., Yuille, A.: Inference and learning with hierarchical shape models. International Journal of Computer Vision, 1–25 (2010)
17. Mumford, D.: Elastica and computer vision. In: Bajaj, C.L. (ed.) Algebraic Geometry and its Applications. Springer, New York (1994)
18. Liu, M.Y., Tuzel, O., Veeraraghavan, A., Chellappa, R.: Fast directional chamfer matching. In: CVPR (2010)
19. Belongie, S., Puzhicha, J., Malik, J.: Shape matching and object recognition using shape contexts. IEEE Transactions. on Pattern Analysis and Machine Intelligence 24, 509–522 (2002)
20. Ferrari, V., Tuytelaars, T., Van Gool, L.: Object Detection by Contour Segment Networks. In: Leonardis, A., Bischof, H., Pinz, A. (eds.) ECCV 2006. LNCS, vol. 3953, pp. 14–28. Springer, Heidelberg (2006)
21. Zhu, Q.-H., Wang, L.-M., Wu, Y., Shi, J.: Contour Context Selection for Object Detection: A Set-to-Set Contour Matching Approach. In: Forsyth, D., Torr, P., Zisserman, A. (eds.) ECCV 2008, Part II. LNCS, vol. 5303, pp. 774–787. Springer, Heidelberg (2008)
22. Riemenschneider, H., Donoser, M., Bischof, H.: Using Partial Edge Contour Matches for Efficient Object Category Localization. In: Daniilidis, K., Maragos, P., Paragios, N. (eds.) ECCV 2010, Part V. LNCS, vol. 6315, pp. 29–42. Springer, Heidelberg (2010)

Superfaces:
A Super-Resolution Model for 3D Faces

Stefano Berretti, Alberto Del Bimbo, and Pietro Pala

University of Firenze, Italy

Abstract. Face recognition based on the analysis of 3D scans has been an active research subject over the last few years. However, the impact of the resolution of 3D scans on the recognition process has not been addressed explicitly yet being of primal importance after the introduction of a new generation of low cost 4D scanning devices. These devices are capable of combined depth/rgb acquisition over time with a low resolution compared to the 3D scanners typically used in 3D face recognition benchmarks. In this paper, we define a super-resolution model for 3D faces by which a sequence of low-resolution 3D scans can be processed to extract a higher resolution 3D face model, namely the *superface* model. The proposed solution relies on the Scaled ICP procedure to align the low-resolution 3D models with each other and estimate the value of the high-resolution 3D model based on the statistics of values of the low-resolution scans in corresponding points. The approach is validated on a data set that includes, for each subject, one sequence of low-resolution 3D face scans and one ground-truth high-resolution 3D face model acquired through a high-resolution 3D scanner. In this way, results of the super-resolution process are evaluated qualitatively and quantitatively by measuring the error between the superface and the ground-truth.

1 Introduction

In recent years, many approaches have been presented to support person recognition by the analysis of 3D face models. In this research area, many challenging issues have been successfully investigated, including 3D face recognition in the presence of non-neutral facial expressions [1, 2], occlusions [3], and missing data [4], to say a few. Typically, the proposed solutions are tested following well defined evaluation protocols on consolidated benchmark data sets that, in order to obtain a reasonable coverage of the many different traits and characteristics of the human face, include 3D face models from several persons differing in terms of gender, age, ethnicity, hair style and accessories (spectacles, nose rings, etc.). The resolution of the 3D face models changes across different data sets, but is always the same within one data set. The issues related to the resolution of the 3D face model and its impact on the recognition accuracy have not been addressed explicitly in the past. Nevertheless, the relevance of these issues is increasing, motivated by the introduction in the marketplace of a new generation of low cost 4D scanning devices (such as Microsoft® Kinect or Asus® Xtion PRO LIVE)

A. Fusiello et al. (Eds.): ECCV 2012 Ws/Demos, Part I, LNCS 7583, pp. 73–82, 2012.

that are capable of combined depth/rgb acquisition over time (30 fps) with a resolution of 18 ppi at a distance of about 30 inches from the scanning device. Evaluating the impact on the recognition accuracy of matching one low-res probe to a high-res gallery is certainly one issue, but an even more challenging issue addresses the study of models to reconstruct one super-resolution face image out of the many low-res depth frames acquired by the 4D scanner.

Formerly introduced for images, super-resolution is the process that aims at recovering one high-resolution image from a set of low-resolution images possibly altered by noise, blurring or geometric warping [5–9]. Approaches proposed in the literature that use super-resolution models in the specific context of 3D data can be grouped in two distinct classes: approaches that apply the super-resolution in the 2D space and then use multiple super-resoluted 2D image to reconstruct a super-resolution 3D object [10]; and approaches that operate directly in the 3D space by applying the super-resolution model on 3D data [11–14]. The approach proposed in [13] is conceived to operate on data provided by time-of-flight cameras. These are upsampled and denoised by using information from a high-resolution image of the same scene that is taken from a viewpoint close to the depth sensor. The denoising module exploits the relations between depth and intensity data, such as the joint occurrence of depth and intensity edges, and smoothness of geometry in areas of largely uniform color. Also the approach proposed in [12] targets processing of data provided by time-of-flight cameras. However, the proposed solution relies on an energy minimization framework that explicitly takes into account the characteristic of the sensor, the agreement of the reconstruction with the aligned low resolution maps and and a regularization term to cope with reconstruction of sparse data points. In general, the approaches that deal with 3D data representing multiple objects in complex scenes focus on the relevance of accurate reconstruction in correspondence to discontinuities of the depth value that are associated with object boundaries. This aspect is less relevant if the 3D data represent a single object with smooth surface such as a face. The approaches proposed in [11, 14] address the specific problem of super-resolution of facial models. In [11], a learning module is trained on high resolution 3D face models so as to learn the mapping between low-res data and high-res data. Given a new low-res face model the learned mapping is used to compute the high-res face model. Differently, in [14] the super-resolution process is modeled as a progressive resolution chain whose features are computed as the solution to a MAP problem.

In this paper we present a model to derive one super-resolution 3D face from several low-res depth images acquired through a Microsoft® Kinect scanner. The proposed approach develops on the super-resolution model proposed in [9] and combines three main processing modules, namely the *face detector*, the *face registration* and the *face sampler*. The face detector processes each frame acquired by the 4D scanner so as to detect and crop the region of the frame where the face is represented. These cropped faces are used to feed the face registration module that performs 3D alignment of all the cropped faces to the first one, used as template. In this way a layered representation is built which provides, for each point on the template several observation values. Based on the statistics of these observation values, the face sampler module resamples the data at a higher resolution.

To validate the proposed approach and estimate the accuracy of the computed superface models we set up a data set of heterogeneous face models, described in detail in Sect. 3.1, that includes, for each individual, one sequence of depth images acquired through a Microsoft® Kinect scanner as well as one high-resolution face model acquired through a 3dMD® scanner. In this way, the accuracy of the reconstructed superface model can be quantitatively measured by comparing the reconstructed model to the corresponding high-res model.

Hence, the contribution of this paper is twofold: we describe a model to extract one super-resolution 3D face model out of a sequence of several low-res depth facial images; we set up and give public access to a data set of heterogeneous face models to be used by researchers working on this topic. The paper is organized as follows: Problem statement and the adopted notation are defined in Sect. 2. The description of the modules for the detection of the facial region in the acquired depth frames, for pairwise alignment of facial data across different frames, and for resampling of facial data are described in Sect. 2.1, Sect. 2.2 and Sect. 2.3, respectively. Finally experimental results and conclusions are discussed in Sect. 3 and Sect. 4.

2   The Superface Model

In the literature, the super-resolution process is typically formalized as an inverse problem: The low resolution images are the observations from slightly different viewpoints of a high resolution image, the underlying scene. It should be noticed that the relative motion between the scene and the camera is a necessary prerequisite to guarantee that pixels in the low-res images represent new samples of the patches in the observed scene. No improvement on resolution (if any, only in terms of SNR) would be possible from images deriving from a fixed camera observing a static scene. Let $\Omega = [1, \ldots, N] \times [1, \ldots, M]$ and $\Phi = [1, \ldots, zN] \times [1, \ldots, zM]$ be the sampling grids of the low and high resolution images, being z a positive integer representing the resolution gain. The forward degradation model, describing the formation of the low-res images can be formalized as follows:

$$X_L^{(k)} = P_k(X_H) \quad k = 1, \ldots, K, \tag{1}$$

being $\left\{ X_L^{(k)} \right\}_{k=1}^{K}$ the set of K low-res images, X_H the high-res image and P_k the operator that maps the high-res image onto the coordinate system and sampling grid of the k-th low-res image. The mapping operated by P_k accounts for four main factors: i) the geometric transformation of X_H to the coordinates of the k-th low-res image $X_L^{(k)}$; ii) blurring introduced by the effect of the atmosphere and camera lens; iii) downsampling and iv) additive noise.

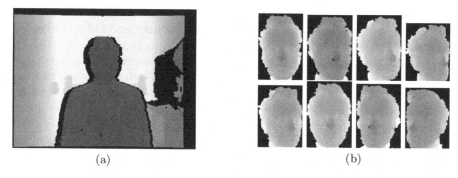

Fig. 1. (a) One sample frame (depth image) acquired by the scanning device. (b) Some cropped faces from the sequence of acquired frames.

The coordinate system of the high-res image X_H is aligned to the coordinate system of the first low-res image $X_L^{(1)}$. Computation of the geometric transformation that maps the coordinate systems of subsequent low-res images is operated by registration of the low-res images. This is accomplished using the Iterative Closest Point procedure, as described in Sect. 2.2.

2.1   Face Cropper

Low-res images correspond to frames (depth images) acquired by a Microsoft® Kinect scanner placed in front of a subject standing at a distance of approx 80 cm from the scanning device. It is assumed that the sequence of acquired frames represents the subject while s/he is slightly rotating the head to the left and right around the vertical axis (the neck). In Fig. 1(a) one sample frame out of the sequence of depth images acquired by the scanner is shown. Acquired frames are processed in order to crop each frame in correspondence to the face of the subject. For this purpose, the Face Tracking function supported by the device SDK has been used. Some representative frames output by the face cropping module for a sample sequence are shown in Fig. 1(b).

2.2   Face Registration

As anticipated before, computation of the geometric transformation that aligns low-res images to a common reference system is accomplished through a variant of the base Iterative Closest Point procedure [15] that jointly estimates the 3D rotation and translation parameters as well as the scaling one [16]. Let $\mathbf{x}_i^{(k)}$ be the 3D coordinates (x, y and the depth value z) of the i-th facial point in the k-th frame $X_L^{(k)}$. Registration of facial data represented in $X_L^{(k)}$ to data represented in the reference frame $X_L^{(1)}$ is accomplished by computing the similarity transform (translation, rotation and scaling) that best aligns the transformed data to the

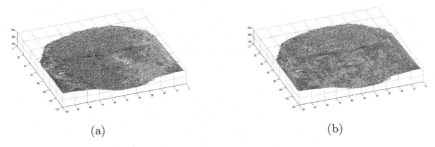

(a)   (b)

Fig. 2. Facial data acquired in two sample frames (one with red and one with blue colors) before (a) and after (b) the application of the adopted ICP procedure

data in the reference frame, that is:

$$\min_{\mathbf{R},\mathbf{S},\mathbf{t},p} \left(\sum_{i_1}^{N_k} \left\| \mathbf{RSx}_i^{(k)} + \mathbf{t} - \mathbf{x}_{p(i)}^{(1)} \right\| \right),$$ (2)

being $\mathbf{R}$ an orthogonal matrix, $\mathbf{S}$ a diagonal scale matrix, $\mathbf{t}$ a translation vector and $p : N_k \mapsto N_1$ a function that maps indexes of facial points across the the k-th and 1-st frames. The solution of Eq. (2), namely $\mathbf{R}^k, \mathbf{S}^k, \mathbf{t}^k$, is computed according to the procedure described in [16]. Fig. 2 shows facial data acquired in two sample frames before and after the application of the adopted ICP procedure.

2.3   Face Sampler

Once facial data from the different frames are aligned to the data in the first frame—used as template—then resampling by interpolation is operated. The goal of this module is to compute a high-res image on the uniformly spaced grid Φ. However, as a result of the alignment of the generic k-th frame to the first one under the effect of Eq. 2, samples on the originally uniform grid Ω distribute irregularly. Therefore, it is necessary to convert this non-uniform raster to a uniformly spaced grid, and this is performed by way of a scattered data interpolation model based on Delaunay triangulation [17, 18]. The interpolation model acts as a function Γ that given the set of N_k scattered points $\left\{ \mathbf{R}^k \mathbf{S}^k \mathbf{x}_i^{(k)} \mathbf{t}^k \right\}_{i=1}^{N_k}$ that are expected to sample a 2D surface in the 3D space, projects this dataset onto a reference plane Π (the (x, y) plane of the first frame) and then estimates the *height* value of the surface for a generic point $p \in \Pi$ within the convex hull of the projected dataset (see Fig. 3).

   In this way, given the super-resolution uniformly spaced grid Φ in Π, it is possible to estimate the value of the 2D surface for each point of Φ enclosed within the convex hull of the projection of the scattered points onto Π. This procedure is operated for each one of the N acquired depth frames so that for each point of Φ, N observations are available. The median of these observations is the estimated value of the superface on the super-resolution grid Φ.

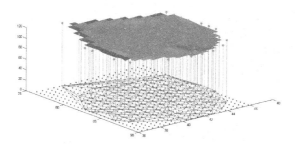

Fig. 3. Projection of data points of a generic frame onto the reference plane associated to the first frame distribute irregularly. Estimation of values of the underlying surface (shown in gray) on a regular grid (blue points) is accomplished by defining a Delaunay triangulation (red lines) on the projection of data points (red stars) and then interpolating the value of the surface within each triangle

3   Experimental Results

To the best of our knowledge, public data sets that provide, at the same time, sequences of low resolution face scans acquired with 3D consumer cameras, and high resolution 3D scans of the same subjects are not available. So, to bypass the lack of benchmark data and test our super-resolution approach, we constructed a proprietary data set which is released to the research community for comparative evaluations (see Sect. 3.1 for details). This data set in used in the tests reported in Sect. 3.2.

3.1   Data Set

In order to experiment the applicability and accuracy of our 3D super-resolution approach, we collected a test data set comprising low-resolution and high-resolution 3D scans. Currently, the data of 20 subjects are included while the subjects enrolling is still going on (we aim a number of about 50 subjects be comprised in the data set). In particular, for each person we captured:

- A 3D high-resolution face model acquired with the *3dMD* scanner. The model comprises a 3D mesh with about 40,000 vertices and 80,000 facets, and a texture stereo image with a resolution of 3341×2027 pixels. The geometry of the mesh is highly accurate with an average RMS error of about 0.2mm or better, depending on the exact pre-calibration and configuration. All 3D models are provided in VRML format;
- A depth-video sequence acquired with the *Kinect* camera. Videos are captured so that the person sits in front of the camera with the face at an approximate distance of 80cm from the sensor. During acquisition, the subject is also asked to slightly move the face around the yaw axis up to an angle

of about 60-70 degrees, so that both the left and right side of the face are visible to the sensor. This results in video sequences lasting approximately 10 to 15 seconds on average. Each depth video is released as a sequence of frames in PNG format and 16 bits gray scale.

The data are released in the same form they are acquired by the sensors, without any processing or annotation[1].

3.2 Error Measures

In order to evaluate the accuracy of the super-resolution process, we compared the 3D geometry of reconstructed face models of sample subjects against the corresponding 3D face models of the same subjects acquired with a high-resolution 3D scanner. This is similar to the problem of measuring the geometric distance between high and low resolution versions of a same triangular mesh, which is a common task in 3D mesh processing providing an indication of the quality of the simplification process that reduces the number of triangles [19]. In our work, the reconstructed mesh of a face originated by the super-resolution process can be regarded as a less accurate 3D representation of a same face acquired with the high-resolution scanner. According to this, we propose to use the error measure introduced in [20], based on the computation of the *Hausdorff* distance.

Given two surfaces S and S', the distance between a point p on S and the surface S' is defined as:

$$d(p, S') = \min_{p' \in S'} d(p, p'), \qquad (3)$$

where $d(p, p')$ is the Euclidian distance between two points in S and S', respectively. The geometric distance, also called one-sided or single-sided *Hausdorff* distance, between two surfaces S and S' is then defined as:

$$d(S, S') = \max_{p \in S} d(p, S'). \qquad (4)$$

This distance is not symmetric (i.e., $d(S, S') \neq d(S', S)$), so that it can underestimate the real distance between two surfaces. Due to this, a more accurate measure of the distance is obtained by using the symmetrical *Hausdorff* distance:

$$d_H(S, S') = \max\{d(S, S'), d(S', S)\}. \qquad (5)$$

The point-to-surface distance of Eq. (3) is also used to define the *mean distance* d_m between two surfaces as the distances between points on S and the surface S', divided by the area of S:

$$d_m(S, S') = \frac{1}{|S|} \sum_{p \in S} d(p, S'). \qquad (6)$$

---

[1] The data set can be accessed at the following link:
http://www.micc.unifi.it/datasets/4d-faces/

The symmetric version of the mean distance is then defined as the average between the two single-sided mean distances, that is, $\bar{d}(S, S') = (d_m(S, S') + d_m(S', S))/2$. Practically, in computing Eq. (4) vertices of the mesh are used as sampling points p of the surface S. In addition, the *Root Mean Square* error (RMS) on the vertices of the two comparing meshes is also computed.

In our experiments, we used the data set described in the previous Section. As an example, Fig. 4 shows the 3D reference frame (i.e., the first frame of the depth-sequence) as triangulated mesh, the 3D reconstructed frame and the 3D high-resolution scan of three sample subjects (named, respectively, #1, #3, and #7) included in the data set. Before evaluating the distance between two face models, they are cropped (i.e., only the points included in a sphere centered on the nose tip and with 95mm of radius are retained), normalized with respect to their center of mass and aligned each other using the ICP algorithm.

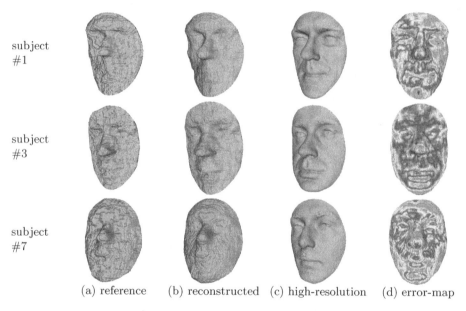

subject #1

subject #3

subject #7

(a) reference   (b) reconstructed   (c) high-resolution   (d) error-map

Fig. 4. Each row reports, for a different sample subject: (a) the 3D reference frame; (b) the 3D reconstructed frame; (c) and the 3D high-resolution scan. In (d), the error map of the Hausdorff distance is reported for the reconstructed model, where the error increases along the red-green-blue color scale.

Results are summarized in Tab. 1. In particular, we reported the average values for the symmetric *Hausdorff* distance (D_H), the symmetric *mean distance* ($\bar{d}$), and the *RMS* error computed between the high-resolution scan and, respectively, the reconstructed frame and the reference frame. In this way, a quantitative evidence of the increased quality of the reconstructed frame with respect to the reference one is obtained. The percentage variation of these error measures when passing from the reference to the reconstructed frame are also reported.

As general behavior, it can be observed that all the three error measures decreases when evaluated on the reconstructed frame instead of the reference one, with a percentage reduction of the error which varies from around 16% up to 23%, respectively, for the symmetric Hausdorff (d_H) and the RMS error. Fig. 4(d) also reports the error map of the Hausdorff distance, where the red-green-blue colors are associated to errors of increasing magnitude. In general, it can be seen that the error is small, with just a few areas of the reconstructed face colored in blue.

Table 1. The average distance measures computed between the 3D high-resolution face scan and, respectively, the reconstructed and the reference frame of each subject. The percentage variation of the distance between the errors for the reconstructed and reference frames is also reported.

average distance	d_H	$\bar{d}$	RMS
reference	14,508231	2.171087	3.112833
reconstructed	12.200201	1.682568	2.393260
% variation	-15.91%	-22.5%	-23,12%

4 Conclusions

In this paper, we have defined a super-resolution approach that permits the construction of a higher-resolution face model starting from a sequence of low-resolution 3D scans acquired with a consumer depth camera. In particular, values of the points of the super resolution model are constructed by iteratively aligning the low-resolution 3D frames to a reference 3D frame using the scaled ICP algorithm, and estimating the statistics of the values in the low-resolution models in corresponding points. Preliminary qualitative and quantitative experiments have been performed on an acquired dataset that includes, for each subject, a sequence of low-resolution 3D frames and one high-resolution 3D scan used to provide the ground truth data of a subject's face. In this way, results of the super-resolution process are evaluated by measuring the distance error between the superface and the ground truth.

Acknowledgment. The authors acknowledge Lorenzo Seidenari for his valuable contribute to the design and development of the software modules for 3D data acquisition through the Kinect scanner.

References

1. Wang, Y., Liu, J., Tang, X.: Robust 3D face recognition by local shape difference boosting. IEEE Trans. on Pattern Analysis and Machine Intelligence 32, 1858–1870 (2010)

2. Berretti, S., Del Bimbo, A., Pala, P.: 3D face recognition using iso-geodesic stripes. IEEE Trans. on Pattern Analysis and Machine Intelligence 32, 2162–2177 (2010)
3. Colombo, A., Cusano, C., Schettini, R.: Gappy PCA classification for occlusion tolerant 3D face detection. Journal of Math. Imaging and Vision 35, 193–207 (2009)
4. Passalis, G., Perakis, P., Theoharis, T., Kakadiaris, I.A.: Using facial symmetry to handle pose variations in real-world 3D face recognition. IEEE Transactions on Pattern Analysis and Machine Intelligence 33, 1938–1951 (2011)
5. Huang, T., Tsai, R.: Multi-frame image restoration and registration. In: Advances in Computer Vision and Image Processing, vol. 1, pp. 317–339 (1984)
6. Hardie, R., Barnard, K., Armstrong, E.: Joint map registration and high-resolution image estimation using a sequence of undersampled images. IEEE Trans. on Image Processing 6, 1621–1633 (1997)
7. Baker, S., Kanade, T.: Limits on super-resolution and how to break them. IEEE Trans. on Pattern Analysis and Machine Intelligence 24, 1167–1183 (2002)
8. Farsiu, S., Robinson, M., Elad, M., Milanfar, P.: Fast and robust multiframe super resolution. IEEE Trans. on Image Processing 13, 1327–1344 (2004)
9. Ebrahimi, M., Vrscay, E.: Multi-frame super-resolution with no explicit motion estimation. In: Proc. of Int. Conf. on Image Processing, Computer Vision, and Pattern Recognition (IPCV), pp. 455–459 (2008)
10. Smelyanskiy, V.N., Cheeseman, P., Maluf, D.A., Morris, R.D.: Bayesian super-resolved surface reconstruction from images. In: Proc. of IEEE Int. Conf. Computer Vision and Pattern Recognition (CVPR), pp. 375–382 (2000)
11. Peng, S., Pan, G., Wu, Z.: Learning-based super-resolution of 3D face model. In: Proc. of IEEE Int. Conf. on Image Processing (ICIP), vol. II, pp. 382–385 (2005)
12. Schuon, S., Theobalt, C., Davis, J., Thrun, S.: Lidarboost: Depth superresolution for tof 3D shape scanning. In: Proc. of IEEE Int. Conf. Computer Vision and Pattern Recognition (CVPR), pp. 343–350 (2009)
13. Yang, Q., Yang, R., Davis, J., Nister, D.: Spatial-depth super resolution for range images. In: Proc. of IEEE Int. Conf. Computer Vision and Pattern Recognition (CVPR), pp. 1–8 (2007)
14. Pan, G., Han, S., Wu, Z., Wang, Y.: Super-Resolution of 3D Face. In: Leonardis, A., Bischof, H., Pinz, A. (eds.) ECCV 2006. LNCS, vol. 3952, pp. 389–401. Springer, Heidelberg (2006)
15. Arun, K., Huang, T., Blostein, S.: Least-squares fitting of two 3-D point sets. IEEE Trans. on Pattern Analysis and Machine Intelligence 9, 698–700 (1987)
16. Du, S., Zheng, N., Xiong, L., Ying, S., Xue, J.: Scaling iterative closest point algorithm for registration of m-D point sets. Journal of Visual Communication and Image Representation 21, 442–452 (2010)
17. Faugeras, O.: Three-dimensional computer vision: A geometric viewpoint. MIT Press, Cambridge (1993)
18. Powell, M.: A review of methods for multivariable interpolation at scattered data points. Cambridge University Press (1996)
19. Aspert, N., Santa-Cruz, D., Ebrahimi, T.: MESH: Measuring errors between surfaces using the Hausdorff distance. In: Proc. of the IEEE Int. Conf. on Multimedia and Expo, vol. I, pp. 705–708 (2002)
20. Cignoni, P., Montani, C., Scopigno, R.: A comparison of mesh simplification algorithms. Computers & Graphics 22, 37–54 (1998)

Stable Spectral Mesh Filtering

Artiom Kovnatsky[1], Michael M. Bronstein[1], and Alexander M. Bronstein[2]

[1] Institute of Computational Science, Faculty of Informatics,
Università della Svizzera Italiana, Lugano, Switzerland
{artiom.kovnatsky,michael.bronstein}@usi.ch
[2] School of Electrical Engineering, Tel Aviv University, Israel
bron@eng.tau.ac.il

Abstract. The rapid development of 3D acquisition technology has brought with itself the need to perform standard signal processing operations such as filters on 3D data. It has been shown that the eigenfunctions of the Laplace-Beltrami operator (manifold harmonics) of a surface play the role of the Fourier basis in the Euclidean space; it is thus possible to formulate signal analysis and synthesis in the manifold harmonics basis. In particular, geometry filtering can be carried out in the manifold harmonics domain by decomposing the embedding coordinates of the shape in this basis. However, since the basis functions depend on the shape itself, such filtering is valid only for weak (near all-pass) filters, and produces severe artifacts otherwise. In this paper, we analyze this problem and propose the fractional filtering approach, wherein we apply iteratively weak fractional powers of the filter, followed by the update of the basis functions. Experimental results show that such a process produces more plausible and meaningful results.

Keywords: Computational Geometry and Object Modeling, Hierarchy and geometric transformations, Laplace-Beltrami operator, 3D Mesh filtering.

1 Introduction

Different operations on the 3D data, such as noise removal, enhancement of specific parts of the object, may be formulated as applying filter $\mathbf{F}$ to the shape. It is well-known that the eigenfunctions of the Laplace-Beltrami operator (manifold harmonics) of a 3D shape (modelled as a 2-manifold) play the role of the Fourier basis in the Euclidean space [14,6]. Methods based on the Laplace-Beltrami operator have been used in a wide range of applications, among them remeshing [5,9], parametrization [2], compression [3], recognition [11,12], clustering, etc. Many methods in computer graphics and geometry processing draw inspiration from the world of physics, finding analogies between physical processes such as heat diffusion or wave equations [1] and the geometric properties of the shape [13]. Several works have studied consistent discretizations of the Laplace-Beltrami operator for the physical problems where this operator is involved [10,8,15]

A. Fusiello et al. (Eds.): ECCV 2012 Ws/Demos, Part I, LNCS 7583, pp. 83–91, 2012.

Original shape   Standard filter   Fractional filter

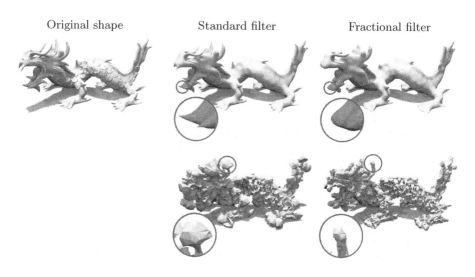

Fig. 1. Low- and band-pass filtering of the dragon shape (first column) using the Laplace-Beltrami filter (second column) and the proposed fractional approach (third column)

The influential paper of Taubin [14] drew the analogy between the classical signal processing theory and the manifold harmonics, showing that standard tools in signal processing such as analysis and synthesis of signals can be carried out on manifolds. This idea was extended in [4] and later in [7], showing a practical framework for shape filtering using the manifold harmonics transform.

One of the problematic issues in this approach is that, unlike the Euclidean case, where the basis functions are fixed, the manifold harmonics depend on the shape itself. Thus, filtering the shape changes the basis in which the filter coefficients are expressed. For strong filter, this may result in severe artifacts and unnatural behaviour.

Main Contribution. In this paper, we analyze this problem and propose the fractional filtering approach, wherein we apply iteratively weak fractional powers of the filter, followed by the update of the basis functions. The rest of the paper is organized as follows. We first review some notions in differential geometry and harmonic analysis in Section 2. In Section 3, we describe the filtering proposed in [7] and our fractional filtering approach. In Section 4 we show experimental results. Finally, Section 5 concludes the paper.

2   Background

In this section we briefly review the concept of manifold harmonics, and how to use it for approximating the shape filtering. For more detailed introduction reader referred to [14,7].

2.1   Manifold Harmonics

We model a shape as a compact two-dimensional manifold X, possibly with a boundary ∂X. Given a smooth scalar field f on the manifold X, the negative divergence of the gradient of a scalar field f, $\Delta f = -\mathrm{div}\,\mathrm{grad}\,f$, is called the *Laplacian* of f. For a general manifold the operator Δ is called the *Laplace-Beltrami* operator, and it generalizes the standard notion of the Laplace operator to manifolds. Note that we define the Laplacian with the negative sign to conform to the computer graphics and computational geometry convention.

Being a positive self-adjoint operator, the Laplacian admits an eigendecomposition

$$\Delta\phi = \lambda\phi \tag{1}$$

with non-negative eigenvalues λ and corresponding orthonormal eigenfunctions ϕ, where orthonormality is understood in the sense of the local inner product induced by the metric on the manifold. Furthermore, due to the assumption that our domain is compact, the spectrum is discrete, $0 = \lambda_1 < \lambda_2 < \cdots$.

In physics, (1) is known as the *Helmholtz equation* representing the spatial component of the wave equation. Thinking of our domain as of a vibrating membrane (with appropriate boundary conditions), the ϕ_i's can be interpreted as natural vibration modes of the membrane, while the λ_i's assume the meaning of the corresponding vibration frequencies. In fact, in this setting the eigenvalues have inverse area or squared spatial frequency units. We will denote the corresponding spatial frequencies as $\omega_i = \sqrt{\lambda_i}$ and use the two interchangeably. The eigenbasis of the Laplace-Beltrami operator is frequently referred to as the *harmonic basis* of the manifold, and the functions ϕ_i as *manifold harmonics*.

Given a square integrable function f on the manifold, satisfying certain boundary conditions when appropriate[1], it is well-established that f can be expanded into a Fourier series

$$f(x) = \sum_{i \geq 1} \hat{f}_i \phi_i(x) \tag{2}$$

with the coefficients

$$\hat{f}_i = \langle f, \phi_i \rangle = \int_X f(x)\phi_i(x)da(x). \tag{3}$$

The process of obtaining the coefficients $\hat{f}_i$ from f is usually referred to as *analysis*; the corresponding linear transformation will be dubbed as the *manifold harmonic transform* (MHT) after [7]. The inverse process obtained via the inverse MHT (IMHT) is known as *synthesis*.

---

[1] If the manifold has a boundary, ∂X, it is typical to enforce Dirichlet boundary conditions of the form $f|_{\partial X} = f_0$, or Neumann boundary conditions of the form $\langle \mathrm{grad} f, n \rangle|_{\partial X} = g_0$, where n denotes the normal to the boundary. Corresponding boundary conditions have to be imposed on the Laplace-Beltrami operator.

2.2 Discrete Manifold Harmonics

In the discretized setting, we represent the manifold X as a triangular mesh built upon the vertex set $\{\mathbf{x}_1, \ldots, \mathbf{x}_n\}$. A function f on the manifold is represented by the vector $\mathbf{f} = (f(\mathbf{x}_1), \ldots, f(\mathbf{x}_n))^{\mathrm{T}}$ of its samples. A common approach to discretizing manifold harmonics is by first constructing a discrete Laplace-Beltrami operator on the mesh, represented as a $n \times n$ matrix, followed by its eigendecomposition.

In our experiments we adopt a standard cotangent scheme [8]. The eigendecomposition results in the following generalized eigenvalue problem:

$$\mathbf{W}\phi_k = \mathbf{D}\lambda_k\phi_k \tag{4}$$

where matrix $\mathbf{D}$ is diagonal, s.t. $D_{ii} = \frac{S_i}{3}$ (S_i - denotes area of all triangles sharing the vertex i), and $\mathbf{W}_{ij} = (\cot(\alpha_{ij}) + \cot(\beta_{ij}))/2, \mathbf{W}_{ii} = -\sum_j \mathbf{W}_{ij}$ (α_{ij}, β_{ij} are the two angles opposite to the edge between vertices i and j in the two triangles sharing the edge). In this case the the resulting eigenfunctions $\mathbf{\Phi}$ are $\mathbf{D}$−orthogonal [4], and the discrete MHT is expressed as multiplication by an $n \times n$ matrix $\mathbf{\Phi}^{\mathrm{T}}\mathbf{D}$, and IMHT is a multiplication by $\mathbf{\Phi}$. In the following we shortly will write $\mathbf{\Phi}^{\mathrm{T}}$ instead of $\mathbf{\Phi}^{\mathrm{T}}\mathbf{D}$, assuming that the appropriate inner product is considered.

3 Shape Filtering

In [7], Vallet and Lévy argued that the *extrinsic geometry* of a shape (i.e., the coordinates of the embedding of the manifold) can be thought of as a vector field $\mathbf{x} : X \to \mathbb{R}^3$ on the manifold and, hence, decomposed into

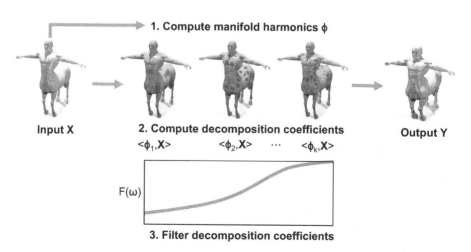

Fig. 2. Pipeline of the Vallet-Lévy method

$$\mathbf{x} = \sum_{i \geq 1} \hat{\mathbf{x}}_i \phi_i \tag{5}$$

using the MHT, with $\hat{\mathbf{x}}_i = (\langle x^1, \phi_i \rangle, \langle x^2, \phi_i \rangle, \langle x^3, \phi_i \rangle)$, x^j denoting the j-th component of the vector $\mathbf{x}$. Since each Fourier coefficient is associated with a spatial frequency, the first coefficients can be interpreted as extrinsic geometric approximation of the shape, while the next ones correspond to the geometric details.

Analogously to the Fourier transform, the MHT separates frequencies, making the application of a filter $F(\omega)$ a simple product,

$$\mathbf{y} = \sum_{i \geq 1} F(\omega_i) \hat{\mathbf{x}}_i \phi_i. \tag{6}$$

The resulting embedding coordinates, $\mathbf{y} : X \to \mathbb{R}^3$, describe a new shape with frequency components changed according to the filter "transmission function" $F(\omega)$.

In practice, the above summation is truncated at some $i = k$ corresponding to ω_i, which is roughly comparable to the sampling radius of the shape. For that reason, fine geometric details do not participate in the analysis and synthesis, creating essentially a low-pass filter on top of $F(\omega)$. To counter this effect, Vallet and Lévy [7] proposed to compute the residual

$$\mathbf{e} = \sum_{i > k} F(\omega_i) \hat{\mathbf{x}}_i \phi_i = \mathbf{x} - \sum_{i=1}^{k} F(\omega_i) \hat{\mathbf{x}}_i \phi_i, \tag{7}$$

and re-inject it into the filtered shape by

$$\mathbf{y} = \sum_{i=1}^{k} F(\omega_i) \hat{\mathbf{x}}_i \phi_i + F_{\mathrm{h}} \mathbf{e}, \tag{8}$$

where F_{h} is the average filter response at $\omega \geq \omega_k$. In this way, the high frequency components are treated as a wave packet and filtered as a whole.

In the discrete setting, we represent the embedding of the shape as the $n \times 3$ matrix $\mathbf{X}$, and the response of the filter by the $k \times k$ diagonal matrix $\mathbf{F}(\omega_{\mathbf{X}}) = \mathrm{diag}\{F(\omega_1), \dots, F(\omega_k)\}$. The discretized filter is given by

$$\begin{aligned} \mathbf{E} &= (\mathbf{I} - \mathbf{\Phi_X}\mathbf{\Phi_X}^{\mathrm{T}})\mathbf{X} \\ \mathbf{Y} &= \mathbf{\Phi_X}\mathbf{F}(\omega_{\mathbf{X}})\mathbf{\Phi_X}^{\mathrm{T}}\mathbf{X} + F_{\mathrm{h}}\mathbf{E}, \end{aligned} \tag{9}$$

or alternatively by

$$\mathbf{Y} = (\mathbf{\Phi_X}\mathbf{F}(\omega_{\mathbf{X}})\mathbf{\Phi_X}^{\mathrm{T}} + F_{\mathrm{h}}\bar{\mathbf{I}}_{\mathrm{h}}^{\mathbf{X}})\mathbf{X}, \tag{10}$$

where $\mathbf{\Phi_X}$ is the $n \times k$ matrix representing the first k frequencies of the MHT and $\bar{\mathbf{I}}_{\mathrm{h}}^{\mathbf{X}} = \mathbf{I} - \mathbf{\Phi_X}\mathbf{\Phi_X}^{\mathrm{T}}$.

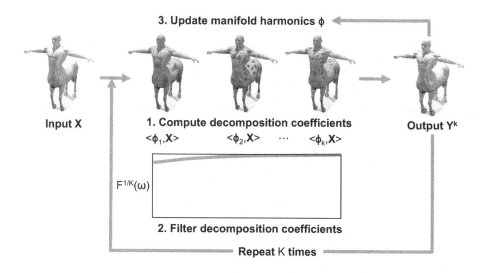

3. Update manifold harmonics φ

Input X

1. Compute decomposition coefficients

$<\phi_1,\mathbf{X}>$ $<\phi_2,\mathbf{X}>$ $\cdots$ $<\phi_k,\mathbf{X}>$

$F^{1/K}(\omega)$

2. Filter decomposition coefficients

Repeat K times

Output Y^k

Fig. 3. Pipeline of our method

3.1 Fractional Filter

It is important to note that the MHT $\boldsymbol{\Phi}_\mathbf{X}$ in (9) actually depends on $\mathbf{X}$ itself and *changes as a result of filtering*. However, Vallet and Lévy [7] do not account for this effect: their approach is correct only for infinitesimal change ($\mathbf{Y} \approx \mathbf{X}$), which is valid only if the filter is "weak" ($\mathbf{F} \approx \mathbf{I}$). For "strong" filters, such processing may result in severe artifacts (see Figure 1).

To counter this effect, we propose computing filters in an iterative manner, using fractional powers $\alpha < 1$ of the transfer function such that $F^\alpha \approx 1$. The fractional filter is computed according to (9) using $F^\alpha(\omega_i)$ as the transfer function; after each application, the Laplace-Beltrami operator and its eigenfunctions are recomputed. Setting $\alpha = 1/K$, the fractional filter is applied K times, resulting in the following intermediate results

$$\mathbf{Y}^{(k+1)} = (\boldsymbol{\Phi}_{\mathbf{Y}^{(k)}}\mathbf{F}^\alpha(\omega_{\mathbf{Y}^{(k)}})\boldsymbol{\Phi}_{\mathbf{Y}^{(k)}}^\mathrm{T} + F_\mathrm{h}^\alpha\bar{\mathbf{I}}_\mathrm{h}^{\mathbf{Y}^{(k)}})\mathbf{Y}^{(k)}, \tag{11}$$

The final result is

$$\mathbf{Y} = (\boldsymbol{\Phi}_{\mathbf{Y}^{(k-1)}}\mathbf{F}^\alpha(\omega_{\mathbf{Y}^{(k-1)}})\boldsymbol{\Phi}_{\mathbf{Y}^{(k-1)}}^\mathrm{T} + F_\mathrm{h}^\alpha\bar{\mathbf{I}}_\mathrm{h}^{\mathbf{Y}^{(k-1)}})\cdots(\boldsymbol{\Phi}_\mathbf{X}\mathbf{F}^\alpha(\omega_\mathbf{X})\boldsymbol{\Phi}_\mathbf{X}^\mathrm{T} + F_\mathrm{h}^\alpha\bar{\mathbf{I}}_\mathrm{h}^\mathbf{X})\mathbf{X}.$$

If all the eigenfunctions are used ($\boldsymbol{\Phi}$ is $n \times n$), the fractional filtering result is

$$\mathbf{Y} = \left(\boldsymbol{\Phi}_{\mathbf{Y}^{(K-1)}}\mathbf{F}^\alpha(\omega_{\mathbf{Y}^{(K-1)}})\boldsymbol{\Phi}_{\mathbf{Y}^{(K-1)}}^\mathrm{T}\right)\cdots\left(\boldsymbol{\Phi}_\mathbf{X}\mathbf{F}^\alpha(\omega_\mathbf{X})\boldsymbol{\Phi}_\mathbf{X}^\mathrm{T}\right)\mathbf{X},$$

as opposed to the standard approach where the eigenfunctions are not updated,

$$\mathbf{Y} = \left(\boldsymbol{\Phi}_\mathbf{X}\mathbf{F}^\alpha(\omega_\mathbf{X})\boldsymbol{\Phi}_\mathbf{X}^\mathrm{T}\right)\cdots\left(\boldsymbol{\Phi}_\mathbf{X}\mathbf{F}^\alpha(\omega_\mathbf{X})\boldsymbol{\Phi}_\mathbf{X}^\mathrm{T}\right)\mathbf{X}$$

$$= \boldsymbol{\Phi}_\mathbf{X}\mathbf{F}(\omega_\mathbf{X})\boldsymbol{\Phi}_\mathbf{X}^\mathrm{T}.$$

Since the fractional filter is infinitesimal, the Laplacain does not change significantly between two applications of the filter; this allows to update efficiently the eigenfunctions Φ as a perturbation of the Laplacian.

4   Results

In this section, we compare the standard filtering approach [7] with the proposed fractional filtering method. As test data, we used the *dragon* and *angel* shapes from the Stanford repository. The models were represented as triangular meshes with 4×10^4 and 5×10^4 vertices, respectively. Cotangent weight scheme was used to compute the discretization of the Laplace-Beltrami operator. In all the experiments, we used the full set of eigenvectors without resorting to the approximation proposed in [7] (treating high frequency components as a wave packet). We used two types of filters: low-pass and band-pass, with cutoff frequencies selected roughly according to the typical feature size on the shape. The fractional power was chosen in each case such that the resulting fractional filter is sufficiently weak.

Figure 5 shows the filtering results of the two shapes. We show the resulting shape after applying several times the fractional filter, without and with recomputation of the eigenbasis after each application. The final (rightmost) image is the filtering result. We can observe severe artifacts caused by the standard approach, such as sharp spikes on the dragon feet (unreasonable for a low-pass filter) and inflated ball-like structures on the dragon tail and angel fingers produced by the band-pass filter (see also Figure 1). Overall, our approach produces much more plausible and logical results: the low-pass filter result is smooth as expected, and the band-pass filter result has the effect of "feature enhancement" or sharpening.

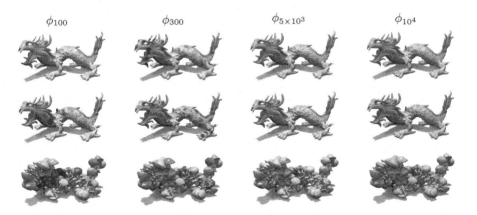

Fig. 4. The eigenfunctions of the Laplace-Beltrami operator of the dragon shape. Top: computed on original shape; middle: after 1/10 of a band-pass filter; bottom: after a full band-pass filter

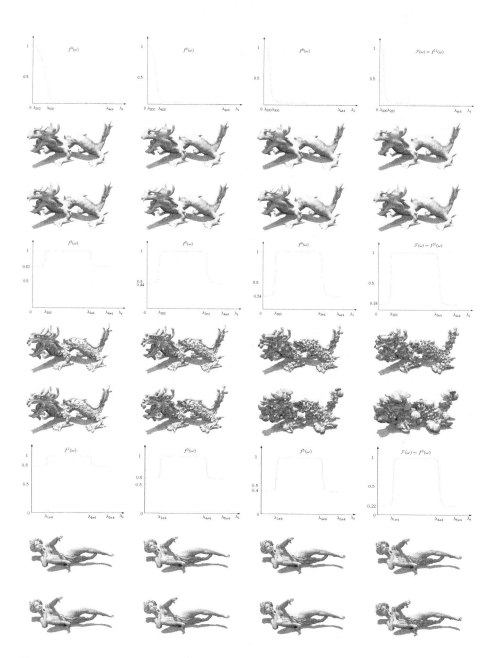

Fig. 5. First, fourth and seventh rows: fractional powers of the filter; fractional filtering results with (second, fifth and eighth row) and without (third, sixth and ninth row) recompilation of the Laplacian basis

5   Conclusions

We analyzed the problem of shape filtering in the manifold harmonic transform domain and presented the fractional filtering method which allows to significantly reduce the artifacts observed when using strong filters. Our approach decomposes the filter into fractional powers and applies it sequentially, recomputing the Laplace-Beltrami eigenbasis after each application. Such a recomputation can be done efficiently as a small perturbation of the eigenvectors. Experimental results show that better results are obtained using this approach compared to direct filtering.

References

1. Coifman, R.R., Lafon, S.: Diffusion maps. Applied and Computational Harmonic Analysis 21, 5–30 (2006)
2. Floater, M., Hormann, K.: Surface parameterization: a tutorial and survey. Advances in Multiresolution for Geometric Modelling 1 (2005)
3. Karni, Z., Gotsman, C.: Spectral compression of mesh geometry. In: SIGGRAPH 2000: Proc. of the 27th Annual Conference on Computer Graphics and Interactive Techniques, pp. 279–286 (2000)
4. Kim, B., Rossignac, J.: Geofilter: Geometric selection of mesh filter parameters. Comput. Graph. Forum 24(3), 295–302 (2005)
5. Kobbelt, L.: Discrete fairing. In: Proc. of the Seventh IMA Conference on the Mathematics of Surfaces, pp. 101–131 (1997)
6. Lévy, B.: Laplace-Beltrami eigenfunctions towards an algorithm that "understands" geometry. In: Proc. SMA (2006)
7. Lévy, B., Zhang, R.H.: Spectral geometry processing. In: ACM SIGGRAPH ASIA Course Notes (2009)
8. Meyer, M., Desbrun, M., Schroder, P., Barr, A.H.: Discrete differential-geometry operators for triangulated 2-manifolds. In: Visualization and Mathematics III, pp. 35–57 (2003)
9. Nealen, A., Igarashi, T., Sorkine, O., Alexa, M.: Laplacian mesh optimization. In: Proc. of the 4th International Conference on Computer Graphics and Interactive Techniques in Australasia and Southeast Asia, pp. 381–389 (2006)
10. Pinkall, U., Polthier, K.: Computing discrete minimal surfaces and their conjugates. Experimental Mathematics 2(1), 15–36 (1993)
11. Reuter, M., Wolter, F.E., Peinecke, N.: Laplace-spectra as fingerprints for shape matching. In: Proc. ACM Symp. Solid and Physical Modeling, pp. 101–106 (2005)
12. Rustamov, R.M.: Laplace-beltrami eigenfunctions for deformation inavriant shape representation. In: Proc. of SGP, pp. 225–233 (2007)
13. Sun, J., Ovsjanikov, M., Guibas, L.J.: A concise and provably informative multi-scale signature based on heat diffusion. In: Proc. SGP (2009)
14. Taubin, G.: A signal processing approach to fair surface design. ACM (1995)
15. Wardetzky, M., Mathur, S., Kälberer, F., Grinspun, E.: Discrete Laplace operators: no free lunch. In: Conf. Computer Graphics and Interactive Techniques (2008)

Analytical Dynamic Programming Matching

Seiichi Uchida, Satoshi Hokahori, and Yaokai Feng

Kyushu University, Fukuoka, Japan

Abstract. In this paper, we show that the truly two-dimensional elastic image matching problem can be solved analytically using dynamic programming (DP) in polynomial time if the problem is formulated as a maximum a posteriori problem using Gaussian distributions for the likelihood and prior. After giving the derivation of the analytical DP matching algorithm, we evaluate its performance on handwritten character images containing various nonlinear deformations, and compare other elastic image matching methods.

1 Introduction

Elastic matching is one of the most fundamental tools for pattern recognition and computer vision. For one-dimensional (i.e., sequential) patterns, elastic matching detects and compensates, for example, any temporal fluctuations. For two-dimensional patterns (i.e., images), elastic matching also detects and compensates various geometric deformations. Owing to these abilities, elastic matching has been applied to recognition tasks, deformation analysis, pattern alignment, image compression, stereo, and so on.

Elastic matching is formulated as an optimization problem of a warping function between two patterns. As such, the property of elastic matching is determined by the problem formulation and the optimization method. These two factors are not independent — the optimization method is selected according to the formulation. For example, if the problem is formulated as a combinatorial optimization problem, a combinatorial optimization method will be used.

Throughout this paper, we focus on dynamic programming (DP) as the optimization method for elastic image matching. As detailed later, DP has promising properties for elastic matching. In fact, DP has undoubtedly been the most established optimization method for sequential patterns since the late 1960s.

For elastic *image matching*, however, DP has not been fully utilized. Consider a combinatorial optimization problem of elastic image matching with a truly two-dimensional warping ability. Unfortunately, as this is an NP-hard problem, DP (as well as other optimizers) cannot solve the problem in polynomial time. Consequently, the warping ability is severely restricted in reducing the computation. This limitation results in so-called pseudo 2D elastic matching that cannot compensate vertical and horizontal deformations simultaneously. In other words, it cannot even compensate rotation.

In this paper, a truly two-dimensional polynomial-time DP matching method, called *analytical DP matching*, is presented, which is very different from the

A. Fusiello et al. (Eds.): ECCV 2012 Ws/Demos, Part I, LNCS 7583, pp. 92–101, 2012.

conventional combinatorial DP matching. The performance thereof is evaluated qualitatively and quantitatively on handwritten character images. The key idea is to formulate the elastic image matching problem as a maximum a posteriori (MAP) problem with a Gaussian likelihood and a Gaussian prior. The quadratic nature of the Gaussian distributions helps us to derive an analytical solution using DP. Consequently, analytical DP matching can obtain the globally optimal solution of the MAP problem with a polynomial-time computation while retaining the truly two-dimensional warping ability.

1.1   Related Work

DP [1–3] has been applied to various tasks in pattern recognition and computer vision. Nowadays, DP is considered a classic optimization method and there are several fascinating alternatives, such as graph cut, belief propagation (or message passing), and so on [4]. Nevertheless, many researchers still choose DP for their current tasks because of its conciseness, versatility, and ability to obtain the globally optimal solution. In fact, DP has recently been employed in studies on tracking [5], stereo [6–8], and elastic image matching [9].

Elastic matching is a typical application of DP. As previously noted, the DP-based matching algorithm, called DP matching or dynamic time warping, has been widely and successfully applied to sequential pattern recognition tasks since the late 1960s. In fact, DP matching (and its stochastic extension, i.e., Hidden Markov Models) is a standard in speech recognition [10, 11] and on-line character recognition [12].

It is quite natural to try to extend the sequential DP matching algorithm to a two-dimensional one. Several researchers [13, 14] have developed DP algorithms for truly two-dimensional elastic image matching, but have encountered the inherent NP-hardness of the problem [15].

Because of this computational intractability, conventional DP-based elastic image matching algorithms employ various approximation strategies, the most popular of which is the limitation of matching flexibility. In fact, we can find many pseudo 2D elastic matching algorithms, such as [9]. Another strategy is partial omission of the mutual dependency between 4-adjacent pixels (e.g., the tree representation in [6, 8, 16]). It is also popular for introducing local search techniques, such as pruning (or beam-search) and coarse-to-fine strategies [17], at the cost of global optimality. Notwithstanding these strategies, there is currently no practical DP algorithm that can provide both globally optimal and truly two-dimensional elastic matching.

All the conventional DP-based elastic matching algorithms (apart from four exceptions noted later) have always used DP as a combinatorial breadth-first search method, i.e., a combinatorial optimization method. This is confirmed by the fact that a very recent survey [3] reported only combinatorial (i.e., discrete) DP algorithms. Even if an optimization problem is originally formulated as a continuous variational problem, it is discretized and then solved by DP as a combinatorial optimization problem [2, 10].

This fact is somewhat peculiar since DP was originally developed as a continuous optimization method to obtain the solution efficiently using an *analytical* strategy [1]. Such analytical solutions have rarely been utilized even in other computer vision and pattern recognition problems. To the best of our knowledge, there are only four studies in which DP has been utilized as an analytical solver. Angel [18] used analytical DP for smooth interpolation. Serra and Berthod [20] and Munich and Perona [21] used it for nonlinear alignment of one-dimensional patterns. Finally, Uchida et al. [22] used it for object tracking.

1.2   Our Contribution

Our main contribution is regenerating the classic DP-based elastic matching algorithm, the combinatorial breadth-first search method that has not been considered since its introduction in the late 1960s. The proposed algorithm, called analytical DP matching, does not include the combinatorial search that becomes intractable for elastic image matching problems. Instead, it utilizes DP to provide an analytical solution, thereby successfully reducing the computational complexity from an exponential order to a polynomial one.

The analytical DP matching algorithm is derived by formulating the elastic matching problem as a MAP problem with Gaussian distributions. The quadratic nature of the Gaussian distributions enables the globally optimal solution of the MAP problem to be obtained with $O(I^4)$ computations for $I \times I$ images. Since this is an analytical solution, it is not necessary to consider either convergence or the initial value issue. It is noteworthy that this algorithm has the potential to be combined with other optimization methods based on a sequential decision process, such as tree-reweighted message passing [19].

Since the problem is formulated as a quadratic optimization problem, it can be solved analytically by a more popular closed-form solution, precisely like least-mean-square (LMS) problems. In this case, the solution requires $O(I^6)$ computations to deal with a large $(O(I^2) \times O(I^2))$ matrix. In contrast, our analytical DP matching algorithm utilizes a column-wise recursive formulation that provides a more efficient solution with $O(I^4)$ computations and a far smaller $(O(I) \times O(I))$ matrix.

2   Formulation of Elastic Image Matching Problem

2.1   Elastic Image Matching as a MAP Problem

Elastic image matching between a pair of $I \times I$ images [1], $\boldsymbol{X} = \{x_{i,j} | i, j = 1, \ldots, I\}$ and $\boldsymbol{Y} = \{y_{u,v} | u, v = 1, \ldots, I\}$, is an optimization problem of the warping function $\boldsymbol{W} = \{\boldsymbol{w}_{i,j}\}$, where $\boldsymbol{w}_{i,j} = (u_{i,j}, v_{i,j})^T$ denotes that pixel $(i,j)^T$ on $\boldsymbol{X}$ corresponds to $(u_{i,j}, v_{i,j})^T$ on $\boldsymbol{Y}$. Hereafter, we assume the boundary conditions, $u_{1,j} = 1, u_{I,j} = I, v_{i,1} = 1, v_{i,I} = I$.

---

[1] We can easily extend the following discussion to arbitrary size images.

We formulate the optimization problem of W as the following MAP problem:

$$\overline{W} = \underset{W}{\operatorname{argmax}} P(W|X,Y). \tag{1}$$

According to Bayes' rule,

$$\underset{W}{\operatorname{argmax}} P(W|X,Y) = \underset{W}{\operatorname{argmax}} P(X,Y|W)P(W), \tag{2}$$

where $P(X,Y|W)$ is a likelihood that evaluates the similarity between X and Y under the warping function W, and $P(W)$ is a prior of W.

We assume the following Gaussian likelihood $P(X,Y|W)$:

$$P(X,Y|W) = \prod_{i,j} \mathcal{N}(w_{i,j};\ \mu_{i,j}, \Sigma_{i,j}), \tag{3}$$

where $\mathcal{N}(\cdot)$ is a two-dimensional Gaussian distribution and $\mu_{i,j}$ and $\Sigma_{i,j}$ are its mean vector and covariance matrix, respectively. Each pixel $(i,j)^T$ on X has its own Gaussian distribution on Y, which evaluates the pixel-wise similarity between $(i,j)^T$ and $w_{i,j} = (u_{i,j}, v_{i,j})^T$. The parameters $\mu_{i,j}$ and $\Sigma_{i,j}$ are estimated before optimizing W. As the prior $P(W)$, we use a smoothness function [2],

$$P(W) = \prod_{i,j} \mathcal{N}(w_{i,j} - w_{i,j-1};\ 0, \lambda I) \cdot \mathcal{N}(w_{i,j} - w_{i-1,j};\ 0, \lambda I). \tag{4}$$

The first and second Gaussian distributions in (4) evaluate intra- and inter-column smoothness, respectively. If the constant λ is set to a larger value, the smoothing effect by the prior becomes weaker. By taking the logarithm of (2), our objective function $F(W)$ is derived as follows:

$$F(W) \equiv \lambda \left[\log P(X,Y|W) + \log P(W) \right] \tag{5}$$

We now introduce the *matrix-vector formulation* [24], or column-wise formulation, where W is treated as a sequence of $2I$-dimensional vectors, $w_1, \ldots, w_i, \ldots, w_I$, where $w_i = (w_{i,1}, w_{i,2}, \ldots, w_{i,j}, \ldots, w_{i,I-1}, w_{i,I})^T$. Then the objective function $F(W)$ becomes

$$F(W) = F(w_1, \ldots, w_I) = \lambda \sum_{i=1}^{I} d_i(w_i) + \sum_{i=1}^{I} \eta(w_i) + \sum_{i=2}^{I} \rho(w_i, w_{i-1}). \tag{6}$$

The first term of (6) is the log likelihood and is defined as

$$d_i(w_i) = \sum_{j=1}^{I} w_{i,j}^T P_{i,j} w_{i,j} + q_{i,j}^T w_{i,j} + r_{i,j} = w_i^T P_i w_i + q_i^T w_i + r_i, \tag{7}$$

---

[2] It is possible to use an arbitrary covariance matrix in these priors instead of λI. It is also possible to use different covariance matrices at different $(i,j)^T$. Although such priors can represent various deformation tendencies, we use the most general prior of (4) throughout this paper to simplify our algorithm derivation.

where $\boldsymbol{P}_i = \text{diag}[\boldsymbol{P}_{i,1}, \ldots, \boldsymbol{P}_{i,j}, \ldots, \boldsymbol{P}_{i,I}]$, $\boldsymbol{q}_i = (\boldsymbol{q}_{i,1}, \ldots, \boldsymbol{q}_{i,j}, \ldots, \boldsymbol{q}_{i,I})^T$, and $r_i = \sum_{i=1}^{I} r_{i,j}$, with these coefficients derived from $\log P(\boldsymbol{X}, \boldsymbol{Y}|\boldsymbol{W})$, i.e., $\boldsymbol{\Sigma}_{i,j}$ and $\boldsymbol{\mu}_{i,j}$. Since $\boldsymbol{\Sigma}_{i,j}$ and $\boldsymbol{\mu}_{i,j}$ are pre-determined as noted above, the coefficients $\boldsymbol{P}_i$, $\boldsymbol{q}_i$, and r_i are also pre-determined. The second and third terms of (6) are the log priors for intra- and inter-column smoothness, respectively:

$$\eta(\boldsymbol{w}_i) = \boldsymbol{w}_i^T \boldsymbol{H} \boldsymbol{w}_i, \tag{8}$$

$$\rho(\boldsymbol{w}_i, \boldsymbol{w}_{i-1}) = (\boldsymbol{w}_i - \boldsymbol{w}_{i-1})^2, \tag{9}$$

where $\boldsymbol{H}$ is a constant matrix.

The minimization problem of (6) is a quadratic (i.e., convex) problem and can thus be analytically solved like LMS problems using a system of $O(I^2)$ linear equations derived by partial differentiation of (6) by each of $2I^2$ variables $\{(u_{i,j}, v_{i,j})\}$. The solution, however, requires $O(I^6)$ computations, because we must deal with a large non-diagonal $O(I^2) \times O(I^2)$ coefficient matrix for the system of linear equations. In the following section, we derive a more efficient $O(I^4)$ algorithm based on DP.

3   Analytical DP Matching

3.1   Derivation of DP Recursion

Similar to Angel [18], we introduce function $f_i(\boldsymbol{w}_{i-1})$, which is defined as

$$f_i(\boldsymbol{w}_{i-1}) = \min_{\boldsymbol{w}_i, \ldots, \boldsymbol{w}_I} \sum_{k=i}^{I} [\lambda d_k(\boldsymbol{w}_k) + \eta(\boldsymbol{w}_k) + \rho(\boldsymbol{w}_k, \boldsymbol{w}_{k-1})]. \tag{10}$$

Note that the minimum value of F is represented using f_2 as follows:

$$\min_{\boldsymbol{w}_1} F(\boldsymbol{W}) = \min_{\boldsymbol{w}_1}[\lambda d_1(\boldsymbol{w}_1) + \eta(\boldsymbol{w}_1) + f_2(\boldsymbol{w}_1)] = \lambda d_1(\overline{\boldsymbol{w}}_1) + \eta(\overline{\boldsymbol{w}}_1) + f_2(\overline{\boldsymbol{w}}_1), \tag{11}$$

where $\overline{\boldsymbol{w}}_1$ denotes $\boldsymbol{w}_1$ giving the minimum of the first equation.

According to the principle of optimality [1], (10) can be rewritten as the following recursive equation, known as *DP recursion*.

$$f_i(\boldsymbol{w}_{i-1}) = \min_{\boldsymbol{w}_i} [\lambda d_i(\boldsymbol{w}_i) + \eta(\boldsymbol{w}_i) + \rho(\boldsymbol{w}_i, \boldsymbol{w}_{i-1}) + f_{i+1}(\boldsymbol{w}_i)]. \tag{12}$$

This recursion indicates that the two-dimensional optimization problem of elastic image matching can be solved as the sequential optimization problem $\boldsymbol{w}_1, \ldots, \boldsymbol{w}_i, \ldots, \boldsymbol{w}_I$ by virtue of the column-wise formulation.

If we use the conventional combinatorial DP algorithm, we first need to discretize $\boldsymbol{w}_i$ as a $2I$-dimensional integer vector, and then calculate the recursion (12) for *all possible* $\boldsymbol{w}_i$ from $i = 1$ to I. Clearly, this is computationally intractable because the number of possible $\boldsymbol{w}_i$ is an exponential order of I. Instead, we use DP as an analytical solver while fully utilizing the fact that the terms of (12) are quadratic in nature and thus differentiable with respect to $\boldsymbol{w}_i$.

Input: Coefficients: $\{P_i, q_i, r_i \mid i = 1, \ldots, I\}$ and $\lambda \in \Re^+$.
Output: $\overline{W} = \overline{w}_1, \ldots, \overline{w}_i, \ldots, \overline{w}_I$ and $\min F$.
Step 1: Initial condition   Obtain (A_I, b_I, c_I).
Step 2: DP recursion
    For $i = I - 1$ downto 2: Obtain (A_i, b_i, c_i) from $(A_{i+1}, b_{i+1}, c_{i+1})$ by (15).
Step 3: Termination
    Obtain $\overline{w}_1$ from $\partial[\lambda d_1(w_1) + \eta(w_1) + f_2(w_1)]/\partial w_1 = 0$.
    $\min F = \lambda d_1(\overline{w}_1) + \eta(\overline{w}_1) + f_2(\overline{w}_1)$.
Step 4: Backtrack   For $i = 2$ to I: Obtain $\overline{w}_i$ by (14) with $w_{i-1} = \overline{w}_{i-1}$.

Fig. 1. Pseudo-code for analytical DP matching

3.2   Solution Using Analytical DP

The most important fact in deriving the proposed method is that all the d_i, as well as η and ρ are quadratic functions of w_i as indicated by (7), (8), and (9), respectively, and thus differentiable with respect to w_i. This means that $f_i(w_{i-1})$ is also a quadratic function [3] and can therefore be represented as

$$f_i(w_{i-1}) = w_{i-1}^T A_i w_{i-1} + b_i^T w_{i-1} + c_i, \tag{13}$$

where A_i is a $2I \times 2I$ matrix, b_i is a $2I$-dimensional vector, and c_i is a scalar, all of which are determined by optimizing $\{w_i\}$. By substituting (13) into (12), and then differentiating with respect to w_i, the optimal $w_i = \overline{w}_i$, which gives the minimum of (12), is derived as:

$$\overline{w}_i = [\lambda P_i + A_{i+1} + H + I]^{-1} (w_{i-1} - (\lambda q_i + b_{i+1})/2), \tag{14}$$

where I is the identity matrix.

By substituting $\overline{w}_i$ into (12) and then comparing with (13), we have the recursive procedure for obtaining (A_i, b_i, c_i) from $(A_{i+1}, b_{i+1}, c_{i+1})$ as follows:

$$\left. \begin{array}{l} A_i = I - [\lambda P_i + A_{i+1} + H + I]^{-1} \\ b_i = [I - A_i](\lambda q_i + b_{i+1}) \\ c_i = -(\lambda q_i + b_{i+1})^T b_i/4 + c_{i+1} + \lambda r_i \end{array} \right\}. \tag{15}$$

The complete algorithm for analytical DP matching is summarized in Fig. 1. After finding the initial value (A_I, b_I, c_I), the value (A_i, b_i, c_i) is calculated from $(A_{i+1}, b_{i+1}, c_{i+1})$ for $i = I - 1$ downto 2 according to the recursive procedure (15). While the derivation of (A_I, b_I, c_I) is not detailed here, it can be derived by comparing (10) with (13) at $i = I$. The optimal correspondence $\overline{w}_i$ is calculated repeatedly by (14) from $\overline{w}_1$. It should be noted that the optimal correspondence $\{\overline{w}_i\}$ is the globally optimal solution of (6). The computational complexity of analytical DP matching is $O(I^4)$, i.e., a polynomial order of I, and is dominated by the $O(I^3)$ computations to obtain the $2I \times 2I$ inverse matrix in (15). Since

---

[3] This can be proved inductively.

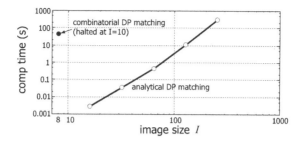

Fig. 2. Comparison of computation times for analytical DP matching and conventional combinatorial DP matching

there are generally fewer than $O(I^4)$ computations for $\boldsymbol{P}_i$, $\boldsymbol{q}_i$, and r_i, the total number of computations is still $O(I^4)$.

Figure 2 shows the average computation times for analytical DP matching at $I = 16, 32, \ldots, 256$ on a personal computer. This graph coincides with the theoretical computational complexity, i.e., $O(I^4)$. The conventional truly two-dimensional DP matching algorithm [14] required 41 s at $I = 8$ and halted at $I = 10$ owing to lack of memory. These comparative results show that analytical DP matching is far more efficient than the conventional DP matching algorithm.

4   Performance Evaluation

For a qualitative and quantitative performance evaluation, several experiments were carried out using handwritten digit images from MNIST [23]. MNIST comprises 60,000 training samples and 10,000 test samples. Each image is gray-scale with size 28×28.

There are several benefits of using handwritten character images for performance evaluation. (i) Elastic matching of character images is often more ambiguous and difficult than general object images because character images are binary patterns showing only curves (i.e., strokes). (ii) Through a character recognition experiment using the elastic matching distance (min F), the "over-fitting" phenomenon can be strictly observed. This is because character images from *different* classes often become similar to each other through over-fitting, and this can be detected as a misrecognition result. (iii) Since handwritten character images have typically been the target of elastic image matching, there are many past results of recognition experiments using the same database, especially MNIST.

Etohfs method [25] was used to determine $\boldsymbol{P}_{i,j}$, $\boldsymbol{q}_{i,j}$, and $r_{i,j}$. Figure 3(a) shows the pixel-wise log-likelihood functions (i.e., $\boldsymbol{w}_{i,j}^T \boldsymbol{P}_{i,j} \boldsymbol{w}_{i,j} + \boldsymbol{q}_{i,j}^T \boldsymbol{w}_{i,j} + r_{i,j}$) for a pair of "2". It is noteworthy that the major axis direction is often similar to the direction of the character stroke. For example, consider the correspondence illustrated by the thick orange arrow in Fig. 3(a). This indicates that point $(i, j)^T$, which lies on the "/"-shaped stroke on $\boldsymbol{X}$, has a high probability of being matched to point $(u, v)^T$ along the "/"-shaped stroke of $\boldsymbol{Y}$.

Figure 3(b) shows the results of analytical DP matching on several handwritten character image pairs. The images at either end are $\boldsymbol{Y}$ and $\boldsymbol{X}$, while

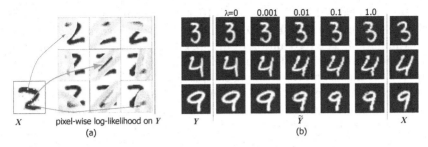

Fig. 3. (a) Pixel-wise log-likelihood for a pair of X and Y. For better visibility, only nine functions are plotted separately. (b) Matching results for different λ values.

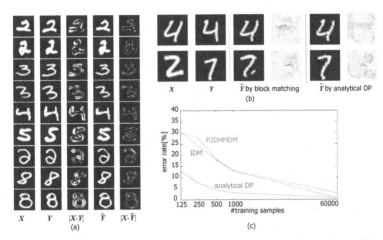

Fig. 4. (a) Visualization of matching accuracy using difference image. (b) Effect of global optimization. (c) Recognition rate of 10,000 handwritten digit images.

the other five images are the matching results $\widetilde{Y} = \{y_{\overline{w}_{i,j}} | i,j = 1,\ldots,I\}$ for five different values of λ. When $\lambda = 0$, the objective function is governed by the smoothness prior η, ρ, and the boundary conditions. Thus, $\widetilde{Y} = Y$. As λ increases, $\widetilde{Y}$ becomes more similar to X.

Figure 4(a) visualizes the accuracy of the proposed algorithm using difference images between X and $\widetilde{Y}$. The fact that $\widetilde{Y} \sim X$ indicates that Y was appropriately fitted to X. It also indicates that the matching flexibility is truly two-dimensional.

Figure 4(b) compares the global optimization result using the proposed algorithm with a local optimization result obtained by block matching. The latter result is equivalent to $(\hat{u}_{i,j}, \hat{v}_{i,j})^T$, which was determined individually at each block. (Thus, it is equivalent to the result obtained by IDM [9].) In Fig. 4(b), the result of matching two images from the same class ("4") is shown. Although the warped images are similar to each other, the pixel correspondences are different. The correspondence by block matching is somewhat scattered and excessive, whereas that by the proposed algorithm is smooth. This result is also confirmed by the other result, where block matching caused over-fitting between different classes ("2" and "7"). For the quantitative performance evaluation, a recognition experiment was carried out. Each of the 10,000 test samples (X) was matched to all the training samples (Y) and their matching distances $\min F$ were used for discrimination. The recognition result of X was finally determined using the 3-nearest neighbor method. The number of training samples was changed from 125 to 60,000, that is, all the training samples in MNIST.

For a comparative evaluation, IDM and P2DHMDM [9] were also used as other promising elastic image matching methods. It was reported in [23] that these methods achieved the best recognition performance on MNIST of all the elastic image matching methods. Their discrimination was done under the same condition [4] as the proposed algorithm. Figure 4(c) shows the recognition rates using IDM, P2DHMDM, and the proposed algorithm. The proposed algorithm outperforms the others especially with fewer training samples. This result indicates that the proposed algorithm can match images with large differences, while at the same time avoiding over-fitting.

5   Conclusion

An analytical DP matching algorithm was proposed for elastic image matching. The proposed algorithm was derived by formulating the matching problem as a MAP problem with a Gaussian likelihood and Gaussian priors. By virtue of the quadratic nature of the Gaussian distributions, DP can be used as an analytical solver that obtains the globally optimal solution of the MAP problem with $O(I^4)$ computations for $I \times I$ images. On the other hand, if DP is used as a conventional combinatorial solver, it requires an exponential number of computations. The computational efficiency of the proposed algorithm was shown through experimental results.

As the discussion in this paper is somewhat general, some specialization would be necessary for each specific image matching problem. In particular, we can apply the proposed algorithm to various images other than handwritten character images. Use of a more sophisticated and less ambiguous pixel value, such as a SIFT image [26], instead of the simple gray-scale value, would be useful to obtain a more reliable pixel-wise likelihood. As noted previously, it is possible to elaborate the prior to incorporate a pattern specific deformation tendency in its covariance matrix. It is also possible to incorporate hard constraints to fix $w_{i,j}$ at arbitrary pixels, like the boundary conditions, by virtue of a property of DP. In other words, given sparse pixel-to-pixel correspondences (by, for example, SIFT matching), the proposed method can provide the remaining correspondences optimally.

References

1. Bellman, R., Dreyfus, S.: Applied Dynamic Programming. Princeton University Press (1962)
2. Amini, A.A., Weymouth, T.E., Jain, R.C.: Using dynamic programming for solving variational problems in vision. PAMI 12(9) (1990)

---

[4] Keysers et al. [9] indicated using Sobel filtered images for better performance. Although this would also be beneficial for the proposed algorithm, gray values were used here for the sake of simpler analysis.

3. Felzenszwalb, P.F., Zabih, R.: Dynamic programming and graph algorithms in computer vision. PAMI 33(4) (2011)
4. Szeliski, R., Zabih, R., Scharstein, D., Veksler, O., Kolmogorov, V., Agarwala, A., Tappen, M., Rother, C.: A Comparative Study of Energy Minimization Methods for Markov Random Fields. In: Leonardis, A., Bischof, H., Pinz, A. (eds.) ECCV 2006. LNCS, vol. 3952, pp. 16–29. Springer, Heidelberg (2006)
5. Buchanan, A., Fitzgibbon, A.: Interactive feature tracking using K-D trees and dynamic programming. In: CVPR (2006)
6. Veksler, O.: Stereo correspondence by dynamic programming on a tree. In: CVPR (2005)
7. Kim, J.C., Lee, K.M., Choi, B.T., Lee, S.U.: A dense stereo matching using two-pass dynamic programming with generalized ground control points. In: CVPR (2005)
8. Lei, C., Selzer, J., Yang, Y.-H.: Region-tree based stereo using dynamic programming optimization. In: CVPR, vol. 2, pp. 2378–2385 (2006)
9. Keysers, D., Deselaers, T., Gollan, C., Ney, H.: Deformation models for image recognition. PAMI 29(8) (2007)
10. Sakoe, H., Chiba, S.: A dynamic programming algorithm optimization for spoken word recognition. IEEE Trans. ASSP 26(1) (1978)
11. Ney, H., Ortmanns, S.: Progress in dynamic programming search for LVCSR. Proc. IEEE 88(8) (2000)
12. Liu, C.-L., Jaeger, S., Nakagawa, M.: Online recognition of Chinese characters: the state-of-the-art. PAMI 26(2) (2004)
13. Levin, E., Pieraccini, R.: Dynamic planar warping for optical character recognition. In: ICASSP (1992)
14. Uchida, S., Sakoe, H.: A monotonic and continuous two-dimensional warping based on dynamic programming. In: ICPR (1998)
15. Keysers, D., Unger, W.: Elastic image matching is NP-complete. Pattern Recog. Lett. 24(1-3) (2003)
16. Mottl, V., Dvoenko, S., Kopylov, A.: Pattern recognition in interrelated data: the problem, fundamental assumptions, recognition algorithms. In: ICPR (2004)
17. Lester, H., Arridge, S.R.: A survey of hierarchical non-linear medical image registration. Pattern Recog. 32(1) (1999)
18. Angel, E.: Dynamic programming for noncausal problems. IEEE Trans. AC 26(5) (1981)
19. Shekhovtsov, A., Kovtun, I., Hlavac, V.: Efficient MRF deformation model for non-rigid image matching. In: CVPR (2007)
20. Serra, B., Berthod, M.: Subpixel contour matching using continuous dynamic programming. In: CVPR (1994)
21. Munich, M.E., Perona, P.: Continuous dynamic time warping for translation invariant curve alignment with applications to signature verification. In: ICCV (1999)
22. Uchida, S., Fujimura, I., Kawano, H., Feng, Y.: Analytical Dynamic Programming Tracker. In: Kimmel, R., Klette, R., Sugimoto, A. (eds.) ACCV 2010, Part I. LNCS, vol. 6492, pp. 296–309. Springer, Heidelberg (2011)
23. http://yann.lecun.com/exdb/mnist/
24. Angel, E., Bellman, R.: Dynamic Programming and Partial Differential Equations. Academic Press (1972)
25. Etoh, M.: Promotion of block matching: parametric representation for motion estimation. In: ICPR (1998)
26. Liu, C., Yuen, J., Torralba, A.: SIFT Flow: dense correspondence across scenes and its applications. PAMI 33(5) (2011)

Correspondences of Persistent Feature Points on Near-Isometric Surfaces

Ying Yang[1,2], David Günther[1,3], Stefanie Wuhrer[3,1], Alan Brunton[3,4], Ioannis Ivrissimtzis[2], Hans-Peter Seidel[1], and Tino Weinkauf[1,*]

[1] MPI Informatik, Saarbrücken, Germany
[2] Durham University, Durham, UK
[3] Saarland University, Saarbrücken, Germany
[4] University of Ottawa, Ottawa, Canada

Abstract. We present a full pipeline for finding corresponding points between two surfaces based on conceptually simple and computationally efficient components. Our pipeline begins with robust and stable extraction of feature points from the surfaces. We then find a set of near isometric correspondences between the feature points by solving an optimization problem using established components. The performance is evaluated on a large number of 3D models from the following perspectives: robustness w.r.t. isometric deformation, robustness w.r.t. noise and incomplete surfaces, partial matching, and anisometric deformation.

1 Introduction

Intrinsic surface correspondence computation is a highly active research area [1,2]. It is a fundamental aspect of applications such as morphing, texture transfer, geometry synthesis and animation. In general, the search space of intrinsic correspondences between two surfaces is too large to be computationally tractable. A well-established way to reduce the search space is to extract distinctive features from both surfaces and compute correspondence between these. Such features typically also have the benefit of being more reliable to match because of their distinctiveness. Consequently, the search space is reduced in a strategic way. We present an algorithmic pipeline that is able to match robustly feature points between two nearly isometric surfaces.

To effectively match feature points, they should not only be distinctive, but also intuitive and visually meaningful. This is important in visually evaluating correspondence quality on real data, where no ground truth correspondence is available for numerical evaluation. We can get a set of points with these properties from Gaussian curvature. However, Gaussian curvature is greatly affected by noise, resulting in minima and maxima of which only a small subset describe meaningful features. With this in mind, we extract reliable feature sets by using topological persistence [3].

* We thank Art Tevs and Michael Wand for helpful discussions. This work has partially been funded by the MMCI within the Excellence Initiative of the German Federal Government.

A. Fusiello et al. (Eds.): ECCV 2012 Ws/Demos, Part I, LNCS 7583, pp. 102–112, 2012.

We extract features using topological persistence and compute correspondences using feature descriptors and near isometric matching. In so doing, we present a novel pipeline for feature matching that has the following properties: (1) it is based on established components; (2) it produces accurate and stable correspondences; (3) it is conceptually direct and simple; and (4) it is computationally efficient. We provide an extensive evaluation of our pipeline.

2   Related Work

There are many recent works on feature extraction and surface correspondence, so for conciseness we will only review the most relevant here. For a more exhaustive comparison of correspondence methods, we refer the reader to a recent survey [1] and a recent competition [2].

Feature Extraction: Heat Kernel Signature (HKS) [4] organizes information about the intrinsic geometry of a shape in a multi-scale way that is stable under perturbations of the shape. Features are detected as local maxima of the HKS for large scales. A later variant used persistent homology to filter out unstable features [5]. While we also use persistence to filter features, we apply discrete Morse theory to Gaussian curvature, thus making our approach less computationally costly and conceptually simpler. The difference of Gaussians and histogram of oriented gradients feature operators have been adapted to meshes [6], and applied to matching. These methods require a multi-scale neighborhood structure, whereas our features are efficient to compute and direct, only needing a fixed neighborhood to compute Gaussian curvature.

Correspondence: Möbius voting [7] uses the observation that isometries are a subset of the Möbius group to devise a method for automatic sparse surface correspondence. A high-order Markov Random Field (MRF) formulation of graph matching based on Möbius transforms has also been proposed for both sparse and dense correspondence [8]. Blended intrinsic maps [9] find per-point blending weights for multiple low-dimensional intrinsic maps computed using Möbius voting; these maps are then blended by linear interpolation. As noted by the authors, this approach is limited in its ability to match partially corresponding surfaces due to its global nature. We use these methods for comparison because they are the current state-of-the-art and have demonstrated equal or superior performance to competing algorithms [9]. A feature-based dense correspondence method [10] starts by computing sparse feature correspondences, and then uses a MRF and front-propagation to compute dense correspondence. It is a well-established technique to extract feature points and explore permutations of matches to find a combination with minimal alignment and deformation error [10,11,12]. Two of these methods [10,12] use the geodesic integral or average to extract features, which are computationally more expensive than Gaussian curvature. The other [11] uses principal curvatures, which are not isometry invariant. Many methods make use of the isometry assumption, often using some kind of embedding [1,13], which are often indirect and expensive to compute. If the embedding is global then the method can be expected to have difficulty with partial matching. Other methods based on the isometry assumption consider HKS as local surface descriptor. Given one pair of corresponding points, full correspondence can be computed for two isometric surfaces using HKS [14].

3 The Matching Pipeline

This section presents our pipeline to find feature point correspondences on two near isometric surfaces S and $\widetilde{S}$. We call two surfaces nearly isometric if the ratio of any corresponding geodesic distances is bounded by a constant threshold τ. The idea of this pipeline is to extract features as the most dominant extrema of the Gaussian curvature in terms of persistence, an established technique in the visualization community (Section 3.1), and to then find near isometric correspondences between these feature sets using modifications of established algorithms in the vision and geometry processing communities (Section 3.2).

3.1 Feature Points and Persistence

In this work, we interpret feature points as extremal points of a curvature field. Since we assume isometry, we use Gaussian curvature. In recent years, several techniques to compute this quantity were proposed. We use a simple quadratic least-square fitting to the underlying point cloud to compute the Gaussian curvature [15]. However, our pipeline does not depend on this choice.

We consider the scalar field formed by the Gaussian curvature on a surface. Points of minimal and maximal Gaussian curvature are critical points of this scalar field. A robust and consistent way to compute critical points is by means of discrete Morse theory [16]. We use the algorithm by Robins et al. [17] to compute the critical points in a combinatorial fashion. Note that the computed critical points are in a one-to-one correspondence to the topological changes of the lower level sets of the formed scalar field [17].

Numerical issues in the curvature computation and noise may create spurious critical points, which challenge the upcoming matching. To distinguish noise-induced and dominant critical points, we make use of an established importance measure for critical points: *persistence* [3]. It measures the "life time" of connected components and loops considering an evolution of the lower level sets. We denote the most dominant minima and maxima of the Gaussian curvature fields on the surfaces S and $\widetilde{S}$ as feature points X and $\widetilde{X}$, respectively.

3.2 Computing Correspondences of Feature Points

Correspondences between feature points are found as follows. For each feature point, we construct a vector based on the geodesic distances between it and a set of sample points on the surface. We measure the similarity of these vectors and find initial correspondences by solving a minimization problem. We then enforce isometric consistency of the set of correspondence pairs using graph matching, pruning inconsistent matches. Finally, a post-matching method finds additional matches that are consistent with the established correspondences.

Initial Correspondences: We first find an initial correspondence between the feature sets by matching the spatial distribution of feature points. Looking from one feature point $\mathbf{x}$ on S to a uniquely defined set of reference points Y, the distribution of those points depends on the point of view of $\mathbf{x}$ and is unique up to intrinsic symmetry. When measuring the distribution with an isometric quantity such as the geodesic distance, this point of view is invariant under isometric transformations. We represent the view point dependent distribution of Y in a quantitative manner by constructing two sets of reference points Y and $\widetilde{Y}$ of cardinality R from S and $\widetilde{S}$ using *geodesic farthest point sampling* [13] and by considering the quantity $f(\mathbf{x}, \mathbf{y}) = 1/(1 + g(\mathbf{x}, \mathbf{y}))$, where $\mathbf{x} \in X$, $\mathbf{y} \in Y$, and $g(\mathbf{x}, \mathbf{y})$ denotes the geodesic distance between $\mathbf{x}$ and $\mathbf{y}$ on S. The function f measures the influence of the reference points on each feature point, and is designed to allow for partial matching as nearby points are weighed more than distant points, and the local neighborhood therefore has a greater influence.

The *feature vector* $\mathbf{f}_Y$ for a given feature point $\mathbf{x} \in X$ is given by the collection of $f(\mathbf{x}, \mathbf{y}_j)$ for all reference points $\mathbf{y}_j \in Y$ in non-decreasing order. Consider two surfaces S and $\widetilde{S}$ and their respective feature points X and $\widetilde{X}$. Assuming $\mathbf{x} \in X$ is the correspondence of $\widetilde{\mathbf{x}} \in \widetilde{X}$, the corresponding feature vectors $\mathbf{f}_Y(\mathbf{x})$ and $\mathbf{f}_{\widetilde{Y}}(\widetilde{\mathbf{x}})$ are expected to be similar. Hence, we measure the dissimilarity Ψ of two feature vectors by their normalized L^1-distance. Computing the dissimilarity between all feature vectors of X and $\widetilde{X}$ yields a dissimilarity matrix. A good correspondence is found if the sum of all its dissimilarities is small. The aim is therefore to find a minimum assignment through column and/or row permutation to minimize the trace of the dissimilarity matrix. To solve this optimization problem, various optimization algorithms, such as [18], can be used. We in this paper use the Hungarian algorithm [19], which results in a set of correspondences Σ_1.

Isometric Correspondences: In the following, we remove the pairs in Σ_1 that are not consistent with the assumption that deformations should be approximately isometric. We aim to find the largest set Σ_2 of consistent correspondences. These correspondences can be found using a kernel extraction method as proposed by Leordeanu and Hebert [20] and used by Huang et al. [11]. Let $(\mathbf{c}_i, \widetilde{\mathbf{c}}_i)$ denote the i-th correspondence in Σ_1. Any two consistent correspondences $\{\mathbf{c}_i, \widetilde{\mathbf{c}}_i\}$ and $\{\mathbf{c}_j, \widetilde{\mathbf{c}}_j\}$ should satisfy the following near-isometry constraint: the minimum c_{ij} of the two ratios $g(\mathbf{c}_i, \mathbf{c}_j)/g(\widetilde{\mathbf{c}}_i, \widetilde{\mathbf{c}}_j)$ and $g(\widetilde{\mathbf{c}}_i, \widetilde{\mathbf{c}}_j)/g(\mathbf{c}_i, \mathbf{c}_j)$ should be larger than the stretching tolerance τ ($0 < \tau < 1$). It is known that a set of correspondences satisfying this condition can be found using a spectral method on a matrix $\mathbf{M}$ that depends on c_{ij} and τ. For more details, refer to [11].

Final Correspondences: As the set Σ_2 might not contain all near-isometric feature point matches, we add additional pairs of feature points in the final step. The additional correspondences are found based on a modified geodesic triangulation technique. Let $X_R \subset X$ and $\widetilde{X}_R \subset \widetilde{X}$ denote the sets of the "rejected" feature points for which correspondences have not been found yet. For each point in X_R, we compute a feature vector w.r.t. the matched points similar to above. The only difference is that the feature vector is now ordered w.r.t. an arbitrary

Table 1. Parameter settings for all models used in the tests

	Cat	Cat (topo. noise)	Centaur	David	Dog	Horse	Wolf	Face 1	Face 2	Face 3
κ	0.05	0.008	0.05	0.05	0.04	0.03	0.05	0.04	0.10	0.02
τ	0.72	0.72	'0.83	0.83	0.72	0.72	0.72	0.72	0.72	0.72

but fixed order of the correspondences in Σ_2. We add a new correspondence pair if the feature vectors of two points are symmetric nearest neighbors under the dissimilarity measure Ψ and the new pair respects the isometric threshold τ w.r.t. all correspondences in Σ_2. All pairs that fulfill these conditions are added to the set Σ_3 of feature correspondences, which is initialized by Σ_2.

4   Evaluation

This section validates the proposed pipeline. We implement the pipeline using MATLAB and C++ and test it on a standard PC. We use code from Surazhsky et al. [21] to compute geodesics and code from Cao[1] for the Hungarian algorithm. Our non-optimized implementation takes about 3 minutes to find corresponding points for the *Cat* model and about 1.5 minutes for the *Centaur* model.

We evaluate the algorithm on a large number of 3D models of the TOSCA [13] database and some models of the BU-3DFE [22] database. Similar to Bronstein et al. [2], we define the correspondence error $\mathcal{C}$ as follows:

$$\mathcal{C} = \frac{1}{|\Sigma_3| \cdot d_g} \min \left\{ \sum_{i=1}^{|\Sigma_3|} g(\mathbf{c}_i, \mathbf{c}_i'), \sum_{i=1}^{|\Sigma_3|} g(\mathbf{c}_i, \mathbf{c}_i'') \right\}, \tag{1}$$

where $|\Sigma_3|$ is the cardinality of Σ_3, d_g is the geodesic diameter of neutral pose S, $(\mathbf{c}_i, \widetilde{\mathbf{c}}_i)$ is a correspondence pair in Σ_3, $\mathbf{c}_i'$ and $\mathbf{c}_i''$ are the ground truth correspondence and the symmetric ground truth correspondence of $\widetilde{\mathbf{c}}_i$ in S, respectively, and the geodesic distances $g(\mathbf{c}_i, \mathbf{c}_i')$ and $g(\mathbf{c}_i, \mathbf{c}_i'')$ are measured on S. Here, the symmetric ground truth $\mathbf{c}_i''$ is defined as the ground truth mapping of $\mathbf{c}_i$ to its intrinsically symmetric part on the shape, given by flipping the left and right sides of the model.

Our algorithm involves three parameters: the persistence threshold κ, the cardinality R of the set Y of sample points and the deformation threshold τ. Regarding parameter settings, we fix $R = 800$ and each of the other two parameters at one consistent value per model, with the exception of the topological noise example, as shown in Table 1.

Fig. 1 (left) shows the influence of the κ and τ parameter values on the results of matching two *Cat* models. A correspondence $\mathbf{c}_i$ is considered close to its ground truth $\mathbf{c}_i'$ if $g(\mathbf{c}_i, \mathbf{c}_i') < 0.05d_g$, close to its symmetric ground truth $\mathbf{c}_i''$ if $g(\mathbf{c}_i, \mathbf{c}_i'') < 0.05d_g$, and a mismatch otherwise. As expected, as the persistence

---

[1] http://www.mathworks.com/matlabcentral/fileexchange/20328, 2008.

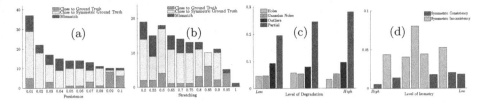

Fig. 1. (a,b): Influence of parameter values on matching two clean *Cat* models. The x-axes show the thresholds and the y-axes show the number of matches. (c,d): Correspondence error $\mathcal{C}$ for the *Cat* model with different types and levels of degradation. Each bar in (c) is the mean over all model pairs, while each bar in (d) is for one pair.

threshold κ increases, the number of features decreases and as the stretching threshold τ increases, the number of matched pairs decreases.

4.1 Synthetic Evaluation

We evaluate the robustness of our algorithm on TOSCA models from four perspectives: isometric deformation, different categories of noise, different object matching and partial matching. Whenever we match two shapes from the same object class, we match the deformed/noisy model to the clean shape of the same object class in neutral pose. To evaluate the robustness against noise, we artificially introduced five different kinds of noise to some models. First, we added three levels of *Gaussian noise* to the deformed versions of the *Cat*, *Centaur*, *David*, *Dog*, *Horse*, and *Wolf* models (38 models total). The variances of Gaussian noise used in the experiments are 20%, 40% and 60% of the model's bounding ball radius. Second, we added three levels of *outliers* to the aforementioned 38 models by moving a vertex in the direction of its outer normal with probability 0.004 by varying the strength of the offset. The outliers are modeled as a type of shot noise that is typically present in scanner data from multi-view camera systems. The models are corrupted by moving a vertex in the direction of its outer normal with probability 0.004. We use three levels of outliers by varying the strength of the offset. Third, we added three levels of *holes* to the deformed versions of the *Cat* model (10 models total). The first level removes the one-ring neighborhood of a set of vertices distributed over the surface. The second and third levels enlarge the holes by removing all triangles that are on the boundary of the model. Fourth, we remove parts of the models in three levels to simulate *partial matching*. For each model in neutral pose, we remove a part by cutting the model with a plane parallel to the symmetry plane of the model. The three levels remove 17%, 33%, and 50% of the model's bounding box, respectively. The partial models are then deformed into all other poses to generate all partial models. Finally, we added *topological noise* to one of the *Cat* models.

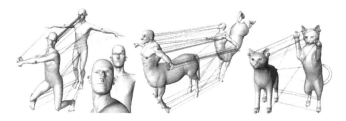

Fig. 2. Matching results for different models, where correspondences are shown in the same color and connected by a line

Fig. 1 (right) shows the correspondence errors $\mathcal{C}$ for the *Cat* models with near-isometric deformations and different types of noise. Note that the correspondence quality does not degrade significantly for increasing levels of Gaussian noise, outliers or holes. As expected, for increasing levels of partial matching, the quality of the correspondence degrades more than for the other types of noise. However, even in case where 50% of the surface was removed, the average correspondence error is below 30% of the geodesic diameter. Similar plots for the other model classes are shown in Appendix B of the supplementary material.

Non-isometric Deformation: Fig. 1 (right) shows $\mathcal{C}$ for the correspondences computed between pairs of *Cat* models. For all of the models that have a mean correspondence error above 0.03, we encounter the following problem. Some points on S correspond to points close to their ground truth correspondences on $\tilde{S}$, while other points on S correspond to their symmetric ground truth correspondences on $\tilde{S}$. Hence, while all correspondences are locally acceptable, the correspondence map is globally inconsistent, which leads to a large value of $\mathcal{C}$. We call this problem *symmetric inconsistency* in the following, and the matching of the legs of the *Dog* and *Wolf* models in Fig. 4 shows an example. However, the symmetric inconsistency only affects very few feature points as can be seen in the bar plots of Fig. 1 (left). The majority of feature points are correctly matched w.r.t. the ground truth or the symmetric ground truth. Fig. 2 shows some qualitative results.

Gaussian Noise: As Gaussian noise will change the intrinsic geometry of the shape, we adjust the parameter τ depending on the specific level of noise. Appendix A of the supplementary material discusses how to relax τ. Basically, τ decreases with the increase of the noise level. This is because stronger noise will create a greater deformation than weaker noise does. Fig. 3 illustrates matching a *Centaur* model degraded by Gaussian noise and its corresponding clean model in neutral pose. As demonstrated by both the small correspondence errors in Fig. 1 (right) and the qualitative results in Fig. 3, our method is able to match feature points even in the presence of Gaussian noise.

Outliers: Fig. 3 shows an example of matching a *Horse* degraded by outliers and its corresponding clean model in neutral pose. Both the numerical evaluation in Fig. 1 (right) and the qualitative results in Fig. 3 demonstrate that our algorithm is able to find high-quality correspondences, when applied to data with outliers.

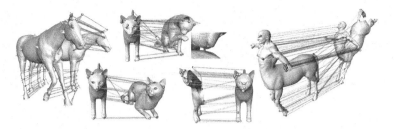

Fig. 3. Matching results for different models corrupted by synthetic noise. From left to right: outliers, holes, topological noise, partial information, and Gaussian noise.

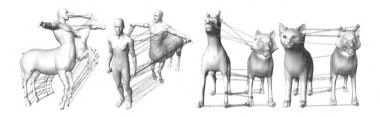

Fig. 4. Matching between different object classes

Holes: Fig. 1 (right) shows that our method still provides comparable performance as for clean models in terms of correspondence quality, although the existence of holes might potentially result in significant changes in geodesic paths. Fig. 3 illustrates qualitatively that feature points are correctly matched.

Partial Matching: Fig. 3 shows an example of matching a partial *Cat* model to a complete *Cat* model. The feature points appearing in both models are visually matched correctly. In a second experiment, we are interested in finding corresponding pairs of vertices for shapes from different object classes. The partial matching results are illustrated in Fig. 4 (left). We observe that feature points describing semantically the same region are correctly matched. For instance, observe the hands and upper body between *Centaur* and *David*. However, feature points could not be matched correctly in regions of the surfaces that are semantically different, as expected. This can be seen in Fig. 4 at the head of *Horse* and the head of *Centaur*.

Topological Noise: Topological noise significantly changes the intrinsic geometry of the surface, and is thus expected to cause problems for our algorithm. Fig. 3 shows the correspondences on a *Cat* model with topological noise.

Different Object Matching: Finding correspondences between two objects of different classes is challenging, since the surfaces are far from isometric. However, our pipeline is able to match most of the feature points correctly, as can be seen in Fig. 4 (right).

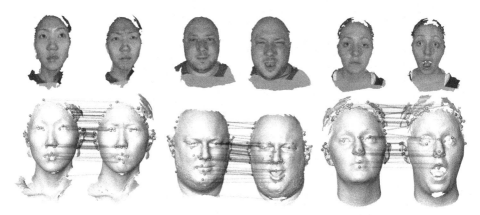

Fig. 5. Correspondences of scans with different facial expressions. The top row shows the textured raw scans and the bottom row shows our results.

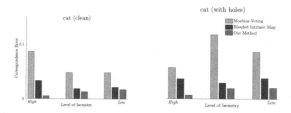

Fig. 6. Comparison for *Cat* without noise and with second level of holes

4.2   Practical and Comparative Evaluation

To assess the real-world applicability of our algorithm, we compute correspondences between different 3D face scans from the BU-3DFE database. These tests are challenging because the meshes have inconsistent topology and different local shape features. The results here are presented visually, as no ground truth is available to evaluate numerically. The matching results are shown in Fig. 5.

We compare the proposed method with two state-of-the-art 3D matching algorithms: Möbius voting [7] and blended intrinsic maps [9] using the code released by the authors[2]. Note that the implementation of Möbius voting may not reflect all the details of the original implementation. We compare to these two methods on pairs of models of the same object from TOSCA for which our method does not encounter the symmetric inconsistency problem. Fig. 6 shows the correspondence errors $\mathcal{C}$ for models with non-isometric deformations and with holes. Note that our method compares favorably to previous approaches. We observed this trend for different models and types of noise.

Limitations of the proposed method include the symmetric inconsistency problem and difficulty handling topological noise and non-isometric deformation. These limitations are due to the heavy dependence on geodesics.

---

[2] http://www.cs.princeton.edu/~vk/CorrsCode/, 2011.

5   Conclusion

We have presented a feature-based approach to find corresponding points for any two given surfaces. The performance is evaluated on a large database, which contains not only clean models, but also data acquired with 3D scanners. We show that our method is robust against isometric deformations and different types of noise, including Gaussian noise, outliers, holes, topological noise and scanner noise. Correct correspondences are found even in the case of partial matching. Future work includes overcoming the symmetric inconsistency issue encountered when matching surfaces with intrinsic symmetries.

References

1. van Kaick, O., Zhang, H., Hamarneh, G., Cohen-Or, D.: A survey on shape correspondence. CGF 30, 1681–1707 (2011)
2. Bronstein, A., Bronstein, M., Castellani, U., Dubrovina, A., Guibas, L., Horaud, R., Kimmel, R., Knossow, D., von Lavante, E., Mateus, D., Ovsjanikov, M., Sharma, A.: SHREC 2010: robust correspondence benchmark. In: 3DOR (2010)
3. Edelsbrunner, H., Letscher, D., Zomorodian, A.: Topological persistence and simplification. DCG 28, 511–533 (2002)
4. Sun, J., Ovsjanikov, M., Guibas, L.: A concise and provably informative multi-scale signature based on heat diffusion. In: SGP, pp. 1383–1392 (2009)
5. Dey, T., Li, K., Luo, C., Ranjan, P., Safa, I., Wang, Y.: Persistent heat signature for pose-oblivious matching of incomplete models. CGF 29, 1545–1554 (2010)
6. Zaharescu, A., Boyer, E., Varanasi, K., Horaud, R.: Surface feature detection and description with applications to mesh matching. In: CVPR, pp. 373–380 (2009)
7. Lipman, Y., Funkhouser, T.: Möbius voting for surface correspondence. TOG (Proc. SIGGRAPH) 28, 72:1–72:12 (2009)
8. Zeng, Y., Wang, C., Wang, Y., Gu, X., Samaras, D., Paragios, N.: Dense non-rigid surface registration using high-order graph matching. In: CVPR, pp. 382–389 (2010)
9. Kim, V., Lipman, Y., Funkhouser, T.: Blended intrinsic maps. TOG 30, 79:1–79:12 (2011)
10. Tung, T., Matsuyama, T.: Dynamic surface matching by geodesic mapping for 3d animation transfer. In: CVPR, pp. 1402–1409 (2010)
11. Huang, Q., Adams, B., Wicke, M., Guibas, L.J.: Non-rigid registration under isometric deformations. In: SGP, pp. 1149–1458 (2008)
12. Zhang, H., Sheffer, A., Cohen-Or, D., Zhou, Q., van Kaick, O., Tagliasacchi, A.: Deformation-driven shape correspondence. CGF (Proc. SGP) 27, 1393–1402 (2008)
13. Bronstein, A., Bronstein, M., Bronstein, M., Kimmel, R.: Numerical geometry of non-rigid shapes. Springer (2008)
14. Ovsjanikov, M., Merigot, Q., Memoli, F., Guibas, L.: One point isometric matching with the heat kernel. CGF (Proc. SGP) 29, 1555–1564 (2010)
15. Cazals, F., Pouget, M.: Estimating differential quantities using polynomial fitting of osculating jets. In: SGP, pp. 177–187 (2003)
16. Forman, R.: Morse theory for cell-complexes. Adv. in Math. 134, 90–145 (1998)
17. Robins, V., Wood, P., Sheppard, A.: Theory and algorithms for constructing discrete morse complexes from grayscale digital images. TPAMI 33, 1646–1658 (2011)

18. Stošić, M., Marques, M., Costeira, J.: Convex solution of a permutation problem. Linear Algebra and its Applications 434, 361–369 (2011)
19. Kuhn, H.: The hungarian method for the assignment problem. Naval Research Logistics Quarterly 2, 83–97 (1955)
20. Leordeanu, M., Hebert, M.: A spectral technique for correspondence problems using pairwise constraints. In: ICCV, pp. 1482–1489 (2005)
21. Surazhsky, V., Surazhsky, T., Kirsanov, D., Gortler, S., Hoppe, H.: Fast exact and approximate geodesics on meshes. TOG (Proc. SIGGRAPH) 24, 553–560 (2005)
22. Yin, L., Wei, X., Sun, Y., Wang, J., Rosato, M.: A 3d facial expression database for facial behavior research. In: FG, pp. 211–216 (2006)

3D Reconstruction of Non-Rigid Surfaces in Real-Time Using Wedge Elements⋆

Antonio Agudo, Begoña Calvo, and J.M.M. Montiel

Instituto de Investigación en Ingeniería de Aragón, Universidad de Zaragoza, Spain
{aagudo,bcalvo,josemari}@unizar.es

Abstract. We present a new FEM (Finite Element Method) model for the 3D reconstruction of a deforming scene using as sole input a calibrated video sequence. Our approach extends the recently proposed 2D thin-plate FEM+EKF (Extended Kalman Filter) combination. Thin-plate FEM is an approximation that models a deforming 3D thin solid as a surface, and then discretizes the surface as a mesh of planar triangles. In contrast, we propose a full-fledged 3D FEM formulation where the deforming 3D solid is discretized as a mesh of 3D wedge elements. The new 3D FEM formulation provides better conditioning for the rank analysis stage necessary to remove the rigid boundary points from the formulation. We show how the proposed formulation accurately estimates deformable scenes from real imagery even for strong deformations. Crucially we also show, for the first time to the best of our knowledge, NRSfM (Non-Rigid Structure from Motion) at 30Hz real-time over real imagery. Real-time can be achieved for our 3D FEM formulation combined with an EKF resulting in accurate estimates even for small size maps.

1 Introduction

The FEM+EKF combination —Finite Element Method to code the deformation model, which is embedded within an Extended Kalman Filter Bayesian estimator— has proven to be able to provide a sequential solution for Non-Rigid Structure from Motion (NRSfM). Agudo et al. [1] propose a simplified 2D thin-plate FEM to code the scene as a deformable surface. In contrast, we propose a full-fledged 3D FEM formulation.

General FEM methods have to discretize a solid into elements defined by the 3D location of their nodes. In our proposal, the elements are wedge-shaped defined by 6 nodes. As the observed solids are opaque, we have to tackle the difficulty of only observing one face of the solid. We propose to extrapolate the solid structure just from its visible face by extrusion. The visible side is modelled as a mesh of triangles, and the mesh is extruded in the normal direction up to a predefined thickness h. The nodes on the hidden side cannot be observed but they define the deformation model. In order to consider their effect, they have to be marginalized out by means of the Schur's complement.

⋆ This work was supported by the Spanish MICINN DIP2009-07130 and DPI2011-15551-E grants. Thanks to Dr. J. Civera and Oscar G. Grasa for fruitful discussion.

A. Fusiello et al. (Eds.): ECCV 2012 Ws/Demos, Part I, LNCS 7583, pp. 113–122, 2012.

The stiffness matrix K is the key to the FEM formulation. Theoretically, K's rank deficiency is 6 because displacements corresponding to rigid body motion [2] do not result in deformation, and hence can happen if no forces are acting on the solid. The thin-plate formulation, due to its approximate nature, does not result in K with 6 rank deficiency [1], so it has to be forced by means of Singular Value Decomposition (SVD). In contrast, our 3D FEM formulation produces K matrices which are 6 rank deficient, showing its theoretical superiority. The 3D FEM can be easier to combine with other FEM models available for the observed structure, such as biomechanical models which are often modelled using 3D elements.

In our approach, all the images are processed, since the estimates are so close a rather simple low cost FEM deformation model is valid. The overall result is that 3D FEM+EKF is able to achieve real-time performance as is experimentally shown. It is also our contribution to provide the first —to the best of our knowledge— experimental validation of a NRSfM system performing in real-time at 30Hz frame-rate using real image sequence.

2   Related Work

NRSfM computes deformable 3D structures from a sequence of images acquired with a monocular camera. It is an ill-posed problem, so additional smoothing constraints or priors are necessary. A relevant class of NRSfM methods are based on closed form factorization, the time varying 3D structure is coded as a linear combination of basis shapes as proposed by Bregler *et al.* [3] for orthographic cameras. Paladini *et al.* [4] propose the first sequential approach for solving NRSfM based on a sequential version of the factorization method over a sliding window. The authors do not report real-time performance.

Bundle Adjustment (BA) has been applied also to solve shape basis approaches to NRSfM. BA can additionally incorporate temporal and spatial smoothness priors both on the deformations and motion [5,6]. Torresani *et al.* [7] introduce an expectation maximization probabilistic linear dynamic model coding deformation weight as Gaussians. Reported experiments, compared with respect to closed form, exhibit better noise rejection and improved accuracy.

In contrast to global models, the piecewise modelling, proposed by Varol *et al.* [8], can more accurately code strong deformations by means of a composition of multiple local deformations. Piecewise methods rely on common features shared between patches to enforce spatial consistency and create a continuous global surface. Taylor *et al.* [9] propose a triangle soup assuming as rigid each triplet of neighbour points. Fayad *et al.* [10] propose quadratic models for each patch.

Template-based methods assume that 2D-to-3D correspondences can be established with a reference image in which the shape is known a priori. These approaches assume isometric deformation for the structure [11]. They have been extended to non-isometric deformations in [12].

Most of the NRSfM methods assume orthographic cameras. Regarding data association can tolerate partial observation of scene points, in any case, the reported experiments rely on given data association instead of embedding the matching within the sequence processing.

FEM was applied in monocular computer vision by Ilić and Fua [13], where an expensive non-linear model accurate for large deformations focused on 1D beam like structures was introduced. The formulation includes the forces and needs to identify boundary points in the image, resulting in a robust and accurate tracking method. In [14] a physical elastic solid model is coded by means of the boundary element method for 2D deformable object tracking, it is not necessary to identify boundary points in the image because 3 rank deficiency is enforced. Agudo *et al.* in [15] extend the EKF-SLAM method [16] to non-rigid scenes, they propose 2D thin-plate FEM model to embed Navier's equations within the EKF estimation. The method can combine both rigid and non-rigid points to estimate 3D reconstruction of deformable scenes and 3D camera trajectory using full perspective cameras. However, prior knowledge about scene point classification as boundary or non-boundary is mandatory. Recently in [1], the boundary points identification prior has been removed, resulting in a method comparable to other NRSfM approaches. FEM models can cope both with isometric and non-isometric scenes without assuming any scene deformation mode. The method is piecewise quadratic and can be considered close to template-based because the shape at rest —not necessarily planar— is needed before coping with the deforming scene. Template-based methods register every image with respect to the initial 3D template, while FEM+EKF sequentially compares the current frame with respect to the 3D scene structure estimated at the previous step.

3   3D FEM Formulation

The partial differential equations for the 3D elasticity problem, known as Navier's equations [2], model the deformation of the solid Ω, with a boundary Γ, under 3D external forces. These equations can be expressed in terms of displacements as:

$$\frac{E}{2(1+\nu)(1-2\nu)}\nabla(\nabla \cdot \boldsymbol{u}) + \frac{E}{2(1+\nu)}\nabla^2\boldsymbol{u} + \boldsymbol{F} = \boldsymbol{0} \ \ in \ \ \Omega, \qquad (1)$$

with $\boldsymbol{u}$ the 3D displacement vector, $\boldsymbol{F}$ the body force applied to the solid, and the material properties of an isotropic linearly elastic solid: the Young's modulus E and the Poisson's ratio ν. $\nabla \cdot (\bullet)$ is the divergence operator, $\nabla(\bullet)$ represents the gradient operator and $\nabla^2(\bullet)$ represents the Laplacian operator. The boundary conditions for Eq. (1) can be expressed as a displacement vector, $\boldsymbol{u} = \bar{\boldsymbol{u}}$, over the boundary Γ_u.

The thin-plate formulation is based on a 2D version of Eq. (1) to model forces and displacements within the plane (membrane effect), and on the Kirchhoff plate to model forces and displacements off the plane (bending effect). The discretized scene elements Ω_e are planar triangles [15,1]. In contrast, our 3D FEM formulation uses Eq. (1) directly to model the solid as a single layer 3D wedge element. The continuous displacements are approximated as $\boldsymbol{u} = \mathbf{N}\boldsymbol{a}$, being $\mathbf{N}$ the matrix of shape functions, then Eq. (1) is rewritten as a sparse linear system:

$$\boldsymbol{K}\,\boldsymbol{a} = \boldsymbol{f}\,, \tag{2}$$

where $\boldsymbol{K}$ is the global stiffness matrix, $\boldsymbol{a}$ is the 3D nodal displacements vector and $\boldsymbol{f}$ is the 3D nodal forces vector. The global $\boldsymbol{K}$ results from the assembling of elemental stiffness matrices $\boldsymbol{K}^e$. The elemental matrix $\boldsymbol{K}^e$, in the normalized element, in natural coordinates (ξ, η, ζ), is computed as:

$$\boldsymbol{K}^e = \frac{1}{E} \int_{-1}^{1} \int_{0}^{1} \int_{0}^{1-\xi} \mathbf{B}^{\top} \mathbf{D} \mathbf{B} \, |\mathbf{J}| \, d\eta \, d\xi \, d\zeta\,, \tag{3}$$

where $\mathbf{B}$ is the strain-displacement matrix for a 3D bilinear wedge element, it depends on the shape functions $\mathbf{N}$. $\mathbf{D}$ is the constitutive matrix which encodes the material properties [2]. $\mathbf{J}$ is the transformation from the normalized to the actual wedge element geometry. E is factorized out of the stiffness matrix to ease the tuning (see Sec. 4). The integrals in Eq. (3) are computed numerically [17].

3.1   3D Wedge Element Definition

We have proposed to model the solid as a single layer of wedge shaped elements. Being an opaque solid, the camera can only detect one surface side, we will call it the visible side. We have to generate the FEM mesh from only the visible side nodes. We propose to extrude each visible side node i along its normal unit vector $\mathbf{d}_i$, up to a fixed thickness h (see Fig. 1(left)). The normal is estimated as a weighted average of the normals of the mesh triangles having the considered node $\mathbf{y}_i$ as a vertex (see Fig. 1(right)). Each normal vector weights according to the corresponding triangle area computed by means of the cross product:

$$\mathbf{d}_i = \frac{\sum_{j=1}^{k}(\mathbf{m}_{ij} - \mathbf{y}_i) \times (\mathbf{m}_{ij+1} - \mathbf{y}_i)}{\left\|\sum_{j=1}^{k}(\mathbf{m}_{ij} - \mathbf{y}_i) \times (\mathbf{m}_{ij+1} - \mathbf{y}_i)\right\|}\,, \tag{4}$$

where $\mathbf{m}_{ij} \in \{\mathbf{m}_{i1}, \mathbf{m}_{i2}, \ldots, \mathbf{m}_{ik}\}$ are the neighbour nodes defining the k Delaunay triangles to which the node $\mathbf{y}_i$ belongs to.

3.2   FEM Linear System Solution

As we assume a single layer of wedge elements, the displacements and forces in linear system Eq. (2) can be reordered to group those corresponding to the visible side, $\boldsymbol{a}^v$, $\boldsymbol{f}^v$, and those corresponding to the hidden side $\boldsymbol{a}^h$, $\boldsymbol{f}^h$:

$$\begin{bmatrix} \boldsymbol{K}_{vv} & \boldsymbol{K}_{vh} \\ \boldsymbol{K}_{vh}^{\top} & \boldsymbol{K}_{hh} \end{bmatrix} \begin{bmatrix} \boldsymbol{a}^v \\ \boldsymbol{a}^h \end{bmatrix} = \begin{bmatrix} \boldsymbol{f}^v \\ \boldsymbol{f}^h \end{bmatrix}. \tag{5}$$

Forces might be acting on both solid faces, however without loss of generality, we can reduce any force acting on the hidden side to an equivalent one on the visible side, then we can safely assume zero forces acting on the hidden side, $\boldsymbol{f}^h = \mathbf{0}$. Hence Schur's complement can be applied to relate $\boldsymbol{a}^v$, $\boldsymbol{f}^v$:

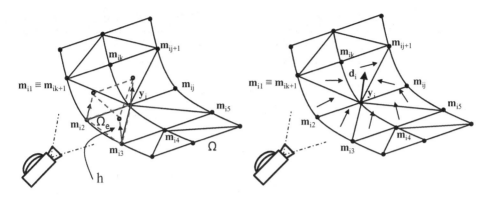

Fig. 1. Left: Extruded wedge element. **Right:** Extrusion normal unit vector $\mathbf{d}_i$, estimated as a weighted average of the normals of the mesh triangles having the considered node $\mathbf{y}_i$ as a vertex.

$$\left[\boldsymbol{K}_{vv} - \boldsymbol{K}_{vh}\boldsymbol{K}_{hh}^{-1}\boldsymbol{K}_{vh}^{\top}\right]\boldsymbol{a}^{v} = \boldsymbol{f}^{v} . \qquad (6)$$

In the absence of boundary conditions, the previous linear system is under-constrained. The full affine solution space can be computed as [1,18]:

$$\boldsymbol{a}^{v} = \boldsymbol{a}_{h} + \boldsymbol{a}_{p}, \qquad \mathcal{K}\,\boldsymbol{a}_{h} = \boldsymbol{0}, \qquad \boldsymbol{a}_{p} = \mathcal{K}^{+}\,\boldsymbol{f}^{v}, \qquad (7)$$

with $\mathcal{K} = \boldsymbol{K}_{vv} - \boldsymbol{K}_{vh}\boldsymbol{K}_{hh}^{-1}\boldsymbol{K}_{vh}^{\top}$. We have verified that $\boldsymbol{K}$ has 6 null singular values as it is theoretically expected. However, $\mathcal{K}$ has 6 singular values significantly smaller than the rest but only 3 of them can be considered null up to numerical accuracy. We attribute this deviation from the theoretical value to the matrix inversion included in the Schur's complement that introduces numerical round-off errors. The particular solution $\boldsymbol{a}_{p}$ is computed by means of the Moore–Penrose pseudoinverse $\mathcal{K}^{+}$ enforcing the matrix $\mathcal{K}$ rank to $3p - 6$, with p the number of nodes.

4   Sequential Approach to NRSfM

The 3D FEM formulation is embedded within the EKF sequential Bayesian estimation cycle. We use a cameracentric EKF-based formulation to estimate the relative pose of the deformable scene with respect to the camera. The 3D FEM formulation free of rigid boundary points permits the displacement of all map points in correlated form by means of the pseudoinverse stiffness matrix $\mathcal{K}^{+}$ and it is embedded in the EKF prediction step.

The state vector $\mathbf{x}_{k}^{C_k} = \left(\mathbf{x}_{rk}^{C_k}{}^{\top}, \mathbf{y}_{k}^{C_k}{}^{\top}\right)^{\top}$ is composed of the camera pose $\mathbf{x}_{rk}^{C_k}$ and the locations of the p map points $\mathbf{y}_{k}^{C_k} = \left(\mathbf{y}_{1k}^{C_k}{}^{\top}, \ldots, \mathbf{y}_{pk}^{C_k}{}^{\top}\right)^{\top}$, coded as cameracentric, i.e. all of them are referenced with respect to the camera frame

$(C_k$ superindex). $\mathbf{x}_{rk}^{C_k}$ is composed of the pose and the corresponding velocity vectors. The dynamics of the pose includes the combined effects of both the camera and scene rigid motions [1] it is assumed to be a constant velocity model.

The state equation for the deformable scene map points is:

$$\mathbf{g}_y = \mathbf{y}_{k+1}^{C_k} = \mathbf{y}_k^{C_k} + \mathcal{K}_k^+ \Delta \mathbf{S}^C, \tag{8}$$

where the incremental non-rigid displacement is modelled as the particular solution for the FEM linear system Eq. (7). The pseudoinverse stiffness matrix $\mathcal{K}_k^+ \left(\hat{\mathbf{y}}_{k-1|k-1}^{C_k} \right)$ depends on the current structure geometry estimate.

The vector of normalized forces $\Delta \mathbf{S}^C$ causes recursively an incremental deformation at each step. We assume $\Delta \mathbf{S}^C$ follows a Gaussian with zero-mean, with $\mathbf{Q_y}$ its covariance. The normalized forces are defined as:

$$\Delta \mathbf{S}_i^C = \frac{1}{E} \left(\Delta f_{xi}^C, \Delta f_{yi}^C, \Delta f_{zi}^C \right)^\top, \tag{9}$$

where E has been factorized out from the stiffness matrix in order to allocate the material tuning parameters within the state noise. In contrast to [1], h thickness parameter cannot be factored out from $\boldsymbol{K}$ and hence cannot be allocated within the normalized forces.

We propose to tune $\mathbf{Q_{y_i}}$ as a diagonal matrix, where the standard deviation codes the normalized forces magnitude. The scene is coded as rigid when $\mathbf{Q_{y_i}} = 0$. Additionally, h and ν have to be defined so as to compute the $\boldsymbol{K}^e$ in Eq. (3). Quasi-incompressible materials are assumed tuning $\nu = 0.499$.

5   Experiments

A Matlab code has been developed to validate the proposed 3D FEM algorithm on real 320×240@30Hz image sequences. The first experiment corresponds to a non-isometrically deforming silicone. Sequence and ground truth taken from [1]. A second experiment corresponds to a waving camera observing an isometrically deforming paper sheet.

We have also developed an optimised C++ code to show the 3D FEM+EKF real-time performance. We process the paper sequences for a 35 feature map to reach real-time at 30Hz on an Intel Core i7 processor at 2GHz based laptop.

For all experiments[1], we assume that the initial sequence frames correspond to a mobile camera observing a rigid scene in order to estimate the structure at rest. We use the proposed method just tuning $\mathbf{Q}_y = 0$ (Sec. 4) to estimate 3D structure at rest.

5.1   Multiply Deformed Silicone Sequence

Data association was automatically computed applying the general matching algorithm. The coded labels for the markers are not considered for the data

---

[1] Videos of the experimental results on website http://webdiis.unizar.es/~aagudo

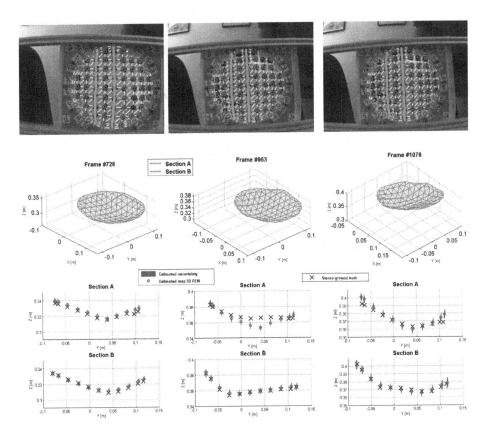

Fig. 2. 3D FEM estimated structure for the multiply deformed silicone. Top: Images with overlaid deformed 3D mesh and elliptical matching acceptance regions: red (predicted&matched), blue (predicted&not matched). **Middle:** General view of the 3D reconstructed deformed scene. **Bottom:** Two cross sections of the reconstructed surface; these represent the estimated points with the 95% acceptance regions according to the estimated covariances, and the stereo ground truth.

association algorithm. Not all the points were detected in all the images. In the video `silicone_sequence.avi`, it can be noticed how non-detection results in map point covariance increase. In any case, non-matched map point locations are updated indirectly from other map point observations via the covariance matrix correlation terms.

The estimated structure provides both the map point locations and the corresponding covariance. The covariance codes the estimation error. The ground truth is included in the 95% acceptance region for the estimated map points (see Fig. 2). We can conclude after a quantitative comparison that the proposed method is accurate, because the ellipses are small, and mostly exact, because the ellipses include the ground truth. It should be noticed that the processed scene does not fulfill the isometric deformation but we can handle it successfully.

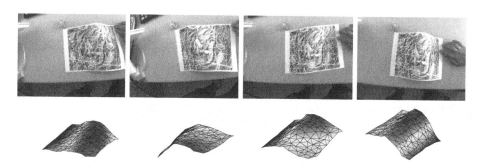

Fig. 3. Estimated structure for the **strong deformation paper**. **Top:** Deformed 3D mesh overlaid on the image sequence. **Bottom:** General view of the 3D deformable surface.

5.2   Deforming Paper Sheet

To display performance under extreme deformations, we used a real image sequence in which there is a strong deformation of a paper sheet observed by a waving camera (see Fig. 3 and `strong_deformation.avi`). FAST interest points in the first image define the map points, the triangular mesh is just the corresponding Delaunay triangulation. Every triangle yields a different stiffness because of its different geometry.

Fig. 3 shows selected frames and the corresponding estimated structure. The tuning, very thin solid and quasi-incompressible material, results in the ability to deal with an isometric scene as a consequence of the generality of our proposal.

5.3   Real-Time Performance

We have implemented the algorithm in C++. Additionally, we have implemented a specialized algorithm for symmetric matrix SVD, to reduce the computational cost from $O\left(21n^3\right)$ to $O\left(12n^3\right)$. We tested the code on the paper sequences (see Fig. 4 and `real_time_sequence.avi`). Given the $O\left(n^3\right)$ complexity, we have limited the map size to 35 features so as to achieve real-time rates at 30Hz. Thus, we show experimentally that the 3D FEM+EKF combination can produce accurate estimates even with small size maps. Note that other methods in the literature use bigger maps, about a hundred points for FEM+EKF in [1], or several hundreds for batch methods in [10]. Taylor *et al.*'s method [9] is only valid for bigger maps. In addition, we must emphasize that our proposal does not use as input the 2D tracking data, but it is computed automatically.

Fig. 5 shows the total cycle time budget identifying: map management and matching, EKF update and EKF prediction. Two phases can be distinguished: rigid initialization and non-rigid estimation. At initialization the map points are coded in inverse depth [16] (6 parameters per point), the prediction cost is negligible and the dominant cost is the cubic update. During the non-rigid estimation map points are coded in Euclidean XYZ (3 parameters per point) with the corresponding reduction in the update stage. However, due to the FEM

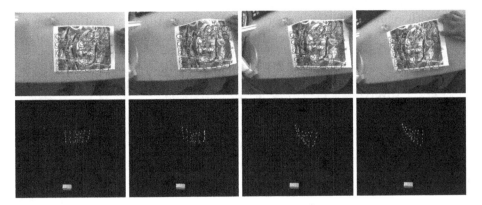

Fig. 4. Estimated structure for the **strong deformation in real-time** at 30Hz. **Top:** Images including elliptical search regions: red (predicted&matched) and blue (predicted&not matched). **Bottom:** General view of the 3D reconstructed deformed scene.

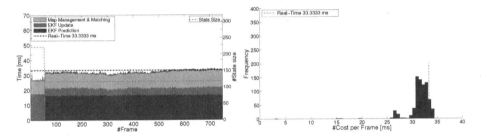

Fig. 5. Left: Real-time computation budget for the strong deformation sequence. Rigid initialization until frame#60 when non-rigid estimation starts. Two scale plots: left-y axis time, right y-axis state size n. **Right:** Per cycle time histogram.

modelling, the prediction stage becomes relevant due to its cubic cost. An increase in the matching during the non-rigid stage is due to the increase in the prediction ellipse size with the corresponding increase in the search time.

6 Conclusions

The 3D FEM+EKF combination has been experimentally validated —for the first time to the best of our knowledge— to be a valid method for sequential real-time at frame-rate NRSfM. It has to be stressed that the 3D FEM+EKF formulation deals with full perspective cameras, and it does not assume prior data association because it is computed within the EKF prediction-match-update cycle. NRSfM can be solved for a low number of scene points, what can be comparatively advantageous for scenes with low texture content.

To reduce the effect of the non-linearities, we are forced to process every single frame in the sequence. In any case, as the EKF handles a dynamic state, the state size does not increase with the number of processed images because we do not have to explicitly represent the scene at previous time steps. All the estimation memory is accumulated in the actual scene estimate and its corresponding covariance matrix. We believe that this is one of key elements to achieve real-time performance.

A new FEM model based on 3D wedge elements have been developed. The novel model is theoretically superior to previous thin-plate FEM formulation [1]. FEM-based NRSfM can be rather effective in considering the rich priors that accurate FEM models can provide. This is particularly relevant for the case of medical images where it is realistic to have available accurate FEM models of the observed scene. This is the goal of our future work.

References

1. Agudo, A., Calvo, B., Montiel, J.M.M.: Finite element based sequential bayesian non-rigid structure from motion. In: CVPR (2012)
2. Zienkiewicz, O.C., Taylor, R.L.: The finite element method, vol. 1: Basic formulation and linear problems. McGraw-Hill, London (1989)
3. Bregler, C., Hertzmann, A., Biermann, H.: Recovering non-rigid 3D shape from image streams. In: CVPR (2000)
4. Paladini, M., Bartoli, A., Agapito, L.: Sequential Non-Rigid Structure-from-Motion with the 3D-Implicit Low-Rank Shape Model. In: Daniilidis, K., Maragos, P., Paragios, N. (eds.) ECCV 2010, Part II. LNCS, vol. 6312, pp. 15–28. Springer, Heidelberg (2010)
5. Bartoli, A., Gay-Bellile, V., Castellani, U., Peyras, J., Olsen, S., Sayd, P.: Coarse-to-fine low-rank structure-from-motion. In: CVPR (2008)
6. Del Bue, A., Llado, X., Agapito, L.: Non-rigid metric shape and motion recovery from uncalibrated images using priors. In: CVPR (2006)
7. Torresani, L., Hertzmann, A., Bregler, C.: Nonrigid structure-from motion: estimating shape and motion with hierarchical priors. PAMI, 878–892 (2008)
8. Varol, A., Salzmann, M., Tola, E., Fua, P.: Template-free monocular reconstruction of deformable surfaces. In: ICCV (2009)
9. Taylor, J., Jepson, A.D., Kutulakos, K.N.: Non-rigid structure from locally-rigid motion. In: CVPR (2010)
10. Fayad, J., Agapito, L., Del Bue, A.: Piecewise Quadratic Reconstruction of Non-Rigid Surfaces from Monocular Sequences. In: Daniilidis, K., Maragos, P., Paragios, N. (eds.) ECCV 2010, Part IV. LNCS, vol. 6314, pp. 297–310. Springer, Heidelberg (2010)
11. Salzmann, M., Fua, P.: Reconstructing sharply folding surfaces: A convex formulation. In: CVPR (2009)
12. Moreno-Noguer, F., Salzmann, M., Lepetit, V., Fua, R.: Capturing 3D stretchable surfaces from single images in closed from. In: CVPR (2009)
13. Ilić, S., Fua, P.: Non-linear beam model for tracking large deformation. In: ICCV (2007)
14. Greminger, M.A., Nelson, B.J.: Deformable object tracking using the boundary element method. In: CVPR (2003)
15. Agudo, A., Calvo, B., Montiel, J.M.M.: FEM models to code non-rigid EKF monocular SLAM. In: Workshop on Dynamic Shape Capture and Analysis (2011)
16. Civera, J., Davison, A.J., Montiel, J.M.M.: Inverse depth parametrization for monocular SLAM. IEEE Transactions on Robotics 24, 932–945 (2008)
17. Stroud, A.H.: Approximate Calculation of Multiple Integrals. Prentice-Hall (1971)
18. Golub, G., Van Loan, C.: Matrix computations. Johns Hopkins Univ. Pr. (1996)

Schrödinger Diffusion
for Shape Analysis with Texture

Jose A. Iglesias and Ron Kimmel

Department of Computer Science
Technion-Israel Institute of Technology, Haifa 32000, Israel

Abstract. In recent years, quantities derived from the heat equation
have become popular in shape processing and analysis of triangulated
surfaces. Such measures are often robust with respect to different kinds
of perturbations, including near-isometries, topological noise and partial-
ities. Here, we propose to exploit the semigroup of a Schrödinger operator
in order to deal with texture data, while maintaining the desirable properties of the heat kernel. We define a family of Schrödinger diffusion
distances analogous to the ones associated to the heat kernels, and show
that they are continuous under perturbations of the data. As an application, we introduce a method for retrieval of textured shapes through
comparison of Schrödinger diffusion distance histograms with the earth's
mover distance, and present some numerical experiments showing superior performance compared to an analogous method that ignores the
texture.

Keywords: Laplace-Beltrami operator, textured shape retrieval, diffusion distance, Schrödinger operators, earth mover's distance.

1   Introduction

There is an ever growing quantity of 3D shapes available, either scanned from
real objects, manually modelled by artists, or acquired from other sources. Adequately classifying them, and being able to find similar and dissimilar models
is therefore increasingly important, and automatic solutions are needed for the
goal of efficient computerized *shape retrieval*.

For a retrieval method to be useful, given the variability of shapes, often
some invariance properties are required. The most obvious one is translation
and rotation (that is, Euclidean) invariance. Their scale is often arbitrary, so
sometimes it is also interesting to enforce invariance with respect to global or
local scaling. More challenging is recognition in classes of non-rigid shapes, like
shapes representing human faces, animals or animated characters. In these cases,
only the intrinsic geometry can be used, thus enforcing invariance to isometries,
and robustness with respect to near-isometries.

Often, geometric models include textures, which are an integral part of the
representation. It is therefore natural to try and use the texture information to
better distinguish between objects, for example in cases like separating between

A. Fusiello et al. (Eds.): ECCV 2012 Ws/Demos, Part I, LNCS 7583, pp. 123–132, 2012.

a horse and a zebra, classifying different species of fish with similar shapes but different colors and patterns, or categorizing archaeological findings.

In this paper, we introduce a representation that incorporates texture data within several recent methods of shape analysis and retrieval, which themselves depend only on intrinsic geometry and hence are appropriate for non-rigid shapes. Our method fully inherits the desirable invariance and robustness properties of these methods, while also utilizing the texture of the shapes.

The paper is organized as follows. In Section 2 we briefly review previous efforts and basic concepts on which our method is based. In Section 3, we define our central quantities, a family of diffusion distances based on diffusion with Schrödinger operators incorporating the texture data, and present some theoretical results about them. Then, in Section 4, we present a system of shape retrieval based on comparison of histograms of Schrödinger diffusion distances with the earth mover's distance. Finally, in Section 5, we present some experimental results obtained with our representation model.

2   Diffusion in Shape Analysis: Previous Works

Adding to a long history of use of Laplace operators in geometry processing applications [1], the spectral decomposition of Laplace-Beltrami operators on surfaces has proven to be useful for tasks of shape analysis and comparison [2].

In [3], diffusion through the heat equation, constructed from the spectral decomposition, was used for comparison of shapes through the introduction of the heat kernel signature (HKS). Since then, many methods have used descriptors for shapes built from the heat kernel [4][5].

Diffusion distances were introduced by Coifman and Lafon in [6] for data analysis of point clouds, under the basic assumption that the sampled points come from an underlying low-dimensional manifold. Recently, diffusion distances have also received considerable attention for shape analysis and retrieval tasks, for example in shape recognition [7] or shape matching [8].

Recently, an approach to shape retrieval including texture data was proposed in [9], introducing three channels of texture (in the Lab color space) through a higher dimensional embedding, similar to the Beltrami framework [10]. In comparison, the method presented here supports a single channel for the texture, yet it has a clear interpretation in terms of diffusion on the original shape. It also requires lower order derivatives of the texture (at most one in our case, versus two for the embedding approach), making it less sensitive to noise.

3   Schrödinger Operators and Diffusion

We will consider our surfaces to be compact two-dimensional manifolds, denoted by M and embedded in $\mathbb{R}^3$, with triangular meshes as discretizations. In terms of a local parametrization and the corresponding first fundamental form g, one can define the Laplace-Beltrami operator through the formula

$$\Delta_g f = (\text{div}_g \circ \text{grad}_g)(f) = \sum_{i,j} \frac{1}{\sqrt{|g|}} \partial_i \left(\sqrt{|g|} g^{ij} \partial_j f \right), \tag{1}$$

where $|g|$ is the determinant of the metric, g^{ij} are the components of the inverse of the metric, and ∂_i denotes partial derivative with respect to the i-th coordinate. It is well known [11] that the Laplace-Beltrami operator doesn't depend on the coordinate functions chosen, and since it's defined in terms of g, it is invariant under transformations that preserve g, that is, isometries. This operator is a generalization of the standard Laplacian in $\mathbb{R}^n$, for many of the processes associated to the former, like diffusion and smoothing.

Consider a function $V : M \to \mathbb{R}$, which we require to be bounded, but without needing any further regularity, in particular not necessarily differentiable or even continuous, to which we will refer as the *potential*. A Schödinger operator on the surface M is an operator of the form $\Delta_g - V$, with V being considered as a multiplication operator, that is, $Vf(x) = V(x)f(x)$.

These operators are referred to as Schrödinger operators, and play a major role in quantum mechanics, where the study of their spectrum is key to understanding the Schrödinger equation. In those cases the potential is usually unbounded, which makes the analysis a challenge of its own. One can also consider the diffusion equation associated to these operators,

$$\begin{cases} \partial_t u(x,t) = \Delta_g u(x,t) - V(x)u(x,t) \\ u(x,0) = u_0(x), \end{cases} \tag{2}$$

which will be the equation defining the quantities that we will use in what follows. Boundary conditions are not needed since M is compact. The following result asserts that for these operators, on the continuous level, everything works as expected, mimicking the situation with the Laplacian and heat kernels:

Theorem 1. *Let (M, g) be a compact Riemannian manifold of class C^2, Δ_g the Laplace-Beltrami operator on (M, g), and $V \in L^\infty(M, \mu_g)$, where μ_g is the measure associated to the Riemannian volume element, with $V \geq 0$. Then, the operator $-\Delta_g + V$ admits a spectral decomposition $\{(\phi_j, \lambda_j)\}_{j=1}^\infty$, such that $\{\phi_j\}_{j=1}^\infty$ is an orthonormal basis for $L^2(M, \mu_g)$, $\lambda_j \geq 0$ and $\lim_{j \to \infty} \lambda_j = +\infty$.*

Moreover, there exists a family of functions $h_t \in L^2(M, \mu_g)$, such that for all $u_0 \in L^2(M, \mu_g)$, the unique solution of (2) is given by

$$u(x,t) = \int_S h_t(x,y)u_0(y)d\mu_g(y), \tag{3}$$

and the following formula holds

$$h_t(x,y) = \sum_{i=1}^\infty e^{-\lambda_i t}\phi_i(x)\phi_i(y). \tag{4}$$

Proof. The proof is essentially the same as in the Laplacian case. We refer to [12] for a standard proof. Let us note, however, that both the hypotheses that the manifold is compact and the potential V is bounded are essential, as otherwise, the discreteness of the spectrum is not guaranteed, since in those cases the involved resolvents could fail to be compact.

Based on this result, a squared diffusion distance [6] can be defined as the L^2 norm of the difference of the kernels for Equation (2), and using Equation (4)

$$d_t^2(x,y) = \|h_t(x,\cdot) - h_t(y,\cdot)\|_{L^2}^2 = \sum_{j=1}^{\infty} e^{-2\lambda_j t}(\phi_j(x) - \phi_j(y))^2. \qquad (5)$$

Note, that the sign in the exponential arises because we have defined $\lambda_j > 0$ to be the eigenvalues of $-(\Delta_g - V)$. These distances enjoy the same properties as those associated to the heat kernel, since all the properties proved in [6], including the fact that the formula above defines a distance, are valid for more general semigroups and not just the one associated to the Laplacian.

We also have that the solutions to the diffusion equation, and therefore any quantities derived from it, in particular our diffusion distances, are continuous with respect to perturbations of the potential. Namely,

Proposition 2. *Consider the problem:*

$$\begin{cases} \partial_t u(x,t) = \Delta u(x,t) - (V(x) + \epsilon N(x))u(x,t) \\ u(x,0) = u_0(x), \end{cases} \qquad (6)$$

where $V, N \in L^\infty(M, \mu_g)$, $V \geq 0$ and $V + \epsilon N \geq 0$ for some $\epsilon \geq 0$. Then, the solutions to of the above problem converge strongly in $L^2(M, \mu_g)$ to the ones of problem 2 as $\epsilon \to 0$, for each fixed $t > 0$.

Proposition 2 can be proved by using standard results in perturbation theory of linear semigroups ([13], IX.2.16), that require convergence of solutions of the resolvents of the operator, which is just the solution of a linear elliptic equation.

3.1   The Feynman-Kac Formula

To shed some light on the behavior of the solutions to Equation (2), we provide an informal discussion on a well-known stochastic interpretation of such solutions.

The Feynman-Kac formula [14] expresses the solution of a diffusion equation in terms of Brownian motion (strictly, the Wiener process on our space, X)

$$u(x,t) = E\left(u_0(X_0) \exp\left(-\int_0^t V(X_\tau)d\tau\right) \mid X_t = x\right), \qquad (7)$$

the conditional expectation meaning that we take averages of all the Wiener paths that reach x at time t, starting from elsewhere. Note that the integral inside the exponential involves the Wiener process itself, and hence needs to be understood in the sense of stochastic integrals. A rigorous treatment of this is beyond the scope of this paper, but can be found in [14].

In the case of the heat equation, $V = 0$, the initial values are transported over random paths, and the expected value over all paths that reach a point at a given time is the value of our solution. This kind of averaging property is the reason behind the robustness to different kinds of noise that diffusion distances and other quantities derived from heat kernels possess.

For Schrödinger operators, one can think of this transported value being modulated exponentially by the potential $V(x) \geq 0$, in a way consistent with what one gets by disregarding the diffusion term to end up with $u_t + Vu = 0$. The transported values will be decreased according to how large V is in the areas that the Brownian motion crosses, on average. Figure 1 illustrates this behavior, for a potential generated from the gradient of the texture on the shape.

4   Textured Shape Retrieval with Schrödinger Diffusion

In our context, all references to textures on shapes will in fact be about vertex colorings. This is because only at that level the notions of a mapping on the surface and the diffusion can have discretizations consistent with one another, as required for our Schrödinger operators. In the case of textures mapped on triangles, one could induce a vertex map by averaging over the Voronoi region corresponding to the vertex in its one-ring neighborhood, for example.

For our shape retrieval application, we intend to define a distance between signatures of the shapes, which in our case will be histograms of Schrödinger diffusion distances between points. The retrieval method would then select from a database the shapes with the smallest distance to the query. In what follows, we assume our texture is a differentiable function $I : M \to \mathbb{R}$ in the continuous model, and a vertex function $I(v_i)$ for the discretized version.

4.1   Operator Discretization

A popular discretization for the Laplace-Beltrami operator of a surface is the so-called cotangent weight scheme [15], where the weights are the sums of cotangents of angles adjacent to the edge, and the normalization coefficients are the Voronoi areas corresponding to the vertex. One of its disadvantages is the fact that for meshes with obtuse angles, the edge weights become negative, making it unsuitable [16] for simulating diffusion processes.

So instead, we chose the 'Mesh Laplacian' discretization of [17], inspired by the one introduced by Belkin and Niyogi for data analysis of point clouds in [18]. For triangular meshes, it is given by

$$\Delta_s f(v_i) = \frac{1}{4\pi s^2} \sum_{\tau \in \mathcal{T}(v_i)} \frac{A(\tau)}{3} \sum_{w \in \tau} e^{\frac{-\|v_i - w\|^2}{4s}} (f(w) - f(v_i)), \qquad (8)$$

where $\mathcal{T}(v_i)$ denotes the set of triangles in a neighborhood of v_i, $A(\tau)$ is the area of the triangle τ and s is a scaling parameter.

This discretization has several advantages. The ones that are the most useful for us are that the weights are nonnegative by definition, and the fact that it converges pointwise to the continuous Laplace-Beltrami operator, when the meshes approximate a smooth surface and $\mathcal{T}(v_i)$ is always the whole shape, as proved in [17]. Spectral convergence in a probabilistic sense, of the point-cloud version of the operator, is proved in [19]. In our case, since it would not be practical to

Fig. 1. Diffusion on a textured shape, with $V = \alpha(1 + \beta|\nabla I|)$. Left to right, row wise: textured shape, modulus of the gradient, snapshot of kernel, diffusion distance. Observe that some of the stripes of the zebra can be seen in the distance and the kernel is shaped by them, since texture edges work against the diffusion. The source is marked in white.

use the whole shape as a neighborhood, we have taken the neighborhoods $\mathcal{T}(v_i)$ to be the one-ring neighborhood of each vertex. The parameter s was choosen in a uniform way, not taking into account the size of the different neighborhoods, as one fifth of the median of the edge lengths over the whole shape.

After discretizing the Laplace-Beltrami operator as above, our discrete operators are defined in the obvious way,

$$((\varDelta_s - V)f)(v_i) = \varDelta_s f(v_i) - V(v_i)f(v_i). \tag{9}$$

4.2   Choice of Potential and Its Discretization

One choice for the potential V would be just to take $V = I$, I corresponding for example to the luminance of the texture. This would have the advantage of not having to explicitly compute any derivative of I, but in turn would make it depend on the reference taken for the texture, that is, on transformations of the kind $\tilde{I} = I + c$, where c is a constant.

Another option is to use an edge indicator for the textures as the potential V, the most straightforward being the modulus of the surface gradient, $V = |\nabla I|$, ∇ being the (Riemannian) gradient on the surface. Other options are $V = \log(1+I)$ or $V = \log(1 + |\nabla I|)$, as a way to mitigate the exponential decay caused by the potential V in Formula (7). In our experiments below, we used this last potential.

Intuitively, from the random walk interpretation and the Feynman-Kac Formula (7), we see that it will be harder to diffuse across edges of the texture, while in constant areas, the behavior will be that of the usual heat equation. This can be appreciated in Figure 1.

We will now describe the approximation of the gradient of a function on the surface that we employed, which is the same as in [20]. Let v be the vertex we are interested in, and $\tau = \{u, v, w\}$ a triangle of the shape having v as a vertex. Denote

$$r_u = \frac{u - v}{|u - v|}, \; r_w = \frac{w - v}{|w - v|}, \; P = \begin{bmatrix} r_u^T \\ r_w^T \end{bmatrix}, \tag{10}$$

where r_u^T, r_w^T denote transposes. Note, that P is the change of basis matrix from the canonical basis to r_u, r_w, which form a basis for the plane that contains the triangle. Also, denote by I_u, I_v, I_w the values of our function on the three vertices. Then, we can consistently approximate the norm of the gradient by

$$(|\nabla I|_v^\tau)^2 = \left(\frac{I_u - I_v}{|u - v|} \; \frac{I_w - I_v}{|w - v|} \right) (PP^T)^{-1} \left(\begin{matrix} \frac{I_u - I_v}{|u - v|} \\ \frac{I_w - I_v}{|w - v|} \end{matrix} \right). \tag{11}$$

Finally, to obtain our discretization, we average this approximation over the one-ring neighborhood of v,

$$|\nabla I|_v = \frac{1}{\#\mathcal{T}(v)} \sum_{\tau \in \mathcal{T}(v)} |\nabla f|_v^\tau. \tag{12}$$

4.3   Point Selection and Histogram Comparison

To obtain a signature based on diffusion distances, one needs to select points between which the distances are computed. In our case, we performed farthest point sampling [21] based on Euclidean ambient distances (for simplicity) to pick 100 points, for which we computed the diffusion distance map to the rest of the shape. Then, the results for each of them are combined in a global histogram, which will serve as descriptor for the shape. The histograms were quantized with 120 bins, and normalized, to compare shapes with any number of vertices.

After obtaining the histograms of diffusion distances to be used as signatures, we need a way to compare them consistently. A popular approach for comparing probability distributions (and hence normalized histograms) is the Earth Mover's Distance, or EMD [22]. We use it to compute distances between the histograms of diffusion distances, as a means of comparing them. Let us note that even if in the one-dimensional continuous case computing the optimal cost is straightforward from the cumulative distribution functions, in the discrete case one still needs to solve a flow network optimization problem, which is computationally expensive, if done naively [23]. In our case, we have used the method and code of Pele and Werman [24] to efficiently approximate the EMD between our histograms.

A similar approach to shape retrieval, but with local descriptors, was used in [25], where the distances used were the inner distances inside planar shapes.

A more sophisticated approach using histograms of geodesic distances and Wasserstein metrics can be found in [26]. We emphasize that we purposefully used a classification method which is far from being state of the art, to be able to better demonstrate the increased performance with just a moderate-sized database.

5   Experimental Results

For our experiments, the shapes were taken from the TOSCA nonrigid shape database [27], and the textures were manually added as vertex colorings. The final database consisted of 73 shapes, belonging to 8 different classes. Inside each class, the shapes differed by an almost-isometric deformation (different 'poses').

The Laplace-Beltrami operators were discretized through the scheme described above, before combining them with the norms of the gradient of the texture data, as described in Section 4. Diffusion distances were computed directly from the definition, using 100 eigenvalues and eigenfunctions, which were in turn computed from the corresponding matrices of the discrete operators.

Then, the EMD between the histograms from each pair of shapes was computed, and finally the two closest matches for each shape were chosen as candidates for retrieval. This whole process was done for $V = 0$ and $V = \alpha \log(1 + \beta|\nabla I|)$, with α and β normalization constants which control the resistance to diffusion induced by the texture.

Results for the distances are shown in Figure 2, and Table 1 shows the amount of correct matches and averages of distances inside and outside the classes, after normalization with respect to the maximum distance between elements.

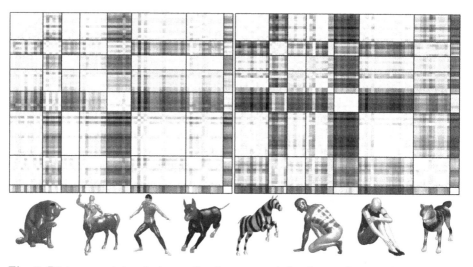

Fig. 2. Distance matrices between the signatures of the shapes. Lines indicate separation between classes. White corresponds to zero distance, black to maximum distance. Left: Results without texture. Right: Results with texture. Lower: Representatives of each class of shapes, in the same order as the matrices.

Table 1. Numerical results for both cases

	$V = 0$	$V = \alpha \log(1 + \beta |\nabla I|)$
Nearest shape belongs to correct class	52/73	65/73
Second nearest shape belongs to correct class	41/73	50/73
Normalized avg. distance for shapes in same class	0.1440	0.1167
Normalized avg. distance for shapes in different classes	0.2905	0.3822

As we can see, the average distance between shapes in the same class is reduced, while the average distance between shapes in different classes increases, providing better separation between the classes. Also, some queries that would produce incorrect matches with just the geometry are correctly matched when also using the texture.

6   Conclusions

We defined a family of diffusion distances based on the diffusion associated to Schrödinger operators, for use in triangulated shapes with textures, where quantities derived from the texture are introduced as the potential part of the operator. These are at least continuous with respect to perturbations of the texture.

The practical usefulness of our method was illustrated by a simple retrieval example using global diffusion distance histograms as descriptors. Using the available texture information resulted in better performance than using only the geometry data through standard heat diffusion.

Our approach could also be useful to incorporate texture data in other methods of shape analysis using Laplacian operators but not heat diffusion explicitly, such as the ones in [28] and [2].

Acknowledgments. This work was supported by the European Commission ITN-FIRST, agreement No. PITN-GA-2009-238702.

References

1. Sorkine, O.: Laplacian mesh processing. In: Eurographics, pp. 53–70 (2005)
2. Rustamov, R.M.: Laplace-beltrami eigenfunctions for deformation invariant shape representation. In: SGP, pp. 225–233 (2007)
3. Sun, J., Ovsjanikov, M., Guibas, L.: A concise and provably informative multi-scale signature based on heat diffusion. In: SGP, pp. 1383–1392 (2009)
4. Bronstein, A.M., Bronstein, M.M., Guibas, L.J., Ovsjanikov, M.: Shape google: Geometric words and expressions for invariant shape retrieval. ACM Trans. Graph. 30(1), 1–1 (2011)
5. Bronstein, M., Kokkinos, I.: Scale-invariant heat kernel signatures for non-rigid shape recognition. In: CVPR, pp. 1704–1711 (2010)
6. Coifman, R., Lafon, S.: Diffusion maps. Appl. Comput. Harmon. Anal. 21, 5–30 (2006)

7. Bronstein, M., Bronstein, A.: Shape recognition with spectral distances. IEEE Trans. Pattern Anal. Mach. Intell. 33, 1065–1071 (2011)
8. Bronstein, A.M., Bronstein, M.M., Kimmel, R., Mahmoudi, M., Sapiro, G.: A gromov-hausdorff framework with diffusion geometry for topologically-robust non-rigid shape matching. Int. J. Comput. Vision 89, 266–286 (2010)
9. Kovnatsky, A., Bronstein, M.M., Bronstein, A.M., Kimmel, R.: Photometric Heat Kernel Signatures. In: Bruckstein, A.M., ter Haar Romeny, B.M., Bronstein, A.M., Bronstein, M.M. (eds.) SSVM 2011. LNCS, vol. 6667, pp. 616–627. Springer, Heidelberg (2012)
10. Sochen, N., Kimmel, R., Malladi, R.: A general framework for low level vision. IEEE Trans. Image Processing 7, 310–318 (1997)
11. Jost, J.: Riemannian geometry and geometric analysis, 5th edn. Springer (2008)
12. Grigoryan, A.: Heat kernel and analysis on manifolds. AMS (2009)
13. Katō, T.: Perturbation theory for linear operators. Springer (1995)
14. Simon, B.: Functional integration and quantum physics. AMS (2005)
15. Pinkall, U., Juni, S.D., Polthier, K.: Computing discrete minimal surfaces and their conjugates. Exper. Math. 2, 15–36 (1993)
16. Wardetzky, M., Mathur, S., Kälberer, F., Grinspun, E.: Discrete laplace operators: no free lunch. In: SGP, pp. 33–37 (2007)
17. Belkin, M., Sun, J., Wang, Y.: Discrete laplace operator for meshed surfaces. In: SODA, pp. 1031–1040 (2009)
18. Belkin, M., Niyogi, P.: Laplacian eigenmaps and spectral techniques for embedding and clustering. In: NIPS, pp. 585–591 (2001)
19. Belkin, M., Niyogi, P.: Convergence of laplacian eigenmaps. In: NIPS (2006)
20. Sethian, J.A., Vladimirsky, A.: Fast methods for the eikonal and related hamilton-jacobi equations on unstructured meshes. PNAS 97, 5699–5703 (2000)
21. Hochbaum, D.S., Shmoys, D.B.: A best possible heuristic for the k-center problem. Math. Oper. Res. 10, 180–184 (1985)
22. Rubner, Y., Tomasi, C., Guibas, L.J.: A metric for distributions with applications to image databases. In: ICCV, pp. 59–66 (1998)
23. Ling, H., Okada, K.: EMD-L_1: An Efficient and Robust Algorithm for Comparing Histogram-Based Descriptors. In: Leonardis, A., Bischof, H., Pinz, A. (eds.) ECCV 2006. LNCS, vol. 3953, pp. 330–343. Springer, Heidelberg (2006)
24. Pele, O., Werman, M.: Fast and robust earth mover's distances. In: ECCV, pp. 460–467 (2009)
25. Ling, H., Jacobs, D.: Using the inner-distance for classification of articulated shapes. In: CVPR, vol. 2, pp. 719–726 (2005)
26. Rabin, J., Peyré, G., Cohen, L.D.: Geodesic Shape Retrieval via Optimal Mass Transport. In: Daniilidis, K., Maragos, P., Paragios, N. (eds.) ECCV 2010, Part V. LNCS, vol. 6315, pp. 771–784. Springer, Heidelberg (2010)
27. Bronstein, A., Bronstein, M., Kimmel, R.: Numerical Geometry of Non-Rigid Shapes. Springer (2008)
28. Aubry, M., Schlickewei, U., Cremers, D.: The wave kernel signature: A quantum mechanical approach to shape analysis. In: ICCV Workshops, pp. 1626–1633 (2011)

Anchored Deformable Face Ensemble Alignment

Xin Cheng[1], Sridha Sridharan[1], Jason Saraghi[2], and Simon Lucey[1,2]

[1] Queensland University of Technology, Australia
[2] The Commonwealth Scientific and Industrial Research Organisation
{x2.cheng,s.sridharan}@qut.edu.au,
{jason.saraghi,simon.lucey}@csiro.au

Abstract. At present, many approaches have been proposed for deformable face alignment with varying degrees of success. However, the common drawback to nearly all these approaches is the inaccurate landmark registrations. The registration errors which occur are predominantly heterogeneous (i.e. low error for some frames in a sequence and higher error for others). In this paper we propose an approach for simultaneously aligning an ensemble of deformable face images stemming from the same subject given noisy heterogeneous landmark estimates. We propose that these initial noisy landmark estimates can be used as an "anchor" in conjunction with known state-of-the-art objectives for unsupervised image ensemble alignment. Impressive alignment performance is obtained using well known deformable face fitting algorithms as "anchors".

1 Introduction

Alignment of deformable faces in an image/video has attracted great interest in the computer vision community motivated by its wide range of applications, such as face recognition, facial expression analysis, facial animation, and audio-visual speech recognition. It is a difficult problem as it involves an optimization in high dimensions where appearance can vary greatly between instances of the object due to lighting conditions, facial hair, pose, age, ethnicity, image noise, and resolution. Many approaches have been proposed for this problem with varying degrees of success. Popular models include Active Appearance Models (AAMs) [1], Active Shape Models (ASMs) [2] and Constrained Local Models (CLMs) [3].

Of particular interest in this paper is the task of performing deformable face fitting across an ensemble of facial images stemming from the same subject. This ensemble of images is not necessary causal, so the facial images can be taken from non-uniform samples in time. Appearance consistency between images in the ensemble is an obvious cue/constraint for this problem. We refer to appearance consistency here as the concept that all faces in an image ensemble are of similar appearance given that they are registered to the same coordinate frame of reference. Employing appearance consistency blindly, however, can lead to poor performance for two reasons. First, an ensemble of face images can be considered aligned to a similar geometric frame of reference without looking like a face

A. Fusiello et al. (Eds.): ECCV 2012 Ws/Demos, Part I, LNCS 7583, pp. 133–142, 2012.

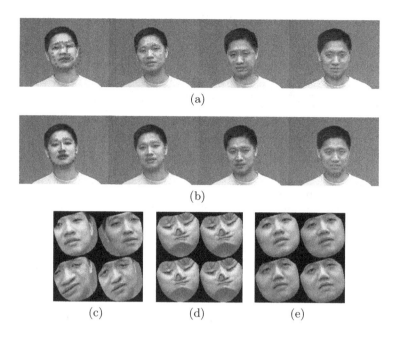

Fig. 1. (a) 4 (out of 40) IJAGS images with very noisy initial alignment. (b) images aligned by the proposed method. (c) faces transformed from the noisy initialization to a reference shape frame. (d) drift (faces aligned without anchoring). (e) faces transformed from the aligned registrations to the reference shape frame.

(see Figure 1(d)), as their is nothing "anchoring" the relative alignment. Second, even though the identity across facial images is constant, other factors are not; including pose, illumination, disappearance/appearance of pixels (e.g. oral cavity opening, eye blinks, occlusions). Due to these problems, most deformable face fitting approaches [1–3] assume appearance independence between frames, instead relying on models / templates learned from offline labelled face datasets. Although providing good performance in general, these approaches often yield imperfect/noisy estimates of landmark positions.

The problem of deformable face fitting across an ensemble of facial images is closely related to the problem of unsupervised image ensemble alignment [4–6]. Recently, an approach referred to as Robust Alignment by Sparse and Low-rank (RASL) decomposition was proposed by Peng et al. [6]. RASL has become of increasing interest to vision researchers as it: (i) can robustly handle variations in illumination through a rank minimization strategy, and (ii) can model outliers and occlusions using an $\mathcal{L}1$ error term. However, RASL cannot manage deformable face fitting in its current framework. In this paper we make three central contributions. First, we introduce an efficient compositional piece-wise affine framework to RASL so as to handle the deformable face fitting task. Second, we propose that noisy estimates from a canonical face fitting algorithm (e.g. AAM, ASM, CLM, etc.) can be introduced into the RASL objective as an "anchoring" term to remove the improper face warping. Third, we demonstrate state of the art performance for deformable face fitting on the IJAGS face datasets (see Figure 1).

2   RASL

RASL is a specific application of an earlier work called Robust Principal Component Analysis [7]. The authors assume the aligned image ensemble $\mathbf{D} \circ \tau$ is formed by sum of the low rank components $\mathbf{A}$ and sparse errors $\mathbf{E}$,

$$\arg \min_{\mathbf{A},\mathbf{E}} \operatorname{rank}(\mathbf{A}) + \lambda ||\mathbf{E}||_0$$
$$s.t. \quad \mathbf{D} \circ \tau = \mathbf{A} + \mathbf{E}, \tag{1}$$

where the image ensemble $\mathbf{D}$ is a matrix where each column is a linearized image, the aligned image ensemble is formed by $\mathbf{D} \circ \tau = [vec(I_1 \circ \tau_1) \cdots vec(I_F \circ \tau_F)]$, in which each $I_i \circ \tau_i$ is image I_i warped by the global transformation τ_i (e.g. similarity, affine and projective transformation). Since both $\operatorname{rank}(\cdot)$ and $||\cdot||_0$ are non-convex and discontinuous functions, the authors relaxed the convexity by replacing $\operatorname{rank}(\cdot)$ with nuclear norm $||\cdot||_*$ and $||\cdot||_0$ with $||\cdot||_1$. The transformation parameter τ is optimized by an additive framework,

$$\arg \min_{\mathbf{A},\mathbf{E},\Delta\tau} ||\mathbf{A}||_* + \lambda ||\mathbf{E}||_1$$
$$s.t. \quad \mathbf{D} \circ (\tau + \Delta\tau) = \mathbf{D} \circ \tau + \mathbf{J}\Delta\tau = \mathbf{A} + \mathbf{E}, \tag{2}$$

where $\mathbf{J}$ is the image Jacobian [8] evaluated at the current transformation τ, $\Delta\tau$ is the additive transformation parameter. In every iteration, the parameters are updated as $\tau = \tau + \Delta\tau$. The conventional RASL method is limited to only global transformations. It is not suitable for face alignment tasks as the global transformations lose the geometric information when applied to non-planar object (i.e. human face). Furthermore, in RASL, the Jacobian matrix $\mathbf{J}$ is evaluated at the updated transformation parameter τ iteratively. This incurs significant cost in computation time, especially for an ensemble with a large number of images.

3   Anchored Deformable Face Alignment

In this Section, we introduce our deformable face ensemble alignment method. We firstly extend RASL by adding a compositional piece-wise-affine transformation function. We then introduce a landmark anchoring penalty to prevent landmarks drift (as shown in Figure 1(d)) after convergence.

3.1   Compositional Alignment

The shape of a deformable subject can be modelled by a mesh, more specifically, by the landmark locations. Mathematically, we define the shape $\mathbf{s}$ with a mesh with v vertices,

$$\mathbf{s} = (x_1, y_1, x_2, y_2, \cdots, x_v, y_v)^{\mathrm{T}}. \tag{3}$$

By applying PCA to a hand labelled face dataset, the shapes of the face can be interpreted by a number of shape parameters $\mathbf{p} = [p_1, p_2, \cdots p_n]^{\mathrm{T}}$, then

$$\mathbf{s} = \mathbf{s}_0 + \sum_{i=1}^{n} p_i \mathbf{s}_i. \tag{4}$$

Each shape $\mathbf{s}$ contains a large number of triangles defined by vertices. Each pair of corresponding triangles from two shapes define a unique affine transformation. To warp a pixel $\mathbf{x}$, we firstly identify which triangle $\mathbf{x}$ belongs to, then we warp it with the affine transformation of that particular triangle. This method is referred to as piece-wise affine transformation. The conventional RASL exploits an additive framework, in which, the Jacobian of the transformation function $\frac{\partial}{\partial \tau} \mathcal{W}(\tau)$ is evaluated at τ. In cases of global transformations as in [6], the Jacobian is constant at all parameters τ. However, for more complicated transformations such as piece-wise affine transformation, the transformation is non-linear, the Jacobian has to be recomputed in every iteration as $\mathbf{p}$ is updated iteratively. This will result in a significant computational cost. The compositional framework provides an alternative to the additive methods. Rather than updating the transformation τ by $\tau + \Delta\tau$, it updates the transformed images $\mathbf{D} \circ \mathbf{p}$ by $\mathbf{D} \circ \mathbf{p} \circ \Delta\mathbf{p}$. In this framework, the objective function Eqn. 2 can be rewritten as,

$$\arg \min_{\mathbf{A}, \mathbf{E}, \Delta\mathbf{p}} ||\mathbf{A}||_* + \lambda ||\mathbf{E}||_1$$
$$s.t. \quad \mathbf{D} \circ \mathbf{p} \circ \Delta\mathbf{p} = \mathbf{D} \circ \mathbf{p} + \mathbf{J}\Delta\mathbf{p} = \mathbf{A} + \mathbf{E}. \tag{5}$$

The image Jacobian matrix $\mathbf{J}$ is formed as,

$$\mathbf{J} = \nabla I(\mathbf{p}) \frac{\partial \mathcal{W}(\mathbf{0})}{\partial \mathbf{p}}, \tag{6}$$

where $\nabla I(\mathbf{p})$ is the image gradient evaluated at $\mathbf{p}$. This gradient has to be recalculated every iteration, however, it is an efficient process compared with recomputing the Jacobian of the piece-wise-affine transformation, $\frac{\partial}{\partial \mathbf{p}} \mathcal{W}$. Fortunately in compositional alignment, since the Jacobian of transformation function is always evaluated at $\mathbf{0}$, it can be precomputed as it only needs to be computed once.

3.2   Anchored RASL

Since there is no prior knowledge of facial appearance exploited, without anchoring, the process will deform the subject's face arbitrarily to find the minimum rank, in nearly all instances resulting in a false alignment. In the proposed method, we introduce a vertex anchoring method using the $\mathcal{L}2$-norm, whose objective function is,

$$\arg \min_{\mathbf{A}, \mathbf{E}, \Delta\mathbf{p}} ||\mathbf{A}||_* + \lambda_1 ||\mathbf{E}||_1 + \lambda_2 ||\mathbf{X} + \boldsymbol{\Phi}\Delta\mathbf{p} - \mathbf{S}||_2^2$$
$$s.t. \quad \mathbf{D} \circ \mathbf{p} \circ \Delta\mathbf{p} = \mathbf{D} \circ \mathbf{p} + \mathbf{J}\Delta\mathbf{p} = \mathbf{A} + \mathbf{E}, \tag{7}$$

where $\mathbf{X}$ is the locations of the current vertices, $\boldsymbol{\Phi}$ is the shape basis matrix (each column in $\boldsymbol{\Phi}$ is a eigenvector of shape), and $\mathbf{S}$ is the anchoring points. In this work we use the initial alignment as anchoring points to avoid the need for additional knowledge. Our experiment shows that although the anchoring points are noisy in terms of landmark locations, they are still able to stabilize the process by stopping alignment from drifting. Our objective function Eqn. 7 can be optimized efficiently by the Augmented Lagrangian Method [6],

$$\mathcal{L}(\mathbf{A}, \mathbf{E}, \Delta\mathbf{p}, \mathbf{Y}) = ||\mathbf{A}||_* + \lambda_1 ||\mathbf{E}||_1 + \lambda_2 ||\mathbf{X} + \boldsymbol{\Phi}\Delta\mathbf{p} - \mathbf{S}||_2^2$$
$$+ <\mathbf{Y}, \mathbf{D} \circ \mathbf{p} + \mathbf{J}\Delta\mathbf{p} - \mathbf{A} - \mathbf{E}> + \frac{\mu}{2} ||\mathbf{D} \circ \mathbf{p} + \mathbf{J}\Delta\mathbf{p} - \mathbf{A} - \mathbf{E}||_2^2, \quad (8)$$

where $\mathbf{Y}$ is the Lagrangian Multiplier, μ is a positive scaler, $< \cdot, \cdot >$ is matrix inner product. Then in every iteration, the new values of $\mathbf{A}$, $\mathbf{E}$, $\Delta\mathbf{p}$ and $\mathbf{Y}$ can be determined by alternating,

$$\mathbf{A}^{k+1} = \arg\min_{\mathbf{A}} \mathcal{L}(\mathbf{A}, \mathbf{E}^k, \Delta\mathbf{p}^k, \mathbf{Y}^k) \quad (9)$$

$$\mathbf{E}^{k+1} = \arg\min_{\mathbf{E}} \mathcal{L}(\mathbf{A}^{k+1}, \mathbf{E}, \Delta\mathbf{p}^k, \mathbf{Y}^k) \quad (10)$$

$$\Delta\mathbf{p}^{k+1} = \arg\min_{\Delta\mathbf{p}} \mathcal{L}(\mathbf{A}^{k+1}, \mathbf{E}^{k+1}, \Delta\mathbf{p}, \mathbf{Y}^k) \quad (11)$$

$$\mathbf{Y}^{k+1} = \mathbf{Y}^k + \mu(\mathbf{D} \circ \mathbf{p} + \mathbf{J}\Delta\mathbf{p}^{k+1} - \mathbf{A}^{k+1} - \mathbf{E}^{k+1}). \quad (12)$$

The $\mathbf{A}^{k+1}$ and $\mathbf{E}^{k+1}$ can be determined using the soft threshold method as described in [7], The update of parameters $\Delta\mathbf{p}$ can be found by,

$$\frac{\partial}{\partial \Delta\mathbf{p}} \mathcal{L}(\mathbf{A}^{k+1}, \mathbf{E}^{k+1}, \Delta\mathbf{p}, \mathbf{Y}) = \frac{\partial}{\partial \Delta\mathbf{p}} (\lambda_2 ||\mathbf{X} + \boldsymbol{\Phi}\Delta\mathbf{p} - \mathbf{S}||_2^2 + \frac{\mu}{2} ||\mathbf{D} \circ \mathbf{p}$$
$$+ \mathbf{J}\Delta\mathbf{p} - \mathbf{A}^{k+1} - \mathbf{E}^{k+1} + \frac{1}{\mu} \mathbf{Y}^k||_2^2) = 0, \quad (13)$$

then we have,

$$\Delta\mathbf{p}^{k+1} = (2\lambda_2 \boldsymbol{\Phi}^{\mathrm{T}}\boldsymbol{\Phi} + \mu\mathbf{J}^{\mathrm{T}}\mathbf{J})^{-1}[2\lambda_2 \boldsymbol{\Phi}^{\mathrm{T}}(\mathbf{S} - \mathbf{X}) + \mu\mathbf{J}^{\mathrm{T}}(\mathbf{A}^{k+1} + \mathbf{E}^{k+1}$$
$$- \frac{1}{\mu}\mathbf{Y}^k - \mathbf{D} \circ \mathbf{p})]. \quad (14)$$

The overall algorithm is described in Algorithm 1.

4   Experiments

In this section, we evaluate the performance of our Anchored RASL method on a variety of face alignment tasks. The face shape model employed in the evaluation was obtained by a training process from all subjects of the IJAGS database and MultiPIE [9] database (5 subjects of IJAGS and 346 subjects in MultiPIE, with varying head poses and facial expressions). The shape model consists of 19 degrees of freedom with 66 landmark points. The image in the

---

Algorithm 1. Face refinement using Anchored RASL

1: **Input:** the initial landmarks $\mathbf{S}$, weights λ_1, λ_2, shape basis $\boldsymbol{\Phi}$, total number of frames F, each frame has P points.
2: Solve for the initial shape parameter, $\mathbf{p} = \mathrm{eval}(\mathbf{S}, \boldsymbol{\Phi})$,
3: Determine warp Jacobian $\frac{\partial \mathcal{W}(\mathbf{0})}{\partial \mathbf{p}}$.
4: **while** not converged **do**
5:    **for** $i = 1$ to F **do**
6:       Warp image, $\widehat{I}_i = I_i \circ p_i$,
7:       Determine gradient, $\nabla \widehat{I}_i = \mathrm{gradient}(\widehat{I}_i)$,
8:       Determine Jacobian, $J_i = \nabla \widehat{I}_i \frac{\partial \mathcal{W}(\mathbf{0})}{\partial \mathbf{p}}$,
9:       Determine ensemble, $\mathbf{Dp}(i,:) = \mathrm{vec}(\widehat{I}_i)'$,
10:      Determine the current mesh, $\mathbf{X} = \boldsymbol{\Phi}\mathbf{p}$.
11:    **end for**
12:    Solve for $\Delta\mathbf{p}$ using

$$\arg\min_{\mathbf{A},\mathbf{E},\Delta\mathbf{p}} ||\mathbf{A}||_* + \lambda_1||\mathbf{E}||_1 + \lambda_2||\mathbf{X} + \boldsymbol{\Phi}\Delta\mathbf{p} - \mathbf{S}||_2^2$$

$$s.t. \quad \mathbf{Dp} + \mathbf{J}\Delta\mathbf{p} = \mathbf{A} + \mathbf{E}, \tag{15}$$

13:    Update shape parameter $\mathbf{p} = \mathbf{p} \circ \Delta\mathbf{p}$.
14: **end while**

---

reference shape frame was scaled to 10,000 RGB pixels. The weight, λ_1 was selected using the same strategy as in [6], $\lambda_1 = 1/\sqrt{m}$, where m is the number of pixels in each aligned image (30,000 in our case). The experiment result shows that the best performance was found when using $\lambda_2 = 0.03/\sqrt{n}$, where n is the number of landmark points in every frame (66 in our implementation). The CLMs tracker we employed in the experiment was implemented by [10]. The shape model and the local features of the CLMs tracker were trained with all subjects of MultiPIE database [9].

4.1 Anchored RASL Vs. Unanchored RASL

To validate the importance of the anchoring term, we evaluated the performance of our anchored RASL method and the conventional RASL on image sequences with synthetic noisy landmark registrations. 40 frames of a single subject with large head pose variations were selected from the IJAGS database. We randomly selected a subset of $n = 32$ frames (equivalent to 80% of the frames), and perturb the annotated ground truth landmarks with synthetic errors. For each selected frame, a random synthetic error $E_i \in \mathcal{N}(0, \sigma^2)$ was added to all landmark points to produce a global alignment offset. In the experiment, we generated test cases with different geometric errors in the anchor points by increasing the standard deviation σ. The performance of our Anchored RASL method and the conventional unanchored RASL method were compared with the RMS geometric errors (shown in Figure 2(a)) and the nuclear norms (shown in Figure 2(b)).

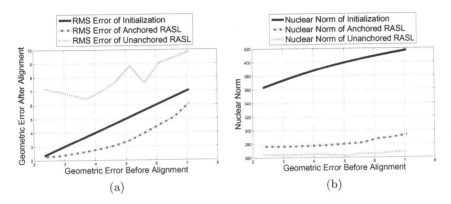

Fig. 2. (a) The RMS geometric errors; (b) The nuclear norms. The conventional RASL is not suitable for deformable face alignment as it searches for the lowest nuclear norm by blindly distorting the faces. To address this problem our anchored approach constrains the landmarks in certain regions to ensure a good alignment.

The experimental results show that the conventional RASL searched the minimum nuclear norm by arbitrarily distorting the faces in each frame. Our anchored RASL method is able to maintain the landmark points in reasonable locations to stop the improper distortions, in order to ensure a good alignment.

4.2   The Efficiency Evaluation

To verify the efficiency improvement of our Compositional Anchored RASL method from the conventional Additive method [6], we compared the computational time and the fitting performance of each method with a sequence of 100 IJAGS face images. The alignment was initialized and anchored by landmark points determined by the state-of-the-art CLMs tracker [3, 10]. The computational time for aligning different number of frames were tracked and presented in Figure 3(a). The fitting performance of the two methods were demonstrated in Figure 3(b). The experimental results show that both the additive method and the compositional method are able to refine the alignment from the state-of-the-art CLMs tracker. The proposed compositional method is able to reduce approximately 99% of the computational cost of the conventional additive method, while maintaining identical fitting performance.

4.3   Visualization

In order to visually inspect the effectiveness of the proposed method, we have selected two simulation results for visualization. The first simulation is conducted using IJAGS database, 40 frames were selected using the same criterion as in the previous section. The σ of the simulated error as defined in Section 4.1 is set to approximately 5% of the average face size. The normalized faces (face transformed from the original image shape frame to the reference shape frame)

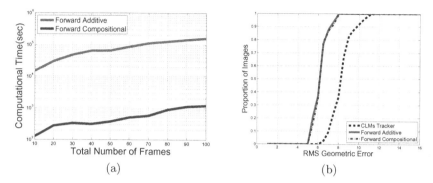

Fig. 3. (a) The computational time with different number of frames; (b) The fitting performance of the two methods when processing 100 frames. It can be observed that the compositional method can reduce the computational cost significantly while maintaining identical fitting performance.

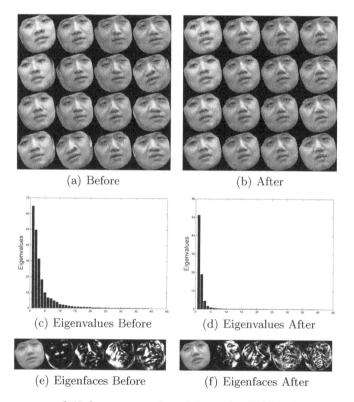

(a) Before   (b) After

(c) Eigenvalues Before   (d) Eigenvalues After

(e) Eigenfaces Before   (f) Eigenfaces After

Fig. 4. A sequence of 40 frames are selected from the IJAGS database. 80% of the frames were perturbed by the Gaussian errors with σ set to approximately 5% of the average face size for initialization and anchoring.

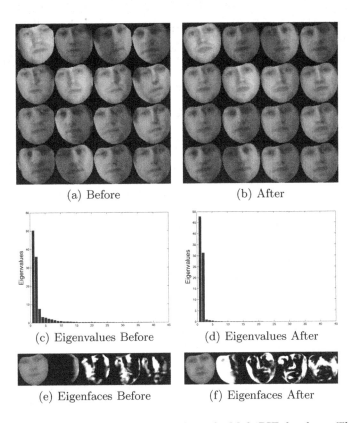

(a) Before   (b) After

(c) Eigenvalues Before   (d) Eigenvalues After

(e) Eigenfaces Before   (f) Eigenfaces After

Fig. 5. A sequence of 40 frames are selected from the MultiPIE database. The sequence was converted to grayscale and blurred by the Gaussian kernel. 80% of the frames were perturbed by the Gaussian errors with σ set to approximately 5% of the average face size for initialization and anchoring.

of the initial alignment and the refined alignment are present in Figure 4(a) and Figure 4(b) respectively. The eigenvalues of the presented normalized faces were determined by principal component analysis and demonstrated in Figure 4(c) and Figure 4(d). The mean face and the first 4 eigenfaces are presented in Figure 4(e) and Figure 4(f). In order to evaluate our approach with low image quality, the second simulation was conducted using 40 frames from the MultiPIE database selected with strong illumination variations. The sequence was converted to grayscale and blurred by Gaussian kernel to lower the image quality. The sequence was initialized by Gaussian errors with σ set to 5% of the average face size. The same set of visualizations are presented in Figure 5.It can be observed that by using our Anchored RASL alignment method, the initial coarse alignments of both dataset are refined. The eigenvalues of the refined sequences are narrowly distributed to the first few Eigenspaces. The mean faces of the refined sequences are very clear whereas the mean faces of the initial alignment are very blurred. The Eigenfaces of the refined sequence is more random.

This is because there are fewer appearance variations of the well aligned faces than the misaligned faces.

5   Conclusion

In this paper, we introduced a new anchored method for deformable image ensemble alignment. This method introduced an efficient compositional piece-wise affine framework to RASL that extends the benefits of RASL to deformable face fitting. This includes robustness to illumination variation through rank minimization and ability to model outliers and occlusions using an $\mathcal{L}$1-norm term. We evaluated our method using a subset of IJAGS database with pose variations and a subset of MultiPIE database with strong illumination variations. Impressive experimental results were demonstrated with different image conditions. The anchoring method demonstrated strong ability to nonrigidly align an ensemble of face images without improper distortion of facial appearance.

References

1. Matthews, I., Baker, S.: Active appearance models revisited. International Journal of Computer Vision 60, 135–164 (2004)
2. Cootes, T.F., Taylor, C.J., Cooper, D.H., Graham, J.: Active shape models their training and application. Comput. Vis. Image Underst. 61, 38–59 (1995)
3. Saragih, J.M., Lucey, S., Cohn, J.: Face alignment through subspace constrained mean-shifts. In: International Conference of Computer Vision, ICCV (2009)
4. Learned-Miller, E.G.: Data driven image models through continuous joint alignment. IEEE Transactions on Pattern Analysis and Machine Intelligence 28, 236–250 (2006)
5. Cox, M., Lucey, S., Sridharan, S., Cohn, J.: Least squares congealing for unsupervised alignment of images. In: IEEE International Conference on Computer Vision and Pattern Recognition, CVPR (2008)
6. Peng, Y., Ganesh, A., Wright, J., Xu, W., Ma, Y.: Rasl: Robust alignment by sparse and low-rank decomposition for linearly correlated images. In: 2010 IEEE Conference on Computer Vision and Pattern Recognition (CVPR), pp. 763–770 (2010)
7. Wright, J., Ma, Y., Ganesh, A., Rao, S.: Robust Principal Component Analysis: Exact Recovery of Corrupted Low-Rank Matrices via Convex Optimization. In: Proceedings of Neural Information Processing Systems, NIPS (2009)
8. Baker, S., Matthews, I.: Lucas-kanade 20 years on: A unifying framework. International Journal of Computer Vision 56, 221–255 (2004)
9. Gross, R., Matthews, I., Cohn, J.F., Kanade, T., Baker, S.: Multi-PIE. Image and Vision Computing (2009)
10. Saraghi, J.: Facetracker (2011),
    http://web.mac.com/jsaragih/FaceTracker/FaceTracker.html

Multiple Object Tracking via Prediction and Filtering with a Sobolev-Type Metric on Curves

Eleonora Bardelli[1], Maria Colombo[1], Andrea Mennucci[1], and Anthony Yezzi[2]

[1] Scuola Normale Superiore, Pisa, Italy
[2] School of Electrical Engineering, Georgia Institute of Technology, Atlanta, USA

Abstract. The problem of multi-target tracking of deforming objects in video sequences arises in many situations in image processing and computer vision. Many algorithms based on finite dimensional particle filters have been proposed. Recently, particle filters for infinite dimensional Shape Spaces have been proposed although predictions are restricted to a low dimensional subspace. We try to extend this approach using predictions in the whole shape space based on a Sobolev-type metric for curves which allows unrestricted infinite dimensional deformations. For the measurement model, we utilize contours which locally minimize a segmentation energy function and focus on the multiple contour tracking framework when there are many local minima of the segmentation energy to be detected. The method detects figures moving without the need of initialization and without the need for prior shape knowledge of the objects tracked.

1 Introduction

We consider the problem of tracking multiple moving shapes in a video sequence, which has been addressed many times in the past and in many different ways.

1.1 Shape Space

Many *Shape Spaces* have been considered in the past. One common approach is to model Shape Space as a finite dimensional space; as in the case of the *B-splines* approach used for the original *snakes* model in [1–3]. Another common approach is the *level set method* [4], where the shape is represented implicitly by the zero level set of a function. Some authors represent *shapes* explicitly as parametric curves, and then decompose the motion of a shape in a finite dimensional *affine* part, and an infinite dimensional *deformation* part [5, 6]. Others model the shape space as an infinite dimensional Riemannian manifold [7, 8]. Some authors do not model the shapes, but rather a (parametric) estimation of their posterior probability distribution (conditional on the images) [9].

Some of the above choices present problems when tracking. The approach with level sets is not well-apt to fast moving shapes: to predict their motion, we

A. Fusiello et al. (Eds.): ECCV 2012 Ws/Demos, Part I, LNCS 7583, pp. 143–152, 2012.

must be able to move the *"shape"* on long range. At the same time, if we model curves as splines, then we must specify the dynamic of the control points, and take care to factor those out of the shape dynamics.

We represent *shapes* as parametric curves. The model that we employ is an Infinite Dimensional Riemannian Manifold, with a Sobolev-type metric $\mathbb{H}$; it has been proposed in [8] and is briefly described in Section 2. The metric can be explained as giving (orthogonal) cost to translation, scaling and deformations of curves. This is a novel approach, in that we will not need, in the tracking model, to address separately the affine and deformation parts: this is implicitly done by the metric $\mathbb{H}$. This also implies that the prediction phase of the tracking algorithm predicts the translation, scaling and deformation parts all together: from the theoretical point of view this improves on previous approaches [6].

1.2 Tracking

We want to track shapes in a series of images I_t, where $t \in \mathbb{N}$, and $I_t \colon \Omega \to \mathbb{R}$ (usually $\Omega = [0,1]^2$). The tracking problem can benefit from prior assumptions: one such prior is the shapes' motion. We model the shapes' dynamics using a simple constant-velocity model. No *a priori* assumption is made on the probability distribution of shapes and of shape velocities.

Tracking is addressed, usually, as a *hidden variable estimation problem*. The tracker has an internal state U_t, usually the *a posteriori* estimate of the position of shape(s) at time t conditional on $I_1 \ldots I_t$. To reduce the complexity, a new estimate U_{t+1} is derived from I_{t+1} and U_t. If the tracker includes a dynamical model of the shape motion, then U_t may estimate the velocity of shapes as well.

To compute the estimate U_t, some authors have employed *(extended) Kalman Filtering* [9]; when the Shape Space is not flat, this has known limitations since the predictor/corrector updates are computed only within a linearized vector space (i.e. the tangent space is used to approximate the relevant neighborhood of the underlying shape space). Moreover this cannot be readily adapted to unsupervised tracking of a large, possibly unknown, number of shapes, since a scene including multiple shapes has inherently a multi-modal posterior.

In [6] the authors propose an approach based on *Particle Filtering*; since this requires sampling and predicting in a (theoretically) infinite dimensional space, they split the motion of shapes in a finite dimensional *affine part* and an infinite dimensional *deformation part*; then they predict the affine part alone. We seek instead to carry out prediction within the entire shape space.

1.3 The Proposed Approach

We try to incorporate a simple simple *particle filtering with importance sampling* scheme in the framework provided by the shape space proposed in [8].

For every frame I_t we consider a set of n curves $\gamma_{t,1} \ldots \gamma_{t,n}$, that represent the objects in image I_t. The update process for the curves on the frame I_{t+1} consists of three steps. In the first step we generate new curves using a prediction-correction scheme, as typical for a particle filtering approach. We first predict the position and shape of objects in I_{t+1} by shooting multiple geodesic trajectories from the curves $\gamma_{t,i}$. Interpolation between all curves at time t and $t-1$ generates approximately n^2 curves and may be interpreted as a *boosting step*.

We then perform a correction step by evolving each predicted curve via the gradient descent flow of an energy $E = F + E_{reg}$ which is made up of a segmentation energy term F (for example the Chan-Vese energy defined in Section 3), plus a regularizing scale and translation invariant term E_{reg}.

In the second step we generate new curves in a random way. The same gradient flow technique as above is applied to evolve m circles of random centers and radii. These random curves are supposed to find new objects entering the frame and could also individuate fast moving objects, on which it is otherwise difficult to initialize the prediction mechanism.

In the final step we select a subset of curves from those generated during the two previous steps by ranking them according to the segmentation energy F. The selection mechanism guarantees also that the selected curves do not cluster around the same local minimum of the segmentation energy but rather track multiple objects in the frame.

The method has been tested on fixed–camera scenes where multiple objects were moving. It was able to track multiple objects, both in translation and deformation, without the need for prior knowledge of the object shapes nor any special initialization. Results are presented in Section 4 and comparisons/relations with previous literature are discussed in Section 5.

An open-source library has been implemented to test the proposed method. It is available at http://mennucci.sns.it/StiefelCurve/. The source code is well commented and documented and fully clarifies all implementation details.

2   The Curve Model

A planar curve γ is a smooth function from $\mathbb{S}^1$ to $\mathbb{R}^2$ (where $\mathbb{S}^1$ is the unit circle); a curve is immersed when $|\gamma'(\theta)| \neq 0 \, \forall \theta \in \mathbb{S}^1$. We define M to be the space of all *smooth planar immersed curves*.

We define $\mathrm{len}(\gamma)$ to be the length of γ. Given a function $g \colon \mathbb{S}^1 \to \mathbb{R}^2$, we let $D_s g := g'/|\gamma'|$ be the derivative with respect to arc length along γ. We define the integral of g along γ and the average of g as

$$\int_\gamma g(s)\,\mathrm{d}s := \int_{\mathbb{S}^1} g(\theta)|\gamma'(\theta)|\,\mathrm{d}\theta \,, \qquad \fint_\gamma g(s)\,\mathrm{d}s := \frac{1}{\mathrm{len}(\gamma)} \int_\gamma g(s)\,\mathrm{d}s.$$

We also define the *centroid* $\overline{\gamma}$ of γ as $\fint_\gamma \gamma(s)\,\mathrm{d}s$.

We endow the space M with a Riemannian metric $\mathbb{H}$ developed in [8]. Suppose that h is a vector field along γ and decompose it as

$$h = h^t + h^l(\gamma - \overline{\gamma}) + \mathrm{len}(\gamma)h^d \,.$$

Setting

$$p(h) := h - (h \cdot D_s\gamma)D_s\gamma - (h \cdot D_s^2\gamma)(\gamma - \overline{\gamma}) \,,$$

the components h^t and h^l of h are defined as

$$h^t := \fint_\gamma p(h) \, ds \in \mathbb{R}^2 \,, \qquad h^l := -\fint_\gamma h \cdot D_s^2 \gamma \, ds \in \mathbb{R} \,.$$

The first component h^t changes the centroid of γ, whereas $h^l(\gamma - \bar\gamma)$ changes the scale of γ, see [8]. The remaining component is intended to deform γ

$$h^d := \frac{1}{\text{len}(\gamma)} [h - h^t - h^l(\gamma - \bar\gamma)] \,.$$

Given $h, k \in T_c M$, decomposed as above, the metric is

$$\langle h, k \rangle_{\mathbb{H}} := h^t \cdot k^t + h^l k^l + \text{len}(\gamma)^2 \fint_\gamma D_s h^d \cdot D_s k^d \, ds \,.$$

The metric $\mathbb{H}$ enjoys the following properties.

- Centroid translations, scale changes and deformations of the curve are orthogonal. Moreover, the space of curves can be decomposed into a product of three spaces representing position, scale, and shape (see Thm 3.4 in [8]).
- Sobolev-type metrics favor *smooth* but otherwise unrestricted infinite–dimensional deformations [10] and they have a coarse-to-fine evolution behavior [11]. They are then quite useful for shape optimization and tracking tasks.
- There is a fast and easy way to compute gradients of commonly used energies with respect to the metric $\mathbb{H}$.
- Geodesics between immersed curves can be numerically computed efficiently. Geodesics connecting immersed curves up to rotation can be computed using simple closed form formulas.

3   The Tracking Algorithm

Given a curve γ, we define its exterior region as the unbounded connected component of $\mathbb{R}^2 \setminus \gamma$ and its interior (denoted by $\mathring\gamma$) as the complement in $\mathbb{R}^2$ of the exterior region. We denote by $F(\gamma, I)$ the standard Chan-Vese energy [12]:

$$F(\gamma, I) = \int_{\mathring\gamma} (I(x) - \text{avg}_{\text{in}} I)^2 \, dx + \int_{\Omega \setminus \mathring\gamma} (I(x) - \text{avg}_{\text{out}} I)^2 \, dx \qquad (1)$$

where $\text{avg}_{\text{in}} I = \fint_{\mathring\gamma} I(x) \, dx$ and $\text{avg}_{\text{out}} I = \fint_{\Omega \setminus \mathring\gamma} I(x) \, dx$.

Let $\{I_t\}_{t=0,\dots,N}$ be the frames of the video to be analyzed and $n \in \mathbb{N}$ a fixed parameter. For every t we define curves $\gamma_{t,1}, \dots, \gamma_{t,n} \in M$, which should outline different objects in the video. We expect more than one curve to estimate each moving object in the video in accordance with the *particle filtering* paradigm.

We also use some auxiliary curves $\delta_{t,1}, \dots, \delta_{t,n} \in M$, which will be defined in the following. The curve $\delta_{t,i}$ represents the state of the curve $\gamma_{t,i}$ in the previous frame. The algorithm also depends on some real parameters $\tau_0, \tau_1, d_0 \geq 0$, and a count parameter $m \in \mathbb{N}$.

We define also a *closeness* function f, which will be used in the third step. Given two curves γ and σ, it is the fraction of the area of $\mathring{\gamma}$ covered by $\mathring{\sigma}$,

$$f(\gamma, \sigma) := \frac{\text{Area}(\mathring{\gamma} \cap \mathring{\sigma})}{\text{Area}(\mathring{\gamma})} \ .$$

Each iteration of the algorithm computes $\gamma_{t+1,i}$ and $\delta_{t+1,i}$ for $i = 1, ..., n$ at time $t + 1$ starting from the previous two sets of curves at time t. To start, we randomly choose curves $\gamma_{0,1}, ..., \gamma_{0,n}$ and define $\delta_{0,i} = \gamma_{0,i}$ for every $i = 1, \ldots, n$. Each full iteration of the algorithm is broken down into three different steps.

Step 1: Generation of New Curves via Prediction and Correction. For every pair $i, j \in \{1, ..., n\}$ let $\Gamma_{i,j} : [-1, 1] \to M$ be a constant speed geodesic such that $\Gamma_{i,j}(-1) = \delta_{t,i}$, $\Gamma_{i,j}(0) = \gamma_{t,j}$ and $\Gamma_{i,j}$ restricted to $[-1, 0]$ is a minimal geodesic between $\delta_{t,i}$ and $\gamma_{t,j}$. An iterative algorithm to compute $\Gamma_{i,j}$ is given in [8]. To shoot a geodesic with a given velocity there is a closed formula, as shown in [13] and [8].

We define the prediction $p_{i,j}$ as the geodesic calculated at time 1, namely

$$p_{i,j} := \Gamma_{i,j}(1) \qquad \forall (i, j) \in \{1, ..., n\}^2 \ .$$

The prediction is made according to a *constant velocity* dynamic of the objects in the video, which is always reasonable on a short time scale. Since geodesics are calculated with respect to the $\mathbb{H}$-metric in M, we do not predict only the position and scale of the new curve, but also its overall shape.

Note that we consider more than n predictions. Since more than one curve is usually tracking any given object, this causes small perturbations in the prediction that give stability to the algorithm. On the other hand we expect predictions made between curves following different objects to be meaningless and to be discarded in the upcoming selection step of the algorithm. Instead of shooting n^2 geodesics, random perturbations may be used but they are difficult to implement in a infinite dimensional shape space.

Then, for every $i, j \in \{1, ..., n\}$, we correct the prediction through a gradient descent flow. We use an energy E_{t+1}, defined as the sum of a Chan-Vese segmentation term F introduced in (1) and a regularizing elastic term with coefficient $k_e > 0$ (which is usually 0.02 in our experiments),

$$E_t(\gamma) := F(\gamma, I_t) + k_e \operatorname{len}(\gamma) \int_\gamma |D_s^2 \gamma|^2 \, ds \ .$$

Let $\operatorname{GF}(\tau, \gamma) : [0, +\infty) \times M \to M$ be the gradient flow of E_{t+1} starting from γ, namely for every $\gamma \in M$ we solve the P.D.E.

$$\begin{cases} \frac{d}{d\tau} \operatorname{GF}(\tau, \gamma) = -\nabla E_{t+1}(\operatorname{GF}(\tau, \gamma)) & \text{for a. e. } \tau \in [0, +\infty) \\ \operatorname{GF}_0(\gamma) = \gamma \end{cases}$$

where ∇E_{t+1} is the gradient of E_{t+1} w.r.t. the metric $\mathbb{H}$. We define the correction as the gradient flow after a fixed flow-time $\tau = \tau_0$,

$$c_{i,j} := \operatorname{GF}(\tau_0, p_{i,j}) \qquad \forall (i, j) \in \{1, ..., n\}^2.$$

Step 2: Generation of Random New Curves. In order to detect new figures which appear in the frames, we consider m random curves $r_1, ..., r_m \in M_i$. Each r_i is a circle of random center and random radius on the image I_{t+1}.

We then correct the random circles with a gradient flow. Taking E_{t+1} and GF as in the previous paragraph, we define c_i as the gradient flow starting from r_i after a fixed flow-time τ_1

$$c_i := \mathrm{GF}(\tau_1, r_i) \qquad \forall i \in \{1, ..., m\}.$$

Step 3: Selection. In this step we select n curves from the large family of new curves generated in the previous steps

$$C_0 := \left\{ c_{i,j} \mid (i,j) \in \{1,..,n\}^2 \right\} \cup \left\{ c_i \mid i \in \{1,..,m\} \right\}.$$

We want to select the curves that best fit the image I_{t+1} according to the segmentation energy F, defined in (1). At the same time we prevent the selected curves from clustering around a single mode of the posterior and ignoring all other modes (as noted in [9]). To avoid this form of "collapsing", we employ a *closeness* function $f \colon M \times M \to [0,1]$, which will be described in the following, and a cut-off value $d_0 \in [0,1]$.

We denote by $F_{t+1}(\gamma) = F(\gamma, I_{t+1})$ the segmentation energy on frame I_{t+1} and by $\gamma_{t+1,1}$ the curve that minimizes F_{t+1} within the set C_0. Then, we consider the set of all curves which have *closeness* to $\gamma_{t+1,1}$ smaller than d_0

$$C_1 := \{c \in C_0 \mid f(\gamma_{t+1,1}, c) < d_0\},$$

and we let $\gamma_{t+1,2}$ be the curve of minimal energy within this set C_1. We repeat the procedure, defining C_2 as the set of curves which have *closeness* to $\gamma_{t+1,1}$ and $\gamma_{t+1,2}$ smaller than d_0; the curve $\gamma_{t+1,3}$ is the one of minimal energy with the set C_2. We repeat this procedure until we have selected n curves $\gamma_{t+1,1}, \ldots, \gamma_{t+1,n}$ or there are no curves left.

Since the sets C_i are decreasing, curves in C_i have F_{t+1} energies greater than $\gamma_{t+1,1} \cdots \gamma_{t+1,i}$. Moreover, a curve $\sigma \in C_i$ is discarded if contains in its interior a curve $\gamma_{t+1,j}$ for some $j \leq i$ because of the definition of f. Indeed, σ is probably a worse segmentation of the same object segmented by $\gamma_{t+1,j}$.

We point out that the energy F_{t+1} used here is different from the energy E_{t+1} used for the gradient flow since we neglect the elastic term in order to select the curves which best segment our moving figures, regardless of their regularity.

Eventually we define the curves $\delta_{t+1,i}$. If $\gamma_{t+1,i} = c_{\tilde{i},\tilde{j}}$ for some $(\tilde{i},\tilde{j})$ (i.e. it was obtained via prediction and correction), we define $\delta_{t+1,i}$ as the curve from which the prediction was generated $\delta_{t+1,i} := \gamma_{t,\tilde{j}}$. Otherwise, $\gamma_{t+1,i} = c_{\tilde{i}}$ (the result of a gradient flow on a random circle), and we define $\delta_{t+1,i} = \gamma_{t+1,i}$.

Optional Splitting of Curves. While tracking, it happens that curves develop self intersection, in particular when a figure is the superposition of two objects whose trajectories deviate after some time (see Figure 1). For this reason the algorithm has provision for an optional *splitting step*, before the selection step. We divide each curve in all its non-self-intersecting parts and those parts substitute it in the pool $\gamma_{t+1,1}, \ldots, \gamma_{t+1,n}$.

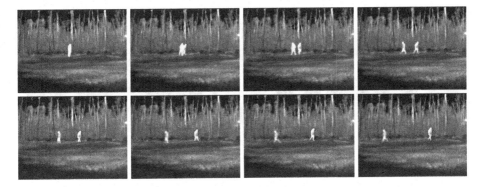

Fig. 1. Evolution with $m = 7$, $n = 3$ without splitting self-intersecting curves

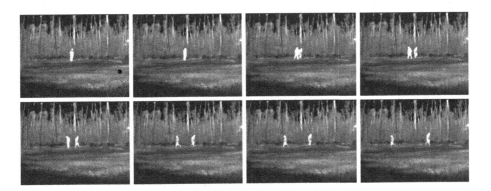

Fig. 2. Evolution with $m = 7$, $n = 3$

4   Experiments

In this section we describe some numerical experiments. Besides testing the algorithm on some simple videos, we run our algorithm disabling some core components, e.g. shape prediction, and present examples of how this affects the quality of the tracking. The variations of the algorithm are the following.

"Gradient flow only". This is the classical Chan-Vese method, implemented on multiple curves. The generation of new curves is made by evolving old curves with a gradient flow on the new frame and selection step is left unchanged.

"Centroid and length prediction". This algorithm differs from the one presented in Section 3 only in the prediction step. In this case the prediction is made about the centroid and length of the curve, leaving the shape unchanged.

Because of the novelty of the shape space and the inherent difficulty of implementing a particle filtering in a infinite dimensional shape space, the main goal of this experimental validation is not to compare the algorithm with the wide literature available nowadays. Instead, we show how the different parts of

Fig. 3. Enlargement of the sixth image in Figure 2, comparison with the same frame obtained without prediction and with prediction of centroid and length only

the algorithm work and what is the contribution of each, hoping that the result presented here might be the first step towards further studies in this direction.

We consider two different sample videos. In the first one there are two overlapping people in the beginning who then walk in opposite directions. The second video shows a bird's eye view of a plaza with many people walking and a motorcycle which enters the video in the right upper corner.

All our sample videos have been preprocessed in order to eliminate the fixed background. The energies are computed on the preprocessed frames. We show here the curves superimposed on the original frames to provide the scene context.

Figures 1, 2, 4 are examples of the program results. In Figure 1, when the two figures cease to be overlapped two new local minima of the Chan-Vese energy appear. They correspond to the two separate figures and are soon captured by the random curves. Other features can be pointed out in Figures 2 and 4.

Multiple Segmentation. The possibility of tracking multiple objects and detecting new objects entering the frame is a key feature of the algorithm. In Figure 2, starting from random circles the central object is detected and then tracked. In Figure 4 there are more objects to follow and because of shadows they have more complex shapes. However, the algorithm works well and the motorcycle which enters the video is quickly detected and followed. Note that only 10 curves are used to follow 5 objects, so the number of needed curves does not grow too much with the number of shapes to track. In both examples once an object has been detected random circles do not influence its tracking any more.

Comparison with "Gradient Flow Only". The prediction produces improvements in the tracking, when compared to simple active-contour based tracking algorithms. For example comparing Figure 4 and 5 we see that figures are detected in both sequences, but in the first they are segmented better than in the second. Indeed, the tracked objects, namely people together with their shadow, have a complicated shape that is quite different from a circle, so it is more difficult for the gradient flow to conform to them after a limited amount of flow time.

Fig. 4. Evolution with $m = 20$, $n = 10$ (only best 5 curves are drawn)

Fig. 5. Evolution with $m = 20$, $n = 10$, without prediction (5 best curves are drawn)

Shape Prediction. The prediction about the shape turns out to be important to delineate small details of the moving shapes. We compared the algorithm with the more limited (and finite dimensional) *"centroid and size prediction"*. Due to space limitation, we omit to include in this paper detailed examples obtained in this way. In Figure 3 we can see a snapshot of the evolution with our algorithm, with *"centroid and size prediction"* and with *"gradient flow only"*. We can observe that the segmentations are much rougher in the last two figures.

5 Conclusions

Our method does not use an a-priori probability model for shapes, as is often done [3, 14], neither *level–set methods*, as is often the case [14] in active contour based trackers. Instead, it uses a metric on curves which allows unrestricted shape deformation and long-range infinite dimensional shape prediction.

The structure of our algorithm overcomes the *motion correspondence problem*. As described in [9], particle filtering is appealing in multiple object tracking because of its ability to carry multiple hypotheses, but establishing the correspondence between objects and observations is not a trivial task.

One current limitation in the proposed algorithm is that it does not enforce temporal coherence in the velocity or the photometry of shapes. This enables the algorithm to easily find and track new objects, but it may be a nuisance in some applications. This is also the reason why the algorithm is applied on pre-filtered, background subtracted frames. However, this limitation is primarily due to our simple choice to use the Chan-Vese model for our segmentation energy and may be significantly improved by using a model that incorporates more photometric details. We are currently testing different choices for the segmentation energy as well as the dynamics so that the algorithm will model and deal with a (possibly non fixed) background, and/or a cluttered scene.

References

1. Kass, M., Witkin, A., Terzopoulos, D.: Snakes: Active contour models. Int. J. Comput. Vis. 1, 321–331 (1987)
2. Blake, A., Yuille, A. (eds.): Active Vision. MIT Press, Cambridge (1992)
3. Isard, M., Blake, A.: Condensation – conditional density propagation for visual tracking. Int. J. Comput. Vis. 1, 5–28 (1998)
4. Sethian, J.A.: Level set methods and fast marching methods. Cambridge University Press, Cambridge (1999)
5. Soatto, S., Yezzi, A.J.: DEFORMOTION: Deforming Motion, Shape Average and the Joint Registration and Segmentation of Images. In: Heyden, A., Sparr, G., Nielsen, M., Johansen, P. (eds.) ECCV 2002, Part III. LNCS, vol. 2352, pp. 32–47. Springer, Heidelberg (2002)
6. Rathi, Y., Vaswani, N., Tannenbaum, A., Yezzi, A.: Tracking deforming objects using particle filtering for geometric active contours. IEEE TPAMI 29, 1470–1475 (2007)
7. Klassen, E., Srivastava, A., Mio, W., Joshi, S.H.: Analysis of planar shapes using geodesic paths on shape spaces. IEEE TPAMI 26, 372–383 (2004)
8. Sundaramoorthi, G., Mennucci, A., Soatto, S., Yezzi, A.: A new geometric metric in the space of curves, and applications to tracking deforming objects by prediction and filtering. SIAM J. Imaging Sci. 4, 109–145 (2011)
9. Chang, C., Ansari, R., Khokhar, A.: Multiple object tracking with kernel particle filter. In: CVPR (2005)
10. Sundaramoorthi, G., Yezzi, A., Mennucci, A.: Sobolev active contours. Int. J. Comput. Vis. 73, 413–417 (2007)
11. Sundaramoorthi, G., Yezzi, A., Mennucci, A.: Coarse-to-fine segmentation and tracking using Sobolev Active Contours. IEEE TPAMI 30, 851–864 (2008)
12. Chan, T., Vese, L.: Active contours without edges. IEEE Trans. Image Process. 10, 266–277 (2001)
13. Edelman, A., Arias, T., Smith, S.: The geometry of algorithms with orthogonality constraints. SIAM J. Matrix Anal. Appl. 20, 303–353 (1999)
14. Zhang, T., Freedman, D.: Tracking objects using density matching and shape priors. In: ICCV, pp. 1056–1062. IEEE Computer Society (2003)

Facial Model Fitting Based on Perturbation Learning and It's Evaluation on Challenging Real-World Diversities Images

Koichi Kinoshita[1,2], Yoshinori Konishi[1], Masato Kawade[1], and Hiroshi Murase[2]

[1] Technology and Intellectual Property HQ, Omron Corporation, Japan
[2] Graduate School of Information Science, Nagoya University, Japan

Abstract. We present a robust and efficient framework for facial shape model fitting. Traditional model fitting approaches are sensitive to noise resulting from scene variations due to lighting, facial expressions, poses, etc., and tend to spend substantial computational effort due to heuristic searching algorithms. Our work distinguishes itself from conventional approaches by employing (a) non-uniform sampling features unified by the shape model that affords robustness, and (b) regression analysis between observed features and underlying shape parameters that allow for efficient model update. We demonstrate the effectiveness of our framework by evaluating its performance on several new and existing datasets including challenging real-world diversities. Significantly higher localization accuracy and speedup factors of 15 have been observed comparing with the traditional approach.

1 Introduction

Facial model fitting methods are expected to fare well under variety of scene conditions resulting, for example, due to lighting changes (e.g., shadows), facial expressions, occlusions, etc. In addition to robustness, practical algorithms also require real time performance for acceptable use. In this work we propose a feature extraction and shape model estimation approach that is robust and computationally efficient.

Previous studies (e.g., [1]) have argued that appropriate combination of local information around each feature point (bottom up) and global information about their layout (top down) is important accurate facial feature localization.

Fig. 1. Robust facial model fitting under variable lighting, complex expressions, and occlusion conditions

A. Fusiello et al. (Eds.): ECCV 2012 Ws/Demos, Part I, LNCS 7583, pp. 153–162, 2012.

Two most significant approaches that realize this concept are namely the Active Shape Model (ASM) [2] and Active Appearance model (AAM) [3], wherein, the local facial features are integrated by a global "Shape Model". These approaches recognized that the facial features lie on a low dimensional linear subspace within the high dimensional feature space.

ASM and AAM approaches have inspired several other facial feature point localization and representation methods. For instance, Li and Ito [4] employ AdaBoosted histogram classifiers that exploit local appearances by means of texture features. STASM [5] improves the model fitting accuracy of ASM by exploiting brightness gradient orthogonal to edge direction as local features, over multiple scales. Building further on the AAM framework, Blanz and Vetter [6, 7] employed 3D shape model and improved fitting performance to non-frontal face images. Matthews and Baker [8, 9] reduced computational time by utilizing the inverse compositional image alignment.

However, in each of these methods the fitting accuracy tends to decrease dramatically when the images contain unexpected variations such as shadow or facial expressions. Additionally, the previously proposed fitting techniques require a large number of iterations, making the real time robust model fitting a difficult problem to solve. In order to address these problems, our work proposes a novel shape model fitting algorithm which has the following main contributions: (a) non-uniform sampling features unified by the shape model that affords robustness, and (b) regression analysis between observed features and underlying shape parameters that allow for efficient model update.

Although [10][11] attempted to control shape parameters by regression, our proposed fitting method correlates the shape model to feature set sampled in a structured layout around each node of the shape model. Therefore, we call our approach as Active Structure Appearance Model (ASAM).

2   Features and Shape Model

2.1   Shape Model

Facial feature point layout can be compactly represented by lower dimensional linear subspace. Let $[x_m, y_m]^T$ represent the coordinates of m-th feature point node in the face image. Taken together, the feature point coordinates form a $2 \times M$-dimensional feature point set for the n-th image, $\hat{\mathbf{x}} = [[x_1, y_1]^T, \ldots, [x_M, y_M]^T] \in \mathcal{R}^{2 \times M}$, where M is the total number of feature points in the image.

Let $\mathbf{x}$ denote the the normalized coordinates of the feature point set, which are related to corresponding $\hat{\mathbf{x}}$ by "pose parameters" $\mathbf{p} = [t_x, t_y, t_\theta, t_s]^T$ corresponding to rotation $\mathbf{R}$, translation $\mathbf{T}$, and scaling t_s,

$$\hat{\mathbf{x}} = \begin{bmatrix} \cos t_\theta & -\sin t_\theta \\ \sin t_\theta & \cos t_\theta \end{bmatrix} \mathbf{x} t_s + \begin{bmatrix} t_x \\ t_y \end{bmatrix} = \mathbf{R}\mathbf{x}t_s + \mathbf{T} \tag{1}$$

The normalized feature point set $\mathbf{x}$ can be compactly represented in a linear subspace of the high $2 \times M$-dimensional feature space. Given $\mathbf{x}$ for several training images, we employ PCA to obtain the reduced orthonormal basis set retaining top k basis vectors corresponding to k largest eigenvalues of the subspace spanned by feature point sets. Let the reduced set of basis vectors be denoted by $\tilde{\Phi}$. Normalized feature $\mathbf{x}$ can be reconstructed from its projection $\mathbf{b}$ as $\mathbf{x} \approx \bar{\mathbf{x}} + \tilde{\Phi}\mathbf{b}$, implying

$$\hat{\mathbf{x}} \approx \mathbf{R}(\bar{\mathbf{x}} + \tilde{\Phi}\mathbf{b})t_s + \mathbf{T} \tag{2}$$

where, $\bar{\mathbf{x}}$ is the average normalized face model and $\mathbf{b}$ is the "shape parameter". The pose and shape parameters together represent the model parameter $\Theta = [\mathbf{p}, \mathbf{b}]$.

2.2   Feature Sampling

Several feature representations have been evaluated in context of faces [5, 8, 12–15]. Face images have been exhaustively scanned by Gabor [13] and Harr-like [14] features for feature extraction. Most of ASM based methods represent features as one dimensional sampling along the edge normal at the feature node [5]. Such a representation is relatively low dimensional and does not robustly capture the underlying feature. Instead, features are easily affected by noise caused by shadow, occlusions, facial expression, etc., and therefore cannot result in reliable shape model fitting.

On the other hand, AAM based methods generally define a homogeneous sampling grid on the average shape model, which is transformed to obtain sampling coordinates for other face images [8]. In these cases, the feature vector tends to be high dimensional, thus requiring high computational cost for shape transformation. Furthermore, such a representation captures unessential information in areas which do contribute to model deformation (e.g. cheek, forehead). In fact, this superfluous information tends to be harmful for model fitting under noisy conditions.

To address these problems, we employ feature sampling method called "Retinotopic Sampling" [12], in which sampling points radiate out from each node of the shape model. In contrast to [12], where sampling was done independently at each feature node, our work associates the non-uniformly sampled features together by means of the shape model. Since the sampling distribution is associated with the shape model structure, we call this sampling method as Structural Retinotopic Sampling. In this work we manually select a particular sampling pattern as shown in fig. 2. A sampling operation given the model parameters Θ will be indicated as:

$$\mathbf{f} = \mathcal{S}(\mathbf{p}) \tag{3}$$

here $\mathbf{f}$ is a sampled feature vector.

3   Feature Perturbation Analysis

In this section we show the relative shift between the ground truth position can be inferred based on a feature subspace learned during off-line training.

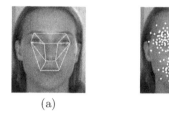

Fig. 2. (a)Shape model and (b) corresponding sampling points

This reduces the required number of search iterations and enables accurate feature localization.

Fig.3(a) shows a test image and selected feature sampling layout. In this experiment the inner corner of the right eye is selected as the basepoint. For training we use 200 images and we extract 5 perturbation samples from each image, resulting in a total of 1000 training examples. Features are perturbed in the following range: shift = within 20% of eye width, rotation = within $+/-$ 30 deg, and scale = 0.5 - 1.5 of the original. For this experiment, we employ pixel brightness at sample locations as feature descriptor. Reduced feature subspace is obtained by applying PCA to this perturbation feature set.

Fig.3(b) shows first two dimensions of the feature subspace, where half the perturbation features are centered to the left of the eye corner and the other half centered on the other side. Samples are obtained from 100 facial images which are different from training examples. Feature perturbation is limited to a distance of 20% of eye width. Similarly, fig.3(c) shows feature subspace spanned by 2nd and 3rd principal components. In this case, half the perturbation feature are sampled at +30 deg orientation with respect to the base feature, and the remaining are sampled at -30 deg orientation.

These examples clearly demonstrate that the perturbation feature subspace is discriminative in terms of the induced perturbations. These results, further reinforces the idea that we can estimate the induced perturbation by utilizing the compact subspace of perturbation features.

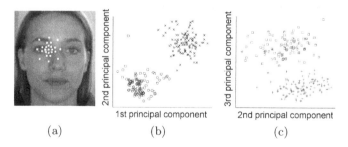

Fig. 3. (a) Sampling points. (b), (c) Feature vector plots on the feature subspace, circle: inside, x: outside, rectangle: -30 deg, +:+30 deg.

4   Shape Model Correlation with Perturbation Features

This section extends the concept and describes an algorithm to estimate the perturbation of the shape model parameters by learning a relationship between perturbed features and perturbation condition of the shape model during training. We employ Canonical Correlation Analysis (CCA) to learn the correlation between sampled features and the shape model parameters.

4.1   Canonical Correlation Analysis

Let $\mathbf{f} = [f_1, \cdots, f_k]^T$ and $\mathbf{p} = [p_1, \cdots, p_l]^T$ denote the k dimensional feature vector and l dimensional parameter vector, respectively. For some vectors, $\mathbf{a}$ and $\mathbf{b}$, $\mathbf{u} = \mathbf{a}^T\mathbf{f}$ and $\mathbf{v} = \mathbf{b}^T\mathbf{p}$ represent arbitrary linear transformations of $\mathbf{f}$ and $\mathbf{p}$, respectively. In order to find optimal values of $\mathbf{a}, \mathbf{b}$ that maximize the correlation between $\mathbf{u}$ and $\mathbf{v}$, the following covariance should be maximized:

$$Cov(\mathbf{u}, \mathbf{v}) = \mathbf{a}^T\boldsymbol{\Sigma}\mathbf{b} \tag{4}$$

where, $\boldsymbol{\Sigma}$ is the cross covariance matrix between $\mathbf{f}$ and $\mathbf{p}$. This problem can be solved as a standard eigenvalue problem by using Lagrange multipliers after normalizing variance of both $\mathbf{u}, \mathbf{v}$ to 1.

Let $(\mathbf{ea}_1, \ldots, \mathbf{ea}_k)$ and $(\mathbf{eb}_1, \ldots, \mathbf{eb}_l)$ denote the k and l eigenvectors, respectively, obtained as a solution to this problem. Assuming, $k > l$, $\mathbf{u}, \mathbf{v}$ can be written as $\mathbf{u} = [\mathbf{ea}_1, \ldots, \mathbf{ea}_l]^T\mathbf{f} = \mathbf{A}^T\mathbf{f}$ and $\mathbf{v} = [\mathbf{eb}_1, \ldots, \mathbf{eb}_l]^T\mathbf{p} = \mathbf{B}^T\mathbf{p}$.

If $\lambda_1, \cdots, \lambda_l$ denote the corresponding eigenvalues, the liner regression from $\mathbf{u}$ to $\mathbf{v}$ can be written as:

$$\mathbf{v} = diag[\lambda_1, \cdots, \lambda_l]\mathbf{u} = \boldsymbol{\Lambda}\mathbf{u} \tag{5}$$

Finally, the mapping $\mathbf{f} \Rightarrow \mathbf{p}$ can be obtained as:

$$\mathbf{p} = \mathbf{Gf}, \quad \text{such that} \quad \mathbf{G} = (\mathbf{B}^T)^{-1}\boldsymbol{\Lambda}\mathbf{A}^T. \tag{6}$$

4.2   Training Procedure and Model Fitting

The training procedure for learning regression model is outline in Algorithm 1. Ground truth feature point locations are assumed to be available for the training images. Briefly, for each training image model parameters, random perturbations are generated and corresponding sampled features are obtained. The relationship between known perturbed model parameters and sampled features is learnt using CCA (Sect. 4.1).

As an example to demonstrate the efficacy of the learning algorithm, fig. 4 shows scatter plots of ground truth values (horizontal axis) versus the estimation result (vertical axis) of model parameters predicted by learned regression model. Correlation coefficient, r, is shown under each plot. All parameters have a positive correlation value greater than 0.5 indicating that transformation matrix, G captures the relationship between features and model parameters effectively.

Input: N Training images with annotated feature point coordinates $\hat{\mathbf{x}}_1, \ldots, \hat{\mathbf{x}}_N$
Output: Regression matrix, $\mathbf{G}$
for $n \leftarrow 1$ **to** N **do**
    Obtain model parameters $\boldsymbol{\Theta}_n$ from $\hat{\mathbf{x}}_n$ as described in Sect. 2.1;
    for $r \leftarrow 1$ **to** R **do**
        Generate, $\boldsymbol{\Theta}_{\mathrm{err}} = \boldsymbol{\Theta}_n + \boldsymbol{\Delta\Theta}_r$, where $\boldsymbol{\Delta\Theta}_r$ is random a perturbation;
        Sample feature $\mathbf{f}_r$ corresponding to $\boldsymbol{\Theta}_{\mathrm{err}}$ according to eqn. 3;
    end
end
Apply CCA to $\{\boldsymbol{\Delta\Theta}\}$ and $\{\mathbf{f}\}$ to obtain $\mathbf{G}$, such that $\boldsymbol{\Delta\Theta} = \mathbf{Gf}$;
return $\mathbf{G}$

Algorithm 1. Training procedure to learn regression function $\mathbf{G}$

At run time the model fitting procedure described in Algorithm 2 is employed. As an input to model fitting, we assume that rough face parameters (location, rotation, and size) are available from the underlying detection method, e.g., [14]. The fitting algorithm starts from the initial model parameters to obtain corresponding sampled features, f. The learned transformation $\mathbf{G}$ (eqn. 6) is used to determine the parameter perturbation $\boldsymbol{\Delta\Theta}$. A correction is applied to update the model parameters and the process is repeated until convergence. Several different convergence criterions are conceivable, e.g., maximum number of iterations, $\|\boldsymbol{\Delta}\mathbf{p}_i\| < \varepsilon$, or use of a trained classifier to evaluate the feature score, etc.

5   Experiments

We conducted exhaustive experimental evaluation of the proposed algorithm on various complex face databases and compared the performance with a state-of-the-art algorithm. The four datasets employed for testing include two public datasets, BioID [16] and the extended Yale face database B [17], and two new datasets INC and Snap. These datasets contain large variations in lighting conditions, facial expressions, occlusions, etc. A summary of dataset composition can be found in table 1. A total of 10,000 images across all datasets were used for training.

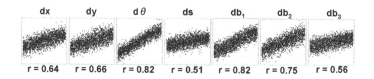

Fig. 4. Scatter plots of model parameters: Ground truth (horizontal axis) vs. estimated values (vertical axis) are shown for pose parameters $(t_x, t_y, t_\theta, t_s)$ and shape parameters (b_1, b_2, b_3). r denotes correlation value in each case.

Input: Face image with rough estimate of pose parameters $\mathbf{p}_0 = [\hat{t}_x, \hat{t}_y, \hat{t}_\theta, \hat{t}_s]$
Output: Optimal model parameters, Θ_{opt}
initialize $i \leftarrow 1$, $\Theta_i = [\mathbf{p}_0, \mathbf{0}^T]$;
repeat
    Sample feature $\mathbf{f}_i$ corresponding to Θ_i according to eqn. 3;
    Obtain parameter perturbation $\Delta\Theta = \mathbf{G}\mathbf{f}_i$;
    Update parameter $\Theta_{i+1} = \Theta_i + \eta\Delta\Theta$ /*η is learning rate */
    $i \leftarrow i + 1$;
until *convergence*;
$\Theta_{opt} \leftarrow \Theta_{i-1}$;
return Θ_{opt}

Algorithm 2. Model fitting procedure estimates optimal model parameters given rough initialization.

Table 1. Evaluation Datasets

	Condition	Facial expression	Number of images
BioID	indoor, homogeneous lighting	including open, closed eyes and mouth	1,521
YaleB	indoor, homogeneous and directional lighting	neutral (frontal pose only)	601
Snap	various lighting condition including indoor room lighting and outdoor natural lighting	various expressions including smile	2,325
INC	indoor, homogeneous lighting	neutral(N), close eyes(E), open mouth(M), smile(S).	300 for each expression

For experiments, Haar-like features [14] with different shapes and orientations were extracted at sampling locations. A total of 6 features at 235 sampling locations resulted in feature dimension of $6 \times 235 = 1410$. The proposed algorithm is compared with the state-of-the-art ASM based STASM [5] approach as baseline. Unlike AAM approaches which estimate appearance, a comparison with ASM based approach used for feature localization is more in line with the proposed framework.

All algorithms are implemented in C/C++ and executed on a Pentium D 3.2GHz PC. Shape model parameters for test images are initialized by face detection algorithm of [18]. Model fitting relies on 6 feature point locations, namely, corners of eyes and mouth. To accommodate for error in ground truth, feature localization results that fall within 10% of eye-to-eye distance are considered positive detections.

Fig. 5 shows the average localization accuracy results for eye and mouth corners for different datasets. For a better perspective, the results for Yale database are broken down as yaleB1, consisting of lighting angles less than 20 deg, and yaleB2, denoting other lighting conditions. Similarly, the INC database is

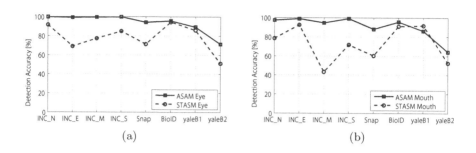

(a)   (b)

Fig. 5. Detection accuracy for (a) Eye and (b) Mouth of the proposed approach (ASAM) compared to the baseline (STASM) on several evaluation datasets

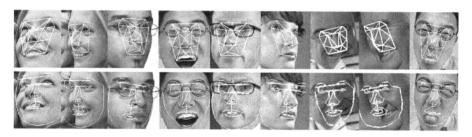

Fig. 6. Qualitative model fitting results comparing the outputs of proposed ASAM (1st row) and baseline STASM (2nd row) algorithms

sub-categorized based on facial expressions. Detection accuracy is defined as the ratio of number images with successful feature localization to the total number of evaluation images.

Detection accuracy for both of ASAM and STASM are similar for datasets which contain only neutral expression and homogeneous lighting (INC_N, BioID, yaleB1). However, ASAM demonstrates significantly superior performance compared to STASM for datasets with complex facial expression (INC_E, INC_M, INC_S). Although both methods show lower performances for extreme directional lighting condition in yaleB2, ASAM still has a better performance than STASM. Lastly, ASAM again outperforms STASM with significant margins on the Snap dataset which includes various facial expressions and lighting conditions.

The average frame processing time for ASAM is 0.017 sec compared to 0.264 sec for STASM. This corresponds to a speedup of 15.

5.1 Discussion

The superior performance and efficiency of the proposed method can be attributed mainly to the novel (1) structural retinotopic sampling integrated by the shape model and (2) perturbation estimation using CCA.

Fig. 7. Model fitting failure results

Structural Retinotopic Sampling: For facial model fitting, areas such as cheek and forehead carry less discriminative information compared to other features such eye, nose, and mouth corners. Homogenous feature sampling approaches get distracted by noise due to shadows, facial expressions (wrinkles), etc., in these relatively unimportant facial regions and tend to result in poor model fitting accuracy. On the other hand, if model fitting approaches only focus on the distinctive features such as eye, nose, and mouth corners, then they are susceptible to minor misalignments and tend to getting stuck in local minima, thus again resulting in poor fitting.

To address the limitations of both global and local feature sampling approaches, our proposed non-uniform feature sampling strategy offers a robust solution. The discriminative corner features are densely sampled to give higher weight to local information, while at the same time modeling semi-global appearance through sparse sampling to allow for smooth search space for model parameters.

Fig. 1 shows fitting results obtained by our proposed approach on several difficult examples including various facial expressions, occlusions, deformations, poses, and lighting variations. Additionally, fig. 6 provides further qualitative assessment by showing examples of model fitting results of ASAM compared with those obtained by STASM. As shown, our method can successfully recover the face model under various challenging, real-world, diversities.

Nevertheless, the approach still has difficulties in obtaining a good model fit under extremely adverse conditions such as sudden contrast variations, substantial occlusions, extreme poses, and their combinations. Some examples of incorrect model estimation are shown in fig.7.

Perturbation Estimation from Feature: Conventional model fitting approaches, including the baseline STASM, refine the model parameters by iteratively searching for individual feature node positions, thus requiring long processing times. In contrast, our proposed framework achieves significant speed up because instead of tracking individual features, it can update the entire shape model quickly by relying on the learned correlation between features and model parameters in a single step matrix multiplication. The model parameters can be refined with fewer iterations.

Although we have found CCA to be very effective in learning the correlations between said features and model parameters, one aspect of our future work involves evaluating other frameworks such as support vector machines, relevance vector machines, etc., for regression modeling.

6   Conclusion

We presented a novel shape model fitting framework which is robust to noise due to structural retinotopic sampling features and is efficient in estimating model parameters by directly obtaining model perturbation based on feature observations. As future work, we will study optimal sampling patterns and investigate into other regression techniques to improve performance even for more extreme conditions.

Acknowledgment. The authors thank Dr. A.Tyagi from Omron STI Corp. for his valuable comments.

References

1. Cristinacce, D., Cootes, T.: Facial feature detection using adaboost with shape constraints. In: Brit. Mach. Vis. Conf. (2003)
2. Cootes, T.F., et al.: Active shape models – their training and application. Computer Vision and Image Understanding 6, 38–59 (1995)
3. Cootes, T.F., Edwards, G.J., Taylor, C.J.: Active Appearance Models. In: Burkhardt, H., Neumann, B. (eds.) ECCV 1998. LNCS, vol. 1407, pp. 484–498. Springer, Heidelberg (1998)
4. Li, Y., Ito, W.: Shape parameter optimization for adaboosted active shape model. In: Proc. Comp. Vis. and Pattern Rec., vol. 1, pp. 251–258 (2005)
5. Milborrow, S.: Active feature models. Master's thesis, University of Cape Town (2007)
6. Blanz, V., Vetter, T.: A morphable model for the synthesis of 3d faces. In: Proc. of the SIGGRAPH 1999, pp. 187–194 (1999)
7. Blanz, V., Vetter, T.: Face recognition based on fitting a 3d morphable model. IEEE Trans. Patt. Analy. and Mach. Intell. 25, 1063–1074 (2003)
8. Matthews, I., Baker, S.: Active appearance models revisited. Int. J. of Comp. Vis. 60, 135–164 (2004)
9. Baker, S., Matthews, I.: Equivalence and efficiency of image alignment algorithms. In: Proc. Comp. Vis. and Pattern Rec. (2001)
10. Donner, R., et al.: Fast active appearance model search using canonical correlation analysis. IEEE Trans. Patt. Analy. and Mach. Intell. 28 (2006)
11. Langs, G.: et al.: Active feature models. In: Proc. Int. Conf. Pat. Rec., vol. 1, pp. 417–420 (2006)
12. Smeraldi, F., Bigun, J.: Retinal vision applied to facial features detection and face authentication. Patt. Recogn. Lett. 23, 463–475 (2002)
13. Wiskott, L., et al.: Face recognition by elastic bunch graph matching. IEEE Trans. Patt. Analy. and Mach. Intell. 19, 775–779 (1997)
14. Viola, P., Jones, M.: Rapid object detection using a boosted cascade of simple features. In: Proc. Comp. Vis. and Pattern Rec. (2001)
15. Kinoshita, K., Konishi, Y., Lao, S., Kawade, M., Murase, H.: Perturbation feature and it's apprication to shape model fitting for facial images. IEICE Trans. D J94-D(4), 721–729 (2011) (in Japanese)
16. Jesorsky, O., et al.: Robust Face Detection using the Hausdorff Distance. Springer (2001), Audio and Video based Person Authentification - AVBPA
17. Lee, K.C., Ho, J., Kriegman, D.: Acquiring linear subspaces for face recognition under variable lighting. IEEE Trans. Patt. Analy. and Mach. Intell. (2005)
18. Yamashita, T.: et al.: A fast omni-directional face detection system. In: Proc. Int. Conf. Comp. Vis. (2005)

Adaptive Rendering for Large-Scale Skyline Characterization and Matching

Jiejie Zhu, Mayank Bansal, Nick Vander Valk, and Hui Cheng

Vision Technologies Lab., SRI International, Princeton, NJ 08540, USA
{jiejie.zhu,mayank.bansal,nicholas.vandervalk,hui.cheng}@sri.com

Abstract. We propose an adaptive rendering approach for large-scale skyline characterization and matching with applications to automated geo-tagging of photos and images. Given an image, our system automatically extracts the skyline and then matches it to a database of reference skylines extracted from rendered images using digital elevation data (DEM). The sampling density of these rendering locations determines both the accuracy and the speed of skyline matching. The proposed approach successfully combines global planning and local greedy search strategies to select new rendering locations incrementally. We report quantitative and qualitative results from synthesized and real experiments, where we achieve a computational speedup of around 4X.

1   Introduction

Skylines, especially in mountainous areas, provide robust and often unique features to characterize an area. Often by looking at the skyline in a photo, such as the half dome in Yosemite, one can recognize the area where the photo was taken. However, to recognize where a photo is taken over a large area of tens or hundreds thousands of square kilometers is very difficult. Based on this observation and previous work [1][2] on skyline analysis, we developed a large-scale skyline characterization and matching system for automated geo-tagging of photos and images.

Given an image, our system automatically extracts the skyline and then matches it to a database of reference skylines extracted from digital elevation data (DEM). The reference skylines are generated through rendering using DEM at locations over the entire area of interest. The selection of these rendering locations determines both the accuracy and the speed of the skyline matching. In addition, it determines the time needed to build the reference skyline database.

We can use a grid on the ground-plane as rendering locations – in this case the distance between two adjacent grid locations is the sampling distance. The larger the sampling distance is, the faster the rendering and the matching algorithms run, but less accurate the skyline matching is. The smaller the sampling distance is, the more accurate the matching is, but the slower the rendering and the matching algorithms run. For example, skyline rendering and extraction over a $10,000 \ km^2$ using 50-100 meters sampling distance can take months to complete. On the other hand, if the sampling distance is large, photos taken close to a mountain or inside a mountain, such as those taken on a hiking trail or a road

A. Fusiello et al. (Eds.): ECCV 2012 Ws/Demos, Part I, LNCS 7583, pp. 163–174, 2012.

Fig. 1. Dramatic skyline change caused by occlusions in complex mountainous terrain

passing through a mountain cannot be found. Fig. 1 depicts such an example where two views that are separated by only 30 meters have very different skylines.

In this paper, we propose an adaptive rendering approach for optimal rendering location selection. By modeling both the rendering process and the skyline matching process, our system can compute the set of optimal rendering locations based on the DEM and a pre-defined matching threshold. The viewpoint selection is optimal in the sense that for a given matching accuracy, it requires far fewer number of renderings than if the rendering locations were uniformly sampled on a dense grid. In the example of Fig. 1 above, a good viewpoint selection algorithm should automatically render densely when close to the mountain and coarsely when far away.

2   Related Work

In recent literature, there has been increasing interest in geo-localization of ground-level imagery using visible skylines by matching them to a database of known skyline shapes. For urban geo-localization, Srikumar et al.[3][2] focused on matching omni-skylines from an upward facing camera to skyline renderings generated on-the-fly from 3D building models of the scene. Our focus in this paper is on geo-localization in natural terrain – in this case, the problem is much harder since we have to match to a specific viewpoint (i.e. the query camera is not upward facing) and we cannot pre-render on sparse road networks like in the urban case. It therefore becomes important to devise a rendering scheme that will render at the fewest number of viewpoints without reducing the localization accuracy achievable.

Lionel et al.[1] recently addressed the problem of automatic photo-to-terrain alignment with a goal of annotating mountain pictures. In their work, high resolution elevation maps are rendered to create synthesized panoramic views which are then matched to the mountain picture using a robust edge matching algorithm. However, their approach assumes that the GPS location and FOV of the query picture are known and then they solve for the unknown camera pose relative to the terrain. In contrast, we would like to address the problem of localization of the query picture itself by matching to a set of terrain renderings obtained from sampled viewpoints. To achieve this, we have to either sample these viewpoints very densely everywhere or we can adopt an adaptive rendering strategy to minimize the search required at the matching stage. In this paper, we focus on such an approach.

Bryan et al.[4] address the problem of automatically aligning historical architectural paintings with 3D models obtained from modern photographs. A key step in their approach is the "view-sensitive retrieval" that aims to find a 3D viewpoint that is sufficiently close to the painting viewpoint. To achieve this, they sample a large (dense) pool of virtual viewpoints around the 3D model and then use a matching procedure to retrieve a small set of nearby matching candidate viewpoints. In this paper, we propose an approach to allow a non-dense rendering of the 3D scene for query localization in the context of natural terrain where dense sampling quickly becomes a computational bottleneck.

There has been some work in the literature on efficient rendering of large terrains. However, the majority of this work has focused on the graphics aspect of rendering including adaptive means to enable faster Google-Earth like renderings served to an end-user. For example, Raphael el al.[5,6] describe a generic data structure to adaptively serve data to the client rendering system and to improve the database loading and rendering speeds independent of the database size. Similarly, a hardware accelerated terrain rendering approach is outlined in [7]. In this paper, we assume that a terrain rendering algorithm is available to us as a black-box and we can use it to render the terrain at any specified location and viewpoint.

3   Skyline Rendering and Matching

In this section, we briefly introduce our skyline rendering and matching algorithms. In skyline rendering, the system takes an area of geo-localized DEM data as input. A ground-level camera location inside this area is specified along with its intrinsic and extrinsic parameters. The system then renders the DEM into a depth image, which is then used to extract a skyline corresponding to the specified viewpoint e.g. Fig. 2.

Given all the rendered skylines, the system extracts features from each of them and saves them in a database for future matching purposes. In feature extraction, a skyline is first approximated by polylines and then the end-points of the line-segments composing these polylines are used as feature points.

Given a query image like in Fig. 3, we use a skyline extraction algorithm [2] to extract the skyline. The polyline approximation-based algorithm described above is then used to extract the query skyline features. For each extracted key feature from the query skyline, the matching process finds a key feature from the rendered skyline that best matches it. The matching score between a keypoint pair is computed as the Chamfer distance between the local skylines centered at these keypoints. This establishes a correspondence between the keypoints of the two skylines following which RANSAC is used to find inliers corresponding to an affine transformation between the two skylines. The overall matching score between the two skylines is computed as the Euclidean distance between the skylines after warping with the computed affine transformation.

Fig. 2. Example of a rendered depth image and its extracted skyline. To extract the skyline, the system looks at the depth image from top to bottom in each column, and labels as skyline pixel the first pixel with a non-infinite depth.

Fig. 3. Example of a query image and its skyline. The contour of the trees are false skyline pixels automatically computed from the skyline extraction model – the RANSAC-based matching process labels them correctly as outliers.

4   Problem Formulation

We assume that we start the adaptive rendering algorithm from a set of pre-rendered viewpoints which are on a uniform but coarsely sampled grid, e.g. at 1 Km spacing. The goal of adaptive rendering is to automatically predict optimal viewpoints c_k (with spacing finer than 1 Km) at which the rendered skyline looks sufficiently different from existing renderings of the same 3D feature (mountain). To achieve this goal, we approach the viewpoint selection process as an incremental algorithm that adds new viewpoints to the set of existing renderings, *but without rendering the new viewpoints first*. Around each already rendered skyline from a viewpoint c_0, we can explicitly compute a "tolerance area" within which the skyline projection from another candidate viewpoint c_k looks similar to c_0. This similarity is defined by an image projection distance between the skylines at c_k and c_0. Thus, for a given threshold on the similarity metric, we can estimate the tolerance area around each existing rendering. Intuitively, the tolerance area specifies the extent within which no additional rendering is required. Thus, for an existing viewpoint inside a complex terrain, we can expect to obtain a much smaller tolerance area than for a simple flat terrain. The tolerance area computation algorithm is described in Sec. 4.2. Given the tolerance areas (and their shape) for each of the existing renderings in our set, in Sec. 4.3, we propose and compare several novel planning strategies to determine the next-best viewpoint that avoids overlap with the existing tolerance areas.

4.1   Camera Configuration

We assume a distortion-free ideal pin-hole camera model for the rendering camera with square pixels and a camera center coincident with the image center. This leads to an ideal camera intrinsic matrix. For our experiments, we cover the 360 degree view surrounding each candidate rendering location using four camera viewpoints $v_1, \ldots, v_4$, each with a horizontal field-of-view of $\theta = 90$ degrees and image resolution of $w = h = 640$. The optical axis for each viewpoint v_i can be described by a pre-defined rotation matrix R_i which fixes a single look-at direction for this viewpoint independent of the rendering location.

In our framework, we represent the 3D points corresponding to the skylines (mountain silhouettes) in world-coordinates by variable $X_i \in \Re^3$. The skyline projection at any viewpoint c_k is then given by:

$$I_k = P_k X_i = K[R|t_k]X_i$$

where $P_k = K[R|t_k]$ is the camera projection matrix for the camera located at displacement t_k w.r.t the world coordinate system origin. The rotation R is one of $R_1, \ldots, R_4$ depending on the viewpoint's look-at direction.

In the following, we will follow the convention that the world coordinate system is defined with XZ as the ground-plane and the Y-axis pointing upwards.

4.2   Tolerance Area Computation

The squared difference between projected skylines I_0 and I_k (at locations c_0 and c_k respectively) can serve as a simple error metric for the estimation of tolerance area. However, the skyline matching algorithm (Sec. 3) accounts for any small distortions of the skyline by an affine transformation model. It therefore makes sense to measure the projection error between skylines visible at two viewpoints after allowing for an affine transformation. Fig. 4 illustrates an example of two projections of a synthetic skyline where the distance between the original skylines does not correctly reflect the difference between their shape. Warping one of the skylines using an affine transformation, however, leads to a much more accurate error metric.

Estimating affine transformation between two images has been studied extensively. Most techniques rely on first applying RANSAC [8] to determine the corresponding pixels and then to recover their geometrical relationships by rejecting outliers. Here, we can apply a similar approach but the computation cost is high considering the huge number of such pair comparisons required in the system.

We propose an analytical approximation approach to compute the affine transformation between the two cameras given their projection matrix. It has merits of requiring much less computation (since it is analytical) while preserving the accuracy compared with the traditional correspondence-based estimation method.

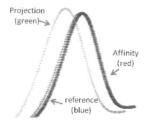

Fig. 4. Example of skyline projection improvement using an affine transformation model from a synthetic experiment. The green and blue curves are two candidate skylines; the red curve is the green curve after warping by an affine transformation that best aligns the candidate skylines. The direct Euclidean distance between the green and blue skylines is around 26 pixels. The corresponding distance between the red and blue curves is 3.6, which is a more accurate estimate of the difference between the skyline shapes than the direct distance.

Affine Transformation. Given two projection matrices $P_1 = K_1[R_1|T_1]$ and $P_2 = K_2[R_2|T_2]$, without loss of generality, we can assume the first camera to be in a canonical form such that $R_1 = I, T_1 = 0$. Instead of selecting all four viewing directions $v_1, \ldots, v_4$ simultaneously for each location, we apply the adaptive rendering selection algorithm to viewpoints facing each direction individually – implying $R_2 = R_1$. Further, for our problem, $K_2 = K_1 = K$. If a 3D point X is visible to both cameras, its projection can be expressed by $U_1 = KX$ and $U_2 = KX + KT$, where $T = T_2 - T_1$. By substituting X using $K^{-1}U_1$, we have

$$U_2 = U_1 + KT \tag{1}$$

By representing U_1 in homogeneous coordinates U_1', $K = [k_1, k_2, k_3]'$ and writing the above equation in a matrix formulation, we have

$$U_2 = \begin{pmatrix} k_3X & 0 & k_1T \\ 0 & k_3X & k_2T \\ 0 & 0 & k_3X + k_3T \end{pmatrix} \begin{pmatrix} \frac{k_1X}{k_3X} \\ \frac{k_2X}{k_3X} \\ 1 \end{pmatrix} \tag{2}$$

If we represent U_2 in homogeneous coordinates U_2', we have

$$U_2' = \frac{U_2}{k_3X + k_3T} = AU_1' \tag{3}$$

$$= \begin{pmatrix} \frac{k_3X}{k_3X+k_3T} & 0 & \frac{k_1T}{k_3X+k_3T} \\ 0 & \frac{k_3X}{k_3X+k_3T} & \frac{k_2T}{k_3X+k_3T} \\ 0 & 0 & 1 \end{pmatrix} U_1' \tag{4}$$

In the above equation, we should note that k_3X is the displacement between the 3D point X and the reference (P_1) camera center, k_3T is the displacement between the 3D point X and the candidate (P_2) camera center. k_3X will be different for each 3D point located on the skyline if their Z-coordinates are different. Building a per-point affine transformation generates the exact transformation between U_1 and U_2, but it is computationally expensive given the large number of 3D points on skylines. Instead, our system chooses a z-value that is representative of the skyline such as the mean or median distance of the skyline points.

Given the above formulation, we now outline our tolerance area computation algorithm: We sample a 10×10 neighborhood around the reference location c_0. At each sampled location, we compute the reprojection error of the skylines between the reference and the sampled location using Eq.4 – if this error is within a given threshold, the sampled location is included in the tolerance area (corresponding to the reference location c_0), otherwise it is excluded.

4.3   Optimal Viewpoint Planning and Selection

Without loss of generality, we assume that we have already computed the tolerance areas for the four corners of a 1 Km $\times$ 1 Km square on the terrain using the algorithm in the previous section. The next step in our pipeline is to select a new location at which the renderer should render so as to cover maximum uncovered ground. In the following, we describe five different strategies to plan the next viewpoint. In the experiments section, we will discuss how each of these strategies performed on our simulation data followed by results of the best performing strategy on real data.

Random Optimistic Viewpoint (ROV). ROV randomly chooses a number of candidate viewpoint locations from the uncovered area. Their tolerance area are computed and ranked based on their overlap with the uncovered area. ROV selects the location with the highest coverage and performs rendering at the selected location. This process will iterate until the coverage reaches an acceptable number, e.g. 90% or 98% used in the experiments.

Approximated Random Optimistic Viewpoint (AROV). The tolerance area computation in ROV is expensive since it requires projecting each 3D skyline point at multiple candidate locations (please refer to the computation cost in the last row of Table 1). To make this process more efficient, AROV interpolates a candidate viewpoint's tolerance area linearly from its nearest rendered viewpoints whose tolerance areas are already computed.

Hierarchy Optimistic Viewpoint (HOV). Different from ROV and AROV, HOV searches optimal viewpoint using a coarse to fine process. At each level, AROV is used to select the next-best viewpoint; when coverage is satisfied at a level, HOV will move to the next finer level.

Shape-Assisted Optimistic Viewpoint (SOV). SOV investigates how the shape of the tolerance area may be used in assisting optimal viewpoint selection. From ROV, AROV and HOV, we noticed that most of tolerance areas can be best described using 2D ellipses. Thus, instead of randomly picking the candidate locations, in SOV we pack them along the minor axes of the ellipse-like tolerance areas so as to achieve a tighter packing over the uncovered area.

Line Planning Optimistic Viewpoint (LPOV). SOV uses independent tolerance areas to select the optimal viewpoint and this strategy may not be optimal for covering the whole area. In order to include more global information in selecting an optimal viewpoint, LPOV pre-locates optimal viewpoints on each line joining a pair of sampled viewpoints. The location of a candidate viewpoint is predicted as a convex combination of the locations of the endpoints; the weights in this convex combination are proportional to the size of each end viewpoint's tolerance area. LPOV encourages sparse optimal viewpoint selection in flat areas since the tolerance areas of the rendered locations are larger in comparison with the rendered viewpoints in clutter areas, such as inside mountains. This line-wise planning and local greedy combined approach contributes to less number of rendered viewpoints with a fast coverage.

5   Experimental Results

This section exhibits our quantitative and qualitative experimental results on i) a synthetic dataset generated by sampling skylines from a parametric model, and ii) a DEM dataset covering around 50 km^2 on a mountainous terrain.

5.1   Simulation Results

We evaluated the five viewpoint selection techniques described in Sec. 4.3 on a synthetic dataset consisting of an area with 100×100 potential (dense) viewpoint locations. All the experiments start with four rendered viewpoints at the corners initially. We evaluate the performance of the algorithms using two criteria:

(A) Total number of viewpoints selected for rendering and,
(B) Size of overlapped area – computed as the number of times the same viewpoint location is included in any of the tolerance areas.

The goal of a good adaptive rendering algorithm is to cover as much area as possible using minimal number of rendered viewpoints where the coverage is defined as the union of tolerance areas from all rendered viewpoints. Thus, our objective is to achieve smaller numbers for both criteria (A) and (B).

Table-1 reports the results of all the methods for the 100×100 grid using the convention x/y where x represents the value of criterion (A) and y the value of criterion (B). We include results from experiments with skylines of different complexity with the reprojection error evaluated with and without the affine transformation model proposed in this paper.

We can conclude the following from the simulation results:

1. Overall, the affine transformation model requires fewer number of renderings, but produces more overlaps, as shown by a comparison between row 1 and rows 2,3.
2. Overall, the number of selected viewpoints is proportional to the complexity of the skylines as observed by comparing row 2 and row 3.

Table 1. Simulation results for viewpoint planning methods using criteria (A)/(B)

Parameters	ROV	AROV	HOV	SOV	LPOV
Non-Affine (p=1, t=15, c=90% r=0)	**240**/1545	286/1636	324/**1210**	275/1941	325/1515
Affine (p=1, t=3, c=98% r=0)	81/6664	**80**/5824	98/6723	100/10043	86/**5489**
Affine (p=2, t=3, c=98%, r=30)	239/9028	217/6991	252/7226	245/9148	**191**/**5943**
Computation Cost (rounded)	45mins	10mins	5mins	30mins	10mins

p: number of peaks on the skyline; t: reprojection error threshold in pixels
r: skyline rotation angle; r=0 represents a skyline that is parallel to the camera plane.
c: coverage percentage at which the adaptive rendering process is terminated.

Table 2. Query geo-localization accuracy results with and without adaptive rendering

	Rendering Resolution/Number of renderings				
	1024m/182	512m/665	256m/2662	128m/10648	Adaptive/2800
Close to mountain	1906m	800m	379m	64m	127m
Medium Range	1609m	703m	402m	102m	98m
Far from mountain	1247m	604m	453m	202m	125m

3. SOV consistently produces the largest size of overlaps which shows that locally optimal algorithms do not achieve good results.

4. ROV requires the highest computation cost. Other algorithms require less computational since the tolerance area is approximated using nearest neighbors. Among them, HOV requires the least computation because a fixed pattern of optimal viewpoint selection is used.

5. LPOV obtains the best performance in the test using skylines with two peaks. This suggests that a planning strategy with a local greedy objective may give good results.

5.2   Experiments Using DEM Data

For experiments with real data, we used an area approximately 5km×10km in size in a moutainous terrain. We select the best performing viewpoint selection method from the simulation (LPOV) for experiments with real data and compare its performance with a hierarchical uniform approach. To characterize the performance of the generated renderings using either approach, we use a set of query images (with known ground-truth geo-location information) shown in Fig. 5 and match each of them to the generated renderings. We selected three groups of query images: close to the mountain (Fig. 5, column-1), medium range from the mountain (Fig. 5, column-2) and far from the mountain (Fig. 5, column-3). We measure the distance between the location of the best matching rendering and the known ground-truth location of the query to showcase the improvement in geo-location using renderings from our adaptive algorithm versus renderings on a uniform grid at four different levels of resolution (1024m, 512m, 256m and 128m).

Fig. 6 shows an example of the viewpoints selected from the proposed adaptive rendering approach with two headings at 0 and 90 degrees (similar results are

Fig. 5. 6 query images used in all the experiments, along with their geo-locations on the overhead view

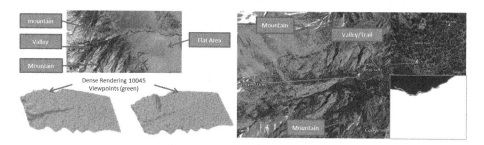

Fig. 6. Left: Example of viewpoints selected from the proposed adaptive rendering approach for heading 0 and 90 degrees. Looking at the terrain area shown on the top, we can see that a large number of viewpoints are selected in the valleys and areas with clutter while a fewer number of viewpoints are selected by our algorithm in flat areas of the terrain. It is also interesting to see that different heading directions will result in different adaptive rendering results given the terrain structure. Right: Result of query 3976. In uniform viewpoint sampling, a 1024m spacing generates best geo-location around 1900m away, while a 128m spacing gives the best geo-localization around 64m away. Adaptive rendering has an error of 174m, but with a 400% system performance improvement. The inlay on the bottom right illustrates the skyline matching result for this query. The green curve indicates the skyline in the query image. The red curve shows the skyline in the rendered image.

obtained from the other two headings). We can see that dense viewpoint sampling is required in cluttered terrain areas such as valley and trails. Incidentally, these areas are critical to skyline matching because occlusions introduce a large number of mismatches.

Skyline matching tests are performed for query images shown in Fig. 5. One of the geo-localization results is shown in Fig. 6. The numerical results are reported in Table 2.

Fig. 7 highlights the important fact that using the proposed adaptive rendering algorith, one can achieve a given matching accuracy using only a small fraction of the number of renderings required by a uniform fixed renderer.

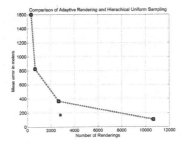

Fig. 7. Comparison of skyline matching accuracy using adaptive rendering and uniform viewpoint sampling at multiple resolution levels. In terms of accuracy, adaptive rendering leads to an improvement of almost 200%. It has a mean error of 200m with the number of renderings around 2500 while the error increases to 400m with the same number of renderings in the case uniform sampling. In terms of the system performance, adaptive rendering achieves 300% improvement as uniform sampling requires more than 7000 renderings to bring the mean error down to 200m.

6 Conclusion

We have proposed an adaptive rendering based approach to enhance geo-localization from 2D skyline images. Using affinity error metric, viewpoint optimality and line-wise planning presented in this paper, our method can successfully reduce overall 4X computational cost while preserving the geo-localization accuracy compared with a uniform sampling approach. In the near future, we would like to explore testing on a larger area. We expect to see even further improvements since terrain surfaces in large areas will likely contain more scattered complex areas where a uniform rendering solution will be infeasible for a desired level of geo-localization accuracy.

References

1. Baboud, L., Cadik, M., Eisemann, E., Seidel, H.: Automatic photo-to-terrain alignment for the annotation of mountain pictures. In: 2011 IEEE Conference on Computer Vision and Pattern Recognition (CVPR), pp. 41–48. IEEE (2011)
2. Ramalingam, S., Bouaziz, S., Sturm, P., Brand, M.: Skyline2gps: Localization in urban canyons using omni-skylines. In: IEEE/RSJ International Conference on Intelligent Robots and Systems (IROS), pp. 3816–3823. IEEE (2010)
3. Ramalingam, S., Bouaziz, S., Sturm, P., Brand, M.: Geolocalization using skylines from omni-images. In: 2009 IEEE 12th International Conference on Computer Vision Workshops (ICCV Workshops), pp. 23–30. IEEE (2009)
4. Russell, B., Sivic, J., Ponce, J., Dessales, H.: Automatic alignment of paintings and photographs depicting a 3d scene. In: 2011 IEEE International Conference on Computer Vision Workshops (ICCV Workshops), pp. 545–552. IEEE (2011)

5. Lerbour, R., Marvie, J., Gautron, P.: Adaptive streaming and rendering of large terrains: A generic solution. In: Proceedings of WSCG (2009)
6. Lerbour, R., Marvie, J., Gautron, P.: Adaptive real-time rendering of planetary terrains. In: Proceedings of WSCG (2010)
7. Röttger, S., Ertl, T.: Hardware accelerated terrain rendering by adaptive slicing. In: Workshop on Vision, Modelling, and Visualization VMV, vol. 1, pp. 159–168 (2001)
8. Choi, S., Kim, T., Yu, W.: Performance evaluation of ransac family. In: BMVC (2009)

Ultra-wide Baseline Facade Matching
for Geo-localization

Mayank Bansal[1,2], Kostas Daniilidis[1], and Harpreet Sawhney[2]

[1] GRASP Lab., University of Pennsylvania, Philadelphia PA, USA
{mayankb,kostas}@cis.upenn.edu
[2] Vision Technologies Lab., SRI International, Princeton NJ, USA
harpreet.sawhney@sri.com

Abstract. Matching street-level images to a database of airborne images is hard because of extreme viewpoint and illumination differences. Color/gradient distributions or local descriptors fail to match forcing us to rely on the structure of self-similarity of patterns on facades. We propose to capture this structure with a novel "scale-selective self-similarity" (S^4) descriptor which is computed at each point on the facade at its inherent scale. To achieve this, we introduce a new method for scale selection which enables the extraction and segmentation of facades as well. Matching is done with a Bayesian classification of the street-view query S^4 descriptors given all labeled descriptors in the bird's-eye-view database. We show experimental results on retrieval accuracy on a challenging set of publicly available imagery and compare with standard SIFT-based techniques.

1 Introduction

In this paper, we propose a novel method for matching facade imagery from very different viewpoints – like from a low flying aircraft and from a street-level camera. The scenario we address entails a database of pre-processed bird's-eye-view (BEV) images and street-view (SV) queries. Such images are characterized by unmitigated differences in local appearance which render any comparison of bags of visual words infeasible. A visual comparison of this imagery ever after rectification testifies to the hardness of the problem. Moreover, a vast majority of facades contain repetitive patterns which make correspondence estimation highly ambiguous. We rather have to rely on comparing the structures of the facade patterns and still account for any transformations between such structures.

The key idea in this paper is to avoid direct matching of features to solve this extreme case of wide-baseline matching. Thus, we formulate the problem as "embeddings" within each respective dataset (SV and BEV) so that large variations are incorporated within the structure of embeddings. This idea has not been explored before especially in the context of air-ground matching. We make the following contributions to the state of the art: (a) we introduce an approach for matching image regions with significant appearance, scale, and viewpoint variations based on a novel *Scale-Selective Self-Similarity (S^4)* feature

A. Fusiello et al. (Eds.): ECCV 2012 Ws/Demos, Part I, LNCS 7583, pp. 175–186, 2012.

that combines intrinsic scale selection with self-similarity descriptors, and (b) we demonstrate a novel system for matching street-level queries to a database of birds-eye views. We show experimental results on the retrieval accuracy from our technique and compare our performance with standard SIFT-descriptors.

We approach the facade detection and matching problem from a combined statistical and structural viewpoint. While other approaches model the lattice structure explicitly [1], we capture the statistical self-similarity (or dis-similarity) of a local patch to its neighbors. By avoiding using a specific feature like SIFT, MSER, or line segments, we can capture this structure at any point – in implementation we do it on a randomly jittered grid. In addition, the self-similarity descriptor also captures the dis-similarity between neighboring elements ignored in lattice approaches but still observed e.g. in [2]. The challenge with self-similarity is to capture the intrinsic local scale governed by the periodicity/generator group of a lattice. We estimate the scale by discovering the closest most salient repetition of a patch which can be centered anywhere. With the exception of [3], other approaches rely on the robustness of interest point or line segment detectors. Having obtained the intrinsic scale enables us to compute the scale-invariant S^4 descriptor and also allows us to **detect** facades as clusters of such points in space that have similar scale and descriptors. Similar descriptors are obtained from the query street-level image as well. At this point, instead of lattice or graph matching [3,2], we apply a labeling approach that labels each query descriptor with the most probable facade label (cluster) in a naive-Bayes sense. This way, we match local lattice structures rather than global ones and the most likely closest database facade is obtained.

2   Related Work

In the discussion of related work, we emphasize two main aspects: **detection** of facades/lattices and **matching**. Chung et al. [2] extract MSER regions in multiple scales which are then clustered w.r.t similarity. Local histograms of gradient similarity, area ratio, and configuration entropy are used to build adjacency matrices which are matched by using a spectral approach comparing only the graph structure. The commonality with our approach is that we never use any direct comparison of appearance across images. On the other hand, their query and model graph structures have to match globally while our approach uses the statistics of the edges of these graphs represented by the self-similarity descriptor and hence exploits the redundancy in features better. Moreover, the self-similarity descriptor is more general and implicit than the concatenation of several neighborhood descriptions (HoG, area ratio, entropy). Park et al. [1] model the lattice discovery as a multi-target tracking problem using Mean-Shift Belief Propagation. Candidates for lattice vertices are interest points that are obtained through clustering. Hays et al. [3] randomly select regions and search for their repetition in two directions in their immediate neighborhood. Lattice discovery is formulated as a graph matching problem with higher-order constraints that model the lattice structure of the region repetitions. The advantage of [1,3] is that they can deal with deformed lattices in the detection step while almost all other approaches including ours remove projective and sometimes affine distortions using vanishing points and ratio constraints. Schindler et al. [4] detect lattices by mapping quadruples of SIFT features to the projective basis and checking the consistency of the rest of the points with respect to this basis. They combine multiple 2D-to-3D pattern correspondences and recover the camera orientation and location as an intersection of the family of solutions obtained using each correspondence.

Recently, Bansal et al. [5] established the feasibility of matching highly disparate street view images to aerial image databases to precisely geo-localize SV images without the need for GPS or camera metadata. Doubek at al. [6] match the similarity of repetitive patterns by comparing the grayscale tiles, the peaks in color histogram, and the sizes of the two lattices. In [7], corners are extracted and grouped according to consistency with the geometric transformations corresponding to the generators of the lattice. Kosecka et al. [8] extract rectangle projections by grouping line segments according to vanishing point consistency. Using [9] they match a query street-view image to a database of geo-tagged street-view images using wide-baseline matching. In [10] and [11], a query street-view image is again matched to a database of street-view images and then used to compute the camera pose. They assume the query image camera internal parameters to be known and use a pyramid to match at multiple scales using geometric consistency. In [12], a viewpoint normalization of planar patches is followed by SIFT computation of the rectified patch. We close our discussion with [13] where omnidirectional views are matched to building outline maps by detecting the tallest vertical corners of the buildings which are matched through 2D to 1D projection.

3   Scale-Selective Self-similarity Features

The viewpoint and appearance difference between oblique Bird's-Eye-View (BEV) and street-view (SV) imagery is too large to be captured by direct matching of descriptors like SIFT and MSER. Therefore, we propose to create a descriptor that captures the structure of repetition of patterns or more generally the relative similarity between local patches within facades. Instead of modeling the structure with a graph or lattice and relying on the robustness of the detection of their nodes, we define a new feature which we call the *Scale-Selective Self-Similarity* or S^4 feature. This feature improves upon the well-known self-similarity descriptor from Shechtman et. al [14] by adding a SIFT-like scale-normalization to allow characterization of the self-similar structure in a scale-invariant manner.

Using the same notation as [14], for a given pixel q, the local self-similarity descriptor d_q is computed as follows. A local image patch of width w_{ss} (e.g., 5 pixels) centered at q is correlated with a larger surrounding image region of radius r_{ss} (e.g., 40 pixels), resulting in a local internal 'correlation surface'. The correlation surface is then transformed into a binned log-polar representation

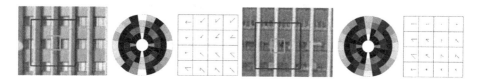

Fig. 1. Example self-similarity and SIFT descriptors for corresponding facades from SV and BEV images respectively

which accounts for increasing positional uncertainty with distance from the pixel q, accounting, thus, for local spatial affine deformations.

Fig. 1 shows a pair of (ortho-rectified) SV and BEV images of a facade that have been manually normalized to the same image scale, and compares how well their self-similarity descriptors match relative to their SIFT descriptors. The self-similarity descriptor at the center of the green ROI (local patch) is computed by correlating within the surrounding support region (blue ROI). The computed descriptors are noticeably quite similar even with the large appearance difference between the images themselves. In comparison, the SIFT descriptors computed using the same support region are dissimilar.

Scale-Selection. While it is clear that the inherent self-similar structure in building facades can serve as a good matching criterion, it is not clear how that structure can be matched if the building is seen at different scales. The basic self-similarity descriptor discussed above assumes a distance binning which is not scale invariant. To account for feature scale differences, Shechtman et al. [14] suggest computing the self-similarity descriptors on a Gaussian image pyramid representation and then searching for the template object across all scales. For the purposes of retrieval, however, such an approach would not work. In particular, for building facades, capturing the self-similar structure at all scales will reduce the discriminability evident at the fundamental scale of the facade. Instead, we would like a SIFT like normalization so that the descriptors between differently scaled buildings can still be matched. The repetitive structure of building facades provides one such normalization scale. However, building facades typically also exhibit *local* periodicity. While recovering this scale will serve the purpose of a valid normalizing scale, it may compromise on the overall discriminability of the computed descriptor by (a) being too local, and (b) by being too dependent on the inherent image scale (the smallest scale structure will be lost first in a noisy query image).

In this paper, we focus on recovering the *motif scale*. We define the motif scale at a pixel in the facade as the smallest wavelength at which any patch in this pixel's local neighborhood repeats. Defined this way, a local window scale would be ignored if it is not consistent with a few other window pixels in its neighborhood – thus making this scale robust against local pattern noise. This motif scale can be measured independently in both horizontal and vertical directions; in our implementation, we have only used the horizontal scale (denoted as λ_x), but the approach is symmetric with respect to using either of the two. Given the motif-scale λ_x value at any pixel, the S^4 descriptor is defined as the self-similarity descriptor computed by setting the patch size w_{ss} to the estimated motif scale λ_x and the correlation radius to $r_{ss} = 2\lambda_x$.

Our approach for motif scale-selection is based on the peaks in the autocorrelation surface in a local neighborhood surrounding a pixel. Consider a pixel (x, y) inside an image $\mathcal{I}$ exhibiting periodic structure and let λ_x be its scale along the x-direction. Now consider a small $w \times h$ patch of pixels around this pixel and correlate it with patches extracted at various offsets (r, θ) in a polar representation. To capture the correlations most relevant to the self-similarity descriptor, we measure the correlation profile using the following SSD measure. Let $\mathcal{J}(s, t) = \mathcal{I}(x + s, y + t)$, then:

$$q(r, \theta) = \sum_{t_y = -\frac{h}{2}}^{\frac{h}{2}} \sum_{t_x = -\frac{w}{2}}^{\frac{w}{2}} (\mathcal{J}(t_x, t_y) - \mathcal{J}(t_x + r\cos(\theta), t_y + r\sin(\theta)))^2 \qquad (1)$$

Then, the correlation profile $p_{(x,y)}(r)$ is computed by integrating the scores $q(r, \theta)$ in a 20° lobe ($\theta_0 = 10^o$) around the horizontal direction:

$$p_{(x,y)}(r) = \exp\left(-\frac{1}{2\theta_0 + 1} \sum_{\theta = -\theta_0}^{\theta_0} q(r, \theta)\right) \qquad (2)$$

where the subscript (x, y) makes explicit the fact that the profile was obtained by correlating the patch around pixel (x, y). The angular integration provides robustness against image distortions and ortho-rectification errors. The value of r is varied such that $r \in \{1, \ldots, S_{max}\}$, where S_{max} is a pre-defined maximum scale value we expect the structure in the input image to exhibit. The correlation profile thus obtained captures the periodicity of the structure by producing the highest correlation for $r \in \{\lambda_x, 2\lambda_x, \ldots\}$. However, depending on the starting location (x, y), the correlation profile can exhibit peaks at r values which are non-integral multiples of λ_x. This will be the case if the patch contains a submotif of the facade which is locally periodic at a higher frequency. The illustration in Fig. 2 depicts this happening for the green and blue profiles obtained from the (black) 1-D signal. The wavelength of both these curves is smaller than the motif scale λ_x by our definition above. To alleviate this issue, we compute multiple correlation profiles by varying the starting offset in an interval $\mathcal{O} = \{(x, y), (x + 1, y), (x + 2, y), \ldots, (x + m, y)\}$. The maximum offset $(x + m, y)$ is set so that the patch around it covers the structure at the maximum scale S_{max} from the starting position i.e. $m + w/2 \geq S_{max}$. The correlation profiles are combined into a single profile $p_{avg}(r)$ by integrating across the offsets, i.e. $p_{avg}(r) = \sum_{o \in \mathcal{O}} p_o(r)$. This removes the higher-frequency peaks in the individual profiles, leaving only the peaks corresponding to the actual wavelength λ_x as depicted in Fig. 2. Furthermore, the scale estimation becomes independent of the choice of the patch dimensions w and h.

To be robust against shallow peak responses, we measure a peakness measure around each peak in the profile $p_{avg}(r)$ and prune peaks which are shallower than a threshold t_{peak}. This threshold is set empirically by running the scale-estimator on textureless and non-repetetive structures. From the locations of

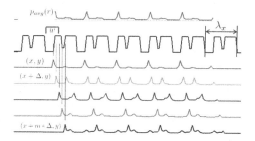

Fig. 2. Scale selection. To determine the scale λ_x of the (black) 1D signal in the second row, if we autocorrelate a patch of width w, we get one of the profiles shown in rows 3-7 depending on the starting offset. However, for a poor offset choice (green and blue curves), one can get comparable peaks in the correlation profile for scale values $< \lambda_x$ making it difficult to extract the correct scale. Integrating across these profiles, however, resolves this issue and results in a well defined profile $p_{avg}(r)$ shown in the first row. The high peaks now correspond to the correct wavelength λ_x.

the remaining peaks, the scale value λ_x can be readily obtained by a discrete Fourier transform. In the absence of any peaks the underlying structure is labeled aperiodic (assigned scale *zero*) – this removes most of the non-facade pixels and serves as an effective building detection mechanism.

4   Facade Extraction and Segmentation

We now describe our general approach for extracting building facade regions which is applicable to both BEV and SV images. The key idea is to exploit the self-similar structure of building facades: ortho-rectify the image, compute motif scales at sampled locations in the given image, compute S^4 descriptors at the computed scales and then cluster the descriptors to group similar structures together.

Motif Scale Computation. In the rectified image, we sample a grid of pixel locations every $\sigma_f = 5$ pixels apart and add uniformly random spatial jitter of amplitude $\sigma_f/2$ at each sample location. This jitter allows us to capture a good sampling of the feature distributions expected from this facade structure at the matching stage. At each sample location, we compute the motif scales using the approach discussed in section 3. An example result at this stage is shown in the left half of Fig. 3 . Note that the scale selection has removed the non-building areas almost completely by labeling them with a *zero* scale value (shown as red dots in the figures). Also note the wide range of motif scales seen across buildings stressing the importance of proper scale selection. At this point, we need a way to segment out individual facades into disjoint groups so that a matching approach can predict labels at the building level.

Facade Segmentation. At each sample location, we compute the S^4 descriptor ($n_\theta = 20$ angular bins and $n_r = 4$ distance bins) by setting the patch size w_{ss}

Fig. 3. Facade Extraction and Segmentation. Rectified BEV images showing, left: the selected horizontal scales with red dots at the locations assigned zero scale value and, right: cluster assignments after K-means.

to the estimated motif scale λ_x and the correlation radius to $r_{ss} = 2\lambda_x$. Now, we perform K-means clustering in this S^4 feature space using L_1 norm as our distance measure. To avoid descriptor grouping across different buildings, we penalize clustering of descriptors which were sampled from far off locations. The desired number of clusters N is set as follows. We manually mark the boundaries of a small number of buildings (5 in our case) in the BEV image and initialize $N = N_0$. Now, we iteratively run K-means with decreasing value for N as long as the following invariant is maintained: clusters on the marked buildings are contained within the marked boundaries. At the end of this process, we obtain a clustering that has the fewest number of clusters within each building and does not merge two different buildings into a single cluster (note that this is not guaranteed for unmarked buildings in general, but due to the descriptor-based grouping, we have not seen any merging of separate buildings into a single cluster in our experiments). For our test BEV set, we typically obtain 1-3 clusters per facade after this procedure. The right half of Fig. 3 shows an example of the clusters obtained after K-means clustering.

Notation. In the following, we will denote the S^4 descriptor vectors obtained from the entire set of BEV imagery by words $\mathcal{V} = \{v_1, v_2, \ldots, v_m\}$, the cluster labels as $\mathcal{C} = \{c_1, c_2, \ldots, c_N\}$ and the labeling function mapping each word to its cluster assignment by the function $\mathcal{L} : \mathcal{V} \to \mathcal{C}$.

5   Facade Matching

Given a query street-view image, we would like to retrieve facades from our BEV database that match the dominant facade(s) in the query. Sec. 6.3 and Fig. 7 illustrate the key steps in our SV-to-BEV matching pipeline. After ortho-rectification, motif scale selection and S^4 descriptor computation, we obtain a set of descriptor vectors $\mathcal{W} = \{w_1, w_2, \ldots, w_n\}$ from the query. For each of these words, we would like to estimate the probability $p(C = c_k | w_i)$ of being assigned to one of the clusters c_k in $\mathcal{C}$. The problem of finding the closest cluster label for each word w_i can be formulated in a Bayesian settings as follows. By Bayes' theorem,

Algorithm 1. BEV processing

1. Ortho-rectify BEV image using vanishing points.
2. Compute motif-scale λ_x at a jittered grid of pixel-locations on the BEV.
3. Compute S^4 descriptors v_i at locations with non-zero scales.
4. Cluster S^4 descriptors v_i using K-means to obtain label-set $\mathcal{C}$ and labeling function $\mathcal{L}$.

Algorithm 2. SV processing

1. Ortho-rectify SV image using vanishing points.
2. Compute motif-scale λ_x at a jittered grid of pixel-locations on the SV.
3. Compute S^4 descriptor-set $\mathcal{W} = \{w_j\}$ at locations with non-zero scales.
4. Compute labels $\mathcal{L}(w_j)$ using Eqn.3.
5. Best matching BEV facade: Facade containing cluster $\mathcal{L}(\mathcal{W})$ (Eqn.6).
6. Top matching facade set: For threshold t, return facades containing clusters k s.t. $f(k) > t$ (Eqn.5).

Table 1. Parameter settings

w	h	S_{max}	σ_f	w_{ss}	r_{ss}
13 px	13 px	48 px	5 px	λ_x	$2\lambda_x$
n_θ	n_r	N_0	$\sigma_{\mathcal{K}}$		
20	4	100	2.5		

Table 2. Facade detection performance

Scene	TP Rate	# Buildings	# FPs
BEV-1	86%	29	8
BEV-2	91%	33	3
BEV-3	86%	21	5

(a) Satellite coverage and sample BEV   (b) Sample queries

Fig. 4. Pittsburgh dataset

$$p(C = c_k | w_i) = \frac{p(w_i | C = c_k) p(C = c_k)}{\sum_{j=1}^{N} p(w_i | C = c_j) p(C = c_j)} \qquad (3)$$

For each word w_i, we estimate the likelihoods $p(w_i | C = c_k)$ by kernel density estimation using a Gaussian kernel $\mathcal{K}(w_i, v_j)$ with wavelength parameter $\sigma_{\mathcal{K}}$. The likelihood is then computed as:

$$p(w_i | C = c_k) = \frac{1}{|c_k|} \sum_{\mathcal{L}(v_j) = c_k} \mathcal{K}(w_i, v_j) \qquad (4)$$

where $|c_k|$ denotes the cardinality of cluster k. The prior probability $p(C = c_k)$ is simply set from the sample proportions: $p(C = c_k) = \frac{|c_k|}{m}$. For each word w_i, we estimate the MAP estimate of the label by choosing the label k with the maximum a-posteriori probability: $\mathcal{L}(w_i) = \arg\max_k p(C = c_k | w_i)$. Given the above word assignments, we can now compute the most probable label for the entire query facade by accumulating the word assignments from each word:

$$f(k) = \sum_i \delta(\mathcal{L}(w_i) = c_k) \tag{5}$$

$$\mathcal{L}(\mathcal{W}) = \arg\max_k \{f(k) \,|\, k = 1, \ldots, N\} \tag{6}$$

where $\delta(.)$ is the indicator function. The label $\mathcal{L}(\mathcal{W})$ identifies a cluster $c^* \in \mathcal{C}$ which, by construction of the clustering algorithm, identifies a single BEV facade.

6   Experiments and Results

Algorithm Parameters. In Table-1, we list all the parameter settings we used in our implementation. The scale estimation process was found robust against different choices of patch-size parameters w and h. S_{max} was set to a number greater than the maximum horizontal building scale for our BEV dataset (manually eyeballed). The S^4 values for n_θ and n_r were set the same as in [14].

BEV and SV Imagery Datasets. Our dataset comprises of BEV imagery (2000×1500 pixels) downloaded using Microsoft's Bing service for an area approximately $2\,\mathrm{Km} \times 1.2\,\mathrm{Km}$ in size (Fig. 4(a)) in downtown Pittsburgh, PA, USA. This dataset is challenging due to a large number (approx. 40) of buildings and very similiar facade patterns. This dataset also covers a much larger area than used in related works in air-ground-based localization e.g. $440m \times 440m$ in [13]. Street-view images downloaded using Panoramio, Flickr, Google Street-View(screenshots), and Microsoft Bing's Streetside(screenshots) were used as queries. For ground-truth purposes, only the SV imagery with geo-tags or visually identifiable facade correspondence (with the BEV) was retained.

Imagery Rectification. We rectify BEV to an orthographic view aligned with the dominant city-block direction. Similarly, the SV imagery is rectified to an orthographic view of the dominant facade in the scene using the Geometric Parsing based vanishing point estimation approach and code [15,16].

6.1   Scale Selection Results

To characterize our scale selection algorithm, we selected a test set of 10 building facades extracted from the Pittsburgh BEV dataset. We manually measured the ground-truth horizontal scale(s) for each facade and compared them to those estimated by our approach. Since we densely estimate these scale values over the facade, we computed a histogram of the estimated scale values and the normalized histogram values are shown as the blue circles (with radii proportional to the histogram values) in the bubble plot of Fig. 5. The red pluses denote the ground-truth scale values – multiple in cases where the facade exhibits more than one motif scale. The comparison shows the accuracy of our scale estimation and the presence of very few outliers.

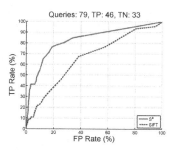

Fig. 5. Evaluation of scale estimation accuracy for 10 BEV building facades

Fig. 6. ROC curve for BEV-to-SV matching on Pittsburgh dataset

(a) Query SV image, and ortho-rectified SV with extracted motif-scales

(b) Matching result with BEV with correspondingly matching clusters shown in same colors.

Fig. 7. Example Street-view (SV) processing

6.2 Facade Detection Evaluation

Table-2 shows results from our facade detection algorithm. For each BEV scene, we looked at the computed horizontal scales – points with non-zero scale values are treated as potential facades. We quantify the performance as follows: for each building facade, if at least 50% of its visible area was assigned a non-zero scale, then we count it as a true detection. If in any 4×4 sub-grid of sampled locations not on a building facade, at least 25% are assigned a non-zero scale, then we count it as a false-positive.

6.3 SV to BEV Matching

Fig. 7 illustrates our typical query SV processing pipeline. The algorithmic steps are outlined in Algorithm-2.

Fig. 8. Qualitative Matching Results. The main tiles show rectified BEV images. The insets show the original and rectified query street-view facades. On the rectified inset, the colored points are a subset of the words $w_1, w_2, \ldots, w_n$ with the top three most frequent recovered labels $\mathcal{L}(w_i)$ shown as red, green and blue points respectively; similarly colored points in the BEV image are words v_j which belong to these three clusters.

Fig. 6 shows the retrieval performance of our approach (along with a comparison with SIFT – details in Sec. 6.4) with a query set of 79 images including 33 true negatives i.e. buildings which were either not part of the BEV database or were significantly occluded. The query set contains challenging images with significant uncorrected image distortions, urban clutter and varied zoom range. A third of these images are high-resolution pictures from Flickr and Panoramio and the remaining are low-resolution screenshots from Google Street-View and Bing Streetside. A few samples from the query set are shown in Fig. 4(b). For generating the ROC curves, instead of using the most probable label from Eqn.6 directly, we treat the vector of frequency of each label $f(k) = \sum_i \delta(\mathcal{L}(w_i) = c_k)$ as a probability distribution. Then, to get a point on the ROC curve, we pick a value between 0.0 and 1.0 and select all the labels with probabilities higher than this value. This becomes our retrieval set which is compared with the ground-truth facade set to compute the TP and FP rates in the usual manner.

Fig. 8 shows two examples of the top three retrieval matches on representative (screen-captured) Google street-view queries. From the amount of perspective (and distortion) in the SV imagery, it is clear that features like MSER and SIFT would hardly find any correspondences.

6.4   Comparison with SIFT Features

Given the prevalence of SIFT features in wide-baseline matching literature, we present experimental comparison of its performance with our approach. To avoid any bias against SIFT due to perspective distortions (and to preclude comparison with SIFT variants like A-SIFT), we extract SIFT features on ortho-rectified BEV and ortho-rectified SV imagery. Next, we use the building clusters found using our S^4-based algorithm and perform an assignment of the SIFT features to these clusters using a nearest-neighbor association on pixel coordinates thus discarding any features on non-building background clutter. The Bayesian classification from Sec. 5 is used on the SIFT clusters to retrieve matching facades for the query images and the quantitative results are shown in the ROC in Fig. 6 which illustrates that we achieve significant improvement in performance using S^4 features instead of SIFT features.

7   Conclusion

We have been able to match query street-level facades to airborne imagery under challenging viewpoint and illumination variation by introducing a novel approach of selecting the intrinsic facade motif scale and modeling facade structure through self-similarity.Using the motif scale, we extract and segment lattice-like facades and construct scale-invariant S^4 descriptors. We localize queries by classifying descriptors, thus matching to facades with semi-local lattice consistency.

References

1. Park, M., Brocklehurst, K., Collins, R., Liu, Y.: Deformed lattice detection in real-world images using mean-shift belief propagation. TPAMI 31, 1804–1816 (2009)
2. Chung, Y., Han, T., He, Z.: Building recognition using sketch-based representations and spectral graph matching. In: ICCV (2010)
3. Hays, J., Leordeanu, M., Efros, A.A., Liu, Y.: Discovering Texture Regularity as a Higher-Order Correspondence Problem. In: Leonardis, A., Bischof, H., Pinz, A. (eds.) ECCV 2006. LNCS, vol. 3952, pp. 522–535. Springer, Heidelberg (2006)
4. Schindler, G., Krishnamurthy, P., Lublinerman, R., Liu, Y., Dellaert, F.: Detecting and Matching Repeated Patterns for Automatic Geo-tagging in Urban Environments. In: CVPR (2008)
5. Bansal, M., Sawhney, H.S., Cheng, H., Daniilidis, K.: Geo-localization of street views with aerial image databases. In: ACM-MM (2011)
6. Doubek, P., Matas, J., Perdoch, M., Chum, O.: Image Matching and Retrieval by Repetitive Patterns. In: ICPR (2010)
7. Schaffalitzky, F., Zisserman, A.: Geometric grouping of repeated elements within images. In: Shape, Contour and Grouping in Computer Vision (1999)
8. Kosecka, J., Zhang, W.: Extraction, matching, and pose recovery based on dominant rectangular structures. In: CVIU, vol. 100, pp. 274–293. Elsevier (2005)
9. Zhang, W., Kosecka, J.: Image Based Localization in Urban Environments. In: 3DPVT (2006)
10. Cipolla, R., Robertson, D., Tordoff, B.: Image-based localisation. In: Proceedings of 10th International Conference on Virtual Systems and Multimedia (2004)
11. Robertson, D., Cipolla, R.: An Image-Based System for Urban Navigation. In: BMVC (2004)
12. Wu, C., Clipp, B., Li, X., Frahm, J., Pollefeys, M.: 3d model matching with viewpoint-invariant patches (vip). In: CVPR (2008)
13. Cham, T., Ciptadi, A., Tan, W., Pham, M., Chia, L.: Estimating camera pose from a single urban ground-view omnidirectional image and a 2D building outline map. In: CVPR (2010)
14. Shechtman, E., Irani, M.: Matching local self-similarities across images and videos. In: CVPR (2007)
15. Barinova, O., Lempitsky, V., Tretiak, E., Kohli, P.: Geometric Image Parsing in Man-Made Environments. In: Daniilidis, K., Maragos, P., Paragios, N. (eds.) ECCV 2010, Part II. LNCS, vol. 6312, pp. 57–70. Springer, Heidelberg (2010)
16. Tardif, J.: Non-iterative approach for fast and accurate vanishing point detection. In: ICCV (2009)

A Memory Efficient Discriminative Approach for Location Aided Recognition

Varsha Hedau[1], Sudipta N. Sinha[2], C. Lawrence Zitnick[2], and Richard Szeliski[2]

[1] Nokia Research, Sunnyvale, CA, USA
varsha.hedau@gmail.com
[2] Microsoft Research, Redmond, WA, USA
{sudipsin,larryz,szeliski}@microsoft.com

Abstract. We propose a visual recognition approach aimed at fast recognition of urban landmarks on a GPS-enabled mobile device. While most existing methods offload their computation to a server, the latency of an image upload over a slow network can be a significant bottleneck. In this paper, we investigate a new approach to mobile visual recognition that would involve uploading only GPS coordinates to a server, following which a compact location specific classifier would be downloaded to the client and recognition would be computed completely on the client. To achieve this goal, we have developed an approach based on supervised learning that involves training very compact random forest classifiers based on labeled geo-tagged images. Our approach selectively chooses highly discriminative yet repeatable visual features in the database images during offline processing. Classification is efficient at query time as we first rectify the image based on vanishing points and then use random binary patterns to densely match a small set of downloaded features with min-hashing used to speedup the search. We evaluate our method on two public benchmarks and on two streetside datasets where we outperform standard bag-of-words retrieval as well as direct feature matching approaches, both of which are infeasible for client-side query processing.

1   Introduction

The ubiquity of cameras on GPS-enabled mobile devices nowadays makes it possible to visually query the identity of a specific landmark in a scene simply by taking a picture and uploading it to a server for processing. The feasibility and accuracy of such applications is rapidly improving as geo-tagged image databases such as Flickr, Google and Bing Maps grow by the day. Recognizing landmarks reliably in streetside photos however poses some challenges. First, streetside buildings exhibit great variations in appearance due to changes in viewpoint, illumination, weather, seasons or even due to changes in the scene structure. Second, clutter in the scene due to the presence of people, vehicles etc can be unavoidable when issuing a query. Finally, not all streetside buildings are easy to recognize. In fact some can be quite difficult to distinguish from one another due to their similar appearance and presence of ambiguous visual features.

A. Fusiello et al. (Eds.): ECCV 2012 Ws/Demos, Part I, LNCS 7583, pp. 187–197, 2012.

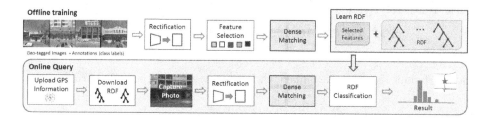

Fig. 1. Overview of our location-aided recognition approach. A device using our method will upload only GPS location to the server at query time; a compact, location specific classifier trained offline will be downloaded to the device and evaluated on the client.

Several recent approaches to location recognition [4,12,15,18,17,19,22,23,28,29] use the query image to retrieve similar images from a geo-registered image database using robust feature matching based on interest points and local feature descriptors. The use of quantized descriptors and bag-of-words (BoW) models are popular due to their scalability [9]. These retrieval methods however require significant memory as they often rely on re-ranking based on a geometric verification step that requires storing all the database image features. When recognition is performed on a server this is less of a concern. However, the latency associated with uploading an image to the server over a slow network can be quite significant. To reduce latency of landmark recognition on mobile devices, we explore an alternative approach where location specific data is downloaded to the device based on its GPS location after which all computation happens on the device. To make this approach feasible the download size must be small and the subsequent processing must be efficient on low-end devices. Our new approach addresses these pertinent issues and we analyze the accuracy and download size tradeoffs of our method and existing methods under these constraints.

In this paper, we propose a memory efficient discriminative approach to landmark recognition that uses the approximate GPS coordinates of the querying device. Instead of storing all the images in a database, we selectively store information necessary to uniquely distinguish each landmark from other landmarks within a reasonable geospatial scope. This is accomplished by training a Random Decision Forest (RDF) classifier [6] to classify each query to the set of possible locations or landmarks within a small region surrounding the GPS location of the querying device. During offline processing, local image features reliably matched across training images of the same landmark are first automatically discovered and matched densely across every training image, yielding features that can be used for landmark classification. During the training stage, a small set of discriminative features are automatically selected from this pool of potential features. For efficient dense matching[1] and for invariance to perspective distortion, all images are rectified prior to matching [4,22] (see Figure 1 for an overview). For fast query processing, we propose using min-hash to further accelerate the dense matching step. We demonstrate our approach on two public benchmarks

---

[1] a patch is compared to patches at all 2d positions across a range of discrete scales.

for landmark recognition and in two urban scenes where all query images are captured on mobile devices. The number of landmarks in these datasets vary between 50–200. In all four cases, our classifiers are quite compact with download size in the range of 150–230 KBytes, with accuracy comparable or better than existing methods which are also impractical for on-device processing.

Our main contribution is a new approach suitable for landmark recognition on the mobile device. We train compact random forest classifiers using geospatial scope of the training images and in the process a small set of discriminative and repeatable local features are discovered. At query classification time, these features are densely matched in the image using binary descriptors. A min-hash technique significantly improves the efficiency of this dense matching step.

1.1   Related Work

Most prior work in landmark recognition has focused on improving keypoint-based retrieval. Knopp et al. [15] remove confusing features in a bag-of-words model, while Li et al. [19] prioritize the matching of repeatable and frequently occurring features. Turcot and Lowe [26] remove features that are not repeatable and merge the remaining features from neighboring images. A vocabulary tree based approach that maximizes the information gain of the visual words was proposed by [23] whereas Jegou et al. [14] developed compact global descriptors for scalable similar image retrieval. Zamir et al. [28] remove noisy matches between images using a variant of the descriptor distance ratio test, and Zhang et al. [29] uses robust motion estimation. Our approach avoids keypoint extraction and instead uses dense matching of a few selective features in the whole image across position and scale. Other methods perform location recognition using scene categorization [12], or using structure from motion point clouds [13,19].

Image rectification is important for wide baseline matching [22,29,5] and also useful for location matching with upright SIFT features [4]. Our work is closely related to [18] that uses a discriminative approach for classifying landmarks using SVMs with histograms of visual words as features. However they rely on text features for obtaining higher classification accuracy. In contrast, we use random decision forest classifiers [6] which are ideal for multi-class classification[2,16,25], can be compactly represented and allow fast evaluation at classification time.

Compact feature descriptors have been proposed for feature extraction on a mobile device [8] and a number of approaches upload a set of feature descriptors instead of the query image [3]. Although this improves the efficiency of the upload, significant latency may still be present. Our use of min-hash for accelerating the dense matching is related to prior work on min-hash for efficient retrieval of near duplicate images from large databases [11,10].

2   Learning Location Classifiers

We recognise the landmark seen in a query image by classifying it as one of the predefined landmark classes. Our training set consists of geo-referenced images annotated with locations labels, typically corresponding to individual buidlings or street intersections. We use random decision forests (RDF) for this multi-class classification task. The input features for RDF are computed from a set of selected patch templates that are densely matched across the image. To ensure that discriminative features are selected during training, we first identify patches that are repeatable within each landmark class [26]. We rectify the images during preprocessing to remove perspective distortion which also makes dense matching more efficient. Our approach is now described in detail.

2.1 Rectification

Planar building facades often undergo severe perspective distortion, based on the camera's orientation and position. Searching over all plausible distortions is computationally prohibitive for dense matching. If the camera's focal length is known and vanishing points can be identified, the degrees of freedom can be reduced using image rectification. Dense patch matching on the rectified image reduces the search to 2d position and scale. Rectification has been used similarly in prior work [4,22]. Our automatic metric rectification method first detects orthogonal vanishing points (VP) using an approximate focal length estimate. By assuming that images have small roll angle, we can easily identify the vertical VP in the image. As in *upright* SIFT [4], the lack of rotational invariance makes our features more discriminative.

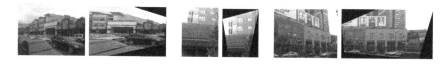

Fig. 2. Three query images and their rectified versions computed by our method

We detect vanishing points in multiple stages. First, the vertical VP is estimated via sequential RANSAC on 2D line segments subtending a small angle to the vertical. For speed and accuracy, longer lines are given preference during the random sampling. When the focal length is known, the vertical VP determines the horizon line in the image. Horizontal VPs are then found using a 1-line RANSAC on non vertical lines that intersect the horizon. When the focal length is unknown, our RANSAC hypothesis also includes a random guess of the focal length, sampled from the normal distribution $N(f, \sigma)$ where $f = 1.5$ is the normalized focal length and $\sigma = 1.0$. If two orthogonal vanishing points are found, we rectify the image using the 2D homography, $H=KR^{-1}K^{-1}$ where, the matrix $K = \text{diag}([f f 1])$ represents camera intrinsics with normalized focal length f and R denotes the 3D rotation with respect to the 3D vanishing directions. The image quad to be rectified is chosen based on a threshold for the maximum distortion induced by H. Figure 2 shows some examples of images rectified using our approach. However, an accurate rectification is not essential for our approach. When only the vertical VP is detected, we only perform roll correction, thereby eliminating one degree of freedom in camera rotation [2].

---

[2] Accelerometers on mobile devices can also provide a vertical VP estimate.

2.2   Feature Selection

A set of repeatable image patches is first extracted from the rectified images. These serve as the input for training the random forest. We densely match each patch in an image, searching for the most similar patch across all position and a few discrete scales. We use the distance between the patch templates and their most similar patches in the image as the input feature F for the classifier.

An ideal pool of features D would contain image patches that are both unique as well as repeatable within a class. To obtain such patches, we extract scale invariant DoG keypoints [20] and DAISY descriptors [27] in the rectified images and perform robust feature matching on image pairs in the training set [20,26]. Outliers are removed using RANSAC and geometric verification after which the correspondences are linked to form multi-view tracks. The set of patches D is then computed by randomly sampling from these tracks [3]. Next, a candidate patch from each track is chosen by selecting the one with the minimum descriptor distance to all other patches in the track. This is added to the set D[4]. For images that did not match any other image, we randomly sample 10 patches corresponding to DoG keypoints in the image. All image patches in our implementation are axis-aligned square patches. They are resampled to 32×32 pixels before computing feature descriptors to be used for dense matching.

We represent the patches using binary (BRIEF) [7] descriptors which allow for very efficient matching. This descriptor is computed by randomly sampling k pixel pairs p_k and p_k' from a 32×32 image patch based on a 2D Gaussian distribution centered on the center pixel, and then setting the k-th bit of the descriptor only if $I(p_k) > I(p_k')$. Based on experiments, we found $k=192$ was a good trade-off between accuracy and speed. Distance between descriptors is measured using Hamming distance, which can be computed very efficiently [7].

2.3   Random Decision Forests

Given a feature vector F computed from densely matching patch descriptors D in the rectified training images, we train a set of random decision trees using standard techniques [6]. The data is recursively split into subsets at each internal node of the binary trees which correspond to binary tests. The leaf nodes of the forest store the class distributions. During classification, the class label is predicted by averaging the class probabilities predicted by all the trees in the forest and selecting the most likely class. We learn binary tests based on single features in F. Thus for each internal node in each tree, we need to learn on which features to make decisions and the corresponding thresholds. The trees are trained independently using standard approaches that randomly selects a subset of potential features from F for training each tree. The best feature at each recursive step is selected as the one which has the largest decrease in Gini impurity. The selection size parameter s (= 20 by default) determines how many random features are considered. No tree pruning is performed in our implementation.

---

[3] Longer tracks are given preference during random sampling.

[4] In our experiments, D had at most 4000 patches, but more patches can be used too.

Random forests have several benefits – trees with axis-aligned splits can be stored very efficiently, since only the feature index and a threshold must be stored at each internal node. The classification step is very fast. Storing the features themselves is efficient, since the set of features F^* actually used by the forest is typically smaller than the size of F. Finally, the random selection of features increases robustness to occlusions. We observed that occasionally features are selected on temporary stationary objects in the scene such as parked cars, which will produce non-informative features at classification time. Random selection reduces the effect of such bias in the training sets. By default, we trained our forests with 50 trees where the number of selected features varied between 200 to 3000. Further discussions on the impact of parameters on accuracy versus storage tradeoffs can be found in Section 3.

2.4   Efficient Dense Matching

Computing the feature vector for the query image prior to classification requires densely matching each patch descriptor in the query image. During training, a subset of features $F^* \subset F$ are selected for the internal nodes of the forest. At query time, we only need to densely match the corresponding descriptors in F^*. However for 500+ descriptors in F^*, brute force Hamming distance computations can be quite expensive. Rectification makes such a dense matching approach more practical, as it restricts the search to 2D translation within multiple scaled version of the image. In practice, we search 10 scales between 0.25X and 1.25X magnification, with a patch size of 32×32 pixels. It is worth noting that no interest points are required by our method.

Significant computational efficiency is obtained using a min-hash approach [11,10] to discard dissimilar patches. With min-hash, we compute a set of hashes for BRIEF descriptors that have a probability of collision equal to the Jaccard similarity of the two binary vectors. If viewed as sets, the Jaccard similarity of two vectors is the cardinality of their intersection divided by their union. Specifically, the min-hash is the minimum index of a positive bit after the vectors are permuted by a random permutation. As in [11], we compute multiple min hashes and concatenate them into sketches for improved discriminability[5].

We compute a set of sketches for each BRIEF descriptor in F^* and construct an inverse lookup table for them. We scan the image, finding potentially similar patches by detecting sketch collisions using efficient lookup (at least $k = 2$ sketches must be identical). The Hamming distance is computed for these descriptors pairs. In practice, we found that no Hamming distances was computed for 80% of all patches at classification time and on average less than ten distance computations were needed for the remaining patches. Since all the bits of the BRIEF descriptor are not required for computing its min-hash sketches, the bits are computed on demand, as needed by the min-hash function. Thus for 80% of the patches, the full BRIEF descriptor is not computed, saving computation. However computing Hamming distance was usually the bottleneck.

---

[5] In our implementation we use 5 sketches each containing 5 sketches.

3   Experimental Results

Datasets: We evaluated our approach on the public ZUBUD [24] and CALTECH building datasets [1], each of which has five images of 200 and 50 buildings respectively. We created random sets of query images using a leave one out strategy for each building. We also report results on two challenging streetside datasets – SUBURB-48 and TOWN-56, collected by us, where the training images comprise of 504 and 464 images corresponding to an area of about four city blocks. For both these datasets, prominent landmarks (classes) such as buildings, restaurants, stores are labeled manually. Our query set contains 200 images captured by cameras on several mobile devices and have strong viewpoint and appearance changes compared to the training images which were acquired during a different season. Table 1 lists the accuracy of our method and the corresponding download sizes for all four datasets. In Figure 3, we show how varying the selection size and the number of decision trees affect the compactness of our classifiers. The accuracy improves as these parameters are increased but starts to converge for a selection size of about 20 and with 50 decision trees.

Comparison with BoW and SIFT: To assess the suitability of our approach for a mobile device, we compare the accuracy and download size tradeoff of our method with SIFT matching [20] and BOW method of [21]. These are considered as state of the art for location recognition when memory footprint and storage is not an issue. The classification accuracy is the percentage of query images correctly recognized. For SIFT, the retrieved images for each query are ranked by the number of matches. The ranked image list is mapped to a list of classes by finding the first occurrence of each class in the sorted list. To force memory/download constraints on SIFT matching, only a fraction of SIFT keypoints were sampled from the database image and used for matching. Further the descriptor vectors were quantized to k-bits entries (k = 1 to 8). Similarly storage constraints were forced on the BoW method by choosing vocabularies with 1K to 100K words and quantizing the histogram entries to use 1 to 16 bits. BOW histogram were represented as sparse vectors. Figure 5 shows that both SIFT and BOW accuracy degrades significantly when the memory/storage size is lowered. In our method, the download size is varied by choosing different RDF parameters. Rectified input images were used in all the comparisons.

Table 1. Datasets used in our experiments and the performance of the proposed approach in terms of compactness of the classifiers and classification accuracy

DATASET	#IMGS	#CLASSES	TRAINING			QUERY STATS	
			#FEATURES	#TREES	DOWNLOAD SIZE	# QUERIES.	ACCURACY
ZUBUD	804	200	4107	50	233 KBYTES	200	92%
CALTECH-50	200	50	2820	50	153 KBYTES	50	90%
SUBURB-48	504	48	2200	60	220 KBYTES	131	50%
TOWN-56	464	56	3138	60	198 KBYTES	62	35.5%

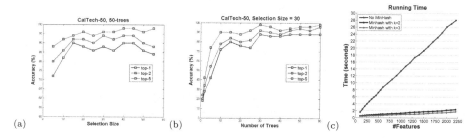

Fig. 3. Accuracy on CALTECH-50 with different RDF parameters – (a) selection size and (b) the number of trees. Accuracy is the fraction of correctly classified queries considering top k results (k = 1, 2 and 5). (c) Feature extraction timings: Brute force distance computation timings shown in blue. Timings for our method is shown in red/black, where Hamming distance is computed only when at least k min-hash sketches collide.

Fig. 4. Four example queries on TOWN-56 and SUBURB-48 datasets. The original and rectified images are shown on the left and the recognized building is shown on the right.

Our method outperforms both BoW and SIFT in accuracy even though our classifiers are one or more orders of magnitude more compact. For example, on TOWN-56 and SUBURB-48 datasets our method had an accuracy of 36% and 49.5% respectively with about 200KB storage size. While SIFT matching did not work at all, BOW methods had an accuracy of approximately 8% and 12% for the two datasets. The best performance with BOW and SIFT was obtained with 2MB+ and 40MB+ storage size in both datasets. The results on CALTECHR-50 is similar; our method has an accuracy of 90% with 100KB of storage whereas BOW methods had an accuracy of 50% when compressed to about 200KB.

Download Size. Each internal node of our decision trees require roughly 5.5 bytes to represent a feature index, an integer threshold and two pointers. The total download size can be approximated as $24N + 6.5TH$ bytes (assuming we have fewer than 1024 classes), where the random forest selects N patches (each of which is represented using 32 bytes). T is the number of trees in the RDF and H is the average tree height. For C classes, we need decision trees with height $\log_2(|C|)$. With hundreds of classes, the storage size is typically dominated by the feature descriptors which are selected during the training stage.

Running Time. For dense matching, we resize the images setting its larger dimension to 512 pixels. When searching 10 levels of scale from 0.25X to 1.25X, the running time varies between 0.5s to 1.5s for most datasets. The time complexity is linear in the number of features. Figure 3(c) shows the running time for performing dense matching on an image of resolution 512 × 420 on a laptop with a single core 2.66GHz processor. For the min-hash based approach, we computed Hamming distance between descriptors only when k out of five sketches matched between a pair of descriptors. Figure 3(c) shows running time for $k = 2$ and 3 and shows how the min-hash produces an order of magnitude speedup.

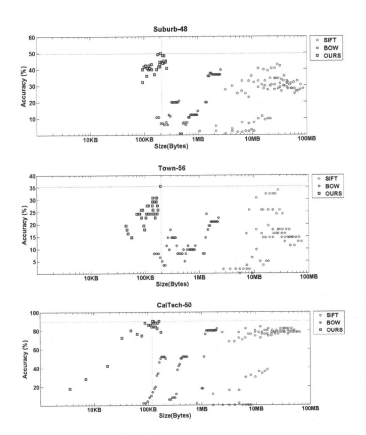

Fig. 5. CLASSIFICATION ACCURACY: On both streetside datasets and CALTECH-50, our method outperforms BoW and SIFT even though our classifiers are 1 or 2 orders of magnitude more compact. Each method was configured with different storage/download sizes to obtain the scatter plots. The X-axes are in log-scale. The best configuration of our method is shown using dotted lines. Our accuracies are reasonable under 100KB whereas BOW performs poorly under 100KB and SIFT matching completely fails.

4 Conclusion

We have proposed a new discriminative method for classifying urban landmarks that exploits geospatial scope to train very compact classifiers with efficient query processing capabilities. Our method is currently less robust to recognizing landmarks across different seasons. In the future we will focus on improving the recognition accuracies using diverse multi-season imagery for training.

References

1. Aly, M., Welinder, P., Munich, M., Perona, P.: Towards automated large scale discovery of image families. In: CVPR Workshop on Internet Vision, pp. 9–16 (2009)
2. Amit, Y., Geman, D.: Shape quantization and recognition with randomized trees. Neural Computation 9 (1997)
3. Arth, C., Wagner, D., Klopschitz, M., Irschara, A., Schmalstieg, D.: Wide area localization on mobile phones. In: ISMAR, pp. 73–82 (2009)
4. Baatz, G., Köser, K., Chen, D., Grzeszczuk, R., Pollefeys, M.: Handling Urban Location Recognition as a 2D Homothetic Problem. In: Daniilidis, K., Maragos, P., Paragios, N. (eds.) ECCV 2010, Part VI. LNCS, vol. 6316, pp. 266–279. Springer, Heidelberg (2010)
5. Bansal, M., Sawhney, H.S., Cheng, H., Daniilidis, K.: Geo-localization of street views with aerial image databases. In: MM 2011, pp. 1125–1128 (2011)
6. Breiman, L.: Random forests. Machine Learning 45 (2001)
7. Calonder, M., Lepetit, V., Strecha, C., Fua, P.: BRIEF: Binary Robust Independent Elementary Features. In: Daniilidis, K., Maragos, P., Paragios, N. (eds.) ECCV 2010, Part IV. LNCS, vol. 6314, pp. 778–792. Springer, Heidelberg (2010)
8. Chandrasekhar, V., Takacs, G., Chen, D., Tsai, S., Grzeszczuk, R., Girod, B.: CHoG: Compressed histogram of gradients a low bit-rate feature descriptor. In: CVPR, pp. 2504–2511 (2009)
9. Chen, D., Baatz, G., Köser, S.T., Vedantham, R., Pylvanainen, T., Roimela, K., Chen, X., Bach, J., Pollefeys, M., Girod, B., Grzeszczuk, R.: City-scale landmark identification on mobile devices. In: CVPR (2011)
10. Chum, O., Perdoch, M., Matas, J.: Geometric min-hashing: Finding a (thick) needle in a haystack. In: CVPR (2009)
11. Chum, O., Philbin, J., Zisserman, A.: Near duplicate image detection: min-hash and tf-idf weighting. In: BMVC (2008)
12. Hays, J., Efros, A.: Im2gps: estimating geographic information from a single image. In: CVPR (2008)
13. Irschara, A., Zach, C., Frahm, J.-M., Bischof, H.: From structure-from-motion point clouds to fast location recognition. In: CVPR, pp. 2599–2606 (2009)
14. Jégou, H., Douze, M., Schmid, C., Pérez, P.: Aggregating local descriptors into a compact image representation. In: CVPR, pp. 3304–3311 (2010)
15. Knopp, J., Sivic, J., Pajdla, T.: Avoiding Confusing Features in Place Recognition. In: Daniilidis, K., Maragos, P., Paragios, N. (eds.) ECCV 2010, Part I. LNCS, vol. 6311, pp. 748–761. Springer, Heidelberg (2010)
16. Lepetit, V., Fua, P.: Keypoint recognition using randomized trees. PAMI 28, 1465–1479 (2006)

17. Li, X., Wu, C., Zach, C., Lazebnik, S., Frahm, J.-M.: Modeling and Recognition of Landmark Image Collections Using Iconic Scene Graphs. In: Forsyth, D., Torr, P., Zisserman, A. (eds.) ECCV 2008, Part I. LNCS, vol. 5302, pp. 427–440. Springer, Heidelberg (2008)

18. Li, Y., Crandall, D., Huttenlocher, D.: Landmark classification in large-scale image collections. In: ICCV (2009)

19. Li, Y., Snavely, N., Huttenlocher, D.P.: Location Recognition Using Prioritized Feature Matching. In: Daniilidis, K., Maragos, P., Paragios, N. (eds.) ECCV 2010, Part II. LNCS, vol. 6312, pp. 791–804. Springer, Heidelberg (2010)

20. Lowe, D.G.: Distinctive image features from scale-invariant keypoints. Int'l J. of Computer Vision 60 (2004)

21. Nister, D., Stewenius, H.: Scalable recognition with a vocabulary tree. In: CVPR, pp. 2161–2168 (2006)

22. Robertson, D., Cipolla, R.: An image based system for urban navigation. In: BMVC, pp. 819–828 (2004)

23. Schindler, G., Brown, M., Szeliski, R.: City-scale location recognition. In: CVPR (2007)

24. Shao, H., Svoboda, T., Gool, L.V.: Zubud-zurich buildings database for image based recognition. Technical report, No. 260, ETH Zurich (2003)

25. Shotton, J., Johnson, M., Cipolla, R.: Semantic texton forests for image categorization and segmentation. In: CVPR (2008)

26. Turcot, P., Lowe, D.G.: Better matching with fewer features: The selection of useful features in large database recognition problems. In: ICCV WS-LAVD (2009)

27. Winder, S., Hua, G., Brown, M.: Picking the best DAISY. In: CVPR, pp. 178–185 (2009)

28. Zamir, A.R., Shah, M.: Accurate Image Localization Based on Google Maps Street View. In: Daniilidis, K., Maragos, P., Paragios, N. (eds.) ECCV 2010, Part IV. LNCS, vol. 6314, pp. 255–268. Springer, Heidelberg (2010)

29. Zhang, W., Kosecka, J.: Hierarchical building recognition. Image Vision Comput 25(5), 704–716 (2007)

Weakly Supervised Learning of Object Segmentations from Web-Scale Video

Glenn Hartmann[1], Matthias Grundmann[2], Judy Hoffman[3], David Tsai[2],
Vivek Kwatra[1], Omid Madani[1], Sudheendra Vijayanarasimhan[1], Irfan Essa[2],
James Rehg[2], and Rahul Sukthankar[1]

[1] Google Research
[2] Georgia Institute of Technology
[3] University of California, Berkeley

Abstract. We propose to learn pixel-level segmentations of objects from
weakly labeled (tagged) internet videos. Specifically, given a large collection of raw YouTube content, along with potentially noisy tags, our
goal is to automatically generate spatiotemporal masks for each object, such as "dog", without employing any pre-trained object detectors.
We formulate this problem as learning weakly supervised classifiers for
a set of independent spatio-temporal segments. The object seeds obtained using segment-level classifiers are further refined using graphcuts
to generate high-precision object masks. Our results, obtained by training on a dataset of 20,000 YouTube videos weakly tagged into 15 classes,
demonstrate automatic extraction of pixel-level object masks. Evaluated
against a ground-truthed subset of 50,000 frames with pixel-level annotations, we confirm that our proposed methods can learn good object
masks just by watching YouTube.

1 Introduction

We are motivated by the question: What could a computer learn about the real
world solely from watching large quantities of internet video? We believe that
internet videos, with their potentially noisy tags, can provide sufficient weak
supervision to learn models of visual concepts. Specifically, our goal is to learn
models that can perform pixel-level spatiotemporal segmentation of objects (*e.g.*,
"dog") when trained only using video-level tags.

To force us to tackle the core challenges, in this paper we adopt an extreme
stance characterized by several desiderata. Our models are *tabula rasa* and must
learn concept models from large numbers of raw, potentially low-quality internet
videos. The only training signals that can be provided to the system must be in
the form of video-level tags, which indicate that the concept occurs somewhere
within the video. Video tags can be corrupted by some degree of label noise
(*e.g.*, some videos labeled "dog" may not contain dogs and there may be videos
containing dogs that are missing the "dog" tag). Although the labels are video-
level, the evaluation is on a spatiotemporal segmentation task with pixel-level
error metrics, such as the precision/recall of pixel masks for a concept, measured

A. Fusiello et al. (Eds.): ECCV 2012 Ws/Demos, Part I, LNCS 7583, pp. 198–208, 2012.
© Springer-Verlag Berlin Heidelberg 2012

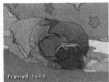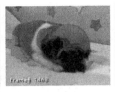

Fig. 1. Video object segmentation: (a) Stabilized frame; (b) Spatiotemporal over-segmentation. (c) Seeds from segment classifier. (d) Spatiotemporal object mask.

on a set of manually annotated ground truth videos. The proposed methods should be capable of scaling, both in the number of training videos and the number of object classes that we recognize.

Figure 1 presents an overview of our object segmentation pipeline. Given a video tagged with a label, say "dog", it is first processed to extract spatiotemporal segments. Then segment-level classifiers (trained from raw video using weakly supervised learning) identify segments for given object categories in the video. These detected segments serve as seeds for extracting pixel-level object masks. The spatiotemporal segments ensure that the target concept is localized in both space and time. This mechanism of going from a tagged YouTube video to a pixel mask summarizes our goal of automatically distilling a large corpus of noisily-tagged video into a smaller collection of spatially- and temporally-segmented object instances with associated high-precision labels. Ours is the first work to tackle weakly supervised training of pixel-level object models solely from large quantities of internet video, where the only labels are potentially noisy video-level tags.

2   Related Work

The area of learning visual concepts from weakly supervised video is still in its infancy. Ramanan et al. [1] construct a single part-based animal model from video. Ommer et al. [2] learn from controlled, hand-recorded video and classify at the frame level. Ali et al. [3] build an appearance model from a single video. Leistner et al. [4] employ weak video primarily to regularize detectors trained using images. Our work is closest in spirit to recent work by Prest et al. [5], which trains on a combination of fully annotated images and manually curated labeled video; the task we address is more extreme as we learn exclusively under weak supervision from raw video with noisy labels.

Our research bears superficial similarity to recent approaches to semi-supervised online learning of object detectors during tracking in video, such as [6]. However, rather than improving the model for a specific tracked object, our goal is to learn broader classes of concepts, without initialization, from raw internet video.

The video segments employed in our work are related to spatiotemporal representations such as Ke et al.'s oversegmented videos [7], Niebles et al.'s human motion volumes [8] and Brendel & Todorovic' 2D+t tubes [9]. We leverage recent

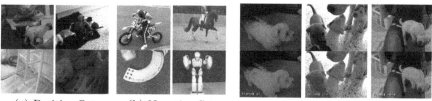

|(a) Positive Set|(b) Negative Set|(c) Inference on "dog" videos|

Fig. 2. We learn to locate objects by training only on video-level labels. (a) samples from "dog" videos; (b) samples from background; (c) sample detections.

work in video segmentation based on motion, such as Xiao & Shah [10], Brox & Malik [11] and Grundmann *et al.* [12,13] to generate our representation.

The weakly supervised learning task bears some similarity to multi-instance learning. In the vision community, related work in this vein includes: Zha *et al.*'s work on multi-label MIL for image classification [14]; Zhou & Zhang's MIML-BOOST and MIML-SVM applied to scene classification; Viola *et al.*'s MILBoost algorithm [15] and Chen *et al.*'s MILES system [16]. However, we focus on high-precision retrieval of instances rather than bag-level classification and are forced to contend with significantly greater label noise *at the bag level*.

Our work contrasts with that of Ren & Gu [17], who employ domain-specific cues (*e.g.*, hands) to segment objects in egocentric video; our methods are most suited for learning models from moving objects in scenes with relatively little background motion. Duchenne *et al.* [18] perform action annotation from weakly labeled data. However, their work is restricted to temporal localization and requires movie scripts that are closely aligned with the scene (and much less noisy than our video-level labels). We differ from existing weakly supervised approaches in video, such as Liu *et al.* [19], which require pixel-level labeling in a sparse set of frames; our work strives to learn object masks without *any* frame-, segment- or pixel-level supervision.

3   Problem Formulation

Our goal can be formalized as the following (see Figure 2). Given a set of object class labels $\mathcal{Y} = \{y_1, y_2, \ldots, y_n\}$ and a large set of weakly tagged videos $\{(v, \mathcal{Y}_v) : \mathcal{Y}_v \subseteq \mathcal{Y}\}$, we seek to learn a model for each concept y_j that can output pixel-level masks for test videos, localized in both space and time. We aim to learn concept models from raw, full-length internet videos containing multiple scenes and several topics. The video-level annotations simply indicate that the given concept y_j occurs somewhere in the video, possibly multiple times, at unspecified spatial and temporal locations. We recognize that each concept can exhibit a diversity of appearances due to intra-class variations (*e.g.*, dog breeds) and that most of the pixels in a video labeled y_j will be unrelated to y_j. While our notion of "concept" is general, our methods are applicable only to semantic labels that correspond to concepts with bounded spatiotemporal extent, such as objects and actions, as opposed to tags that demand scene-level understanding or higher-level domain-specific knowledge. Figure 2 gives a high-level idea of our framework.

To bound our exploration and to enable direct comparisons, in this paper we focus on a restricted set of approaches to our problem. Specifically, all of our proposed methods strictly adhere to the following general strategy:

1. We assume that while label noise can be significant (*e.g.*, 20%), it is independent of the given video v or concept y_j;
2. We learn each concept y_j separately, allowing any given video v to contain multiple concepts $\mathcal{Y}_v \subseteq \mathcal{Y}$;
3. We assume that each video v can be partitioned into a set of spatiotemporal segments $\mathcal{S}_v$, that each segment $s_i \in \mathcal{S}_v$ can be represented by aggregations of a variety of local features, and that each s_i can be independently classified;
4. Rather than directly incorporating the spatiotemporal dependencies between segments in our models (*e.g.*, using a CRF), we account for these in a more computationally scalable object mask refinement phase.

These principles guide us to computationally efficient algorithms that learn from large quantities of video ($> 10^8$ frames) using parallelized implementations. Specifically, our weakly supervised learning operates independently on instances that are spatiotemporal segments, represented using a set of features (bags of quantized features, with responses aggregated over the segment). In other words, the core problem can be formulated as a segment selection task, where the set of selected segments can be converted to pixel-level object masks.

In the following discussion, for a given concept y_j, the term *positive videos* refers to those videos in the labeled set that have the clip-level tag y_j and *negative videos* to those that do not.

4   Training Segment Classifiers and Object Segmentation

We tackle this weakly supervised problem using the two establised approaches, described below. The learning techniques take as input segments that are either positive or negative, that is each segment inherits the binary label of the video it is in. The learned models then score and rank the segments of a given test video. Each segment is described by bags of local features. We also present a training variant based on one-vs-one class comparisons and a post-processing technique that takes as input the individually ranked segments and improves the final object masks by exploiting spatiotemporal consistency

4.1   Discriminative Segment Classifier

The most direct approach to learning under weak supervision is to train a discriminative one vs. rest model for a segment from each concept using all of the available data (labeled segments), which effectively treats the background segments present in each positive video as label noise. The intuition is that since similar background segments are present in both positive and negative data, a linear model (with its limited capacity) should largely ignore such segments and focus more on the desired concept (whose segments are unlikely to appear in the negative videos). The challenge is whether such an approach can work even if the fraction of segments that relate to the concept is small (*e.g.*, 20% of the total). Thus, the input to the classifier is the set of features for a given segment and the ouput is a single real-valued output indicating the classifier's confidence that this segment is an instance of the concept.

We employ Fan *et al.*'s LIBLINEAR (linear SVM) classifier [20], trained independently (one vs. rest) on each concept using 200,000 positive and 400,000 negative segments, sampled uniformly from concept and background (negative) videos, respectively (sampling enables us to retain the training set in memory).

4.2   Multiple Instance Learning (MIL)

To explore MIL on our task, We adapt the MILBoost algorithm with ISR criterion [15]. We use sparse boosting with decision stumps [21] as the base classifier. All of the instance (segment) weights are updated by multiplying with the corresponding bag weights. Viola *et al.* noted [15] that the ISR criterion can lead to competition among instances in the same bag, but this is a reasonable choice for our problem because: 1) the target concept can occur in only a very small fraction of the pixels in a positive video, and 2) the tags for our videos are themselves noisy. We train using 500,000 positive and 50,000 negative segment instances.

4.3   One-vs-One Training Variant

Many of the segments within the positive videos (tagged by a specific desired concept, the target of learning) belong to concepts that *co-occur* with the desired concept. Such segments, may help detect the desired concept, but they are not *part* of the desired concept. When we take as the negative videos a subset of all videos, these frequently associated concepts tend to be learned, because they are not sufficiently represented in the negative videos. The problem of associated or co-occurring concepts is pervasive to weakly-supervised learning. Focusing the learner on what makes the concept what it is, by showing videos drawn randomly from different distributions corresponding to other concepts should help focus the learner on the desired concept.

We realize this idea by training one-versus-one linear classifiers for each class pair. Let $s_{i,j}(\mathbf{x})$ denote the score that the binary classifier, trained on segments from video tagged by concepts i and j, assigns to class i when applied to a segment with feature vector $\mathbf{x}$ of a segment. Then, when scoring segments from a video tagged by class i, the score of a segment x is defined as the minimum over all classifier scores:

$$s_i(x) = \min_{j \neq i} s_{i,j}(\mathbf{x}).$$

For each class pairing i and j, the segments are taken from videos tagged with i and j only (about 100,000 segments each in our experiments), and raw classifier scores are calibrated (to obtain probabilities) on 20% of such segments. Taking the minimum score is intuitive, as we seek those segments that are least like any other concept. Note that this is slightly different from traditional 1-vs-1 multi-class SVM training, which votes across many pairs of subsets of classes.

4.4 Object Segmentation from Ranked Segments

The segment-level classifiers described above output a set of segments for each video ranked by the likelihood of being instances of the concept.[1] Given such a list of segment "seeds" for a video, our goal is now to refine these into object masks using both appearance and spatial consistency. To construct such a dense labeling, we adopt a graph-cut based segmentation formulation, summarized briefly due to space considerations.

Our formulation employs a unary appearance (color and local texture) potential that is obtained using two Gaussian Mixture Models trained on foreground (pixels in selected seeds) and background (pixels sampled far from seeds). The pairwise term is standard and designed to enforce smoothness. The energy function is efficiently minimized using [22] for each frame in the test video.

5 Evaluation

We present both qualitative and quantitative evaluations of our method on a large corpus of partially groundtruthed internet video. Additional results examining the role of different features, type of video over-segmentation and comparisons with other weakly supervised classifiers are omitted here due to space limitations.

Table 1. Summary of weakly supervised internet video dataset

Concept	Summary	Number
bike	motorbikes and bicycles, often with a rider	1,671
boat	a variety of watercraft including ships, boats and jetskis	1,283
card	playing cards, featured in magic tricks and card games	937
dog	dogs of various breeds, indoors & outdoors	1,336
helicopter	includes both full-size and toy helicopters in outdoors scenes	1,189
horse	typically horses being ridden in equestrian events	1,800
robot	a variety of robots, including toys, research & industrial machines	601
transformer	shape-shifting toys, often occluded by hands manipulating them	1,283
background	(from a variety of other tags detailed in text)	12,207

---

[1] The common application case for object segmentation is that the given category occurs somewhere within the tagged test video; our method can be applied to untagged test videos by requiring a high-precision threshold on segment-level seeds and dropping videos without insufficient seed segments.

5.1   Dataset

Our dataset consists of full-length internet videos that are several minutes in length and contain multiple shots. To remain true to our goals, we perform no manual filtering or selection of the content. We have collected 20,000 public videos from YouTube, summarized in Table 1 along with additional background videos from several other tags, such as "stadium", "protest", "flower", "mountain", and "running". Additionally, a set of test videos from different classes has been manually annotated (at the pixel level) to generate a ground truth set of approximately 50,000 frames to generate precision/recall curves.

5.2   Experiments

We process each of the videos in the training set as follows to ensure uniformity. First, we scale each video to a consistent width of 240 pixels, maintaining its original aspect ratio. Next, we perform video stabilization [11,13] to reduce camera motion that could corrupt motion features and shapes of spatiotemporal segments. We then perform hierarchical spatiotemporal segmentation[2] to identify segments (at multiple scales) that capture contiguous parts of objects and the background. To better understand the role of segmentation, we also repeat our experiments using a tesselation of *cuboids* (spatiotemporal generalization of patches), where each image is divided into 12×9 patches, 10 frames deep.

We represent each segment (and cuboid) using the following features: 1) RGB color histogram, quantized over 20 bins; 2) histogram of local binary patterns computed on 5×5 patches [23,24]; 3) histogram of dense optical flow [25], with an additional fifth bin for near-zero flow; 4) heatmaps computed over a 8×6 grid to represent the (x, y) shape of each segment, summed over its temporal extent; 5) histogram of quantized SIFT-like local descriptors extracted densely within each segment.

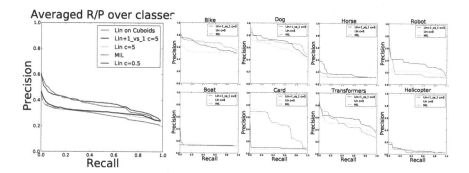

Fig. 3. Averaged & per-class results. Random pixel baseline precision: 16%.

---

[2] Using the web-based segmentation service at http://videosegmentation.com [12].

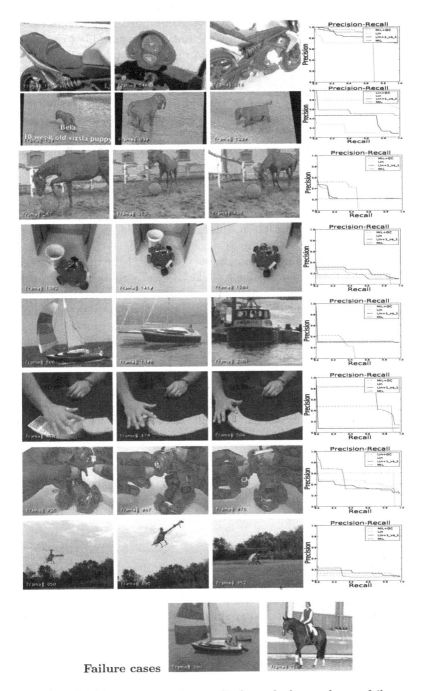

Fig. 4. Sample object segmentation results for each class and some failure cases

Computational Details: It is a challenging task to process videos at such a large scale. We distribute the job of video stabilization, spatiotemporal segmentation and feature extraction for each video to different machines using the MapReduce framework. Using our implementation, we are able to process our 20,000 videos using a cluster of 5000 nodes in less than 30 hours.

For the liblinear classifier, we present results based on a few regularization (C) values (and compare the classifiers using the same C). For MIL, we set the regularization term of sparse boost to 1.0 and used 1000 decision stumps.

Figure 3 presents pixel-level precision/recall curves[3] (overall and per class) for segment-level classification. Surprisingly, the choice of segment-level classifier is not critical. In particular, posing this problem in a multiple-instance learning (MIL) framework does not result in clear gains. Using the one-vs-one variant generates significant improvement over one-vs-rest, and in paired (per groundtruth video) tests, comparing precision at each of 5%, 10%, and 20% recall levels, we observe 17 or more wins vs. 9 or fewer losses.

The use of video segmentation also dominates cuboids in a similar fashion, both on average and in paired comparisons.

Weakly supervised learning of some visual concepts at the individual segment level is easier than others. For instance, "bike", "dog", "robot" and "transformers" seem to have sufficiently distinctive features that they can be separated from the background class, at the segment level, under weak supervision. Among the difficult classes, spatiotemporal segmentation often undersegments helicopters. "Horse", "boat" and "card" seem to be difficult because of the problem of associated segments (e.g., water in the case of boat).

Figure 4 shows examples of object masks (magenta overlay) for each of the eight classes, as well as precision-recall curves for the corresponding video. These results include object mask refinement (dashed lines in P-R curves) as well as the raw P-R curves using individual segment classifiers. We see that, the object masks localize objects from different classes, even under challenging conditions: dog at the beach, complicated close-up of motorbike, etc. Object mask refinement works best for high-precision individual segment results. We note that rare objects, such as the beach ball in the horse video, are occasionally highlighted (false positives). Additional failure cases are shown in Figure 4 (last row).

6   Conclusion

This paper proposes the idea of learning spatiotemporal object models, with minimal supervision, from large quantities of weakly and noisily tagged video. Since we are the first to tackle this problem, particularly at large scale, we conduct an evaluation of several computationally scalable approaches to weakly supervised learning. We believe that weakly supervised learning from internet video has the potential to radically transform object and action recognition. This paper is just the first step towards that goal.

---

[3] Precision is the fraction of correctly classified pixels to classified pixels; recall is the fraction of correctly classified to groundtruth concept pixels.

In future work, we plan to explore several directions. First, our current framework implicitly uses segment-level loss whereas the evaluation is at the pixel level; directly optimizing the latter is worth exploring. Second, we plan to investigate how our approach scales to thousands of concepts. Finally, we plan to use our object segmentation masks as strongly supervised training data for training traditional object detectors in both image and video domains.

Acknowledgments. We thank C. Cortes, S. Kumar, K. Murphy, M. Ruzon, E. Sargin, G. Toderici, J. Weston, and J. Yagnik for many helpful discussions.

References

1. Ramanan, D., Forsyth, D., Barnard, K.: Building models of animals from video. PAMI 28 (2006)
2. Ommer, B., Mader, T., Buhmann, J.: Seeing the objects behind the dots: Recognition in videos from a moving camera. IJCV 83 (2009)
3. Ali, K., Hasler, D., Fleuret, F.: FlowBoost—Appearance learning from sparsely annotated video. In: CVPR (2011)
4. Leistner, C., Godec, M., Schulter, S., Saffari, A., Werlberger, M., Bischof, H.: Improving classifiers with unlabeled weakly-related videos. In: CVPR (2011)
5. Prest, A., Leistner, C., Civera, J., Schmid, C., Ferrari, V.: Learning object class detectors from weakly annotated video. In: CVPR (2012)
6. Kalal, Z., Matas, J., Mikolajczyk, K.: P-N Learning: Bootstrapping binary classifiers by structural constraints. In: CVPR (2010)
7. Ke, Y., Sukthankar, R., Hebert, M.: Event detection in crowded videos. In: ICCV (2007)
8. Niebles, J.C., Han, B., Ferencz, A., Fei-Fei, L.: Extracting Moving People from Internet Videos. In: Forsyth, D., Torr, P., Zisserman, A. (eds.) ECCV 2008, Part IV. LNCS, vol. 5305, pp. 527–540. Springer, Heidelberg (2008)
9. Brendel, W., Todorovic, S.: Learning spatiotemporal graphs of human activities. In: ICCV (2011)
10. Xiao, J., Shah, M.: Motion layer extraction in the presence of occlusion using graph cuts. PAMI 27, 1644–1659 (2005)
11. Brox, T., Malik, J.: Object Segmentation by Long Term Analysis of Point Trajectories. In: Daniilidis, K., Maragos, P., Paragios, N. (eds.) ECCV 2010, Part V. LNCS, vol. 6315, pp. 282–295. Springer, Heidelberg (2010)
12. Grundmann, M., Kwatra, V., Han, M., Essa, I.: Efficient hierarchical graph-based video segmentation. In: CVPR (2011)
13. Grundmann, M., Kwatra, V., Essa, I.: Auto-directed video stabilization with robust L1 optimal camera paths. In: CVPR (2011)
14. Zha, Z.J., Hua, X.S., Mei, T., Wang, J., Qi, G.J., Wang, Z.: Joint multi-label multi-instance learning for image classification. In: CVPR (2008)
15. Viola, P., Platt, J., Zhang, C.: Multiple instance boosting for object detection. In: NIPS (2005)
16. Chen, Y., Bi, J., Wang, J.: MILES: Multiple-instance learning via embedded instance selection. PAMI 28, 1931–1947 (2006)
17. Ren, X., Gu, C.: Figure-ground segmentation improves handled object recognition in egocentric video. In: CVPR (2010)

18. Duchenne, O., Laptev, I., Sivic, J., Bach, F., Ponce, J.: Automatic annotation of human actions in video. In: ICCV (2009)
19. Liu, D., Hua, G., Chen, T.: A hierarchical visual model for video object summarization. PAMI 32, 2178–2190 (2010)
20. Fan, R.E., Chang, K.W., Hsieh, C.J., Wang, X.R., Lin, C.J.: LIBLINEAR: A library for large linear classification. JMLR 9, 1871–1874 (2008)
21. Duchi, J., Singer, Y.: Boosting with structural sparsity. In: ICML (2009)
22. Boykov, Y., Veksler, O., Zabih, R.: Fast approximate energy minimization via graph cuts. PAMI 23, 1222–1239 (2001)
23. Ojala, T., et al.: Performance evaluation of texture measures with classification based on Kullback discrimination of distributions. In: ICPR (1994)
24. Wang, X., Han, T.: An HOG-LBP human detector with partial occlusion handling. In: ICCV (2009)
25. Chaudhry, R., et al.: Histograms of oriented optical flow and Binet-Cauchy kernels on nonlinear dynamical systems. In: CVPR (2009)

Classifier Ensemble Recommendation

Pyry Matikainen[1], Rahul Sukthankar[2,1], and Martial Hebert[1]

[1] The Robotics Institute, Carnegie Mellon University
[2] Google Research
{pmatikai,rahuls}@cs.cmu.edu, hebert@ri.cmu.edu

Abstract. The problem of training classifiers from limited data is one that particularly affects large-scale and social applications, and as a result, although carefully trained machine learning forms the backbone of many current techniques in research, it sees dramatically fewer applications for end-users. Recently we demonstrated a technique for selecting or *recommending* a single good classifier from a large library even with highly impoverished training data. We consider alternatives for extending our recommendation technique to *sets* of classifiers, including a modification to the AdaBoost algorithm that incorporates recommendation. Evaluating on an action recognition problem, we present two viable methods for extending model recommendation to sets.

1 Introduction

Classifiers continue to be impractical for web-scale uses, and when they are used, they tend to be in the form of *generic* classifiers (*e.g.*, face detectors) rather than the carefully tuned custom classifiers seen in research applications. The reasons for this are twofold. First, properly training a classifier is a surprisingly difficult affair — aside from the amount of data required (which might be substantial), methodological issues such as cross-validation for appropriate SVM parameters and the production of appropriately 'hard' negative examples complicate the neat theoretical story. Second, classifiers are computationally expensive to run and train when compared to web-scale technologies like approximate nearest neighbor methods and hashing techniques.

While this second concern will likely be alleviated in time by advances in the amount of available computing power, the first concern, that classifiers are in practice difficult to produce, must be given more care.

Our recent work [1] suggests a way out: rather than requiring end users to train classifiers, we recast the problem as a *selection* problem from a *pre-trained* library of classifiers. Instead of an end-user trying to directly learn a classifier from limited training data, the training data should be instead be used *select* a classifier from a pre-trained library according to which classifier had the best accuracy. But of course there is no "free lunch": with limited labeled training data, it is also hard to even *measure* the accuracy of a classifier. What we realized is that if many users are attempting to perform such a selection at the same time, then this problem of selecting the best classifier from a large library

A. Fusiello et al. (Eds.): ECCV 2012 Ws/Demos, Part I, LNCS 7583, pp. 209–218, 2012.

is *exactly analogous* to that addressed by collaborative filtering techniques for recommender systems, such as Netflix and Amazon.com! While any one user's measured classifier accuracies will be inaccurate, when considered jointly, there are correlations between classifier accuracies across different tasks that collaborative filtering methods can exploit to improve the classifier accuracy estimates for individual tasks. We were able to show that it is possible in practice to select a better classifier than by directly trying *every* option on the limited *training* set.

That technique, termed "model recommendation", can naturally be adapted to web-scale, since it is built around collaborative filtering techniques that were designed with web-scale data (*e.g.*, the Netflix ratings database) in mind. Furthermore, the formulation has a number of other benefits: it allows powerful classifier techniques to be used; in fact, any type of underlying classification machinery can be used, because the recommendation only uses the measured ratings or accuracies of those classifiers, and does not need to know anything about their underlying implementations. The work can be distributed: because the most computationally expensive step (evaluating the classifiers) can be performed by the users themselves in parallel. Additionally, since the users can evaluate classifiers locally and only return the ratings, some measure of privacy is preserved, since the raw samples (*e.g.*, videos) do not need to be sent to the recommendation system.

Although model recommendation might naturally be applied to banks of classifiers such as in exemplar SVMs [2] or Action Bank [3], the major limitation of the technique is that in the original formulation it is only designed to recommend a *single* model or classifier from the library. This naturally raises the question of how to extend the method to jointly recommend sets or ensembles of classifiers, and in this paper we evaluate several alternatives for doing so. Our key contribution in this paper is to demonstrate that the model recommendation framework can be extended to recommending sets of models, and that this ensemble recommendation outperforms both an AdaBoost baseline and a direct training baseline.

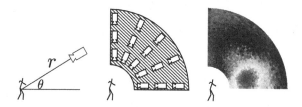

Fig. 1. We adopt the same illustrative example as [1] for visualization purposes. A library of classifiers produced by training SVMs to detect walking, where each SVM is trained only on samples from a narrow viewpoint, defined by its elevation θ and mean to subject r (left). The accuracies of all 1600 classifiers on a training set can be visualized as a heat map (right).

To help visualize model recommendation and our extensions to it, throughout the paper we use the illustrative example from [1], which is a scenario where the problem is to select a set of classifiers to detect the action "walking" from a fixed camera with an unknown vantage point. Since the camera is fixed, it can be described in terms of its mean distance r to the subject and its angle from the horizon θ (see Fig. 1). A library of 1600 "walking" classifiers is arranged in a 40×40 polar grid of possible viewing locations, and each is trained from synthetic data (rendered motion capture videos of people walking) generated for its assigned viewing location. Then, given a small training set of data from a new camera at an *unknown* viewing point, the goal is then to select a *set* of classifiers from the library which when combined gives the best classification accuracy.

2   Related Work

This work combines our model recommendation technique [1] and boosting, and is loosely related to multi-task learning. In particular, common multi-task learning techniques attempt to enforce sparsity in the selection of features [4,5], or support vectors [6], or kernels [7], across multiple tasks in order to enforce the sharing of some kind of information across tasks. Unlike these sparsity based approaches, there is no explicit forced sharing of features in model recommendation; indeed, it is possible to recommend a model for a target task that is not shared with any other task. This distinction is important because multi-task learning is known to fail when the tasks jointly learned are insufficiently related to one another, and hence an open area of research in multi-task learning is how to select which tasks to learn together [8].

Given the popularity of boosting, it has unsurprisingly been applied to multi-task learning as well. These methods tend to follow the standard multi-task approach of enforcing sparsity, such as in Chapelle *et al.* [9] where boosting selects a common set of weights for weak learners across all tasks, and then individual tasks are allowed to sparsely deviate from that common weighting. Wang *et al.* [10] take a slightly different approach, where the sparsity is enforced by learning a partitioning (clustering) of the tasks, where all the tasks in a cluster are forced to share the same weights for the weak learners. Faddoul *et al.* [11] take yet another approach, in which the weak learners are joint classifiers of two tasks, and so the boosting naturally selects a compromise between two tasks. However, the limitation of their approach is that it does not easily scale to more than two tasks, and these techniques generally need closely related tasks.

3   Method

Since model recommendation is a new and unconventional technique, we start with a brief functional overview of what it requires as input and what it accomplishes. Then, we briefly review the standard AdaBoost algorithm, and we describe how it can be modified to incorporate model recommendation.

(a) Camera view   (b) Raw accura-   (c) Predicted
                          cies

Fig. 2. An illustration of the model recommendation technique [1]. A set of 1600 viewpoint-tuned classifiers are evaluated (rated) on a dataset of 12 labeled samples from a particular camera viewpoint (Fig. 2(a)). Because there are only 12 training samples, there is quantization noise in measuring the accuracy of the classifiers (Fig. 2(b)), since the accuracies can only vary in increments of $\frac{1}{12}$. Model recommendation is able to take these noisy estimates of the accuracies and predict improved estimates (Fig. 2(c)). We adopt this display convention to aid comparison to [1].

3.1   Recommendation in Brief

Model recommendation is a method for selecting an item from a library, where the goal is to return an item ("model") which is likely to be *rated* highly for a specific task. More formally, suppose there is some problem-specific rating function $r(c_j, d_k)$ which returns a numerical score rating item c_j on task d_k; if the items in the library are classifiers and the tasks are labeled sets of samples, then the rating function can be the accuracy of a given classifier on a dataset.

As a notational convenience we denote $r(c_j, d_k) = r_{jk}$. In order to make recommendations, a ratings matrix R (or "ratings store") is needed; the entries of this matrix are the ratings of items on different tasks, where $R_{j,k} = r_{jk}$, which is the rating of item j on task k.

Model recommendation takes a subset of ratings of items on a task, and uses that subset of rated items along with the ratings store to predict the ratings of other items. Functionally, supposing that A is a vector of item ratings for a target task, then model recommendation returns a prediction of a given classifier j's rating on that task $r'_j = \text{RecommendPredictAccuracy}(c_j, R, A)$. We perform the prediction using the factorization method presented in [1].

Note that this "subset" of probe ratings might very well be the entire set of classifiers. For example, in Fig. 2, all 1600 classifiers are used as probes on a small training set of 12 samples, producing a very noisy heat map of accuracies. When this full set of accuracies is fed into model recommendation, the returned predicted accuracies are a de-noised version of the input.

3.2   Ensemble Recommendation Methods

Here we present four options for selecting classifier ensembles. The simplest, top-k recommendation, just selects the top-k classifiers according to their predicted accuracies from model recommendation. AdaBoost is an unmodified, standard boosting algorithm. Recommendation boosting takes AdaBoost, but uses model recommendation to select the classifier at each iteration. Recommendation boosting+ uses the same underlying mechanism as recommendation boosting, but afterwards combines its selection with the top-k selection to add more variation to the selected set. Note that we use the boosting methods as feature selection mechanisms and discard the final weights of the selected classifiers in favor of simply training an SVM on the selection; this use of AdaBoost is common in vision [12,13] and occasionally sees use in other domains [14,15].

Top k Recommendation. Given the predicted ratings r' according to recommendation, rather than selecting only the top one, we select the top k, where k is the size of the desired set to be recommended. This is the obvious way of recommending multiple classifiers, but the downside is that it can potentially recommend a highly redundant set.

AdaBoost. Although the AdaBoost has been extended to more than two classes, for simplicity in this paper we consider only a binary classification problem. The algorithm learns a classifier from a training set, where X_i is the ith data sample in the training set of a target task, and $y_i \in \{-1, 1\}$ is the associated binary label for that sample, and where n is the number of training samples.

AdaBoost is an iterative algorithm, where each iteration considers a different weighted version of the training set; we denote the weight of data sample i in iteration t by w_{it}. Then, given a classifier f_j, the weighted error of that classifier at an iteration is given by WeightedErr$(f_j, W, X, y) = \frac{\sum_i I(f_j(X_i) \neq y_i) \cdot w_{it}}{\sum_i w_{it}}$, where $I(.)$ is an indicator function. The weighted accuracy of the classifier is simply WeightedAccuracy$(f_j, W, X, y) = 1 -$ WeightedErr$(.)$.

At each iteration the classifier with the lowest weighted error is selected, and the weights modified to increase the weights of misclassified samples and decrease the weights of correctly classified ones. The algorithm is given in Alg. 1.

Recommendation Boosting. We modify AdaBoost to incorporate recommendation using the the key insight that boosting algorithms can be seen as a series of tasks, and therefore model recommendation can be used to pick the weak learner at each iteration of the algorithm

Recommendation boosting simply replaces the selection of the classifier with the lowest weighted error with a model recommendation step. That is, instead of using the weighted errors of the classifiers to directly select the classifier for an iteration, the measured accuracies (along with a ratings matrix R of the accuracies of classifiers in the library evaluated on other action recognition tasks) are fed into model recommendation to predict the accuracies for the classifiers, and the classifier with the highest predicted accuracy selected. This modified algorithm is given in Alg. 2.

Input   : Classifiers $F = \{f_1, f_2, \ldots, f_j, \ldots\}$
Input   : Training-samples and labels X, y
Output: A selected set $S \subseteq F$
$\forall w_i \in W, w_i \leftarrow \frac{1}{n}$;
$S \leftarrow \{\}$;
for $t = 1, \ldots, k$ **do**
     $s_t \leftarrow \text{argmin}_{f_j} \text{WeightedErr}(f_j, W, X, y)$;
     $e_t \leftarrow \text{WeightedErr}(s_t, W, X, y)$;
     $\alpha_t \leftarrow \frac{1}{2} \log \frac{1-e_t}{\max(e_t, \epsilon)}$;
     $\forall w_i \in W, w_i \leftarrow w_i \cdot e^{-\alpha_t \cdot \text{sign}(y_i \cdot s_t(X_i))}$;
     $W \leftarrow \text{Normalize}(W)$;
     $S \leftarrow S \cup \{s_t\}$;
end

Algorithm 1. AdaBoost

Recommendation Boosting+ As explained in [16], eventually AdaBoost will converge to a 'limit cycle' in which the same weak learners are cyclically selected. If the number of training samples is small, this convergence can happen very quickly. As a result, in the quantitative experiments performed later, AdaBoost only selects a mean of 11 unique classifiers over 20 iterations, while recommendation boosting only selects 10 unique classifiers over those same 20 iterations.

In recommendation boosting+ we add variety to the set of classifiers selected by recommendation boosting– if recommendation boosting only selects b unique classifiers, but a set of k is desired, then the remaining $k-b$ classifiers are selected as the $k - b$ classifiers with the highest predicted accuracies according to model recommendation.

4   Evaluation

We evaluate our alternatives on action recognition in two ways. First, we consider a simplified qualitative example (Fig. 1) using synthetic data (rendered videos of motion capture data using the same viewing angle setup as in [1], with histogram of optical flow descriptors).

For quantitative results we consider an action recognition problem on the UCF50 dataset [17] using limited training data (10.2 training samples on average, compared to the approximately 100 per action that are available when UCF is evaluated as a single task). We use STIP [18] plus HOG3D [19] bag-of-words histograms as our low-level representation; this is commonly used as the foundation for action recognition systems and often performs similarly to more complex approaches [20]. The UCF50 dataset is a difficult dataset of videos of various actions harvested from YouTube; for this setup, we limit the amount of training data by splitting the dataset into a number of tasks. UCF50 contains approximately 5500 videos, divided into 50 actions, with each action further subdivided into groups of videos, where each group comprises a set of related videos. We

---

Input : Classifiers $F = \{f_1, f_2, \ldots, f_j, \ldots\}$
Input : Training-samples and labels X, y
Input : Ratings matrix R of classifier accuracies on other tasks
Output: A selected set $S \subseteq F$
$\forall w_i \in W, w_i \leftarrow \frac{1}{n}$;
$S \leftarrow \{\}$;
for $t = 1, \ldots, k$ **do**
$\quad A = [\texttt{WeightedAccuracy}(f_j, W, X, y) \text{ for } f_j \in F]$;
$\quad s_t \leftarrow \text{argmax}_{f_j} \texttt{RecommendPredictAccuracy}(f_j, R, A)$;
$\quad e_t \leftarrow \texttt{WeightedErr}(s_t, W, X, y)$;
$\quad \alpha_t \leftarrow \frac{1}{2} \log \frac{1-e_t}{\max(e_t, \epsilon)}$;
$\quad \forall w_i \in W, w_i \leftarrow w_i \cdot e^{-\alpha_t \cdot \text{sign}(y_i \cdot s_t(X_i))}$;
$\quad W \leftarrow \texttt{Normalize}(W)$;
$\quad S \leftarrow S \cup \{s_t\}$;
end

Algorithm 2. Recommendation Boosting

produce each task by merging 1-3 groups of the same action, dedicating 2/3 of the video groups to training data, and the remaining 1/3 to testing data. We augment each group with an equal number of negative samples drawn at random from the other actions, so that each task is then a one vs. all binary classification problem with an equal number of positive and negative samples (so that chance is 50% accuracy). The mean number of training samples per task is 10.2, and the mean number of testing samples 24.3. Each group may be used in multiple training or test tasks (but there is no overlap between test and training).

We use the training groups to generate a library of 1000 classifiers trained on different groups, and also to generate a ratings store of those 1000 classifiers rated on 1000 tasks. Thus, the ratings store has size 1000×1000. Ideally, different data would be used to train the classifier library and build the ratings store, as rating a classifier against the same group from which it was trained results in an overly optimistic accuracy (rating) and possibly distorts the computed factorization. For testing, we use a set of 250 tasks with no videos or video groups in common with the set used to generate the classifiers and store. This is the same general setup as in [1], but randomized train/test partitions mean that results cannot be exactly compared. However, model recommendation [1] can be compared to our proposed ensemble recommendation by noting that ensemble recommendation degenerates to model recommendation if a set of size one is to be recommended.

5 Results

Qualitative results for the viewing angle situation can be seen in Fig. 3. Note how top-k recommendation chooses a very redundant set of classifiers, where all five classifiers are tightly clustered around the predicted maximum. AdaBoost, on the other hand, is confused by the spurious classifiers that appear to have 100%

accuracy on the training set. Recommendation boosting picks a few classifiers near the predicted maximum, but then spreads the remainder out for better coverage of the region near the maximum. Thus the recommendation boosted set is more likely to be robust to variations in the action.

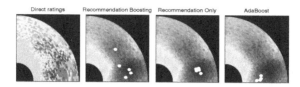

Fig. 3. A comparison of the selected classifiers according to top-k recommendation, AdaBoost, and recommendation boosting. Top-k recommendation selects a highly redundant set of classifiers, while AdaBoost is led astray by a few erroneously good classifiers. Recommendation boosting selects a nice spread of classifiers.

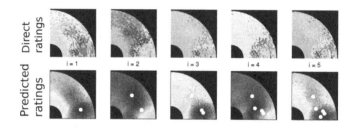

Fig. 4. Progression of the classifiers selected by recommendation boosting; note how each iteration's reweighting of the training samples shifts the distribution of predicted accuracies so that the selected classifiers do not all clump near one location, as in top-k recommendation (see Fig. 3).

A visualization of how recommendation boosting selects its classifier each iteration can be seen in Fig. 4. At the first iteration, the selected classifier is the same as the top recommended classifier, but then in subsequent iterations, as misclassified samples are more strongly weighted, the distribution of classifier ratings changes to promote the selection of classifiers other than those at the original maximum. At each iteration the method is able to smooth over the extremely noisy measured accuracies for the iteration to produce a better estimate of where the maximum accuracy is obtained for that iteration.

Quantitative results on the UCF50 dataset are shown in Fig. 5, where it can be seen that recommendation boosting outperforms both AdaBoost and direct training. Interestingly, the straightforward top-k recommendation method does better than basic recommendation boosting, suggesting that for this evaluation domain, redundancy in the classifier library is not as large a concern as expected. It is likely that the 1000 classifier library samples the space of possible classifiers so sparsely that there is too little redundancy in the classifiers to be detrimental.

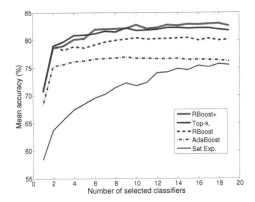

Fig. 5. Mean accuracy of the selected set of classifiers vs. the size of the selected set. Top-k recommendation and recommendation boosting+ have the best performance, with recommendation boosting+ having a slight edge at larger set sizes. The accuracy obtained by directly training each task on the low-level STIP+HOG inputs is 77%.

For this experiment, the direct training baseline (in each task, directly train an SVM on the input STIP+HOG bag-of-words histograms, rather than appealing to the library) obtains an accuracy of 77%, which only AdaBoost fails to exceed. Recommendation boosting+ exhibits a slight improvement over top-k selection (this difference is statistically significant to $p < 0.05$ for set sizes ≥ 18).

All of the selection strategies show large gains at first and then quickly plateau, indicating that they front-load their selections with the strongest classifiers. Indeed, the difference between the recommendation variants largely manifests after the first two selected classifiers.

6   Conclusions

In this paper we have evaluated several alternatives for extending model recommendation to recommending sets. Out of these alternatives, recommendation boosting+ and top-k recommendation methods are the clear victors.

Between these two alternatives, however, the distinction is less clear. In terms of quantitative performance, the two are very similar, with recommendation boosting+ having a narrow edge at larger recommended set sizes. Furthermore, qualitative results suggest that the top-k selection strategy should be prone to selecting redundant classifiers if the classifier library contains them.

Acknowledgments. This work was partially funded by the Army Research Laboratory under Cooperative Agreement #W911NF-10-2-0061. The U.S. Government is authorized to reproduce and distribute reprints for government purposes notwithstanding any copyright notation.

References

1. Matikainen, P., Sukthankar, R., Hebert, M.: Model recommendation for action recognition. In: CVPR (2012)
2. Malisiewicz, T., Shrivastava, A., Gupta, A., Efros, A.: Exemplar-svms for visual object detection, label transfer and image retrieval. In: ICML (2012)
3. Sadanand, S., Corso, J.: Action bank: A high-level representation of activity in video. In: CVPR (2012)
4. Obozinski, G., Taskar, B.: Multi-task feature selection. In: ICML Workshop on Structural Knowledge Transfer for Machine Learning (2006)
5. Argyriou, A., Evgeniou, T., Pontil, M.: Multi-task feature learning. In: NIPS (2007)
6. Evgeniou, T., Micchelli, C.A., Pontil, M.: Learning multiple tasks with kernel methods. JMLR 6, 615–637 (2005)
7. Rückert, U., Kramer, S.: Kernel-based inductive transfer. In: ECML (2008)
8. Kang, Z., Grauman, K., Sha, F.: Learning with whom to share in multi-task feature learning. In: ICML (2011)
9. Chapelle, O., Shivaswamy, P., Vadrevu, S., Weinberger, K., Zhang, Y., Tseng, B.: Multi-task learning for boosting with application to web search ranking. In: ACM SIGKDD (2010)
10. Wang, X., Zhang, C., Zhang, Z.: Boosted multi-task learning for face verification with applications to web image and video search. In: CVPR (2009)
11. Faddoul, J., Chidlovskii, B., Torre, F., Gilleron, R.: Boosting multi-task weak learners with applications to textual and social data. In: Machine Learning and Applications (2010)
12. Shen, L., Bai, L.: Adaboost gabor feature selection for classification. In: Proceedings of the Image and Vision Computing Conference, New Zealand (2004)
13. Zhou, M., Wei, H.: Face verification using gabor wavelets and adaboost. In: ICPR (2006)
14. Zhou, X., Zhuang, X., Liu, M., Tang, H., Hasegawa-Johnson, M., Huang, T.: HMM-Based Acoustic Event Detection with AdaBoost Feature Selection. In: Stiefelhagen, R., Bowers, R., Fiscus, J.G. (eds.) RT 2007 and CLEAR 2007. LNCS, vol. 4625, pp. 345–353. Springer, Heidelberg (2008)
15. Morra, J., Zhuowen, T., Apostolova, L., Green, A., Toga, A., Thompson, P.: Comparison of adaboost and support vector machines for detecting alzheimer's disease through automated hippocampal segmentation. IEEE Transactions on Medical Imaging 29, 30–43 (2010)
16. Rudin, C., Daubechies, I., The, R.S.: dynamics of adaboost: Cyclic behavior and convergence of margins. JMLR 5 (2004)
17. University of Central Florida: UCF50 action recognition dataset (2011), http://server.cs.ucf.edu/~vision/data.html#UCF50
18. Laptev, I., Lindeberg, T.: Space-time interest points. In: ICCV (2003)
19. Kläser, A., Marszałek, M., Schmid, C.: A spatio-temporal descriptor based on 3d-gradients. In: British Machine Vision Conference, pp. 995–1004 (2008)
20. Kovashka, A., Grauman, K.: Learning a hierarchy of discriminative space-time neighborhood features for human action recognition. In: CVPR (2010)

Towards Exhaustive Pairwise Matching in Large Image Collections

Kumar Srijan and C.V. Jawahar

Center for Visual Information Technology, IIIT, Hyderabad
kumar.srijan@research.iiit.ac.in, jawahar@iiit.ac.in
http://cvit.iiit.ac.in

Abstract. Exhaustive pairwise matching on large datasets presents serious practical challenges, and has mostly remained an unexplored domain. We make a step in this direction by demonstrating the feasibility of scalable indexing and fast retrieval of appearance and geometric information in images. We identify unification of database filtering and geometric verification steps as a key step for doing this. We devise a novel inverted indexing scheme, based on Bloom filters, to scalably index high order features extracted from pairs of nearby features. Unlike a conventional inverted index, we can adapt the size of the inverted index to maintain adequate sparsity of the posting lists. This ensures constant time query retrievals. We are thus able to implement an exhaustive pairwise matching scheme, with linear time complexity, using the 'query each image in turn' technique. We find the exhaustive nature of our approach to be very useful in mining small clusters of images, as demonstrated by a 73.2% recall on the UKBench dataset. In the Oxford Buildings dataset, we are able to discover all the query buildings. We also discover interesting overlapping images connecting distant images.

1 Introduction

The easy accessibility of large collections of images has opened opportunities for mining them. These datasets are excellent resources for location recognition[1], browsing[2], summarization[3], reconstruction[4] or creating walkthroughs[5] of various popular destinations. Given the current techniques for harvesting these large collections, they tend to be highly unordered and have a lot of irrelevant images. Hence, the automatic organization of these datasets is very much required. We present a method to organize these datasets as Image Match Graphs. This will allow the discovery of interesting intermediate images to connect distant images, as shown in Figure 1, and small clusters of matching images.

The match graph construction problem is to produce a graph denoting matches between any pair of images in the dataset. This problem is related to the image retrieval problem, where the user supplies a query image and the system returns a ranked list of similar images. Many of the recent techniques [6] for image retrieval utilize the Bag-of-Words(BoW) framework to implement a filtering stage whereby a large number of images are rejected. In this framework, visual

A. Fusiello et al. (Eds.): ECCV 2012 Ws/Demos, Part I, LNCS 7583, pp. 219–228, 2012.

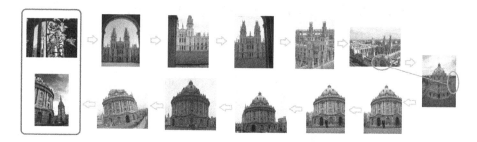

Fig. 1. A path discovered from an image of All Souls Building to an image of Radcliffe Camera in Oxford in our match graph

words are cluster centers extracted by clustering a large collection of descriptors extracted from various images. These visual words are used to quantize feature descriptors, such as SIFT [7], SURF [8] etc. To speedup the matching process, an inverted index is built which maps the visual words to a posting list of images which contain them. For every visual word in the query image, a vote is given to all the images which contain that visual word. A shortlist is obtained by taking into account the top scoring images. A geometric verification is performed on the images in the shortlist for reranking and rejecting non matching images.

Many of the recent techniques for image retrieval [9–11] try to bring geometry into the filtering stage to obtain more precise posting lists. Zhang et al. [9] use the geometry preserving visual words which captures both cooccurences, and local and long-range spatial layouts of the visual words to outperform even the BOW model using RANSAC for geometry verification. Similarly, [10] incorporate the neighborhood statistics of features into the vocabulary tree and in the spatial domain to improve the discriminative power of the features.

Efficient solutions for match graph construction also use techniques use for efficient image retrieval, such as feature quantization, indexing etc., to limit the amount of data that needs to be dealt with. Image retrieval also provides an immediate solution to the match graph construction problem: 'query each image in turn' and create a link from every image to each of its verified retrieved images [12]. Query expansion is used on these verified images to discover more overlapping images. Similarly, *Image webs* [2] use Image retrieval techniques to identify the skeleton of clusters, and complete the clusters by verifying potential links within a connected component with a focus on maximizing the *algebraic connectivity* of the cluster.

Chum et al. introduced Minhash based techniques [11, 13] which employ random sampling of the visual words using MinHash functions to obtain image signatures, similar to image histograms in the BoW framework. The signatures are sampled to obtain sketches, which become more discriminative than an individual visual word. Hence, all the sketch collisions, which are detected using a hash table, are verified. This makes the chance of discovery of a matching pair of images independent of the size of the database. The verified matches, called

Fig. 2. A sampling of High Order Features(yellow) extracted in a pair of images. Geometric parameters(s_p/s_s , D/s_p , α and θ) are computed for a primary feature(red) with respect to all its secondary features(blue). s_p and s_s denote the scales of the primary and secondary features respectively. Vectors point towards the dominant orientation of the features. Four matching high order features are shown(green) which correspond to the primary features highlighted in the images.

seeds, are grown using query expansion to obtain full clusters. One disadvantage of this technique is that the chance of discovery of small clusters is not very high.

Notwithstanding, the success of the above techniques, it can be seen that the ideal solution for match graph construction is matching every image in the database to every other, that is, exhaustive pairwise matching. We explore the feasibility of doing this for building match graphs for large datasets. For this, we build upon the advantages of the above techniques: First, we employ an inverted index based retrieval scheme which provides direct access to the list of relevant images for a given query. Second, similar to the sketches used by Minhash based techniques, we use high ordered features, extracted from pairs of nearby features, to do feature matching in a more discriminative space. The indexing of geometry allows us to do match verification directly from index retrievals. We are thus able to implement 'query each image in turn' for exhaustive pairwise matching in linear time complexity.

2   High Order Features for Exhaustive Pairwise Matching

The direct implementation of 'query each image in turn' for building match graphs is not applicable due to its quadratic matching cost. In [12] and [2], the number of images needed to be taken into consideration for a query visual word is proportional to the size of the database. The number of such queries needed to be issued is proportional to the size of the database, making the overall timing complexity of the whole process quadratic in the number of images. Also, the need for keeping a shortlist of candidates from the filtering stage has the potential to miss out some of the matching images, thereby missing the quality of exhaustive pairwise matching. This issue becomes serious in the presence of a large number of distractor features, like those coming from trees, water etc., which dilute the contribution of visual words coming from the object in the image. This leads to relevant images not being able to make into the shortlist.

Min Hashing based techniques are able to bring down the computation cost by computing *sketches* which lead to lesser number of random matches than visual words. However, at a time, only one sketch per image is taken for matching as compared to a histogram level matching in [2, 12]. This affects the chance of discovery of matching images having only a few visual words in common. The chance of discovering a match also depends upon the size of the sketch. Choosing a low sketch size would find many matching images, but would also lead to many irrelevant sketch collisions in large datasets. In [13], using a sketch size of 3 for Oxford 100K Oxford Landmark database, 38.4 sketch collision were generated per image which lead to only 441 verified seeds in total. Therefore, a high sketch size is used in practice, but this leads to missing out seeds in smaller clusters and in clusters having low average image similarity. Moreover, since query expansion is used for completing the clusters, the success of these techniques is indirectly affected by the size of the database. The effect of these phenomenon is observed in the cluster representing the landmark "Magdalen Tower" in the Oxford Buildings Dataset [6], where only 3 of the 54 valid images were discovered, and no other image could be discovered through query expansion.

We identify scalable exhaustive pairwise matching as a feasible paradigm to overcome aforementioned issues. It can be seen that the inverted indexing technique could be made scalable if the size of the inverted index could grow with the size of the database, making the average size of the posting lists constant to allow querying in constant time. This is, however, not possible given the fixed domain of visual words. Therefore, we extract high order features by combining a feature with its nearby features and encoding their respective geometric configuration. This provides an extensive domain which is much more discriminative than visual words, and can be easily reprojected to a required size, using hash functions, based on the size of the database to obtain constant average size of the list. Zhang et al. have used a similar notion of high order spatial features in [14] to find all the cooccuring feature occurences under translation in a pair of images.

To address the problem of missing potential matches outside the shortlist, we design a match verification criteria which can be implemented on-the-fly from the index retrievals. This works well in practice as our high order features capture geometric information. Moreover, we match all high order features in a query image with all other high order features in the database, unlike [13], where only one sketch is pooled at a time per image for matching. This greatly enhances the chance of discovering small clusters.

Extracting High Order Features: We extract Hessian Affine regions and compute SIFT [7] descriptors of these regions for all the images in the database. These SIFT descriptors are quantized to a visual word vocabulary, using a kdtree built over the vocabulary. We choose nearby features for creating high order features, as their perspective projection into a matching image can be well modelled using a much simpler affine geometry. Next, we bin every image into bins of size 100 pixels. For each bin, we select upto 30 features, called *primary* features, by shortlisting features with the highest value of the scale parameter. Each *primary*

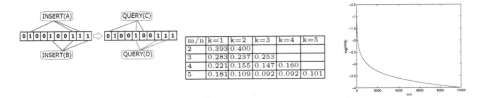

Fig. 3. (a)[left] The process of insertion and querying in a Bloom filter of size 10bit with 3 hash functions. [right] The first query is is not present in the Bloom filter. The second query is a false positive. (b) Table showing the False positive rates(FPR) for various combinations of parameters m(size of the Bloom filter)/n(number of elements to be indexed) and k(number of hash functions). (c) Table showing the variation of $log(FPR)$ with m/n for one hash function($k = 1$).

feature is paired with upto 20 of their nearest neighbours, within a radius of 80 pixels, to create high order features. Since our high order features are confined to local regions, we expect thier correspondences to follow affine geometry. Next, we compute the geometric parameters corresponding to the four grammar rules enlisted in [15]. Figure 2 gives a detailed description of these parameters. These grammar rules define invariants with respect to affine transformations. A high order feature is represented as a tuple enlisting visual words of the primary and the secondary feature, and the quantized values of the geometric parameters.

3   Indexing High Order Features Using Bloom Filters

The domain of high order features is obained by the cross product of the domain of visual words with itself and the domain of geometric parameters. Given a 1M vocabulary, the size of the domain of our high order features is 10^{12} even while neglecting the geometric parameters. This makes it possible to reproject our domain to a custom size, in accordance with the size of the database, to obtain sparse posting lists in the inverted index. To do this, we design an indexing scheme inspired from Bloom filters which minimize memory usage and provide constant time retrievals.

Bloom Filters: Bloom Filter [16] is a space efficient data structure for doing set membership queries. It allows constant time insertions and set membership queries. The downside of this scheme is that it occasionally identifies a non member query element as present. These are called false positives. Hence, the output for each query can be either "present in set, but can be wrong" or "certainly not in set".

A Bloom filter is composed of a bit array, A, and a fixed set of associated hash functions, H. For inserting an element, e into the set S, all $h \in H$ are evaluated for e, and the bit positions corresponding to the resulting hash values are set to 1. For doing a membership query, $h \in H$ are evaluated on the query element, and all the bit positions corresponding to the resulting hash values are checked for their set value. If any one of these bit positions is not set in the bit array, then the element is definitely not in the set, otherwise the element is deemed present. A false positive occurs when *all* the bit positions corresponding to the hash values of a query element have already been set by other elements inserted before.

Given the number of hash functions(k), the size of the bit vector(m) and the number of elements indexed(n), it is possible to determine the false positive rate by:

$$(1 - e^{-kn/m})^k$$

Figure 3 shows a simplified representation of Bloom filter operations, followed by a table showing false positive rates for low values of m/n and k. This is accompanied by a log plot of false positive rate with m/n for $k = 1$.

Indexing Using an Inverted Index over Bloom Filters: A simple indexing scheme can be built for N images, by allocating equally sized Bloom filters, $A_1 \ldots A_N$, with identical hash functions, and inserting the respective high order features of each of the N images. A query high order feature, q can now be resolved by evaluating all $h \in H$, and checking the corresponding bit positions in all the Bloom filters. It is easy to see that this process can be speeded up by storing the bit arrays of the Bloom filters as an inverted index over the bit positions. Retrieval can now be done easily by taking intersections of the posting lists of bit positions corresponding to evaluations of all $h \in H$ on q.

In the above framework, it is interesting to note that, keeping $k = 1$, that is, using only a single hash function, would eliminate any need of computing list intersections, making the retrieval process similar to that of BoW framework. However, unlike standard BoW, there is no restriction on the size of the inverted index, which is determined by the size of the bit array used. We can thus control the size of the inverted index in accordance to the size of the database to ensure a constant average length of the posting lists. This ensures constant time query retrievals. Only one hash function was also used by Mitzenmacher in [17] to make Bloom filters compressible.

One should, however, take care to always choose a big enough size of the inverted index so that the false positive rate while querying is low. Figure 3 shows the variation of false positive rate with m/n for $k = 1$. For a given maximum number, c, of high order features for any image in the database, it is easy to see that a false positive rate better than 10^{-3} can be easily achieved by allocating an inverted index of size $1000c$. Assuming 20k high order features in a query and database images, this implies generation of $20 \times 10^3 \times 10^{-3} = 20$ false matches on an average with every image.

Spatial Verification: We consider two primary features in different images a true correspondce only if they have at least v high order features originating from them in common. This criteria can be evaluated directly from inverted index retrievals, by querying all the high order features from a primary feature in succession and selecting images which claim to have v of these features. We consider an image level match verification to be passed if w such truly

Fig. 4. Two of the objects retrieved by our method for creating match graphs on the UKBench Dataset

corresponding primary features are found. This works well in practice as the high order features come from a very discriminative domain, resulting in very few mismatching of primary features across images. We keep the maximum number of secondary features per primary feature high at 20, to provide sufficient redundancy for finding common high order features with other primary features.

Given the susceptibility of our retrieval scheme to errors, it necessary for our spatial verification criteria to be robust to occasional mismatches. It is not difficult to see that our spatial verification scheme is robust to the introduction of a such few spurious mismatchings, because a single high order feature mismatch at random is not likely make the corresponding query primary feature truly correspond to another in a non matching image. Similarly, the event of multiple spurious high order mismatches corresponding to a single primary feature is also unlikely.

Match Graph Construction: We start by choosing an appropriate size, m, of the inverted index as discussed earlier. For Match Graph construction, we use a three-pass strategy, where we start by declaring a counter array of the size m to keep a count of high order features getting a certain hash value. In the first pass, we compute high order features and their corresponding hash value for all the images, while also updating the counter array. Now, precise memory allocations can be made for the posting lists of the inverted index based on the counter array. In the second pass, we index all the images by inserting their hash values computed earlier into the inverted index. In the final pass, we query each image in turn, and note down all the correspondences in an adjacency list.

4   Results

We use a standard image retrieval benchmark dataset, the University of Kentucky dataset(UKBench), introduced by Nister et al. [18], to measure our detection rate in small clusters. This dataset has 4 images each of 2550 objects making a total of 10200 medium resolution images. We used a vocabulary of 100K visual words for this experiment. On an average, 1048 features were extracted per image from this databset. An average of 413 primary features were selected for every image, which resulted in an average of 7436 high order features per image. This implies every primary feature combines with 18 secondary features on an average. A total of around 76m high order features were indexed using a simple FNV hash function. We defined the size of the inverted index to be 2^{25}, while the highest number of highorder features in a image was 23598. This corresponds to a maximum expected false positive rate of querying an image at 7×10^{-4}. This implies a maximum of 16.6 mismatches are expected to be generated between any pair of images.

The timing breakdown of the whole execution was as follows: Extraction the high order features and computation of their hash value took an average of 0.1 seconds per image. Building the inverted index over Bloom filters took 39 seconds. Querying the database took around 0.073 seconds per image. The total time required for the whole process was 23.6 minutes. The number of bytes required for indexing is equal to the sum of size of the inverted index and the number of high order features, that is, $8 \times 32 + 4 \times 76 = 560$Mb.

For the purpose of measuring our efficiency in detecting small clusters, we choose our match verification criteria as finding one primary feature with 3 high order features identical. We were able to find 1868 object clusters, corresponding to 73.2% recall, as compared to 49.6% recall reported in [13]. Figure 4 shows 2 of our retreived objects.

We have tested our approach on the challenging Oxford 5k dataset, introduced in [6]. It contains 5062 high resolution images of various buildings in Oxford, obtained by querying for building names on Flickr. Since, labels given to images tend not to be very accurate, this dataset contains a lot of distractors. Groundtruth is available for 11 of these buildings in the form of *Good, Ok*, and *Junk* images. Out of these *Good* and *Ok* images are considered true positives and the *Junk* images are considered as "don't care" samples.

For Oxford Buildings dataset, the maximum amount of high order features which got extracted for an image was 45k. The size of the inverted index used was 2^{29}. This gives a false positive rate of 8×10^{-5} for indexing 45k elements. This imples a maximum of 3.6 mismatches are expected to be generated between any pair of images. A total of 78 million high order features were extracted leading to a total memory requirement for indexing at $8 \times 512 + 4 \times 78 = 4408$Mb. The total time taken for extracting high order features and querying each image was $25 + 2 = 29$ minutes. For the high order features queried, the average length of the posting list was 1.16.

We kept the match verification criteria as finding atleast 3 primary features having atleast 4 high order features each identical between a query and a database image. We have computed the clusters as the connected component on the graph of matching images. In all 317 clusters were discovered containing a total 1367 images in them. The largest cluster has 362 images showing nearby All Souls building and Radcliffe Camera from various viewpoints. We were also able to find many interesting smaller clusters. These results are shown in Figure 6. We got mismatches, mostly in the form of text images, as shown in Figure 5.

We tested the scalability of our approach using the Oxford 105K dataset used in [13]. A total of 1480 million high order features were extracted. We used an inverted index of size 2^{29}, which resulted in an average length of posting list for the queried high order features at 6.8. The effect of larger average length of posting list can be seen at the average query time per image, which increased from 0.024 seconds to 0.086 seconds. A faster average query time can be obtained by using a larger inverted index. The total time taken for extracting features and querying was $9 + 2.5 = 11.5$ hours. The memory requirement for indexing was $8 \times 512 + 4 \times 1480 = 10016$Mb. We used the verification criteria as finding

Fig. 5. Text is is the most common source of errors in our scheme. In this particular case, a text image got matched to the window structure in the final image, which contains the landmark Radcliffe Camera. Hence, these images also become a part of the cluster containing Radcliffe Camera and All Souls Building.

Fig. 6. Top two rows show small clusters identified by our method. Bottom row shows the cluster corresponding to 'difficult' Magdalen Tower.

atleast 6 primary features having atleast 4 high order features in common. We were able to obtain 2147 clusters involving 7198 images, with the largest cluster having 2265 images. Eyeballing this cluster revealed mismatches due to repeating patterns such as text, doors and windows which lead to coalescing of many smaller clusters.

5   Discussion and Conclusions

We show that it is feasible to index sufficient high order features capturing the appearance and geometric characteristics in an image, to an extent that there is no need for doing explicit geometrical verification. This is very advantageous as it eliminates any need for random disk accesses to fetch information required for doing geometrical verification. This is made possible as our geometric match verification criteria is computable directly from inverted index retrievals. We design an inverted indexing scheme which can adapt to the size of the database to ensure adequate sparsity of the posting lists to ensure constant time retrievals. The space savings are made by exploiting the behavior of an oversized Bloom filter using only one hash function. The extreme amounts of memory used by the Bloom filter is then shared efficiently using an inverted index structure for indexing multiple images. Our match verification is robust to the introduction of occasional spurious matches generated by our indexing scheme. Indexing high order features coming from an extensive domain would create problems for all the popular indexing schemes used for image retrieval or match graph construction, but we turn this to our advantage, by devicing an indexing scheme based on Bloom filters, which uses constant storage per entry irrespective of the size or complexity of the entry.

In conclusion, our contributions can be summarized as: (i) introducing a novel indexing scheme suited for indexing and querying the geometrical and appearance information in images (ii) implementing an exhaustive pairwise matching scheme to build an image match graph for moderately large datasets in linear time (iii) introducing a geometric verification criteria verifiable at index.

Acknowledgement. This work is supported by the Department of Science and Technology, Government of India.

References

1. Li, Y., Snavely, N., Huttenlocher, D.P.: Location Recognition Using Prioritized Feature Matching. In: Daniilidis, K., Maragos, P., Paragios, N. (eds.) ECCV 2010, Part II. LNCS, vol. 6312, pp. 791–804. Springer, Heidelberg (2010)
2. Heath, K., Gelfand, N., Ovsjanikov, M., Aanjaneya, M., Guibas, L.J.: Image webs: Computing and exploiting connectivity in image collections. In: CVPR, pp. 3432–3439 (2010)
3. Simon, I., Snavely, N., Seitz, S.M.: Scene summarization for online image collections. In: ICCV, pp. 1–8 (2007)
4. Snavely, N., Seitz, S.M., Szeliski, R.: Photo tourism: exploring photo collections in 3d. ACM Trans. Graph. 25(3), 835–846 (2006)
5. Srijan, K., Ishtiaque, S.A., Sinha, S., Jawahar, C.V.: Image-based walkthroughs from incremental and partial scene reconstructions. In: BMVC (2010)
6. Philbin, J., Chum, O., Isard, M., Sivic, J., Zisserman, A.: Object retrieval with large vocabularies and fast spatial matching. In: CVPR (2007)
7. Lowe, D.G.: Distinctive image features from scale-invariant keypoints. International Journal of Computer Vision 60(2), 91–110 (2004)
8. Bay, H., Tuytelaars, T., Van Gool, L.: SURF: Speeded Up Robust Features. In: Leonardis, A., Bischof, H., Pinz, A. (eds.) ECCV 2006. LNCS, vol. 3951, pp. 404–417. Springer, Heidelberg (2006)
9. Zhang, Y., Jia, Z., Chen, T.: Image retrieval with geometry-preserving visual phrases. In: CVPR, pp. 809–816 (2011)
10. Wang, X., Yang, M., Cour, T., Zhu, S., Yu, K., Han, T.X.: Contextual weighting for vocabulary tree based image retrieval. In: ICCV, pp. 209–216 (2011)
11. Chum, O., Perdoch, M., Matas, J.: Geometric min-hashing: Finding a (thick) needle in a haystack. In: CVPR, pp. 17–24 (2009)
12. Philbin, J., Zisserman, A.: Object mining using a matching graph on very large image collections. In: ICVGIP, pp. 738–745 (2008)
13. Chum, O., Matas, J.: Large-scale discovery of spatially related images. IEEE Trans. Pattern Anal. Mach. Intell. 32(2), 371–377 (2010)
14. Zhang, Y., Chen, T.: Efficient kernels for identifying unbounded-order spatial features. In: CVPR, pp. 1762–1769 (2009)
15. Xu, Y., Madison, R.: Robust object recognition using a cascade of geometric consistency filters. In: AIPR 2009, pp. 1–8 (2009)
16. Bloom, B.H.: Space/time trade-offs in hash coding with allowable errors. Commun. ACM 13(7), 422–426 (1970)
17. Mitzenmacher, M.: Compressed bloom filters. IEEE/ACM Trans. Netw. 10(5), 604–612 (2002)
18. Nistér, D., Stewénius, H.: Scalable recognition with a vocabulary tree. In: CVPR (2), pp. 2161–2168 (2006)

Large Vocabularies for Keypoint-Based Representation and Matching of Image Patches

Andrzej Śluzek

Khalifa University, Abu Dhabi, UAE
andrzej.sluzek@kustar.ac.ae

Abstract. In large visual databases, detection of prospectively similar contents requires simple and robust methods. Keypoint correspondences are a popular approach which, nevertheless, cannot detect (using typical descriptions) similarities in a wider image context, e.g. detection of similar fragments. For such capabilities, the analysis of configuration constraints is needed. We propose keypoint descriptions which (by using sets of words from large vocabularies) represent semi-local characteristics of images. Thus, similar image patches (including similarly looking objects) can be preliminarily retrieved by straightforward keypoint matching. A limited-scale experimental verification is provided. The approach can be prospectively used as a simple mid-level feature matching in large and unpredictable visual databases.

Keywords: keypoint description, keypoint correspondences, visual vocabulary, near-duplicate patches, affine invariance.

1 Introduction

In large visual databases of unknown and unpredictable contents, one of the critical problems is a fast detection of prospectively similar pieces of data. BoW techniques are relatively successful in retrieval of near-duplicate images (using descriptions of detected keypoints) and *the-same-category* scenes (using dense sampling instead of keypoint detection).

Retrieval of near-duplicate patches (located on different backgrounds) is another important problem in visual datasets. The results can be used for detection of similar objects located in random scenes, for the identification of typical/popular objects in visual collections, etc. Unfortunately, it is still a challenging problem, primarily because of its computational complexity. In random images, keypoint correspondences seldom indicate locations which are similar in a wider context. Thus, typical methods combine keypoint matching with the analysis of configuration constraints (often modeled by affine transformations). Such methods have limited applicability to large databases because each pair of images has to be separately processed to identity groups of similar keypoints satisfying the configuration constraints.

Configuration constraints have been analyzed using diversified techniques. RANSAC-based algorithmss ([1,2]), hashing ([3,4]), the Hough transform ([5,6]),

A. Fusiello et al. (Eds.): ECCV 2012 Ws/Demos, Part I, LNCS 7583, pp. 229–238, 2012.

topological constraints ([7,8]) are examples of the most popular approaches. Nevertheless, if the verification of constraints is needed, the size of processed visual databases cannot grow beyond certain limits (in spite of recent improvements, e.g., [9,10]).

Our goal, motivated by the recent results presented in [11], is to introduce and evaluate an alternative representation of individual keypoints. We propose large vocabularies of words invariantly characterizing keypoints in a semi-local context (i.e. a word represents both a keypoint and its neighborhood). By using such vocabularies, similar patches can be prospectively identified by straightforward keypoint matching. At the low level, we use typical tools, i.e. Harris-Affine keypoint detector ([12]) and SIFT descriptor ([5,13]), but any affine-invariant keypoint detector and any keypoint descriptor can be alternatively applied.

Section 2 of the paper contains fundamentals of the proposed approach. First, we briefly review TERM features, their descriptors and the corresponding vocabularies introduced in [11] to affine-invariantly characterize configurations of elliptical keypoints. TERM3 features (the main tool used in [11]) are built from triplets of keypoints. This is a disadvantage because even in images with artificially reduced numbers of keypoints, the numbers of TERM3 can be very large. Therefore, we show in Subsection 2.2 how to embed similar data into descriptions of *individual* keypoints using several novel vocabularies.

A limited-scale experimental validation is presented in Section 3. First, it is verified how reliably a match between two keypoints indicates that these keypoints belong to near-duplicate patches. Secondly, we investigate whether images with near-duplicate patches can be retrieved using just a presence of keypoint correspondences as the criterion. The results on publicly available databases are not perfect, but they are encouraging. Section 4 concludes the paper.

2   Principles of the Method

2.1   TERM Features and Their Descriptors

TERM3/TERM2 features, [11], characterize configurations of three/two elliptical keypoints. Given E_0 ellipse (with p_0 origin) and two external points p_1 and p_2 (which are origins of two other ellipses E_1 and E_2) we can build a trapezoid using the intersections of E_0 with $[p_0, p_1]$ and $[p_0, p_2]$ vectors, and with the diameters parallel to the corresponding tangent lines (Fig. 1).

Similar trapezoids are built in E_1 and E_2 ellipses. Then, such triplets of $Q_{0(12)}$, $Q_{1(02)}$ and $Q_{2(01)}$ trapezoids are refereed to as TERM3 features for three-ellipse configurations (Figs 2a,b,c,d). In order to avoid ambiguities, the ellipses are arranged in a tuple according to their areas.

If the ellipses are jointly transformed by an affine mapping, the configuration of trapezoids is correspondingly reshaped, Figs 2b,d. Thus, similar values of affine-invariant descriptors of TERM3 would indicate the affine covariance of three-ellipse configurations.

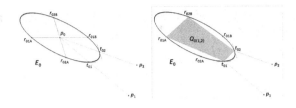

Fig. 1. A trapezoid built in E_0 ellipse based on two external points p_1 and p_2

Affine-invariant TERM2 features (which play only a supplementary role) consist of three quadrilaterals Q_T, Q_B and Q_L (see the bottom row of Fig. 2) defined by a configuration of two ellipses.

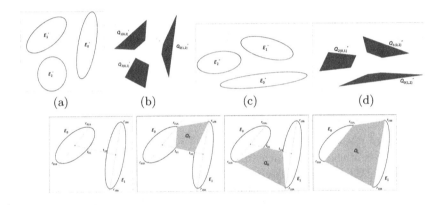

Fig. 2. Principles of TERM3 features(a,b,c,d) and TERM2 features (bottom row)

Descriptors of TERM3 and TERM2 features (referred to as T3 and T2, correspondingly) are built using a simple affine-invariant moment expression $Inv = \frac{\mu_{20}\mu_{02} - \mu_{11}^2}{\mu_{00}^4}$, where μ_{pq} indicates a central moment of $(p+q)^{th}$ order. T2 descriptor consist of the Inv values computed separately for Q_T, Q_B and Q_L quadrilaterals (i.e. T2 is a $3D$ vector). For T3, the values of Inv are obtained for individual trapezoids $Q_{0(12)}$, $Q_{1(02)}$ and $Q_{2(01)}$, for their pairs and for the union of all of them. Therefore, T3 is a $7D$ vector.

High performances of TERM3 matching in retrieval of near-duplicate patches are reported in [11]. The most successful variant (over 90% of correct matches) is a combination of T3, T2 and SIFT words, i.e. two TERM3 are matched if: (a) their T3 words are identical, (b) SIFT words of the contributing keypoints are correspondingly identical, and (c) T2 words for pairs of contributing keypoints are also correspondingly identical. Fig. 3 shows an example of correspondences found by such a method (the standard O2O SIFT-based matching is also presented for a reference).

(a)   (b)

Fig. 3. Exemplary correspondences found by TERM3 matching (a) and keypoint matching by using SIFT-based mutual nearest neighbor O2O (b)

2.2 Vocabularies for Keypoint Description and Matching

The major disadvantage of TERM3 is the number of such features in typical images. Even if the numbers are reduced (first, by reducing the numbers of keypoints and, secondly, by building the features over keypoint neighborhoods of limited size) more than $10,000$ TERM3 can be frequently formed in images containing just 200-300 keypoints. As an alternative, we propose the incorporation of TERM-related data into descriptions of individual keypoints. Then, although the complexity of keypoint description increases, the number of records remains the same and all extracted keypoints can be used (if necessary).

Consider a TERM3 feature with the largest (dominant) E_0 elliptical keypoint. As explained earlier, its description includes:

- T3 word of the whole TERM3 feature;
- SIFT words of the dominant ellipse E_0 and the other ellipses E_1, E_2;
- T2 words of TERM2 features built over (E_0, E_1), (E_0, E_2) and (E_1, E_2) pairs of ellipses.

Assume the cardinalities of SIFT, T3 and T2 vocabularies are, correspondingly, $\|SV\|$, $\|TV_3\|$ and $\|TV_2\|$. Then, E_0 keypoint can be described by various vocabularies (only selected options are mentioned) representing both the keypoint and the configuration of its neighborhood:

- **VocA:** SIFT word of E_0. Two keypoints are matched if they have the same SIFT words. $\|VocA\| = \|SV\|$. Each keypoint is described by a single word only (in this case no neighborhood data are used).
- **VocB:** SIFT word of E_0 and SIFT word of either E_1 or E_2. Two keypoints are matched if they have the same SIFT words and some of their neighbors have the same SIFT words. $\|VocB\| = \|SV\|^2$. Each keypoint is described by a *set of words* (SoW). A similar idea was proposed in the pioneer work [7].
- **VocC:** SIFT word of E_0 and T3 word TERM3. Two keypoints are matched if they have the same SIFT words and they belong to TERM3 features with the same T3 words. $\|VocC\| = \|SV\| \times \|TV_3\|$. Each keypoint is described by SoW.
- **VocD:** SIFT word of E_0, SIFT word of either E_1 or E_2 and T3 word of TERM3. Two keypoints are matched if they have the same SIFT words, some of their neighbors have the same SIFT words and these neighbors belong to

TERM3 features with the same T3 word. $\|VocD\| = \|SV\|^2 \times \|TV_3\|$. Each keypoint is described by SoW.

- **VocE:** SIFT words of E_0, E_1 and E_2, T3 word of TERM3, T2 words of TERM2 built over (E_0, E_1), (E_0, E_2) and (E_1, E_2). Two keypoints are matched only if they are dominant keypoints of two TERM3 matched according to Subsection 2.1. $\|VocE\| = \|SV\|^3 \times \|TV_3\| \times \|TV_2\|^3$. Each keypoint is described by SoW.

In general, two keypoints are considered a match (within a selected vocabulary) if their SoW's (*sets of words*) intersect. The objective of the conducted experiments is to evaluate applicability of keypoint matching defined by such vocabularies to near-duplicate patch detection and to verify how effective this simple approach is in the retrieval of images containing near-duplicate patches.

3   Experiments

The main experiment has been conducted using a publicly available VISIBLE[1] dataset which consists of 100 images containing diversified views on varying backgrounds of 1, 2 or 3 objects from over 30 types of objects. Because the objects are approximately piecewise planar, outlines of their shapes can be naturally used as the ground truth for near-duplicate patches (see examples in Fig. 4). With 100 images, there are 4,950 image pairs in this dataset, and 512 pairs share at least one near-duplicate patch. The objective is to detect/locate such patches and, subsequently, to retrieve pairs of images containing near-duplicate patches.

Fig. 4. Exemplary images and the outlines of near-duplicate patches from VISIBLE dataset

In the other experiment, images from popular databases (PASCAL2007, Caltech101, 15 Scenes, INRIA, etc.) have been used. Unfortunately, in these images the required ground truth is not available (e.g., in PASCAL2007 outlines of *the-same-class* objects are provided, but classes are defined semantically so that such outlines seldom share near-duplicate patches). Thus, the results of this experiment are used for a general evaluation rather than for a systematic analysis of performances.

We are certainly aware of a limited scale of the conducted experiments. However, databases where the ground truth is provided as outlines of near-duplicate *patches* (instead of *the-same-class* objects) are not easily available (we hope to build such a database but this is an extremely tedious process).

---

[1] http://www.ii.pwr.wroc.pl/~visible/data/upload/FragmentMatchingDB.zip

3.1 Methodology

Keypoints are extracted using Harris-Affine detector, [12]. The SIFT vocabulary for keypoint description contains 500 words (i.e. $\|SV\| = 500$) built from almost $1,000,000$ keypoints found in 800 diversified images. In the preprocessing phase, TERM features are formed in all images. We basically follow the methodology of [11] where more details can be found. Similarly to many other works (e.g. [6,14,15]), neighborhoods of limited size are considered (with a non-standard definition of neighborhoods which include only keypoints of sizes proportional to the distance between keypoints). The small-size vocabularies describing TERM features are built using over $30,000,000$ triplets of keypoints from 1000 images. T3 vocabulary contains 128 words ($\|TV_3\| = 128$) and there are only 27 words in T2 vocabulary ($\|TV_3\| = 27$). Thus, the cardinalities of the proposed vocabularies are: $\|VocA\| = 500$, $\|VocB\| = 250,000$, $\|VocC\| = 64,000$, $\|VocD\| = 32,000,000$ and $\|VocE\| = 314,928,000,000,000$. Note that some vocabularies require **long integer** representation.

With large numbers of image pairs to be matched, it is almost impossible to manually verify the ground truth of keypoint correspondences. Thus, we use an approximate method where a match is considered a true correspondence if in both images the keypoints belong to the outlines of near-duplicate patches. This may generate some false positives (matching different parts of near-duplicates) and false negatives (similar fragments which are outside the outlined patches) but, in general, the results have been found fairly accurate.

Therefore, performances of keypoint matching can be measured using only *precision*. The results of image pair retrieval are evaluated using three popular metrics, i.e. *precision*, *recall* and *F-measure*. Instead of the ordinary *F-measure*, we use F_β (with a small value $\beta = 0.3$) which highlights a higher importance of *precision*. It can be argued that in very large databases users are more interested in fairly small sets of mostly relevant objects (even if some relevant objects are not retrieved) than in large sets of mostly irrelevant objects (even though almost all relevant objects are included).

3.2 VISIBLE Database

TERM3 matching has been tested on VISIBLE database in [11]. Using limited numbers of keypoints to reduce the numbers of TERM3 features (which, nevertheless, exceed $10,000$ in some images) a high 93% *precision* of feature matching is obtained. We first match the same keypoints represented by the sets of words proposed in Subsection 2.2. Note that the numbers of data records are now very small (all images contain less than 300 keypoints). The results for selected vocabularies are given in Table 1 (in one case we use the intersection of correspondences provided by two vocabularies).

It can be noted that matching by **VocE** (which incorporates all data used to match TERM3) is almost as good as TERM3 matching; a minor deterioration is because we limit the size of SoW's to 100 (while actually some keypoints appear in more than 100 TERM3). However, even for smaller vocabularies the results

Table 1. Precision of feature matching for selected vocabularies ([11] results provided for reference)

Vocabulary	VocA	VocB	VocC	VocB∩VocC	VocD	VocE	[11]
total matches	2, 202, 689	434, 774	148, 667	90, 970	53, 862	616	n.a.
correct matches	75, 429	28, 528	9, 532	8, 902	6, 643	555	n.a.
precision	3.64%	6.56%	6.41%	9.78%	12.33%	90.10%	93%

can be improved if we accept only matches with sufficiently large intersections of SoW's. For example, using 5 as the threshold, *precision* of **VocB**, **VocB∩VocC** and **VocD** increases to 44%,70% and 41%, correspondingly.

Subsequently, we retrieve a pair of images as prospectively containing near-duplicate patches if at least one keypoint match is found. For **VocB**, **VocC**, **VocB∩VocC** and **VocD**, a keypoint match requires at least 5 elements in SoW intersections. For **VocE** any non-empty intersections are accepted. Again, we use the [11] results as the reference compared to the results provided in Table 2. It should be noted that VISIBLE dataset contains 512 image pairs sharing similar objects/patches but only 311 of them share any keypoints within the outlines of patches (because of a limited number of keypoints used). Thus, *recall* of image pair retrieval cannot exceed $311/512 = 60.74\%$ and the *recall* values in Table 2 should be seen in this context.

Table 2. Retrieval of image pairs sharing near-duplicate patches

Vocabulary	VocA	VocB	VocC	VocB∩VocC	VocD	VocE	[11]
returned	4950	340	3685	31	747	259	272
correct	311	92	210	162	135	233	248
precision	6.68%	27.06%	5.70%	48.94%	18.07%	89.96%	91.17%
recall	60.74%	17.97%	41.02%	31.64%	26.37%	45.51%	48.23%
$F_{0.3}$	7.21%	25.98%	6.13%	46.83%	18.55%	83.25%	84.98%

When we considered ALL extracted keypoints (note that for the [11] method it would be prohibitively costly) the results are qualitatively similar (see Tables 3 for selected details). The *precision* values might be slightly lower (with the corresponding increase of *recall*) because less prominent keypoints contribute a number of additional correspondences (often incorrect).

Table 3. Selected results by using ALL keypoints extracted in VISIBLE images

Vocabulary	keypoints matched(correct)	precision	image pairs(correct)	precision/recall/$F_{0.3}$
VocA	9, 027, 281(190, 145)	2.11%	4950(510)	10.30%/99.61%/11.12%
VocB∩VocC	40, 941(22, 748)	55.56%	653(263)	40.27%/51.37%/41.01%
VocD	25, 459(10, 847)	42.61%	795(138)	17.36%/26.95%/17.88%

Altogether, we can conclude that vocabularies incorporating TERM-related data into words describing individual keypoints are prospectively a useful tool for a preliminary search in large and complex databases. **VocE** vocabulary is clearly superior (because it inherits many properties of the original TERM3 matching). However, if the memory footprint is an issue, **VocB∩VocC** can be alternatively used (with the corresponding drop of performances). Exemplary matches (including one example which is partially incorrect) obtained by using **VocE** are given in Fig. 5.

Fig. 5. Exemplary matches in VISIBLE dataset by using **Method D**

3.3 Other Databases

A random collection of over $1,000$ images from several popular databases have been used in the second experiment. Initially, we hoped that near-duplicate patches would be retrieved from pairs of images sharing *the-same-class* objects, especially for man-made objects with some configurational consistency (e.g. *cars*, *trains*, etc.) but is has not been confirmed. In PASCAL2007 (where the ground truth outlines of *the-same-class* objects are available) *precision* of image pair retrieval was at the level of random choice. Nevertheless, some conclusions can be drawn from almost $500,000$ image matches performed (although only some of them have been later visually inspected).

The general observations support results of the first experiment. In particular, approx. 90% of keypoint correspondences (returned by both **VocE** and **VocB∩VocC** matching) actually represent visually identifiable similar patches. If clusters of several correspondences are found, images usually contain larger patches. A few examples (shown either locally or in the image context) are provided in Fig. 6.

Fig. 6. Exemplary retrievals of near-duplicate patches shown in the context of whole images (top rows) and locally (bottom). The outlines are approximate.

4   Final Remarks

The paper argues that detection of near-duplicate patches in images of random contents is feasible at the level of individual keypoint matching (i.e. without any verification/analysis of configuration constraints). Large-size vocabularies are proposed for this purpose (each keypoint is described by a set of words). In contrast to other keypoint-related large vocabularies (e.g., [4]) we use words representing both visual and geometric characteristics of keypoint neighborhoods,

The preliminary experimental verification has been conducted on a small database (which provides the ground truth in the required form). A larger-scale evaluation (without the ground truth data) on image from popular databases provides qualitatively similar results. Because of its very low computational costs (word-based matching), the method can be instrumental in building mid-level features (e.g. [16]) for large databases and in visual data mining, [17].

References

1. Fischler, M., Bolles, R.: Random Sample Consensus: a Paradigm for Model Fitting with Applications to Image Analysis and Automated Cartography. In: Buxton, B.F., Cipolla, R. (eds.) ECCV 1996. LNCS, vol. 1064, pp. 683–695. Springer, Heidelberg (1996)
2. Chum, O., Matas, J.: Matching with prosac - progressive sample consensus. In: Proc. IEEE Conf. CVPR 2005, San Diego, CA, pp. 220–226 (2005)
3. Wolfson, H., Rigoutsos, I.: Geometric hashing: An overview. IEEE Comp. Science and Engineering 4, 10–21 (1997)
4. Chum, O., Perdoch, M., Matas, J.: Geometric min-hashing: Finding a (thick) needle in a haystack. In: Proc. IEEE Conf. CVPR 2009, pp. 17–24 (2009)
5. Lowe, D.G.: Object recognition from local scale-invariant features. In: Proc. 7th IEEE Int. Conf. Computer Vision, vol. 2, pp. 1150–1157 (1999)
6. Paradowski, M., Śluzek, A.: Local Keypoints and Global Affine Geometry: Triangles and Ellipses for Image Fragment Matching. In: Kwaśnicka, H., Jain, L.C. (eds.) Innovations in Intelligent Image Analysis. SCI, vol. 339, pp. 195–224. Springer, Heidelberg (2011)
7. Schmid, C., Mohr, R.: Object recognition using local characterization and semi-local constraints. Technical report, INRIA (1996)
8. Tell, D., Carlsson, S.: Combining Appearance and Topology for Wide Baseline Matching. In: Heyden, A., Sparr, G., Nielsen, M., Johansen, P. (eds.) ECCV 2002, Part I. LNCS, vol. 2350, pp. 68–81. Springer, Heidelberg (2002)
9. Perd'och, M., Chum, O., Matas, J.: Efficient representation of local geometry for large scale object retrieval. In: Proc. IEEE Conf. CVPR 2009, pp. 9–16 (2009)
10. Jegou, H., Douze, M., Schmid, C.: Improving bag-of-features for large scale image search. International Journal of Computer Vision 87, 316–336 (2010)
11. Śluzek, A., Paradowski, M.: Detection of Near-Duplicate Patches in Random Images Using Keypoint-Based Features. In: Blanc-Talon, J., Philips, W., Popescu, D., Scheunders, P., Zemcik, P. (eds.) ACIVS 2011. LNCS, vol. 7517, pp. 301–312. Springer, Heidelberg (2012)
12. Mikolajczyk, K., Schmid, C.: Scale and affine invariant interest point detectors. International Journal of Computer Vision 60, 63–86 (2004)
13. Lowe, D.G.: Distinctive image features from scale-invariant keypoints. International Journal of Computer Vision 60, 91–110 (2004)
14. Schmid, C., Mohr, R.: Local grayvalue invariants for image retrieval. IEEE Trans. PAMI 19, 530–535 (1997)
15. Yang, D., Śluzek, A.: A low-dimensional local descriptor incorporating tps warping for image matching. Image and Vision Computing 28, 1184–1195 (2010)
16. Boureau, Y.L., Bach, F., LeCun, Y., Ponce, J.: Learning mid-level features for recognition. In: Proc. IEEE Conf. CVPR 2010, pp. 2559–2566 (2010)
17. Han, J.: Data mining for image/video processing: A promising research frontier. In: Proc. Int. Conf. on Content-based Image and Video Retrieval CIVR 2008, pp. 1–2 (2008)

Linearized Smooth Additive Classifiers

Subhransu Maji

Toyota Technological Institute at Chicago,
Chicago, IL 60637, USA
smaji@ttic.edu

Abstract. We consider a framework for learning additive classifiers based on regularized empirical risk minimization, where the regularization favors "smooth" functions. We present representations of classifiers for which the optimization problem can be efficiently solved. The first family of such classifiers are derived from a *penalized spline* formulation due to Eilers and Marx, which is modified to enabled linearization. The second is a novel family of classifiers that are based on classes of *orthogonal basis* functions with *othogonal derivatives*. Both these families lead to explicit feature embeddings that can be used with off-the-shelf linear solvers such as LIBLINEAR to obtain additive classifiers. The proposed family of classifiers offer better trade-offs between training time, memory overhead and classifier accuracy, compared to the state-of-the-art in additive classifier training.

1 Introduction

Additive classifiers are a generalization of linear ones and arise naturally in many applications. These include SVM classifiers based on additive kernels, i.e., kernels of the form, $\mathbf{K}(\mathbf{x}, \mathbf{y}) = \sum_i K_i(x_i, y_i)$. Such classifiers frequently arise in computer vision applications where images are represented as a histogram or counts of low-level features, such as color or texture, and a similarity measure, such as the intersection kernel or the χ^2 kernel [2–4] is used to compare them. Although these non-linear kernels provide significant improvements in accuracy over their linear counterparts, it often comes at the expense of higher computational and memory requirements during training and testing.

In recent years, methods for training kernel SVMs that are based on training linear SVMs on feature maps that approximately preserve the kernel dot product have become popular. This includes the work of Rahimi and Recht [5] who proposed such feature maps for shift-invariant kernels, such as the Gaussian kernel. For additive kernels the scheme is easier since the one dimensional decomposition of the kernel allows independent computation of feature maps in each dimension. This direction has been explored by us in our earlier work [3] to construct approximate feature embeddings for the min kernel that results in a piecewise linear approximation of the function in each dimension. For γ-homogenous additive kernels [6] Vedaldi and Zisserman [4] propose feature maps that enable similar efficient training. The resulting efficiencies during training

A. Fusiello et al. (Eds.): ECCV 2012 Ws/Demos, Part I, LNCS 7583, pp. 239–248, 2012.

and testing make additive classifiers the classifiers of choice for many computer vision applications.

In this work we revisit the additive modeling literature to obtain feature maps that enable similar efficient training. The Penalized-Spline (P-Spline) formulation due to Eilers and Marx [1] has emerged as a practical approach for training additive models for the regression setting ever since Generalized Additive Models (GAMs) were introduced by Hastie and Tibshirani [7]. However, it does not directly apply to the classification setting, nor does it scale to the size of datasets and features typical in computer vision applications. Nevertheless, we show that with a small modification to the original formulation, one can derive feature maps that can be directly used with fast linear SVM solvers, such as LIBLINEAR, to solve the optimization problem in the classification setting. These feature maps inherit the advantages of the P-Spline formulation, which is that it allows explicit control over the smoothness of the estimated function.

The perspective of learning smooth additive classifiers offers a general recipe for learning. Consider a scheme where the functions in each dimension are expanded using an orthonormal basis set, and smoothness is ensured by penalizing the norm of the function derivatives. We identify a family of orthogonal basis functions for which the additive learning problem reduces an equivalent linear problem. These basis functions have an additional property that they are differentiable and have orthogonal derivatives.

Experiments on various image classification datasets show that the proposed techniques can offer orders of magnitude reduction in training time over standard kernel SVM training, often with almost no memory overhead and within a small constant multiple of the time required to train a linear SVM. These classifiers offer better trade-offs between training time, memory overhead and classifier accuracy, compared to the state-of-the-art in additive classifier training.

2   Generalized Additive Models

Given training data, $(\mathbf{x}^k, y^k)$, $k = 1, \ldots, m$ with $\mathbf{x}^k \in \mathbb{R}^D$ and $y^k \in \{-1, +1\}$, we are interested in learning functions based on the following optimization problem:

$$\min_{f \in F} \sum_k l\left(y^k, f(\mathbf{x}^k)\right) + \lambda R(f) \tag{1}$$

where, l is a loss function and $R(f)$ is a regularization term. In the classification setting, a commonly used loss function l is the hinge loss function:

$$l\left(y^k, f(\mathbf{x}^k)\right) = \max\left(0, 1 - y^k f(\mathbf{x}^k)\right) \tag{2}$$

When, $f(\mathbf{x}) = \mathbf{w}^T \mathbf{x}$ and $R(f) = \mathbf{w}^T \mathbf{w}$, this reduces to the standard linear SVM formulation. In the additive modeling setting, a typical regularization is the norm of the dth order derivative of the function, i.e., $R(f) = \sum_i \int_{-\infty}^{\infty} f_i^d(t)^2 dt$. Motivated by the analysis in our earlier work [3], we consider representations of the function f for which the optimization problem can be efficiently solved. For further discussion, we assume that the features are one dimensional, because the analysis can be done for each dimension independently for additive functions.

3   Linearized Spline Embeddings

Eilers and Marx [1] proposed a practical modeling approach for GAMs where they represent the functions in each dimension using a relatively large number of uniformly spaced B-Spline bases. The smoothness of these functions is ensured by penalizing the first or second order differences between the adjacent spline coefficients. Let $\Phi(x^k)$ denote the vector with entries $\Phi_i(x^k)$, the projection of x^k on to the ith basis function. The P-Spline optimization problem for the classification setting with the hinge loss function consists of minimizing $c(\mathbf{w})$:

$$c(\mathbf{w}) = \frac{\lambda}{2}\mathbf{w}^T \mathbf{D}_d^T \mathbf{D}_d \mathbf{w} + \frac{1}{n}\sum_k \max\left(0, 1 - y^k\left(\mathbf{w}^T \Phi(x^k)\right)\right) \tag{3}$$

where, $\mathbf{w}$ is a vector of weights for the basis functions representing the underlying function. The matrix $\mathbf{D}_d$ constructs the dth order differences of $\mathbf{w}$, $\mathbf{D}_d\mathbf{w} = \Delta^d\mathbf{w}$. The first difference of $\mathbf{w}$, $\Delta^1\mathbf{w}$, is a vector of elements $w_i - w_{i+1}$. Higher order difference matrices can be computed by repeating the differencing. For a n bases, the difference matrix $\mathbf{D}_1$ is a $(n-1) \times n$ matrix with $d_{i,i} = 1$, $d_{i,i+1} = -1$ and zero everywhere else.

To enable a reduction to the linear case, we modify the matrix $\mathbf{D}_1$ by adding one more row to the top. Now $\mathbf{D}_1$ is a $n \times n$ matrix with $s_{i,i} = 1, s_{i,i-1} = -1$. The resulting difference matrices $\mathbf{D}_1$ and $\mathbf{D}_2 = \mathbf{D}_1^2$ are shown below:

$$\mathbf{D}_1 = \begin{pmatrix} 1 & & & \\ -1 & 1 & & \\ & -1 & 1 & \\ & & \cdots & \\ & & -1 & 1 \end{pmatrix}, \mathbf{D}_2 = \begin{pmatrix} 1 & & & \\ -2 & 1 & & \\ 1 & -2 & 1 & \\ & & \cdots & \\ & 1 & -2 & 1 \end{pmatrix}$$

The first row of $\mathbf{D}_1$ has the effect of penalizing the norm on the first coefficient of the spline bases, which plays the role of regularization in the linear setting (e.g. ridge regression, linear SVMs, etc). Alternatively, one can think of this as an additional basis at left most point whose coefficient is set to zero. The key advantage is that the matrix $\mathbf{D}_d$ is invertible and has a particularly simple form which allows us to linearize the whole system by re-parametrizing $\mathbf{w}$ by $\mathbf{D}_d^{-1}\mathbf{w}$, resulting in the following optimization problem :

$$c(\mathbf{w}) = \frac{\lambda}{2}\mathbf{w}^T\mathbf{w} + \frac{1}{n}\sum_k \max\left(0, 1 - y^k\left(\mathbf{w}^T \mathbf{D}_d^{-T} \Phi(x^k)\right)\right) \tag{4}$$

Since the whole classifier is linear on the features $\Psi^d(x^k) = \mathbf{D}_d^{-T}\Phi(x^k)$, the underlying additive classifier can be learned by using a fast linear solver on the transformed feature space Ψ. The inverse matrices $\mathbf{D}_1^{-T}$ and $\mathbf{D}_2^{-T}$ are both upper triangular – the matrix $\mathbf{D}_1^{-T}$ has entries $s_{i,j} = 1, j \geq i$ and $\mathbf{D}_2^{-T}$ has entries $s_{i,j} = j - i + 1, j \geq i$. We will show in Section 5, that this structure can be exploited in a custom solver to further reduce the memory and computational requirements during training.

Let us define the implicit kernel between data points as the dot product of their feature maps $\boldsymbol{\Psi} = \mathbf{D}_d^{-T}\boldsymbol{\Phi}$. For uniformly spaced B-Splines of degree d denoted by $\boldsymbol{\Phi}_d$, with $\mathbf{D}_1$ regularization, the implicit kernel $K_d = \boldsymbol{\Psi}_d^T\boldsymbol{\Psi}_d$, where $\boldsymbol{\Psi}_d = \mathbf{D}_1^{-T}\boldsymbol{\Phi}_d$, resembles the smooth versions of the min kernel $K_{\min}(x,y)$, where $K_{\min}(x,y) = \min(x,y)$, as shown in Figure 1. In fact, in our earlier work [3] we motivated the use of linear spline basis as an approximation to the min kernel. Higher order regularizations lead to features that resemble the truncated polynomial kernels [8, 9] which consist of uniformly spaced knots $\tau_1, \ldots, \tau_n$ and truncated polynomial features, $\Phi_i(x) = (x - \tau_i)_+^p$. However these features are less numerically stable than the B-Spline basis (see [10] for a comparison).

$K_{\min}$ K_1 $K_{\min} - K_1$ K_2 $K_{\min} - K_2$ K_3 $K_{\min} - K_3$

Fig. 1. Spline Kernels. $K_{\min}(x,y), x, y \in [0,1]$ along with K_d for $d = 1, 2, 3$ corresponding to linear, quadratic and cubic B-Spline basis shown as a heat map (yellow is high, black is low). Using 10 uniformly spaced bases, these kernels closely approximate the min kernel.

4 Generalized Fourier Embeddings

Generalized Fourier expansion of the functions in each dimension provides an alternate way of fitting additive models. Let $\Psi_1(x), \Psi_2(x), \ldots, \Psi_n(x)$ be an orthogonal basis system in the interval $[a, b]$, wrt. a weight function $w(x)$, i.e., we have $\int_a^b \Psi_i(x)\Psi_j(x)w(x)dx = 0, i \neq j$. Given a function $f(x) = \sum_i a_i\Psi_i(x)$, the regularization can be written as:

$$\int_a^b f^d(x)^2 w(x)dx = \int_a^b \left(\sum_{i,j} a_i a_j \Psi_i^d(x)\Psi_j^d(x) \right) w(x)dx$$

Consider an orthogonal family of basis functions which are differentiable and whose derivatives are also orthogonal. One can normalize the basis such that $\int_a^b \Psi_i^d(x)\Psi_j^d(x)w(x)dx = \delta_{ij}$. In this case the regularization has a simple form:

$$\int_a^b f^d(x)^2 w(x)dx = \int_a^b \left(\sum_{i,j} a_i a_j \Psi_i^d(x)\Psi_j^d(x) \right) w(x)dx = \sum_i a_i^2$$

One again the problem of learning a regularized additive classifier reduces to a linear classifier in the embedded space $\boldsymbol{\Psi}(x)$. We identify two such bases:

Trigonometric Basis. The classic trigonometric basis functions:

$$\{1, \cos(\pi x), \sin(\pi x), \cos(2\pi x), \sin(2\pi x), \ldots\} \tag{5}$$

are orthogonal in $[-1, 1]$, wrt. the weight function $w(x) = 1$. The derivatives are also in the same family (except the constant function), hence are also orthogonal. The normalized feature embeddings for $d = 1, 2$ are shown in Table 1.

Hermite Basis. Hermite polynomials are an orthogonal basis system with orthogonal derivatives wrt. the weight function $e^{-x^2/2}$. Using the following identity:

$$\int_{-\infty}^{\infty} H_m(x) H_n(x) e^{-x^2/2} dx = \sqrt{2\pi} n! \delta_{mn} \tag{6}$$

and the property that $H'_n = nH_{n-1}$ (Apell sequence), one can obtain closed form features for $d = 1, 2$ as shown in Table 1. It is also known that the family of polynomial basis functions that are orthogonal with orthogonal derivatives belong to one of three families: Jacobi, Laguerre or Hermite [11]. The extended support of the weight function of the Hermite basis makes them well suited for additive modeling.

Although both these bases are complete, for practical purposes one can approximate the scheme using the first few basis functions. The quality of approximation depends on how well the underlying function can be approximated by these chosen bases. For e.g., low degree polynomials are better represented by Hermite basis.

Table 1. Trigonometric and Hermite embeddings $\boldsymbol{\Psi}^d$ penalizing the dth derivative

Trigonometric $x \in [-1, 1]$, $w(x) = 1$	Hermite $x \in N(0, 1)$, $w(x) = e^{-x^2/2}$
$\Psi_n^1(x) = \{\frac{\cos(n\pi x)}{n}, \frac{\sin(n\pi x)}{n}\}$	$\Psi_n^1(x) = \frac{H_n(x)}{\sqrt{n n!}}$
$\Psi_n^2(x) = \{\frac{\cos(n\pi x)}{n^2}, \frac{\sin(n\pi x)}{n^2}\}$	$\Psi_1^2(x) = \Psi_1^1(x)$, $\Psi_n^2(x) = \frac{H_n(x)}{\sqrt{n(n-1)n!}}$, $n > 1$

5 Learning Additive Classifiers

The proposed embeddings can be used with a fast linear SVM solver to train the underlying additive classifier. However, when the embedded feature space is large there can be a significant memory overhead in storing these features. For better memory efficiency, one could compute the embeddings "on the fly", i.e., in the inner loop of the training algorithm. This scheme is particularly attractive for the B-spline basis since it is relatively cheap to compute the embeddings. Moreover, the sparsity structure of the basis functions and the regularization can be exploited to further reduce the computational and memory overhead.

Most learning methods are sequential – they repeatedly evaluate the classifier at a point and update the classifier if the prediction is incorrect. The number of classifier evaluations, $\mathbf{w}^T \mathbf{D}_d^{-T} \boldsymbol{\Phi}(x)$, can be significantly larger than the number of updates. Hence, it is computationally efficient to maintain $\mathbf{w}_d = \mathbf{D}_d^{-1} \mathbf{w}$, and use sparse vector multiplication to evaluate the classifier. Updates to the weight vector $\mathbf{w}$ and $\mathbf{w}_d$ are of the form:

$$\mathbf{w} \leftarrow \mathbf{w} - \eta \mathbf{D}_d^{-T} \boldsymbol{\Phi}(x^k), \qquad \mathbf{w}_d \leftarrow \mathbf{w}_d - \eta \mathbf{L}_d \boldsymbol{\Phi}(x^k) \tag{7}$$

Where η is a step and $\mathbf{L}_d = \mathbf{D}_d^{-1} \mathbf{D}_d^{-T}$. Unlike the matrix $\mathbf{D}_d^T \mathbf{D}_d$, the matrix $\mathbf{L}_d$ is dense. Hence, updates to $\mathbf{w}_d$ can change all its entries. Even though $\mathbf{L}_d$ is dense, one can compute $\mathbf{L}_d \boldsymbol{\Phi}(x)$ in $2dn$ steps instead of n^2 steps by exploiting the structure of $\mathbf{D}_d^{-T}$. This can be done by initializing $a_i = \boldsymbol{\Phi}_i(x)$, and then repeating step A d times, followed by step B d times, to compute $\mathbf{L}_d \boldsymbol{\Phi}(x)$.

$$\text{Step A} : a_i = a_i + a_{i+1}, i = n - 1 \text{ to } 1$$
$$\text{Step B} : a_i = a_i + a_{i-1}, i = 2 \text{ to } n$$

For input features that are sparse and non-negative, which often arise in "bag-of-words" representations of text documents or images, it is important to preserve the sparsity of the features in the embeddings for computational and memory efficiency. Formally, we need the property that $\boldsymbol{\Psi}(0) = \mathbf{0}$. For the B-Spline basis, one can achieve this by removing basis functions that have support at 0. For the generalized Fourier features, one could consider an expansion using only the bases that evaluate to zero when the input is zero, i.e., $\boldsymbol{\Psi}(0) = 0$.

6   Experiments

Often on large datasets consisting of very high dimensional features, to avoid the memory bottleneck, one may compute the embedding in the inner loop of the training algorithm. We call this the "online" method. We modify LIBLINEAR to enable this online computation, but other solvers such as PEGASOS [12], which was used in our previous work [3], can also be easily modified to do the same. The custom solver allows us to exploit the sparsity of embeddings (Section 5).

A practical regularization is $\mathbf{D}_0 = \mathbf{I}$ with the B-Spline embeddings, where $\mathbf{I}$ is the identity matrix, which leads to sparse features. This makes it difficult to estimate the weights for basis functions which have few data points, but one can use a higher order B-Spline basis to somewhat mitigate this problem.

We present image classification experiments on two image datasets, MNIST [13] and Daimler Chrysler (DC) pedestrians [14]. On these datasets, SVM classifiers based on histogram intersection kernel outperform linear SVM classifiers [3, 15], when used with features based on a spatial pyramid of histogram of oriented gradients [2, 16]. The MNIST dataset has 60K instances and the features are 2172 dimensional and dense, leading to 130 million non-zero entries. The DC dataset has three training sets and two test sets. Each training set has 19.8K instances and the features are 656 dimensional and dense, leading to 13 million non-zero entries. These sizes are typical of image datasets, and training kernel SVM classifiers requires several hours on a single machine.

Effect of B-Spline Embedding Parameters. Table 2 shows the accuracy and training times as we vary the number of basis functions, regularization $\mathbf{D}_d, (d = 0, 1, 2)$, and the B-Spline degree $\in \{1, 2, 3\}$ on the first split of the DC pedestrian dataset. We set $C = 1$ and the bias term $B = 1$ for training all the models. On this dataset, we find that $\mathbf{D}_0$ and $\mathbf{D}_1$ regularization is as accurate and significantly faster than $\mathbf{D}_0$. This suggests that first order smoothness is sufficient for this dataset. In addition, $\mathbf{D}_0$ regularization leads to sparse features, which can be directly used with any linear solver that can exploit this sparsity. The training time for B-Splines scales sub-linearly with the number of basis functions, hence better fits can be obtained without significant loss in efficiency.

Table 2. The effect of spline parameters on training time/test accuracy on DC dataset

Spline	Regularization		
	$\mathbf{D}_0$	$\mathbf{D}_1$	$\mathbf{D}_2$
	5 basis functions		
Linear	**6.60s** (89.55%)	**20.27s** (89.68%)	**41.60s** (89.93%)
Quadratic	8.74s (**90.45%**)	30.47s (**90.20%**)	80.25s (**89.94%**)
Cubic	11.68s (90.03%)	49.85s (89.93%)	143.50s (88.57%)
	10 basis functions		
Linear	**5.61s** (90.42%)	**23.06s** (90.86%)	**77.99s** (**89.43%**)
Quadratic	8.10s (**90.69%**)	29.97s (**90.73%**)	126.03s (89.23%)
Cubic	11.59s (90.48%)	42.26s (90.67%)	193.47s (89.14%)
	20 basis functions		
Linear	**5.96s** (90.23%)	**32.43s** (**91.20%**)	**246.87s** (**89.06%**)
Quadratic	7.26s (90.34%)	34.99s (91.10%)	328.32s (88.89%)
Cubic	10.08s (**90.39%**)	42.88s (91.00%)	429.57s (88.92%)

Effect of Fourier Embedding Parameters. Table 3 shows the accuracy and training times for various Fourier embeddings on DC dataset. The raw features, are first normalized so that the data in each dimension $\in [-1, 1]$. The experiments are performed by precomputing the embeddings and using LIBLINEAR to train various models, as it is relatively more expensive to compute the embeddings online. The training times and accuracies are similar to that of B-Spline models.

Comparison of Various Additive Models. Table 4 shows the accuracy and training times of various additive models compared to linear and the more expensive min kernel SVM on all the 6 combinations of training and test sets of the DC dataset. The optimal parameters were found on the first training and test set. The additive models are up to $50\times$ faster to train and are as accurate as the min kernel SVM. The B-Spline additive models significantly outperform a linear SVM, require a small additional training time and almost *no* memory overhead.

Table 5 shows the accuracies and training times of various additive models on the MNIST dataset using the online method. We train one-vs-all classifiers

Table 3. The effect of Fourier parameters on training time/test accuracy on DC dataset

#Basis	Trigonometric				Hermite			
	$d = 1$		$d = 2$		$d = 1$		$d = 2$	
	Accuracy	Time	Accuracy	Time	Accuracy	Time	Accuracy	Time
1	88.94%	**07.0s**	88.94%	**07.0s**	84.17%	**02.8s**	84.17%	**02.8s**
2	89.59%	10.2s	89.64%	10.2s	88.01%	04.6s	88.01%	04.6s
3	88.99%	12.7s	89.77%	12.8s	88.22%	07.7s	88.70%	09.9s
4	**89.77%**	16.0s	**89.84%**	15.9s	**89.00%**	12.6s	**89.05%**	11.9s

for each digit, and the classification scores are normalized to $\in [0, 1]$ by Platt's scaling. During testing, each example is assigned the label of the classifier with the highest response. The optimal parameters for training were found using 2-fold cross validation on the training set. Once again, the additive models significantly outperform the linear classifier and match the accuracy of the min kernel SVM, while being $50\times$ faster. The spline embeddings once again perform the best, requiring a small multiple of the time required to train a linear SVM, without requiring additional memory since the features are computed online.

Table 4. Training time/test accuracy of various additive classifiers on DC dataset

Method	Test Accuracy	Training Time	
SVM (linear) + LIBLINEAR	81.49 (1.29)	3.8s	
SVM (min) + LIBSVM	89.05 (1.42)	363.1s	
		online	batch
B-Spline ($\mathbf{D}_0$, Linear, $n = 05$)	88.51 (1.35)	**5.9s**	-
B-Spline ($\mathbf{D}_0$, Cubic, $n = 05$)	89.00 (1.44)	10.8s	-
B-Spline ($\mathbf{D}_1$, Linear, $n = 10$)	**89.56** (1.35)	17.2s	-
B-Spline ($\mathbf{D}_1$, Cubic, $n = 10$)	89.25 (1.39)	19.2s	-
Fourier ($d = 1$, $n = 4$)	88.44 (1.43)	159.9s	12.7s ($4\times$ memory)
Hermite ($d = 1$, $n = 4$)	87.67 (1.26)	35.5s	12.6s ($4\times$ memory)

Table 5. Training time/test error of various additive classifiers on MNIST dataset

Method	Test Error	Training Time
SVM (linear) + LIBLINEAR	1.44%	6.2s
SVM (min) + LIBSVM	0.79%	~ 2.5 hours
B-Spline ($\mathbf{D}_0$, Linear, $n = 20$)	0.88%	31.6s
B-Spline ($\mathbf{D}_0$, Cubic, $n = 20$)	0.86%	51.6s
B-Spline ($\mathbf{D}_1$, Linear, $n = 40$)	**0.81%**	157.7s
B-Spline ($\mathbf{D}_1$, Cubic, $n = 40$)	0.82%	244.9s
Hermite ($d = 1, n = 4$)	1.06%	358.6s

7 Comparison to Previous Work

The spline embeddings proposed in this work are a generalization of our earlier work [3](MB). The ϕ_2-sparse and ϕ_2 classifiers proposed in MB are equivalent to the embeddings obtained by using a linear spline basis with $\mathbf{D}_0$ and $\mathbf{D}_1$ regularization respectively. The family of spline embeddings offers finer-grained control over the training time and accuracy than MB. For example, one can use $\mathbf{D}_0$ regularization with quadratic B-Spline basis to obtain a classifier with intermediate accuracy and training time as the ϕ_2-sparse and ϕ_2 classifiers as seen in Table 4. The other approach related to our work is that of Vedaldi and Zisserman [4] (VZ). We compare our approach to theirs in terms of memory overhead and training time, since the accuracies of all these methods are similar to the exact kernel SVM classifier.

Memory Overhead. The VZ method has similar memory overhead as the Fourier embeddings since both these result in dense embeddings of similar dimension. When used in the offline case, i.e., with precomputed embeddings, this can lead to an order of magnitude increase in memory requirement, which may be impractical for large datasets. In comparison, the spline embeddings have lower memory overhead since the projected features are sparse regardless of the number of basis functions. The Fourier and VZ methods can be easily modified to compute features online to reduce their memory overhead, but this comes at the expense of training time.

Training Time. The training times of Fourier embeddings and VZ are similar, both for the online and offline case, since both these embeddings are dense and involve similar computations. Even though the B-Spline basis can be much higher dimensional, the training time remains small because of the optimizations we presented in Section 5. If we restrict ourselves to the online case, which is of practical importance, the training time is dominated by the time taken to compute the embeddings. The B-Spline embeddings are the fastest to compute as they involve fewer arithmetic operations than trigonometric functions or higher order polynomials. The Fourier embeddings or VZ can be sped up using precomputed tables, but are unlikely to be faster than the B-Spline embeddings.

8 Conclusion

Motivated by the additive modeling literature, we propose two families of embeddings that enable efficient learning of additive classifiers. Spline embeddings can be derived by a simple modification of the P-Spline formulation of Eilers and Marx [1] and generalize our earlier work [3]. These classifiers can be trained using a custom solver, with almost no memory overhead, and within a small constant multiple of the training time compared to a linear classifier, and are as accurate as an additive kernel SVM classifier. We also propose a family of generalized Fourier features that can be used with an off-the-shelf linear solver such as LIBLINEAR to efficiently train additive classifiers.

Acknowledgements. The work was done when the author was a graduate student at the University of California at Berkeley. The author would also like to thank Alex Berg for helpful discussions.

References

1. Eilers, P., Marx, B.: Generalized linear additive smooth structures. Journal of Computational and Graphical Statistics 11(4), 758–783 (2002)
2. Lazebnik, S., Schmid, C., Ponce, J.: Beyond bags of features: Spatial pyramid matching for recognizing natural scene categories. In: CVPR (2006)
3. Maji, S., Berg, A.C.: Max margin additive classifiers for detection. In: ICCV (2009)
4. Vedaldi, A., Zisserman, A.: Efficient additive kernels via explicit feature maps. In: CVPR (2010)
5. Rahimi, A., Recht, B.: Random features for large-scale kernel machines. In: NIPS (2007)
6. Hein, M., Bousquet, O.: Hilbertian metrics and positive definite kernels on probability measures. In: AISTATS (2005)
7. Hastie, T., Tibshirani, R.: Generalized Additive Models. Chapman & Hall/CRC (1990)
8. Pearce, N., Wand, M.: Penalized splines and reproducing kernel methods. The American Statistician 60(3), 233–240 (2006)
9. Wahba, G.: Spline models for observational data, vol. 59. Society for Industrial Mathematics (1990)
10. Eilers, P., Marx, B.: Splines, knots, and penalties. Wiley Interdisciplinary Reviews: Computational Statistics (2005)
11. Webster, M.: Orthogonal polynomials with orthogonal derivatives. Mathematische Zeitschrift 39, 634–638 (1935)
12. Shalev-Shwartz, S., Singer, Y., Srebro, N.: Pegasos: Primal estimated sub-gradient solver for svm. In: ICML (2007)
13. LeCun, Y., Cortes, C.: The mnist database of handwritten digits (1998)
14. Munder, S., Gavrila, D.M.: An experimental study on pedestrian classification. IEEE TPAMI 28(11) (2006)
15. Maji, S., Berg, A.C., Malik, J.: Classification using intersection kernel support vector machines is efficient. In: CVPR (2008)
16. Dalal, N., Triggs, B.: Histograms of oriented gradients for human detection. In: CVPR (2005)

Ask'nSeek: A New Game for Object Detection and Labeling

Axel Carlier[1], Oge Marques[2], and Vincent Charvillat[1]

[1] IRIT-ENSEEIHT, University of Toulouse, France
{Axel.Carlier,Vincent.Charvillat}@enseeiht.fr
[2] Florida Atlantic University, USA
omarques@fau.edu

Abstract. This paper proposes a novel approach to detect and label objects within images and describes a two-player web-based guessing game – Ask'nSeek – that supports these tasks in a fun and interactive way. Ask'nSeek asks users to guess the location of a hidden region within an image with the help of semantic and topological clues. The information collected from game logs is combined with results from content analysis algorithms and used to feed a machine learning algorithm that outputs the outline of the most relevant regions within the image and their names. Two noteworthy aspects of the proposed game are: (i) it solves two computer vision problems – object detection and labeling – in a single game; and (ii) it learns spatial relations within the image from game logs. The game has been evaluated through user studies, which confirmed that it was easy to understand, intuitive, and fun to play.

1 Introduction

There are many open problems in computer vision (e.g., object detection) for which state-of-the-art solutions still fall short of performing perfectly. The realization that many of those tasks are arduous for computers and yet relatively easy for humans has inspired many researchers to approach those problems from a 'human computation' viewpoint, using methods that include crowdsourcing ("a way of solving problem based on a large number of small contributions from a large number of different persons") and games – often called, more specifically, "games with a purpose (GWAPs)" [1].

In this paper we propose a novel approach to solving a subset of computer vision problems – namely *object detection and labeling*[1] – using games and describe Ask'nSeek, a two-player web-based guessing game targeted at the tasks of object detection and labeling. Ask'nSeek asks users to guess the location of a small rectangular region hidden within an image with the help of semantic and topological clues (e.g., "to the right of the bus"), by clicking on the image location which they believe corresponds to (one of the points of) the hidden region. Once enough games have been played using a given image, our novel machine learning algorithm combines user-provided input (coordinates of clicked points and spatial relationships between points and regions – 'above', 'below', 'left', 'right', 'on', 'partially on', or 'none') with results from off-the-shelf computer vision algorithms applied to the image, to produce the outline (bounding

---

[1] In this paper we use the phrase *object labeling* to refer to the process of assigning a textual label to an object's bounding box.

A. Fusiello et al. (Eds.): ECCV 2012 Ws/Demos, Part I, LNCS 7583, pp. 249–258, 2012.

box) of the most relevant regions within the image and their associated labels. These results can be compared against manually generated ground-truth (if such information is available) or used as semi-automatically generated ground truth for researchers in associated fields. Figure 1 shows examples of object detection and labeling results for two images from the PASCAL VOC 2007 dataset.

Fig. 1. Examples of object detection and labeling results obtained with the game-based approach described in this paper: (left) four objects /regions were detected and their bounding boxes were labeled as 'woman', 'sky', 'motorbikes', and 'man'; (right) two objects ('cat' and 'dog') were detected and labeled

2   Related Work

The idea of using games with the purpose of collecting useful data for computer vision has been brought first by Luis von Ahn and his ESP game [2]. In that game, two players are paired randomly and assigned the task of looking at the same image and typing keyword descriptions of the image. They score points when they manage to type the same keyword; in that case the word becomes part of the tags describing the image. This game has been initially devised to address the problem of constructing ground truth database for training computer vision algorithms. In the same spirit, Peekaboom [3], a subsequent and complementary game, goes a step further since it consists in locating objects (labeled by ESP) in a given image. Two players are again paired randomly: while one player reveals parts of the image, the other (who initially sees nothing from the image) has to guess the correct associated label.

In 2009, Ho et al. postulated that the cooperative nature of the ESP game has a number of limitations, including the generation of less specific or diverse labeling results, and proposed a competitive game for image annotation: KissKissBan [4]. Their game uses a *couple*, whose objective is the same as the players in the ESP Game (i.e., to guess what the partner is typing), but introduces the role of *blocker*, a third party who has 7 seconds to provide a list of blocked words, which contains the words he thinks couples might match on. They show that the results from their game have higher entropy than the ones produced by the ESP game (used as baseline for comparison), and are, therefore, more diverse.

More recently, Steggink and Snoek [5] presented the Name-It-Game, an interactive region-based image annotation game, whose labels are semantically enhanced by means of the WordNet ontology. Name-It is a two-player game in which players switch roles (either *revealer* or *guesser*) after each turn. The revealer is shown an image and a list of words, from which he selects an object name, chooses the definition (obtained via WordNet) that best describes the sense in which that word is used in that particular image, and outlines the object of interest using a combination of polygonal and freehand segmentation, in order to progressively reveal an object in an image to the guesser. The guesser has to guess the name of the object (or a synonym) and may ask for hints during the guessing process.

In another recent effort, Ni et al. [6] have designed P-HOG (Purposive Hidden-Object-Game), a single-player game in which the goal is to locate an object that has been artificially embedded (i.e., hidden) within an image by drawing a bounding box around it.

The main difference between Ask'nSeek and all of the above-mentioned games is that it does not require any player to explicitly outline regions or objects (or draw bounding boxes around them). Most importantly, Ask'nSeek is better than any of its predecessors in the sense that our game was designed to conceal the desired tasks expected to be performed by the users (labeling regions, clicking on relevant points within the image, and establishing meaningful spatial relationships between points and regions) while keeping it quick and entertaining.

3   The Game

3.1   Basic Structure, Terminology, and Rules

Ask'nSeek is a two-player, web-based, game that can be played on a contemporary browser without any need for plug-ins. One player, the *master* (Figure 2(b)) hides a rectangular region somewhere within a randomly chosen image. The second player (*seeker*) (Figure 2(a)) tries to guess the location of the hidden region through a series of successive guesses, expressed by clicking at some point in the image. What makes the game more interesting is that, rather than just blindly clicking around, the seeker must ask the master for clues relative to some meaningful object within the image before each and every click. Once the master receives a request for a clue from the seeker containing a label, it is *required* to provide a spatial relation, which is selected from a list: {above, below, to the right of, to the left of, on, partially on, none of the above}. These *indications* – in the form of (spatial relation, label), e.g., "below the dog" – accumulate throughout the game and are expected to be jointly taken into account by the seeker during game play. Based on the previously selected points and the indications provided by the master, the seeker can refine their next guesses and – hopefully – guess the hidden region after relatively few attempts. The game is played in *cooperative mode*, i.e., the master wants the seeker to locate the region as quickly as possible, which usually leads to accurate clues and game logs with high quality information.

According to the classification in [1], Ask'nSeek is an "Inversion-Problem game", because "given an input, Player 1 (in our case, called *master*) produces an output, and Player 2 (the *seeker*) guesses the input". More specifically, the *input* in question is the location of the hidden region within an image and the *outputs* produced by Player 1 are what we call *indications*.

(a)   (b)

Fig. 2. Screenshots of the Ask'nSeek game: (a) seeker's screen; (b) master's screen

- **Initial Setup:** Two players are randomly chosen by the game itself.
- **Rules:** The master produces an input (by hiding a rectangular region within an image). Based on this input, the master produces outputs (spatial clues, i.e., indications) that are sent to the seeker. The outputs from the master should help the seeker produce the original input, i.e., locate the hidden box.
- **Winning Condition:** The seeker produces the input that was originally produced by the master, i.e., guesses the correct location by clicking on any pixel within the hidden bounding box.

3.2   Interpretation of Game Logs through a Machine Learning Algorithm

The machine learning strategy adopted in our work lies within the "semi-supervised clustering with constraints" framework. It combines data from two main sources: game logs and output of suitable computer vision algorithms. The game logs contain labels as well as 'on', 'partially on' and 'left-right-above-below' relations. Examples of labels include foreground objects (e.g., dog, bus) as well as other semantically meaningful regions within the image (e.g., sky, road).

We employ various content analysis algorithms (e.g., bottom-up saliency maps, interest point detectors) to derive a set of points that we will try to cluster in our model. For example, if we take as an input a saliency map, we randomly choose points following the distribution described by the saliency map. The goal of our algorithm is then to estimate a mixture of Gaussians that best describes our set of points, in which each resulting 2D Gaussian is assigned a label obtained from the game logs.

The indications given by players are used in different ways, depending on their type:

- the 'left-right-above-below' relations are used to create starting bounding boxes and can be seen as "hard constraints", i.e., the associated Gaussian can never be contradictory with these relations;
- the 'on' relations help us initialize the position for a Gaussian; and
- the 'partially on' relations can be seen as a "soft constraint" and provide information on the limits of a Gaussian. We use it to limit the size of the corresponding Gaussian, i.e. to constrain to the growth of the associated bounding boxes.

We grow the Gaussians and force them to respect the constraints described above. When the algorithm stops we compute a bounding box for each Gaussian and (for visualization purposes) overlay it on the image with its associated label.

4   Evaluation

In this section we describe several steps used to evaluate the feasibility of the approach, the minimum number of games needed to produce enough information for the underlying machine learning algorithm, and the quality of results obtained on images for which enough games have been played.

4.1   Simulating Game Logs – Experiments with Synthetic Data

After having conceived, designed, and implemented the Ask'nSeek game and performed a preliminary user study that showed that it is potentially fun to play, we proceeded to assess the quality of the data that can be collected and inferred from game logs. To do so, we decided to simulate a large number of game logs and analyze the generated traces, first by taking everything into account and then by limiting ourselves to a tiny fraction of the total number of simulated games.

Simulation Principles. We designed a game simulator whose goal was to enable us to quickly acquire a large amount of ready-to-use data (i.e., game logs) without having to deploy the game at a large scale and collect data from many users. Moreover, as a bonus, we might achieve a deeper understanding of how the game data enables our machine learning algorithm to do its job which, consequently, might lead to improvements and refinements of the game itself. The game simulator makes several important assumptions, among them: (i) the master never lies about the spatial relationship between the hidden region and a labeled region in the image; (ii) the seeker never makes mistakes, such as clicking on a pixel that should be ruled out due to previously received clues (this assumption also implies that the seeker has "perfect memory" and takes *all* previous clues into account before guessing the location for the next click); (iii) we have complete control over the labels, i.e., they come from a preselected vocabulary (consistent with the ground truth annotations for the PASCAL VOC dataset) and they do not contain any noise, misspellings, etc.; and (iv) neither master nor seeker "gives up" before having attempted all feasible options.

The first step of the simulation consists in the generation of a ground truth segmentation and labeling of the image. We have adopted the same conventions and terminology used in the PASCAL VOC dataset to associate each object to its surrounding bounding box and a label, and extended it to background elements such as sky, road, etc. This was based on observations from the first user study, where users reported that they tend to use *all the information present in the image* – rather than just the objects associated with PASCAL VOC object detectors – to find the hidden region more easily and quickly.

Once we have produced ground truth for an image, we generate simulated player traces for each simulated game, using an algorithm that models all the typical steps during game play, from the master's choice at the beginning, to the game logic used to determine if there is a winner or not and whether there is any clue that the master may still provide to the seeker.

Assessing the Impact of the Number of Games. We generated 10,000 game simulations for every test image. Each entry in the game log associates the coordinates of a point, a spatial relation, and a label.

First we considered only the game logs that use the spatial relations "above", "below","on the left of" and "on the right of". We then used that information to build a bounding box limiting the region that respects all the constraints defined by these relations, within which the object must reside. Figure 3(a) plots in black all the points that fall outside this bounding box for the 'dog' object.

(a)   (b)

Fig. 3. Analysis of simulation logs with different number of simulated games: (a) 10,000 games; (b) 7 games. See text for details

Second, we augmented the amount of information provided by the bounding box by incorporating the spatial relation "on". The information provided by these points is very strong, because they state with certainty that a point which is "on" an object is actually part of it. Rather than just using the (x,y) coordinates of the "on" points, we use the SLIC superpixel segmentation algorithm implementation from [7] to split the image into subregions, i.e., to "grow" each "on" point to its corresponding superpixel. By doing so, we consider not only the point, but the entire segmented region it belongs to, as being "on" the object. Such regions are plotted in red on Figure 3. We apply the same treatment to "partially on" points and plot the corresponding superpixels in green on Figure 3.

Figure 3(a) shows that the combination of superpixels corresponding to "on" and "partially on" points from 10,000 game logs produces an almost perfect rectangular bounding box. For the sake of comparison, Figure 3(b) shows the equivalent points if only a very small subset of our simulated game logs, in this case seven games, is taken into account.

4.2   Examples of Results from Actual Game Logs

After deploying the game and collecting actual game logs, we performed a preliminary (mostly qualitative) evaluation of the object detection and labeling results obtained using the proposed approach. Figure 4 shows the direct outputs of our model (where the

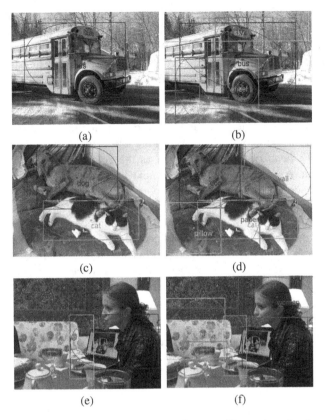

Fig. 4. Representative outputs of our model for three images of increasing visual complexity: (left column) dominant labels only; (right column) 5 most frequent labels. See text for details.

final bounding boxes enclose the Gaussian ellipses produced by the machine learning algorithm), once it has been applied to real traces for three different PASCAL VOC images: 2007_003137, 2007_002597, 2007_002914. In a sense, these three images present an increasing visual richness: one bus, two pets and many objects. We collected 19 games and 56 indications for the bus image, 17 games and 44 indications for the cat and dog image and 19 games and 57 indications for the woman. As an example, the 44 indications for the cat and dog image are made of 2 'above' indications, 13 'below', 10 'left', 5 'right', 9 'on' and 5 'partially on'. The average length of the games is $44/17 = 2.6$ indications which actually shows that Ask'n'Seek finishes rather quickly on this image. The average number or indications per game is 3.0 for the two other images.

Figure 4 allows us to compare the results produced by our model in two distinct cases: using only the most cited labels (on the left column) and with the 5 most cited labels (on the right). For the bus image, the most cited label is *bus* (24 occurrences), followed by *wheel* (8), *door* (7), *sky* (5) and *"ecolier"* (5 occurrences). Figure 4(a)-(b) highlight the existing interactions between clusters: when five labels are used (b), the size and shape of the dominant cluster (*bus*) changes a bit, when compared to the result for only one label (a). For the cat and dog image, the most cited labels, by far, are *dog* (used 16 times) and *cat* (16 times as well). By only handling these two dominant labels (the next most cited labels are cited 5 times or less), we obtain the result shown in Figure 4(c). In addition, we extracted richer labels from the game data, namely: 5 occurrences of *head* (2 *cat's head*, 3 *dog's head*), as well as 5 *legs* and 2 *nose* labels combined with *cat, dog, front, back* in a more complex way, which naturally corresponds to multiple instances (of heads, noses, etc.). In our current implementation, we don't handle these composite labels for 'parts of objects'. When the label *cat's head* is cited, it increases the count of *cat's head* occurrences as well as the count for *cat*, since this label is already dominant. As a consequence, the 3 next labels presented in Figure 4(d) are *paper* (4 occurrences), *wall*, and *pillow* (3 occurrences each). The results for label *wall* are reasonably good despite the fact that we didn't collect any 'on' points for it, i.e., the Gaussian cluster for *wall* simply fits within its bounding box. Figure 4(e)-(f) show the result for an image for which no obvious object emerges. Many labels are cited with almost the same frequency. We collected 8 occurrences of *computer*, 7 of *cake*, 6 of *woman*, 6 for *couch* and 5 for *glass* as well as fewer occurrences of *tea pot, cup of coffee, carpet, nose, head* etc. We chose to highlight the two most frequent ones (*computer* and *cake*) in part(e), and extend to include *woman, couch* and *glass* in part(f).

4.3   Comparison against a Baseline Object Detector

In this subsection we show a preliminary visual (i.e., qualitative) comparison between the results obtained with the Ask'nSeek game (with information from only 17 games) and the results produced by a state-of-the-art object detection algorithm, namely the "Discriminatively Trained Deformable Part Models" approach [8][2]. Figure 5 show representative results for the 'dog' and 'cat' objects and illustrate how our approach reduces the total number of false positives and improves the overall quality (i.e., size and location) of the bounding boxes.

5   User Studies

In this section we report the results of a preliminary evaluation after having enlisted 40 users to play the game, and highlight results obtained from these game logs.

Here is the protocol we followed for the user study.

1. The game is web-based and implemented in HTML5, i.e., no plug-in is required to play. We use a classical client/server architecture, in which the server handles the communications between the players (i.e., the clients) as well as the flow of the game and persists players' interactions into a database.

---

[2] We used the MATLAB code available at [9], which contains the official implementation of [8]. We followed the instructions provided by the authors and left the threshold parameter unspecified (default option).

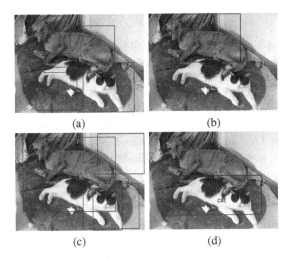

(a)   (b)

(c)   (d)

Fig. 5. Representative representative results: (a) baseline dog detector from [9]; (b) result from our approach for label 'dog'; (c) baseline cat detector from [9]; (d) result from our approach for label 'cat'

2. We used ten images from the PASCAL VOC dataset. This dataset was chosen because of its popularity for benchmarking in object detection and related tasks and for its public availability. After a sequence of games is played, we randomly permute the images.

3. We had a tutoring process, during which the game was explained to users (in a computer lab setting). Both master and seeker roles were described in detail, and game aspects such as the exact meaning of each spatial relation were carefully explained.

4. We collected data from 40 participants (25 males and 15 females), with ages ranging from 18 to 62. Each game requires a pair of participants. Each pair is allowed to play as many games as they desire. The total number of games played in this first user study was 148, with an average of 3.1 indications per game.

5. Players made use of all the spatial relations they were provided with. 'On the left' represents 18% of the indications, 'on the right' 19%, 'above' 15%, 'below' 19%, 'on' 13%, 'partially on' 12% and finally 'can't relate' 4%.

6. At the end of the process, users were asked to evaluate the game on four major aspects – enjoyability, simplicity, ergonomics and clarity – using a Likert scale, ranging from 'very good' (5) to 'very bad' (1). These are the results: enjoyability: 3.6; simplicity: 3.9; ergonomics: 3.4; and clarity: 3.7. In addition, users were asked if they would be interested in playing again at a later time, to which 40% answered "Yes", 45% said "Why not?", and 15% replied "No".

In summary, most of the players found the game enjoyable and fun to play.

6 Conclusions

This paper proposed a novel approach to solving a selected subset of computer vision problems using games and described Ask'nSeek, a novel, simple, fun, web-based guessing game based on images, their most relevant regions, and the spatial relationships among them. Two noteworthy aspects of the proposed game are: (i) it does in *one game* what ESP [2] and Peekaboom [3] do in *two* games (namely, collecting labels and locating the objects associated with those labels); and (ii) it avoids explicitly asking the user to map labels and regions thanks to our novel semi-supervised learning algorithm.

We also described how the information collected from *very few* game logs per image was used to feed a machine learning algorithm, which in turn produces the outline of the most relevant regions within the image and their labels.

Our game can also be extended and improved in several directions, among them: different game modes, timer(s), addition of a social component (e.g., play against your Facebook friends), extending the interface to allow touchscreen gestures for tablet-based play, and incorporation of incentives to the game, e.g., badges or coins, which should – among other things – encourage switching roles (master-seeker) periodically.

References

1. von Ahn, L., Dabbish, L.: Designing games with a purpose. Commun. ACM 51, 58–67 (2008)
2. von Ahn, L., Dabbish, L.: Esp: Labeling images with a computer game. In: AAAI Spring Symposium: Knowledge Collection from Volunteer Contributors, pp. 91–98 (2005)
3. von Ahn, L., Liu, R., Blum, M.: Peekaboom: a game for locating objects in images. In: CHI, pp. 55–64 (2006)
4. Ho, C.J., Chang, T.H., Lee, J.C., Jen Hsu, J.Y., Chen, K.T.: Kisskissban: a competitive human computation game for image annotation. SIGKDD Expl. 12, 21–24 (2010)
5. Steggink, J., Snoek, C.G.M.: Adding semantics to image-region annotations with the name-it-game. Multimedia Systems 17, 367–378 (2011)
6. Ni, Y., Dong, J., Feng, J., Yan, S.: Purposive hidden-object-game: embedding human computation in popular game. In: ACM MM 2011, pp. 1121–1124 (2011)
7. Vedaldi, A., Fulkerson, B.: VLFeat: An open and portable library of computer vision algorithms (2008), http://www.vlfeat.org/
8. Felzenszwalb, P., Girshick, R., McAllester, D., Ramanan, D.: Object detection with discriminatively trained part-based models. IEEE Trans. PAMI 32, 1627–1645 (2010)
9. Felzenszwalb, P., Girshick, R., McAllester, D.: Discriminatively trained deformable part models, release 4, http://people.cs.uchicago.edu/~pff/latent-release4/

Learning to Match Images in Large-Scale Collections

Song Cao and Noah Snavely

Cornell University
Ithaca, NY, 14853

Abstract. Many computer vision applications require computing structure and feature correspondence across a large, unorganized image collection. This is a computationally expensive process, because the graph of matching image pairs is unknown in advance, and so methods for quickly and accurately predicting which of the $O(n^2)$ pairs of images match are critical. Image comparison methods such as bag-of-words models or global features are often used to predict similar pairs, but can be very noisy. In this paper, we propose a new image matching method that uses discriminative learning techniques—applied to training data gathered automatically during the image matching process—to gradually compute a better similarity measure for predicting whether two images in a given collection overlap. By using such a learned similarity measure, our algorithm can select image pairs that are more likely to match for performing further feature matching and geometric verification, improving the overall efficiency of the matching process. Our approach processes a set of images in an iterative manner, alternately performing pairwise feature matching and learning an improved similarity measure. Our experiments show that our learned measures can significantly improve match prediction over the standard *tf-idf*-weighted similarity and more recent unsupervised techniques even with small amounts of training data, and can improve the overall speed of the image matching process by more than a factor of two.

1 Introduction

A key problem in recent Web-scale vision systems is to take a large, unstructured image collection (e.g., a large set of Internet photos) and discover its visual connectivity structure, i.e., determine which images overlap which other images, in the form of an *image graph*, and find feature correspondence between matching images. Finding this structure often involves testing many pairs of images, by matching SIFT features and performing geometric verification. For example, 3D reconstruction methods for large-scale Internet photos—such as all photos of Rome—require finding feature correspondence by matching many pairs of images [1, 2], and other applications, such as summarizing photo collections [3] and unsupervised discovery of objects [4] require similar connectivity information. The computational cost for such feature matching and geometric verification can be quite high, especially if more than a small fraction of the total $O(n^2)$ possible image pairs in a set of n images are matched. However, many large image collections exhibit sparse visual connectivity—only a fraction of possible image pairs overlap. The question is then: how can we compute a good approximation of the image connectivity graph, as efficiently as possible? We present a method that

A. Fusiello et al. (Eds.): ECCV 2012 Ws/Demos, Part I, LNCS 7583, pp. 259–270, 2012.

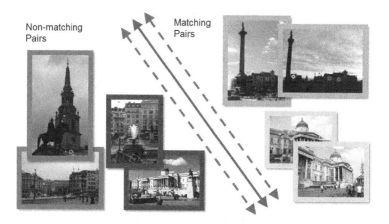

Fig. 1. Training an SVM classifier with positive and negative image pairs. Although each image pair (images with borders of the same color) shown above contain images with many common visual words (shown as boxes with same colors each pair), some pairs are true matches (top right), while others are false matches (bottom left). Accordingly, some visual words are more discriminative (or confusing) than others. Our goal is to learn a weighting of different visual words to better predict matching and non-matching image pairs. This weighting is shown here as a max-margin separating hyperplane. The images shown above are from the **Trafalgar** dataset.

Fig. 2. Two example visual words with different discriminative power. The three images on the left contain a common visual word (in green), which is highly weighted by our learned model. In contrast, the three images on the right also share a common visual word (in red), but do not match; this word is given low weight.

learns a good measure for comparing images during such an image matching process, improving this measure as it discovers the structure of the image graph.

To avoid exhaustive feature matching on all $O(n^2)$ image pairs, recent work has used fast, whole-image similarity measures, such as bag-of-words (BoW) [5, 1, 2, 4] or GIST features [6], to predict a smaller set of candidate image pairs on which to perform detailed matching. BoW methods in particular, often used in image retrieval [7], have had increasing success for this image matching problem. However, BoW similarities are quite noisy, due to quantization error and imperfect feature detections. As a result, when used to predict image pairs for matching, many cycles are wasted matching features between non-overlapping images, making the matching process unnecessarily time-consuming.

In this paper, we explore a new, iterative approach that learns to predict which pairs of images in an input dataset match, and which do not, using discriminative learning of BoW models. Our method adapts over time in the process of discovering the structure of the image graph; as it attempts to match pairs of input images, the results are used as training data to learn a model specific for that dataset. Motivating our approach is the observation that some visual words are inherently more reliable for measuring image similarity than others, and that these good features seem to be specific to a given dataset (e.g., images of Times Square). For example, some visual words might be more stable across viewpoint and illumination, or less sensitive to quantization errors, than others (Figure 2). This suggests that if each visual word is correctly weighted, then our ability to predict whether two images match can improve. While there are many unsupervised ways to define such weights—e.g., *tf-idf* weighting [5], burstiness [8], co-occurrence measures [9]—we explore the use of supervised learning to find a good set of weights, given example pairs of matching and non-matching image pairs from an image set. Unlike prior heuristic approaches, our method is free to leverage whatever structure is present in the data to learn to separate matching image pairs from non-matching pairs.

Given a collection of images (represented as BoW histograms) of a place, our method starts with an unsupervised similarity measure (e.g., *tf-idf*) and automatically generates training data by first finding a small number of image pairs with high similarity, then applying relatively expensive feature matching and verification steps on these pairs. This results in both positive image pairs (successful matches) and negative pairs (unsuccessful matches). We then use discriminative learning (e.g., SVMs), to learn a new similarity measure on features derived from these example image pairs, by posing this as a linear classification problem. Unlike many classification problems, these features are formed from image *pairs*, rather than individual images, as illustrated in Figure 1. This process iterates, alternating between proposing more images to match, and learning a better similarity measure. We show that, even with very small amounts of training data, our learned models consistently outperform recent unsupervised techniques. Moreover, the overhead of learning is quite low; the linear SVMs we use are extremely efficient to compute, even when using a vocabulary of 1M visual words.

Our contributions are two-fold. First, we propose a fast, simple method for using discriminative learning to classify image pairs in large-scale matching problems, showing significant improvement over state-of-the-art unsupervised methods; we also show that a modified form of regularization, as well as drawing negative training examples from unrelated datasets, can improve our learned models. Second, we propose a new iterative image matching method, based on this learning approach, that can reduce the amount of time needed to find matches in large image sets by a factor of more than two on average.

2 Related Work

Bag-of-Words Models and Image Retrieval. In BoW models, features such as SIFT [10] are extracted from an input image, then vector-quantized according to a vocabulary of visual words learned from a large set of features (ideally from a related dataset). An image is then represented as a histogram over visual words. Often *tf-idf* weighting is applied to these histograms [5], inspired by techniques from text retrieval. The similarity of an image pair can then be computed as, say, the dot product or histogram intersection of their weighted histograms. BoW models are often used in image retrieval, but are also common in object classification problems [11], where they have been shown to work well combined with discriminative methods. Our problem differs from traditional classification problems in that we seek to classify *pairs* of images of some scene as matching or non-matching, rather than classifying images into categories. This fits our goal of discovering the structure of a large input collection; such collections are often better described as a graph of pairwise connections, rather than a set of discrete categories. While our problem is related to image retrieval, it differs in that the database and query images are one and the same, and we want to discover the structure of the database from scratch—we aren't matching to a database known in advance. However, we build on methods of computing weights for visual words proposed in the retrieval literature. Many such methods are, like *tf-idf* weighting, unsupervised; Jegou et al. downweight confusing features by modeling burstiness in BoW models [8], while Chum et al. downweight highly correlated sets of visual words ("co-ocsets") [9]; sparse methods have also been applied to identifying informative features [12]. Although such unsupervised weighting schemes improve retrieval performance, we find that supervised learning can exploit structure in the data for our image matching problem much more effectively (Figure 4). Other methods use a form of supervision, but in a more limited way. For instance, Mikulik et al. create a very fine visual vocabulary and compute a probabilistic model of correlations between similar words [13]; others use image geo-tags [14, 15] to select important features. Probably most related to our work is that of Turcot and Lowe, who also gauge feature importance by performing image matching [16]. However, their approach requires matching every image to k other database images, then modifying each database vector individually. In contrast, our discriminative learning approach can generalize much more efficiently, learning a useful metric before touching much of the database, which is key to our goal of quickly predicting matching images in large collections. Supervised learning has also been applied to learn better features through non-linear projection of feature descriptors [17]. We instead learn linear classifiers in the high-dimensional BoW feature space.

Distance Metric Learning. Our problem can be considered as treating images as high-dimensional feature vectors, and learning a distance metric between images [18–20]. We forumulate this as learning a classifier over pairs of images, predicting a binary variable (matching/non-matching) for each pair. Although online similarity learning over images has been considered before [21, 22], these formulate the learning problem using triplets of training images; in our problem setting, however, matching or non-matching image *pairs* are more readily available as training data, motivating our formulation. While our automatic training data generation procedure is related to that of [4], we use it in an iterative manner to achieve a different objective than learning topic models.

3   Our Approach

Given a set of images $\mathcal{I}$ of a location, our goal is to efficiently compute an image graph on $\mathcal{I}$ with edges linking overlapping images, by performing detailed SIFT matching and geometric verification on some set of image pairs (edges). Through this matching process, we can determine whether or not the pair overlaps (and which features correspond), by thresholding on the number of geometrically consistent matches. For large collections, we wish to check a small subset of the $O(n^2)$ possible edges, yielding an approximate graph; hence, we want to intelligently select a subset of edges to match, so as to quickly compute as complete a graph as possible. Our approach seeks an efficient way to predict whether or not a given image pair will match, by learning over time how to classify pairs of images as matching or non-matching. In this section, we formulate this problem as a one of discriminative learning, and propose an iterative approach that alternates between detailed images matching and learning a discriminative model using the matching results.

3.1 Discriminative Learning of a Classifier for Image Pairs

Consider two images represented as *tf-idf* weighted, sparse, normalized BoW histograms a and b, each with dimension n (with n equal to, say, 1 million). A typical similarity measure $sim(a, b)$ is the cosine similarity, i.e., the dot product $sim(a, b) = a^T b$. A more general way to define a similarity function is $sim(a, b) = a^T M b$, where M is a symmetric $n \times n$ matrix. When M is the identity matrix, this definition reduces to the *tf-idf*-weighted similarity (since a and b are "pre-weighted" with their *tf-idf* weights).[1] At the other extreme, one could learn a full matrix M; however, this would be expensive given the high dimensionality of the histograms. In our case, we restrict our method to learning a diagonal matrix W, which results in a *weighted* dot product of the histograms: $sim(a, b) = a^T W b = \sum_i w_i a_i b_i$, where the w_i's are the diagonal entries of W. Note that we do not enforce that the w_i's are non-negative, hence $sim(a, b)$ not a true metric; nonetheless, we can still use the output as a decision value for prediction. While forcing M to be diagonal is somewhat limiting, our results suggest that this method still works well in the high-dimensional space of BoW histograms.

Our goal, then, is to learn a weighting w_i on different dimensions of the visual vocabulary specific to a given dataset; for this, we use the tools of discriminative learning. For a pair of images (a, b), we define a feature vector $x^{a,b}$ as the vector of pair-wise products of corresponding dimensions of a and b: $x_i^{a,b} = a_i b_i$. Given these features, $sim(a, b)$ is simply the dot product of the weight vector w with the feature vector $x^{a,b}$.[2] Given this representation, there is a natural formulation of the learning problem as that of learning a hyperplane—or equivalently a set of weights w_i—that separate positive (matching) pairs with negative (non-matching) pairs of images. For this problem, we can automatically generate training data by checking if two images match using detailed SIFT matching and geometric verification: pairs (a, b) that pass become positive training examples $x^{a,b}$ with label $y = 1$; pairs (c, d) that do not match become negative training examples $x^{c,d}$ with label $y = -1$. Figure 1 illustrates this formulation.

---

[1] We found that such preweighting works better than raw histograms for our learning method.

[2] Other features defined on an image pair could also be used; e.g., defining the features as the element-wise *min* of the two vectors results in a weighted histogram intersection similarity, and creating a feature vector from all n^2 products of word pairs results in learning a full matrix M.

Fig. 3. Correct predictions of non-matching pairs. Due to challenging differences in contrast, illumination and viewpoints, these two image pairs both failed the SIFT matching and verification process, despite exhibiting visual overlap (as well as common visual words, which are marked with boxes of the same color). In contrast, our model is able to correctly highly rank these images, as they happen to have very discriminative visual words (in red). Note that the common visual words may not always imply exact correspondence (e.g., because of repeating patterns).

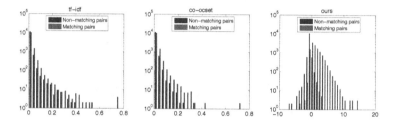

Fig. 4. Histograms of matching vs. non-matching testing pairs. From left to right: histograms of *tf-idf* similarity, co-ocset similarity [9] and our output values ($\sim$100K training pairs) respectively, for matching and non-matching test pairs. Note the log scale on the y-axis. The test pairs consist of randomly chosen unseen image pairs from the **TateModern** dataset.

We use L_2-regularized L_2-loss SVMs for learning, which in our problem optimize:

$$\min_w \frac{1}{2} w^T w + C \sum_{(a,b) \in S} (\max(0, 1 - y^{a,b} w^T x^{a,b}))^2, \qquad (1)$$

where S is the set of training pairs (a, b). The output weight vector w defines a separating hyperplane, but we also interpret it as a similarity measure (a weighted dot product).

While we find that standard linear SVMs work well given sufficient training data, in our setting we start out with no training data, as it is only generated once we start matching images. Given small amounts of training data, standard SVMs can severely overfit the data, performing worse than *tf-idf* weighting. We propose two extensions to address this problem. First, if negative examples from other image collections are available, we find that these can boost the performance when combined with current training data (though positive examples don't seem to help). Second, we utilize a *modified regularization* for SVMs that uses the *tf-idf* weights as a prior. In particular, our modified approach regularizes the weight vector w to be close to a vector of all ones, w_0 (representing *tf-idf* weighting). To regularize, we substitute w in the regularization term in (1) with $w - w_0$, and solve this modified optimization problem. This smoothly transitions between the original *tf-idf* weights and our learned weights, and softly enforces positiveness of the weights, which helps in preventing overfitting and showing significant improvement over both approaches given limited amounts of training data (Section 4).

Compared to the feature selection method of Turcot and Lowe [16], we do not rely on explicit correspondence found by SIFT, and instead allow the SVMs to choose the weights as they see fit. Interestingly, although our training data is defined by the output of feature matching, in some cases feature matching fails to identify truly matching image pairs, that our learned model can correctly predict (Figure 3). Figure 4 demonstrates the predictive power of our method, by comparing histograms of similarities for matching and non-matching pairs generated by our approach and two unsupervised methods (*tf-idf* and the co-ocset method [9]) on the TateModern dataset (Section 4). Our method can significantly improve separability of matching and non-matching pairs.

3.2 Iterative Learning and Matching

In practice, given a new set of images, there is initially no training data to learn from. However, given even a relatively small amount of training data, our algorithm can still boost performance in predicting matching and non-matching image pairs. Thus, we can bootstrap by matching a small subset of pairs, then learning a better similarity measure from the outcome of matching. We start by using the vanilla *tf-idf* weighted image similarities to rank, for each image, all other images. Then our method performs SIFT matching and verification on a small number of highly-ranked image pairs, and trains a linear SVM using the resulting training data. We use the resulting classifier weights to recompute a similarity measure, to re-rank the candidate lists for all images. The system then resumes the image matching process using the new rankings, and repeats.

Given a learned similarity measure, there are many ways to decide the order in which to attempt to match image pairs. We considered two simple strategies: one is to match all image pairs with similarity values above some threshold; the other is to go down re-ranked candidate lists of each images "layer by layer", matching each image to its most similar candidate in turn. These two strategies have different impacts on the overall system behaviour. In general, the threshold-based strategy generates a higher percentage of true matching pairs out of all pairs tested, while the layer-based strategy "grows" the image graph more uniformly. In our experiments, we adopt the layer-based strategy, as it is less biased towards parts of the image set that are initially ranked as very similar.

4 Experiments

To evaluate our approach, we collected 5 image datasets from Flickr, each corresponding to a popular landmark and consisting of several thousand images, as summarized in Table 1. The sets were chosen so that each contains a diversity of views, rather than a single dominant view that would be relatively easy to learn an appearance model for. In addition, each dataset contains images that are not pertinent to the scene itself, such as close-ups of people and photos of water. We created a vocabulary of 1M visual words [23] on SIFT features from a separate set of images of Rome, used for all 5 datasets. We also tested our method on two standard image retrieval datasets, Oxford5K and Paris [7, 24]; for each we learned specific vocabularies from the database images. We used LIBLINEAR and SVM-LIGHT[3] to learn our SVMs.

4.1 Performance of Discriminative Learning

First, there are a few key questions that we'd like to answer: How much training data do we need to see an improvement, and how quickly does performance improve with more training data? How much do our two proposed extensions help given limited data? In the limit, given large amounts of training data, how good of a similarity function can we learn for a given location? To answer these questions, we devised an experiment testing how well our approach can separate matching and non-matching pairs in each dataset, given different amounts and types of training data. A perfect similarity measure will, for any given image in the dataset, rank all of the matching images in the rest of the dataset above all of the non-matching ones. To measure this, we selected 50 images for each dataset as "queries" and created ground truth by performing SIFT matching and geometric consistency check between these images and all of the other images in that set (for Oxford5K and Paris, however, the standard query images and ground truth are used). We compare our performance with two unsupervised baseline methods: raw *tf-idf* [5] and co-occurrence set (co-ocset) [9] similarities. We measure the quality of the ranking of the rest of the dataset for each query by the average precision (AP), and performance of each model is measured by its mean AP (mAP) over our test set (higher is better).

We trained SVMs with 200, 1,000, and 2,000 randomly sampled image pairs (with no test query images involved in the training), using equal numbers of positive and negative pairs, and determining the regularization parameter C through cross-validation. To gauge how well our method can perform in the limit, we also trained models with a much larger training set (around 100K training pairs) for each dataset. We also test the effect of our proposed two extensions: modified regularization and adding negative training pairs from an unrelated image set; for the latter, we used the same set of about 1M negative examples from several other datasets.[4]

The results are shown in Table 1. For our 5 Flickr datasets, our models trained with 200 examples (with standard regularization) are slightly worse on average than *tf-idf* similarity, probably due to overfitting to insufficient training data, but both extensions of our approach prove effective in dealing with this issue, each exceeding our baselines on average. Unsupervised co-ocset similarity also shows improvement over *tf-idf* similarity, but our models consistently outperform both; even our unmodified method trained with 1,000 examples outperforms both baselines, and with 2,000 examples the mAP improves even further. The performance of models trained with ~100K examples jumps by a significant margin, illustrating the large potential improvement of our discriminative learning approach over time. Note that 100K examples is still a small

---

[3] http://www.csie.ntu.edu.tw/~cjlin/liblinear/,
http://svmlight.joachims.org/

[4] We only test adding such negative data for our 5 Flickr sets, as they share a common vocabulary.

Table 1. mAP performance of models trained with various training data sizes. The baselines are the mAP scores for rankings using *tf-idf* similarity and co-ocset similarity [9]. Columns marked with **200**, **1000**, **2000**, and **∼100K** show the performance of models trained with corresponding number of examples. N**+neg** corresponds to models trained with the same set of N examples combined with large amounts of negative examples from other datasets; N**+mr** denotes models trained with the same set of N examples using our modified regularization.

Dataset	#img	tf-idf	co-ocset	200	200+neg	200+mr	1000	1000+neg	1000+mr	2000	2000+neg	2000+mr	∼100K
Trafalgar	6981	0.558	0.563	0.620	0.629	0.653	0.689	0.703	0.698	0.719	0.733	0.725	0.794
LondonEye	7047	0.621	0.629	0.586	0.632	0.657	0.650	0.676	0.677	0.673	0.694	0.687	0.783
TateModern	4813	0.712	0.716	0.771	0.793	0.813	0.828	0.835	0.836	0.839	0.851	0.846	0.884
SanMarco	7792	0.577	0.601	0.518	0.535	0.618	0.606	0.633	0.636	0.637	0.658	0.658	0.766
TimesSquare	6426	0.491	0.492	0.410	0.446	0.503	0.474	0.535	0.511	0.498	0.563	0.518	0.617
Average		0.592	0.600	0.581	0.607	0.649	0.650	0.676	0.672	0.673	0.700	0.687	0.769
Oxford5K [7]	5062	0.592	0.608	0.303	-	0.615	0.354	-	0.626	0.397	-	0.629	0.655
Paris [24]	6412	0.635	0.636	0.505	-	0.652	0.620	-	0.668	0.632	-	0.676	0.695
Average		0.613	0.622	0.404	-	0.633	0.487	-	0.647	0.514	-	0.652	0.675

fraction of the total number of possible pairs in each set (e.g., the **Trafalgar** dataset, with 6,981 images, has over 24M image pairs). Comparing our two extensions, we find that the improvement by modified regularization is more significant when there is very little training data (e.g. 200 examples), while adding unrelated negative examples gives a larger improvement when more data is available (e.g. 2,000 examples). Because Oxford5K and Paris each encompass several disparate landmarks, they require more training data, and hence modified regularization is essential for these two datasets. With modified regularization, models trained with only 200 examples outperform the baselines. We also tested with much lower amounts of training data; we found that with as few as 20 training examples, our method can consistently outperform both baselines in all datasets.

The mAP score above is also used in image retrieval, though we emphasize that we address a different problem in that we seek to discover the connectivity of an entire image set. Our method focuses on learning similarity measures, and as such is orthogonal to other popular methods for improving image retrieval, such as query expansion [25], Hamming embedding [26], or using better feature detectors than the DoG detector. Hence, while our baseline is not as good as that achieved in [7] (e.g. 0.618 for Oxford5K), our method could be combined with others to achieve even better performance.

4.2   System Evaluation

While the experiment above illustrates that our learning framework can yield better similarity measures, how well does our iterative matching system work in practice? The training pairs we get while matching will be different from the random ones selected above. Hence, we also evaluate the performance of our iterative matching system as a whole by running it on the datasets described above. As a reminder, our algorithm matches images in rounds, initially using *tf-idf* similarity to rank candidate pairs for matching, but learning a better model over time. Learning initially takes place once a certain number N of image pairs have been processed. We observe that the margin

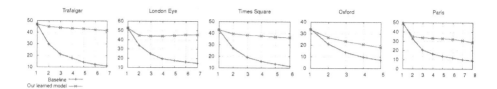

Fig. 5. Per-round _match success rates_ for five datasets. The x-axis is the round number, and the y-axis is the percentage of image pairs tested so far found to be true matches. Since we use _tf-idf_ similarity in the first round, the corresponding percentages are the same for that round.

of performance improvement decreases as the number of training instances (rounds) increases, so at each round we match more image pairs than last round by a factor of β before training. This increases overall efficiency, as learning and re-ranking take time. In our experiments, we use $\beta = 1.5$ and $N = 2000$. We compare to a baseline system that does not rerank image pairs, and simply processes each image's most similar candidates in the order computed by _tf-idf_ similarity. This mimics current similarity-based large scale image matching methods [1, 4]. We terminate when ≥ 40 candidates are processed for each image. For this experiment, _efficiency_ is the key metric—how quickly can we find matches, and what percent of the image pairs we try turn out to be true matches (meaning we didn't waste effort matching them)? Hence, we evaluate performance after each round of matching using the percentage of image pairs tested so far that were found to be true matches. A higher _match success rate_ indicates better efficiency.

Match success rate over time for five datasets are shown in Figure 5; the other datasets show a similar trend. Aside from the initial round (where we use _tf-idf_ similarity), our system significantly improves the match success rate. For instance, for the Trafalgar dataset, after seven rounds of matching, our method has a success rate of over 40%, while the baseline method has a success rate of just over 10%. We also found the mAP metric used in Section 4.1 also improves gradually over time.

We found that the overhead of training and re-ranking between rounds is much less than the time spent on image matching. For the Oxford5K dataset, our measured CPU time for matching was 2,621 minutes, while training and re-ranking took 17 and 118 minutes respectively (0.66% and 4.49% of image matching time). To obtain 7,000 matching image pairs, the _tf-idf_ similarity-based image matching method checked over 90K image pairs (≥ 1525 CPU minutes) while our approach checked fewer than 31K (<707 CPU minutes including training and re-ranking overhead), more than a factor of two improvement in efficiency. We also observed similar speedups with other datasets.

5   Conclusions and Discussion

In conclusion, we have shown that even with small amounts of training data, our learned SVM models can predict matching and non-matching image pairs significantly better than _tf-idf_ and co-ocset methods for large-scale image matching. Our image matching algorithm iteratively learns a better model of image similarity using accumulated image matching results, in turn improving the efficiency of the matching process.

We find that in our datasets, there are often a small number of reliable, discriminative, highly weighted features. We tried using training data from other datasets to predict them, but found this didn't work well; these "good" features seem specific to each dataset. One limitation of our approach is that discriminative learning is biased towards visual words that appear frequently, which could lead to good classification for canonical images in a dataset, but worse results for rarer ones. This relates to a trade-off between generality and specificity. The more specific the dataset, the easier to learn a good similarity measure. On the other hand, recent work has proposed learning per-image classifiers or similarity functions [27, 28]. It would be interesting to explore what level of granularity of similarity measure (global, local, or something in between) works best.

References

1. Agarwal, S., Snavely, N., Simon, I., Seitz, S., Szeliski, R.: Building Rome in a day. In: ICCV (2009)
2. Frahm, J.-M., Fite-Georgel, P., Gallup, D., Johnson, T., Raguram, R., Wu, C., Jen, Y.-H., Dunn, E., Clipp, B., Lazebnik, S., Pollefeys, M.: Building Rome on a Cloudless Day. In: Daniilidis, K., Maragos, P., Paragios, N. (eds.) ECCV 2010, Part IV. LNCS, vol. 6314, pp. 368–381. Springer, Heidelberg (2010)
3. Simon, I., Snavely, N., Seitz, S.: Scene summarization for online image collections. In: ICCV (2007)
4. Philbin, J., Sivic, J., Zisserman, A.: Geometric latent dirichlet allocation on a matching graph for large-scale image datasets. IJCV (2010)
5. Sivic, J., Zisserman, A.: Video google: A text retrieval approach to object matching in videos. In: ICCV (2003)
6. Li, X., Wu, C., Zach, C., Lazebnik, S., Frahm, J.-M.: Modeling and Recognition of Landmark Image Collections Using Iconic Scene Graphs. In: Forsyth, D., Torr, P., Zisserman, A. (eds.) ECCV 2008, Part I. LNCS, vol. 5302, pp. 427–440. Springer, Heidelberg (2008)
7. Philbin, J., Chum, O., Isard, M., Sivic, J., Zisserman, A.: Object retrieval with large vocabularies and fast spatial matching. In: CVPR (2007)
8. Jegou, H., Douze, M., Schmid, C.: On the burstiness of visual elements. In: CVPR (2009)
9. Chum, O., Matas, J.: Unsupervised discovery of co-occurrence in sparse high dimensional data. In: CVPR (2010)
10. Lowe, D.: Distinctive image features from scale-invariant keypoints. IJCV (2004)
11. Zhang, J., Lazebnik, S., Schmid, C.: Local features and kernels for classification of texture and object categories: a comprehensive study. IJCV (2007)
12. Naikal, N., Yang, A., Sastry, S.: Informative feature selection for object recognition via sparse PCA. In: ICCV (2011)
13. Mikulík, A., Perdoch, M., Chum, O., Matas, J.: Learning a Fine Vocabulary. In: Daniilidis, K., Maragos, P., Paragios, N. (eds.) ECCV 2010, Part III. LNCS, vol. 6313, pp. 1–14. Springer, Heidelberg (2010)
14. Schindler, G., Brown, M., Szeliski, R.: City-scale location recognition. In: CVPR (2007)
15. Knopp, J., Sivic, J., Pajdla, T.: Avoiding Confusing Features in Place Recognition. In: Daniilidis, K., Maragos, P., Paragios, N. (eds.) ECCV 2010, Part I. LNCS, vol. 6311, pp. 748–761. Springer, Heidelberg (2010)
16. Turcot, P., Lowe, D.: Better matching with fewer features: The selection of useful features in large database recognition problems. In: Workshop on Emergent Issues in Large Amounts of Visual Data, ICCV (2009)

17. Philbin, J., Isard, M., Sivic, J., Zisserman, A.: Descriptor Learning for Efficient Retrieval. In: Daniilidis, K., Maragos, P., Paragios, N. (eds.) ECCV 2010, Part III. LNCS, vol. 6313, pp. 677–691. Springer, Heidelberg (2010)
18. Xing, E., Ng, A., Jordan, M., Russell, S.: Distance metric learning with application to clustering with side-information. In: NIPS (2003)
19. Schultz, M., Joachims, T.: Learning a distance metric from relative comparisons. In: NIPS (2003)
20. Frome, A., Malik, J.: Learning distance functions for exemplar-based object recognition. In: ICCV (2007)
21. Chechik, G., Sharma, V., Shalit, U., Bengio, S.: An online algorithm for large scale image similarity learning. In: NIPS (2009)
22. Bai, B., Weston, J., Grangier, D., Collobert, R., Sadamasa, K., Qi, Y., Chapelle, O., Weinberger, K.: Supervised semantic indexing. In: CIKM (2009)
23. Nister, D., Stewenius, H.: Scalable recognition with a vocabulary tree. In: CVPR (2006)
24. Philbin, J., Chum, O., Isard, M., Sivic, J., Zisserman, A.: Lost in quantization: Improving particular object retrieval in large scale image databases. In: CVPR (2008)
25. Chum, O., Philbin, J., Sivic, J., Isard, M., Zisserman, A.: Total recall: Automatic query expansion with a generative feature model for object retrieval. In: ICCV (2007)
26. Jégou, H., Douze, M., Schmid, C.: Improving bag-of-features for large scale image search. IJCV 87, 316–336 (2010)
27. Frome, A., Singer, Y., Sha, F., Malik, J.: Learning globally-consistent local distance functions for shape-based image retrieval and classification. In: ICCV (2007)
28. Malisiewicz, T., Gupta, A., Efros, A.A.: Ensemble of exemplar-SVMs for object detection and beyond. In: ICCV (2011)

Efficient Mining of Repetitions in Large-Scale TV Streams with Product Quantization Hashing

Jiangbo Yuan[1], Guillaume Gravier[2], Sébastien Campion[2],
Xiuwen Liu[1], and Hervé Jégou[2]

[1] Florida State University, Tallahassee, FL 32306, USA
[2] INRIA-IRISA, 35042 Rennes Cedex, France

Abstract. Duplicates or near-duplicates mining in video sequences is of broad interest to many multimedia applications. How to design an effective and scalable system, however, is still a challenge to the community. In this paper, we present a method to detect recurrent sequences in large-scale TV streams in an unsupervised manner and with little *a priori* knowledge on the content. The method relies on a product k-means quantizer that efficiently produces hash keys adapted to the data distribution for frame descriptors. This hashing technique combined with a temporal consistency check allows the detection of meaningful repetitions in TV streams. When considering all frames (about 47 millions) of a 22-day long TV broadcast, our system detects all repetitions in 15 minutes, excluding the computation of the frame descriptors. Experimental results show that our approach is a promising way to deal with very large video databases.

1 Introduction

Mining repetitions in video data consists in finding occurrences of repeating segments, also referred to as motifs or repetitions, within the video. In the most general setup, no prior knowledge of the relevant motifs is available. A motif is solely characterized by the fact that it is repeated with very limited variability. Finding out such repeated segments in an automatic manner is of interest for several applications, in particular for TV stream structuring where repeating inter-programs—e.g., advertisements, jingles, credits—are key elements [1–3] to be identified. Motif discovery in video is also used for commercial detection [4] or to analyze news video [5]. However, most methods proposed in the literature do not scale up and can hardly deal with more than a few million frames.

In this paper, we focus on efficiently discovering unknown and repeating sequences in very long TV streams, where the targeted repetitions are either short repeating clips or more complex sequences such as commercials, trailers, or longer programs. A naive approach to the problem consists in using an off-the-shelf video retrieval system to index all the frames and retrieve repeated ones by submitting each frame in turn as a query. The efficiency of such query-based approaches is improved by using approximate nearest neighbor search techniques [6, 5], yet this approach is tractable only on a limited scale as the

A. Fusiello et al. (Eds.): ECCV 2012 Ws/Demos, Part I, LNCS 7583, pp. 271–280, 2012.
© Springer-Verlag Berlin Heidelberg 2012

complexity is quadratic in the amount of data. Frame sub-sampling is usually performed to skirt the scale issue, with typically one frame extracted per shot in a repeatable manner, however at the cost of a reduced temporal precision. A better way to find all cross-neighbors consists in directly constructing a k-nearest neighbor graph. But even state-of-the-art algorithms [7, 8] are limited to a few million vectors and cannot deal with week-long TV streams, in particular because of memory requirements for such methods where a temporary version of the graph must be stored in memory during the construction phase.

As an alternative to indexing, clustering [9, 10] or hashing [11, 4, 12, 3] techniques are used to discover repeating segments by grouping similar frames. Clustering and hashing methods are close in spirit as they share the same underlying goal of mapping frame-level features to integers, based on a partition of the feature space [13]. Clustering approaches better fit the data distribution, but traditional clustering methods produce a relatively coarse partition, which is detrimental for the precision of the matching and for the complexity of the subsequent stages. In contrast, hashing-based methods enable fast projection with a reasonable large hash table. It is however difficult, if possible, to balance the recall and precision of the projection, in particular because the lack of data adaptation leads to unevenly group the vectors [13].

In this work, we propose a method for efficient discovery of repeated segments in large TV streams, bridging the gap between quantization techniques and hashing techniques. In particular, we show the interest of a hashing scheme based on *product quantization hashing* to combine the efficiency of hashing techniques to produce hash keys with the possibility to better fit the data distribution offered by clustering. The scheme is inspired by previous work on the use of product quantization (PQ) as a descriptor encoding approach for approximate nearest neighbor search in the compressed domain [14]. In our case, product quantization is used for hashing purposes to overcome the efficiency and scalability limitations of traditional clustering approaches. Compared to k-means and hierarchical k-means, product quantization is able to implicitly generate a large number of cells (as large as 2^{64} or even larger) with a very fast learning stage, and, as importantly, with a very compact representation of the centroids. As a consequence, the resulting partition is of significantly better quality than in traditional hashing-methods with comparable hash-table size.

In the context of repetition mining, product quantization hashing is used to assign each frame in a video stream to some bucket based on the resulting code with a typical size of 32 bits. As a result of the hashing step, each bucket contains visually similar frames—as defined by the representation selected for frames, GIST features in our case—from which repeated sequences are searched.

The paper is organized as follows. After describing the frame representation used, Section 2 describes the proposed product quantization hashing scheme. Section 3 describes the discovery procedure used to extract maximal-length repeated patterns from the hash table. Experimental results on three weeks of annotated TV data (47 million frames) are reported in Section 4. Finally, concluding remarks are given in Section 5.

2   Product Quantization Hashing

As previously mentioned, we want to consider all video frames in the problem of discovering repeated patterns so as to maintain good temporal localization. Clearly, this choice is possible only if one defines a representation of a frame that is both compact, discriminative and exhibit an efficient indexing structure. To this end, we use global descriptors for each frame. Product quantization is then used to efficiently map global descriptors to a very large number of clusters. Finally, a hash code is derived from the product quantization. We describe in turn each step of the process.

2.1   Frame Representation

Similar to previous work on TV stream description [12, 3], frames are represented by color GIST descriptors [15] which are especially effective to cope with compression artifacts if an image has undergone no or limited geometrical distortion [16], as is typically the case in video. A GIST feature is a low-dimensional representation that captures the global layout of a scene, and is specifically successful at recognizing different categories of scenes that avoids the recognition of individual objects or regions. The components of the description aim at reflecting the so-called spatial envelope of the images, which is related to a set of perceptual dimensions (naturalness, openness, roughness, expansion, ruggedness) representing the dominant spatial structure of a scene.

In this work, the image is divided into a 4x4 spatial resolution grid at 3 different scales, and orientation histograms are computed in each of the scale/spatial positions. Given that the description is computed for the three RGB channels, a frame is finally described by a 960-dimensional vector representation. Finally, PCA is applied, reducing the final dimension from 960 to 64.

2.2   Product Quantization

Product quantization refers to the process of separately quantizing parts of a vector. It is a compromise between a component-wise scalar quantization and a vector quantizer applied to the full vector. By encoding the subspaces independently, a product quantizer can efficiently map the input vectors to a very large number of clusters while keeping, to some extent, the advantage of a vector quantizer. Recently, a k-means version of product quantization was proposed in an approximate nearest neighbor search algorithm [14]. The structure of the quantizer allows the estimation of the Euclidean distance between two vectors directly from the quantized indexes at query time.

Here, we use the product quantization step to assign GIST-PCA vectors representing similar visual content to a unique cluster from which a compact hash code will be derived. Given a collection of D-dimensional descriptors, the product k-means clustering step works as follows:

○ Divide the space into m subspaces of dimension d each ;
○ Quantize each subspace with k-means assuming the same number of clusters k for each subspace ;
○ Encode each vector as an index of m integers $\in [1, k]$, known as a PQ code of length $m \times \lceil \log_2 k \rceil$ bits.

In the context of repetition discovery, product quantization offers several advantages compared to traditional clustering algorithms (e.g., flat k-means, BIRCH). In particular, the quantizers operate on low dimensional subspaces and are trained with limited number of training vectors. In our case, 20,000 vectors randomly selected from the first day of the TV stream were used to learn the codebooks. Most importantly, PQ generates a very large number of clusters with low assignment complexity. In this paper, the regular k-means was trained on one million vectors to produce K cells, resulting in a $K \times D$ assignment complexity. In comparison, PQ was trained on 20,000 vectors for $K = k^m$ clusters with an assignment complexity of $k \times D$.

In this work, product quantization is used so that frames in the same cluster are visually similar and are thus expected to be from sequentially close segments or from repeating segments. In other words, each frame in a cluster should belong to one of the occurrences of the same repeated pattern. While increasing the number of bits per code provides smaller quantization error leading in better approximate nearest neighbor search, this is not a desirable property here. Indeed, in the discovery problem as we formulate it, having all visually similar frames as part of the same cluster is a necessity. Within each cell, contrary to nearest neighbor search, we therefore target high recall rather than high precision. We therefore chose $m = 8$ and $k = 8$ or 32, i.e., 24 bits or 40 bits codes, instead of the 64 bits typically used in [14].

2.3   Hashing PQ Codes

Even though the PQ codes are compact, the space of possible codes remain sparsely populated, even for real-world video sizes. In practice, they are further hashed to gain additional memory and computational efficiency. For instance, PQ-codes with $m = 8$ and $k = 32$ partitions the space into 32^8 distinct cells. This number is significantly larger than the total number of frames in a 24-hour long video stream, which comprises approximately 2×10^6 frames. The m-dimensional PQ-code is therefore subsequently hashed (with any good hashing function such as a universal hash function) and the resulting key is used within a regular hashing scheme. As a result, each frame is represented by a 32 bits signature, with visually similar frames sharing with high probability the same signature and therefore assigned to the same bucket. Obviously, as with any non reversible hashing functions, collisions might appear.

3   Discovering Repetitions Using Temporal Consistency

We exploit the structure of the hash table resulting from product quantization hashing to discover a set of repeated patterns (a.k.a. repetitions) in each bucket.

Algorithm 1. Find initial small repeated segments

$\rightarrow$ RepSets $\leftarrow$ {}
for each bucket **do**
    if bucket size $> b_{min}$ **then**
        $\rightarrow$ append a new entry to RepSets
        $\rightarrow$ sort frames by their temporal indexes in ascending order
        for each segment of contiguous frames with length $> l_{min}$, where contiguous
        means that the distance between two neighboring frames $< g_{max}$ **do**
            $\rightarrow$ append the start and end frame of the segment to the current RepSets
            entry
        end for
    end if
end for
$\rightarrow$ remove all entries in RepSets within only one segment
$\rightarrow$ return RepSets

As discussed above, high recall was preferred to high precision. Filtering out noise from the bucket is therefore a necessity before identifying small repeated sequences. As a final stage, boundary refinement is applied before merging the small sequences to form maximal ones.

3.1 Extracting Small Repeated Sequences from the Hash Table

The first step in identifying maximal length repeated sequences is to find in each bucket short repeated sequences. As the hashing scheme was designed to ensure high recall within each bucket to the expense of precision, finding such sequences in each bucket must cope in some way with outliers. This is performed by sorting frames within the bucket according to their time stamp in order to identify sequences of contiguous frames, allowing for small gaps between consecutive frames to deal with noise and outliers. As all frames in a bucket are visually similar, the short repeated sequences identified are deemed to be occurrences of the pattern.

The procedure is given in Algorithm 1 where the output, RepSets, of the algorithm is the list of all sets of repeated segments. The threshold b_{min} is used to avoid searching in very small buckets while l_{min} filters out very short repetitions. Finally, g_{max} is the maximum temporal gap tolerated for two frames to be considered contiguous. The use of g_{max} mostly reflects that the recall in each bucket is not perfect even if good.

The size of the RepSets list usually is considerably large: In our experiments, with $b_{min} = 8$, $l_{min} = 4$ and $g_{max} = 25$ (i.e., 1 s), between 20,000 to 40,000 sets where found for a 24 hours long TV stream. This number is reduced to a few thousands after removing all singletons. However, these short repeated segments detected by the initial stage of the algorithm are far from the maximal length repeated sequences one wants to discover. The next steps therefore aim at extending each individual segment and refining their boundaries before merging related sets to form longer repeated sequences.

Algorithm 2. Segment boundary optimization

---

for each segment $S_i \in$ RepSets **do**
$\quad \rightarrow$ find the monochrome segment $M_k \in$ right before S_i
$\quad$ **if** start_ID(S_i) − end_ID$(M_k) < b_{max}$ **then**
$\quad\quad \rightarrow$ start_ID$(S_i) \leftarrow$ end_ID(M_k)
$\quad$ **end if**
$\quad \rightarrow$ find the monochrome segment $M_l \in$ right after S_i
$\quad$ **if** start_ID(M_l) − end_ID$(S_i) < b_{max}$ **then**
$\quad\quad \rightarrow$ end_ID$(S_i) \leftarrow$ start_ID(M_l)
$\quad$ **end if**
$\quad \rightarrow$ label S_i with $<M_k, M_l>$
end for

3.2   Segment Boundary Optimization

In the particular case of advertisements in TV streams, one can take advantage of specific markers such as inter-commercial monochrome segments as in [4, 17]. Inter-commercial markers are usually very short sequences, i.e., less than 1 s, which consist of monochrome frames with no audio signal. A large majority of the repeated sequences in TV streams corresponds to advertisements which intuitively provide an appealing feature for TV stream structuring [10]. Moreover, taking benefit from product quantization hashing, inter-commercial markers can be detected at almost no extra cost. These facts justify that specific processing be devoted to inter-commercial monochrome frames to adjust boundaries of short repeating segments.

As inter-commercial monochrome short segments are numerous in TV streams and are by definition visually very similar, they all fall into the same bucket after product quantization hashing and therefore generate an entry in the RepSets list easily identifiable by its many occurrences. The set of monochrome repeated segments is therefore characterized and identified by its abnormally large population.

Based on the location of monochrome segments, one can refine the boundaries of the repeated segments: Whenever a monochrome segment appears near the beginning (respectively, the end) of an occurrence of a repeated segment, the starting (respectively, ending) frame ID of the latter is modified to match the corresponding boundary in the monochrome segment. This procedure is formally described by Algorithm 2, where b_{max} is set to 200. The use of a threshold reflects the fact that monochrome segments appear with commercials, thus reducing the probability of optimizing the boundaries of a non commercial repeated segment.

3.3   Finding Out Maximal Length Repeated Segments

The previous steps enable to identify short repeated segments which are then merged to yield longer repeated segments. For sake of comparison with other methods, the fusion stage was limited to basic operations to avoid over-fitting problems and application specific solutions. The fusion successively takes place

Table 1. Datasets and statistics of the reference repeated segments

Name	#frames	length	#rep seg
TV-DAY1	2,160,026	24 h	133
TV-DAY2	2,159,920	24 h	148
TV-22	47,517,004	528 h	1,502

at two levels. An inner-set fusion is first performed independently within each entry of the RepSets list before merging across all entries.

Inner-set fusion indicates that, in a list of short repeated segments, several may belong to a continuous program but somehow are cut by the detection. For each entry in the RepSets list, two segments with a gap (say, S_i S_{i+1}) less than a threshold $g'_{max} = 1,000$ are merged. When we take advantage of monochrome segments, we increase $g'_{max} = 10,000$ if the two segments have the same labels (say, $<M_k, M_{k+1}>$, as defined in Algorithm 2).

Inter-set fusion is expensive since it has to exhaustively check all identical sets. The basic idea is the following: Given two entries r_1 and r_2 in RepSets (assume the size of r_1 is larger than the size of r_2), we mix and merge their segments together by using a gap threshold $g''_{max} = 500$, then we accept the returned set if its size is equal or smaller than r_2. All the accepted new repSets form the final RepSets that will be evaluated.

4   Experimental Results

4.1   Dataset and Ground-Truth

Experiments are carried out on a 22-day long TV stream. The dataset was manually annotated using the individual TV programs as basic units. Each unit is identified by its start and end times, a title and a genre (e.g., program, jingle). A ground truth reference is built from these annotations by considering all units with the same title as repeated segments/events. Note that such repetitions vary in genre, in length and in the number of occurrences.

Experiments are carried out either on the entire dataset or on small portions identified as TV-DAY1 and TV-DAY2 (see Tab. 1), corresponding to respectively the first and second day of the stream. The former is used to train the product quantizers and to tune parameters while the latter is used for sake of comparison to existing approaches which cannot scale to the 22 days.

All the algorithms have been developed in C and Matlab (for and only for the detection part). Experiments have been performed on a single core machine under Unix.

4.2   Evaluation Measures

Performance measures were designed to assess the detection of repeated segments both in terms of purity and temporal localization. Given the detected list of repeated segments—i.e., RepSets—and the ground truth list, there is often a many-to-one mapping between the lists because of the difficult sets fusion. We therefore map each entry in the ground truth list to the best corresponding entry in RepSets. Each detected segment is then mapped to at most one occurrence of the corresponding event in the ground truth, assuming two segments coincide if they overlap by more than $\theta \times l$ where l is the length of the longer segment and θ a user defined parameter. Relying on the mapping above, the detection is evaluated by the F1-score for a particular repeating segment, i.e., the harmonic mean of precision and recall defined as

- recall=(# correctly detected reference segments)/(# of reference segments)
- precision=(# correctly detected segments)/(# of detected segments)

The measurements are averaged over all repeating events to yield global measures denoted as AF (for a single-day data) and mAF (for the 22-day data).

4.3   Results

Experiments are performed with different hashing and clustering techniques, namely: standard k-means (KM), hashing (STDHASH), locality sensitive hashing (LSH), and our product quantization hashing (PQH) with 24 or 40 bits keys. Comparative results are reported in Fig. 1 for the TV-DAY2 subset for varying values of the overlap threshold θ. Final results on the entire corpus are given in Fig. 2 for PQ hashing and LSH which are the only scalable methods. In both cases, results are reported with and without boundary optimization using monochrome frames.

Standard k-means and hashing are special cases of our method: Setting $m = 1$ results in a standard k-means while defining $m = 64$ and $k = 2$ (or a small value) yields an approach very similar to standard hashing schemes as used in [11, 4, 12, 3]. LSH use random projections with a hash function defined as

$$h_r(x) = \begin{cases} 1, \text{ if } r^T x \geqslant 0 \\ 0, \text{ otherwise} \end{cases} \tag{1}$$

where r is a random vector subject to a $\mathcal{N}(0, I)$ distribution. See [18] for more details. The length of binary codes (b) depends on how many hash functions are used. From the results in Fig. 1, we observe that longer codes (e.g., LSH-128) are less adapted as they allow very limited frame distortion.

Fig. 1 shows that the standard hashing method, though the fastest, provides poor results. On the opposite, the methods based on regular k-means clustering are effective, especially for large values of k. However, the learning and assignment steps are too expensive for real-time purpose, and even infeasible for the very large values of k needed for the purpose of hashing because of the lack of sufficient amount of training data. Therefore, these two methods are not adapted to process large-scale streams. In contrast, PQH-24, PQH-40, and LSH-64 provide overall competitive results with reasonable processing time. PQH-40 achieved the best timing performance (about 20 s for encoding and hashing, and 17 s for

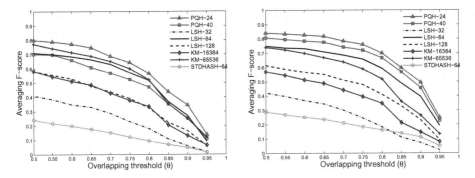

Fig. 1. Detection performance on TV-DAY2 without (left) and with (right) monochrome segments for boundary refinement

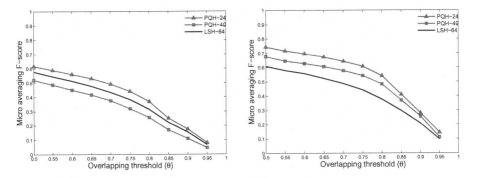

Fig. 2. Detection performance on TV-22 without (left) and with (right) monochrome segments for boundary refinement

detection). The accuracy of PQH-24 is slightly better however with a slower processing time, in particular in the detection step (9 s for encoding and hashing, and 42 s for detection). LSH-64 is faster than PQH-24 on encoding but takes about 230 s for detection. Note that the timing performance highly depends on the size of the candidate RepSets.

Performance measures on the 22 days long TV stream, as reported in Fig. 2, demonstrate the effectiveness of our approach to accurately discover repeating segments in very large data streams.

5 Conclusion

In this paper, we have proposed a new method for efficiently and effectively detecting repeated sequences in large TV streams, without requiring prior knowledge. By hashing PQ-codes to produce compact but effective frame-signatures, our method is scalable in terms of both storage and complexity. Several directions can be envisioned to further refine the method. Boundary refinement using shot boundaries might be considered when monochrome frames are not available.

Using key-frames is an option to drastically speed-up the process that needs to be explored. Finally, the PQ hashing scheme proposed meets the needs of other applications. For instance, we plan to extend the work for web-based near duplicate video detection by encoding entire video clips in order to fetch a higher-level signature for video retrieval/mining.

References

1. Naturel, X., Gros, P.: Detecting repeats for video structuring. Multimedia Tools and Applications 38, 233–252 (2007)
2. Manson, G., Berrani, S.A.: Automatic tv broadcast structuring. International Journal of Digital Multimedia Broadcasting, 16 pages (2010)
3. Ibrahim, Z.A.A., Gros, P.: Tv stream structuring. ISRN Signal Processing, 17 pages (2011)
4. Gauch, J.M., Shivadas, A.: Finding and identifying unknown commercials using repeated video sequence detection. Computer Vision and Image Understanding 103, 80–88 (2006)
5. Yang, X., Tian, Q., Member, S., Xue, P.: Efficient short video repeat identification with application to news video structure analysis. IEEE Transactions on Multimedia 9, 600–609 (2007)
6. Yuan, J., Wang, W., Meng, J., Wu, Y., Li, D.: Mining repetitive clips through finding continuous paths. In: ACM MM 2007, pp. 289–292. ACM, New York (2007)
7. Dong, W., Charikar, M., Li, K.: Efficient k-nearest neighbor graph construction for generic similarity measures. In: WWW (2011)
8. Wang, J., Wang, J., Zeng, G., Tu, Z., Li, S.: Scalable k-nn graph construction for visual descriptors. In: Conf. on Vision and Pattern Recognition (2012)
9. Goh, K.S.: Audio-visual event detection based on mining of semantic audio-visual labels. In: Proceedings of SPIE, vol. 5307, pp. 292–299 (2003)
10. Berrani, S., Manson, G., Lechat, P.: A non-supervised approach for repeated sequence detection in tv broadcast streams. Signal Processing Image Communication 23, 525–537 (2008)
11. Pua, K.M., Gauch, J.M., Gauch, S.E., Miadowicz, J.Z.: Real time repeated video sequence identification. Computer Vision and Image Understanding 93, 310–327 (2004)
12. Döhring, I., Lienhart, R.: Mining tv broadcasts for recurring video sequences. In: ACM CIVR 2009, pp. 28:1–28:8. ACM, New York (2009)
13. Paulevé, L., Jégou, H., Amsaleg, L.: Locality sensitive hashing: a comparison of hash function types and querying mechanisms. Pattern Recognition Letters (2010)
14. Jégou, H., Douze, M., Schmid, C.: Product quantization for nearest neighbor search. PAMI 33, 117–128 (2011)
15. Oliva, A., Torralba, A.B.: Modeling the shape of the scene: A holistic representation of the spatial envelope. IJCV 42, 145–175 (2001)
16. Douze, M., Jégou, H., Singh, H., Amsaleg, L., Schmid, C.: Evaluation of GIST descriptors for web-scale image search. In: CIVR (2009)
17. Naturel, X., Gravier, G., Gros, P.: Fast Structuring of Large Television Streams Using Program Guides. In: Marchand-Maillet, S., Bruno, E., Nürnberger, A., Detyniecki, M. (eds.) AMR 2006. LNCS, vol. 4398, pp. 222–231. Springer, Heidelberg (2007)
18. Charikar, M.S.: Similarity estimation techniques from rounding algorithms. In: Proc. of 34th STOC, pp. 380–388. ACM (2002)

An Efficient Parallel Strategy for Matching Visual Self-similarities in Large Image Databases

Katharina Schwarz, Tobias Häußler, and Hendrik P.A. Lensch

Computer Graphics, Tübingen University
72076 Tübingen, Germany

Abstract. Due to high interest of social online systems, there exists a huge and still increasing amount of image data in the web. In order to handle this massive amount of visual information, algorithms often need to be redesigned. In this work, we developed an efficient approach to find visual similarities between images that runs completely on GPU and is applicable to large image databases. Based on local self-similarity descriptors, the approach finds similarities even across modalities. Given a set of images, a database is created by storing all descriptors in an arrangement suitable for parallel GPU-based comparison. A novel voting-scheme further considers the spatial layout of descriptors with hardly any overhead. Thousands of images are searched in only a few seconds. We apply our algorithm to cluster a set of image responses to identify various senses of ambiguous words and re-tag similar images with missing tags.

1 Introduction

Finding similarities between images is a computational intensive task that is necessary in many computer vision applications, e.g., image retrieval and organization, object detection or recognition. Typically, the comparison is based on extracted features representing important image properties. Mostly, it is assumed that multiple similar images share the same properties as well as the extracted features. A major challenge is the extraction of suitable features because they should be classified as looking similar if captured under varying lighting conditions, from slightly different viewpoints, or with partially occluded objects.

Fig. 1. Images retrieved from Google Images querying "apple" sorted by similarity to the template (left). Decreasing similarity from top left to bottom right.

A. Fusiello et al. (Eds.): ECCV 2012 Ws/Demos, Part I, LNCS 7583, pp. 281–290, 2012.
© Springer-Verlag Berlin Heidelberg 2012

The features have to account for changes in rotation, scale, illumination, color, texture, etc. Moreover, the set of common properties can vary drastically when taking images of various domains (photographs, drawings, sketches) into account.

In order to search for similar images, large image databases such as Flickr or search engines like Google Images typically use meta-data, tags, and textual search queries specified by users while ignoring the visual content. Flickr, e.g., contains millions of images and a simple search often yields millions of results. The quality of the results is largely based on the search term and the quality of the meta-data. Improvement on the quality of answers can only be achieved by taking, besides textual data, also the visual appearance of images into account. The local self-similarity descriptor introduced by Shechtman and Irani [1] encodes local similarities within an image region and successfully finds templates in other images. Unfortunately, since the computation of this descriptor is very expensive, applying it to large databases is a big challenge.

We present a variation of a self-similarity algorithm that makes it applicable to huge image databases. Descriptor generation and matching run completely on a modern GPU using CUDA. Due to our suitable representation of the descriptor database as well as a new voting-scheme considering the spatial arrangement with hardly any overhead, our implementation scales to databases with thousands of images that can be searched in only a few seconds. Further, no additional pre-processing steps like learning or quantization are needed. Evaluation is performed with ETHZ, Caltech 101 and MIRFLICKR datasets as well as over one million images downloaded from Flickr. Even for matching a template with the large Flickr sets, we can compute over 1400 full image comparisons per second. We apply our algorithm to cluster a given set of image responses to identify various meanings of ambiguous words and re-tag images with similar shapes but missing tag. It also could be used for real-time analysis of video streams.

2   Related Work and Background

Descriptors on Large Databases. Different descriptors and matching strategies have been used for large-scale image retrieval and similarity matching. Local descriptors such as SIFT [2] were used in the bag-of-visual-words (BOV) approach [3], ignoring the global shape and spatial arrangement of an image. Zhang et al. [4] group multiple visual words to encode spatial arrangement in the inverted file structure. Another approach is based on global descriptors such as GIST [5]. Because of its low memory requirements it scales up to very large databases [6]. Johnson et al. [7] used GIST to organize large photo collections on the GPU with a SIFT-based geometric verification to further refine the ranking generated by the global descriptor.

Whereas images of similar scenes do not necessarily show the same objects with similar geometric layout, a certain combination of features is typical. So, learning and classification methods have been used in combination with local and global descriptors. Xiao et al. evaluated such descriptors on a large database ("SUN database") [8]. Shrivastava et al. [9] proposed a computationally intensive method to find visual similar images over different domains learning features that are most important for a particular image. In contrast, we aim at efficiently finding similar images across various domains without any prior learning steps.

Self-similarities. The local self-similarity descriptor, on which our work is based, was introduced by Shechtman and Irani [1]. It was developed on the observation that similar images do not necessarily share properties like colors, textures, or edges. So, measuring them is not always sufficient for comparison. These images are similar because their local intensity pattern is repeated in nearby image locations in a similar relative geometric layout which is captured in this descriptor.

The self-similarity descriptor is generated by measuring the similarity of an image patch within its surrounding region. The sum of squared differences (SSD) between a 5×5 image patch centered at an image pixel and all 5×5 patches in the surrounding region is calculated and normalized, leading to a correlation surface that is subsequently transformed into a binned log-polar representation with 80 bins. Some of the descriptors are non-informative, because they do not capture any local self-similarity or they capture too much. Non-informative descriptors are discarded and the remaining descriptors of an image form a global ensemble. Ensembles are similar if the distance between the descriptor values is small and the spatial arrangement of the descriptors is similar. Boiman and Irani used the self-similarity descriptor to detect objects in images based on both freehand sketches and real images with an optimized ensemble matching strategy [10]. Their elimination of comparison calculations at locations where the similarity is probably very low leads to a scattered memory access pattern that does not fit well onto the GPU. Therefore, we developed a different GPU-optimized strategy.

Chatfield et al. [11] use the self-similarity descriptor to retrieve deformable shapes. They refine the sparsification of descriptors and study the influence of quantization on matching performance for large-scale retrieval using a BOV approach. In contrast, we do not need any quantization and, thus, avoid errors therefrom. Moreover, time-consuming generation of vocabulary is not necessary.

3   Approach and Implementation

Based on the self-similarity descriptor [1], we developed a simple approach that enables searching for similar images to a given template or calculate similarity values for an image set (e.g. Fig. 1) also in huge databases. Our system first creates the self-similarity descriptors of an image that form an ensemble (Fig. 2(a)) and stores the ensembles of all images in a database suitable for parallel GPU-based comparison (Fig. 2(b)). This database of ensembles is only created once and matching then operates directly on the database without any further pre-processing steps by comparing ensembles (Fig. 2(c)). Our efficient implementation is able to compare more than 1400 images in only one second.

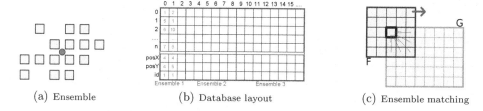

(a) Ensemble   (b) Database layout   (c) Ensemble matching

Fig. 2. Approach. (a) Ensemble is formed by informative descriptors (rectangles) capturing the spatial arrangement around the center (red dot). (b) Layout for storage of ensembles in device memory. (c) All descriptors in ensemble F are compared to all descriptors in the database. Matching descriptors cast a vote on the spatial arrangement.

Database Handling. The first step is to compute the spatial ensembles as given in [1]. This step can be trivially parallelized on the GPU using CUDA. The ensemble of the descriptors of a 256×265 image occupy about 600 KB, typically containing 440 descriptors. In order to handle large databases a caching strategy is proposed. Ensembles residing in GPU device memory are swapped out to host memory if the device memory becomes exhausted. As the same strategy is used for host memory, ensembles are finally swapped out to disk which is determined by a simple LRU (least recently used) strategy. The ensembles are stored in a 2D array with one descriptor per column (Fig. 2(b)) ensuring fast access to same values in different descriptors in subsequent CUDA threads. As the ensemble a descriptor belongs to as well as its position within the ensemble have to be known in the matching stage, a second array stores additional information.

Matching Ensembles. In the matching stage, the ensemble of a template is compared to all ensembles in the database, yielding a similarity measure. The detailed comparison of ensembles is described in the following. We can either compare one query image to all images stored in the database or compute a weighted similarity graph between each pair of images in a cluster. In each case, multiple scales are supported. As already mentioned, the approach presented by Boiman and Irani [10] does not fit well onto the GPU. Thus, we decided to use a simple brute-force voting of first identifying the potential center and then calculating the score of an ensemble. Our approach is similar to a 2D cross-correlation (Fig. 2(c)). Every descriptor in the query ensemble is compared to the descriptors of all ensembles in the database. For small distance, the template descriptor casts a vote for a certain central position in a database ensemble. Votes indicate how many template descriptors are similar to database descriptors in the same spatial arrangement. Then, the votes are weighted by a number denoting how scattered the voting template descriptors are.

Details of the Matching Strategy. When querying for an image, the template ensemble I is compared to the whole database with ensembles I'_k ($k = 1..K$, with K images in database). Thus, at first the squared distance t between descriptor d_i

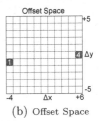

(a) Similar descriptors in different images   (b) Offset Space

Fig. 3. Voting in offset space. Lines connect similar descriptors (a). Red descriptors share same offsets and vote in offset space at corresponding positions. Blue descriptors vote for another offset. Maximum in offset space indicates best matching positions (b).

of I and descriptor d'_{kj} of I'_k ($i, j = 1..80$ bins) is calculated by one CUDA thread per combination of template and database descriptor. If t is below some threshold T, the spatial offset between d_i and d'_{kj} is used to vote for an ensemble offset in offset space $S^s_k(\Delta x, \Delta y)$ (Fig. 3). This offset space exists for each ensemble in the database. In order to account for small deformations and variations in scale, each bin in offset space contains 3×3 offsets. As soft-weighting would require many memory accesses, we only increase $S^s_k(\Delta x, \Delta y)$ by 1 if distance t is below T. Because this is rarely the case, the number of memory accesses is very small. Thus, an atomic instruction is used that operates directly on global memory. The offset for which most descriptors voted indicates the displacement where the template image fits best to the database image.

However, the number of votes does not contain any information about the arrangement of the voting descriptors in the template ensemble. If only descriptors in a small region of I cast a vote, then the similarity is smaller than if descriptors were uniformly distributed over I (Fig. 4). In order to incorporate the spatial arrangement, we decided to include the position of the voting descriptors into the matching results. Therefore, we partition I into rectangular regions R_m (e.g. 5×5) and assign each descriptor to such a region by its position in the ensemble. In addition to $S^s_k(\Delta x, \Delta y)$, a second offset space $S^r_k(\Delta x, \Delta y)$ stores information about the regions where the voting descriptors are located. $S^r_k(\Delta x, \Delta y)$ is organized as 2D 32-bit integer array. Bits b_0 to b_{24} are connected

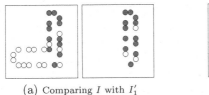
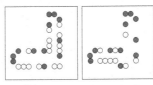

(a) Comparing I with I'_1 (b) Comparing I with I'_2

Fig. 4. Regions in voting. Both times the same number of descriptors cast a vote (red). This would result in the same similarity, although shape of I is more similar to I'_2 than to I'_1. We increase the comparison score by taking the position into account (b).

Algorithm 1. Voting in offset space (pseudo-code)

for all i, j, k in parallel **do**
   if $(t \leftarrow \|d_i - d'_{kj}\|^2) < T$ **then**
      $\Delta \mathbf{x} \leftarrow \mathbf{x}_{d'_{kj}} - \mathbf{x}_{d_i}$
      $S^s_k(\Delta \mathbf{x}) \leftarrow S^s_k(\Delta \mathbf{x}) + 1$
      $S^r_k(\Delta \mathbf{x}) \leftarrow S^r_k(\Delta \mathbf{x}) \mid (1 << \nu)$
   end if
end for

to a region. The bit b_ν is set if a descriptor in region R_ν casts a vote (Alg. 1). Then, offset $\Delta \mathbf{x} = \arg\max_{\Delta x \Delta y} m(\Delta x, \Delta y)$ and similarity $s = \frac{\max(m(\Delta x, \Delta y))}{r \cdot \max(c_I, c_{I'_k})}$ are calculated with $m(\Delta x, \Delta y) = S^s_k(\Delta x, \Delta y) \cdot \text{popcnt}(S^r_k(\Delta x, \Delta y))$. While r describes the number of informative descriptors in the template ensemble I, c_I and $c_{I'_k}$ is the number of descriptors in I and I'_k, respectively. The number of set bits in x is counted with $\text{popcnt}(x)$.

For comparison on various scales, the query is scaled to different sizes before comparing it with the database. Matching all ensembles in the database with each other needs K^2 comparisons. For L scales, the database must contain ensembles in L scales. Consequently, $(LK)^2$ comparisons have to be performed. Due to redundant comparisons, the complexity can be reduced to $(L + 1)K^2$.

4   Evaluation

In order to analyze accuracy, speed, and memory requirements of our approach, we performed experiments on the datasets ETHZ Extended Shape Classes [12] (383 images in 7 categories) and Caltech 101 [13] (9145 images in 101 categories, we removed "BACKGROUND" and "Faces_easy"). For testing on larger image counts, we used MIRFLICKR [14] containing 1 M Flickr images and additionally downloaded over a million images from Flickr with some random categories.

Visual Results. The self-similarity descriptor already works well for finding similar forms over various domains. To validate our changes in the algorithm, we performed tests with the ETHZ and Caltech datasets. Thus, a database is searched for each image yielding a similarity value between the query and all images. The results are sorted by their similarity and the average precision (AP) is calculated from this list. The mean average precision (mAP) is calculated for each category. The results for ETHZ (Fig. 5(a)) as well as for Caltech dataset vary a lot depending on the different categories. Categories with images sharing a distinct shape work best (e.g. Caltech: Airplanes (mAP=0.84), Motorbike (0.71), Faces (0.58)). Other categories (Pyramid (0.17)) contain images with very cluttered background that are not well suited as a template image. So, they have negative impact on the mAP of a category. Our results for ETHZ are similar to [11]. For measuring cross-domain matching, we applied several effects to the templates (Fig. 5(b)) without changing the images in the database. As expected, the AP remains for every effect nearly the same as for the original image.

(a) mAPs for ETHZ categories   (b) APs for various domains (Effects applied to templates only)

Fig. 5. Visual evaluation on ETHZ dataset. Approach works well for different domains.

Performance. We measured performance on a NVIDIA GeForce GTX 580 with 1,5 GB VRAM. The host system uses Intel Xeon X5660 CPU and 48 GB RAM. First, we only consider the generation of all descriptors of a single image, comparing our GPU version against the OpenCV implementation on CPU (Fig. 6). The CPU test was performed on an AMD Phenom II X4 965 CPU with an OpenMP-optimized version. For every image size, our GPU descriptor generation algorithm performs about ten times faster than the CPU implementation.

As already mentioned, we created the database such that our matching is performed very fast and can also be applied to very large image datasets without waiting for hours or even days. Results are shown in Table 1. Images were downscaled to 256×256 pixels. Times for creating the database as well as for matching vary depending on size of the image set and number of descriptors. For the Caltech set we even retrieved 2849 full image comparisons in only 1 sec. (load DB: 0.89 sec., match: 2 sec.). In order to compensate for variations, we also tested two larger datasets with images of varying sizes and content from Flickr: MIRFLICKR and images we downloaded for random categories. Both times, matching an image still resulted in over 1400 comparisons per sec.

This indicates a great speedup contrasted to [11], where comparing a single pair of VGA images with quantized descriptors took at least 20 sec. on a 2.4 GHz Pentium. Further, compared to [7], our method promises performance benefits while performing not only geometric verification, but also advanced shape

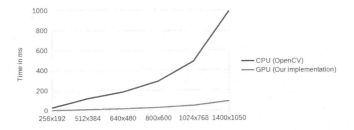

Fig. 6. Runtime comparison: OpenCV vs. our GPU version for descriptor generation

Table 1. Performance measurements for ETHZ, Caltech and two larger datasets

	Images	Descriptors		Create DB	Matching one image	
		Total	Informative	[h:min:s.ms]	[h:min:s.ms]	Img. Comp./ sec.
ETHZ	383	533,280	165,784	00:00:06.11	00:00:00.23	1644
Caltech	8,242	10,675,016	3,936,554	00:01:13.71	00:00:02.89	2849
MIRFLICKR	999,997	1,331,604,604	446,570,589	09:06:30.17	00:11:51.48	1407
Flickr Images	1,087,007	1,430,601,920	486,668,007	07:38:55.78	00:12:52.31	1406

matching. In their work, verifying about 4,000 clusters of 30,000 images takes 40 minutes. Our implementation is also faster than various methods based on locality sensitive hashing functions, implemented for CPU [15]. As, on average, only about 30% descriptors in an image are informative, more than half are discarded. The memory required to store the informative ones was 48MB for ETHZ, 1.1GB for Caltech 101 and even 139GB for our Flickr dataset. Thus, memory requirements are larger than with a quantized approach.

5 Applications

Large-scale image databases normally allow to search by textual queries which often are ambiguous and lead to images with different visual appearance. Due to our efficient implementation, the search results can be improved by taking the shape of the objects shown in images into account and clustering many similar images (around 800 images in about 10 min) or even re-tagging a large database.

Clustering. Based on the calculated similarity values of our implementation, we generate clusters of similar looking images. The database is created with images retrieved from Google Images by searching for a single word. Then, comparing all images with each other results in a distance graph. The nodes represent images, the edge weight corresponds to the distance $(1 - similarity)$. In this graph, cluster centers are found by searching for the node that has the most neighbors with a distance smaller than a threshold. This threshold is based on the average distance of all nodes in the graph. Finally, a cluster consists of the center and all its neighbors in a certain range. By repeating this process multiple times

Fig. 7. Detected clusters in search results for "heart", "glass" (Google Images)

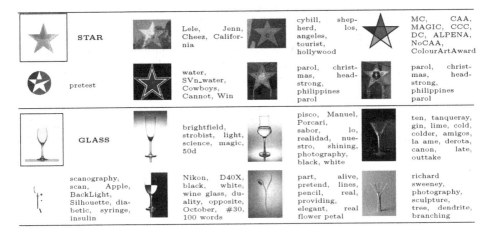

Fig. 8. Images (attached: tag-lists) retrieved in our Flickr set containing similar shape as template (framed) but not according tag. Images not necessarily show same object.

while removing the previously found centers and neighbors, several clusters are extracted. It is amazing what different clusters are found within some categories showing the ambiguity of the words. For example various meanings of "glass": different forms of glasses for drinking, windows or even glass wash liquids (Fig. 7).

Re-tagging. As our implementation works very efficient, it can be used to quickly find multiple images containing a shape similar to a template image in a large photo database. The test photo collection with about one million images we downloaded from Flickr is enriched with a tag-list we also obtained from Flickr (textual information describing the image and added by Flickr users). Searching for a template image in the photo database may lead to a number of images that contain visual similarity to the template although not containing the according query in their tag-list (Fig. 8). In this case, an additional tag is added to the list which leads to a more complete tag-list. If the photo collection is then searched in a textual way, more true positive images are returned.

6   Conclusion

We present an efficient approach to find similar images in large datasets based on the local self-similarity descriptor and an ensemble matching strategy that runs completely on GPU using CUDA. We made some effort such that the descriptor database only has to be generated once for all images and, afterwards, enables efficient matching that works directly on it. New images can be directly added. Based on a novel voting-scheme to compare the spatial arrangement of descriptors, our GPU implementation searches the content of thousands of images in only a few seconds without any further pre-processing steps. Thus, images can be searched nearly instantly. Evaluation is performed with several datasets. Depending on the image size and content, on average about 1800 image comparisons are carried out per second. Applying our implementation to clustering of a given set of images retrieved for a textual query leads to fascinating identifications of various meanings of ambiguous words and extending tag-lists of similar images can further improve retrieval based on textual search.

Acknowledgments. This work has been partially funded by the DFG Emmy Noether fellowship (Le 1341/1-1) and an NVIDIA Professor Partnership Award.

References

1. Shechtman, E., Irani, M.: Matching Local Self-Similarities across Images and Videos. In: IEEE Conf. on Comp. Vis. and Pat. Recogn, CVPR (2007)
2. Lowe, D.G.: Object Recognition from Local Scale-Invariant Features. In: Proc. of Int. Conf. on Comp. Vis., ICCV (1999)
3. Sivic, J., Zisserman, A.: Video Google: A Text Retrieval Approach to Object Matching in Videos. In: Proc. of Int. Conf. on Comp. Vis (ICCV), vol. 2, pp. 1470–1477 (2003)
4. Zhang, Y., Jia, Z., Chen, T.: Image Retrieval with Geometry-Preserving Visual Phrases. In: IEEE Conf. on Comp. Vis. and Pat. Recogn (CVPR), pp. 809–816 (2011)
5. Oliva, A., Torralba, A.: Modeling the Shape of the Scene: A Holistic Representation of the Spatial Envelope. Int. Journal of Comp. Vis. 42, 145–175 (2001)
6. Douze, M., Jégou, H., Sandhawalia, H., Amsaleg, L., Schmid, C.: Evaluation of GIST descriptors for web-scale image search. In: Proc. of ACM Int. Conf. on Image and Video Retrieval, CIVR (2009)
7. Johnson, T., Georgel, P., Raguram, R., Frahm, J.M.: Fast Organization of Large Photo Collections using CUDA. In: Wksp. on Comp. Vis. on GPUs, ECCV (2010)
8. Xiao, J., Hays, J., Ehinger, K.A., Oliva, A., Torralba, A.: SUN database: Large-scale scene recognition from abbey to zoo. In: IEEE Conf. on Comp. Vis. and Pat. Recogn, CVPR (2010)
9. Shrivastava, A., Malisiewicz, T., Gupta, A., Efros, A.A.: Data-driven Visual Similarity for Cross-domain Image Matching. ACM Trans. Graph. 30 (2011)
10. Boiman, O., Irani, M.: Detecting Irregularities in Images and in Video. Int. Journal of Comp. Vis. 74, 17–31 (2007)
11. Chatfield, K., Philbin, J., Zisserman, A.: Efficient Retrieval of Deformable Shape Classes using Local Self-Similarities. In: Wksp. on Non-rigid Shape Analysis and Deformable Image Alignment, ICCV, pp. 264–271 (2009)
12. Schindler, K., Suter, D.: Object Detection by Global Contour Shape. Pattern Recogn. 41, 3736–3748 (2008)
13. Fei-Fei, L., Fergus, R., Perona, P.: Learning Generative Visual Models from Few Training Examples: An Incremental Bayesian Approach Tested on 101 Object Categories, vol. 12, p. 178. IEEE Computer Society, Los Alamitos (2004)
14. Mark, J., Huiskes, B.T., Lew, M.S.: New Trends and Ideas in Visual Concept Detection: The MIR Flickr Retrieval Evaluation Initiative. In: MIR 2010: Proc. of the 2010 ACM Int. Conf. on Multimedia Information Retrieval, pp. 527–536. ACM, New York (2010)
15. Aly, M., Munich, M., Perona, P.: Indexing in Large Scale Image Collections: Scaling Properties and Benchmark. In: IEEE Wksp. on Applications of Comp. Vis., WACV (2011)

Atomic Action Features:
A New Feature for Action Recognition

Qiang Zhou[1] and Gang Wang[1,2]

[1] Advanced Digital Sciences Center, Singapore
Zhou.Qiang@adsc.com.sg
[2] Nanyang Technological University, Singapore
wanggang@ntu.edu.sg

Abstract. We introduce an atomic action based features and demonstrate that it consistently improves performance on human activity recognition. The features are built using auxiliary atomic action data collected in our lab. We train a kernelized SVM classifier for each atomic action class. Then given a local spatio-temporal cuboid of a test video, we represent it using the responses of our atomic action classifiers. This new atomic action feature is discriminative, and has semantic meanings. We perform extensive experiments on four benchmark action recognition datasets. The results show that atomic action features either outperform the corresponding low level features or significantly boost the recognition performance by combining the two.

1 Introduction

Low level local spatio-temporal features such as HOG and HOF [1–8] have been shown very successful for action recognition in the past. In a "bag of words" representation scheme, these local features are directly clustered to build a visual dictionary and then represented as visual words. During this process, neither semantic nor discriminative cues are utilized. Hence redundant or non-informative visual patterns might be kept. We argue that representing local features in a semantic, discriminative space may offer extra advantages and provide complementary information to that of the low level features.

In this paper, we propose atomic action features, a new representation of local spatio-temporal cuboids based on atomic actions. Atomic actions are basic units of human actions, such as "raising a hand", "one-arm waving". Many atomic actions can be characterized by local motion, and complex actions such as "playing basketball" can be considered as compositions of atomic actions. Intuitively, we can categorize an action based on what atomic actions are observed and how frequent they are. Our idea is to encode local features in atomic action space. Figure 1 illustrate the framework of extracting our atomic action feature representation. The implementation is simple: we train a number of discriminative atomic action classifiers (kernelized SVM classifiers are employed in this paper), then for a local spatio-temporal cuboid, we apply the learned classifiers. A classification score denotes the confidence that a cuboid belongs to an atomic

A. Fusiello et al. (Eds.): ECCV 2012 Ws/Demos, Part I, LNCS 7583, pp. 291–300, 2012.

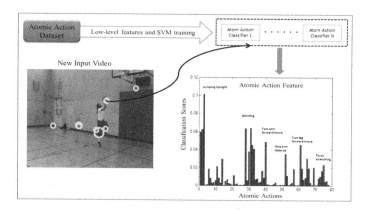

Fig. 1. Illustration of the atomic action feature extraction process. We first collect an atomic action dataset. For each atomic action class, we train a kernelized SVM based on low level features. Given a new action video, for each local spatio-temporal cuboid, we run all the atomic action classifiers. The classification scores are used as the atomic action features to represent the cuboid.

action. Then the set of classification scores are used to represent the cuboid, which shows how likely the cuboid belongs to each of the atomic actions. The new feature representation is complementary to the low-level features, as shown by our experiments.

We build this feature representation based on two insights. First, the representation is discriminative. We train our atomic action SVM classifiers using many positive and negative training examples. In the training process, discriminative visual patterns that are beneficial for classification are preserved, while the others are abandoned. By mapping a local spatio-temporal cuboid to this space, we explicitly exploit its affinity with these discriminative visual patterns. Second, the representation has semantic meanings, and is well aligned with human interpretation.

As a result, though the methodology is conceptually simple, we find it works very well on most of the popular action recognition databases. It either outperforms the corresponding low level features or boosts the performance by combining it with the low level features. And interestingly, our atomic action classifiers have very strong generalization ability. We collect atomic action videos in our lab, with around 10 subjects. The same atomic actions classifiers are applied to four datasets: KTH [9], Hollywood2 [10], Olympic Sport [5] and Youtube [2]. All the results show the effectiveness of our method without adapting the atomic action classifiers. This is very useful, since we don't have to manually annotate atomic action examples for a specific dataset when applying this idea.

1.1 Related Work

Our work is most relevant to the line of work which uses many object categories as the basic representation for image annotation, retrieval, and classification [11, 12, 6, 13]. Our works differs from theirs in two senses. First, we develop this representation for action representation, while they tackle image analysis. Second, our atomic action features are local features. In contrast, [14, 12] build global image features, and [11] detects object instances based on sub-windows, which are still semi-local. In [6], Liu et al. proposed a middle level representation: a video sequence is represented with responses to a set of attribute classifiers. In this paper, we represent each local spatio-temporal cuboid using atomic action features. Local features are expected to be more robust to clutter, occlusion, etc.

We learn atomic action features using positive and negative examples. Recently, there has been growing interest in learning features for action recognition [15, 16]. These works learn spatio-temporal features in a unsupervised manner, to replace the HOG/HOF features, and show promising results. Our work is complementary to theirs, since we can build our atomic action features based on their learned representation.

Atomic actions are studied before by various researchers [17, 18]. They usually aim to reliably detect atomic actions, or build models to model the composition of atomic actions. Different from their work, we encode local features in the semantic atomic action space and can apply it to various action recognition tasks including sports recognition and movie clip recognition.

2 Approach

Our approach is to build atomic action features for human action recognition. The atomic action features are expected to capture the semantic meanings of local spatio-temporal cuboids, and are discriminative. We have training and test videos, we also collect a dataset with atomic action clips. We train a kernelized SVM classifier for each atomic action based on the conventional low level features Then given a local spatio-temporal cuboid, we extract the same low level features, and apply our atomic action classifiers to produce atomic action features, which are the classification responses. We train classifiers based on these new atomic action features. We also combine atomic action features with the original low level features in a multiple kernel learning framework.

2.1 Collecting an Atomic Action Dataset

To our best knowledge, there are no atomic action datasets available. We collect an atomic action dataset in our lab to train the atomic action classifiers. We choose 26 common atomic actions, including "one-hand waving", "two-hands up", "stretching", "stand up", and so on. For each atomic action class, we invite around 10 volunteers to perform it. Then we can run a saliency detector to detect clean local spatio-temporal cuboid to represent these actions. In order to deal with view variance, we capture each atomic action in three different views. In total, our dataset includes about 1300 videos.

2.2   Training Atomic Action Classifier to Generate Atomic Action Features

We train atomic action classifiers based on local features, as atomic actions are usually characterized by local motion. For each atomic action video, we run the STIP [19] detector to find local spatio-temporal cuboids which contain the salient information. We choose histogram of oriented gradient (HOG) and histogram of optical flow (HOF) [1] to describe local appearance and motion, due to their popularity and the superior performance [1–3, 5]. Following [1], we concatenate HOG and HOF descriptors as a single feature vector For each atomic action category, we randomly choose 2000 cuboids as positive training examples, we also randomly choose 2000 negative samples from all the other categories. A binary SVM classifier with the chi-square kernel is trained based these positive and negative training examples. Note that each atomic action class has three different views. We train a classifier for each view independently due to the big inter-view variation. At the end, we have 78 classifiers in total.

We want to use classification scores as the feature representation, then classification scores of different classifiers must be calibrated. We do this by converting the SVM decision values into probabilistic scores by using the sigmoid mapping function:

$$g(x) = \frac{1}{1 + \exp\left(af(x) + b\right)} \tag{1}$$

where $f(x)$ is the classification score of an atomic action classifier on a local cuboid x, a and b are sigmoid function parameters. We directly use the LIBSVM [20] software to generate probabilistic outputs.

Then given a new local cuboid x_t, we run all the atomic action classifier on it and get an atomic action feature (AAF) vector.

$$AAF(x_t) = [g_1(x_t), \ldots, g_N(x_t)] \tag{2}$$

where $g_i(x)$ is the probabilistic score of the ith atomic action classifier. We use ℓ_2 normalization scheme to normalize the feature vector.

2.3   Using Atomic Action Features to Recognize Actions

We apply our atomic action features to general action recognition. We adopt the most popular "bag of words" scheme to make a fair comparison with the original low level features. But note that our features can also be used with other complex models.

Two types of global representation are tested. The first one is the original bag of words representation. No spatio-temporal information is exploited. In the second method, we follow [1] to partition a video into several spatio-temporal grids. We use three types of spatio-temporal grids: $1 \times 1\ t1$, $1 \times 1\ t2$ and $h3 \times 1\ t1$. More details can be found in [1]. We call the first method BoW and the second methods SPM in the rest of this paper.

Again, we use the SVM classifier with the chi-square kernel to recognize actions.

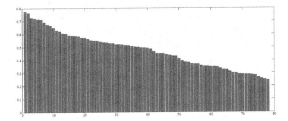

Fig. 2. The average precision (AP) score of the 78 atomic action classifiers on a validation set. The three atomic action classes which have the highest AP values are: torso bending, torso stretching, and one-arm raise up; the three classes which have the lowest AP values are: body whirling, jumping upright and one-arm forward raise up.

For each type of low-level features (such as the HOG/HOF), we can produce the corresponding atomic action features. These two features are expected to be complimentary. We also combine these two features together in the multiple kernel learning framework. We construct a chi-square kernel for each, and then add the two kernels with weights. The weights are learnt via cross validation. Our experimental results show that the combined kernel always works better than the kernel constructed using the original low-level features. This is interesting, as for a low-level feature, we can use this method to boost its performance.

3   Experiments

3.1   Evaluating the Trained Atomic Action Classifiers

We first evaluate the performance of our atomic action classifiers on a validation set. For a particular atomic action classifier, there are 350 positive test samples (cuboids) and 14000 negative test samples (cuboids). An average precision (AP) score is calculated for each atomic action classifier. Figure 2 shows the AP of all categorizes. The mean AP over all classifiers is 0.473. It shows our atomic action classifiers can do reasonably well on classification.

3.2   Performance of the Atomic Action Features on Different Dataset

The same atomic action classifiers are applied to four benchmarks dataset to produce atomic action features for recognition.

The KTH Action Dataset. This dataset is firstly introduced in [20]. We follow a previous experiment setup [9, 3] and train a multi-class classifier and the average accuracy is used to evaluate the performance.

We report the performances of different types of feature on the KTH dataset in Table 1. For all the compared features, the visual dictionary size is 1024.

Table 1. Average Accuracy values on the KTH dataset. "HOG" shows the results of only using the HOG features to represent each local spatio-temporal cuboid. "HOF" shows the results of only using the HOF features to represent each local spatio-temporal cuboid. "HOG/HOF" shows the results of concatenating HOG and HOF features (162 dimensions in total) to represent each local spatio-temporal cuboid. "Atom" shows the results of only using our atomic action features to represent each local spatio-temporal cuboid. "HOG/HOF+Atom" shows the results of combing "HOG/HOF" and atomic action features with a multiple kernel SVM classifier. "Bow" means the standard bag of word scheme; "SPM" means spatio-temporal grids are used, and each grid is represented as a bag of words histogram.

Feature	HOG	HOF	HOG/HOF	Atom	HOG/HOF+Atom
BoW	81.1%	91.4%	89.6%	88.3%	93.2%
SPM	81.6%	90.7%	88.5%	87.5%	93.0%

We use the same size for all the other four datasets. And a chi-square kernelized SVM classifier is applied. The performance of atomic action features is comparable to that of "HOF/HOF". Combining the two significantly boosts the performance.

The Hollywood2 Dataset. This is a dataset of 12 action classes collected from 69 Hollywood movies [10]. We follow the experiment setup of [3] and train a binary classifier for each action class. We first compute the average precision (AP) for each action class. And the mean average precision over all the action classes is reported, as in [10, 3].

Table 2. Average Precision (AP) values on the Hollywood2 Dataset. (Please refer to table 1 for notation definition.)

Feature	HOG	HOF	HOG/HOF	Atom	HOG/HOF+Atom
BoW	31.8%	40.3%	41.3%	43.1%	46.3%
SPM	37.6%	42.2%	44.0%	45.9%	49.4%

A comparison of our atomic action feature against other feature for each action category on the HOllywood2 dataset is shown in Table 2. For both BOW and SPM methods, our atomic action feature outperform HOG, HOF, and the corresponding HOG/HOF features. Atomic action features outperform the others on 7 categories with BOW, and on 8 categories with SPM over all the action classes. Combining "HOG/HOF" and atomic actions features obtains around 5% improvement on mean average precision, for both the BOW and SPM methods.

Olympic Sports Dataset. This dataset is created by Niebles et al. [5]. We follow their experimental setting in [5] and train a binary classifier for each action class. Similar to the Hollywood2 dataset, average precision (AP) is calculated for each action class, and mean average precision values over all the action classes are reported.

Table 3. Average Precision (AP) values on the Olympic Sports Dataset. (Please refer to table 1 for notation definition.

Feature	HOG	HOF	HOG/HOF	Atom	HOG/HOF+Atom
BoW	55.1%	57.2%	59.2%	63.1%	68.4%
SPM	61.9%	59.5%	63.9%	64.5%	71.0%

Table 4. Average Accuracy values for the classification task in YouTube Action dataset.(Please refer to table 1 for notation definition.)

Feature	HOG	HOF	HOG/HOF	Atom	HOG/HOF+Atom
BoW	61.7%	56.0%	61.9%	59.3%	68.4%
SPM	65.9%	57.7%	65.9%	62.7%	72.7%

In table 3, we show the performance of different features on the Olympic Sport dataset. Our atomic action feature achieve the best results on the mean average precision over all the categories, compared to HOG, HOF, and HOG/HOF. This shows our atomic action representation is very discriminative on this dataset. On most categorizes (12/16 for BOW and 11/16 for SPM), our atomic action features outperform the corresponding low-level HOG/HOF features. Combing the two types of features results in about 9% and 7% gain in mean AP for BOW and SPM methods, respectively. We shows two examples of our atomic action features on the Olympic Sport dataset in Figure 3, which are very descriptive.

YouTube Action Dataset. This dataset is published in [2] for evaluating action recognition in unconstrained videos. We follow their leave on out cross validation (LOOCV) method for these 25 groups in our experiments. Average accuracy scores over all the classes are compared.

The results are compared in table 4. From the table, we can see a gain of about 7% is achieved by combining our atomic action features with "HOG/HOF", compared to only using "HOF/HOF". Interestingly, "HOF/HOF+Atom" outperforms a more complicated approach proposed by Liu et al. [2], whose average accuracy number is 71.2%.

Table 5. Comparison of using the "HOG/HOF + Atom" feature with other methods in the literature

KTH		Olympic Sports		Hollywood2	
Niebles et al. [5]	91.3%	Niebles et al. [5]	72.1%	Alexander et al. [21]	45.3%
Laptev et al. [1]	91.8%	Liu et al. [6]	74.3%	Laptev et al.[1]	47.7%
Liu et al. [6]	91.6%				
Our Method	93.2%	Our Method	71.0%	Our Method	49.4%

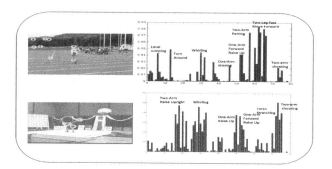

Fig. 3. Two examples of our atomic action feature on the Olympic Sports dataset. Left : local spatio-temporal cuboid (indicated in red), right : the corresponding atomic action features.

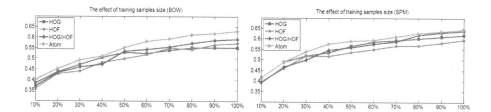

Fig. 4. The performance of different features on the Olympic Sports dataset, with different number of training samples. Our atomic action feature representation always outperform HOG, HOF and HOG/HOF features.

3.3   Comparison with Previous Work

In table 5, we compare our results with those of several previous papers on the KTH, Olympic Sports, and Hollywood2 datasets. Even only using a less sophisticated model (SPM), we find our approach "HOG/HOF+atom" works reasonably well compared to many previous, more sophisticated models.

3.4   The Effect of Training Sample Size

In this section, we investigate the effect of training sample size, when using the proposed atomic action features. We test the performance of atomic action features with different number of training samples on the Olympic Sports dataset. We randomly select 10%, 20%, 30%, 40%, 50%, 60%, 70%, 80%, 90% of the positive and negative videos respectively in the training data for each category to do the experiments. For each size, we repeat the experiments 10 times by randomly selecting training examples. The results are averaged and compared in Figure 4. We can see from the figure that the atomic action features always perform better than the other features (HOG, HOF, and HOG/HOF), with varying number of training samples.

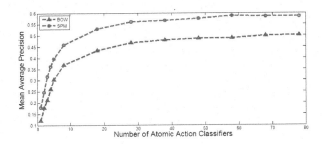

Fig. 5. The performance with different atomic action classifiers sizes on Olympic Sports dataset. For each classifier size, we repeat the experiments 30 times by randomly selecting classifiers. Averaged score is reported and compared.

3.5   The Effect of Atomic Action Classifier Size

We also investigate the effect of the number of atomic action classifiers, on the Olympic Sports datasets. We perform experiments with different numbers of atomic action classifiers: 1, 2, 3, 4, 5, 8, 18, 28, 38, 48, 58, and 68 respectively. For each number, we repeat the experiments 30 times, by randomly choosing a subset of atomic action classifiers. Averaged results are reported. Figure 5 shows the mean average precision values with varying number of atomic action classifiers. The improvement is not so significant when the size of atomic action classifiers reaches 30.

4   Conclusions and Discussions

In this paper, we have presented a simple method to build atomic action features for action recognition. Our extensive results on four action recognition benchmark datasets show the effectiveness of this method. There are two interesting things about this new type of feature. First, for a state-of-the-art low level feature (HOG/HOF), our method can at least help improving its performance by combing it with the atomic action features. Second, our atomic action classifiers have very strong generalization ability because they only capture local motion information. We build the atomic action classifiers using a dataset collected in our lab, but can successfully apply it to various datasets.

Acknowledgments. This study is supported by the research grant for the Human Sixth Sense Programme at the Advanced Digital Sciences Center from Singapore's Agency for Science, Technology and Research (A*STAR).

References

1. Laptev, I., Marszalek, M., Schmid, C., Rozenfeld, B.: Learning realistic human actions from movies. In: Proc. CVPR (2008)

2. Liu, J., Luo, J., Shah, M.: Recognizing realistic actions from videos "in the wild". In: Proc. CVPR (2009)
3. Wang, H., Ullah, M.M., Kläser, A., Laptev, I., Schmid, C.: Evaluation of local spatio-temporal features for action recognition. In: Proc. BMVC (2009)
4. Ni, B., Yan, S., Kassim, A.A.: Recognizing human group activities with localized causalities. In: Proc. CVPR (2009)
5. Niebles, J.C., Chen, C.-W., Fei-Fei, L.: Modeling Temporal Structure of Decomposable Motion Segments for Activity Classification. In: Daniilidis, K., Maragos, P., Paragios, N. (eds.) ECCV 2010, Part II. LNCS, vol. 6312, pp. 392–405. Springer, Heidelberg (2010)
6. Liu, J., Kuipers, B., Savarese, S.: Recognizing human actions by attributes. In: Proc. CVPR (2011)
7. Ni, B., Wang, G., Moulin, P.: Rgbd-hudaact: A color-depth video database for human daily activity recognition. In: ICCV Workshops (2011)
8. Zhang, T., Xu, C., Zhu, G., Liu, S., Lu, H.: A generic framework for event detection in various video domains. In: ACM Multimedia (2010)
9. Schüldt, C., Laptev, I., Caputo, B.: Recognizing human actions: A local svm approach. In: Proc. ICPR (2004)
10. Marszalek, M., Laptev, I., Schmid, C.: Actions in context. In: Proc. CVPR (2009)
11. Li, L.-J., Su, H., Lim, Y., Fei-Fei, L.: Objects as attributes for scene classificcation. In: ECCV Workshop (2010)
12. Rasiwasia, N., Vasconcelos, N.: Scene classification with low-dimensional semantic spaces and weak supervision. In: Proc. CVPR (2008)
13. Sadanand, S., Corso, J.J.: Action bank: A high-level representation of activity in video. In: Proc. CVPR (2012)
14. Torresani, L., Szummer, M., Fitzgibbon, A.: Efficient Object Category Recognition Using Classemes. In: Daniilidis, K., Maragos, P., Paragios, N. (eds.) ECCV 2010, Part I. LNCS, vol. 6311, pp. 776–789. Springer, Heidelberg (2010)
15. Taylor, G.W., Fergus, R., LeCun, Y., Bregler, C.: Convolutional Learning of Spatio-temporal Features. In: Daniilidis, K., Maragos, P., Paragios, N. (eds.) ECCV 2010, Part VI. LNCS, vol. 6316, pp. 140–153. Springer, Heidelberg (2010)
16. Le, Q.V., Zou, W.Y., Yeung, S.Y., Ng, A.Y.: Learning hierarchical invariant spatio-temporal features for action recognition with independent subspace analysis. In: Proc. CVPR (2011)
17. Gaidon, A., Harchaoui, Z., Schmid, C.: Actom sequence models for efficient action detection. In: Proc. CVPR (2011)
18. Ryoo, M.S., Aggarwal, J.K.: Recognition of composite human activities through context-free grammar based representation. In: Proc. CVPR (2006)
19. Laptev, I.: On space-time interest points. IJCV 64(2-3), 107–123 (2005)
20. Chang, C.C., Lin, C.J.: LIBSVM: A library for support vector machines. ACM Transactions on Intelligent Systems and Technology 2, 27:1–27:27 (2011), Software, http://www.csie.ntu.edu.tw/~cjlin/libsvm
21. Kläser, A., Marszalek, M., Schmid, C.: A spatio-temporal descriptor based on 3d-gradients. In: Proc. BMVC (2008)

Spatio-temporal SIFT and Its Application to Human Action Classification

Manal Al Ghamdi[1], Lei Zhang[2], and Yoshihiko Gotoh[1]

[1] University of Sheffield, UK
[2] Harbin Engineering University, PRC

Abstract. This paper presents a space-time extension of scale-invariant feature transform (SIFT) originally applied to the 2-dimensional (2D) volumetric images. Most of the previous extensions dealt with 3-dimensional (3D) spacial information using a combination of a 2D detector and a 3D descriptor for applications such as medical image analysis. In this work we build a spatio-temporal difference-of-Gaussian (DoG) pyramid to detect the local extrema, aiming at processing video streams. Interest points are extracted not only from the spatial plane (xy) but also from the planes along the time axis (xt and yt). The space-time extension was evaluated using the human action classification task. Experiments with the KTH and the UCF sports datasets show that the approach was able to produce results comparable to the state-of-the-arts.

1 Introduction

Consider a task of detecting humans and their motions in a video stream. It is a challenging task and requires identification of different levels of features that represent human presence and activities. It has been shown that a number of interest point based approaches can deal with this task [1–3]. They typically used a bag-of-features (BoF) model for feature representation, and proved their robustness to location changes and to noises. However, they depended mainly on the descriptor phase to produce discriminative representation of a video, discarding information relevant to the distribution of interest points in the spatio-temporal domain. As a consequence, the features produced often lacked temporal information for describing smooth motions. Furthermore, they were not able to address the scale and location invariance in the temporal domain.

Since its original development by Lowe [4], scale invariant feature transform (SIFT) has been successful in various image processing applications for locally detecting and describing interest points. It has proved its efficiency with tasks in a 2D space such as image similarity and classification. Recently its extension to higher dimensional spaces has been explored in order to represent more complex data. In this paper we present a SIFT extension for detecting interest points that can have significant local variations in both the spatial and temporal domains. Identified features are invariant to scale, location and orientation changes. The work is related to two recent studies: firstly Dorr *et al.* constructed spatio-temporal pyramids as a multi-resolution representation for video streams [5].

A. Fusiello et al. (Eds.): ECCV 2012 Ws/Demos, Part I, LNCS 7583, pp. 301–310, 2012.

They applied these pyramids to visualise dynamic gaze density maps. The second one was presented by Lopes *et al.* for human action recognition application [6]. They collected 2D SIFT and 2D SURF (speeded up robust features) interest points on the xy plane along the spatial domain and on the xt and yt planes along the spatio-temporal domain.

The approach consists of two stages: transformation of 3D (2D space and time) video signal to spatio-temporal pyramids, followed by extraction of interest points from the spacial and the spatio-temporal planes. The spatio-temporal SIFT (ST-SIFT) detector is presented in Section 3. To describe the region around the detected points we use the 3D SIFT descriptor developed by [7] that calculates the spatio-temporal gradient for each pixel in the given cuboid. The approach leads to local regions that are invariant to scale and location in both the spatial and the temporal domains. The contribution of this paper can be summarised as follows:

* Construction of multi-resolution space-time Gaussians and difference-of-Gaussian (DoG) pyramids, where each level contains a 3D smoothed and subsampled version of the previous level;
* Provision of an interest point detection schema from three different planes along the spatial and the temporal axes;
* Formulation of the space-time detector that is scale and location invariant;
* Application of the developed ST-SIFT on a human action classification task, with comparison to other state-of-the-art approaches.

2   Related Work

Recently, local features have received a great deal of attention in video-processing applications. They are extended to take into account the spatio-temporal nature of video data. Laptev and Lindeberg [8] extended the well-known Harris-Laplace detector in the spatial domain to the spatio-temporal domain. Schuldt *et al.* presented a video representation based on detected interest points combined with a support vector machine (SVM) classification schema for action recognition [3]. Motivated by these studies, Dollar *et al.* developed an approach to behaviour recognition, extracting local maxima from the space and the temporal domains based on responses of the Gaussian filter convolved with a pair of 1D Gabor filters [1].

SIFT extension can be categorised into three groups: (1) extension of the descriptor part only, combined with 2D detectors, (2) a full 3D spatial extension, and (3) a combination of different approaches to separately describing motion and appearance. One example of the first category is by Scovanner *et al.*, who extended the descriptor to the time domain and dropped the scale and location invariance covered by the detector [7]. In the second category Cheung and Hamarneh generalised SIFT to n-dimensional space (n-SIFT) with 2^{5n-3} dimensional features vector [9]. Allaire *et al.* also developed a full 3D extension, addressing two important issues not previously solved, namely, extracted points with low contrast and the full 3D orientation invariance [10]. Unlike the other groups Chen and Hauptmann handled the spatial and the temporal domains separately [11]. Their MoSIFT descriptor contained two parts: describing the spatial domain with a histogram of gradient (HOG) and the temporal domain with a histogram of optical flow (HOF) that captured moves of interest points.

3   Spatio-temporal SIFT Detector

3.1   Conventional 2D SIFT Detector

The 2D SIFT detector maps the spacial content of an image to a coordinate of scale, location and orientation invariant feature. This is achieved using a scale-space kernel function such as the Gaussian, which is a continuous function to capture stable features in different scales. The Gaussian function on a point (x, y) at scale σ can be defined as

$$G(x, y, \sigma) = \frac{1}{2\pi\sigma^2} \exp\left(-\frac{x^2 + y^2}{2\sigma^2}\right) \tag{1}$$

The scale-space function $L(x, y, \sigma)$ for the input image $I(x, y, \sigma)$ can be

$$L(x, y, \sigma) = G(x, y, \sigma) * I(x, y, \sigma) \tag{2}$$

where $*$ is the convolution operation. The following $D(x, y, \sigma)$ indicates stable locations in the scale-space, derived by convolution of the input image with the DoG functions:

$$D(x, y, \sigma) = (G(x, y, K\sigma) - G(x, y, \sigma)) * I(x, y, \sigma) \tag{3}$$
$$= L(x, y, K\sigma) - L(x, y, \sigma) \tag{4}$$

where the DoG function is the difference between two neighbours with the constant scale factor K. Finally the maxima and the minima of $D(x, y, \sigma)$ give scale-invariant points in the scale-space.

3.2   Spatio-temporal Difference of Gaussian Pyramid

To achieve the invariance in both space and time, we first calculate a spatio-temporal DoG pyramid. Interest points are extracted in three different planes — xy, yt, and xt — from the DoG. Points that are common in three planes carry vital information in both the spatial and the temporal domains. The DoG pyramid is a bandpass version of the original signal, which serves a scale-space of video to detect invariant interest points [5]. Unlike the previous works for SIFT extension where they constructed 3D spatial pyramids, we treat both the spatial and the temporal domains equally. The spatio-temporal Gaussian pyramid was originally introduced by Uz et al. in 1991, where downsampling was performed separately in the spatial and the temporal domains [12]. This means that every lower level in the pyramid is generated by dropping every other pixel in the spatial domain followed by dropping every other frame in the temporal domain.

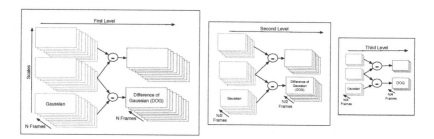

Fig. 1. Video pyramids. Each level is spatially and temporally downsampled from the previous level, and convolution with the 3D Gaussian is calculated to create a Gaussian pyramid. The DoG is then constructed by subtracting the adjacent Gaussian scales.

For a video sequence with a frame size of $W \times H$, let $I(x, y, t)$ denote a pixel at location (x, y) in frame t. We construct the Gaussian pyramid of N levels where N is determined by the frame size. G_i ($i = 0, \ldots, N - 1$) represents each level of the pyramid, where the highest level $G_0(t)$ corresponds to the original video frame sequence. This process leads to the multi-level spatio-temporal Gaussians and the DoG pyramids shown in Figure 1. Incremental convolution of video signal I with the 3D Gaussian filter G results in the scale space L of the first level:

$$L(x, y, t, \sigma, \tau) = G(x, y, t, \sigma, \tau) * I(x, y, t, \sigma, \tau) \tag{5}$$

with multiple scales S separated by a constant value of $K = 2^{1/S}$. The spatio-temporal Gaussian function with the spatial and the temporal scale parameters, σ and τ, is given by

$$G(x, y, t, \sigma, \tau) = \frac{1}{(2\pi)^{\frac{3}{2}} \sigma^2 \tau} \exp\left(-\frac{x^2 + y^2}{2\sigma^2} - \frac{t^2}{2\tau^2}\right) \tag{6}$$

Following Lowe [4], $S + 3$ scales are generated for each level to guarantee that local extrema detection will cover the complete octave. To produce a lower level the signal is spatially and temporally downsampled with the Gaussian at scales σ and τ. This yields a level with the lower frame rate and frames of the smaller size (illustrated on the left side in each box of Figure 1). The frame size at level G_i is $W/2^i \times H/2^i$, and $G_i(t)$ matches $G_0(2^i t)$ at time t (see this in Figure 2). The next step is to construct a DoG pyramid; for each level in the Gaussian pyramid, a DoG of one lower octave is derived by subtracting the Gaussian of the adjacent scales:

$$D(x, y, \sigma, \tau) = (G(x, y, K\sigma, \tau) - G(x, y, \sigma, \tau)) * I(x, y, \sigma, \tau) \tag{7}$$
$$= L(x, y, K\sigma, \tau) - L(x, y, \sigma, \tau) \tag{8}$$

This is shown on the right side in each box of Figure 1.

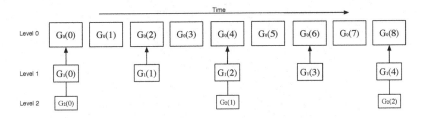

Fig. 2. Mapping strategy between three levels in the spatio-temporal Gaussian pyramid. A pixel $G_i(t)$ at level G_i maps to a pixel $G_0(2^i t)$. For example, $G_1(3)$ mapped to $G_0(6)$ and $G_2(1)$ mapped to $G_0(4)$.

3.3 Interest Points Detection

Once the DoG pyramid is constructed, local extrema of the adjacent scales in the xy, xt and yt planes are compared. The assumption here is that spatio-temporal events can be described by common interest points between the spatial axis (appearance information) and the temporal axis (motion information). Lopes *et al.* presented an approach to forming a spatio-temporal volume by stacking a set of frames from a video signal [6]. There are three directions to slice this volume into planes, as illustrated in Figure 3. One can slice through the spatial axis to create xy planes. Alternatively one can create a sequence of planes from the temporal axis combined with either the x or y spatial axis.

Extrema are detected from each slice of the spatio-temporal pyramid separately, and the union of common extrema in three directions are selected as interest points. It may be required to introduce some tolerance controlled by some threshold. This is because identified extrema may not be a pixel at exactly the same position although close to each other. Similar to the original 2D SIFT by Lowe [4], local extrema are detected by comparing each sample point to its eight neighbours in the current scale and the nine neighbours in the scales above and below. This is performed at each level within the DoG pyramid. In the end

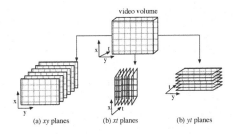

(a) *xy* planes   (b) *xt* planes   (b) *yt* planes

Fig. 3. The video volume and the generated planes along different directions. Three axes of each DoG scale volume represent x and y in the spacial and t in the temporal dimensions, creating three planes, xy, xt, and yt.

Fig. 4. Comparison between the interest points extracted with the 2D-SIFT (left) and the proposed ST-SIFT (right). The 2D-SIFT defines the spatial points only from the moving objects and the background, while the ST-SIFT defines the spatial points from different scales that have motion information.

filtering may be applied to remove noisy points and edges. Figure 4 shows the difference between the interest points extracted, from the KTH hand-waving action, using the traditional 2D-SIFT and the proposed ST-SIFT.

4   Experiments

We evaluated the ST-SIFT detector using the human action classification task.

4.1   Implementation

To extract interest points from the spatio-temporal video cube, ST-SIFT was built on a 2D-SIFT based image classifier in the *VLFeat toolbox* [13]. A BoF model implemented in this toolbox was an open library containing various algorithms for computer vision applications. The spatio-temporal regions around the interest points were described by the 3D HOG [7]. Publicly available code by Scovanner *et al.* was used, which is slightly different from what was described in [7]. The descriptor length was 640-dimensional for each interest point, which was determined by the number of bins to represent angles, θ and ϕ, in the sub-histograms.

The next was the vocabulary learning; descriptors generated for interest points were clustered to a pre-specified number of visual words. We used Elkan's k-means clustering algorithm, which was faster than the standard Lloyd's k-means. Centres of the generated clusters were referred to as 'visual words' while the set of these words was known as the 'spatio-temporal word vocabulary'. Based on the vocabulary, a frequency histogram was created where visual descriptors were mapped to the visual words. The word frequency in each video was accumulated onto a histogram known as a signature. A support vector machine (SVM) classifier was used to learn a model from signatures for each action. We used a non-linear SVM with a χ^2-kernel.

Table 1. Confusion matrix for the KTH dataset

	Walk	Jog	Run	Box	Wave	Clap
Walk	100	0	0	0	0	0
Jog	0	78	11	0	0	11
Run	0	11	89	0	0	0
Box	0	0	0	100	0	0
Wave	0	0	0	0	100	0
Clap	0	0	11	0	11	78

4.2 Experimental Setup

Two publicly available human actions datasets were employed. The first was known as the KTH dataset developed by Schuldt *et al.* [3]. It contained six different human activities — walking, jogging, running, hand-waving, boxing and hand-clapping. Each action was performed by 25 persons in 4 different scenarios with monotone background. Following the studies conducted by [2] and [14], we divided the dataset into two parts, 16 persons for training and 9 persons for testing.

The second one was the UCF sports dataset, more realistic but challenging data collected from broadcast sport videos by Ahmed *et al.* [15]. There were nine actions in the publicly available part of this dataset, consisting of diving, golf swinging, kicking, lifting, horseback riding, running, skating, swinging, walking[1]. Following the original paper [15], we used a leave-one-out cross validation training method.

When constructing a Gaussian pyramid, the number of scales was set to three for each of four levels in the KTH dataset, and three for each of three levels in the UCF sports dataset. The codebook size was a key parameter for BoF models. We followed the experiment procedure in [14], and the best performance was obtained for both datasets with the codebook size of 1500 words. A single SVM classifier was built for each action using all training samples.

4.3 Results

This section presents the performance of the ST-SIFT interest points detector using two datasets. Tables 1 and 2 show confusion matrices for human action classification experiments with the KTH and the UCF sports datasets. The overall accuracy of each was 90.74% and 80.56%, respectively. The approach using the ST-SIFT detector was able to clearly distinguish between similar actions such as walking and running.

In the second set of experiments, ST-SIFT was compared with two conventional SIFT algorithms. One was the combination of the original 2D DoG detector and the 2D HOG descriptor by Lowe [4], with which each frame was

---

[1] The tenth action, pole vaulting, was not publicly available.

Table 2. Confusion matrix for the UCF sports dataset

	Dive	Golf	Kick	Lift	Rid	Run	Skate	Swing	Walk
Dive	75	25	0	0	0	0	0	0	0
Golf	0	75	25	0	0	0	0	0	0
Kick	0	0	100	0	0	0	0	0	0
Lift	0	0	0	100	0	0	0	0	0
Rid	0	0	0	25	50	25	0	0	0
Run	0	0	0	0	0	100	0	0	0
Skate	0	0	25	0	0	25	50	0	0
Swing	0	0	0	0	0	0	25	75	0
Walk	0	0	0	0	0	0	0	0	100

represented separately. Another representation consisted of the 2D DoG detector and the 3D HOG descriptor developed in [7]. Table 3 shows that the ST-SIFT detector followed by the 3D HOG descriptor outperformed the other two representations. This indicates that ST-SIFT is able to (1) capture the interest points that have vital information in both the spatial and the temporal domains, which were missed by the conventional approaches, and to (2) represent events in real video sequences.

4.4   Comparison of ST-SIFT with the Recent State-of-the-Art

We compare the performance of ST-SIFT with approaches to interest points extraction published recently using KTH and UCF sports data. Note that some groups applied pre-processing and object tracking steps before extracting interest points while other groups combined multiple techniques to improve the performance. The purpose of this comparison is to show the rough position of ST-SIFT among the recent state-of-the-art techniques in the context of action classification task. ST-SIFT was not the best but among the state-of-the-art in the field.

The KTH dataset has been experimented with various techniques for action recognition task. In 2004, Schuldt *et al.* [3] combined Laptev [8] local space-time features with spatio-temporal jets to recognising complex motion patterns. Their experiment reported a 71.7% accuracy. In 2005, Dollar *et al.* [1] proposed sparse spatio-temporal features extended from the 2D corner detector and described the interest points region using the spatio-temporal cuboid and achieved a recognition accuracy of 81.2%. Laptev *et al.* [16] improved the accuracy to 91.8% by describing interest points with the histograms of oriented gradient (HoG) and

Table 3. Comparison of ST-SIFT and conventional detectors

detector	descriptor	KTH	UCF
ST SIFT	3D HOG	90.74%	80.56%
2D DoG	3D HOG	77.00%	77.78%
2D DoG	2D HOG	72.22%	58.52%

the optic flow (HoF). Niebles *et al.* [2] on the other hand achieved a lower performance of 83.3% than Dollar *et al.* [1] by describing the Dollar interest points with a spatial-temporal gradient cube.

For the UCF sports dataset, Rodriguez *et al.* [15] achieved 69.2% accuracy in 2008 by extending the traditional Maximum Average Correlation Height (MACH) filter to 3D volume and combining it with Spatio-temporal Regularity Flow (SPREF). In 2009, Liu *et al.* [17] reported a recognition rate of 74.5% by combining different detectors including Harris-Laplacian (HAR), Hessian-Laplacian (HES) and MSER and then they described the region of interest using Dollar *et al.* [1]. Wang *et al.* [18] outperformed them with 85.6% by dense sampling to extract video blocks and a 3D-HOG descriptor. Recently, Kläser *et al.* boosted the recognition accuracy to 86.7% by employing object localisation in the bag-of-visual-features representation [19]. An even better result of 87.3% accuracy was reached by Kovashka *et al.* by learning the space-time neighbourhoods in a BoF representation [20].

5 Conclusion

In this paper we presented a spatio-temporal extension to the 2D SIFT approach and demonstrated its performance using the task of human action classification. We combined the ST-SIFT detector with the 3D-HOG descriptor and applied to the KTH and the UCF sports datasets. The results showed that ST-SIFT was able detect local features for human activities. The purpose of this development was to extract local features that were invariant to location, scale, orientation and temporal changes. The KTH and the UCF sports datasets did not involve significant scaling and orientation changes; however, ST-SIFT should be able to deliver better performance when such changes are observed. They have been chosen to build a comparison level with the existing approaches that are usually tested on these datasets for this task. Future work includes application to video searching and retrieval using video data with high variation in scale, location and rotation.

Acknowledgements. The first author would like to thank Umm Al-Qura University, Makkah, Saudi Arabia for funding this work as part of her PhD scholarship program. This work is partly sponsored by National Natural Science Foundation of China #60702053, and Young Teacher Supporting Plan by Harbin Engineering University and Heilongjiang Province, China #1155G17.

References

1. Dollar, P., Rabaud, V., Cottrell, G., Belongie, S.: Behavior recognition via sparse spatio-temporal features. In: IEEE International Workshop on Visual Surveillance and Performance Evaluation of Tracking and Surveillance (2005)
2. Niebles, J., Wang, H., Fei-Fei, L.: Unsupervised learning of human action categories using spatial-temporal words. International Journal of Computer Vision 79 (2008)

3. Schuldt, C., Laptev, I., Caputo, B.: Recognizing human actions: a local SVM approach. In: International Conference on Pattern Recognition, vol. 3 (2004)
4. Lowe, D.G.: Distinctive image features from scale-invariant keypoints. International Journal of Computer Vision 60 (2004)
5. Dorr, M., Jarodzka, H., Barth, E.: Space-variant spatio-temporal filtering of video for gaze visualization and perceptual learning. In: Symposium on Eye-Tracking Research & Applications, New York (2010)
6. Lopes, A., Oliveira, R., de Almeida, J., de Araujo, A.A.: Spatio-temporal frames in a bag-of-visual-features approach for human actions recognition. In: Brazilian Symposium on Computer Graphics and Image Processing (2009)
7. Scovanner, P., Ali, S., Shah, M.: A 3-dimensional sift descriptor and its application to action recognition. In: International Conference on Multimedia (2007)
8. Laptev, I., Lindeberg, T.: Space-time interest points. In: International Conference on Computer Vision (2003)
9. Cheung, W., Hamarneh, G.: N-sift: N-dimensional scale invariant feature transform for matching medical images. In: International Symposium on Biomedical Imaging: From Nano to Macro (2007)
10. Allaire, S., Kim, J., Breen, S., Jaffray, D., Pekar, V.: Full orientation invariance and improved feature selectivity of 3d sift with application to medical image analysis. In: Computer Vision and Pattern Recognition Workshops (2008)
11. Chen, M.Y., Hauptmann, A.: Mosift: Recognizing human actions in surveillance videos. Transform (2009)
12. Uz, K., Vetterli, M., LeGall, D.: Interpolative multiresolution coding of advance television with compatible subchannels. IEEE Transactions on Circuits and Systems for Video Technology 1 (1991)
13. Vedaldi, A., Fulkerson, B.: Vlfeat: an open and portable library of computer vision algorithms. In: International Conference on Multimedia, New York (2010)
14. Shao, L., Mattivi, R.: Feature detector and descriptor evaluation in human action recognition. In: International Conference on Image and Video Retrieval (2010)
15. Rodriguez, M., Ahmed, J., Shah, M.: Action mach a spatio-temporal maximum average correlation height filter for action recognition. In: Conference on Computer Vision and Pattern Recognition (2008)
16. Laptev, I., Marszalek, M., Schmid, C., Rozenfeld, B.: Learning realistic human actions from movies. In: Conference on Computer Vision and Pattern Recognition (2008)
17. Liu, J., Luo, J., Shah, M.: Action recognition in unconstrained amateur videos. In: International Conference on Acoustics, Speech and Signal Processing (2009)
18. Wang, H., Ullah, M.M., Kläser, A., Laptev, I., Schmid, C.: Evaluation of local spatio-temporal features for action recognition. In: British Machine Vision Conference (2009)
19. Kläser, A., Marszałek, M., Laptev, I., Schmid, C.: Will person detection help bag-of-features action recognition? Technical Report RR-7373, INRIA Grenoble, France (2010)
20. Kovashka, A., Grauman, K.: Learning a hierarchy of discriminative space-time neighborhood features for human action recognition. In: Conference on Computer Vision and Pattern Recognition (2010)

Statistics of Pairwise Co-occurring Local Spatio-temporal Features for Human Action Recognition

Piotr Bilinski and Francois Bremond

INRIA Sophia Antipolis, STARS Team
2004 Route des Lucioles, 06902 Sophia Antipolis, France
{Piotr.Bilinski,Francois.Bremond}@inria.fr
www.inria.fr

Abstract. The bag-of-words approach with local spatio-temporal features have become a popular video representation for action recognition in videos. Together these techniques have demonstrated high recognition results for a number of action classes. Recent approaches have typically focused on capturing global statistics of features. However, existing methods ignore relations between features and thus may not be discriminative enough. Therefore, we propose a novel feature representation which captures statistics of pairwise co-occurring local spatio-temporal features. Our representation captures not only global distribution of features but also focuses on geometric and appearance (both visual and motion) relations among the features. Calculating a set of bag-of-words representations with different geometrical arrangement among the features, we keep an important association between appearance and geometric information. Using two benchmark datasets for human action recognition, we demonstrate that our representation enhances the discriminative power of features and improves action recognition performance.

1 Introduction

In recent years, recognition of human actions has became one of the most popular topic in computer vision domain. It has many potential applications, such as video surveillance, video indexing, retrieving and browsing, sport event analysis, human-computer interface and virtual reality. Although various methods have been proposed and much progress has been made, action recognition still remains a challenging problem. The main issues are: variations in visual and motion appearance of both people and actions, occlusions, noise, enormous amount of video data and changes in viewpoint, scale, rotation and illumination.

Over the last decade, there have been many studies on the recognition of human actions in videos. Most of the state-of-the-art approaches can be divided into four categories depending on the type of features used. The first group of methods uses silhouette information [1–5]. The second category of techniques analyses object or motion trajectories [6–9]. However, both of these groups require precise algorithms, which is often very difficult to achieve due to such challenges as:

A. Fusiello et al. (Eds.): ECCV 2012 Ws/Demos, Part I, LNCS 7583, pp. 311–320, 2012.
© Springer-Verlag Berlin Heidelberg 2012

low discriminative appearance, illumination changes, camera movement, occlusions, noise and drifting problems. The third group of methods uses local spatio-temporal features [10–14]. Local spatio-temporal features have recently become a very popular video representation for action recognition. They have demonstrated promising recognition results for a number of action classes. They are able to capture both motion and visual appearance. Moreover, they are robust to scale variations, viewpoint changes and background clutter. Over the last decade, many algorithms have been proposed to detect local spatio-temporal interest points (e.g. Harris3D [10], Cuboid [15], Hessian [16] or Dense sampling [17]) and represent them using spatio-temporal descriptors (e.g. HOG [18], HOG3D [12], HOF [18], Cuboid [15] or ESURF [16]). One of the most frequently used detectors in the literature is the Harris3D [10], which is a space-time extension of the Harris operator. This algorithm is usually applied with Histogram of Oriented Gradients (HOG) and Histogram of Oriented Flow (HOF) descriptors [18]. The former describes local visual appearance and the latter characterizes local motion appearance of an interest point.

Local spatio-temporal features have been mostly used with the bag-of-words model. Together, these techniques have shown to achieve high recognition rate across various datasets. The bag-of-words model encodes global statistics of features, computing histogram of feature occurrences in a video sequence. This technique also has its own limitations. One of the main drawbacks of the bag-of-words model is that it ignores local pairwise relations among the features. To overcome this limitation, contextual features from the fourth category could be used. Contextual features can capture human-object interactions [19], scene context information [20, 21], figure-centric features [22–25], or pairwise relations between features [24, 26, 27]. Oikonomopoulos et al. [26] have proposed to construct class-specific codebooks of local features and encode spatial co-occurrences of pairs of codewords. Then, the action model is classified based on the probabilistic voting framework. Liu et al. [14] have explored the correlation of the compact video-word clusters using a modified correlogram. Banerjee et al. [24] have proposed to learn local neighbourhood relationships between local features, and train a CRF based human activity classifier. The neighbourhood relationships are modelled in terms of pairwise co-occurrence statistics. However, these methods are restricted using discriminative power of individual local features and ignoring association between appearance and geometric information. Thus, the performance of these techniques mainly depends on a single type of applied features. Ta et al. [27] have proposed to encode both appearance and spatio-temporal relations of local features. However, by calculating two independent codebooks (one codebook per feature type), this method ignores important association between appearance and geometric information.

To differ from those ideas, we propose a novel representation based on local spatio-temporal features and bag-of-words technique. Recent methods have typically focused on capturing global statistics of features. However, existing approaches ignore relations between the features, and thus may not be discriminative enough. Therefore, we propose a novel feature representation which captures statistics of pairwise co-occurring local spatio-temporal features. Our representation captures not only global distribution of features but also focuses on geometric and appearance (both visual and motion) relations among the features. Calculating a set of bag-of-words representations with different geometrical arrangement among the features, we keep an important association between appearance and geometric information. We evaluate our approach on two publicly available datasets for human action recognition (KTH and UCF-ARG datasets). We show that the proposed representation enhances the discriminative power of local features and improves action recognition performance.

The rest of the paper is organized as follows. In section 2, we present our novel action recognition approach. In section 3, we present obtained results from our extensive set of experiments. Finally, in section 4, we conclude with future directions of work.

2   Proposed Approach

We propose a novel feature representation which captures statistics of pairwise co-occurring local spatio-temporal features. Firstly, we detect local interest points and capture both motion and visual appearance around extracted points. Then, we create a set of bag-of-words representations with different geometrical arrangement among the features. Our representation captures not only global distribution of features but also focuses on geometric and appearance (both visual and motion) relations among the features. Moreover, calculating a set of bag-of-words representations, we keep an important association between geometric and appearance information. The technique presented in this section enhances the discriminative abilities of features and improves action recognition performance.

2.1   Feature Extraction

Local spatio-temporal features have demonstrated high recognition results for a number of action classes. Therefore, we use them as basic features for our approach.

For each video sequence, we extract local spatio-temporal points of interest and their local spatio-temporal descriptors. To detect interest points, we use the sparse Harris3D corner detector [10]. To enhance the probability of capturing relevant information, we apply an algorithm searching over multiple spatial and temporal scales. Then, for each detected point, we compute HOG and HOF descriptors.

We highlight here that, all the mentioned algorithms in this section were selected based on their use in the literature and provide a good baseline for comparison with state-of-the-art techniques. However, our action representation method is independent of the type of detector and descriptor, and can be used together with any other algorithm.

2.2 Statistics of Pairwise Co-occurring Local Spatio-temporal Features

In this section, we present our novel feature representation which captures statistics of pairwise co-occurring local spatio-temporal features. The following steps are applied for each video sequence independently.

Firstly, we extract local spatio-temporal interest points $\mathbb{P} = \{P_1, ..., P_n\}$ (where $P_l = (x_l, y_l, t_l)$) in a video sequence (Section 2.1). Then, for every point P_i we find its n-nearest neighbouring points from the extracted set of points $\mathbb{P}$:

$$\mathbb{F}(\mathbb{P}) = \{(P_i, P_j) \in \mathbb{P}^2 : i_{nn}(\mathbb{P}, i, j) \leq n\}, \tag{1}$$

where $i_{nn}(\mathbb{P}, i, j) = m$ means that point P_j is the m-th nearest neighbour in order to point P_i. To calculate the distance between two points, we use the Euclidean metric.

Then, to differentiate pairs of points between those that are close to each other from those that are far away from each other, we split the set $\mathbb{F}(\mathbb{P})$ to several smaller subsets based on the value of the function i_{nn}:

$$\mathbb{S}(\mathbb{P}, a, b) = \{(P_i, P_j) \in \mathbb{F}(\mathbb{P}) : i_{nn}(\mathbb{P}, i, j) \in \langle a, b \rangle\}, \tag{2}$$

where $0 \leq a \leq b \leq n$.

As we mentioned in the previous section, each point P_i is represented not only by its $3D$ position but also by the HOG-HOF descriptor. For simplicity, we indicate a HOG-HOF descriptor assigned to point P_i as $\mathfrak{D}(P_i)$. Therefore, to capture appearance (both visual and motion) relationship between two points, we represent each pair of points from the set $\mathbb{S}(\mathbb{P}, a, b)$ as a concatenation of their descriptors:

$$\mathbb{D}(\mathbb{P}, a, b) = \{\mathfrak{D}(P_i) || \mathfrak{D}(P_j) : (P_i, P_j) \in \mathbb{S}(\mathbb{P}, a, b)\}, \tag{3}$$

where $||$ is the concatenation operator.

Finally, we represent each video sequence as a collection of sets of features $\mathbb{D}(\mathbb{P}, a, b)$:

$$\mathbb{V}(\mathbb{P}, \mathbb{K}) = (\mathbb{D}(\mathbb{P}, k_1, k_2), \mathbb{D}(\mathbb{P}, k_2, k_3), ..., \mathbb{D}(\mathbb{P}, k_{|\mathbb{K}|-1}, k_{|\mathbb{K}|})), \tag{4}$$

where $\mathbb{K} = (k_1, k_2, ..., k_{|\mathbb{K}|})$. These sets vary in different geometrical arrangement among the features.

Our novel representation of features captures geometric and appearance (both visual and motion) relations among the features. Moreover, calculating sets of features $\mathbb{D}(\mathbb{P}, a, b)$, we keep an important association between geometric and appearance information. Thus, by using suitable designed features, we are able to overcome the limitation of the bag-of-words approach.

2.3   Action Representation

To represent videos, we apply the bag-of-words model for each feature class (*i.e.* HOG-HOF and $\mathbb{D}(\mathbb{P}, ., .))$ independently. We construct visual vocabularies from training videos clustering computed features. Then, we assign each feature to its closest visual world. The obtained histograms of visual world occurrences over video forms the final representation.

The amount of features $\mathbb{D}(\mathbb{P}, ., .)$ extracted from all the training videos can be large. Therefore, to speed-up the approach, we propose to perform clustering in the following hierarchical manner. In the first step, we process each video sequence independently. To reduce the computational cost, we limit the number of features for each video sequence to F_{MAX} using random sampling. Then, the obtained features are clustered. In the second step, we process all the training videos together and re-cluster all the obtained groups of features to create a final codebook representation.

2.4   Action Classification

To recognize an action, we use Multiple Kernel Learning (MKL) formulated for multi-class classification problem. We use MKL because it provides a natural method to combine different types of features. Given a list of base kernel functions, MKL searches for their linear combination which maximizes a performance measure. MKL considers a convex combination of n kernels:

$$K(H_i, H_j) = \sum_{z=1}^{n} \beta_z K_z(H_i, H_j), \tag{5}$$

with $\beta_z \geq 0$ and $\sum_{z=1}^{n} \beta_z = 1$.

To compare two m-bins histograms $H_i = [H_i(1), ..., H_i(m)]^T$ and $H_j = [H_j(1), ..., H_j(m)]^T$, we apply a χ^2 distance:

$$\chi^2(H_i, H_j) = \frac{1}{2} \sum_{z=1}^{m} \left(\frac{(H_i(z) - H_j(z))^2}{H_i(z) + H_j(z)} \right), \tag{6}$$

This distance is then converted into a χ^2 kernel using a multi-channel generalized Gaussian kernel:

$$K_z(H_i, H_j) = exp(-\frac{1}{A_z}\chi^2(H_i, H_j)), \tag{7}$$

where A_z is the normalization parameter set as in [18].

3   Experiments

Our experiments demonstrate the effectiveness of the proposed representation for a various of action categories. We evaluate our approach on two benchmark datasets for human action recognition - KTH and UCF-ARG datasets. Sample frames from video sequences of these datasets are presented in Figure 1. The performed experiments demonstrate that our representation enhances the discriminative power of features and improves action recognition accuracy.

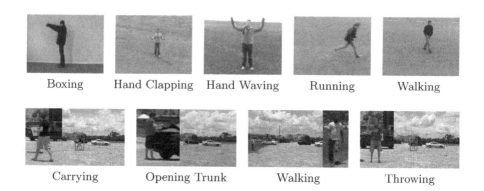

| Boxing | Hand Clapping | Hand Waving | Running | Walking |

| Carrying | Opening Trunk | Walking | Throwing |

Fig. 1. Sample frames from video sequences of the KTH (first row) and UCF-ARG (second row) datasets

3.1 Implementation Details

In order to quantize local features, we use the k-means clustering technique. We use the L_2 norm to calculate the distance between features and visual words. We set the maximum amount of features extracted from a single video sequence to $F_{MAX} = 10^5$, which is a good compromise between the amount of data obtained from a video sequence and the time needed for clustering. We set the size of the codebook to 1000, which has shown empirically to give good results. In order to create statistics of pairwise co-occurring local spatio-temporal features, we set the parameter $\mathbb{K}$ to $(1, 2, 4, 8, 16)$, which has shown empirically to give good results.

In all our experiments, we apply the cross-validation technique to both gauge the generalizability of the proposed approach, and select the most discriminative statistics of pairwise co-occurring local spatio-temporal features. We use the Leave-One-Out Cross-Validation (LOOCV) technique, where videos of one person are used as the validation data, and the remaining videos as the training data. This is done repeatedly so that the videos of each person are used once as the validation data.

3.2 KTH Dataset

The KTH [28][1] dataset contains six types of human actions: walking, jogging, running, boxing, hand waving and hand clapping. Each action is performed several times by 25 different subjects in four different scenarios: outdoors (s1), outdoors with scale variation (s2), outdoors with different clothes (s3) and indoors (s4). The dataset contains 599 video files. All sequences were recorded with 25 fps frame rate.

---

[1] http://www.nada.kth.se/cvap/actions/

The dataset contains a set of challenges like: scale changes, illumination variations, shadows, different scenarios, cloth variations, inter and intra action class speed variations and low resolution (160×120 pixels spatial resolution).

We follow recent evaluations on the KTH dataset [29–33] using LOOCV scheme. In general, LOOCV assesses the performance of an approach with much more reliability than splitting-based evaluation schemes because it is much more comprehensive. Results from the experiments are presented in Table 1. Comparison of our approach with state-of-the-art methods in the literature using LOOCV technique is presented in Table 2. For scenarios $s1$, $s2$, $s3$ and $s4$, our approach obtains the recognition rate of 98.67%, 95.33%, 93.20% and 98.00% respectively. Overall, our approach obtains 96.30% recognition rate. The results clearly show that our representation enhances the discriminative power of features, improves action recognition performance and outperforms state-of-the-art techniques.

Table 1. KTH dataset: Evaluation of our approach. The table shows the recognition rate overall and for each scenario independently.

KTH	Recognition Rate
s1	98.67%
s2	95.33%
s3	93.20%
s4	98.00%
s1-s4	**96.30%**

Table 2. KTH dataset: Comparison of our approach with state-of-the-art methods in the literature

Method	Year	Recognition Rate
Ta *et al.* [27]	2010	93.0%
Liu *et al.* [29]	2009	93.8%
Wu *et al.* [30]	2011	94.5%
Kim *et al.* [31]	2007	95.33%
Wu *et al.* [32]	2011	95.7%
Lin *et al.* [33]	2011	95.77%
Our method		**96.30%**

3.3   UCF-ARG Dataset

The UCF-ARG[2] (University of Central Florida - Aerial camera, Rooftop camera and Ground camera) is a multiview human action dataset. It contains 12 actors performing ten types of human activities: boxing, carrying, clapping, digging, jogging, open-close trunk, running, throwing, walking and waving. Except for open-close trunk, all the other actions are performed 4 times by each actor in different directions. The open-close trunk action is performed 3 times by each actor. In total, we use 468 video sequences from the ground camera. The dataset is recorded using a high-definition camcorder (Sanyo Xacti FH1A camera) with 60 fps frame rate and spatial resolution of 1920×1080 pixels.

The dataset contains a set of challenges like: different shapes, sizes and ethnicities of people, scale changes, shadows, cloth variations, inter and intra action class speed variations, and different scenarios.

To the best of our knowledge there are no publicly available results for this dataset. Therefore, we compare our approach with popular baseline approach [18]. We use Harris3D to detect local spatio-temporal interest points and HOG-HOF descriptors to represent 3D video patches in the neighbourhood of detected points. Then, we apply bag-of-words model to represent video sequences and SVM for classification. The results from the experiments are presented in Table 3. The baseline approach obtains 80.98% recognition rate. Our proposed statistics of pairwise co-occurring local spatio-temporal features improve action recognition rate achieving 82.05% accuracy. We observe that also on this dataset, our representation enhances the discriminative power of local features and improves action recognition performance.

Table 3. UCF-ARG dataset: Comparison of our approach with baseline state-of-the-art method

Method	Year	Recognition Rate
Laptev *et al.* [18]	2008	80.98%
Our method		**82.05%**

4   Conclusions and Future Work

We have proposed a novel feature representation which captures statistics of pairwise co-occurring local spatio-temporal features. Our representation captures not only global distribution of features but also focuses on geometric and appearance (both visual and motion) relations among the features. Calculating a set of bag-of-words representations with different geometrical arrangement among the features, we keep an important association between appearance and geometric information. The proposed approach has been evaluated on two public benchmark datasets for human action recognition. Obtained results have demonstrated

---

[2] http://vision.eecs.ucf.edu/data/UCF-ARG.html

that our technique enhances the discriminative power of features and improves action recognition performance. In the future work, we intend to evaluate our technique using different interest point detectors and descriptors. We also intend to examine different machine learning techniques to combine various types of features.

Acknowledgements. This work was supported by the Région Provence-Alpes-Côte d'Azur. However, the views and opinions expressed herein do not necessarily reflect those of the financing institution.

References

1. Davis, J.: Hierarchical motion history images for recognizing human motion. In: IEEE Workshop on Detection and Recognition of Events in Video (2001)
2. Ahad, M., Tan, J., Kim, H., Ishikawa, S.: Motion history image: its variants and applications. Machine Vision and Applications (2010)
3. Aggarwal, J.K., Cai, Q.: Human motion analysis: a review. CVIU (1999)
4. Kim, T.-S., Uddin, Z.: In: Silhouette-based Human Activity Recognition Using Independent Component Analysis, Linear Discriminant Analysis and Hidden Markov Model. InTech (2010)
5. Lin, Z., Jiang, Z., Davis, L.S.: Recognizing actions by shape-motion prototype trees. In: ICCV (2009)
6. Messing, R., Pal, C., Kautz, H.: Activity recognition using the velocity histories of tracked keypoints. In: ICCV (2009)
7. Raptis, M., Soatto, S.: Tracklet Descriptors for Action Modeling and Video Analysis. In: Daniilidis, K., Maragos, P., Paragios, N. (eds.) ECCV 2010, Part I. LNCS, vol. 6311, pp. 577–590. Springer, Heidelberg (2010)
8. Kaaniche, M.-B., Bremond, F.: Gesture recognition by learning local motion signatures. In: CVPR (2010)
9. Wang, H., Klaser, A., Schmid, C., Cheng-Lin, L.: Action recognition by dense trajectories. In: CVPR (2011)
10. Laptev, I.: On space-time interest points. IJCV (2005)
11. Rapantzikos, K., Avrithis, Y., Kollias, S.: Dense saliency-based spatiotemporal feature points for action recognition. In: CVPR (2009)
12. Klaser, A., Marszalek, M., Schmid, C.: A spatio-temporal descriptor based on 3d-gradients. In: BMVC (2008)
13. Gilbert, A., Illingworth, J., Bowden, R.: Fast realistic multi-action recognition using mined dense spatio-temporal features. In: ICCV (2009)
14. Liu, J., Shah, M.: Learning human actions via information maximization. In: CVPR (2008)
15. Dollar, P., Rabaud, V., Cottrell, G., Belongie, S.: Behavior recognition via sparse spatio-temporal features. In: Joint IEEE International Workshop on Visual Surveillance and Performance Evaluation of Tracking and Surveillance, in Conjunction with ICCV (2005)
16. Willems, G., Tuytelaars, T., Van Gool, L.: An Efficient Dense and Scale-Invariant Spatio-Temporal Interest Point Detector. In: Forsyth, D., Torr, P., Zisserman, A. (eds.) ECCV 2008, Part II. LNCS, vol. 5303, pp. 650–663. Springer, Heidelberg (2008)

17. Wang, H., Ullah, M.M., Klaser, A., Laptev, I., Schmid, C.: Evaluation of local spatio-temporal features for action recognition. In: BMVC (2009)
18. Laptev, I., Marszalek, M., Schmid, C., Rozenfeld, B.: Learning realistic human actions from movies. In: CVPR (2008)
19. Gupta, A., Davis, L.S.: Objects in action: An approach for combining action understanding and object perception. In: CVPR (2007)
20. Li, L.J., Fei-Fei, L.: What, where and who? classifying events by scene and object recognition. In: ICCV (2007)
21. Marszalek, M., Laptev, I., Schmid, C.: Actions in context. In: CVPR (2009)
22. Sun, J., Wu, X., Yan, S., Cheong, L.F., Chua, T.-S., Li, J.: Hierarchical spatio-temporal context modeling for action recognition. In: CVPR (2009)
23. Wang, J., Chen, Z., Wu, Y.: Action recognition with multiscale spatio-temporal contexts. In: CVPR (2011)
24. Banerjee, P., Nevatia, R.: Learning neighborhood co-occurrence statistics of sparse features for human activity recognition. In: AVSS (2011)
25. Kovashka, A., Grauman, K.: Learning a hierarchy of discriminative space-time neighborhood features for human action recognition. In: CVPR (2010)
26. Oikonomopoulos, A., Patras, I., Pantic, M.: An implicit spatiotemporal shape model for human activity localisation and recognition. In: Workshop on Human Communicative Behaviour Analysis, in Conjunction with CVPR (2009)
27. Ta, A.P., Wolf, C., Lavoue, G., Baskurt, A., Jolion, J.-M.: Pairwise features for human action recognition. In: ICPR (2010)
28. Schuldt, C., Laptev, I., Caputo, B.: Recognizing human actions: A local svm approach. In: ICPR (2004)
29. Liu, J., Luo, J., Shah, M.: Recognizing realistic actions from videos "in the wild". In: CVPR (2009)
30. Wu, X., Xu, D., Duan, L., Luo, J.: Action recognition using context and appearance distribution features. In: CVPR (2011)
31. Kim, T.-K., Wong, S.-F., Cipolla, R.: Tensor canonical correlation analysis for action classification. In: CVPR (2007)
32. Wu, S., Oreifej, O., Shah, M.: Action recognition in videos acquired by a moving camera using motion decomposition of lagrangian particle trajectories. In: ICCV (2011)
33. Jiang, Z., Lin, Z., Davis, L.: Recognizing human actions by learning and matching shape-motion prototype trees. PAMI (2011)

Visual Code-Sentences: A New Video Representation Based on Image Descriptor Sequences

Yusuke Mitarai and Masakazu Matsugu

Canon Inc. Digital System Technology Development Headquarters, Tokyo, Japan

Abstract. We present a new descriptor-sequence model for action recognition that enhances discriminative power in the spatio-temporal context, while maintaining robustness against background clutter as well as variability in inter-/intra-person behavior. We extend the framework of Dense Trajectories based activity recognition (Wang *et al.*, 2011) and introduce a pool of dynamic Bayesian networks (e.g., multiple HMMs) with histogram descriptors as codebooks of composite action categories represented at respective key points. The entire codebooks bound with spatio-temporal interest points constitute intermediate feature representation as basis for generic action categories. This representation scheme is intended to serve as *visual code-sentences* which subsume a rich vocabulary of basis action categories. Through extensive experiments using KTH, UCF Sports, and Hollywood2 datasets, we demonstrate some improvements over the state-of-the-art methods.

1   Introduction

We have seen great improvements in the domain of action recognition in videos over the past few decades, especially in modeling of as well as feature representation for action categories [1]. In regard to local features, the most notable advancement is the proposal of spatio-temporal interest points by Laptev and Lindeberg (2003) [9], which provides a substrate of stable representations of actions, and the original local feature and its variants are now widely used by researchers in the field of action recognition.

Stable representation of action categories in cluttered scenes is still a challenging problem that needs to be solved with a representation framework rich discriminative power. For example, we need the ability to distinguish similar categories like running and jogging, while we also need to neglect individualities observed as personal differences that are typically measured by speed and appearance (e.g., body shape, clothing, and personal belongings). Background clutter and view-point diversity further challenge action recognition.

Recently, methods using trajectories, extracted based on spatio-temporal interest points and tracking scheme, have been very successful in recognizing actions [5, 14, 15, 23, 25]. Despite their success, they have difficulty in discriminating spatio-temporal contexts, albeit maintaining stability and robustness in recognition.

A. Fusiello et al. (Eds.): ECCV 2012 Ws/Demos, Part I, LNCS 7583, pp. 321–331, 2012.

In this paper, we address these problems with a trajectory-based approach. The main contributions of this paper are twofold: 1) Introduction of a pool of dynamic Bayesian networks or DBNs (e.g., multiple HMMs) bound with positional information in respective trajectories. Each HMM is organized to provide an intermediate representation of basis action primitives as a *code-sentence*, a set of *code words* with temporal dependency. This repository of DBN enhances discriminative power in the spatio-temporal context since each DBN can capture the spatio-temporal ordering of composite action primitives. 2) Introduction of histogram-based description of trajectory-bound intermediate features that inherit robustness and stability of BoW-like representation.

Thus, in the proposed framework of Dense Trajectories based action recognition, we seek balance between discriminability in spatio-temporal dependencies and stability against intra and inter-person behavioral variations as well as background clutter.

2   Related Work

Local spatio-temporal words/features have been exploited to recognize actions ([6, 8, 9, 11, 18, 22]). Models of human actions based on key point descriptors have been shown to perform well in action recognition from videos.

Modeling efforts in action recognition have a long history. Bag-of-words models devoid of spatio-temporal ordering information have also been exploited in action recognition [4, 10, 13]. Because of independence on spatio-temporal relationships, BoW-based approaches are limited in their ability to represent and differentiate such dependencies. Several models attempt to alleviate this limitation; new types of features capture spatio-temporal correlation [21], modeling spatio-temporal relationships by coarse spatio-temporal grid regions.

One of the standard approaches for recognizing human actions uses dynamic Bayesian networks [19, 28]. The simplest form of this approach is HMM. For modeling complex behaviors, several extensions of HMM have been advocated: coupled hidden semi Markov models [16], hierarchical HMM [12, 17], and hidden CRF [29]. Hierarchical approaches have been taken in modeling complex activities: probabilistic topic models [26], hierarchical spatio-temporal context in trajectories [23], and hierarchical HMM ([12, 17]).

Trajectory-based approaches in human action recognition have recently attracted attention in research communities and demonstrate the state-of-the-art method [25] for the challenging datasets UCF Sports, Hollywood2, and YouTube.

For modeling the dynamic structure of trajectory-aligned features, a few approaches using like a dynamic Bayesian networks as the models of trajectory-aligned features were proposed: modeling velocity histories of tracked key points [15], and trajectory transition descriptor based on a Markov stationary distribution of quantized displacement vectors [23].

3   Visual Code-Sentences

We model arbitrary actions by a set of hypothetical action primitives as *visual code-sentences* in the sense that *sentences* correspond to actions, while the *visual code-sentences* constitute visual code-words necessary to represent meaningful action categories. Here, *sentences* are defined as descriptor-sequences along the trajectories extracted from video, and each *sentence* is hypothetically generated from a certain component model, *code-sentence,* capturing the temporal order of state transitions. It is well known that such a model is generally given by dynamic Bayesian networks (DBN). We note that each *sentence* is position-bound (e.g., bound with key points along specific trajectory) and a generative model of a *sentence* is represented as a mixture of *code-sentences* that capture a dynamic structure of *sentences*. Entire *code-sentences* are pooled in a repository so we can generate arbitrary *sentences*.

We will show that, in the Dense Trajectories based approach, a histogram based description of the trajectory bound component models can also be used for the stability and robustness of action recognition. Changes in the dynamic structure of spatio-temporal ordering as categorical changes in actions are assumed to be distinguishable based on histogram representation, while suppressing inter- or intra-person variations.

3.1   Summary of Our Representation and Classification System

To extract the *code-sentence* representation, we need to extract a number of *sentences* from video by aligning descriptors at each key point along trajectories [25]. The component model which presumably generated the *sentence* is determined based on the likelihood of the *sentence* corresponding to each component model. Each component is modeled by a generative model of DBN that represents dynamical properties of *code-sentence*. We use HMM a simple DBN. A pool of HMMs is learned with a video dataset (see 3.3). Finally, a BoW-like representation is constructed based on the histogram of each component model which possibly generated the *sentence*.

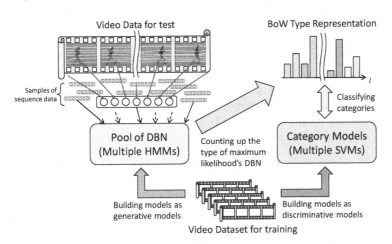

Fig. 1. Illustration of our representation and classification system summary

In the classification stage, we similarly extract *visual code-sentences* and the associated histogram description from the Dense Trajectories of the input data. The resulting BoW-like representation from the input video is finally classified using multiple SVMs.

3.2   Model Definition of Code-Sentences

The *visual code-sentences* (VCS) as generative models of spatio-temporal sequence shall be defined so as to serve as basis features of actions in the sense that any action categories can be represented by such composite, intermediate-level description of actions. For a given L length trajectory extracted from video, the continuous-valued descriptor (e.g. HOG, MBH, etc. as shown in subsection 4.1) sequence along the trajectory, $x_1, x_2, ..., x_L$, and $X = \{x_1, x_2, ..., x_L\}$ is assumed to be generated from latent states $\{z_t\}$, so that the sequence can be described by continuous HMMs. Using a parameter vector, $\theta = \{\pi, A, \varphi\}$, the probability of observing the sequence $X=\{x_t\}$, is given by:

$$p(X|\pi, A, \varphi) = \sum_{z_1} p(z_1|\pi)p(x_1|z_1, \varphi) \prod_{t=2}^{L} \sum_{z_t, z_{t-1}} p(z_t|z_{t-1}, A)p(x_t|z_t, \varphi). \quad (1)$$

$\theta = \{\pi, A, \varphi\}$ is a set of parameters of probability functions, $p(z_1|\pi)$, $p(z_t|z_{t-1}, A)$ and $p(x_t|z_t, \varphi)$. Let $\Theta = \{\theta_1, \theta_2, ..., \theta_M\}$ be a set of M parameter vectors of each HMM. Then, using these parameters, we consider a *sentence*, indexed by $l(X)$, for a given video sequence is represented by a VCS that gives the highest probability:

$$l(X) = \underset{m}{\operatorname{argmax}}\ p(X|\theta_m). \quad (2)$$

In the proposed framework, a VCS is given by a set of indices, $l(X)$, that represents a primitive action category in a vector quantized state space. Thus we quantize each sequence data not based on the Markov stationary distribution [23] but based on the above generative models (HMMs) which are directly modeling sequence data.

3.3   Learning Visual Code-Sentences Method

Let $\{X_1, X_2, ..., X_N\}$ be a set of N sequences extracted from various sets of video data. We propose to learn VCSs by generating a pool of HMMs for sequences of data. In contrast to [27], the procedure for obtaining VCS begins by random initialization of all labels, $\{l(X)\}$, and all parameter vectors, Θ. We then update the parameter of each HMM based on sequences of data to obtain the approximate estimate of the following parameter (3)

$$\theta_m^{new} = \underset{\theta}{\operatorname{argmax}} \prod_{l(X)=m} p(X|\theta_m) \quad (3)$$

$p(X|\theta_m)$ is defined as in Eq. (1). This step is intended to obtain approximate cluster centers of the sequences of data like a cluster center calculation step of the k-means clustering algorithm. Next, the labels of respective sequence data are updated in a manner (2). This step is assumed to be an assignment to cluster step of the k-means. After all labels are updated, the parameter of each HMM is updated similarly to approximate (3). These two steps are repeatedly performed until the update step converges. This approach is similar to modeling a set of varied sequence data by HMM mixture models. We do not exploit ordinary EM algorithms to obtain HMM mixture models. Instead, we generate a set of parameters of HMMs to explore diversity and completeness in the resulting models and avoid obtaining only similar models.

VCSs as multiple HMMs are learned with a plurality of sequence data from training video sequence, yielding 2,000 HMMs with 480,000 sequences sampled randomly from video for each descriptor type. These 2,000 HMMs include three types of HMMs: 1) Ergodic HMMs with two latent states for cyclic action primitives, 2) Left-to-Right HMMs with four latent states for action primitives corresponding to slow motions and 3) Left-to-Right HMMs with six latent states for action primitives corresponding to fast motions. The last type is permitted to skip one latent state. We obtained 400 Ergodic HMMs and 800 x 2 Left-to-Right HMMs, respectively.

The learning phase typically converges after by repeating the assignment and update step about 100 times. When too many pieces of sentence data are assigned to a particular component label in the learning phase, we divided such agglomerated data to obtain 'hard-assignments' to different class labels. The resulting VCSs as repository of multiple HMMs are used for video representations.

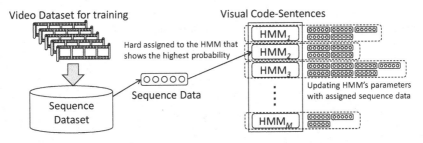

Fig. 2. Learning system for VCSs. The Sequence Dataset is constructed from various sets of video data. (Assign Step): Generating probability for each HMM is calculated, and each sequence is assigned to the most probable HMM. (Update Step): Each HMM's parameter is updated independently by sequence data assigned to each HMM. The 'Assign' and 'Update' steps are performed repeatedly until the HMM parameters converge.

4   Experimental Setup

In this section, we describe the experimental setup, which uses visual code-sentences to evaluate the performance of our video representation method.

4.1   Extracting Sentence Data from Video

We use the trajectory base feature extraction method (Dense Trajectories recently proposed by Wang *et al.* [25]) to extract sentences from video. Trajectories are extracted by tracking points located on grid points till each length becomes L (we use a length $L = 15$) with a dense optical flow field in multiple spatial scales. In their original setup, the trajectories are removed if tracked points exist in the neighborhood of the start points of the trajectories. In our framework, we do not remove these trajectories to avoid heterogeneous sampling.

Descriptions on tracked points of the trajectories which constitute the sentences are the same descriptors as the ones in Dense Trajectories, i.e., motion descriptors for tracked points [25], HOG [2], HOF [10] and MBH [3]. We also use the same descriptors directly as in [25], but do not perform temporal integration and concatenation as in [25]. We treat them as sequence data so that the temporal context is retained and discriminated in the classification stage.

4.2   Video Representation with Visual Code-Sentences

We use a bag-of-features type of video representation with visual code-sentences. The representation data is a histogram with bins of each feature type's HMMs, such as motion descriptors for tracked points, HOG, HOF, X-direction MBH, and Y-direction MBH. There are 2,000 HMMs for each feature-type, so the representation data is obtained by concatenating five histograms each of which consists of 2,000 bins. Sequences of data are extracted from the video, and the generating probabilities of each sequence data are computed with each HMM of each type. We assume that the obtained sequence data corresponds to the most probable HMM.

We use a non-linear SVM with a χ^2-kernel [10] for predicting action category. A χ^2-kernel $K(h_i, h_j)$ is described as follows:

$$K\left(\boldsymbol{h_i}, \boldsymbol{h_j}\right) = exp\left[-\sum_{\gamma} \frac{1}{\rho A^{\gamma}} \sum_{bin} \frac{\left\{h_i^{\gamma}(bin) - h_j^{\gamma}(bin)\right\}^2}{h_i^{\gamma}(bin) + h_j^{\gamma}(bin)}\right] \tag{4}$$

$h_j^{\gamma}(bin)$ is the bin-th element of histogram for feature type γ. A^{γ} is the mean value of χ^2 distances of the training data about feature type γ [30], and ρ is a parameter for adjusting kernel width.

We perform the estimate of the action categories based on the following category score $S_c(h)$ corresponding to category c:

$$S_c(\boldsymbol{h}) = \sum_{h_{i,c} \in SV_c} \alpha_{i,c} K\left(\boldsymbol{h}, \boldsymbol{h_{i,c}}\right) + \beta_{SVM_c} + b_c \tag{5}$$

where $h_{i,c}$ is i-th support vector corresponding to category c, and $\alpha_{i,c}$ is the coefficient for the i-th support vector. β_{SVM_c} is a bias parameter obtained by learning SVM for category c, and b_c is a second bias parameter particular to category c to adjust unevenness of the number of training data. In classification task, the test data is classified to the category which gave the highest category score. In the retrieval task, the result lists categories in descending order of the scores.

4.3   Datasets

Video representation with visual code-sentences is evaluated on three standard human action datasets: KTH [22], UCF Sports [20] and Hollywood2 [13] shown in Figure 3. We describe each dataset in this section.

KTH Dataset. The learning process is performed with the training dataset, and hyper parameters (i.e., soft margin parameter of SVMs and parameter to adjust kernel width) are optimized with the validation dataset. Based on the original experimental setup, we evaluate average accuracy over all categories.

UCF Sports Dataset. We evaluate average accuracy over all categories by a leave-one-out setup. In training we use horizontal flipped data. Because the amount of training data per category is uneven, we optimize the second bias parameter. Thus, soft margin, kernel width, and second bias parameter are optimized.

Hollywood2 Dataset. The dataset is treated for retrieval task, and we evaluate the performance by the mean average precision. In this case, two hyper parameters are optimized, as in the case the KTH Dataset.

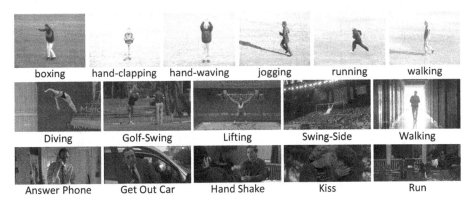

Fig. 3. Some example frames from video pulled from KTH (*first row*), UCF Sports (*second row*) and Hollywood2 (*last row*) datasets

5   Evaluation Results

In this section, we report evaluation results of the datasets, and compare our method with the state-of-the-art methods shown in Table 1.

We note that, for KTH, our method gives a slightly worse result than the state-of-the-art methods. Most failures came from the confusion between similar categories like "running" and "jogging", probably due to robustness of VCS representation for variation in motion speed. We demonstrated improved performance over the state-of-the-art method in Gaidon *et al.* [5] on UCF Sports with parameter tuning to each category.

In the case of Hollywood2, our method yielded the best result of 58.3%. We obtained average accuracy of 93.75%, 93.28% and 93.17% for the size of VCS 1000, 500, and 250 respectively on KTH dataset. Thus, for the larger size of VCS, recognition

Table 1. Recognition performance

KTH		UCF Sports		Hollywood2	
Laptev *et al.* [10]	91.8%	Kläser *et al.* [7]	86.7%	Gilbert *et al.* [6]	50.9%
Kovashka *et al.* [8]	94.53%	Wang *et al.* [25]	88.2%	Ullah *et al.* [24]	55.3%
Wang *et al.* [25]	**95.0%**	Gaidon *et al.* [5]	90.3%	Wang *et al.* [25]	**58.3%**
Our method	93.98%	Our method	**91.1%**	Our method	**58.3%**

performance tended to be slightly higher. We also compare average precision pre action categories for Hollywood2 dataset shown in Table 2. Our method achieved the best results for 5 out of 12 action categories.

Table 2. Average Precision pre action categories for Hollywood2 dataset

	Our Method	Wang *et al.* [25]	Ullah *et al.* [24]
AnswerPhone	27.9%	**32.6%**	24.8%
DriveCar	**92.7%**	88.0%	88.1%
Eat	**66.2%**	65.2%	61.4%
FightPerson	80.9%	**81.4%**	76.5%
GetOutCar	44.9%	**52.7%**	47.4%
HandShake	33.5%	29.6%	**38.4%**
HugPerson	49.9%	**54.2%**	44.6%
Kiss	63.7%	**65.8%**	61.5%
Run	**84.9%**	82.1%	74.3%
SitDown	**66.0%**	62.5%	61.3%
SitUp	20.1%	20.0%	**25.5%**
StandUp	**69.0%**	65.2%	60.4%
mAP	**58.3%**	**58.3%**	55.3%

To gain a more concrete view on the functionality of the proposed VCS based representation, we investigate the contribution of specific VCS in the KTH dataset. Some of the VCSs act as specific components to represent a class of particular action categories. The specific VCSs are shared to represent similar categories. Some VCSs are specific to a particular category, while other VCSs are specific to discriminate small differences among similar categories. For example, "hand-waving" includes a composite action of "lifting-up right hand", and we actually found a corresponding type of motion descriptor sequence as VCS, shown in Figure 4 (a). Figure 4 (b) represents a sequence for upper body motion that does not include information on swinging arm motion (this can be used to discriminate "running" from "walking"), which is given by MBH based descriptor sequence modeled as a VCS. We also found some shared basis of action categories for foot movement commonly used in representing "running" and "walking" in MBH-based VCSs (Figure 4 (c)).

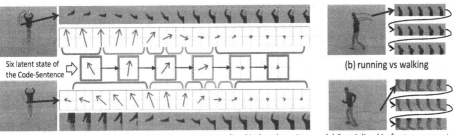

(a) The details of the behavior about Code-Sentence specialized in hand waving   (b) running vs walking   (c) Specialized in foot movement

Fig. 4. Example of some specific VCSs and trajectories corresponding to each VCS

Table 3 gives 'Assignment Rate' that represents the probability of VCS found in a sentence extracted from a video of a certain category.

Table 3. 'Assignment Rate' that show exemplary VCSs found in specific action datasets

category / VCS type	boxing	hand clapping	hand waving	jogging	running	walking
(a) hand-waving	7.7E-5	2.2E-5	**6.7E-3**	1.3E-6	5.0E-6	1.4E-5
(b) running vs walking	7.9E-4	5.6E-4	2.3E-4	1.2E-3	3.9E-4	**4.4E-3**
(c) foot movement	3.6E-4	1.6E-4	1.3E-4	**2.7E-3**	**2.8E-3**	1.7E-3

6   Conclusion

We proposed a method of video representation with *visual code-sentences* and demonstrated its validity through extensive experiments with several challenging datasets. We achieved competitive performance using a code book half the size of the method by proposed Wang *et al.* [25] with approximately 3% improvement in performance for a challenging dataset (e.g., UCF Sports). We also validated the proposed framework with supporting evidences to show that VCS can be shared and used as a basis for representing a variety of action categories.

The proposed method can be poor in distinguishing categories that differ only by motion speed (e.g., distinguishing "jogging" from "running"), however it is effective in identifying categories with inter-/intra- person variations in motion speed. In the experiments, we did not optimize descriptor parameters suitable for VCSs, and further performance improvement through parameter optimization is left for future work.

References

1. Aggarwal, J.K., Ryoo, M.S.: Human Activity Analysis: A Review. ACM Computing Surveys 43(16) (2011)
2. Dalal, N., Triggs, B.: Histograms of Oriented Gradients for Human Detection. In: CVPR (2005)

3. Dalal, N., Triggs, B., Schmid, C.: Human Detection Using Oriented Histograms of Flow and Appearance. In: Leonardis, A., Bischof, H., Pinz, A. (eds.) ECCV 2006. LNCS, vol. 3952, pp. 428–441. Springer, Heidelberg (2006)
4. Dollár, P., Rabaud, V., Cottrell, G., Belongie, S.: Behavior Recognition via Sparse Spatio-Temporal Features. In: VS-PETS (2005)
5. Gaidon, A., Harchaoui, Z., Schmid, C.: A time series kernel for action recognition. In: BMVC (2011)
6. Gilbert, A., Illingworth, J., Bowden, R.: Action Recognition using Mined Hierarchical Compound Features. TPAMI 33(5) (2009)
7. Kläser, A., Marszałek, M., Laptev, I., Schmid, C.: Will person detection help bag-of-features action recognition. Technical Report, INRIA Grenoble - Rhone-Alpes (2010)
8. Kovashshka, A., Grauman, K.: Learning a Hierarchical of Discriminative Space-Time Neighborhood Features for Human Action Recognition. In: CVPR (2010)
9. Laptev, I., Lindeberg, T.: Space-time Interest Points. In: ICCV (2003)
10. Laptev, I., Marszałek, M., Schmid, C., Rozenfeld, B.: Learning realistic human actions from movies. In: CVPR (2008)
11. Liu, J., Yang, Y., Shah, M.: Learning Semantic Visual Vocabularies Using Diffusion Distance. In: CVPR (2009)
12. Loy, C.C., Xiang, T., Gong, S.: Detecting and Discriminating Behavioural Anomalies. Pattern Recognition 44 (2011)
13. Marszałek, M., Laptev, I., Schmid, C.: Actions in Context. In: CVPR (2009)
14. Matikainen, P., Hebert, M., Sukthankar, R.: Trajectons: Action Recognition Through the Motion Analysis of Tracked Features. In: ICCV Workshop on Video-Oriented Object and Event Classification (2009)
15. Messing, R., Pal, C., Kautz, H.: Activity recognition using the velocity histories of tracked keypoints. In: ICCV (2009)
16. Natarajan, P., Nevatia, R.: Coupled Hidden Semi Markov Models for Activity Recognition. In: WMVC (2007)
17. Nguyen, N.T., Phung, D.Q., Venkatesch, S., Bui, H.H.: Learning and Detecting Activities from Movements Trajectories Using Hierarchical Hidden Markov Model. In: CVPR (2005)
18. Niebles, J.C., Wang, H., Fei-Fei, L.: Unsupervised Learning of Human Action Categories Using Spatial-temporal Words. In: BMVC (2006)
19. Park, S., Aggarwal, J.K.: A hierarchical Bayesian network for event recognition of human actions and interactions. Multimedia Systems 10(2) (2004)
20. Rodriguez, M., Ahmed, J., Shah, M.: Action MACH: A Spatio-temporal Maximum Average Correlation Height Filter for Action Recognition. In: CVPR (2008)
21. Savarese, A., Pozo, A.D., Niebles, J.C., Fei-Fei, L.: Spatial-temporal correlations for unsupervised action classification. In: Motion and Video Computing (2008)
22. Schüldt, C., Laptev, I., Caputo, B.: Recognizing Human Actions: A Local SVM Approach. In: ICPR (2004)
23. Sun, J., Wu, X., Yan, S., Cheong, L.F., Chua, T.S., Li, J.: Hierarchical Spatio-Temporal Context Modeling for Action Recognition. In: CVPR (2009)
24. Ullah, M.M., Parizi, S.N., Laptev, I.: Improving Bag-of-Features Action Recognition with Non-local Cues. In: BMVC (2010)
25. Wang, H., Kläser, A., Schmid, C., Liu, C.: Action Recognition by Dense Trajectories. In: CVPR (2011)
26. Wang, X., Ma, X., Grimson, W.E.L.: Unsupervised Activity Perception in Crowded and Complicated Scenes Using Hierarchical Bayesian Models. TPAMI 31(3) (2009)
27. Xiang, T., Gong, S.: Video Behaviour Profiling for Anomaly Detection. TPAMI 30(5) (2008)

28. Zeng, Z., Ji, Q.: Knowledge Based Activity Recognition with Dynamic Bayesian Network. In: Daniilidis, K., Maragos, P., Paragios, N. (eds.) ECCV 2010, Part VI. LNCS, vol. 6316, pp. 532–546. Springer, Heidelberg (2010)
29. Zhang, J., Gong, S.: Action categorization with modified hidden conditional random field. Pattern Recognition 42(1) (2010)
30. Zhang, J., Marszałek, M., Lazebnik, S., Schmid, C.: Local Features and Kernels for Classification of Texture and Object Categories: A Comprehensive Study. IJCV 73(2) (2007)

Action Recognition Robust to Background Clutter by Using Stereo Vision

Jordi Sanchez-Riera, Jan Čech, and Radu Horaud

INRIA Grenoble Rhône-Alpes, Montbonnot Saint-Marin, France
{jordi.sanchez-riera,jan.cech,radu.horaud}@inria.fr

Abstract. An action recognition algorithm which works with binocular videos is presented. The proposed method uses standard bag-of-words approach, where each action clip is represented as a histogram of visual words. However, instead of using classical monocular HoG/HoF features, we construct features from the scene-flow computed by a matching algorithm on the sequence of stereo images. The resulting algorithm has a comparable or slightly better recognition accuracy than standard monocular solution in controlled setup with a single actor present in the scene. However, we show its significantly improved performance in case of strong background clutter due to other people freely moving behind the actor.

1   Introduction

An extensive research has been done in action recognition throughout recent years, which is well documented in survey papers [1,2]. Most of the methods work with monocular videos only. Very successful methods use image retrieval techniques, where each video sequence is represented as a histogram of visual words [3], and large margin classifier is then used for recognition.

In particular, spatiotemporal interest points [3] are detected in the image sequence. These points are described by a descriptor HoG (Histogram of Gradients)/HoF (Histogram of Optical Flow) [4] which capture surrounding of an interest point. The descriptors are quantized by K-means clustering and each videoclip is represented as a histogram with K bins. Support Vector Machine is then used for classification.

Further research to improve the recognition accuracy went in the direction of densifying the interest points and enhancing the local descriptors. The interest points employed in [3] are spatiotemporal extensions of a Harris corner detector, i.e. locations in a video stream having large local variance in both spatial and temporal dimensions, representing abrupt events in the stream. This is in order to achieve high repeatability of the detection. However, such points are quite rare and important relevant information can be missed. Therefore there were alternatives to these interest points, e.g. based on Gabor filters [5,6], or even simply using a regular dense sampling [7] to reach higher coverage, or a hybrid scheme by [8], which start by dense sampling and optimize the position and scale within a bounded area in order to increase the coverage and preserve the

A. Fusiello et al. (Eds.): ECCV 2012 Ws/Demos, Part I, LNCS 7583, pp. 332–341, 2012.

repeatability of the interest points. An extension of the original HoG/HoF descriptor was proposed e.g. by spatiotemporal gradients [9], or motion boundary histograms [10].

However these methods can be quite sensitive to background clutter present in populated scenes, since interest points are detected not only in the actor but on the background as well. This causes the global histogram representation to be corrupted and the accuracy is significantly decreased.

Stereo vision or multiple view vision have not been much used in action recognition. Using stereo, the existing methods typically try to make the algorithm insensitive to a camera viewpoint [11]. Similarly [12] uses a special room and a multi-camera setup to construct viewpoint invariant action representation, and [13] incorporate temporal information to the multi-view setup. Work [14] uses the depth map obtained by stereo matching to fit an articulated body model and use joint trajectories for action recognition.

An alternative to stereo vision is using RGB-D sensor, which provides a depth image besides the color/intensity image. It is based on time-of-flight or structured light technology. This research is vivid nowadays due to the recent irruption of Kinect device. For instance [15] constructs 3D motion primitives from a cloud of 3D points. Work [16] extends 2D silhoutte by projection of the point cloud into three orthogonal planes. In [17] the authors uses local interest point descriptors which are computed from spatiotemporal image and depth gradients for each pixel of a spatiotemporal neighbourhood of interest points. Since the neighbourhood is large, they use PCA for dimensionality reduction prior to quantization. In [18], spatiotemporal interest points are divided into different layers based on depth and a multichannel histogram is created. Another direction is to estimate the body skeleton from the depth data. Commercially successful real-time game controller uses skeleton model from body part labelling of depth data of Kinect [19]. Joint trajectories are used for action or gesture recognition in e.g. [20,21]. However, for some applications such active sensors are not suitable. For example, in outdoor setup or in a scenario with multiple autonomous robots whose active sensors would interfere to each other.

Therefore we propose a simple stereo vision based method, which can focus the algorithm to an active actor while disregarding the background activity based on completely passive system, see Fig. 1. Our contribution is extending the original successful action recognition framework [3] with descriptors based on stereo-vision and the scene-flow. We observed a significant improvement of the proposed method in the robustness to the perturbations due to the uncontrolled motion of other people behind the actor.

The rest of the paper is structured as follows: The proposed method is described in detail in Sec. 2. Experimental validation which includes a comparison with the state-of-the-art algorithm is presented in Sec. 3. Finally, Sec. 4 concludes the paper.

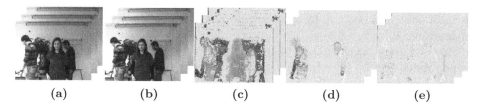

(a)   (b)   (c)   (d)   (e)

Fig. 1. Example of data for one sequence. The input data consists of sequences of (a) Left and (b) Right images. The maps of (c) disparity, (d) horizontal, (e) vertical component of the optical flow computed by algorithm [22]. The maps are color-coded: gray color means unassigned value, for disparity warmer colors corresponds to points closer to the camera, for optical flow warmer colors corresponds to motion to the left and up respectively.

2   Method Description

Before we give details on the proposed descriptor, we briefly revise the bag-of-words (BoW) paradigm for action recognition. Following [3] it requires to:

1. Collect a set of local descriptors associated to the interest points for image frames of all training action video clips.
2. Apply clustering algorithm to these descriptors, for instance, K-means.
3. Quantize the descriptor to get the 'visual words'. For each descriptor, assign label according to its nearest cluster centroid.
4. Represent a video clip as a K-bins histogram of the quantized descriptor ('bag of words').
5. Train a classifier with these histograms, for instance, SVM.

In Steps 1–3, the the visual word vocabulary (or the codebook) is constructed. The dimensionality of the local descriptor is typically high and the space is consequently sparse, that is why it is represented by K clusters of observed data. In Steps 4–5, a compact (K-length vector) representation of training videoclips with annotated labels is used to train a classifier. The 'bag of words' representation encodes a relative frequence of occurences of the quantized desriptors and it turns out to be discriminative among action classes. Later for recognition, an unknown videoclip is first represented as the K-length histogram and then it is fed to the classifier which assigns the class label.

We follow exactly this framework, except for the Step 1. Unlike the monocular HoG/HoF descriptor [3], we introduce a new descriptor based on the Scene-Flow [22].

2.1   Local Descriptor Based on the Scene-Flow

The Scene-flow is a 3D extension of the optical flow. We represent a scene-flow as depth and optical flow, which together with a camera calibration is equivalent to

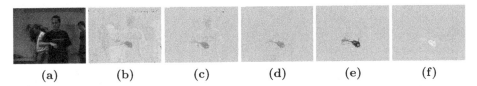

$$\text{(a)} \qquad \text{(b)} \qquad \text{(c)} \qquad \text{(d)} \qquad \text{(e)} \qquad \text{(f)}$$

Fig. 2. Construction of the proposed descriptor. The actor's face is detected from the left input image (a). The raw disparity map (b) is segmented, such that all pixels having the lower disparity than the actor's face are discarded (c). The descriptor is then computed for all remaining pixels undergoing non-zero motion, such that it consists of the pixel's position relative to the face, it's disparity (d), and horizontal (e) and vertical (f) components of optical flow.

a vector field of 3D position and associated 3D velocities of reconstructed surface points. This intrinsic representation is potentially less sensitive to the changes of texture and illumination in the action dataset than the representation which relies solely on the intensity images. Moreover, with the notion of depth, it is straightforward to focus the actor performing the action to be recognized while discarding any activity from the background clutter.

We assume the action performing actor is the person which is the closest to the camera. We believe this is a reasonable assumption, which is typically the case of human-robot interaction or movies.

The proposed descriptor is constructed as follows, see Fig. 2:

1. Get the synchonized sequences of the left $\mathbf{I}_l$ and right images $\mathbf{I}_r$. For each frame compute the disparity map $\mathbf{D}$ and optical flow maps $\mathbf{F}_h, \mathbf{F}_v$ by the algorithm [22].
2. Find the actor's face with a face detector [23]: $(x_0, y_0) = \mathrm{FD}(\mathbf{I}_l)$. In case of multiple faces detected, the one with the highest disparity $d_0 = \mathbf{D}(x_0, y_0)$ is selected[1]. In case no face is detected, if the actor turns or the detector miss the face, we simply assume a previous face position.
3. Segment the scene using disparity and optical flow: (1) Only pixels with magnitude of optical flow greater than zero are considered, (2) Only pixels with disparity greater or equal to the disparity of the actor's face are considered. So the set of valid pixels

$$S = \{(x, y) : \mathbf{F}_h(x, y)^2 + \mathbf{F}_v(x, y)^2 > 0 \text{ and } \mathbf{D}(x, y) > d_0 - \mu\},$$

where $\mu = 5$ is a small margin to ensure the entire actor's body is included.
4. At each reconstructed pixel passing the above test $(x, y) \in S$, the local descriptor is 5-dimensional only:

$$L(x, y) = \Big(x - x_0, y - y_0, \mathbf{D}(x, y) - d_0, \mathbf{F}_h(x, y), \mathbf{F}_v(x, y)\Big).$$

---

[1] The disparity of the face is estimated as an average disparity inside the bounding box obtained from the face detection. The center of the bounding box is the pixel (x_0, y_0).

Fig. 3. Histograms of visual words and corresponding assignment to pixels for frames of two actions: clap (top) and turn-around (bottom). The color encodes the indices of visual words $1, \ldots, K$. The coloring is such that similar visual words have similar color. We can see typical visual words occuring during the actions.

Notice the face-normalized position of the pixels, brings a kind of global information into the local descriptor.

Following the BoW procedure described above, after building the codebook and subsequent quantization of pixel descriptors, the resulting histograms of their occurrences in the action video sequence intuitively encodes the activity of actor's body parts in the sense of 3D motion. See Fig. 3 for an illustration.

3   Experiments

To evaluate the performance of the proposed binocular method and compare it with a state-of-the-art monocular method [3], we use the Ravel[2] dataset [24]. The Ravel dataset consists of 7 actions (talk phone, drink, scratch head, turn around, check watch, clap, cross arms) performed by 12 actors in 6 trials each. First 3 trials are with stable static background without other people in the scene (we denote as 'Controlled'), while next 3 trials are performed with motion background clutter due to arbitrary activity of the people behind the actor (we denote as 'Clutter'). See Fig. 4 and Fig. 5 for respective examples. The dataset is challenging due to the strong intra-class variance, strong dynamic background in the 'Clutter', and unstable lighting conditions.

We will show results of two baseline algorithms. The first one is the algorithm described in [3] works with monocular (left camera) stream only and uses the sparse spatiotemporal interests points and HoG/HoF descriptors, we denote as 'STIPs'. The other baseline is the same algorithm, however we ran it in both left and right camera sequences, matched the detected points along the epipolar lines, and removed the interest points which have smaller disparity than the

---

[2] http://ravel.humavips.eu

Fig. 4. Ravel dataset examples - controlled setup. Note that different actors perform the same action quite differently as for example in "cross arms". Actions: "cross arms", "check watch", "scratch head", "cross arms", "talk phone", "cross arms", "scratch head", "clap".

disparity of the actor's face. The motivation behind is to remove the irrelevant interest points detected on the background clutter. The rest of the algorithm [3] remains the same. We call this algorithm 'STIPs-stereo'. The proposed method described in Sec. 2, is denoted as '5DF'.

The codebook was built in a sequence of a single actor, namely 'character-09'. This actor was not later used either for learning a classifier or for testing. We believe a single actor performing the same set of actions as all other actors sweeps the space of local descriptors is enough and also K-means algorithm is run only once and not in the leave-one-out loop (see later), which would be too time consuming. The size of the codebook K was optimized for all the methods in the logarithmic range from $K = 10$ to $K = 10000$ and the optimum was found for $K = 1000$, the same for all the methods.

Learning a classifier and testing was performed in a standard leave-one-actor-out scenario. One actor was removed from the set, the linear SVM classifier was trained in the sequences of remaining actors and then tested on the sequence of the left actor and this was repeated for all actors. The recognition rate reported is the average error over all actors.

Results are shown in Tab. 1. We can see the proposed method (5DF) performs comparably in the setup when there is a single actor in the scene only. This proves the proposed descriptor computed in the meaningful semi-dense locations is informative. Furthemore, we can see the recognition accuracy of the proposed method does not drop much in cases of the background clutter of other people freely moving behind the actor. This demonstrates that the algorithm can properly focus the active actor while disregarding the background activity using the depth information from stereo. The monocular baseline method [3] (STIPs) is naturally very sensitive to this type of the background clutter. The algorithm cannot distinguish the informative interest points of the clutter from corresponding descriptors on other people in the scene, which contaminates the

Fig. 5. Ravel dataset examples - cluttered setup. Actions: "turn around", "clap", "talk phone", "talk phone", "turn around", "drink", "check watch", "drink". Note different illumination conditions.

Table 1. Recogntion accuracy of the tested methods. The proposed (5DF) method has comparable results with state-of-the-art method (STIPs) in the controlled setup with only one actor in the scene, while it much less sensitive to the strong dynamic background clutter. The other baseline (STIPs-stereo) is less sensitive to the background by using the stereo information, however due to insufficient coverage of interest points the recognition accuracy is lower.

Algorithm	Controlled	Clutter
STIPs [3]	0.6883	0.4675
STIPs-stereo	0.6537	0.5238
5DF (the proposed method)	0.6840	0.6494

histograms and the recognition accuracy drops significantly. The second baseline (STIPs-stereo), which attempts to remove the interest points detected on the background by stereo matching, is less sensitive to the background clutter, however its recognition accuracy is slightly lower for 'controlled' setup. The reason is that the sparse spatiotemporal interest points become even sparser, since the stereo matching may discard also points on the foreground due to matching ambiguity. Notice that in STIPs method, we have about 10 interest points per frame, but in our method we have about 10000 locations per frame where descriptors are computed.

For more insight, we show confusion matrices of both methods for both 'controlled' and 'clutter' setups, see Fig. 6–8. For instance, we can see that scratch head is confusing with talk phone. This is not so surprising since these actions starts with the hand at the level of the pocket and is directed to the head, where the difference is whereas it remains static (talk phone) or moving (scratch head). Again, there is significantly much less confusion in case of the background

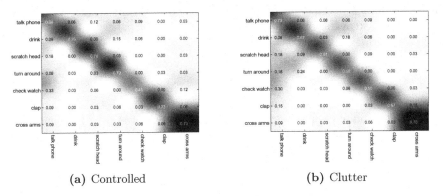

(a) Controlled   (b) Clutter

Fig. 6. Confusion Matrix for the proposed method (5DF) for a) Controlled and b) Cluttered setup

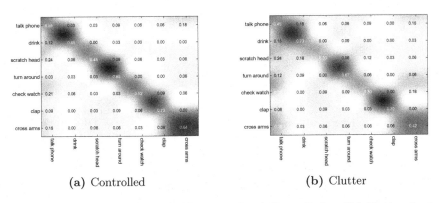

(a) Controlled   (b) Clutter

Fig. 7. Confusion Matrix for the STIPs-stereo for a) Controlled and b) Cluttered setup

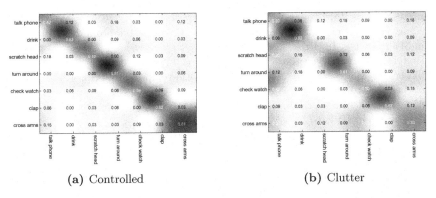

(a) Controlled   (b) Clutter

Fig. 8. Confusion Matrix for the state-of-the-art method [3] (STIPs) for a) Controlled and b) Cluttered setup

clutter in the proposed binocular method compared to the state-of-the-art method which only uses a monocular video. This corroborates that stereo vision brings an important extra information.

4   Conclusion

We presented an action recognition method which uses the scene-flow computed from binocular video sequences. Experimentally we proved that the extra information from stereo significantly improves the recognition accuracy in the presence of strong background clutter.

The proposed method requires the actor's face is detected in majority of the frames. We expect that a tracker with a motion model would help to localize the face if it is turned away. Future work includes an elaboration on the design of the local descriptor. Combination of the local descriptor with the proposed one could further improve the recognition accuracy.

Acknowledgements. This research was supported by EC project FP7-ICT-247525-HUMAVIPS.

References

1. Weinland, D., Ronfard, R., Boyer, E.: A survey of vision-based methods for action representation, segmentation and recognition. CVIU 115, 224–241 (2011)
2. Poppe, R.: A survey on vision-based human action recognition. IVC 28, 976–990 (2010)
3. Laptev, I.: On space-time interest points. IJCV 64 (2005)
4. Dalal, N., Triggs, B.: Histograms of oriented gradients for human detection. In: Proc. CVPR (2005)
5. Dollár, P., Rabaud, V., Cottrell, G., Belongie, S.: Behavior recognition via sparse spatio-temporal features. VS-PETS (2005)
6. Bregonzio, M., Gong, S., Xiang, T.: Recognising action as clouds of space-time interest points. In: Proc. CVPR (2009)
7. Wang, H., Klaser, A., Laptev, I., Schmid, C.: A spatio-temporal descriptor based on 3D-gradients. In: Proc. BMVC (2009)
8. Tuytelaars, T.: Dense interest points. In: Proc. CVPR (2010)
9. Klaser, A., Marszalek, M., Schmid, C.: A spatio-temporal descriptor based on 3D-gradients. In: Proc. BMVC (2008)
10. Wang, H., Kläser, A., Schmid, C., Liu, C.L.: Action recognition by dense trajectories. In: Proc. CVPR (2011)
11. Roh, M.C., Shin, H.K., Lee, S.W.: View-independent human action recognition with volume motion template on single stereo camera. Pattern Recognition Letters 31, 639–647 (2010)
12. Weinland, D., Boyer, E., Ronfard, R.: Action recognition from arbitrary views using 3D exemplars. In: Proc. ICCV (2007)
13. Yan, P., Khan, S.M., Shah, M.: Learning 4D action feautre models for arbitrary view action recognition. In: Proc. CVPR (2008)

14. Uddin, M.Z., Thang, N.D., Kim, J.T., Kim, T.S.: Human activity recognition using body joint-angle features and hidden Markov model. ETRI Journal 33, 569–579 (2011)
15. Holte, M.B., Moeslund, T.B., Fihl, P.: View-invariant gesture recognition using 3d optical flow and harmonic motion context. CVIU 114, 1353–1361 (2010)
16. Li, W., Zhang, Z., Liu, Z.: Action recognition based on a bag of 3D points. In: Proc. CVPR Workshop on Human Communicative Behaviour Analysis (2010)
17. Zhang, H., Parker, L.E.: 4-dimensional local spatio-temporal features for human activity recognition. In: Proc. IROS (2011)
18. Ni, P.B., Wang, G., Moulin: RGBD-HuDaAct: A color-depth video database for human daily activity recognition. In: Proc. ICCV Workshop on Consumer Depth Cameras for Computer Vision (2011)
19. Shotton, J., Fitzgibbon, A., Cook, M., Sharp, T., Finocchio, M.: Real-time human pose recognition in parts from single depth images. In: Proc. CVPR (2011)
20. Sung, J., Ponce, C., Selman, B., Saxena, A.: Unstructured human activity detection from rgbd images. In: Proc. ICRA (2012)
21. Xia, L., Chen, C.C., Aggarwal, J.K.: View invariant human action recognition using histograms of 3D joints. In: Proc. CVPR Workshop on Human Activity Understanding from 3D Data (HAU3D) (2012)
22. Cech, J., Sanchez-Riera, J., Horaud, R.P.: Scene flow estimation by growing correspondence seeds. In: Proc. CVPR (2011)
23. Šochman, J., Matas, J.: Waldboost – learning for time constrained sequential detection. In: CVPR (2005)
24. Alameda-Pineda, X., Sanchez-Riera, J., Franc, V., Wienke, J., Cech, J., Kulkarni, K., Deleforge, A., Horaud, R.P.: Ravel: An annotated corpus for training robots with audiovisual abilities. Journal on Multimodal User Interfaces (2012)

Recognizing Actions across Cameras by Exploring the Correlated Subspace

Chun-Hao Huang, Yi-Ren Yeh, and Yu-Chiang Frank Wang

Research Center for IT Innovation, Academia Sinica, Taipei, Taiwan
{paulchhuang,yryeh,ycwang}@citi.sinica.edu.tw

Abstract. We present a novel transfer learning approach to cross-camera action recognition. Inspired by canonical correlation analysis (CCA), we first extract the spatio-temporal visual words from videos captured at different views, and derive a correlation subspace as a joint representation for different bag-of-words models at different views. Different from prior CCA-based approaches which simply train standard classifiers such as SVM in the resulting subspace, we explore the *domain transfer ability* of CCA in the correlation subspace, in which each dimension has a different capability in correlating source and target data. In our work, we propose a novel SVM with a correlation regularizer which incorporates such ability into the design of the SVM. Experiments on the IXMAS dataset verify the effectiveness of our method, which is shown to outperform state-of-the-art transfer learning approaches without taking such domain transfer ability into consideration.

1   Introduction

Action recognition has been an active research topic for researchers in the areas of computer vision and image processing. However, in practical scenarios, one typically needs to deal with multiple cameras with different lighting, depression angle, etc. conditions. Moreover, actions of interest might not be seen by a particular camera in advance, and thus no training data for that action is available. Therefore, it is expected that most existing single-view action recognition approaches cannot be easily extended for cross-view action recognition due to poor generalization [1].

While some researchers proposed to extract view-invariant representations for cross camera action recognition (e.g., [2,3]), *transfer learning* [4] has recently been applied to address this problem [5,6]. The purpose of transfer learning is to transfer the knowledge observed from one or few source domains to the target domain, so that the task in the target domain (e.g., predicting the action of interest captured by a new camera) can be solved accordingly.

Based on canonical correlation analysis (CCA) [7], we present a transfer learning based approach (via CCA) for cross camera action recognition. Our method aims at determining a correlation subspace as a shared representation of action models captured by different cameras. However, the correlation between the projected source and target view data will be different in each dimension of

A. Fusiello et al. (Eds.): ECCV 2012 Ws/Demos, Part I, LNCS 7583, pp. 342–351, 2012.

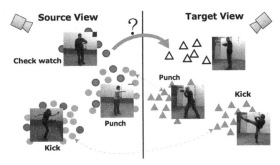

Fig. 1. The scenario of cross-camera action recognition. Note that instances in circles and triangles are actions captured by the source and target view camera, respectively. Our approach aims at utilizing labeled training data (colored circles) at the source view and unlabeled data pairs (in gray) from both views for recognizing unseen actions (in white) at the target view.

this subspace, depending on the corresponding correlation coefficient. Therefore, we need to take such *domain transfer ability* into consideration when designing the classifier in this joint subspace. We propose a novel SVM formulation, which incorporates such ability into classification in the joint subspace, so that the unseen actions at the target view can be projected and recognized accordingly. As shown in Figure 1, we focus on the scenario of using labeled data captured by the source camera for training (i.e., colored instances in Figure 1), and *no* training data is available at the target view. The unlabeled instance pairs (shown in gray in Figure 1) are collected from both views for transfer learning purposes ([5,6] also have this requirement). Later in our experiments, the effectiveness of our proposed method will be verified.

2   Related Work

2.1   Action Recognition

One can divide existing works on action recognition into two categories: human body modeling and action representation [8]. The former aims at tracking joints of human body model and recognizing actions by predicting poses [9], while the latter utilizes spatial and temporal information for recognizing the associated action (e.g., spatiotemporal curvatures of 2D trajectories [2] or space-time volumes [10]). Inspired by the use of bag-of-words models for image classification, researchers also advocate the extraction of spatio-temporal descriptors [11,12] for constructing the corresponding bag-of-words model for recognition. In such cases, actions are thus described by histograms of *visual words*.

2.2   Cross-View Action Recognition

For cross camera/view action recognition, only labeled instances collected by one or multiple source view cameras are available for training. Since *both* training and test data at the target view cannot be seen in advance, this scenario makes cross-view action recognition very challenging. Some researchers aim at designing view-invariant representation [2,3]. Alternatively, one can approach this problem as solving a matching task according to the quality of recovered geometry [13].

Recently, transfer learning has attracted the attention from researchers, and it has been successfully applied to cross-camera action recognition. The goal of transfer learning is to first learn a model to distinguish between different actions using training (labeled) data $\mathcal{D}_l^s$ from the source view domain $\mathcal{X}^s \in \mathbb{R}^{d_s}$. Once this model is observed, transfer learning aims at mapping this model into the target view domain $\mathcal{X}^t \in \mathbb{R}^{d_t}$ by utilizing unlabeled instance pairs $(\mathcal{D}_u^s, \mathcal{D}_u^t)$ collected by cameras at both source and target views. Generally, these approaches focus on determining a *shared representation* for both views when representing a data instance. For example, Farhadi and Tabrizi [5] propose to learn split-based features for source-view frames based on local data structure. They convert such features to the corresponding frames at the target view, so that actions at the target view can be encoded and recognized accordingly. However, their method requires the assumption that the local data structures at two domains are consistent, which might not be practical. Li and Zickler [14] characterize the source and target domains as two points on a Grassmann manifold, and they take the sampled points between them (along the geodesic) as the shared feature representation. Their approach considers data in different feature spaces lie on a low-dimensional manifold, and thus implicitly assumes their local structures are similar. Besides the implicit assumption of similar local structures for both domains, another concerns for the above methods is the requirement of $d_s = d_t$, i.e., the feature dimensions of source and target domains must be the same, which also limits their practical uses. Recently, Liu *et al.* [6] advocate to construct a bilingual codebook as a shared feature representation for both domains. With unlabeled data collected from both domains, their approach learns a shared codebook for two views in terms of a bipartite graph, and the bilingual words are obtained by spectral clustering. Although this approach does not require similarities of local data structure and allows features dimensions of the two views to be different, the shared feature attributes are considered to be *equally important*, which may not be preferable if the (shared) features extracted from each domain have uncoordinated contributions.

3   Our Proposed Method

3.1   Learning Correlation Subspace via CCA

The idea of applying transfer learning for cross-view action recognition is to determine a common representation (e.g., a joint subspace) for features extracted from source and target views, so that the model trained from the source-view data can be applied to recognize test data observed at the target view. Among existing methods [15,5,16,6], canonical correlation analysis (CCA) is a very effective technique. It aims at maximizing the correlation between two variable sets [15,16] and thus fits the goal of this work.

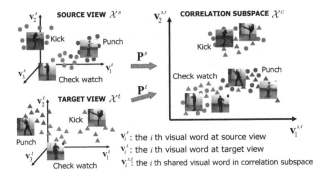

Fig. 2. Transfer learning via CCA [15]. Note that $\mathbf{P}^s$ and $\mathbf{P}^t$ are the projection matrices derived by CCA.

For the sake of completeness, we briefly review CCA as follows. Given two sets of n centered unlabeled observations $\mathbf{X}^s = [\mathbf{x}_1^s, \ldots, \mathbf{x}_n^s] \in \mathbb{R}^{d_s \times n}$ and $\mathbf{X}^t = [\mathbf{x}_1^t, \ldots, \mathbf{x}_n^t] \in \mathbb{R}^{d_t \times n}$ ($\mathbf{x}_i^s \in \mathcal{D}_u^s$ and $\mathbf{x}_i^t \in \mathcal{D}_u^s$) in source and target views respectively, CCA learns the projection vectors $\mathbf{u}^s \in \mathbb{R}^{d_s}$ and $\mathbf{u}^t \in \mathbb{R}^{d_t}$, which maximizes the correlation coefficient ρ:

$$\max_{\mathbf{u}^s, \mathbf{u}^t} \rho = \frac{\mathbf{u}^{s\top} \mathbf{\Sigma}_{st} \mathbf{u}^t}{\sqrt{\mathbf{u}^{s\top} \mathbf{\Sigma}_{ss} \mathbf{u}^s} \sqrt{\mathbf{u}^{t\top} \mathbf{\Sigma}_{tt} \mathbf{u}^t}}, \tag{1}$$

where $\mathbf{\Sigma}_{st} = \mathbf{X}^s \mathbf{X}^{t\top}$, $\mathbf{\Sigma}_{ss} = \mathbf{X}^s \mathbf{X}^{s\top}$, $\mathbf{\Sigma}_{tt} = \mathbf{X}^t \mathbf{X}^{t\top}$, and $\rho \in [0, 1]$. As suggested by [16], $\mathbf{u}^s$ in (1) can be solved by a generalized eigenvalue decomposition problem:

$$\mathbf{\Sigma}_{st} (\mathbf{\Sigma}_{tt})^{-1} \mathbf{\Sigma}_{st}^\top \mathbf{u}^s = \eta \mathbf{\Sigma}_{ss} \mathbf{u}^s. \tag{2}$$

Once $\mathbf{u}^s$ is obtained, $\mathbf{u}^t$ can be calculated by $\mathbf{\Sigma}_{tt}^{-1} \mathbf{\Sigma}_{st} \mathbf{u}^s / \eta$. In practice, regularization terms $\lambda_s \mathbf{I}$ and $\lambda_t \mathbf{I}$ need to be added into $\mathbf{\Sigma}_{ss}$ and $\mathbf{\Sigma}_{tt}$ to avoid overfitting and singularity problems. As a result, one solves the following problem instead:

$$\mathbf{\Sigma}_{st} (\mathbf{\Sigma}_{tt} + \lambda_t \mathbf{I})^{-1} \mathbf{\Sigma}_{st}^\top \mathbf{u}^s = \eta (\mathbf{\Sigma}_{ss} + \lambda_s \mathbf{I}) \mathbf{u}^s. \tag{3}$$

Generally, one can derive more than one pair of projection vectors $\{\mathbf{u}_i^s\}_{i=1}^d$ and $\{\mathbf{u}_i^t\}_{i=1}^d$ with corresponding ρ_i in a descending order (i.e., $\rho_i > \rho_{i+1}$). Thus, the source (target) view data $\mathbf{X}^s$ ($\mathbf{X}^t$) projected onto $\mathbf{u}^s$ ($\mathbf{u}^t$) will lie in the *correlation subspace* $\mathcal{X}^c \in \mathbb{R}^d$, which is spanned by $\{\mathbf{v}_i^{s,t}\}_{i=1}^d$.

Figure 2 shows a CCA example for cross-view action recognition. Given data of three action classes in source and target views ($\mathcal{X}^s$ and $\mathcal{X}^t$), CCA determines projection matrices $\mathbf{P}^s = [\mathbf{u}_1^s, \ldots, \mathbf{u}_d^s] \in \mathbb{R}^{d_s \times d}$ and $\mathbf{P}^t = [\mathbf{u}_1^t, \ldots, \mathbf{u}_d^t] \in \mathbb{R}^{d_t \times d}$. Once the correlation subspace $\mathcal{X}^c \in \mathbb{R}^d$ is derived, unseen test data at the target view can be directly recognized by the model trained from the source view data projected onto $\mathcal{X}^c$.

3.2   Domain Transfer Ability of CCA

As discussed in Section 3.1, unseen test at the target view can be first projected onto the CCA correlation subspace $\mathcal{X}^c$, and thus the model learned from the source view data at this subspace can be applied for recognition. It is worth repeating that each dimension $\mathbf{v}_i^{s,t}$ in this subspace is associated with a different correlation coefficient ρ_i; the higher ρ_i is, the closer the projected data from different domains are. It is obvious that, a better *domain transfer ability* is resulted for the dominant dimensions $\mathbf{v}_i^{s,t}$ with larger ρ_i, and thus one should take such ability into consideration when designing a classification model in this correlation subspace.

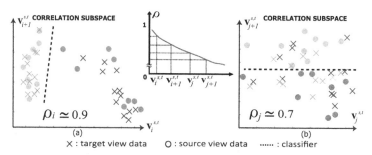

X : target view data   O : source view data   ······ : classifier

Fig. 3. Projecting source and target view instances from the IXMAS dataset into different correlation subspaces using projection vectors with different ρ

Figure 3 illustrates this issue by projecting source and target view data onto different 2D correlation subspaces, in which one subspace is associated with ($\mathbf{v}_i^{s,t}$ and $\mathbf{v}_{i+1}^{s,t}$) with higher ρ, and the other one is constructed by ($\mathbf{v}_j^{s,t}$ and $\mathbf{v}_{j+1}^{s,t}$) with smaller ρ values. The dash lines represent the classifier learned from projected source view data (since no labeled data in the target domain is available). From Figure 3(a), we see that the location of projected source and target data with the same label are close to each other, since the two basis vectors correspond to larger ρ values. On the other hand, as shown in Figure 3(b), the distributions of projected source and target view data are different due to a lower ρ. As a result, the classifier learned from projected source view data (i.e., the dash lines) cannot generalize well to the projected target view ones. In other words, poorer domain transfer ability will result in increased recognition error, even the classifier is well designed using the projected source view data.

To overcome such limitations for CCA in transfer learning, we advocate the *adaptation* of the learning model based on the domain transfer ability. Based on the formulation of support vector machine (SVM), we propose a new SVM formulation which takes such ability into account, and it can be applied to address cross-view recognition.

3.3   The Proposed SVM Formulation

Generally, if the ith feature attribute exhibits better discrimination ability, the standard SVM would produce a larger magnitude for the corresponding model (i.e., a larger $|w_i|$). As discussed earlier, transfer leaning via CCA does not take the domain transfer ability into account when learning the classifiers in the correlation subspace and thus degrades the recognition performance. To address this problem, we introduce a correlation regularizer and propose a novel SVM formulation which integrates the domain transfer ability and class discrimination in a unified framework. Due to the introduction of such ability, the generalization of our SVM for transfer leaning will be significantly improved.

The proposed SVM solves the following problem:

$$\min_{\mathbf{w}} \frac{1}{2}\|\mathbf{w}\|_2^2 + C \sum_{i=1}^{N} \xi_i - \frac{1}{2}\mathbf{r}^\top \text{Abs}(\mathbf{w}) \tag{4}$$

$$\text{s.t.} \ \ y_i(\langle \mathbf{w}, \mathbf{P}^{s\top}\mathbf{x}_i^s\rangle + b) + \xi_i \geq 1, \ \xi_i \geq 0, \ \forall(\mathbf{x}_i^s, y_i) \in \mathcal{D}_l^s,$$

where $\text{Abs}(\mathbf{w}) \equiv [|w_1|, |w_2|, \ldots, |w_d|]$ and $\mathbf{r} \equiv [\rho_1, \ldots, \rho_d]$ is the correlation vector in which each element indicates the correlation coefficient of CCA for each projection dimension. Note that only labeled source domain data $\mathbf{x}_i^s \in \mathcal{D}_l^s$ is available for training (not target domain data), and y_i is the associated class label. Parameters C and ξ are penalty term and slack variables as in the standard SVM. We have $\mathbf{P}^{s\top}\mathbf{x}_i^s$ as the projection of source domain data $\mathbf{x}_i^s$ onto the correlation subspace $\mathcal{X}_c$. The proposed term $\mathbf{r}^\top \text{Abs}(\mathbf{w})$, which is introduced for model adaptation based on CCA, can be regarded as a similarity measure for $\mathbf{r}$ and $\mathbf{w}$. More precisely, a smaller correlation coefficient ρ_i would enforce the shrinkage of the corresponding $|w_i|$, and thus suppresses the learned model along the ith CCA projection vector; on the other hand, a larger ρ_i favors the contribution of the associated $|w_i|$ when minimizing (4).

Since it is not straightforward to solve the minimization problem in (4) with $\text{Abs}(\mathbf{w})$, we seek the approximated solution by relaxing the original problem into the following form:

$$\min_{\mathbf{w}} \frac{1}{2}\|\mathbf{w}\|_2^2 + C \sum_{i=1}^{N} \xi_i - \frac{1}{2}(\mathbf{r} \odot \mathbf{r})^\top (\mathbf{w} \odot \mathbf{w}) \tag{5}$$

$$\text{s.t.} \ \ y_i(\langle \mathbf{w}, \mathbf{P}^{s\top}\mathbf{x}_i^s\rangle + b) + \xi_i \geq 1, \ \xi_i \geq 0, \ \forall(\mathbf{x}_i^s, y_i) \in \mathcal{D}_l^s,$$

where $\odot$ indicates the element-wise multiplication. We can further simplify (5) as:

$$\min_{\mathbf{w}} \frac{1}{2}\sum_{i=1}^{d}(1 - \rho_i^2)w_i^2 + C \sum_{i=1}^{N} \xi_i \tag{6}$$

$$\text{s.t.} \ \ y_i(\langle \mathbf{w}, \mathbf{P}^{s\top}\mathbf{x}_i^s\rangle + b) + \xi_i \geq 1, \ \xi_i \geq 0, \ \forall(\mathbf{x}_i^s, y_i) \in \mathcal{D}_l^s.$$

We refer to (6) as our proposed SVM formulation. Recall that $0 < \rho_i < 1$ in CCA, so that the convexity of the proposed objective function is guaranteed. It can be seen that, depending on the derived correlation coefficients, the formulation in (6) is effectively weighting each component of the regularization term accordingly. As a result, this modified SVM automatically adapt the derived classification model $\mathbf{w}$ based on the domain transfer ability of CCA, and thus it exhibits better generalization in recognizing projected unseen test data in the correlation subspace (as confirmed by our experiments). The decision function for classifying unseen test data at target domain is shown as follows:

$$f(\mathbf{x}) = \text{sgn}\left(\langle \mathbf{w}, \mathbf{P}^{t\top}\mathbf{x}^t\rangle + b\right), \tag{7}$$

where $\mathbf{P}^t$ projects the input test data $\mathbf{x}^t$ from the target domain onto the correlation subspace $\mathcal{X}_c$.

4   Experiments

4.1   Dataset and Experiment Settings

We consider the IXMAS multiview action dataset [3] which contains action videos of eleven action classes. Each action video is performed three times by twelve actors, and the actions are synchronically captured by five cameras, as shown in Figure 4. For a fair comparison with recent works such as [6], we extract descriptors defined by [11] and describe each action video as a group of spatio-temporal cuboids (at most 200). For each view these cuboids are quantized into $N = 1000$ visual words. As for data partition, we randomly choose two thirds of the video instances in each class as unlabeled data, and the rest are labeled data for training purposes. We follow the leave-one-action-out strategy as [6] did, which means we consider only one unseen action class at the target view to be recognized, and we exclude all instances of that class at both views when selecting the unlabeled data. The regularization terms λ_s and λ_t in (3) are both empirically set as 50. Instead of using a predetermined dimension number d (as [16] did), we select $\mathbf{v}_i^{s,t}$ with the corresponding correlation coefficient ρ_i above 0.5 for spanning the correlation subspace, and only the labeled data projected from the source view to this subspace are used for training. We repeat the above setting for each action class of interest, and report the average recognition performance in Figure 5.

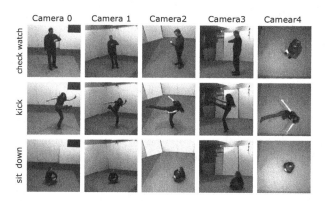

Fig. 4. Example actions of the IXMAS dataset. Each row represents an action at five different views.

4.2   Discussions

To compare our performance with other approaches, we consider the methods of direct prediction using classifiers learned at the source view (i.e., standard BoW without transfer learning), and the bag-of-bilingual-words (BoBW) model proposed in [6]. We note that, the above two approaches apply the standard linear SVM after deriving the feature representation for training/testing. Besides CCA [15], to argue that our SVM can be extended to other methods based on joint feature representations, we also consider a variant of BoBW [6]. We first compute the correlation between the source and target view data in terms of the derived BoBW, and apply our SVM with the correlation regularizer using the associated correlation coefficients (i.e., BoBW + our SVM in Figure 5).

	camera0						camera1						camera2					
	A	B	C	D	E	F	A	B	C	D	E	F	A	B	C	D	E	F
cam0			-				9.29	60.96	63.03	63.18	63.23	**64.90**	11.62	41.21	50.76	56.97	56.67	**60.61**
cam1	10.71	58.08	59.70	66.72	65.40	**70.25**			-				7.12	33.54	38.03	57.83	**61.97**	59.34
cam2	8.79	52.63	49.34	57.37	58.33	**62.47**	6.67	50.86	45.79	59.19	59.60	**61.87**			-			
cam3	6.31	40.35	44.44	65.30	61.87	**66.01**	9.75	33.59	33.27	46.77	48.43	**52.68**	5.96	41.26	43.99	61.36	**63.74**	61.36
cam4	5.35	38.59	40.91	54.39	51.52	**55.76**	9.44	37.53	37.00	53.59	49.24	**55.00**	9.19	34.80	38.28	57.88	57.88	**60.15**
avg.	7.79	47.41	48.60	60.95	59.28	**63.62**	8.79	45.73	44.77	55.68	55.13	**58.61**	8.47	37.70	42.77	58.51	60.06	**60.37**

	camera3						camera4					
	A	B	C	D	E	F	A	B	C	D	E	F
cam0	7.78	39.65	41.36	**63.64**	57.37	62.17	7.12	24.60	37.02	43.69	42.22	**48.23**
cam1	12.02	35.91	39.14	48.59	46.92	**54.85**	8.89	26.87	22.22	44.24	41.36	**49.29**
cam2	6.46	41.46	42.78	60.00	61.31	**61.46**	10.35	28.03	33.43	45.05	46.11	**51.82**
cam3			-				8.89	27.53	28.28	40.66	41.01	**41.06**
cam4	9.60	27.68	34.60	48.03	45.51	**48.89**			-			
avg.	8.96	36.17	39.47	55.06	52.78	**56.84**	8.81	26.76	30.24	43.41	42.68	**47.60**

Fig. 5. Performance comparisons on the IXMAS dataset. Note that each row indicates the source view camera (for training), and each column is the target view camera for recognizing the unseen action class. We consider the methods of A: BoW without transfer learning [11], B: BoBW [6], C: BoBW + our SVM, D: CCA + linear SVM [15], E: CCA + nonlinear SVM, and F: our proposed framework (CCA + our SVM).

From Figure 5, we see that the method without transfer learning (i.e., columns A) achieved the poorest results as expected. While the BoBW model (columns B) and the approach of CCA (columns D) remarkably improved the performance by determining a shared representation for training/test, the use of our SVM for BoBW (columns C) produced comparable or better results than the simple use of BoBW did, and the integration of CCA with our proposed SVM (columns F) achieved the best performance. Comparing the results shown in columns C and F, although our SVM taking the correlation of the source and target view data was able to improve the recognition performance, it would still be desirable to derive such correlation from a correlation-based transfer learning approach such as CCA. This explains why our approach combining CCA and imposing the resulting correlation coefficient into the proposed SVM formulation achieved the best recognition performance.

We further investigate the effectiveness of the proposed SVM over the standard one in terms of domain transfer ability. Figure 6(a) and (b) show the averaged value $|w_i|$ of each attribute in the standard and our SVM models using the

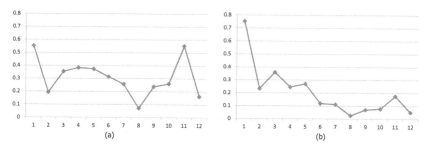

Fig. 6. Comparisons of the averaged $|w_i|$ values: (a) standard SVM and (b) our proposed SVM. The horizontal axis indicates the index of the dimension in the correlated subspace (arranged according to the associated correlation coefficients in a descending order). The vertical axis shows the associated $|w_i|$ values. The recognition rates for the two SVMs on recognizing the action "get-up" are 47.22% and 77.78%, respectively.

IXMAS dataset, respectively. From Figure 6(a), we see that the standard SVM aims at separating data the in the correlated subspace without considering the domain transfer ability (i.e., the correlation between projected data), and thus we still observe prominent $|w_i|$ values at non-dominant feature dimensions (i.e., the 11th dimension). On the other hand, in Figure 6(b), our proposed SVM suppresses the contributions of non-dominant feature dimensions in the correlated subspace, and thus only results in large $|w_i|$ values for dominant feature dimensions. The actual recognition rates for the two models were 47.22% and 77.78% for the action "get-up." Such a significant recognition improvement verifies that the leaning and enforcement of domain transfer ability of our proposed SVM model are preferable for transfer learning based cross-view action recognition.

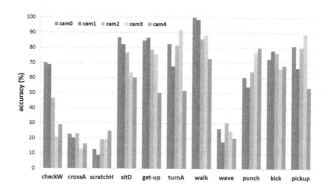

Fig. 7. Average recognition rates at different target views for each action category

Figure 7 compares the recognition performance of each action for different target views. As expected, we observe that the transfer of recognition models is more challenging for certain actions/views (e.g., cross-arms, wave, etc. actions only with movements of arms). In general, camera 4 (top view) obtains the lowest recognition rate, and it is mainly due to the ambiguity between different torso-associated actions observed at this view.

5 Conclusions

We proposed a transfer learning based approach to cross-camera action recognition. By exploring the correlation subspace derived by CCA using unlabeled data pairs of source and target view data, we presented a novel SVM formulation with a correlation regularizer. The proposed SVM takes the domain transfer ability into consideration when designing the classifier at the correlation subspace. As a result, only projected and labeled training data from the source view are required when designing the classifier in the resulting subspace (i.e., no training data at the target view is needed). Experimental results on the IXMAS dataset confirmed the use of our proposed framework for improved recognition, and we verified that our approach outperformed state-of-the-art transfer learning algorithms which did not take such domain transfer ability into consideration.

References

1. Holte, M., Tran, C., Trivedi, M., Moeslund, T.: Human action recognition using multiple views: a comparative perspective on recent developments. In: ACM MM Joint Workshop on HGBU (2011)
2. Rao, C., Yilmaz, A., Shah, M.: View-invariant representation and recognition of actions. IJCV 50, 203–226 (2002)
3. Weinland, D., Ronfard, R., Boyer, E.: Free viewpoint action recognition using motion history volumes. CVIU 104, 249–257 (2006)
4. Pan, S.J., Yang, Q.: A survey on transfer learning. IEEE TKDE 22, 1345–1359 (2010)
5. Farhadi, A., Tabrizi, M.K.: Learning to Recognize Activities from the Wrong View Point. In: Forsyth, D., Torr, P., Zisserman, A. (eds.) ECCV 2008, Part I. LNCS, vol. 5302, pp. 154–166. Springer, Heidelberg (2008)
6. Liu, J., Shah, M., Kuipers, B., Savarese, S.: Cross-view action recognition via view knowledge transfer. In: CVPR (2011)
7. Hotelling, H.: Relations between two sets of variates. Biometrika 28, 321–377 (1936)
8. Poppe, R.: A survey on vision-based human action recognition. IVC 28, 976–990 (2010)
9. Tran, C., Trivedi, M.: Human body modelling and tracking using volumetric representation: Selected recent studies and possibilities for extensions. In: ICDSC (2008)
10. Blank, M., Gorelick, L., Shechtman, E., Irani, M., Basri, R.: Actions as space-time shapes. In: ICCV (2005)
11. Dollár, P., Rabaud, V., Cottrell, G., Belongie, S.: Behavior recognition via sparse spatio-temporal features. In: ICCV Joint Workshop on VS-PETS (2005)
12. Laptev, I.: On space-time interest points. IJCV 64, 107–123 (2005)
13. ul Haq, A., Gondal, I., Murshed, M.: On dynamic scene geometry for view-invariant action matching. In: CVPR (2011)
14. Li, R., Zickler, T.: Discriminative virtual views for cross-view action recognition. In: CVPR (2012)
15. Blitzer, J., Foster, D., Kakade, S.: Domain adaptation with coupled subspaces. In: AISTATS (2011)
16. Hardoon, D.R., Szedmak, S., Shawe-Taylor, J.: Canonical correlation analysis: An overview with application to learning methods. Neural Computation 16, 2639–2664 (2004)

Chinese Shadow Puppetry with an Interactive Interface Using the Kinect Sensor

Hui Zhang[1,2], Yuhao Song[1], Zhuo Chen[1], Ji Cai[1], and Ke Lu[1]

[1] Dept. of Computer Science, United International College, 28, Jinfeng Road,
Tangjiawan, Zhuhai, Guangdong, China
[2] Shenzhen Key Lab of Intelligent Media and Speech, PKU-HKUST Shenzhen Hong
Kong Institution, Shenzhen, China

Abstract. This paper addresses the problem of using body gestures to control the Chinese shadow puppets with the Microsoft Kinect sensor. By analyzing the motion of the actors in the Chinese famous drama, Wu-song Fights the Tiger, we propose a general framework for controlling two shadow puppets, a human model and an animal model. A performer can conduct simple actions such as turning the head, stretching the arms or kicking the legs. However, it is more difficult for a normal performer to simulate more complicated movements, for example, back flips and splits. Therefore we define some special postures to represent these difficult movements. Besides, in order to be compatible with the Chinese drama style, we use water color to paint the background scenery and the foreground characters. We show some preliminary results which demonstrate the effectiveness of this work.

Keywords: Kinect, shadow puppetry, gesture.

1 Introduction

The Chinese shadow play, or shadow puppetry, is an ancient form of story-telling in which sticks and flat puppets are manipulated behind an illuminated background to create moving pictures [1]. It is a popular means of entertainment being regarded as a predecessor of animation and movies. The shadow puppet is a cut-out figure operated by the puppeteer between a light source and a translucent screen. By moving both the puppets and the light source, various effects can be achieved. A talented puppeteer can make the figures perform all kinds of actions, such as walk, dance, fight, nod and laugh. However, it is not that easy for a normal user to control the movements of the puppets. A more friendly interface for them is to manipulate directly using their body gestures [2] so that the puppets can mimic the performers' motion. Although action and gesture recognition [3][4][5][6][7] is an extensively studied research field, controlling the movements of puppets is still a challenging problem because of the diversity of the movements of the puppets and the mapping between performers and puppets.

Recently, a lot of works have been carried out on digital puppetry [8]. The first live animated computer graphics puppetry is probably the Waldos [9], which is

A. Fusiello et al. (Eds.): ECCV 2012 Ws/Demos, Part I, LNCS 7583, pp. 352–361, 2012.

manipulated through a mechanical arm controlled by a puppeteer. Puppeteers could also use multimodal systems, with data gloves, joysticks, motion capture and midi devices, to control the digital puppets [10]. Shin proposed to transfer motion capture data to animated characters using the notion of dynamic importance of an end effecter [11].

However, all of these mentioned works are based on 3D characters. The solution of animation performed by two dimensional puppets appears only recently. In [12], Hsu et al. introduced a motion planning technique which automatically generates the animation of 2D puppets. Tan et al. presented a method for interactive animation of 2D shadow play puppets by real-time visual simulating the shadow using texture mapping, blending techniques, and lighting and blurring effects [13]. Inspired by traditional Chinese shadow puppetry, the project ShadowStory [14] allows the users to design their own puppets with a tablet PC and animate them with orientation sensors. In [15], a 2D shape deformation of the triangulated cartoon is driven by its skeleton and the animation can be obtained by retargeting the skeleton joints to the shape.

With the emergence of Microsoft Kinect, the Xbox 360 video game console Kinect, people start to use it to control the puppet. Kinect is composed of a depth sensor, a color camera sensor and a four-element microphone array [16]. Through a natural user interface using gestures and spoken commands, it enables users to control and interact with the computer without touching a game controller. Kinect has the capability to track the skeleton image of one or two people moving within the Kinect field of view for gesture-driven applications.

People use different ways to control puppets. Gobeille and Watson developed a prototype of directly mapping the movement of one hand to the motion of the puppetry bird mouth [17]. Walther controlled a 3D puppet's motion only by the movements of two hands [18]. Instead of only one puppeteer controlling one puppet, Boyle proposed a collaborative interface of two puppeteers using their body movements [19]. However, all these state-of-the-art works only provide preliminary results for controlling puppets. Lots of puppet movements could not be easily mapped to the gestures of an actor, such as splits and somersaults, which are quite normal in Chinese Kungfu Shadow Play. Therefore we study the movie in which the puppeteer manipulates the shadow puppets and then recognize the hand and body movements of the actors by making use of Kinect. Furthermore, in addition to the body movement, the shadow puppet would have some subtle face expressions, such as moving its lower jaw and eyebrow when it speaks, moving eyeballs when it thinks, etc. Therefore we propose to control the simple movements of the shadow puppets directly by users' gestures and trigger the animation of complicated puppet movements by pre-defined user postures or by voice. Besides, in order to be compatible with the Chinese drama style, we use water color to paint the whole scenery.

The remainder of the paper is organized as follows. Section 2 describes details of the puppeteer gestures and how to control the puppets. Section 3 introduces implementation details of the proposed technique. Section 4 presents the experimental results, followed by discussions and conclusions in Section 5.

2   Gesture Control

Kinect scans the user's skeleton for further interactions with the computers. Therefore, it is easy to directly map the human gesture to the puppet gesture. However, this is only true for simple human movements, such as moving legs, jumping. Those complicated actions, e.g., back flips and splits, could not be performed by the normal user.

Fig. 1. The backfilp (the first row) and the standing splits (the second row) gesture of the puppet Wusong

Furthermore, the shadow puppet is of two dimensions whose movement is in the screen plane, while the skeleton and its motion are three dimensional. Considering the difficulty of transforming 3D behaviors of the skeleton into the movement and rotation of 2D puppets, we prefer using the data-driven method instead of the mechanism method (i.e. the physical model). For example, the behavior of forearms is transformed into rotation angles by Kinect. Those series of angles are read time by time and mapped into the user-controlled character in program. Therefore for the definition of the action movement, our solution is to use event listener to trigger the character movement, such as walk, splits and rolling.

According to the characteristic of motion of the Wusong and the Tiger puppets, we found that they require different means of representation. We classified them as a human model and an animal model, and introduced different ways for controlling their puppets in below.

2.1 Actions of Human Models

As the structure of the Wusong puppet is similar to the user, it is easy to directly map the Kinect skeleton to its model, parts by parts [2]. We propose to use the above mentioned data-driven method to implement those complicated gestures. However, since the range of Kinect detection is limited, a displacement might not be captured and we have to define the puppet walking by making use of pre-defined gestures.

- *Back flips.* When the user hands stretch to up-backward, the animation of back flips will be triggered. The top row of figure 1 shows the screenshots of the puppet Wusong's back flips.
- *Standing splits.* When the user rising the calf of one leg backward with a $\geq$ 90° angle to the thigh, the back flips animation will be triggered. The bottom row of figure 1 shows the screenshots of the puppet Wusong's standing splits.
- *Walking.* When the user's left foot steps to left and has a certain distance to the right foot, the walking animation of the Wusong model would be triggered. Figure 2 shows the screenshots of the puppet Wusong's walking animation.

Fig. 2. The puppet Wusong walks

Additionally, for subtle movements such as the opening of the mouse, we use Kinect audio control. The performer's voice drives the mouse movement of the puppet Wusong (see figure 3 for details).

2.2 Actions of Animal Models

Let's use the Tiger puppet as an example of an animal model. Since animal models and human models are very different, we cannot directly map the Kinect scanned skeleton to the corresponding Tiger puppet. Especially in the shadow play, Wusong Fights the Tiger, most of the action of the Tiger has relatively large range of movements, such as somersaults, rolling. These actions are difficult to mimic by human. Therefore we have proposed three methods to solve the problems.

(a)   (b)

Fig. 3. The mouse movement of the puppet Wusong is triggered by the voice of the performer. (a) The puppet Wusong's mouth is closed. (b) The puppet Wusong's mouth is opened.

The first solution is to define a number of gestures to achieve these movements of the Tiger. The advantage of this approach is that the animation can be very real to mimic the tiger's action, especially for some subtle movements. The figure 4 shows three images in the animation of the Tiger's idle state.

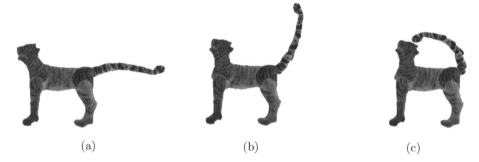

(a)   (b)   (c)

Fig. 4. The animation of the Tiger's idle state

However, the drawback of this method is obvious. These gestures can only be applicable for the Tiger in this shadow play, and the more the number of gestures, the longer the cycle of producing the animation.

The second possible solution is to bind the tiger model with two control points. These two control points are the points which the puppeteer manipulates when they play the puppet Tiger. Figure 5.(a) shows the location of the control points. As the control points move, various parts of the Tiger will move due to the inertia and the traction. Kinect only gets the skeleton position of the two hands in order to manipulate the shadow play and it will be easy for players. However, relying solely on the two control points cannot completely achieve all the tiger actions, such as the Tiger squatting on the ground. The Tiger's legs will bend after colliding with the underground (see figure 5.(b) for detail).

The third solution that we currently conceive is the best one. It is similar to the human model mapping in the first approach. The difference is that we map the joints on left and right part of the human skeleton to those on the Tiger's front and rear. Figure 6 illustrates the joints on the human skeleton captured by Kinect and their correspondences on the tiger model.

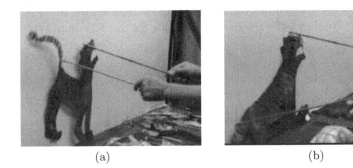

(a)   (b)

Fig. 5. (a) The puppeteer uses two sticks to control the movement of the Tiger, through two control points. (b) The Tiger squatting on the ground. The Tiger's legs will bend after colliding with the underground.

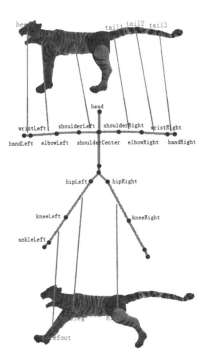

Fig. 6. The joints on the human skeleton scanned by Kinect are mapped to their corresponding joints on the tiger model

2.3   Gesture Mapping

To summarize, there are some important gestures to be represented in the Chinese Kungfu drama. We shows the gesture mapping list for the Tiger and Wusong puppet in table 1.

Table 1. Gesture mapping list for (a) the Tiger and (b) Wusong. The postures captured will trigger the corresponding puppet actions.

Actions of the puppet	Postures to be recognized
To turn around	Nod.
To move left	Moving the leg one step to right.
To move right	Moving the leg one step to left.
To roll forward	Preparatory action of rolling forward.
To roll backward	Preparatory action of rolling backward.
Legs in the air	Surrender

(a)

Actions of the puppet	Postures to be recognized
To walk left	Moving the leg one step to right.
To walk right	Moving the leg one step to left.
To roll forward	Preparatory action of rolling forward.
To roll backward	Preparatory action of rolling backward.
Backward somersault	Arms stretching up-backward.
Front somersault	Arms stretching up-forward.
Splits	Splitting the two legs with an angle $\geq 60^{\circ}$.
Standing splits	Rising the calf of one leg backward, with an angle $\geq 90^{\circ}$ to the thigh.
Single-Handspring	Putting two hands on one foot while keeping the legs straight.

(b)

3   Implementation

In our system we use the official Microsoft Windows SDK for posture detection instead of the other cracked SDK such as the very popular OpenNI. This is due to the reason that the Windows SDK provides the best recognition accuracy and furthermore, the Windows SDK supports audio driven interaction. Therefore different from OpenNI, we can use it for controlling the subtle face expression of the shadow puppets. By integrating SDK and the sensor Kinect into Unity3D, our method can control the 2D shadow puppet through a multimodal interface with depth, rgd and voice inputs.

We designed the 3D scenery by Autodest 3DMax and put the puppets model into it. To generate a more traditional Chinese style in the screen, we render the final result with the method of watercolor painting in [20]. By making use of Shading language, we implemented several steps of processing such as blurring, edge strokes, sharpening. Some extra elements were also added into the scene, for example the waterfall and the wave effect, generated with the particle system in the Unity engine. By controlling the emission, the size and the energy of the particles, effects such as the water splash and the waterfall are imitated veritably. Additionally the texture of the water-drop is refined for a higher reality.

4   Experimental Results

In our experiment, Wusong and the tiger of the famous Chinese novel "Outlaws of the Marsh" are the two puppets to be controlled. We took separate pictures of their body parts as the textures and create their models by assembling them respectively in 3D Max. Figure 7 shows the separate parts of the tiger and figure 4 shows the Tiger puppet.

Fig. 7. The separate parts of the tiger

We detected Wusong and the Tiger with a single Kinect at the same time. However, since a human and an animal has different structures of the skeleton, we have to use different mapping strategies for controlling them. The Wusong puppet was mapped with a normal human skeleton and the Tiger puppet was mapped with the skeleton shown in figure 6.(b). Figure 8.(a) shows that two players are posing in front of Kinect and figure 8.(b) shows that their gestures are mapped to the Wusong and the Tiger puppets, respectively.

(a)   (b)

Fig. 8. (a) Two players are captured by Kinect. (b) The players' gestures are mapped to the Wusong and the Tiger puppets, respectively.

(a)   (b)

Fig. 9. (a) One of the scenes in the shadow display. (b) The water colored version of the scene.

Figure 9.(a) shows the 3D scenery we designed, in which there stands the puppet Wusong. After several steps of processing, such as blurring, edge strokes, sharpening, we added a background with the rice paper. Figure 9.(b) shows the final result after our rendering.

5   Conclusions and Future Works

This paper presents using body gestures to control the Chinese shadow puppets with the Microsoft Kinect sensor. By analyzing the motion of the actors in the Chinese famous drama, Wusong Fights the Tiger, we propose a general framework for controlling two shadow puppets, a human model and an animal model. A performer can conduct simple actions such as turning the head, stretching the arms or kicking the legs. However, it is more difficult for a normal performer to simulate more complicated movements, for example, back flips and splits. Therefore we define some special postures to represent these difficult movements. Besides, in order to be compatible with the Chinese drama style, we use water color to paint the background scenery and the foreground characters. Some preliminary results demonstrate the effectiveness of this work.

However, we had only introduced controlling the human and animal puppets in this paper. We still need to map the human skeleton to other categories of models, such as birds, plants, or arbitrary shaped puppets. Another possible work is to directly capture the puppeteer's movements of manipulating the puppets and use these gestures to control the puppet movements.

Acknowledgments. The work described in this article was partially supported by the National Natural Science Foundation of China (Project No. 61005038) and an internal funding from United International College.

References

1. Chen, F.P.L.: Visions for the Masses; Chinese Shadow Plays from Shaanxi and Shanxi. Cornell University (2004)

2. Leite, L., Orvalho, V.: Shape your body: Control a virtual silhouette using body motion. In: Proceedings of ACM SIGCHI Conference on Human Factors in Computing Systems (2012)
3. Zhang, Z.R.M.Y.: Robust hand gesture recognition with kinect sensor. In: Proceedings of the 19th ACM International Conference on Multimedia, pp. 759–760 (2011)
4. banovic Volkan Isler Linnda R. Caporeal Jeff Trinkle, E.M.M.: Shadowplay: A generative model for nonverbal human-robot interaction. In: Proceedings of the 4th ACM/IEEE International Conference on Human Robot Interaction, pp. 117–124 (2009)
5. Shao, L., Ji, L., Liu, Y., Zhang, J.: Human action segmentation and recognition via motion and shape analysis. Pattern Recognition Letters 33, 438–445 (2012)
6. Shao, L., Gao, R., Liu, Y., Zhang, H.: Transform based spatio-temporal descriptors for human action recognition. Neurocomputing 74, 962–973 (2011)
7. Wu, D., Shao, L.: Silhouette analysis based action recognition via exploiting human poses. IEEE Transactions on Circuits and Systems for Video Technology (2012)
8. Sturman, D.: Computer puppetry. IEEE Computer Graphics and Applications 18, 38–45 (1998)
9. Graham, W.: Course Notes: 3D Character Animation by Computer. In: Course Notes: 3D Character Animation by Computer, ACM SIGGRAPH, pp. 6–79 (1989)
10. Tardif, H.: Character animation in real time. In: Panel Proceedings: Applications of Virtual Reality I, ACM SIGGRAPH (1991)
11. Shin, H., Lee, J., Shin, S.Y., Gleicher, M.: Computer puppetry: An importance-based approach. ACM Trans. Graph., 67–94 (2001)
12. Hsu, W.S., Ye, T.: Planning character motions for shadow play animations. In: Proc. CASA, pp. 184–190 (2005)
13. Tan, K.L., Talib, A.Z., Osman, M.A.: Real-time simulation and interactive animation of shadow play puppets using opengl. International Journal of IJCIE 4, 1–8 (2010)
14. Lu, F., Tian, F., Jian, Y., Ca, X., Lu, W., Li, G., Zhang, X., Dai, G., Wang, H.: Shadowstory: creative and collaborative digital storytelling inspired by cultural heritage. In: Proc. of the ACM Conference on Human Factors in Computing Systems, pp. 1919–1928 (2011)
15. Pan, J., Zhang, J.J.: Sketch-Based Skeleton-Driven 2D Animation and Motion Capture. In: Pan, Z., Cheok, A.D., Müller, W. (eds.) Transactions on Edutainment VI. LNCS, vol. 6758, pp. 164–181. Springer, Heidelberg (2011)
16. Kean, S., Hall, J.C., Perry, P.: Meet the Kinect: An Introduction to Programming Natural User Interfaces. Springer-Verlag New York Inc. (2011)
17. Emily Gobeille, T.W.: Interactive puppet prototype with xbox kinect (2011)
18. Walther, J.: Kinect digital puppeteering with openkinect (2010)
19. Boyle, C., Foster, A.: We be monsters: A collaborative kinect puppet (2011)
20. Lei, S.I.E., Chang, C.-F.: Real-Time Rendering of Watercolor Effects for Virtual Environments. In: Aizawa, K., Nakamura, Y., Satoh, S. (eds.) PCM 2004. LNCS, vol. 3333, pp. 474–481. Springer, Heidelberg (2004)

Group Dynamics and Multimodal Interaction Modeling Using a Smart Digital Signage

Tony Tung, Randy Gomez, Tatsuya Kawahara, and Takashi Matsuyama

Kyoto University,
Academic Center for Computing and Media Studies
and Graduate School of Informatics, Japan
tung@vision.kuee.kyoto-u.ac.jp,
{randy-g,kawahara}@ar.media.kyoto-u.ac.jp, tm@i.kyoto-u.ac.jp

Abstract. This paper presents a new multimodal system for group dynamics and interaction analysis. The framework is composed of a mic array and multiview video cameras placed on a digital signage display which serves as a support for interaction. We show that visual information processing can be used to localize nonverbal communication events and synchronized with audio information. Our contribution is twofold: 1) we present a scalable portable system for multiple people multimodal interaction sensing, and 2) we propose a general framework to model A/V multimodal interaction that employs speaker diarization for audio processing and hybrid dynamical systems (HDS) for video processing. HDS are used to represent communication dynamics between multiple people by capturing the characteristics of temporal structures in head motions. Experimental results show real-world situations of group communication processing for joint attention estimation. We believe the proposed framework is very promising for further research.

1 Introduction

Over the last decades electronic displays have become ubiquitous and have participated in many everyday life activities. Digital advertising displays, video games or poster presentations trigger group discussions which generally contain lots of interactions, and therefore lots of information on human communication and behavior. Here, we present a novel multimodal system to capture and analyze multiple people dynamics and interaction. The system detects and recognizes verbal and non-verbal communication signals, and returns human readable feedbacks on a display screen. Visual information processing is used to detect communication events that are synchronized with audio information (e.g., head motion and speech). The system could potentially be adapted for various applications such as entertainment (multiplayer interactive gaming device), education or edutainment (virtual support for lecturer), medicine, etc.

Multimodal Audio/Video systems designed for human behavior and interaction analysis usually consist of multiple video cameras and microphones placed in a dedicated room, and oriented towards the participants. To date, these systems are still very tedious to setup and often require wearable equipments that

A. Fusiello et al. (Eds.): ECCV 2012 Ws/Demos, Part I, LNCS 7583, pp. 362–371, 2012.
© Springer-Verlag Berlin Heidelberg 2012

Fig. 1. Smart digital signage tested during poster presentation for group dynamics and multimodal interaction analysis

prevent them to be used casually or in an uncontrolled environment. Hence, we propose a scalable portable system (i.e., all the devices are transportable while their number can be increased) that employs state-of-the-art techniques in graphics (GPU), vision, and speech processing for multimodal interaction sensing and analysis. Non-verbal signals from head motions are identified and correlated with speech data, and their dynamics are modeled using hybrid dynamical systems (HDS). We show that HDS can be used to obtain temporal structures (i.e., duration, overlaps, etc.) of multimodal events for interaction analysis. The current system has been setup for multiple subjects interacting in front of a large digital display at a short distance, out of the range of consumer depth cameras (see Fig. 1). Real poster presentations as well as casual discussions were captured using the system for joint attention estimation. The next sections present related work, a description of the framework, A/V multimodal interaction modeling using speaker diarization and hybrid linear dynamical systems, experimental results, and a conclusion about our contribution.

2   Related Work

Interaction modeling has been a very attractive research topic since decades due to its multidisciplinary aspect. For example, human-to-human and human-computer interaction have been studied in numerous fields of science such as psychology [1], computer graphics [2], communication [3,4], etc. In group communication, humans use visual and audio cues to convey and exchange information. Hence video and audio data have been naturally extensively used to study human behavior in communication. For example, several corpus such as VACE [5], AMI [6], Mission Survival [7], IMADE [8] were created to capture multimodal signals in multi-party conversation and interaction. Speech is often used to detect dominant speakers based on turn-taking and behavior analysis, while non-verbal cues provide feedbacks to understand communication patterns and behavior subtleties (e.g., smile, head nodding or gaze direction change) and can be used as back-channels to improve communication [9]. Nevertheless heavy equipments (e.g., headsets) are often required, visual information processing is usually limited (due to video resolution), and no solution is given for automatic multimodal information analysis.

As shown in the literature, the Hidden Markov Models (HMM) are very popular for speech and gesture modeling and recognition [10,11]. However, limitations lie in the lack of flexibility for timing structure manipulation (e.g., duration of states and transitions), which makes the modeling of some real-world events impractical, whereas event dynamics can be crucial to characterize human communication mechanisms. Hence, we propose to use linear dynamical systems (LDS) to model communication event dynamics. LDS have been applied for dynamic texture modeling [12], facial movement synchronization [13], human action recognition [14], etc. In our framework, we use hybrid dynamical systems (HDS) to model nonverbal behaviors which are synchronized with speech.

To our knowledge no similar framework has been proposed in the literature that aims at multi-people interaction modeling using multimodal (audio and video) signals to study human behavior in group communication (e.g., to detect and analyze joint attention of audience). Other systems using digital signage, like the moodmeter from MIT, usually require only one video camera that performs *only* face detection/classification. Audio is not used and they do not consider human-human interaction. Commercial systems, like Samsung Smart TVs, use single-human gestures as remote control and do not handle interaction between multiple people.

3   Multimodal Sensing Framework

3.1   Audio/Video System Setting

Audio. We employ a hands-free speech communication setup in the capture environment to give subjects more degrees of freedom in interacting with each other. This setup precludes holding or wearing a physical microphone. Although signal-to-noise (SNR) ratio is significantly lower in the hands-free setup as compared to the close-distant talking microphones, we mitigate this issue by using a microphone array. The increase in microphone count results in an improvement of the SNR. In our setup, we use 19-channel microphone array in a linear configuration attached on top of a 65-inch digital display (see Fig 1). Each signal from the microphone is sampled with 16KHz sampling rate, which is sufficient to cover the frequency band of the speech signal.

Video. Multiple video cameras are employed to capture nonverbal communication and interaction between multiple people. 6 HD video cameras are placed on a pole mounted on the display to obtain wide field of view (270 deg) and dense 3D face reconstruction. To keep the design simple, only one PC with a single GPU is used for video capture and processing. Videos are recorded simultaneously in SXGA at 15fps using Point Grey 1394b cameras with wide angle

3.5mm lenses. Note that to date, hardware synchronization of HR cameras with standard depth cameras is still not possible.

3.2 Multimodal Signal Capture

Audio. Aside from mere convenience, hands-free speech communication through microphone array offers meaningful signal processing tools. Data from the different channels can be processed to suppress contaminants emanating from noisy sources in real environment condition through beamforming [15]. Moreover, microphone array processing can also be used to effectively focus the microphone sensitivity to the party of interest, and further enhance the speech signal. This minimizes cross talk from the other speech sources or unwanted noise coming from the environment. Then, nonlinear processing technique is introduced in which the speech from other sources (other than that of the party of interest) is transformed to noise [16]. For example, in a poster presentation scenario, the party of interest is either the presenter or the audience, thus we transform either one of these to noise and enhance the other. As a result, the processed audio stream contains both the enhanced speech of the party of interest and noise (transformed speech).

Video. The proposed system detects and tracks multiple people faces from multiple views. As we use HD cameras, appearance-based methods return reliable detection results [17]. Face detection is combined with face feature detection (e.g., nose) for the sake of robustness, and computed on GPU to speed up calculations. To achieve simultaneous detections from multiple views with a single GPU, we first build a composite image by concatenation of regions of interests from multiview frames, and then transfer the image to the GPU; e.g., a consumer graphics card (GeForce NVIDIA GTX) can easily handles 3 frames simultaneously in real-time. Our face tracker employs a Bayesian model and online learning for continuous tracking [18]. Here, face feature coordinates, face templates, detection scores, and depth distributions are used as priors to estimate posterior probabilities of face positions. Dense 3D face reconstruction from stereo and point cloud noise removal using spatio-temporal joint bilateral filtering are also computed online (see Fig.2). Head pose can therefore be estimated by a geometrical approach (model fitting) to derive head motion and gaze direction. See Fig. 3 (bottom) for an overview of the process.

4 Multimodal Interaction Dynamics

Temporal structures in speech and head motion play a crucial role in natural human communication. While speech processing from audio data allows speaker turn diarization, dynamic features from visual information processing can be modeled using an interval-based representation of hybrid dynamical systems (IHDS) that model human communication event dynamics [13]. The proposed strategy allows the identification of behavior patterns in multimodal interaction such as when joint attention occurs (see Fig. 3).

Fig. 2. Video processing: (Left) Real-time depth map from stereo; (Center and Right) multi-people face detection, tracking, and 3D face for head pose estimation

4.1 Speaker Diarization

Diarization of speaker turns involves classifying one speaker from the other: e.g. in the case of a poster presentation, identifying the presenter-audience turn. When considering speech as the mode of input in the diarization task, the performance of the system primarily depends on separating the presenter's speech from that of the audience. However, separation is not straightforward since speech itself shares a common subspace even when spoken by different people. This is the reason why speech recognition technology is usually speaker-independent (e.g. speech from different people can still be recognized even if not enrolled during training). Thus, the technique in the microphone array processing circumvents this problem by treating the speech-speech classification approach into speech-noise classification.

We note that speech and noise subspaces are distinct, which minimizes classication ambiguity. In our framework, we design two Gaussian mixture model (GMM) classiers (e.g., λ_S for speech and λ_N for noise). Depending on the size of the training data, Gaussian components are increased to improve subspace discrimination. This process is terminated when the classification accuracy reaches the saturation value. Specically, we use 256 Gaussian components for each model. The two GMMs are trained by means of Expectation-Maximization [19]. The microphone array-processed data is windowed using a 25-ms frame. Then, mel cepstrum, energy and delta energy features are extracted, which are used in the training phase. These features suciently capture the relevant speech information with reduced dimensionality. In the actual diarization scheme shown inFig. 3 (top), identication of the speaker turn is implemented by processing the 19-channel mic array signals resulting to $\bar{x}$. The processed data contain the enhanced speech (party of interest) and noise (unwanted party). Then, likelihood score is evaluated using the mic array-processed stream against the 2 GMMs (λ_S and λ_N). Finally, the GMM that results to a higher likelihood score is selected as the corresponding class.

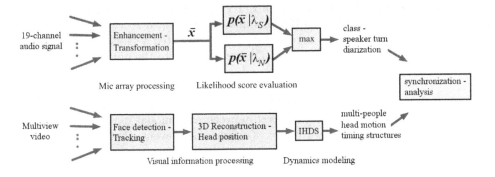

Fig. 3. Processing scheme for multimodal interaction analysis

4.2 Hybrid Linear Dynamical System

Definition. A hybrid linear dynamical system (HDS) integrates both dynamical and discrete-event systems. Dynamical systems are described by differential equations and are suitable for modeling smooth and continuous physical phenomena, while discrete-event systems usually describe discontinuous changes in physical phenomena and in subjective or intellectual activities.

Assuming a *signal* can be discretized in atomic entities (or dynamic primitives), then any complex human behavior can be modeled by: (1) a set of N linear dynamical systems (LDS) $\mathcal{D} = (D_1 \ldots D_N)$, and (2) a finite state machine (FSM) that represents states and state transitions. Let us denote a temporal sequence of an observed signal $Y = \{y(t)\}_{t=1\ldots T}$, $y(t) \in \mathbf{R}^m$, and its hidden states $X = \{x(t)\}_{t=1\ldots T}$, $x(t) \in \mathbf{R}^n$ belonging to a continuous state space. D_i can then be defined as:

$$\begin{cases} x(t+1) = F_i x(t) + g_i + v_i(t) \\ y(t) \quad\;\; = H x(t) + w(t), \end{cases} \tag{1}$$

where $F_i \in \mathbf{R}^{n \times n}$ is the state transition matrix which models the dynamics of D_i, g_i is a bias vector and $H \in \mathbf{R}^{m \times n}$ is the observation matrix which maps the hidden states to the output of the system by linear projection. $v_i(t) \sim \mathcal{N}(0, Q_i)$ and $w(t) \sim \mathcal{N}(0, R)$ are process and measurement noises modeled as Gaussian distributions with null averages and Q_i and R as covariances respectively. In order to control the system state changes between two events, an FSM having a discrete set of states $\mathcal{S} = \{s_i\}_{i=1\ldots N}$ is coupled to $\mathcal{D}$, where each s_i corresponds to an LDS D_i. The number N of LDS and their parameters $\{\theta\}$ can be estimated by clustering of LDS and optimization of $\{\theta\}$ by Expectation-Maximization [13].

Interval Representation. Interval-based representation of HDS (IHDS) is used to describe event timing structures (see Fig. 3 (bottom)) and can be used for event classification or recognition [13]. Let us denote $I_k = <s_i, \tau_j>$ an interval identified by a state (or mode) $s_i \in \mathcal{S}$ and a duration $\tau_j = e_k - b_k$, where b_k and

e_k are the starting and ending time of I_k respectively. Complex human behavior can then be modeled using an IHDS, similar to a musical score where $\{I_k\}$ are notes and N is the scale. As s_i, and thus D_i, is activated a sequence of continuous states can be generated from $\{x(t)\}$ and mapped to the output observation space as $\{y(t)\}$.

Interaction Analysis. Let us define an interaction event as an action-reaction pair. Particularly, the *interaction level* between multimodal signals can then be defined by the number of occurrences of synchronized events that happen within a delay (i.e., reaction time), and can characterize reactivity. Synchronized events can be identified by computing temporal differences between the beginning and ending of each interval. Hence, signal synchronization Z of two signals Y_k and $Y_{k'}$ can then be estimated by identifying all overlapping intervals (i.e., synchronized events) in the signal $\mathcal{I} = \{(I_k, I_{k'}) : [b_k, e_k] \cap [b_{k'}, e_{k'}] \neq \emptyset\}$, and by considering the following distribution:

$$Z(Y_k, Y_{k'}) = Pr(\{b_k - b_{k'} = \Delta_b, e_k - e_{k'} = \Delta_e\}_{\mathcal{I}} | \{[b_k, e_k] \cap [b_{k'}, e_{k'}] \neq \emptyset\}_{\mathcal{I}}), \quad (2)$$

The distribution can be modeled as a 2D Gaussian centered in $Z_0 = \frac{\sum \Delta(I_k, I_{k'})}{N_{kk'}}$, where $N_{kk'}$ is the number of overlapping intervals in $\mathcal{I}$ and $\Delta(I_k, I_{k'}) = ((b_k - b_{k'}), (e_k - e_{k'}))$ is the temporal difference between I_k and $I_{k'}$. Z contains information about reactivity with respect to reaction time (especially where $|b_k - b_{k'}| < 1s$). If $\{(b_k - b_{k'}) \to 0\}$ and $\{(e_k - e_{k'}) \to 0\}$, then all pairs of overlapping intervals are synchronized.

5   Experimental Results

To assess the performance of our framework, the setup was tested in real-world situations such as a conference hall and a meeting room. Despite fairly cluttered backgrounds and various illumination conditions, the system was effective and poster presentations as well as casual discussions between 3-4 people were held to evaluate joint attention of subjects from multimodal event interaction analysis (see Fig. 1,2). Audio and multiview video are captured simultaneously, and an offline process outputs multimodal interaction levels within seconds.

In Figure 4, we show the results obtained with two sequences with some ground-truth hand-made annotations : a) a poster presentation involving a presenter and 2-people audience (2000 frames), and b) a casual discussion between 3 subjects commenting photos displayed on the screen (2500 frames). Head motion dynamics were modeled using HDS from head positions (x, y) (see plots). We show interval-based representations of HDS model states (IHDS) with $N = 4$ modes. Here, state changes correspond to head motions (e.g., turning, nodding, etc.). Presenter in a) and Subject 1 in b) who were closer to the display did numerous head movements towards the screen and other subjects (26.5/min v 32.3/min). In a) Audience 2 produced much more nonverbal communication signals than Audience 1 (32/min v 19.5/min), whereas in b) Subject 2 and Subject

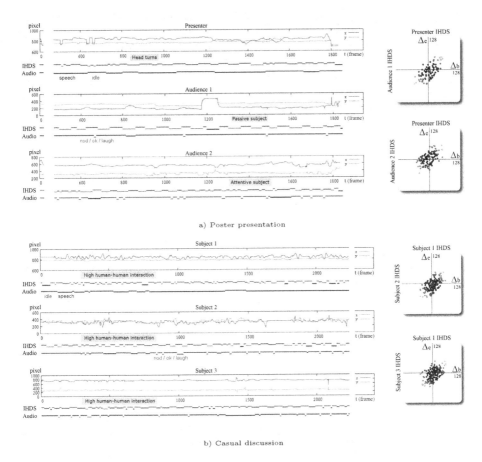

a) Poster presentation

b) Casual discussion

Fig. 4. Group dynamics and multimodal interaction modeling for: a) Poster presentation and b) Casual discussion. From the top: head position (x, y) in pixels, IHDS modeling with 4 modes, and speaker diarization (red: idle, blue: speech, green: nod/ok/laugh). Right: IHDS synchronization distributions.

3 performed similarly (25.3/min v 27.3/min). As can be observed, interactions between participants were more frequent during the casual discussion in b). Also, face tracking of Audience 1 in a) was lost around frame 1200 during the processing due an implementation issue. Nevertheless the unexpected tracking behavior has been successfully identified as a separate state by the HDS model.

Signal synchronizations (see right in a) and b)) show all synchronized interval disparities between Presenter and Audience 1 and 2, and between Subject 1 and Subject 2 and 3 respectively. The temporal difference distributions have a maximum $|\Delta b|$ and $|\Delta e|$ of 60f (4s). The centers of the distributions are close to the center (red circle), meaning mere synchronization. Note that in the context of poster presentation, the position of the subjects does not change a lot. Hence, we could consider global head motions without cancelling the body motions.

Therefore, reactions to signals from the head include as well reactions from body motions (e.g., body translation can create reaction).

In both scenarios, one participant is more active than the others: the Presenter in a) with 62.5% of speech, and the Subject 1 in b) with 73.5%. (Audience 1 and 2 have 3.1% and 9.4% of speech respectively, and Subjects 2 and 3 have 14.2% and 12.3.) Hence, we propose to use Eq. 4.2 to evaluate joint attention of the other participants by analyzing multimodal interactions and measuring interaction levels. Figure 5 shows interaction levels between the main speaker and each participants, i.e., the number of reactions with respect to reaction time. In a) and b), we show: (Left) head reactions in response to audio stimuli for all participants (main speaker included), and (Right) head reactions of participants other that the main speaker in response to visual stimuli from him. In a), we can see again that Audience 2 has much more reactions than Audience 1 for both audio and visual stimuli. More reactions are found with the visual stimuli: Audience 2 (46 reactions per minute) v Audience 1 (33rpm), The audio stimuli return: Audience 2 (8rpm) v Audience 1 (5rpm). In b), the number of reactions are similar, showing equal interaction level between Subject 2 and 3. Audio: 13rpm v 11rpm, and video: 83rpm v 87rpm. As human reaction time to audio and visual stimuli is usually below 1s (15 frames), the level of attention of each participant can be derived by the behavior of the curves near the origin. Interestingly we can observe that reaction times of Audience 2 and Subject 2 are very good, which is reconfirmed by checking the videos.

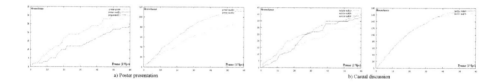

Fig. 5. Multimodal interaction level with respect to reaction time: a) Poster presentation, and b) Casual discussion

6   Conclusion

This paper presents a new framework for group dynamics and multimodal interaction modeling. The proposed system is portable and scalable and consists of a smart digital signage display equipped with a mic array and multiview video cameras. We capture multiple human interaction events and analyze them automatically using audio and visual information processing. We show that communication dynamics can be used to estimate joint attention using an interval-based representation of hybrid dynamical systems and speaker turn diarization. To our knowledge, no similar framework has been proposed yet.

Acknowledgments. This work was supported in part by the JST-CREST project "Creation of Human-Harmonized Information Technology for Convivial Society", and the Japan Society for the Promotion of Science (Wakate-B No. 23700170). The authors would like to thank Dr. Hiroaki Kawashima for his inspirational work on IHDS.

References

1. Newcomb, T.M., Turner, R.H., Converse, P.E.: Social psychology: The study of human interaction. Routledge and Kegan Paul (1966)
2. Cassell, J., Vilhjálmsson, H., Bickmore, T.: Beat: the behavior expression animation toolkit. In: SIGGRAPH (2001)
3. Buchanan, M.: Secret signals. Nature (2009)
4. Pentland, A.: To signal is human. American Scientist (2010)
5. Chen, L., Rose, R., Qiao, Y., Kimbara, I., Parrill, F., Welji, H., Han, T., Tu, J., Huang, Z., Harper, M., Quek, F., Xiong, Y., McNeill, D., Tuttle, R., Huang, T.: Vace multimodal meeting corpus (2006)
6. Poel, M., Poppe, R., Nijholt, A.: Meeting behavior detection in smart environments: Nonverbal cues that help to obtain natural interaction. In: FG (2008)
7. Pianesi, F., Zancanaro, M., Lepri, B., Cappelletti, A.: A multimodal annotated corpus of concensus decision making meetings. In: Language Resources and Evaluation, pp. 409–429 (2007)
8. Sumi, Y., Yano, M., Nishida, T.: Analysis environment of conversational structure with nonverbal multimodal data. In: ICMI-MLMI (2010)
9. White, S.: Backchannels across cultures: A study of americans and japanese. Language in Society 18, 59–76 (1989)
10. Rabiner, L.R.: A tutorial on hidden markow models and selected applications in speech recognition. IEEE 77, 257–286 (1989)
11. Liu, C.D., Chung, Y.N., Chung, P.C.: An interaction-embedded hmm framework for human behavior understanding: With nursing environments as examples. IEEE Trans. Information Technology in Biomedecine 14, 1236–1246 (2010)
12. Doretto, G., Chiuso, A., Wu, Y., Soatto, S.: Dynamic textures. IJCV 51 (2003)
13. Kawashima, H., Matsuyama, T.: Interval-based modeling of human communication dynamics via hybrid dynamical systems. In: NIPS Workshop on Modeling Human Communication Dynamics (2010)
14. Chaudhry, R., Ravichandran, A., Hager, G., Vidal, R.: Histograms of oriented optical flow and binet-cauchy kernels on nonlinear dynamical systems for the recognition of human actions. In: CVPR (2009)
15. Jani, E., Heracleus, P., Ishi, C., Nagita, N.: Joint use of microphone array and laser range finders for speaker identification in meeting. Japanese Society for Artificial Intelligence (2011)
16. Gomez, R., Lee, A., Saruwatari, H., Shikano, K.: Robust speech recognition with spectral subtraction in low snr. In: Int'l Conf. Spoken Language Processing (2004)
17. Viola, P., Jones, M.: Robust real-time object detection. IJCV (2001)
18. Pérez, P., Hue, C., Vermaak, J., Gangnet, M.: Color-Based Probabilistic Tracking. In: Heyden, A., Sparr, G., Nielsen, M., Johansen, P. (eds.) ECCV 2002, Part I. LNCS, vol. 2350, pp. 661–675. Springer, Heidelberg (2002)
19. Gomez, R., Kawahara, T.: Robust speech recognition based on dereverberation parameter optimization using acoustic model likelihood. IEEE Trans. Audio, Speech and Language Processing (2010)

Automated Textual Descriptions for a Wide Range of Video Events with 48 Human Actions⋆

Patrick Hanckmann, Klamer Schutte, and Gertjan J. Burghouts

TNO, The Hague, The Netherlands

Abstract. Presented is a hybrid method to generate textual descriptions of video based on actions. The method includes an action classifier and a description generator. The aim for the action classifier is to detect and classify the actions in the video, such that they can be used as verbs for the description generator. The aim of the description generator is (1) to find the actors (objects or persons) in the video and connect these correctly to the verbs, such that these represent the subject, and direct and indirect objects, and (2) to generate a sentence based on the verb, subject, and direct and indirect objects. The novelty of our method is that we exploit the discriminative power of a bag-of-features action detector with the generative power of a rule-based action descriptor. Shown is that this approach outperforms a homogeneous setup with the rule-based action detector and action descriptor.

1 Introduction

This paper proposes a method to generate textual action descriptions from general videos. The action descriptions are centered around 48 verbs such as walk, bury, approach, give, etc [1].

The amount of video data is increasing daily, both on the internet (e.g. YouTube) and for surveillance applications. This poses a challenge on extracting information from this huge bulk of data. In this paper, we consider the automated search for relevant event in videos. One determinant of an event's relevancy, is the action that is performed by humans in the scene. We argue that most events are characterized by multiple actions, and not a single one. A typical event is that one person approaches the other, walks up to the other person, and gives something. These actions, 'walk', 'approach', 'give' and 'receive', occur in a particular order, and are partially overlapping. Moreover, there are two persons in this event. In general, events may consist of multiple actions and performed by one or more persons. Such events are the topic of this paper. Therefore, we progress beyond single-actor datasets such as KTH [2] and Weizmann [3]. The UCF Sports [4], Hollywood2 [5] and YouTube [6] datasets are much more challenging as they involve interactions with other people and items and the recording conditions are harder. Yet they lack the realistic property of having video events which comprise multiple actions. We consider the DARPA dataset

⋆ This work has been sponsored by DARPA, Mind's Eye program.

A. Fusiello et al. (Eds.): ECCV 2012 Ws/Demos, Part I, LNCS 7583, pp. 372–380, 2012.
© Springer-Verlag Berlin Heidelberg 2012

[1] in which videoclips are annotated in terms of 48 human actions, where each event consists of on average 7 actions.

In this paper, we consider the automated tagging of realistic video events. We propose a method that produces textual descriptions. The reason for this is that text is intuitive: the popularity of the Google search engine is that it enables a user to perform a text-based search. Our method produces descriptions that cover a wide range of events, they are not limited to a particular domain, and they are based on 48 generic human actions. Figure 1 illustrates the textual descriptions.

Ground truth examples:
Man flees while woman chases him.
A man and woman stand side by side,
　the man begins running and the woman follows him.
One person is running and leaving.
　The other person starts chasing.
Our system response:
Person 4 goes.
Person 4 leaves.
Person 4 walks.
Person 7 flees from person 4.

Fig. 1. The image shows two people who chase each other. Next to the image the ground truth provided by 3 different people is printed. Our system response provides the detected actions as verbs in a short sentence with their connected subject and object. It shows that our system response captures the essence of the action as described in the ground truth.

Prior research on creating textual descriptions from video has been focused on:

- using speech recognition to generate video subscriptions [7],
- detecting and extracting text which is present in the video [7],
- detecting patterns in a restricted environment and use the detected patterns to generate a description [8,9].

The first two options generate a description based on what can be read or heard in a video. In this paper we rather aim to deduct these description from the video data itself. The third option has only been applied in action restricted environments (e.g. video data from sports in which strict rules apply). Detecting the state of the game directly translates in a description. Behavior seen in general videos is not as structured. The proposed method in this paper includes a detector for 48 human actions and a generic descriptor that generates sentences for a wide range of events based on these actions. The approach in [10] is also generic, but there are three limitations compared to our method: (1) it has a strong focus on describing the environment and describing the subjects' emotional states, where in this paper we do not exploit emotional states as they do not occur in the considered 48 human actions, (2) it assumes that the subject is always a person, our method generalizes subjects to both people and vehicles, and (3) we extend the set from 5 actions to 48 actions: approach, arrive, attach, bounce, bury, carry, catch, chase, close, collide, dig, drop, enter, exchange, exit, fall, flee, fly, follow, get, give, go, hand, haul, have, hit, hold, jump, kick, leave, lift, move, open, pass, pick up, push, put down, raise, receive, replace, run, snatch, stop, take, throw, touch, turn, and walk.

The contributions of our work are the action classifier and the description generator. The novelty of our work is that we take advantage of the discriminative power of 48 bag-of-features action detectors [11] to identify the subset of likely actions, and to subsequently describe them with a rule-based method that relates the actions to entities in the scene. Important aspects of our method are classification of actions, detection of actors, and connecting the actions to the relevant actors in the video. An actor can be a person or an object. The proposed method is a combination of an action classifier and a description generator.

This paper will introduce the system generating the video descriptions, including the action classifier and description generator, in section 2. In section 3 the experimental setup is discussed, followed in section 4 with the results. Finally our conclusions will be presented in section 5.

2   Method

The action classifier, and the description generator are part of our system. Our system is a video processing system using a pipeline to process the videos. It takes video data as input, and provides the action descriptions as output. An overview of the system components is depicted in figure 2. In subsection 2.1 an overview of the system is presented. The actual action classifier and description generator are described in more depth in subsections 2.2 and 2.3 respectively.

Fig. 2. The processing pipeline

2.1   System Overview

Our method is part of a larger system in which objects in the scene are detected, tracked and their features are captured. This overall system is described in [12,13] and it is summarized here. It consists of five building blocks (see figure 2): visual processing, fusion engine, event description, action classifier, and the description generator.

The **visual processing** [14] incorporates three steps. First the extraction of meaningful objects and their properties from video by (1) detection of moving objects [15], (2) a trained object detector for specific classes like persons and cars [16,17], and (3) computation of other features (e.g. description of pose and body part movements) [18]. After detection it combines items into tracks.

The **fusion engine** [19] filters and fuses tracked objects in order to form entities. Only entities - a subset of the detected and tracked objects - are selected for further processing.

The **event description** generates a more abstract description. From the low-level object features, information at situation level [20] is created. There are three types of event properties:

1. Single-entity event properties, which describe properties of one entity (e.g. "the entity is moving fast").
2. Relations, properties about the relation between two entities (e.g. "the distance between two entities is decreasing").
3. Global properties of the scene, which present information about the scene that is not exclusively related to one or more entities (e.g. "there is only one entity present").

A belief value is assigned to each property.

The **action classifier** assigns to all 48 human actions a probability (see also [1]). We consider two types of action classifiers, which we will compare in our experiments. The first type is a discriminative bag-of-features classifier. The second type is a generative rule-based classifier. The two classifiers will be described in more detail in section 2.2. In section 2.3, we experimentally establish the best classifier to generate textual descriptions for video.

The **description generator** uses the events from the Event Description to build hypothesis about what happened in the video. The most likely hypothesis are selected based on the classified actions combined with the information from the hypothesis. The selected hypothesis connect the actions to entities and objects. If there are entities or objects that can be connected with the action, then a textual description is generated.

2.2 Action Classifier

The aim of the action classifier is to recognize the verbs that are used for the description generator. The Random-Forest Tag-Propagation (RF_TP) and multi-hypotheses Rule Based System (RBS) classifiers are considered. The choice is based on performance: the RF_TP performs best [21] and the RBS performed second best as actions classifiers in previous research [13] on the DARPA dataset under investigation (see section 3 for details).

The RF_TP classifier [11] is a rule-based classifier which learns its rules from an abundant set of decision trees (i.e. a random forest) [22]. In order to deliver a list of actions with their probability, the similarity distributions over the actions is calculated [23]. The core of the RF_TP method is that it models the probability of a verb (in a video) as a consequence of the similarities with all of the previously seen videos and the actions that are active in those. The training of the RF-TP is described in [11]. The RF_TP outputs a vector containing a belief value for each action present in the video.

The RBS classifier is a Rule Based System. World knowledge, coded in the rules, describes the actions. There are currently 73 rules describing 48 actions. The rules are essentially a set of conditions. The conditions are based on the beliefs and relations as generated by the event description (see example 1). In the example, *E1*, *T1*, etc. are placeholders for actual entity identifiers and timestamps. As more than one entity can be present at any time, and as actions might happen multiple times by one or different entities, the RBS builds multiple hypotheses. The belief value of the action is calculated by taking the sum of the beliefs of the triggered conditions (and if the condition is not triggered, it's belief is zero), divided by the maximum possible performance: $B(hypothesis) = \frac{\sum B(conditions)}{number\ of\ conditions}$. In this way an inexact match between the rules and noisy input data is allowed. For every action, the top hypothesis is selected. For each hypothesis, a belief value is calculated. There are 73 hypotheses in total, so we have 73 beliefs. These belief values are matched to the 48 human actions. We use a simple linear mapping obtained from a least-squares fit as a linear L2 norm optimization.

Example 1. Rule representing the catch action.

action = chase
condition(1) = object(E1) moving at time(T1)
condition(2) = object(E2) moving at time(T2)
condition(3) = object(E1) is a person
condition(4) = object(E2) is a person
condition(5) = time(T1) and time(T2) overlap
Resulting sentence = "Person E1 chases Person E2"

2.3   Description Generator

The RBS is also used to generate descriptions. It can be applied as description generator due to the generative properties and the structure of the rules which connects entities and objects to actions. When applied as a description generator the RBS builds the hypotheses and selects for every rule the hypothesis with the highest belief value. Based on the actions classified by the action classifier, a selection is made among the rules (and their top hypothesis). For every action a rule is chosen that represents that action. Then, from the list of actions the description generator selects a number of actions based on: (1) the action probability, (2) the hypothesis score generated by the RBS, and (3) if an entity or object is present in the best hypothesis (which implies that the action is connected to an entity or object). For the selected actions, the hypothesis are used to extract the subject and objects (see example 1). The actions are used as the verbs. A sentence is considered to at least contain a subject and a verb (e.g. person *E1* catches). However, the rule can also provide the direct and indirect object (e.g. person *E1* catches object *E2*). Additionally the hypothesis provides temporal information for the action, which can be used to order the actions in time. Finally, a compact sentence is generated for each action using a template filling approach. The template provides information about what prepositions are used in combination with specific verbs, the order of the words in the sentence, and the conjugation of the verbs.

Ground truth examples:
A man catches a box that is flying through the air.
The person caught the box.
Man catches box flying through the air.
Our system response:
Entity 11 goes.
Entity 11 catches person 6.
Person 6 has.

Fig. 3. The image shows one person catching a box. Next to the image the ground truth provided by 3 different people is printed. Our system response provides the detected actions as verbs in a short sentence with their connected subject and object. It shows that our system response captures the essence of the action as described in the ground truth. However, it confuses the subject and the direct object.

3   Experimental Setup

The description generator is evaluated on 241 short videos (available at [1]). For all videos ground truth is available. The ground truth consist of 10 sentences per video, written by 10 different people. The ground truth can contain complex sentences (see the examples in figure 3, and note the confusion of the subject and object in the video) and therefore describe multiple actions. Per video at minimum 1, at maximum 10, and at average 4.9 different actions are present in the ground truth.

For each ground truth sentence we extract, using the Stanford Natural Language Parser [24,25], the verb, subject, and object(s). The subject and objects are labeled with one of the four categories: person, car, bike, or other. The description generator constructs a sentence containing a verb and subject, and (if detected) a direct and indirect object. Its subject and objects are also labeled with one of the four categories.

The experiment will compare the following action classifier - description generator combinations: RBS + RBS, and the RF_TP + RBS. Both setups of the description generator use the same event description data. The RBS + RBS uses the RBS both for action classification and description generation. The RF_TP + RBS uses the RF_TP to classify actions and the RBS to generate descriptions. For the RF_TP + RBS the rule set was optimized to gather information about the subject and objects to generate a sentence. For the RBS + RBS setup the rule set was optimized for the classification of actions.

We calculate two performance measures: a union and a percentage score. For each clip we compare the ground truth sentences to the generated sentences. The clip's *union score* is the best match for all sentence pairs (i.e. the percentage of clips where there is at least one agreement between ground truth and generated sentences); its *percentage score* is the mean match corrected for the minimum number of the amount of ground truth sentences and the amount of generated sentences (i.e. the agreement between the sets of ground truth and generated sentences). We report the average over all clips, for verbs, subjects and objects as well as an overall score (the overall score is the mean of the verb, subject and object scores).

4   Experimental Results

The performance for both the RBS + RBS and RF_TP + RBS is given in table 1. Both on union and the percentage score we see the better performance for the RF_TP + RBS compared to the RBS + RBS, supported by an increase for the descriptions' Verb, Subject and Object components.

Table 1. Performance of the description generator

RBS + RBS				
Score	Overall	Verb	Subject	Objects
union	61.6%	86.1%	52.3%	51.7%
percentage	25.4%	38.6%	18.6%	18.9%
RF_TP + RBS				
Score	Overall	Verb	Subject	Objects
union	68.3%	92.3%	62.0%	67.8%
percentage	40.4%	59.3%	30.5%	31.5%

The performance gain for the verb classification on the union score is 6.2%, thus more correct verbs have been reported by the RF_TP + RBS. For the percentage score the improvement is 20.7%, so we also have an improved accuracy of the classified verbs.

The performance on the subjects increased as well for both the union and the percentage score, with resp. 9.7% and 11.9%. Every generated sentence does at least contains a verb and a subject. The performance gain of the subject score is less than the verbs performance gain, while it would be expected to be similar or higher. Both the object and the subject score suffer from too restrictive threshold on the person, car and bike detectors leading to many entities labeled 'other'.

The performance on the objects increased for the union and the percentage score by 16.1% and 12.6%. It shows that the RF_TP + RBS is better in detecting and connecting the direct and indirect objects in a video.

The results show that the discriminative bag-of-features based RF_TP is better used as verb classifier than the RBS when creating descriptions. Although

[13] already showed that the RF_TP is a good stand alone verb classifier, here we see it also performs well when applied to a description task. Even though the RF_TP classifier is not optimized for the description generator (e.g. the set of frequently occurring actions may be different) we conclude that a dedicated action classifier improves the performance significantly.

5   Conclusions and Future Work

This paper shows that a dedicated action classifier in addition to a description generator improves the description performance significantly. Although not perfect, a percentage score of almost 60% on correctly reported verbs is quite good.

The performance on the subject and objects classification is currently low. The issue is misclassification of the actors in the video and as a result reporting "other" as classification too often. Still, we showed a significant increase in the subject and object recognition scores. This increase can be attributed to a better understanding of the scene from the description generator.

The percentage score of the current action classifier is expected to improve further if we can train the action classifier on the description ground truth. The classification of the subject and objects in the description generator should be improved by adjusting the classifiers in visual processing and by relying more on world knowledge coded in rules in the RBS. Furthermore, the number of track-breaks in the visual processing should be reduced, possibly by using multi-hypotheses tracking, as the current rule set is quite sensitive to track break errors. We expect that these latter two improvements will significantly boost the recognition performance for the subject and objects.

Acknowledgement. This work is supported by DARPA (Mind's Eye program). The content of the information does not necessarily reflect the position or the policy of the US Government, and no official endorsement should be inferred. The authors acknowledge the Cortex team for their contributions.

References

1. DARPA: Hosting corpora suitable for research in visual activity recognition, in particular, the video corpora collected as part of DARPA's Mind's Eye program (2011), http://www.visint.org
2. Schüldt, C., Laptev, I., Caputo, B.: Recognizing human actions: A local svm approach. In: Proc. of ICPR, pp. 32–36 (2004)
3. Gorelick, L., Blank, M., Shechtman, E., Irani, M., Basri, R.: Actions as space-time shapes. IEEE Trans. Pattern Anal. Mach. Intell. 29, 2247–2253 (2007)
4. Ali, S., Shah, M.: Floor Fields for Tracking in High Density Crowd Scenes. In: Forsyth, D., Torr, P., Zisserman, A. (eds.) ECCV 2008, Part II. LNCS, vol. 5303, pp. 1–14. Springer, Heidelberg (2008)
5. Marszalek, M., Laptev, I., Schmid, C.: Actions in context. In: CVPR (2009)
6. Liu, J., Luo, J., Shah, M.: Recognizing realistic actions from videos "in the wild". In: CVPR (2009)

7. Gagnon, L.: Automatic detection of visual elements in films and description with a synthetic voice- application to video description. In: Proceedings of the 9th International Conference on Low Vision (2008)
8. Gupta, A., Srinivasan, P., Shi, J., Davis, L.: Understanding videos, constructing plots learning a visually grounded storyline model from annotated videos. In: IEEE Conference on Computer Vision and Pattern Recognition, CVPR 2009, pp. 2012–2019 (2009)
9. Kojima, A., Tamura, T., Fukunaga, K.: Natural language description of human activities from video images based on concept hierarchy of actions. International Journal of Computer Vision 50, 171–184 (2002)
10. Khan, M.U.G., Zhang, L., Gotoh, Y.: Towards coherent natural language description of video streams. In: ICCV Workshops, pp. 664–671. IEEE (2011)
11. Burghouts, G., Bouma, H., de Hollander, R., van den Broek, S., Schutte, K.: Recognition of 48 human behaviors from video. in Int. Symp. Optronics in Defense and Security, OPTRO (2012)
12. Ditzel, M., Kester, L., van den Broek, S.: System design for distributed adaptive observation systems. In: IEEE Int. Conf. Information Fusion (2011)
13. Bouma, H., Hanckmann, P., Marck, J.-W., Penning, L., den Hollander, R., ten Hove, J.-M., van den Broek, S., Schutte, K., Burghouts, G.: Automatic human action recognition in a scene from visual inputs. In: Proc. SPIE, vol. 8388 (2012)
14. Burghouts, G., den Hollander, R., Schutte, K., Marck, J., Landsmeer, S., Breejen, E.d.: Increasing the security at vital infrastructures: automated detection of deviant behaviors. In: Proc. SPIE, vol. 8019 (2011)
15. Withagen, P., Schutte, K., Groen, F.: Probabilistic classification between foreground objects and background. In: Proc. IEEE Int. Conf. Pattern Recognition, pp. 31–34 (2004)
16. Laptev, I.: Improving object detection with boosted histograms. Image and Vision Computing, 535–544 (2009)
17. Felzenszwalb, P., Girshick, R., McAllester, D., Ramanan, D.: Object detection with discriminatively trained part based models. IEEE Trans. Pattern Analysis and Machine Intelligence 32(9), 1627–1645 (2010)
18. Ferrari, V., Marin-Jimenez, M., Zisserman, A.: Progressive search space reduction for human pose estimation. In: IEEE Computer Vision and Pattern Recognition (2008)
19. van den Broek, S., Hanckmann, P., Ditzel, M.: Situation and threat assessment for urban scenarios in a distributed system. In: Proc. Int. Conf. Information Fusion (2011)
20. Steinberg, A.N., Bowman, C.L.: Rethinking the JDL data fusion levels. In: NSSDF Conference Proceedings (2004)
21. Burghouts, G., Schutte, K.: Correlations between 48 human actions improve their detection. In: ICPR 2012 (2012)
22. Breiman, L.: Random forests. Machine Learning 45, 1 (2001)
23. Guillaumin, M., Mensink, T., Verbeek, J., Schmid, C.: Tagprop: Discriminative metric learning in nearest neighbor models for image auto-annotation. In: ICCV (2009)
24. Klein, D., Manning, C.D.: Accurate unlexicalized parsing. In: Proceedings of the 41st Annual Meeting of the Association for Computational Linguistics, pp. 423–430 (2003)
25. The Stanford Natural Language Processing Group: The Stanford parser: A statistical parser (2003), http://nlp.stanford.edu/software/lex-parser.shtml

Learning Implicit Transfer
for Person Re-identification

Tamar Avraham, Ilya Gurvich, Michael Lindenbaum, and Shaul Markovitch

Computer Science Department, Technion - I.I.T., Haifa 32000, Israel

Abstract. This paper proposes a novel approach for pedestrian re-identification. Previous re-identification methods use one of 3 approaches: invariant features; designing metrics that aim to bring instances of shared identities close to one another and instances of different identities far from one another; or learning a transformation from the appearance in one domain to the other. Our *implicit* approach models camera transfer by a binary relation $R = \{(x,y)|x$ and y describe the same person seen from cameras A and B respectively$\}$. This solution implies that the camera transfer function is a multi-valued mapping and not a single-valued transformation, and does not assume the existence of a metric with desirable properties. We present an algorithm that follows this approach and achieves new state-of-the-art performance.

1 Introduction

The re-identification problem has received increasing attention in the last five to six years, especially due to its important role in surveillance systems. It is desirable that computer vision systems will be able to keep track of people after they have left the field of view of one camera and entered the field of view of the next, even when these fields of view do not overlap.

We make the distinction between the *general re-identification* problem, in which the goal is to re-identify a person in any new location, and the *camera-specific re-identification* problem, in which the goal is to provide a solution for a specific site. In this work we tackle the second goal. Given a pair of stationary cameras, A and B, capturing two non-overlapping regions, and a training set of annotated people captured by those two cameras, our objective is to recognize correspondence between the appearance of a never-before-seen person in camera A and his or her appearance in camera B. As can be seen in the examples in Fig. 1, learning the domain of the camera-specific transformations may be very informative. Each camera is associated with a limited variety of backgrounds, illumination conditions, and sometimes human poses. We propose an algorithm that exploits these properties. Our algorithm is based on the observation that the transfer between two cameras is a multi-valued mapping which can be estimated using implicit function learning.

Previous re-identification methods have used solutions that belong to one of three families of methods: those that seek for invariant features; those that seek for a metric in which instances associated with the same person are close and

A. Fusiello et al. (Eds.): ECCV 2012 Ws/Demos, Part I, LNCS 7583, pp. 381–390, 2012.
© Springer-Verlag Berlin Heidelberg 2012

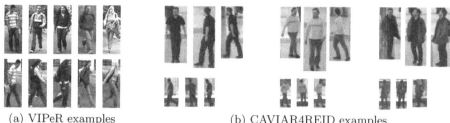

(a) VIPeR examples   (b) CAVIAR4REID examples

Fig. 1. (a) Examples from the VIPeR dataset: five people captured by one camera (top row) and another camera (second row). (b) Examples from the CAVIAR4REID dataset: three people captured by one camera in multi-shots (top), and the same three people captured by a second camera (bottom). We see that the background, illumination, resolution and sometimes pose are camera dependent.

instances associated with different people are far; and those that try to learn a transformation, i.e., a function, that transfers the descriptors of people as they 'move' from one camera to the other. Our *implicit* approach models camera transfer by a binary relation $R = \{(x, y)|x$ and y describe the same person seen from cameras A and B respectively}. This solution implies that the camera transfer function is a multi-valued mapping and not a single-valued transformation. Moreover, it does not assume the existence of a metric that can bring all instances of shared identities close to one another and instances of different identities far from one another. Instead, given a person's appearance described by a feature vector of length k, the binary relation models a (not necessarily continuous) sub-space in $\mathbb{R}^{2k}$. That is, we divide the $\mathbb{R}^{2k}$ space to 'positive' regions (belonging to the relation) and 'negative' regions (not belonging to the relation). As a result, this modeling does not build only on a feature-by-feature comparison, but models also dependencies between different features.

Our algorithm, denoted *ICT* (short for *Implicit Camera Transfer*), models the binary relation by training a (non-linear) binary classifier with concatenations of pairs of vectors, the first describing an instance associated with camera A, and the second describing an instance associated with camera B. One class includes the *positive pairs* – pairs of instances capturing the same person with the two different cameras, and the second class includes the *negative pairs* – pairs of instances whose members are associated with two different people and two different cameras. This algorithm, although so simple, provides state-of-the-art results. It can work for single-shots per person as well as for multi-shots (video).

We consider the optimal number of negative examples to use for training and show that utilizing the more abundant negative examples allows us to learn the transfer associated with two cameras from rather small sets of inter-camera example pairs. The ICT algorithm simultaneously learns to distinguish between changes that are camera and location dependent and those that depend on the person's identity. This allows the use of simple features extracted from the bounding boxes surrounding the people, without incorporating high-level, risky, and time consuming, preprocesses.

In Sec. 2 we review related work, in Sec. 3 we describe the ICT algorithm, and in Sec. 4 we describe the experiments on the VIPeR [1] and the CAVIAR4REID [2] datasets. Sec. 5 concludes.

2   Related Work

Object re-identification is a challenge that has been receiving increasing attention (e.g., face re-identification [3, 4], car re-identification [5]). Person, or pedestrian, re-identification is a special focus of recent research, mainly due to its important role in surveillance systems. One common approach proposes *invariant* features that are stable to illumination, resolution, pose, and background changes. A 'same' or 'not-same' decision is then made using some fixed distance measure. In [6], for instance, normalized color and salient edgel histograms are the basis for matching segmented parts. In [7] a similarity measure based on principal axis correspondence is used. In [8] the similarity between two sets of signatures, each describing a person's video track, is measured by the width of the margins of a linear SVM. In [9] features extracted from a person's track are compacted with an epitomic analysis that recognizes the presence of recurrent local patterns. In [10] each semantic body part is described by a signature composed of features that are stable to changes in pose, viewpoint, resolution and illumination.

Some recent methods focus on learning characteristics of the similarity between feature vectors describing two instances of the same person against that of two vectors describing instances of different people. These similarity-based methods usually use the absolute distance as the characteristic to be learned. The ELF method [11] models the feature-wise difference distribution using Adaboost for feature selection and classification. In [12] it is observed that what matters is not the similarity itself, but the relative similarity: positive pairs should be ranked higher than negative pairs. The goal is to weigh the features in a way that maximizes the difference between absolute differences of negative pairs and absolute differences of positive pairs. The method in [13] takes a similar approach using probabilistic modeling. In contrast to these methods, we do not assume that greater similarity implies 'same'. Moreover, as opposed to methods that use the absolute distances as a starting point, or that compare histograms bin-by-bin, we do not perform a feature-by-feature comparison, and allow dependencies between any two features in the two input descriptors.

Most of the aforementioned methods try to solve the *general re-identification* setup. When two specific cameras are considered, the correlation between the cameras' identities and the expected background, illumination, and human pose may be exploited. The following situation may then be considered: An instance associated with person i in camera A undergoes a transformation function T and is then captured as an instance in camera B. In [14] it was shown that the domain of possible transformations between color histograms lies in a low-dimensional subspace. This paper is based on modeling the transformation as well. We take a different approach and argue that the transformation is a multi-valued function (or a binary relation). Moreover, unlike the approach in [14], which uses only positive examples, our approach allows the utilization of negative examples to better model the transformation domain.

Some methods start with a pre-process for separating the people from the background (e.g., [6, 8, 10]) and some also attempt to divide the person into semantic parts. For instance, [6] begins with a spatio-temporal segmentation process and then searches for correspondence between different segments. In [10], regions are separated into parts corresponding to head, torso and legs by vertical asymmetries. In [2] pictorial structures are extracted in order to fit corresponding body parts. These high-level processes indeed lead to more accurate recognition but may also lead to mistakes that will then be dragged into the training and classification stages. In our work we use bounding boxes surrounding the people and yet achieve very good performance. This is because our algorithm is implicitly trained to filter out the background by recognizing the background associated with each camera as person-independent. This approach is not limited to re-identifying people as it does not rely on a specific model for their appearance. As a result, it also allows items carried by the people (e.g., bags) to be used as cues without additional explicit analysis. Note that high-level semantic analysis requires processing time that is unlikely to allow real-time performance, while the method proposed here can be used for real-time re-identification.

3   Implicitly Learning Inter-camera Transfer

In this section we describe the ICT algorithm. Given that there are two stationary cameras A and B, covering two non-overlapping regions of a site, our algorithm is trained to find correspondence between people captured by the two cameras. Let $V_{i,k}^A$ describe the k'th appearance of a person with identity i captured by camera A, and let $V_{j,l}^B$ describe the l'th appearance of a person with identity j captured by camera B. Given a pair $(V_{i,k}^A, V_{j,l}^B)$, the goal is to distinguish between *positive* pairs with the same identity $(i = j)$, and *negative* pairs $(i \neq j)$. Our algorithm trains a binary classifier using concatenations of such positive and negative pairs of vectors coming from training data. Then it classifies new such pairs by querying the classifier on their concatenations. See Fig. 2. A detailed description of the algorithm follows.

The ICT Algorithm

The Training Stage:

The Input:

- A set $\{V_{i,k}^A | i = 1, ..., n; k = 1, ..., m_i^A\}$ of vectors describing instances of n people captured by camera A.
- A set $\{V_{i,k}^B | i = 1, ...n; k = 1, ..., m_i^B\}$ of vectors describing instances of the same n people captured by camera B.

That is, for each person and each camera we may be provided with a few descriptor vectors, each associated with his or her appearance in a different video frame.

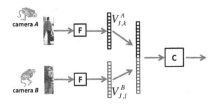

Fig. 2. Illustration of the classification stage of the ICT algorithm. From each of the instances captured by cameras A and B, features are extracted (F). The concatenation of those two feature vectors, $V_{I,k}^A$ and $V_{J,l}^B$, is the input to the classifier C.

Let $[a \| b] = (a_1, ..., a_n, b_1, ..., b_m)$ denote the concatenation of vectors $a = (a_1, ..., a_n)$ and $b = (b_1, ..., b_m)$. The training input for the binary classifier is:

- A set of positive examples $\{[V_{i,k}^A \| V_{i,l}^B] \mid, i \in \{1, ..., n\}, k \in \{1, ..., m_i^A\}, l \in \{1, ..., m_i^B\}\}$.
- A set of negative examples $\{[V_{i,k}^A \| V_{j,l}^B] \mid i \neq j, i, j \in \{1, ..., n\}, k \in \{1, ..., m_i^A\}, l \in \{1, ..., m_j^B\}\}$.

For the type of descriptors used and for details about the classifiers used in our experiments, see Sec. 4. Note that there are $\sum_{i=1}^n m_i^A m_i^B$ positive examples, while there is a quadratic number $\sum_{i=1}^n \sum_{j=1, j \neq i}^n m_i^A m_j^B$ of negative examples. We do not use all the negative examples but show that even a fraction of them significantly contribute to the success of the algorithm. See Sec. 4.2.

The Classification/Decision Stage:

The Input:

- A set $\{V_{I,k}^A \mid k = 1, ..., m_I^A\}$ of vectors describing a person's track as captured by camera A.
- A set $\{V_{J,l}^B \mid l = 1, ..., m_J^B\}$ of vectors describing a person's track as captured by camera B.

The Decision: Apply the trained classifier on each of the concatenations $[V_{I,k}^A \| V_{J,l}^B]$, $k = 1, ..., m_I^A$, $l = 1, ..., m_J^B$. One possibility is to use the binary classifications and to output a binary decision by their majority. However, more informative is to output a continuous score that allows different candidate matches to be ranked. The way to obtain such a score depends on the classifier used. In our experiments we use an SVM as the classifier and output the average of the decision values: let $y_{k,l}$, $k = 1, ..., m_I^A$, $l = 1, ..., m_J^B$ be the decision values obtained from the classifier. The algorithm returns the mean $Y = \sum_{k=1}^{m_I^A} \sum_{l=1}^{m_J^B} y_{k,l} / m_I^A m_J^B$.

4   Experiments

After providing additional implementation details (Sec. 4.1), we test ICT's performance as a function of the number of negative examples utilized for training

(Sec. 4.2). Then we compare its performance to that of the latest state-of-the-art for the single-shots case on the VIPeR dataset (Sec. 4.3). In Sec. 4.4 we compare ICT's performance to that of recent state-of-the-art for multi-shot setups on the CAVIAR4REID dataset[1][2].

4.1   Implementation Details

Features. We use a common and simple description of bounding boxes surrounding the people: each bounding box is divided into five horizontal stripes. Each stripe is described by a histogram with 10 bins for each of the color components H, S, and V. This results in feature vectors with 150 dimensions. We did not focus on finding optimal features. Any alternative descriptors (e.g., textural descriptors [13], temporal features [6], or semantic features [2, 10]) can be easily used as well, and may further improve the algorithm's performance.

Classifiers. We use an RBF kernel binary SVM as the classifier for the concatenated vectors. In one of our experiments below we test the use of a one-class-SVM also with an RBF kernel. We use the implementation provided by LibSVM [16].

Evaluation Methods. In the experiments described below we output and compare average Cumulative Match Characteristic (CMC) curves. This is the most widely accepted way to evaluate re-identification algorithms. For each person in the test set, each algorithm ranks the matching of his or her appearance in camera A with the appearances of all the people in the test set in camera B. The CMC curve summarizes the statistics of the ranks of the true matches. For quantitative comparison we use the measure rank(i), which denotes the percentage of true matches found within the first i ranked instances, the CMC-expectation measure, which is the mean rank of the true match, and the nAUC (normalized Area Under Curve).

4.2   The Role of Negative Examples

As mentioned in Sec. 3, the number of negative examples that can be used for training is quadratic in the number of positive examples. Using all the negative examples can lead to a strong bias and is computationally expensive. Do we need all the negative examples? Do we need negative examples at all? In our first set of experiments we tested the contribution of the negative examples by checking the algorithm's performance as a function of the number of negative examples used for training. These experiments use the VIPeR dataset, the most commonly used dataset for evaluating re-identification methods. It contains 632 pedestrian image pairs. Each pair contains two images of the same individual seen from different

---

[1] The Matlab source code used in all the experiments is available in
http://www.cs.technion.ac.il/~tammya/Reidentification.html.

[2] We are aware of the set of data annotated by [15] and corresponding to 119 people appearing in the i-LIDs videos. That set includes a few instances for each person without indication of the camera's identity. It was thus unsuitable for our setup.

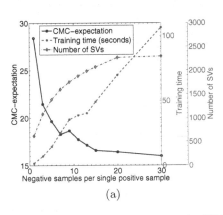
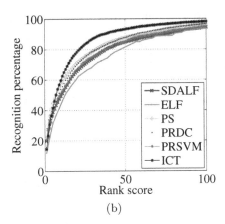

(a)   (b)

Fig. 3. (a) ICT's performance on the VIPeR dataset as a function of κ, the number of negative examples per single positive example, measured by the CMC expectation, the training time, and the support-vectors used by the SVM. (b) CMC curves comparing ICT's results on VIPeR with recent state-of-the-art reported in [2, 10–13].

viewpoints by two cameras. See examples in Fig. 1(a). We perform a 2-fold cross-validation, dividing the 632 pedestrians into equal-size training and test sets. We repeat this process four times with different random choices for the sets. The number of positive examples available for training is $P = 316$ (one concatenated pair for each person). We test the performance of ICT for different numbers of negative examples $N = \kappa P$, where $\kappa = 1, 3, 5, 7, 9, 11, 13, 15, 20, 30$. That is, for each positive example associated with person i, κ of the $N - 1$ negative examples involving person i's appearance in camera A are randomly selected. Each training involves a parameter learning stage: we learn the optimal c and γ parameters for the RBF SVM by a 4-fold cross-validation inside the training set, searching for the parameters that result in the lowest CMC-expectation.

See Fig. 3(a) for ICT's performance as a function of κ. It reports the CMC expectation, the training time, and the number of support vectors found by the SVM. We see that the expectation drops as κ increases, at a high slope for small κ's and at an almost zero slope for $\kappa > 15$. We also see a similar convergence in the number of support vectors, which means that adding more than a certain number of negative examples does not add information. Note that the computation time for training grows linearly with κ. We also tested a variation of the algorithm that learns only from positive examples using one-class-SVM (i.e, $\kappa = 0$). The one-class SVM test, which followed a similar procedure, yields a CMC expectation value of 45.6, which is worst than the CMC expectation achieved by the binary SVM for $\kappa = 1$.

We learned that (a) not all negative examples are essential and training time can be saved by selecting only some of them; (b) the negative examples play an important role in compensating for the usually small number of positive examples, by helping in defining the borders of the "cloud" formed by the positive transformations.

Table 1. Results of ICT on the VIPeR dataset compared to the models in [2, 10–13].

method	expectation	rank(1)	rank(10)	rank(20)	nAUC
SDALF	25.5	19.9	49.4	65.7	92.2
ELF	28.9	12	44	61	91.2
PS	21.2	**21.8**	57.2	71.2	93.6
PRDC	21.5	15.7	53.9	70.1	93.5
PRSVM	27.9	14.6	50.9	66.8	91.4
ICT	**15.9**	14.4	**59.7**	**78.3**	**95.3**

4.3   Comparing to State-of-the-Art on VIPeR

In order to compare ICT's performance on the VIPeR dataset with that of recent work we repeated the above experiment, this time performing cross validations for 10 random splits, using $\kappa = 30$. See Fig. 3(b). The results of the ELF [11] and the SDALF [10] algorithms were kindly provided by the authors of [10]. The results of PRDC were kindly provided by the authors of [13]. The results of the PS based algorithm were kindly provided by the authors of [2]. The results of PRSVM are those presented in [12]. See Table 1 for a comparison of the CMC expectation, rank(1), rank(10), rank(20), and nAUC of the different methods. The CMC-expectation and the nAUC are much better for ICT than for all previous methods. ICT does not achieve the best rank(1) performance, but performs best for all ranks 8 and up.

The different measures show different aspects of the algorithm's performance. We argue that while the lower ranks are desirable, they are not achievable for the majority of the cases, which makes the higher ranks and the CMC expectations at least as important. The few lower ranks only reflect the algorithm's performance on the easy cases, while the CMC-expectation reflects the average human operator effort, and together with higher ranks, measures the algorithm's performance for average and difficult cases. The higher ranks on the VIPeR data may be more relevant for realistic applications in which the set of candidates contain only a few people. Consider, for example, a common surveillance scenario in which a suspect is recognized as he is captured by a certain camera, and we wish to continue tracking him. Yet the tracker has lost him because of a short occlusion, or because he passed through a 'blind' area not covered by any camera. Now, we can define a set of possible candidates for this 'lost' suspect. The number of candidates in such a case will be rather small. Hence, instead of 316 candidates (as tested in the VIPeR experiment setup), we may have, say, 8 candidates on whom we can apply a re-identification algorithm. If we scale the CMC curves accordingly, we may expect, on the average, that rank(1) for 8 candidates is approximately equivalent to rank(40) for 316 candidates. In this case ICT promises 91% success, while the next runner up promises success of only 84%.

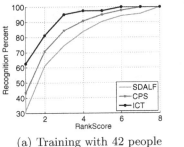 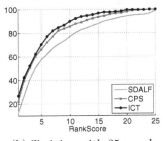

(a) Training with 42 people and an 8-person test set

(b) Training with 25 people and a 25-person test set

Fig. 4. CMC curves comparing ICT's results on CAVIAR4RfEID with those of SDALF [10] and CPS [2]

4.4 Comparing to State-of-the-Art on CAVIAR4REID

In this section we compare the performance of ICT with that of state-of-the-art on the newly released CAVIAR4REID dataset. This dataset includes 50 pedestrians captured by two different cameras. For each person in each camera there are 10 available appearances. We report results for two setups in Fig. 4, demonstrating the relative performance as a function of the size of the training data available. In the first setup (Fig. 4(a)), 42 people are included in the inter-camera training set and 8 others in the test set. In the second setup (Fig. 4(b)), the 50 people are equally divided into a training set of 25 and a test set of 25. For each setup, we average results on 10 random divisions. Our results are compared to those of SDALF and CPS reported in [2]. In [2] the test set consists of all 50 inter-camera people. We estimated the performance for test sets of 25 and 8 by normalizing the CMC curves reported in [2][3]. We see that for training sets of 25 people our algorithm meets the state-of-the-art performance of CPS, and outperforms SDALF and CPS for larger training sets. Note that the SDALF and CPS methods include high-level semantic analysis that requires heavy processing during the classification stage, while our classification stage includes very basic feature extraction and classifier calls that can run in real-time.(For instance, the runtime of an SVM RBF classifier with $\sim$ 1000 support vectors on one concatenated vector is 0.8 milliseconds on a standard laptop.)

5   Discussion

This paper considers the re-identification task and contributes the observation that the transfer between two cameras is a multi-valued mapping (a binary relation) which can be estimated using implicit function learning. We show that utilizing the more abundant negative examples allows us to learn the transfer

---

[3] If a person's true match was rated m among n people, then on the average it will be ranked $(m - 1) * (k - 1)/(n - 1) + 1$ among k people.

associated with two cameras from rather small sets of inter-camera example pairs. The algorithm yields an extremely fast classifier. We present new state-of-the-art re-identification performance.

The paper focuses on the camera-specific context, which enables the algorithm to implicitly "filter out" the irrelevant, person-independent, features without high-level semantic analysis. Yet we intend to test the utility of combining analysis of this sort in our algorithm, with the goal of finding the optimal combination that will bring maximum performance with minimum training.

Acknowledgments. This work was supported by the VULCAN consortium, a Magnet project administrated by the Office of the Chief Scientist at the ministry of Industry and Trade, Israel. The authors would like to thank Loris Bazzani, Dong Seon Cheng, and Wei-Shi Zheng for sharing their data and/or results.

References

1. Gray, D., Brennan, S., Tao, H.: Evaluating appearance models for recognition, reacquisition, and tracking. In: PETS Workshop in Conjunction with ICCV (2007)
2. Cheng, D.S., Cristani, M., Stoppa, M., Bazzani, L., Murino, V.: Custom pictorial structures for re-identification. In: BMVC (2011)
3. Pinto, N., DiCarlo, J., Cox, D.: How far can you get with a modern face recognition test set using only simple features? In: CVPR (2009)
4. Wolf, L., Hassner, T., Taigman, Y.: Descriptor based methods in the wild. In: ECCV (2008)
5. Ferencz, A., Learned-miller, E., Malik, J.: Learning to locate informative features for visual identification. IJCV 77, 3–24 (2008)
6. Gheissari, N., Sebastian, T., Hartley, R.: Person reidentification using spatiotemporal appearance. In: CVPR (2006)
7. Hu, W., Hu, M., Zhou, X., Tan, T., Lou, J.: Principal axis-based correspondence between multiple cameras for people tracking. PAMI 28, 663–671 (2006)
8. Cong, D., Khoudour, L., Achard, C., Meurie, C., Lezoray, O.: People re-identification by spectral classification of silhouettes. Signal Processing 90 (2010)
9. Bazzani, L., Cristani, M., Perina, A., Farenzena, M., Murino, V.: Multiple-shot person re-identification by HPE signature. In: ICPR, pp. 1413–1416 (2010)
10. Farenzena, M., Bazzani, L., Perina, A., Murino, V., Cristani, M.: Person re-identification by symmetry-driven accumulation of local features. In: CVPR (2010)
11. Gray, D., Tao, H.: Viewpoint Invariant Pedestrian Recognition with an Ensemble of Localized Features. In: Forsyth, D., Torr, P., Zisserman, A. (eds.) ECCV 2008, Part I. LNCS, vol. 5302, pp. 262–275. Springer, Heidelberg (2008)
12. Prosser, B., Zheng, W., Shaogang, G., Xiang, T.: Person re-identification by support vector ranking. In: BMVC (2010)
13. Zheng, W., Gong, S., Xiang, T.: Person re-identification by probabilistic relative distance comparison. In: CVPR (2011)
14. Javed, O., Khurram, S., Mubarak, S.: Appearance modeling for tracking in multiple non-overlapping cameras. In: CVPR (2005)
15. Zheng, W., Gong, S., Xiang, T.: Associating groups of people. In: BMVC (2009)
16. Chang, C., Lin, C.: LIBSVM: a library for support vector machines (2001), Software, http://www.csie.ntu.edu.tw/~cjlin/libsvm

Person Re-identification:
What Features Are Important?

Chunxiao Liu[1], Shaogang Gong[2], Chen Change Loy[3], and Xinggang Lin[1]

[1] Dept. of Electronic Engineering, Tsinghua University, China
[2] School of EECS, Queen Mary University of London, UK
[3] Vision Semantics Ltd., UK

Abstract. State-of-the-art person re-identification methods seek robust person matching through combining various feature types. Often, these features are implicitly assigned with a single vector of global weights, which are assumed to be universally good for all individuals, independent to their different appearances. In this study, we show that certain features play more important role than others under different circumstances. Consequently, we propose a novel unsupervised approach for learning a bottom-up feature importance, so features extracted from different individuals are weighted adaptively driven by their unique and inherent appearance attributes. Extensive experiments on two public datasets demonstrate that attribute-sensitive feature importance facilitates more accurate person matching when it is fused together with global weights obtained using existing methods.

1 Introduction

Appearance-based person re-identification is a non-trivial problem owing to visual ambiguities and uncertainties caused by illumination changes, viewpoint and pose variations, and inter-object occlusions [1]. Under such stringent constraints, most existing methods [2, 3] combine different appearance features, such as colour and texture, to improve reliability and robustness in person matching. Typically, the feature histograms are concatenated and weighted in accordance to their *importance*, i.e. their discriminative power in distinguishing a target of interest from other individuals.

State-of-the-art approaches [4–7] implicitly assume a feature weighting or selection mechanism that is *global*, by assuming a single weight vector (or a linear weight function) that is globally optimal across all circumstances, e.g. colour is the most important and universally good feature across all individuals. In this study, we term this weight as global feature importance. They can be learned either through boosting [7], rank learning [4], or distance metric learning [5]. Scalability is the main bottleneck of such approaches as the learning process requires exhaustive supervision on pairwise individual correspondence.

We believe that certain appearance features can be more important than others in describing an individual and distinguishing him/her from other people. For instance, colour is more informative to describe and distinguish an individual

A. Fusiello et al. (Eds.): ECCV 2012 Ws/Demos, Part I, LNCS 7583, pp. 391–401, 2012.
© Springer-Verlag Berlin Heidelberg 2012

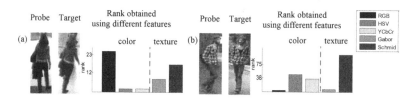

Fig. 1. We show the probe image and the target image, together with the rank of correct matching by using different feature types separately

wearing textureless bright red shirt, but texture information can be equally or more critical for a person wearing plaid shirt (Fig. 1).

Thus, it is desired not to bias all the weights to the features that are universally good for all individuals but also *selectively distribute some weights to informative feature given different appearance attributes*, which refer to appearance characteristics of individuals, e.g. dark shirt, blue jeans. This intuition is well motivated by the study in human visual attention [8], of which results suggest that visual attention is not only governed by top-down global feature importance, but also affected by bottom-up salient features of individual objects as a result of attentional competition between features.

To this end, we first investigate what features are more important under what circumstances. In particular, we show that selecting features specifically for different individuals can yield more robust re-identification performance than feature histogram concatenation with uniform weighting [9, 10]. Motivated by this observation, we propose an effective approach based on the random forest [11] to adaptively determine the feature importance of an individual driven by his/her inherent appearance attributes. Extensive experiments conducted on two challenging person re-identification datasets demonstrate that person matching can benefit from complementing existing 'global weighting' approaches with the proposed attribute-sensitive feature importance.

Related Work - Most existing approaches [4–7] can be considered as 'global weighting' approaches. For example, the RankSVM method in [4] aims to find a linear function to weight the absolute difference of samples via optimisation given pairwise relevance constraints. The Probabilistic Relative Distance Comparison (PRDC) [5] maximises the probability of a pair of true match having a smaller distance than that of a wrong matched pair. The output is an orthogonal matrix that essentially encodes the global importance of each feature.

The method proposed in [12] shares a similar spirit to our work, i.e. it aims to discover what is important given specific appearance. In contrast to [12] that requires labelled gallery images to discover gallery-specific feature importance, our method is fully unsupervised. Importantly, our method is more flexible since the feature importance is attribute-driven, thus it is not limited to specific gallery. A more recent work in [13] starts to explore prototype relevance for improving processing time in re-identification problem. In contrast, we systematically investigate salient feature importance mining for improving matching accuracy.

Contributions - (1) we draw insights into what features are more important under what circumstances. To our best knowledge, this is the first study that systematically investigates the role of different feature types given different appearance attributes; and (2) we formulate a novel unsupervised approach for on-the-fly mining of attribute-sensitive feature importance. Combining it with global feature importance leads to more accurate person re-identification while requiring no more supervision cost than existing learning-based approaches.

2   Attribute-Sensitive Feature Importance

The summary of our approach is depicted in Fig. 2. The three main steps are: (1) discovering prototypes by a clustering forest; (2) attribute-sensitive feature importance mining; (3) determining the feature importance of a probe image on-the-fly.

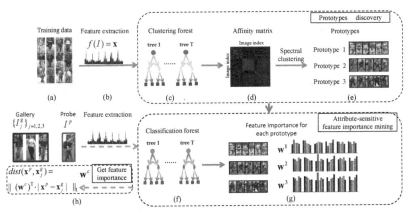

Fig. 2. Overview of attribute-sensitive feature importance mining. Training steps are indicated by red solid arrows and testing steps are denoted by blue slash arrows.

Prototypes Discovery - The first step of our method is to cluster a given set of unlabelled images into several *prototypes*, each of which compose of images that possess similar appearance attributes, e.g. wearing colorful shirt, with backpack, dark jacket (Fig. 2(e)).

Formally, given an input of n unlabelled images $\{I_i\}$, where $i = 1, \ldots, n$, feature extraction $f(\cdot)$ is first performed on every image to extract a D-dimensional feature vector, that is $f(I) = \mathbf{x} = (x_1, \ldots, x_D)^\mathsf{T} \in \mathbb{R}^D$ (Fig. 2(b)). We wish to discover a set of prototypes $c \in \mathcal{C} = \{1, \ldots, K\}$, i.e. low-dimensional manifold clusters that group images $\{I\}$ with similar appearance attributes. We treat the prototype discovery problem as a graph partitioning problem, which requires us to first estimate the pairwise similarity between images.

To estimate the similarity between images, we construct a clustering forest[14], an ensemble of T_{cluster} clustering trees (Fig. 2(c)). Each clustering tree t defines a partition of the input samples $\mathbf{x}$ at its leaves, $l(\mathbf{x}) : \mathbb{R}^D \to \mathcal{L} \subset \mathbb{N}$, where l

represent a leaf index and $\mathcal{L}$ is the set of all leaves in a given tree. For each tree, we compute an $n \times n$ affinity matrix A^t, with each element A^t_{ij} defined as

$$A^t_{ij} = \exp^{-\text{dist}^t(\mathbf{x}_i, \mathbf{x}_j)}, \tag{1}$$

where

$$\text{dist}^t(\mathbf{x}_i, \mathbf{x}_j) = \begin{cases} 0 & \text{if } l(\mathbf{x}_i) = l(\mathbf{x}_j) \\ \infty & \text{otherwise} \end{cases} . \tag{2}$$

Following the Eqn. (2), we assign closest affinity=1 (distance=0) to samples $\mathbf{x}_i$ and $\mathbf{x}_j$ if they fall into the same leaf node, and affinity=0 (distance=∞) otherwise. To obtain a smooth forest affinity matrix, we compute the final affinity matrix as $A = \frac{1}{T_{\text{cluster}}} \sum_{t=1}^{T_{\text{cluster}}} A^t$. This method offers a few advantages as compared to conventional similarity measuring approaches: (1) avoiding manual definition of distance function since the pairwise affinities are defined by the tree structure itself, and (2) implicit selection of optimal features and corresponding forest parameters via optimisation of the well-defined clustering information gain function [11].

Given the affinity matrix, the normalised cuts algorithm [15] is employed to partition the weighted graph into K prototypes. Thus, each unlabelled probe image $\{I_i\}$ is assigned to a prototype c_i(Fig. 2(e)). In this study, K is predefined but one can estimate the cluster number automatically using alternative methods such as [16].

Attribute-Sensitive Feature Importance - As discussed in Sec. 1, unlike the global weight vector that is assumed to be universally good for all images, attribute-sensitive feature importance is specific to prototype characterised by different appearance characteristics. That is each prototype c has its own attribute-sensitive weighting $\mathbf{w}^c = (w^c_1, \ldots, w^c_D)^\mathsf{T}$, of which high value should be assigned to unique features of that prototype. For example, texture features gain higher weights than others if the images in the prototype have rich textures but less bright colours.

Based on the above intuition, we compute the importance of a feature according to its ability in discriminating different prototypes. Specifically, we train a classification random forest [11] using $\{\mathbf{x}\}$ as inputs and treating the associated prototype labels $\{c\}$ as classification outputs (Fig. 2(f)). For each tree t, we reserve $\frac{1}{3}$ of the original training data as out-of-bag (oob) validation samples. First, we compute the classification error $\epsilon^{c,t}_d$ for every dth feature in prototype c. Then we randomly permute the value of the dth feature in the oob samples and compute the $\tilde{\epsilon}^{c,t}_d$ on the perturbed oob samples of prototype c. The importance of the dth feature of prototype c is then computed as the error gain [11]

$$w^c_d = \frac{1}{T_{\text{class}}} \sum_{t=1}^{T_{\text{class}}} (\tilde{\epsilon}^{c,t}_d - \epsilon^{c,t}_d), \tag{3}$$

where T_{class} is the total number of trees in the classification forest. Higher value in w^c_d indicates higher importance of the dth feature in prototype c. Intuitively, the dth feature is important if perturbing its value in the samples causes a drastic increase in classification error, which suggests its critical role in discriminating between different prototypes.

Ranking - Given feature vector of an unseen probe image $\mathbf{x}^p$, our method will determine its feature importance on-the-fly driven by its appearance. First, we classify $\mathbf{x}^p$ using the learned classification forest to obtain its prototype label c (Fig. 2(h)). Then we compute the distance $\mathbf{x}^p$ against a feature vector of a gallery/target image $\mathbf{x}^g$ using the following function

$$\text{dist}(\mathbf{x}^p, \mathbf{x}^g) = \|(\mathbf{w}^c)^\mathsf{T}|\mathbf{x}^p - \mathbf{x}^g|\|_1. \tag{4}$$

The matching ranks of $\mathbf{x}^p$ against a gallery of images can be obtained by sorting the distances computed from Eqn. (4). A smaller distance results in a higher rank.

Fusion with Global Feature Weight Vector - We investigate the fusion between the global feature weight matrix $\mathbf{V}$ obtained from existing methods [4, 5] and our attribute-sensitive feature importance vector $\mathbf{w}$ to gain more accurate person re-identification performance. We adopt a weighted sum scheme as follows

$$\text{dist}_{\text{fusion}}(\mathbf{x}^p, \mathbf{x}^g) = \alpha\|(\mathbf{w}^c)^\mathsf{T}|\mathbf{x}^p - \mathbf{x}^g|\|_1 + (1-\alpha)\|\mathbf{V}^\mathsf{T}|\mathbf{x}^p - \mathbf{x}^g|\|_1, \tag{5}$$

where α is a parameter that controls the weight between global attribute-sensitive importances.

3   Experiments

In Sec. 3.1, we first investigate the re-identification performance of using different features given individuals with different inherent appearance attributes. In Sec. 3.2, the qualitative results of prototype discovery are presented. We then compare feature importances produced by our unsupervised bottom-up solution and two top-down global weighting methods, namely RankSVM [4] and PRDC [5], in Sec. 3.3. Finally, we report the results on combining these two types of feature importance.

Datasets - Two publicly available person re-identification datasets, namely VIPeR [7] and i-LIDS Multiple-Camera Tracking Scenario (MCTS) [17] were used for evaluation. The VIPeR dataset contains 632 persons, each of which has two images captured in outdoor views. The dataset is challenging due to drastic appearance difference between most of the matched image pairs caused by viewpoint variations and large illumination changes at outdoor environment (see Fig. 3). The i-LIDS MCTS dataset was captured in a busy airport arrival hall using multiple cameras. It contains 119 people with a total of 476 images, with an average of four images per person. Apart from the illumination changes and pose variations, many images in this dataset are also subject to severe inter-object occlusions (Fig. 3(f)).

Features - We employed a mixture of colour and texture histograms similar to those employed in [4, 5]. Specifically, we divided an image of a person equally

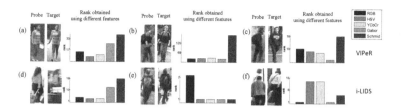

Fig. 3. In each subfigure, we show the probe image and the target image, together with the rank of correct matching by using different feature types separately.

into six horizontal stripes, to roughly capture the head, upper and lower torsos, and leg regions. In each stripe, we considered 8 colour channels (RGB, HSV and YCbCr)[1] and 21 texture filters (8 Gabor filters and 13 Schmid filters) applied to luminance channel [4]. Each channel was represented by a 16-dimensional vector. Concatenating all the feature channels resulted in 2784-dimensional feature vector for each image.

Evaluation - We used the $\ell1$-norm as the matching distance metric. The matching performance was measured using the averaged cumulative match characteristic (CMC) curve [7] over 10 trials. The CMC curve represents the correct matching rate at the top r ranks. We selected all the images of p person to build the test set. The remaining data was used for training. In the test set of each trial, we randomly chose one image from each person to set up the test gallery set and the remaining images were used as probe images.

3.1 Performance of Using Different Features

We believe that certain features can be more important than others in describing an individual and distinguishing him/her from other people. To validate our hypothesis, we analysed the matching performance of using different features individually.

We first provide a few examples in Fig. 3 (also presented in Fig. 1) to compare the ranks returned by using different feature types. It is observed that no single feature type was able to constantly outperform the others. In the VIPeR dataset, for individuals wearing textureless but colourful and bright clothing (e.g. Fig. 3(a)), the colour features yielded a higher rank. For person wearing clothing with rich texture or with a logo, e.g. Figures 3 (b) and (c), texture features especially the Gabor features tend to dominate. The results suggest that certain features can be more informative than others given different appearance attributes.

The overall matching performance is presented in Fig. 4. In general, HSV and YCbCr features exhibited very close performances, which were much superior

---

[1] Since HSV and YCbCr share similar luminance/brightness channel, dropping one of them results in a total of 8 channels.

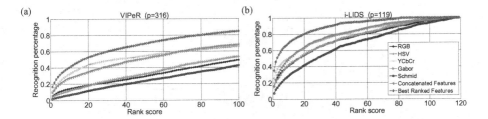

Fig. 4. The CMC performance comparison of using different features on the VIPeR and i-LIDs datasets. 'Concatenated Features' refers to the concatenation of all feature histograms with uniform weighting. In the 'Best Ranked Features' strategy, ranking for each individual was selected based on the best feature that returned the highest rank during matching.

over all other features. This observation of colours being the most informative features agreed with the past studies [7]. Simply concatenating all the feature histograms with uniform weighting did not necessary yield better performance, as can be observed in Fig. 4. The results suggest a more careful feature weighting according to their level of informativeness is necessary. The 'Best Ranked Features' strategy yielded the best performance, i.e. 13.97% and 11.31% improvement of AUC (area under curve) on the VIPeR and i-LIDS datasets, respectively, in comparison to 'Concatenated Features'. In the 'Best Ranked Features' strategy, the final rank was obtained by selecting the best feature that returned the highest rank for each individual, e.g. selecting HSV feature for Fig 3(a) whilst choosing Gabor feature for Fig 3(c). This is a heuristic way. Nevertheless, the results suggest that the overall matching performance can potentially be boosted by weighting features selectively according to the inherent appearance attributes.

3.2   Prototype Discovery

To weigh features in accordance to the inherent appearance attributes, our method first discovers prototypes, i.e. low-dimensional manifold clusters that model similar appearance attributes (see Sec. 2). The number of cluster K is set to 10 and 5 for the VIPeR and i-LIDS datasets, respectively, roughly based on the amount of training samples. We set $T_{cluster} = T_{class} = 200$. The minimum forest node size was set to 1.

Some examples of prototype discovered on the VIPeR dataset are depicted in Fig. 5. Each colour-coded row represents a prototype. A short list of possible attributes discovered in each prototype is given next to it. Note that these inherent attributes were neither pre-defined nor pre-labelled, but automatically discovered by the unsupervised clustering forest. As shown by the example members in each prototype, images with similar attributes were likely to be categorised into the same cluster. For instance, a majority of attributes in the second prototype can be characterised with bright and high contrast colour appearance. In the forth prototype, the key attributes are 'carrying backpack' and 'side pose'.

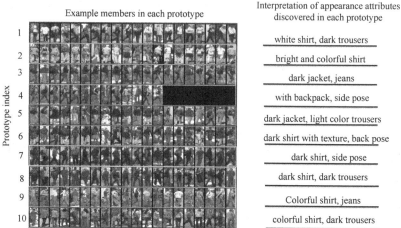

Fig. 5. Example of prototypes discovered on the VIPeR dataset. Each prototype represents a low-dimensional manifold cluster that models similar appearance attributes. Each image row in the figure shows a few examples of images in a particular prototype, with their interpreted unsupervised attributes listed on the right.

The results demonstrate that our method is capable of generating reasonably good clusters of inherent attributes, which can be employed in subsequent step for attribute-sensitive feature importance mining.

3.3   Attribute-Sensitive vs. Global Feature Importance

Comparing Global and Attribute-Sensitive Importance: The aim of this experiment is to compare the feature importances produced by existing approaches [4, 5] and the proposed attribute-sensitive feature importance mining method. Two state-of-the-art methods, i.e. the RankSVM [4] and the PRDC [5] (see Sec. 1), were evaluated using the authors'code. The global feature importances/weights were learned using the labelled images, and averaged over 10-fold cross validation. We set the penalty parameter C in RankSVM to 100 for both datasets and used the default parameter values for PRDC.

The left pane of Fig. 6 shows the feature importance discovered by both RankSVM and PRDC. For PRDC, we only show the first learned orthogonal projection, i.e. feature importance. Each region in the partitioned silhouette images were masked with the labelling colour of the dominant feature. In the feature importance plot, we show in each region the importance of each type of features. The importance of a certain feature type is derived by summing the weight of all the histogram bins belong to this type. The same steps were repeated to depict the attribute-sensitive feature importance on the right pane.

In general, the global feature importance emphasised more on the colour features for all the regions, whereas the texture features were assigned higher

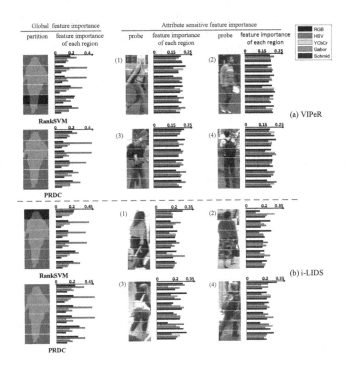

Fig. 6. Comparison of the global feature importance/weights produced by the RankSVM[4], PRDC[5], and the attribute-sensitive feature importance discovered using the proposed method

weights in the leg region than the torso region. This weight assignment or importance was applied universally to all images. In contrast, the attribute-sensitive feature importance are more person-specific. For example, for image regions with colourful appearance, e.g. Fig. 6(a)-1, the colour features in torso region were assigned with higher weights than the texture features. For image regions with rich texture, such as the stripes on the jumper (Figure. 6(a)-3), flower skirt (Figure. 6(b)-2), and bag (Figure. 6(b)-4), the importance of texture features increased. For instance, in Fig. 6(b)-2, the weight of gabor feature in the fifth region was 36.7% higher than that observed in the third region.

Table 1. Comparison of top rank matching rate (%) on the VIPeR and i-LIDS datasets. r is the rank and p is the size of gallery set.

Methods	VIPeR ($p = 316$)				i-LIDS ($p = 50$)			
	$r = 1$	$r = 5$	$r = 10$	$r = 20$	$r = 1$	$r = 5$	$r = 10$	$r = 20$
Uniform weight[9, 10]	9.43	20.03	27.06	34.68	30.40	55.20	67.20	80.80
Our method	9.56	22.44	30.85	42.82	27.60	53.60	66.60	81.00
RankSVM[4]	14.87	37.12	50.19	65.66	29.80	57.60	73.40	84.80
Our method+RankSVM	**15.73**	**37.66**	**51.17**	**66.27**	**33.00**	**58.40**	**73.80**	**86.00**
PRDC[5]	16.01	37.09	**51.27**	**65.95**	32.00	58.00	71.00	83.00
Our method+PRDC	**16.14**	**37.72**	50.98	**65.95**	**34.40**	**59.20**	**71.40**	**84.60**

Integrating Global and Attribute-Sensitive Importance: As shown in Table. 1, in comparison to the baseline uniform feature importance, our method yielded improved matching rate on the VIPeR dataset. No improvement was observed on the i-LIDS dataset. A possible reason is the small training size in the i-LIDS dataset, which leads to suboptimal prototype discovery. This can be resolved by collecting more unsupervised images during prototype discovery. We integrated both global and attribute-sensitive feature importance following the method described in Sec. 2 by setting $\alpha = 0.1$. An improvement as much as 3.2% on rank 1 matching rate can be obtained when we combined our method with RankSVM [4] and PRDC [5] on these two datasets. It is not surprised to observe that the supervised learning-based approaches [4, 5] outperformed our unsupervised approach. Nevertheless, the global approaches benefited from slight bias of feature weights driven by specific appearance attributes of individuals. The results suggest that these two kinds of feature importance are not exclusive, but can complement each other to gain improved matching rate.

4   Conclusion

In this study, we have shown that certain appearance features can be more important than others in describing an individual and distinguishing him/her from other people. The results suggested that instead of biasing all the weights to features that are universally good for all individuals, selectively distributing some weights to informative feature specific to certain appearance attributes can lead to better re-identification result. Future work include the investigation of better integration strategy of both global and attribute-sensitive feature importance, and incremental update of prototypes.

Acknowledgments. Chunxiao Liu was supported by NSF 61132007.

References

1. Doretto, G., Sebastian, T., Tu, P., Rittscher, J.: Appearance-based person reidentification in camera networks: problem overview and current approaches. Journal of Ambient Intelligence and Humanized Computing 2(2), 127–151 (2011)
2. Farenzena, M., Bazzani, L., Perina, A., Cristani, M., Murino, V.: Person re-identification by symmetry-driven accumulation of local features. In: CVPR, pp. 2360–2367 (2010)
3. Bazzani, L., Cristani, M., Perina, A., Murino, V.: Multiple-shot person re-identification by chromatic and epitomic analyses. Pattern Recognition Letters (2011)
4. Prosser, B., Zheng, W., Gong, S., Xiang, T.: Person re-identification by support vector ranking. In: BMVC, pp. 21.1–21.11 (2010)
5. Zheng, W., Gong, S., Xiang, T.: Person re-identification by probabilistic relative distance comparison. In: CVPR, pp. 649–656 (2011)
6. Mignon, A., Jurie, F.: PCCA: A new approach for distance learning from sparse pairwise constraints. In: CVPR (2012)

7. Gray, D., Tao, H.: Viewpoint Invariant Pedestrian Recognition with an Ensemble of Localized Features. In: Forsyth, D., Torr, P., Zisserman, A. (eds.) ECCV 2008, Part I. LNCS, vol. 5302, pp. 262–275. Springer, Heidelberg (2008)
8. Yantis, S.: Control of visual attention. Attention 1, 223–256 (1998)
9. Wang, X., Doretto, G., Sebastian, T., Rittscher, J., Tu, P.: Shape and appearance context modeling. In: ICCV, pp. 1–8 (2007)
10. Loy, C.C., Xiang, T., Gong, S.: Time-delayed correlation analysis for multi-camera activity understanding. IJCV 90(1), 106–129 (2010)
11. Breiman, L.: Random forests. Machine Learning 45(1), 5–32 (2001)
12. Schwartz, W., Davis, L.: Learning discriminative appearance-based models using partial least squares. In: Proc. the 22nd Brazilian Symposium on Computer Graphics and Image Processing, pp. 322–329 (2009)
13. Satta, R., Fumera, G., Roli, F.: Fast person re-identification based on dissimilarity representations. Pattern Recognition Letters (2012)
14. Criminisi, A., Shotton, J., Konukoglu, E.: Decision forests: A unified framework for classification, regression, density estimation, manifold learning and semi-supervised learning. Foundations and Trends in Computer Graphics and Vision 7(2-3), 81–227 (2012)
15. Shi, J., Malik, J.: Normalized cuts and image segmentation. IEEE TPAMI 22(8), 888–905 (2000)
16. Perona, P., Zelnik-Manor, L.: Self-tuning spectral clustering. In: NIPS, pp. 1601–1608 (2004)
17. Zheng, W., Gong, S., Xiang, T.: Associating groups of people. In: BMVC, pp. 23.1–23.11 (2009)

Towards Person Identification
and Re-identification with Attributes

Ryan Layne, Timothy M. Hospedales, and Shaogang Gong

School of EECS, Queen Mary University of London, UK

Abstract. Visual identification of an individual in a crowded environment observed by a distributed camera network is critical to a variety of tasks including commercial space management, border control, and crime prevention. Automatic re-identification of a human from public space CCTV video is challenging due to spatiotemporal visual feature variations and strong visual similarity in people's appearance, compounded by low-resolution and poor quality video data. Relying on re-identification using a probe image is limiting, as a linguistic description of an individual's profile may often be the only available cues. In this work, we show how mid-level semantic attributes can be used synergistically with low-level features for both identification and re-identification. Specifically, we learn an attribute-centric representation to describe people, and a metric for comparing attribute profiles to disambiguate individuals. This differs from existing approaches to re-identification which rely purely on bottom-up statistics of low-level features: it allows improved robustness to view and lighting; and can be used for identification as well as re-identification. Experiments demonstrate the flexibility and effectiveness of our approach compared to existing feature representations when applied to benchmark datasets.

1   Introduction

Person re-identification, or *inter-camera entity association*, is the task of recognising an individual in diverse scenes obtained from non-overlapping cameras. In particular, for long-term people monitoring over space and time, when an individual disappears from one view they need be differentiated from numerous possible targets and re-identified in another view, potentially under a different viewing angle and lighting condition and subject to variable degrees of occlusion.

Relying on manual re-identification in large camera networks is prohibitively costly and inaccurate. Operators are often assigned more cameras to monitor than is optimal and manual matching can also be prone to attentive gaps [1]. Moreover, human performance is subjectively determined by individual operator's experience therefore is often difficult to transfer and also subject to operator bias [2]. For these reasons, there has been extensive work in the computer vision community on automated re-identification. These efforts have primarily focused on developing feature representations which are discriminative yet invariant to view angle and lighting [3], and improved learning methods to better discriminate identity [4]. Nevertheless, despite extensive research, automated re-identification

A. Fusiello et al. (Eds.): ECCV 2012 Ws/Demos, Part I, LNCS 7583, pp. 402–412, 2012.
© Springer-Verlag Berlin Heidelberg 2012

is still a largely unsolved problem. This is due to the underlying challenge that most features are still either insufficiently discriminative for cross-view entity association, especially with low resolution images, or insufficiently robust to view angle and lighting changes.

Contemporary approaches to re-identification typically exploit low-level features [5, 6, 3], because they can be relatively easily measured. In this paper, we take inspiration from the operating procedures of human experts [7–9], and recent research in attribute learning [10] to introduce a new class of mid-level *attribute* features. When performing person re-identification, human experts seek and rely upon matching appearance or functional attributes that are unambiguous in interpretation, such as hair-style, shoe-type or clothing-style [7]. This attribute-centric representation is also used when a description is provided verbally (e.g., by an eye-witness) to an operator. We term this process attribute-profile identification, or zero-shot re-identification. Many of these mid-level attributes can be measured reasonably reliably with modern computer-vision techniques. This provides both a mechanism for attribute-profile identification as well as a valuable new class of features for re-identification. Crucially, attributes and low-level features provide very different types of information – effectively separate modalities. We will show how, with appropriate data fusion, attributes and low-level features can provide powerful re-identification as well as attribute-profile identification capabilities.

1.1   Related Work and Contributions

Re-identification. Contemporary approaches to re-identification typically exploit low-level features such as colour, texture, spatial structure [3], or combinations thereof [6, 11]. Once a suitable representation has been obtained, nearest-neighbour [3] or learning-based matching algorithms such as ranking [6] may be used for re-identification. In each case, a distance metric (e.g., Euclidean or Bhattacharyya) must be chosen to measure the similarity between two samples. It is also be possible to discriminatively optimise the distance metric [4]. Other complementary aspects of the problem have also been pursued to improve performance, such as improving robustness by combining multiple frames worth of features along a tracklet [11] and learning the topology or activity correllations of the camera network [12] to cut down the matching space.

Attributes. Attribute based modelling has recently been exploited to good effect in object [10] and action [13] recognition. To put this in context, in contrast to low-level features, or high-level classes / identities, attributes are the mid-level *description* of a class or instance. There are various unsupervised (e.g., PCA or topic-models) or supervised (e.g., neural network) modelling approaches which produce data-driven mid-level representations. These techniques aim to project the data onto a basis set defined by the assumptions of the particular model (e.g., maximisation of variance, likelihood, or sparsity). In contrast, attribute learning focuses on representing data instances by projecting them onto a basis set defined by domain-specific axes which are semantically meaningful to humans.

Semantic attribute representations have various benefits: (i) If data is sparse (as in re-identification, which can be seen as one-shot learning) they can be more powerful than low level features [10, 14, 13] because they provide a form of transfer learning since attributes can be learned from a larger dataset apriori; (ii) they can be used in conjunction with raw data for greater effectiveness [13] and (iii) they are a suitable representation for direct human interaction, therefore allowing searches to be specified or constrained by attributes [10, 14, 15].

Attributes in Identification and Surveillance. One view of attributes is as a type of transferrable context [16] in that they provide auxiliary information about an instance to aid in (re)-identification. Here they are related to the study of soft-biometrics, which aims to enhance biometric identification performance with ancillary information [17, 18]. Alternatively they can be used for semantic attribute-profile identification (zero-shot learning [10]) in which early research has aimed to retrieve people matching a verbal attribute description from a camera network [8]. However, this has so far only been illustrated on relatively simple data with a small set of equally-reliable facial attributes. We will illustrate that one of the central issues for exploiting attributes for general automated (re)-identification is dealing with their unequal and variable informativeness and reliability of measurement from raw data.

Contributions. In this paper, we move towards leveraging semantic mid-level attributes for automated person identification and re-identification. Specifically, we make four main contributions: (i) We introduce and evaluate an ontology of useful attributes which can be relatively easily measured using computer vision methods from the set of attributes used by human experts . (ii) We show how to learn an attribute-space distance metric to leverage attributes for re-identification. (iii) We evaluate the resulting approach and improve state of the art re-identification performance on standard benchmark datasets. (iv) We show how attributes and raw-data can also be used together for zero-shot re-identification.

2   Quantifying Attributes for Re-identification

In this section, we first describe our space of defined attributes (Section 2.1), then how to train detectors for each attribute (Section 2.2). Finally, we show how to learn a distance-metric for attribute space, and fuse these attributes with raw low-level features for re-identification (Section 2.3).

2.1   Attributes

Based on the operational procedures of human experts [7], we define the following space of $N_a = 15$ binary attributes for our study: *shorts, skirt, sandals, backpack, jeans, logo, v-neck, open-outerwear, stripes, sunglasses, headphones, long-hair, short-hair, gender, carrying-object.* Twelve of these are related to attire, and three are soft biometrics. Figure 1 shows an example of each attribute[1].

---

[1] We provide our annotations here: http://www.eecs.qmul.ac.uk/~rlayne/

Fig. 1. Example positive images for each attribute in our ontology. From left to right: *shorts, sandals, backpack, open-outerwear, sunglasses, skirt, carrying-object, v-neck, stripes, gender, headphones, short-hair, long-hair, logo, jeans.*

2.2 Attribute Detection

Low-level Feature Extraction. To detect attributes, we first extract an 2784-dimensional low-level colour and texture feature vector denoted $\mathbf{x}$ from each person image I following the method in [6]. This consists of 464-dimensional feature vectors extracted from six equal sized horizontal strips from the image. Each strip uses 8 colour channels (RGB, HSV and YCbCr) and 21 texture filters (Gabor, Schmid) derived from the luminance channel. We use the same parameter choices for γ, λ, θ and σ^2 as [6] for Gabor filter extraction, and for τ and σ for Schmid extraction. Finally, we use a bin size of 16 to describe each channel.

We train Support Vector Machines (SVM) to detect attributes.

We use Maji et al.'s implementation [19] of LIBSVM and investigate Linear, RBF, χ^2 and Intersection kernels. We select the Intersection kernel as it compares closely with χ^2 but can be trained much faster For each attribute, we perform cross validation to select SVM slack parameter C from $C \in [-10, 5]$. SVM scores are probability mapped, so each attribute detector i outputs a posterior $p(a_i|\mathbf{x})$.

Attribute Training and Representation. The prevalence of each attribute (e.g., jeans, sunglasses) varies dramatically so some attributes have a limited number of positive examples. To avoid bias due to imbalanced data, we train each attribute detector with all the positive examples, and obtain a matching number of negative examples by regularly subsampling the rest of the data.

Given the learned bank of attribute detectors, any person image can now be represented in a semantic attribute space by stacking the posteriors from each attribute detector into a N_a dimensional vector: $A(\mathbf{x}) = [p(a_1|\mathbf{x}), \ldots, p(a_{N_a}|\mathbf{x})]^T$.

2.3 Re-identification

Model and Fusion. In order to use our attributes for re-identification, we choose a base re-identification method, and investigate how attributes can be fused to enhance performance. In particular we choose to build on *Symmetry-Driven Accumulation of Local Features* (SDALF), introduced by Farenzena et al. [3]. SDALF provides a low-level feature and Nearest Neighbour (NN) matching strategy giving state-of-the-art performance for a non-learning NN approach, and can be fused with additional sources of information.

Farenzena et al. introduces a state of the art distance metric d_{SDALF} to compare person images I_p and I_q. Within this nearest neighbour strategy, we can integrate our attribute-based distance d_{ATTR} as follows:

$$d(I_p, I_q) = (1 - \beta_{ATTR}) \cdot d_{SDALF}(SDALF(I_p), SDALF(I_q)) \qquad (1)$$
$$+ \beta_{ATTR} \cdot d_{ATTR}(ATTR(I_p), ATTR(I_q)). \qquad (2)$$

Here Eq. (1) corresponds the SDALF distance and Eq. (2) fuses our attribute-based distance metric. For our attribute representation, we will learn a Mahalanobis $L2$ distance metric d_{ATTR}, detailed next.

Attribute Metric Learning. Since attributes are unequal due to variability in number of training samples, how reliably they are measured, and how informative they are, we need to decide how to weight the attributes. To address this, we exploit the information theoretic distance metric learning strategy from [20]. We define the distance (Eq. (2)) between attribute profiles $A(\mathbf{x})$ as the following Mahalanobis distance, parameterized by positive definite matrix Λ:

$$d_{ATTR}(I_p, I_q; \Lambda) = (A(\mathbf{x}_p) - A(\mathbf{x}_q))^T \Lambda (A(\mathbf{x}_p) - A(\mathbf{x}_q)). \qquad (3)$$

A distance metric paramaterized by Λ can be represented by the corresponding multi-variate Gaussian $p(\mathbf{x}; \Lambda, \mu) \propto \exp(-d_\Lambda(\mathbf{x}, \mu)/2)$. The Kullback-Leibler divergence $\mathcal{KLD}(\Lambda||\Lambda)$ between two such Gaussians thus provides a well-founded measure of the similarity between two Mahalanobis distance metrics. Building on this measure of similarity between distance metrics, choosing a distance metric to optimise the separability of person images via attributes can be expressed via the following large-margin constraint satisfaction problem [20]:

$$\min_\Lambda \mathcal{KLD}\left(p(\mathbf{x}; \Lambda_0)||p(\mathbf{x}; \Lambda)\right) \ s.t. \qquad (4)$$
$$d_A(\mathbf{x}_i, \mathbf{x}_j) \leq u \qquad if \qquad (i, j) \in S,$$
$$d_A(\mathbf{x}_i, \mathbf{x}_j) \geq l \qquad if \qquad (i, j) \in D,$$

where Λ_0 is a regulariser representing a simple identity-matrix metric, $(i, j) \in S$ indicates instances i and j are images of the same person, and $(i, j) \in D$ indicates images of different people. The matrix Λ obtained by optimising Eq. (4) provides the optimal distance metric via Eq. (3) and hence Eq. (1).

2.4   Attribute-Profile Identification / Zero-Shot Re-identification

In addition to re-identification based on a probe image, we can also directly identify a person given solely their semantic attribute description (aka zero-shot learning [10] or attribute search [8]). Given an attribute description in the form of a binary vector $\mathbf{a}$, we can attempt to find this person by NN matching $\mathbf{a}$ against the attribute profiles $A(\mathbf{x}_i)$ of each person i in the dataset.

Surprisingly, in a multi-camera context, we can also use raw-data to improve attribute-profile identification [21]. The intuition is if searching for a given profile

a in view A, we also can use the match from another view B (or multiple matches from A if available) to obtain an estimated appearance/low level feature $\hat{\mathbf{x}}$ as additional context. This then provides an additional source of information from view B which can be used together with **a** in the full framework (Eq. (1)). Of course the matching within view B is imperfect, so we take $\hat{\mathbf{x}}$ as $\hat{\mathbf{x}} = \frac{1}{K} \sum_l \mathbf{x}_{\mathbf{a},l}^B$, averaging over the top K matches $\mathbf{x}_{\mathbf{a},l}^B$ to prototype **a** in view B.

3 Experiments and Discussion

Datasets We select three challenging datasets with which to validate our model, VIPeR [5], i-LIDS pedestrians [22] and ETHZ [23]. **VIPeR** contains 632 pedestrian image pairs from two cameras with different viewpoint, pose and lighting. Images are scaled to 128x48 pixels. We follow [5, 3] in considering Cam B as the gallery set and Cam A as the probe set. Performance is evaluated by matching each test image in Cam A against the Cam B gallery. **i-LIDS** [22] contains 479 images of 119 pedestrians captured from non-overlapping cameras observing a busy airport hall. In addition to pose and illumination variations, images are also subject to occlusion. Images are scaled to 128x64 pixels. We follow [3] in randomly selecting one image for each pedestrian to build a gallery, while the others form the probe set, averaging results over 10 trials. **ETHZ** was developed using a mobile camera and contains high variations in person appearance; but low pose variation. As in [3], images are normalised to 64x32 pixels and we test on SEQ. 1 only which consists of 83 persons with 4,857 detections. Since the number of people here is too small to split separate metric training and testing sets we report figures for vanilla attributes instead.

Conditions. For each dataset, we select a portion for training, while re-identification performance is reported on the held out test portion. There are two phases to training: attribute detector learning (Section 2.2) and attribute distance metric learning (Section 2.3). Because VIPeR contains the largest amount of data, and the most diversity in attributes, we train the attribute detectors for all experiments on this dataset. This is important because it highlights the value of attributes as a source of transferrable information [16].

For the metric learning, we learned on the training portion of each dataset. We quantify re-identification performance in the standard way [5, 3]: recognition rate is visualised with Cumulative Matching Characteristic (CMC) curves, which indicate the probability of the correct match appearing in the top n.

We compare the following re-identification methods: **SDALF** [3] using code provided by the authors (note that SDALF is already shown to decisively outperform [24]); **Attr** vanilla attribute based re-identification (euclidean distance); **AccMI** attribute based re-identification with a weighting given by product of accuracy and mutual information with identity [25]; **MLA** attribute based-reidentification with discriminatively learned distance metric; **SDALF+MLA** SDALF fused with MLA (weight β_{ATTR} determined by optimisation on training set).

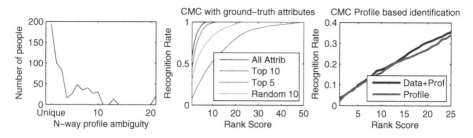

Fig. 2. (a) Most people are uniquely identifiable by attributes. (b). VIPeR re-indentification with perfect attribute classifiers (p=632). (c) Attribute search / zero-shot re-identification (p=168).

Table 1. Attribute Detection Performance

Attribute	Abs	Mean	Attribute	Abs	Mean	Attribute	Abs	Mean
shorts	0.79	0.74	sandals	0.64	0.58	backpacks	0.66	0.52
jeans	0.76	0.73	carrying	0.75	0.50	logo	0.59	0.58
vnecks	0.44	0.53	openouter	0.64	0.56	stripes	0.41	0.47
sunglasses	0.66	0.60	headphones	0.74	0.58	shorthair	0.52	0.52
longhair	0.65	0.55	male	0.68	0.68	skirt	0.67	0.76

3.1 Attribute Analysis

We first analyse the potential of our attribute ontology with regards to the VIPeR dataset. Fig. 2(a) shows a histogram of the number of individuals against degree of attribute profile uniqueness or ambiguity. Clearly the majority of people can be uniquely or almost uniquely identified by their profile, while there are a small number of people with a very generic profile. The CMC curve (for gallery size p=632) that would be obtained assuming perfect attribute classifiers is shown in Fig. 2(b). This impressive result highlights the potential for attribute-based re-identification. Also shown are the results with top 5 or 10 attributes (sorted by mutual information with identity), and a random 10 attributes. This shows that: (i) as few as 10 attributes are sufficient if they are good (high MI) and perfectly detectable, while 5 is too few; and (ii) attributes with high MI are significantly more useful than low MI (always present or absent) attributes.

Attribute Detection. Attribute detection in VIPeR achieves an average accuracy of 64%, with 11 detectors performing greater than 60% (Table 1). This highlights the issue of inequality of attributes and the importance learning a good distance metric to focus on the most reliable and discriminative attributes.

Zero-shot identification. We next evaluate the novel task of identification based solely on the manual attribute profile of a target (instead of the standard re-identification approach of providing a probe image) using VIPeR. This corresponds to the task of identifying an individual in a surveilled space based on an, e.g. radioed, textual description of their attributes. This is challenging both

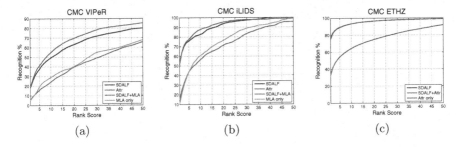

Fig. 3. Averaged CMC curves for (a) VIPeR (gallery size $p = 250$), (b) iLIDS (gallery size $p = 60$) and (c) ETHZ1 (gallery size $p = 80$)

(a) VIPeR   (b) i-LIDS

Fig. 4. Examples where MLA (green) increases the re-id rank of the correct match vs SDALF (red)

because of profile ambiguity (Fig. 2(a)) and limited accuracy of the attribute detectors (Table 1). Performing zero-shot identification enhanced with data from other camera (Section 2.4), we raise the CMC nAUC from 67% to 68% and double the Rank 1 match rate from 2% to 4% (Fig. 2(c)).

3.2   Re-identification

Quantitative Evaluation The re-identification performance of all models is summarised in Figure 3 and Table 2. In each case, optimisation with of the distance metric improves re-identification over vanilla attributes (MLA vs Attr). Optimised attributes in conjunction SDALF outperforms vanilla SDALF (SDALF+MLA vs SDALF). Importantly, at the most valuable low rank $r = 1$

Table 2. Breakdown of re-identification rates at specified ranks, and area under CMC

ILIDS	Attr	MLA	SDALF	SDALF+MLA	ETHZ1		Attr	MLA	SDALF	SDALF+Attr
R1	15.42	10.75	51.33	52.92	R1		32.92	35.27	75.86	75.86
R5	43.83	43.58	75.75	77.42	R5		53.73	55.90	88.82	88.82
R10	56.42	60.75	82.58	87.75	R10		63.43	65.64	92.77	92.77
R25	76.25	83.50	96.00	97.17	R25		78.27	79.70	96.76	96.78
nAUC	77.42	80.58	92.96	93.73	nAUC		83.64	84.48	96.84	96.93

VIPER	Attr	MLA	SDALF	SDALF+MLA	AccMI
R1	5.40	5.06	18.02	18.78	6.40
R5	15.80	19.24	37.38	40.94	15.86
R10	24.34	29.06	49.38	54.94	26.02
R25	44.94	48.06	68.44	74.28	46.86
nAUC	80.72	82.90	86.56	90.15	81.00

(perfect match), SDALF has re-identification rates of 18.0%, 51.3% and 75.9% while our full method has rates of 18.8%, 52.9% and 76% (for VIPeR, iLIDS and ETH respectively; gallery size $p = 250$, $p = 60$, $p = 80$). We note that a simpler attribute weighting baseline based on accuracy and mutual information with identity (AccMI,[25]) does not improve much on vanilla unweighted attributes. Moreover, this method requires ground-truth for attributes (so we can only test it on VIPeR), which is not a limitation shared by our approach.

Some examples of re-identification using MLA and SDALF are shown in Figure 4 (a) and (b) for VIPeR and i-LIDS respectively. These illustrate how attributes can complement low-level features. In the first examples for VIPeR and iLIDS the detectors for *backpacks* and *carrying* respectively push the true match up the rankings compared to SDALF.

4   Conclusions

We have shown how state-of-the-art low-level feature representations for automated re-identification can be further improved by taking advantage of a mid-level attribute representation reflecting semantic cues used by human experts [7]. Existing approaches to re-identification [3, 6, 5] focus on high-dimensional low-level features which are assumed invariant to view and lighting. However, their simple nature and invariance also limits their discriminative power for identity. In contrast, attributes provide a low-dimensional mid-level representation which makes no invariance assumptions (Variability in appearance of each attribute is learned by the classifier). Importantly, although individual attributes vary in robustness and informativeness, attributes provide a strong cue for identity. Their low-dimensional nature means they are also amenable to discriminatively learning a good full-covariance distance metric in order to take into account inter-attribute correlations. In developing a separate cue-modality, our approach is potentially complementary to most existing approaches, whether focused on low-level features [3], or learning methods [4].

The proposed attribute-centric model provides an important contribution and novel research direction for practical re-identification: by providing a complementary and informative mid-level cue, as well as opening up new applications such as zero-shot identification within the same framework. As a novel application, consider how semantic attributes could potentially be used to constrain or relax re-identification, for example by specifying invariance to whether or not the target has removed or added a hat.

The most promising direction for future research is improving the attribute-detector performance, as evidenced by the excellent results in Fig. 2(b) using ground-truth attributes. The more limited empirical performance is due to lack of training data, which could be addressed by transfer learning to bring attribute detectors trained on large databases (e.g., web-crawls) to re-identification.

Acknowledgements. Ryan Layne is supported by a EPSRC CASE studentship supported by UK MOD SA/SD. The authors also wish to thank Toby Nortcliffe of the Home Office CAST for insights on human expertise.

References

1. Keval, H.: CCTV Control Room Collaboration and Communication: Does it Work? In: Proceedings of Human Centred Technology Workshop, pp. 11–12 (2006)
2. Williams, D.: Effective CCTV and the challenge of constructing legitimate suspicion using remote visual images. Journal of Investigative Psychology and Offender Profiling 4(2), 97–107 (2007)
3. Farenzena, M., Bazzani, L., Perina, A., Murino, V., Cristani, M.: Person re-identification by symmetry-driven accumulation of local features. In: Computer Vision and Pattern Recognition (2010)
4. Zheng, W.S., Gong, S., Xiang, T.: Person re-identification by probabilistic relative distance comparison. In: Computer Vision and Pattern Recognition (2011)
5. Gray, D., Brennan, S., Tao, H.: Evaluating appearance models for recognition, reacquisition, and tracking. In: Performance Evaluation of Tracking and Surveillance (2007)
6. Prosser, B., Zheng, W.S., Gong, S., Xiang, T.: Person Re-Identification by Support Vector Ranking. In: British Machine Vision Conference, pp. 21.1–21.11 (2010)
7. Nortcliffe, T.: People Analysis CCTV Investigator Handbook. Home Office Centre of Applied Science and Technology (2011)
8. Vaquero, D.A., Feris, R.S., Tran, D., Brown, L., Hampapur, A., Turk, M.: Attribute-based people search in surveillance environments. In: Workshop on the Applications of Computer Vision, pp. 1–8 (2009)
9. Cheng, D.S., Cristani, M., Stoppa, M., Bazzani, L.: Custom Pictorial Structures for Re-identification. In: British Machine Vision Conference (2011)
10. Lampert, C., Nickisch, H., Harmeling, S.: Learning to detect unseen object classes by between-class attribute transfer. In: Computer Vision and Pattern Recognition (2009)
11. Bazzani, L., Cristani, M., Perina, A., Farenzena, M., Murino, V.: Multiple-shot Person Re-identification by HPE signature. In: International Conference on Pattern Recognition, pp. 1413–1416 (2010)
12. Loy, C.C., Xiang, T., Gong, S.: Time-Delayed Correlation Analysis for Multi-Camera Activity Understanding. International Journal of Computer Vision 90(1), 106–129 (2010)
13. Liu, J., Kuipers, B.: Recognizing human actions by attributes. In: CVPR (2011)

14. Siddiquie, B., Feris, R.S., Davis, L.S.: Image ranking and retrieval based on multi-attribute queries. In: Computer Vision and Pattern Recognition (2011)
15. Kumar, N., Berg, A., Belhumeur, P.: Describable visual attributes for face verification and image search. IEEE Transactions on Pattern Analysis and Machine Intelligence 33(10), 1962–1977 (2011)
16. Zheng, W.S., Gong, S., Xiang, T.: Quantifying and Transferring Contextual Information in Object Detection. IEEE Transactions on Pattern Analysis and Machine Intelligence 1(8), 1–14 (2011)
17. Jain, A.K., Dass, S.: Soft biometric traits for personal recognition systems. In: Biometric Authentication, pp. 1–7 (2004)
18. Dantcheva, A., Velardo, C., D'Angelo, A., Dugelay, J.L.: Bag of soft biometrics for person identification. Multimedia Tools and Applications 51(2), 739–777 (2010)
19. Maji, S., Berkeley, U.C., Berg, A.C.A., Malik, J.: Classification using intersection kernel support vector machines is efficient. In: Computer Vision and Pattern Recognition (2008)
20. Davis, J.V., Kulis, B., Jain, P., Sra, S., Dhillon, I.S.: Information-Theoretic Metric Learning. In: International Conference on Machine Learning (2007)
21. Fu, Y., Hospedales, T.M., Xiang, T., Gong, S.: Attribute Learning for Understanding Unstructured Social Activity. In: Fitzgibbon, A., Lazebnik, S., Perona, P., Sato, Y., Schmid, C. (eds.) ECCV 2012, Part IV. LNCS, vol. 7575, pp. 521–534. Springer, Heidelberg (2012)
22. Zheng, W.S., Gong, S., Xiang, T.: Associating Groups of People. In: British Machine Vision Conference (2009)
23. Schwartz, W.R., Davis, L.S.: Learning discriminative appearance-based models using partial least squares. In: Brazilian Symposium on Computer Graphics and Image Processing (2009)
24. Gray, D., Tao, H.: Viewpoint Invariant Pedestrian Recognition with an Ensemble of Localized Features. In: Forsyth, D., Torr, P., Zisserman, A. (eds.) ECCV 2008, Part I. LNCS, vol. 5302, pp. 262–275. Springer, Heidelberg (2008)
25. Yang, Y., Pedersen, J.O.: A comparative study on feature selection in text categorization. In: International Conference on Machine Learning (1997)

Local Descriptors Encoded by Fisher Vectors for Person Re-identification

Bingpeng Ma, Yu Su, and Frédéric Jurie

GREYC — CNRS UMR 6072, University of Caen Basse-Normandie, Caen, France
{bingpeng.ma,yu.su,frederic.jurie}@unicaen.fr

Abstract. This paper proposes a new descriptor for *person re-identification* building on the recent advances of Fisher Vectors. Specifically, a simple vector of attributes consisting in the pixel coordinates, its intensity as well as the first and second-order derivatives is computed for each pixel of the image. These local descriptors are turned into Fisher Vectors before being pooled to produce a global representation of the image. The so-obtained Local Descriptors encoded by Fisher Vector (LDFV) have been validated through experiments on two person re-identification benchmarks (VIPeR and ETHZ), achieving state-of-the-art performance on both datasets.

1 Introduction and Related Works

In recent years, person re-identification in unconstrained conditions have attracted more and more research interest. Person re-identification consists in recognizing an individual through different images (e.g. coming from cameras in a distributed network or from the same camera at different time). The key issue of such systems is their ability to measure the similarity between two person-centered bounding boxes and predict if they represent to the same person, despite changes in illumination, viewpoint, background, occlusions and low resolution.

In order to tackle this problem, many researchers have concentrated on (i) the design of visual features to describe individual images, and (ii) the use of adapted distance measures (e.g. obtained by metric learning), to predict if two images represent the same person.

The visual features applied in person re-identification can be roughly categorized into global and local features. While global features encode the holistic configuration of body parts, local features encode the detailed traits within body parts. The typical features for person re-identification are: color (widely used since the color of clothing constitutes simple but efficient visual signatures) [1], HOG like signatures [2,3], texture [4,5,6], differential filters [6], Haar-like filters [7], co-occurrence matrices [3], interest points [8], e.g. SURF and SIFT [9,10] or the signatures of image regions [2,1]. In addition, these features can be combined as they play different roles. For example, [4] combined 8 color features with 21 texture filters (Gabor and differential filters). [1] and [11] combined Maximally Stable Color Regions (MSCR) descriptors with weighted color histograms, achieving the state-of-the-art results on several wildly-used person re-identification datasets under unsupervised setting.

A. Fusiello et al. (Eds.): ECCV 2012 Ws/Demos, Part I, LNCS 7583, pp. 413–422, 2012.

Perhaps the most common approach for combining local features for producing a global signature of the image is the Bag-of-Words (BoW) model [12], in which local features extracted from an image are first mapped to a set of visual words and then the image is represented as a histogram of visual word occurrences. The BoW model has been used for person re-identification in [10], where the authors builds groups of descriptors by embedding the visual words into concentric spatial structures and by enriching the BoW description of a person by the contextual information coming from the surrounding people. Recently, the BoW model has been greatly enhanced by the introduction of the Fisher vector [13] which encodes higher order statistics of local features. It has been shown that the resultant Fisher vector gives excellent performance for several challenging object recognition and image retrieval tasks [14,15].

In addition, metric learning can be used to further improve the performance by providing a metric adapted to the task (e.g. [16,10,4]). Most distance metrics learning approaches learn a Mahalanobis-like distance, such as Large Margin Nearest Neighbors (LMNN) [17], Information Theoretic Metric Learning (ITML) [18] and Logistic Discriminant Metric Learning (LDML) [19], and Pairwise Constrained Component Analysis (PCCA) [20].

Building on these advances, this paper proposes to combine Fisher vectors with a new very simple 7-d local descriptor adapted to the representation of persons images, and to use the resultant representation (*Local Descriptors encoded by Fisher Vector* or LDFV) to describe persons images. Specifically, in LDFV, each pixel of an image is converted into a 7-d local feature, which contains the coordinates, the intensity, the first-order and second-order derivative of this pixel. Then, the local features are encoded and aggregated into a global Fisher vector, *i.e.* the LDFV representation. Finally, we learn the distance between LDFV representations using the metric learning approach proposed by [20].

The proposed representation has been experimentally validated on two person re-identification databases (VIPeR and ETHZ), which are challenging since they contain pose changes, viewpoint and lighting variations, and occlusions. Furthermore, these datasets have been used in the recent literature, allowing comparisons with recent approaches.

2 Description of the Proposed Approach

2.1 LDFV: Local Descriptor Encoded by Fisher Vector

In order to capture the local properties of images, we have designed a very simple 7-d descriptor inspired by [21]:

$$f(x, y, I) = (x, y, I(x,y), I_x(x,y), I_y(x,y), I_{xx}(x,y), I_{yy}(x,y)) \qquad (1)$$

where x and y are the pixel coordinates, $I(x,y)$ is the raw pixel intensity at position (x,y), I_x and I_y are the first-order derivatives of image I with respect to x and y, while I_{xx} and I_{yy} are the second-order derivatives.

Let $M = \{m_t, t = 1, \ldots, T\}$ be the set of the T local descriptors extracted from an image. The key idea of Fisher vectors [13] is to model the data with a generative model and compute the gradient of the likelihood of the data with respect to the parameters of the model, i.e. $\nabla_\lambda \log p(M|\lambda)$. We model M with a Gaussian mixture model (GMM) using Maximum Likelihood (ML) estimation. Let $\hat{u}_\lambda$ be the GMM model: $\hat{u}_\lambda(m) = \sum_{i=1}^{K} w_i u_i(\mu_i, \sigma_i)$, where K is the number of Gaussian components. The parameters of the models are $\lambda = \{w_i, \mu_i, \sigma_i, i = 1, \ldots, K\}$, where w_i denotes weight of the i-th component, while μ_i and σ_i are its mean and its standard deviations. We assume the covariance matrices are diagonal and σ_i represent the vector of standard deviations of the i-th component of the model. It worth pointing out that, considering the computational efficiency, for each image in the training set, only a randomly selected subset of local features is used to train the GMM model.

After getting the GMM, image representations are computed using Fisher vector, which is a powerful method for aggregating local descriptors and has been demonstrated to outperform the BoW model by a large margin [22]. Let $\gamma_t(i)$ be the soft assignment of the descriptor m_t to the component i:

$$\gamma_t(i) = \frac{w_i u_i(m_t)}{\sum_{j=1}^{K} w_j u_j(m_t)} \tag{2}$$

$G_{\mu,i}^M$ and $G_{\sigma,i}^M$ are the 7-dimensional gradients with respect to μ_i and σ_i of the component i. They can be computed using the following derivations:

$$G_{\mu,i}^M = \frac{1}{T\sqrt{w_i}} \sum_{t=1}^{T} \gamma_t(i)\left(\frac{m_t - \mu_i}{\sigma_i}\right) \tag{3}$$

$$G_{\sigma,i}^M = \frac{1}{T\sqrt{2w_i}} \sum_{t=1}^{T} \gamma_t(i)\left[\frac{(m_t - \mu_i)^2}{\sigma_i^2} - 1\right] \tag{4}$$

where the division between vectors is as a term-by-term operation. The final gradient vector G is the concatenation of the $G_{\mu,i}^M$ and $G_{\sigma,i}^M$ vectors for $i = 1, \ldots, K$ and is therefore $2 \times 7 \times K$-dimensional.

LDFV on color images. Previous works have shown that using color is a useful cue for person re-identification. We use the color information by splitting the image into 3 color channels (HSV), extract the proposed descriptor on each channel separately and finally concatenate the 3 descriptors into a single signature.

Similarity between LDFV representations Finally, the distance between two images I_i and I_j can obtained by computing the Euclidean distance between their representations :

$$d(I_i, I_j) = ||LDFV_i - LDFV_j|| \tag{5}$$

2.2   LDFV Extensions

bLDFV: Using Spatial Information

To provide a rough approximation of the spatial information, we divide the image into many rectangular bins and compute one LDFV descriptor per bin. Please note that for doing this we compute one GMM per bin. Then, the descriptors of the different bins are concatenated to form the final representation. It is denoted by bLDFV, for bin-based LDFV.

It must be pointed out that our method does not use any body part segmentation. However, adapting the bins to body parts would be possible and could make the results even better.

eLDFV: Combining LDFV with Other Features.

As mentioned in the introduction, combining different types of image descriptors is generally useful. In this paper, we combine our bLDFV descriptor with two other descriptors: the Weighted Color Histograms (wHSV) and the MSCR, shown to be efficient for this task [1]. We denote this combination as eLDFV (enriched LDFV). In eLDFV, the difference between two image signatures $eD_1 = (HA_1, MSCR_1, bLDFV_1)$ and $eD_2 = (HA_2, MSCR_2, bLDFV_2)$ is computed as:

$$d_{eLDFV}(eD_1, eD_2) = \frac{1}{6}d_{wHSV}(HA_1, HA_2) + \frac{1}{6}d_{MSCR}(MSCR_1, \\ MSCR_2) + \frac{2}{3}d_{bLDFV}(bLDFV_1, bLDFV_2); \tag{6}$$

Regarding the definition of d_{wHSV} and d_{MSCR}, we use the ones given in [1]. For simplicity reason and because it's not the central part of the paper, we have set the mixing weights by hand, giving more importance to the proposed descriptor. Learning them could certainly improve the results further.

sLDFV: Using Metric Learning.

In addition to the unsupervised similarity function (Eq. 5), we have also evaluated a supervised similarity function in which we use PCCA [20] to learn the metric. This variant is denoted sLDFV for supervised bLDFV. PCCA learns a projection into a low-dimensional space where the distance between pairs of data points respects the desired constraints, exhibiting good generalization properties in presence of high dimensional data. Please note that the bLDFV descriptors are pre-processed by applying a whitened PCA before PCCA. In sLDFV, PCCA is used with a linear kernel, for making the computations faster.

3   Experiment

The proposed approach has been experimentally validated on two person re-identification datasets (VIPeR [16] and ETHZ [3,23]). After introducing the datasets, we present several experiments showing the efficiency of our simple LDFV descriptor and its extensions.

3.1   Datasets and Performance Evaluation

The VIPeR [16] dataset contains $1,264$ images (normalized to 128×48 pixels) of 632 persons. There are exactly two images per person, taken from two non-overlapping viewpoints. As shown Fig. 1, VIPeR's images have a high degree of viewpoint and illumination variations: for most pairs there are 90 degrees from one of the other viewpoints. The VIPeR dataset has been widely used in the literatures, and is now considered as the benchmark of reference for person re-identification.

The ETHZ [3,23] dataset contains three video sequences of crowded street scenes captured by two moving cameras mounted on a chariot. The three sequences are as follows: $4,857$ images of 83 pedestrians in SEQ. #1, $1,961$ images of 35 pedestrians in SEQ. #2, and $1,762$ images of 28 pedestrians in SEQ. #3. The most challenging aspects of ETHZ are illumination changes and occlusions.

For both datasets, the performance is measured by the Cumulative Matching Characteristic (CMC) curve [24], which is the standard metric for person re-identification. The CMC curve represents the probability of finding the correct match over the first n ranks.

3.2   Evaluation of the Proposed Image Descriptor

In this section, our motivation is to evaluate the intrinsic properties of the descriptor. For this reason we don't use any metric learning but simply measure the similarity between two persons using the Euclidean distance between their representations.

Evaluation of the Simple 7-d Feature Vector. The core of our descriptor is the 7-d simple feature vector given Eq. (1). This first set of experiments aims at validating this feature vector by comparing it with several alternatives, the rest of the framework being exactly the same. We did experiments with (i) SIFT features (reduced to 64 dimensions by PCA) and (ii) Gabor features [25] (with 8 scales and 8 orientations). For these experiments, we divide the bounding box into 12 bins (3×4) and the number of GMM components is set to 16. For each bin and each one of the 3 color channels (HSV), we compute the FV model and concatenate the 12 descriptors for obtaining the final representation. The size of the final descriptor is $7 \times 16 \times 12 \times 2 \times 3$ for our 7-d descriptor, $64 \times 16 \times 12 \times 2 \times 3$ for both the SIFT and Gabor descriptor based FV. We then compute CMC normalized Area under Curves (nAUC) on VIPeR get respectively 83.17, 86.37 and 91.60 for SIFT, Gabor and bLDFV using our 7-d feature vector. Consequently, the proposed descriptor, in addition of being compact and very simple to compute, gives much better results than SIFT and Gabor filters for this task.

We have evaluated the performance of our descriptor for different number of GMM components (16, 32, 50 and 100), and have observed that the performance is not very sensitive to this parameter. Consequently, we use 16 components in all of our experiments, which is a good tradeoff between performance and efficiency.

Fig. 1. VIPeR dataset: images of the same subjects from different viewpoint

As set of representative images is required to learn the GMM, we conducted a set of experiments in order to evaluate how critical the choice for these images is. Out experiments have shown that using the whole dataset or only a smaller training set independent from the test set makes almost no difference, showing thereby that, in practice, a small set of representative images is more than enough for learning the GMM.

Single-Shot Experiments. Single-shot means that a single image is used as the query. We first present some experiments on the VIPeR dataset, showing the relative importance of the different components of our descriptor. As explained in Sec. 2 the full descriptor (eLDFV) is based on a basic Fisher encoding of the simple 7-d feature vector (LFDV) computed on the 3 color channels (HSV) and its two extensions, *i.e.* the spatial encoding (bLFDV) and the combination with two other features (namely wHSV and MSCR).

Fig. 2 gives the performance of eLDFV as well as the performance of wHSV, MSCR and bLDFV alone. We follow the same experimental protocol used in [1] and report the average performance over 10 random split of 316 persons. The figure also gives the performance of the state-of-the-art SDALF [1]. We can draw several conclusions: (i) LDFV alone performs much better than MSCR and wHSV (ii) using spatial information (bLFDV) improves the performance of LDFV (iii) combining the three components (eLDFV) gives a significant improvement over bLDFV and any of the individual components (iv) the proposed approach outperforms SDALF by a large margin. For example, the CMC score at rank 1, 10 and 50 for eLDFV are respectively of 22.34%, 60.04% and 88.82% while those of SDALF are of 19.84%, 49.37 and 84.84%.

We have also tested the proposed descriptor on the ETHZ database, in the single shot scenario ($N = 1$). Here again we follow the evaluation protocol proposed by [1]. Fig. 3 shows the CMC curves for the three different sequences. In the figure, dashed results come from [1]. The solid line are given by the proposed method. We can see that the performances of LDFV, bLDFV and eLDFV are all much better than that of the ones of SDALF, on all the three sequences, and

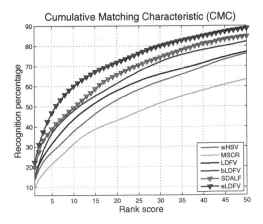

Fig. 2. VIPeR dataset: CMC curves of LDFV, bLDFV, eLDFV and SDALF

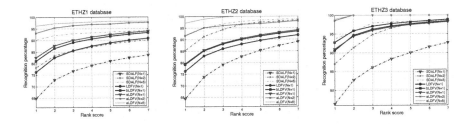

Fig. 3. CMC curves for the ETHZ dataset

improvements are even more visible than on VIPeR. Especially, on SEQ. 1 and 3, the performances of eLDFV are much worse than those of bLDFV though eLDFV is the combination of bLDFV, wHSV and MSCR. We attribute this to the low accuracy of wHSV and MSCR. In particular, on SEQ. 1, the minimum and maximum of the matching rate between the eLDFV and SDALF is about 10% and 18%, respectively. In SEQ. 2, rank 1 matching rate is around 80% for eLDFV and 64% for SDALF. The mean matching rate differences between eLDFV and SDALF on 7 ranks are about 10% in SEQ. 3.

Multi-shot Experiments on ETHZ. Besides the single-shot case, we also test our descriptors in the multi-shot case. In this case $N \geq 2$ images are used as queries. We also follow the evaluation framework proposed by [1], the number of query images N being set to 2 and 5. Results are also shown Fig. 3. We can see that on SEQ. 1 and 3, eLDFV gives almost perfect results. Especially, on SEQ. 3, the performance of eLDFV is 100% with $N = 2, 5$, for ranks greater than 2.

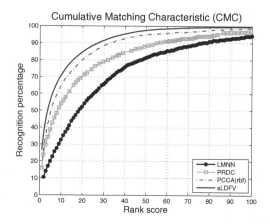

Fig. 4. VIPeR dataset: CMC curves with 316 persons

Table 1. VIPeR dataset: Top ranked matching rates (%) with 316 persons

Method	r=1	r=5	r=10	r=20
PRDC [26]	15.66	38.42	53.86	70.09
MCC[26]	15.19	41.77	57.59	73.39
ITML[26]	11.61	31.39	45.76	63.86
LMNN[26]	6.23	19.65	32.63	52.25
CPS [11]	21.00	45.00	57.00	71.00
PRSVM [4]	13.00	37.00	51.00	68.00
ELF [6]	12.00	31.00	41.00	58.00
PCCA-sqrt n^-=10 [20]	17.28	42.41	56.68	74.53
PCCA-rbf n^-=10 [20]	19.27	48.89	64.91	80.28
sLDFV n^-=10	**26.53**	**56.38**	**70.88**	**84.63**

3.3   Comparison with Recent Approaches

In this section we compare our framework with recent approaches. For making comparison fair, we use here the metric learning algorithm described Sec. 2.2.

We first present some experiments done on the VIPeR dataset. Following the standard protocol for this dataset, the dataset is split into a train and a test set by randomly selecting 316 persons out of the 632 for the test set, the remaining persons being in the train set. Like in [20], one negative pairs is produced for each person, by randomly selecting one image of another person. We produce 10 times more negative pairs than positive ones. The process is repeated 100 times and the results are reported as the mean/std values over the 100 runs.

Fig. 4 and Tab. 1 compare our approach (sLDFV) with three different approaches using metric learning: PRDC [26], LMNN [17] and PCCA [20]. The results of PRDC and LMNN are taken from [26] while the ones of PCCA come from [20]. For PRDC and LMNN, the image representation is the combination of RGB, YCbCr and HSV color features and two texture features extracted by local derivatives and Gabor filters on 6 horizontal strips. For PCCA, the feature descriptor is a 16 bins color histograms in 3 color spaces (RGB, HSV and YCrCb) as well as texture histograms based on Local Binary Patterns (LBP) computed on 6 non overlapping horizontal strips. PCCA [20] reports state-of-the-art results for person re-identification, improving over Maximally Collapsing Classes [27], ITML [18] or LMNN-R [28].

Fig. 4 and Tab. 1 shows that the proposed approach (sLDFV) performs much better than any previous approaches. For example, if we compare sLDFV with PCCA, we can see that matching rates for rank 1, 10 and 20 are of 26.53%, 70.88% and 84.63% for sLDFV while those of PCCA are only 19.27%, 64.91% and 80.28%. It must be pointed out that sLDFV is not using any non-linear kernel, from which we can expect further improvements.

4 Conclusion

In this paper, we have addressed the problem of person re-identification by proposing a novel descriptor, which is based on a simple seven-dimensional feature representation and the Fisher vector method. We test our descriptor on two challenging public datasets (VIPeR and ETHZ), outperforming the current state-of-the-art performance on both datasets.

There are several aspects to be further improved in the future, such as the weights of different features which are fixed by hand at the moment and should be learnt, or the seven-dimensional feature, based on pixels intensities, which can be made more robust to noise.

Acknowledgments. This work is a part of the Quaero Program funded by OSEO, French State agency for innovation and by the ANR, grant reference ANR-08-SECU-008-01/SCARFACE. The first author is partially supported by National Natural Science Foundation of China under contract No. 61003103.

References

1. Farenzena, M., Bazzani, L., Perina, A., Murino, V., Cristani, M.: Person re-identification by symmetry-driven accumulation of local features. In: Proc. IEEE Conf. on Comp. Vision and Pattern Recognition (2010)
2. Oreifej, O., Mehran, R., Shah, M.: Human identity recognition in aerial images. In: Proc. IEEE Conf. on Comp. Vision and Pattern Recognition (2010)
3. Schwartz, W., Davis, L.: Learning discriminative appearance based models using partial least squares. In: Brazilian Symp. on Comp. Graphics and Im. Proc. (2009)
4. Prosser, B., Zheng, W., Gong, S., Xiang, T.: Person re-identification by support vector ranking. In: BMVC (2010)
5. Zhang, Y., Li, S.: Gabor-LBP based region covariance descriptor for person re-identification. In: Int. Conf. on Image and Graphics, pp. 368–371 (2011)
6. Gray, D., Tao, H.: Viewpoint Invariant Pedestrian Recognition with an Ensemble of Localized Features. In: Forsyth, D., Torr, P., Zisserman, A. (eds.) ECCV 2008, Part I. LNCS, vol. 5302, pp. 262–275. Springer, Heidelberg (2008)
7. Bak, S., Corvee, E., Bremond, F., Thonnat, M.: Person re-identification using haar-based and DCD-based signature. In: Proc. Int. Workshop on Activity Monitoring by Multi-Camera Surveillance Systems (2010)

8. Gheissari, N., Sebastian, T., Tu, P., Rittscher, J., Hartley, R.: Person re-identification using spatiotemporal appearance. In: Proc. IEEE Conf. on Comp. Vision and Pattern Recognition (2006)

9. Kai, J., Bodensteiner, C., Arens, M.: Person re-identification in multi-camera networks. In: Proc. IEEE CVPR Workshops (2011)

10. Zheng, W., Gong, S., Xiang, T.: Associating groups of people. In: BMVC (2009)

11. Cheng, D.S., Cristani, M., Stoppa, M., Bazzani, L., Murino, V.: Custom pictorial structures for re-identification. In: BMVC (2011)

12. Sivic, J., Zisserman, A.: Video google: a text retrieval approach to object matching in videos. In: Proc. IEEE Conf. on Comp. Vision and Pattern Recognition (2003)

13. Perronnin, F., Dance, C.: Fisher kernels on visual vocabularies for image categorization. In: Proc. IEEE Conf. on Comp. Vision and Pattern Recognition (2007)

14. Perronnin, F., Sánchez, J., Mensink, T.: Improving the Fisher Kernel for Large-Scale Image Classification. In: Daniilidis, K., Maragos, P., Paragios, N. (eds.) ECCV 2010, Part IV. LNCS, vol. 6314, pp. 143–156. Springer, Heidelberg (2010)

15. Perronnin, F., Liu, Y., Sánchez, J., Poirier, H.: Large-scale image retrieval with compressed Fisher vectors. In: Proc. IEEE Conf. on Comp. Vision and Pattern Recognition (2010)

16. Gray, D., Brennan, S., Tao, H.: Evaluating appearance models for recognition, reacquisition, and tracking. In: IEEE International Workshop on Performance Evaluation of Tracking and Surveillance (2007)

17. Weinberger, K., Saul, L.: Distance metric learning for large margin nearest neighbor classification. Journal of Machine Learning Research 10, 207–244 (2009)

18. Davis, J.V., Kulis, B., Jain, P., Sra, S., Dhillon, I.S.: Information-theoretic metric learning. In: Proc. International Conference on Machine Learning, pp. 209–216 (2007)

19. Guillaumin, M., Verbeek, J., Schmid, C.: Is that you? metric learning approaches for face identification. In: Proc. IEEE International Conference on Computer Vision (2009)

20. Mignon, A., Jurie, F.: PCCA: a new approach for distance learning from sparse pairwise constraints. In: Proc. IEEE Conf. on Comp. Vision and Pattern Recognition (2012)

21. Tuzel, O., Porikli, F., Meer, P.: Pedestrian detection via classification on riemannian manifolds. IEEE Trans. on PAMI 30, 1713–1727 (2008)

22. Chatfield, K., Lempitsky, V., Vedaldi, A., Zisserman, A.: The devil is in the details: an evaluation of recent feature encoding methods. In: BMVC (2011)

23. Ess, A., Leibe, B., Schindler, K., van Gool, L.: A mobile vision system for robust multi-person tracking. In: Proc. IEEE Conf. on Comp. Vision and Pattern Recognition (2008)

24. Moon, H., Phillips, P.: Computational and performance aspects of PCA-based face-recognition algorithms. Perception 30, 303–321 (2001)

25. Fisher, R.A.: The use of multiple measures in taxonomic problems. Ann. Eugenics 7, 179–188 (1936)

26. Zheng, W., Gong, S., Xiang, T.: Person re-identification by probabilistic relative distance comparison. In: Proc. IEEE Conf. on Comp. Vision and Pattern Recognition (2011)

27. Globerson, A., Roweis, S.: Metric learning by collapsing classes. In: Advances in Neural Information Processing Systems (2006)

28. Dikmen, M., Akbas, E., Huang, T.S., Ahuja, N.: Pedestrian Recognition with a Learned Metric. In: Kimmel, R., Klette, R., Sugimoto, A. (eds.) ACCV 2010, Part IV. LNCS, vol. 6495, pp. 501–512. Springer, Heidelberg (2011)

Re-identification of Pedestrians in Crowds Using Dynamic Time Warping

Damien Simonnet, Michal Lewandowski, Sergio A. Velastin,
James Orwell, and Esin Turkbeyler

Digital Imaging Research Centre, Kingston University
Kingston-upon-Thames KT1 2EE, UK
{damien.simonnet,m.lewandowski}@kingston.ac.uk,
sergio.velastin@ieee.org, j.orwell@kingston.ac.uk
Roke Manor Research, Romsey, Hampshire SO51 0ZN, UK
esin.turkbeyler@roke.co.uk

Abstract. This paper presents a new tracking algorithm to solve on-line the 'Tag and Track' problem in a crowded scene with a network of CCTV Pan, Tilt and Zoom (PTZ) cameras. The dataset is very challenging as the non-overlapping cameras exhibit pan tilt and zoom motions, both smoothly and abruptly. Therefore a tracking-by-detection approach is combined with a re-identification method based on appearance features to solve the re-acquisition problem between non overlapping camera views and crowds occlusions. However, conventional re-identification techniques of multi target trackers, which consist of learning an online appearance model to differentiate the target of interest from other people in the scene, are not suitable for this scenario because the tagged pedestrian moves in an environment where pedestrians walking with them are constantly changing. Therefore, a novel multiple shots re-identification technique is proposed which combines a standard single shot re-identification, based on offline training to recognize humans from different views, with a Dynamic Time Warping (DTW) distance.

1 Introduction

Tracking pedestrians in surveillance videos is an important task, not only in itself but also as a component of pedestrian counting, activity and event recognition, and scene understanding in general. Robust tracking in crowded environments remains a major challenge, mainly due to occlusions and interactions between pedestrians. This paper reports work with a network of Pan, Tilt and Zoom (PTZ) cameras, viewing unstructured crowded scenes [1] where the crowd is relatively free to move over time and space, which corresponds to real scenarios in public spaces such as airports, railway stations or pedestrian streets. A new tracking algorithm is presented to solve on-line the 'Tag and Track' problem, where one pedestrian is nominated (tagged) and then tracked as they are observed from multiple cameras. The dataset[1], illustrated by Fig. 1, is very

---

[1] Available upon request from the authors.

A. Fusiello et al. (Eds.): ECCV 2012 Ws/Demos, Part I, LNCS 7583, pp. 423–432, 2012.

Fig. 1. Network of PTZ cameras dataset. Samples of the person which is tracked with three PTZ cameras (C6, C7 and C34) in a crowded scene during 1 minute and 40 seconds. This dataset is very challenging because the scene is crowded, cameras can move and pedestrians are seen from different non-overlapping viewpoints.

challenging: the non-overlapping cameras exhibit pan tilt and zoom motions, both smoothly and abruptly. Our approach is a novel combination of tracking-by-detection and re-identification using Dynamic Time Warping (DTW) of the resulting appearance features.

The proposed method can be used on arbitrary and diverse input sources: an important advantage is that it does not require the initialization of a background image. Furthermore, it is suitable for integration alongside automatic control of the PTZ cameras, to monitor a scene for the presence of a specific individual. This aspect is not included here. Similarly, a full implementation would require relational details of the cameras in the network to be either specified or learned. These relations will condition the probability density estimate, and are not included here: a uniform prior is assumed.

The rest of the paper is organized as follows. Related work is presented in section 2. Section 3 presents the Tag and Tracker with a network of PTZ cameras. Evaluation is performed in section 4. Finally, the conclusion is given in section 5.

2   Related Work

The proposed approach uses a pipeline process of detection, tracking and re-identification: these aspects are considered in turn below. To detect observations of individuals in a crowded scene, methods based on foreground-background segmentation are not applicable, and are not considered further here. Methods to detect pedestrians in single image frames [2–6] are becoming increasingly accurate, and therefore directly applicable to a (multi-)tracking framework in cluttered conditions. Tracking individuals in a crowded scene must first be distinguished from methods which consider the crowds themselves as global entities [7], which are not considered further here.

Benfold and Reid [8] apply a tracking-by-detection algorithm to data from a high definition fixed camera in a crowded pedestrian street, aiming to obtain a precise location of the pedestrians' heads. First, a combined head/full body detector is applied to detect pedestrians in crowds. This is then combined with a Markov Chain Monte Carlo Data Association (MCMCDA) and a KLT tracker.

The former makes the data association more robust as it is performed over a short time window. The latter uses motion feature, based on appearance, to reinforce the kinematic data association process. For example, the velocity of the target and the observation should be similar, hence many false alarm observations can be removed.

Kuo and Nevatia [9] present a multi-target tracker for crowded scenes from a single camera. First, pedestrian locations in each frame are indicated by a human detector [5]. Then, tracklets (i.e. short sequences of these locations reliably referring to the same individual) are built based on position, size, appearance and motion. These tracklets are then associated using motion, time and an appearance model. This model, learnt with Adaboost, selects the most discriminative pedestrian subparts, using colour (RGB histogram), shape (HOG [2]) and texture (covariance matrix) features. There is a high system latency because the whole sequence is processed before obtaining the results, in contrast to [8].

To re-identify pedestrians, three different types of algorithms can be found in the literature: *short-term*, *contextual long-term*, and *non-contextual long-term* re-identification. *Short-term* re-identification is used by tracking algorithms to associate the data frame by frame and is generally based on appearance features (e.g. colour histogram, texture, edges). *Contextual long-term* re-identification methods [9] use the context of a single static camera to learn online models to differentiate the subject from other pedestrians in the scene and is used to solve the track fragmentation problem. *Non-contextual long-term* re-identification methods [10, 11] are applied across arbitrary cameras and views. The third approach has not yet been applied to the problem of re-identifying pedestrians in a crowded scene with a network of moving cameras. Doretto et al. [10] present such a method for a network of static calibrated cameras in a non crowded environment: this is generalised to non-static, non-calibrated cameras in a crowded environment. In [10], two approaches for re-identification are used, the first called *single shot* bases its re-identification on a single image, and the second called *multiple shots* uses a sequence of images and is therefore more robust.

In this paper, a novel *non-contextual long-term multiple shots* re-identification method is proposed.

3   Tracking in a Network of PTZ Cameras

In this section, a novel algorithm is presented and illustrated by Fig. 2, to solve the 'Tag and Track' requirement. It has three three main steps: human detection, multi-target tracking, and association of the resulting tracklets. First, pedestrians are detected in each frame based on a HOG detector [2]. Then, short reliable tracklets for the pedestrians are built, using spatial multi-target tracker. Then, a *non-contextual long-term* re-identification technique is applied to link tracklets corresponding to the tracked target.

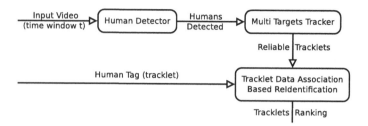

Fig. 2. Flow chart for the Tag and Tracker based on tracklet data association. First, given a tag pedestrian (tracklet), short reliable tracklets are built with a multi-target tracker which uses human detections in each frame during the time window t. Then, a tracklet data association is performed to rank the candidate tracklets. This is intended as one component of a fully automatic system for automatic control of CCTV PTZ cameras.

3.1 Spatial Multi Target Tracker by Detection

As no multi-target tracking methodology prevails for crowded scenes with a moving camera, the Nearest Neighbour Standard Filter (NNSF) [12] is chosen. It is based on a Kalman Filter, consisting of the usual steps: prediction, selection of the validated measurement, and update of the tracker state. Its specificity is the selection of the valid measurement via a Mahalanobis distance.

The measurement and state vector are respectively defined as $Z = \{x, y, h\}$ and $X = \{x, y, h, v_x, v_y, v_h\}$ where x, y represent the position of the pedestrian centre in the image space, h the pedestrian height, and v_x, v_y, v_h are their corresponding speeds. The system transition matrix is defined as a constant velocity model with Gaussian noise to represent acceleration, as this has proved effective for static cameras. As tracking is performed in the image space, the process noise Q and the measurement noise R depend on pedestrian height and are Gaussian.

Then, valid measurements are selected by using the validation volume defined in Eq. (1) where z is a measurement, $S(k + 1)$ and $\hat{z}(k + 1|k)$ represent respectively the innovation covariance and the measurement prediction, and γ is the normalized innovation square which defines the probability of a measurement to be in the validation volume, based on the Mahalanobis distance. The parameter γ, depending on a probability p to be in the validation volume and the degree of freedom d of the measurement vector, will be used to define what is a reliable tracklet.

$$\mathcal{V}(k + 1, \gamma) = \{z, \ [z - \hat{z}(k + 1|k)]^t S(k + 1)^{-1}[z - \hat{z}(k + 1|k)] \leqslant \gamma\} \quad (1)$$

Finally, the measurement with the smallest Mahalanobis distance is selected to update the state vector. Multiple measurements could have been used for updating the filter. However, the aim of the tracker is to build reliable tracklets and the human detector has removed multiple detections per object during its non maximal suppression stage, so there is no need to use complex methods to update the filter state (e.g. using appearance features to select multiple detected instances of one pedestrian and then updating the state with multiple measurements). It is noted that this selection process can lead to no measurement. In this case the measurement noise is formally infinity, and so the Kalman filter sets the state to be the predicted state and the a posteriori covariance as the a priori covariance.

This NNSF is designed to track one person in clutter, and needs an external initialization to indicate which one person that should be [12]. So, this tracking algorithm needs to be extended for tracking multiple targets whose number is unknown, and to start and stop tracks automatically, and is referred to as the JNNSF (Joint Nearest Neighbour Standard Filter). JNNSF uses a variable number of NNSF filters with a joint data association step, and is composed of three main steps: *track formation*, *track maintenance* and *track termination*.

Track formation occurs when an observation, output by the human detector, has not been associated to any of the current NNSF trackers and when the detection confidence exceeds a high threshold. Then, the *track maintenance* component associates the detection responses with the NNSF trackers. A lower threshold for the detection confidence is used for this stage. The tracker states are first predicted and then updated, using these associated measurements. When no measurement is associated (e.g. due to failure of the detector with occluded pedestrians), the prediction alone is applied. If, after several iterations, the covariance is too big, then a *track termination* step is invoked.

Up to this point, we have presented the underlying detection and tracking process that results in tracklets for different people in the scene. Under favourable circumstances (e.g. low clutter) these tracklets accurately represent the trajectories of each person. However, in many cases, and especially in clutter, these tracklets will be segmented, have swapping ids etc. and a further process is needed as explained in the next section.

3.2 Re-identification of Tracklets across Multiple Shots

Conventional re-identification techniques [8, 9] applied in crowded scenes are not suitable for a multi-camera scenario because they generally learn an on-line model to differentiate the target pedestrian of interest from the other pedestrians in the scene. However, the tagged pedestrian moves in an environment where pedestrians walking with them are also constantly changing. Consequently, a *non-contextual long-term* re-identification method, based on the work of Dikmen et al. [11] (that uses a viewpoint invariant metric based a Large Margin Nearest Neighbour classifier trained on the Viewpoint Invariant Pedestrian Recognition (VIPeR [13]) dataset) is proposed to solve this problem. Moreover, a novel *multiple shots* re-identification technique (more robust than a *single shot* technique which uses only one sample per tracklet) is introduced. Based on the observation that pedestrian walking is a cycling activity which may vary in time and speed, the Dynamic Time Warping (DTW) distance [14] is combined with the similarity distance introduced in [11] to associate tracklets.

More formally, given a target's tracklet T_r, the objective is to identify the most similar subsequent tracklet among a set of N_t candidate tracklets $(T_{c,k})_{k \in [\![1, N_t]\!]}$, generated during a time window t (if $t \to \infty$ then this is a global approach, else a finite t effectively dictates a trade-off between latency and the achievable performance of an on-line system). This is achieved by first extracting and assembling a temporal sequence $F_T = (x_i)_{i \in [\![1, S_T]\!]}$ for each tracklet T where S_T is the size of the tracklet and x_i is an appearance feature obtained from the target at frame i. As a consequence, the similarity of these high dimensional series can be measured by a Dynamic Time Warping distance [14] which minimises the effects of shifting and distortion in time by allowing 'elastic' transformation of series in order to detect similar shapes with different phases.

Given two tracklets (T_a, T_b of respective size S_a and S_b), the re-identification problem is cast as the task of aligning two sequences of observations ($F_a = (x_i)_{i \in [\![1, S_a]\!]}$ and $F_b = (x_j)_{j \in [\![1, S_b]\!]}$) in order to generate the most representative distance measure of their overall difference represented as a a symmetric cost distance matrix $E = \{D(x_i, x_j)\}$ where D is a metric. Afterwards, the algorithm finds the best alignment path (i.e. warping path) between tracklets by satisfying the *boundary, monotonicity* and *continuity* conditions which respectively assigns first and last elements of tracklets to each other, preserves the time-ordering of pedestrians, and limits the warping path from long jumps (shifts in time) while aligning tracklets. The final distance between tracklets is given by the end point $P(S_a, S_b)$ of an accumulated global cost matrix P normalised by the sum of tracklets lengths ($S_a + S_b$), where P has been initialised by Eq. (2) and then updated by a cost function associated based on a warping path defined by Eq.(3).

$$\forall i \in [\![1, S_1]\!], P_{i,1} = \sum_{k=1}^{i} E_{k,1}, \ \forall j \in [\![1, S_2]\!], P_{1,j} = \sum_{k=1}^{j} E_{1,k} \qquad (2)$$

$$\forall (i,j) \in [\![2, S_1]\!] \times [\![2, S_2]\!], P(i,j) = \min\{P_{i-1,j-1}, P_{i-1,j}, P_{i,j-1}\} + E_{i,j} \qquad (3)$$

In this work, the appearance feature x_i is a vectorized image using 8-bin histograms for each channel of RGB and HSV colour space, but the general approach could be applied to other types of features. To compensate observation differences due to view changes between tracklets, pedestrians are compared with a specialised view-invariant distance metric [11] (distance metric D).

Finally, given any tracklet T_r (corresponding to the tagged target), the multiple shots re-identification is performed by ranking all other tracklets $(T_{c,k})_{k \in [\![1, N_t]\!]}$ within the t seconds time slot according to the distance obtained by the introduced metric. Therefore, the proposed Tag and Tracker is an online tracking algorithm which gives a response with at most t seconds of latency.

4   Evaluation

This section presents an evaluation of the Tag and Track algorithm proposed here on the challenging dataset illustrated in Fig. 1, which involves constantly moving PTZ cameras and contains two complete changes of camera view. The aim of an uncalibrated Tag and Tracker with a network of cameras is not to be able at any time to give the precise location of the pedestrian e.g. in real-world coordinates, but to be able from a starting position (i.e. when a pedestrian is tagged by an operator) to follow the pedestrian through the camera network, localising it in a given camera and to a given image location in that camera.

To our best knowledge, no results have been reported to track a pedestrian in crowded scenes in a network of PTZ cameras. Therefore, here we evaluate the re-identification part our algorithm, because this is key for achieving the aim of the algorithm outlined above. Before going into this aspect, on Fig. 5 we illustrate that the JNNSF tracker is able to build long and reliable tracklets with a moving camera in a crowded scene. Tracklets were built with the normalized innovation square $\gamma = 16.2662$ which corresponds to a probability of true measurement $p = 0.999$ with a measurement degree of freedom $d = 3$ (x, y and h). For the re-identification part, RGB and HSV histograms were extracted from 8×24 rectangular regions, which in turn are densely collected from a regular grid with 4 pixels spacing in vertical and 12 pixels spacing in horizontal direction. This step size is equal to half the width and length of the rectangles resulting in an overlapping representation. The final appearance feature vector x_i is obtained by concatenation of all histograms. Finally, a PCA is applied to obtain a better space for the learning of the metric. The training model for [11] is then retrained with the VIPeR [13] dataset and it uses a vector dimension of 100 after PCA.

The method incorporating Dynamic Time Warping is compared against a single shot re-identification method [11] and its straightforward multiple-shot extension which sums all the similarity scores obtained by [11]. In the rest of the section, we will refer respectively to these three algorithms as *DTW Multiple-Shot*, *Single Shot* and *Simple Multiple-Shot*. The evaluation process is as follows. A pedestrian observation is tagged in a single frame, and the tracker is started with a fixed time window $t = 20s$. The tracklet that includes this observation is designated T_r, and the other tracklets in this window are ranked in order of association. Then, we report the rank of that tracklet which truly represents this pedestrian. However, if the rank is not rank 1, we re-initialize (i.e. re-tag) the correct tracklet, so as not to unduly penalise the method. So ideally, an on-line Tag and Tracker which perfectly satisfies the Tag and Track requirement for a network of cameras will have a rank 1 for each tracklet association.

This evaluation process (tracklet re-identification ranking) for a Tag and Track problem is seen as an extension of Cumulative Matching Characteristics (CMC) [13] used in the evaluation of pedestrian recognition methods with different viewpoints which plots the recognition percentage against the ranking. In the tracklet re-identification evaluation, the height of the bar indicates the ranking of the true tracklet, so a height of 1 indicates a perfect match and higher rankings indicate progressively poorer matching. The results are not displayed as percentages (as in CMC curves) because the number of candidates is not fixed and in fact depends on the number of tracklets generated by the tracker. Consequently, Fig. 3 shows that the DTW Multiple-Shot method significantly outperforms the Single Shot and Simple Multiple-Shot methods and is able to track the target from the first frame tagged until the end of the

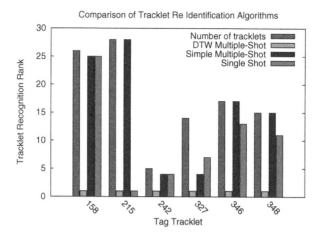

Fig. 3. Comparison of the three tracklet re-identification methods: DTW Multiple-Shot (ours), Single Shot and Simple Multiple-Shot. The JNNSF multiple target tracker was able to build automatically seven independent tracklets (158, 215, 242, 327, 346, 348 and 374) corresponding to the tracked target (plus many others corresponding to other people). The number of tracklets corresponds to the total number of candidate tracklets generated by the JNNSF tracker in a time window of $t = 20s$ and it also represents the worse possible ranking, the best being 1. Our method outperformed the others and is able to track the tagged target from the beginning to the end of the scene.

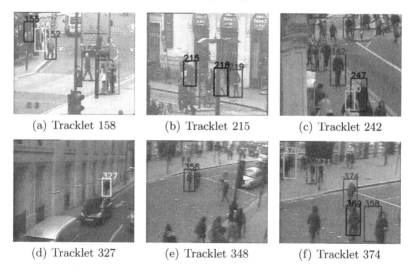

(a) Tracklet 158   (b) Tracklet 215   (c) Tracklet 242

(d) Tracklet 327   (e) Tracklet 348   (f) Tracklet 374

Fig. 4. An illustrative time sequence to show that the Tag and Track algorithm is able to link tracklets in a challenging scenario: it first links tracklets 158 and 215, (a) and (b) from the same camera after significant occlusion and challenging camera move. Then it also links tracklets between different camera (i.e. tracklet 215, 242 and 327, (b)-(d)) and also links tracklets after occlusion when the camera is moving (i.e. tracklet 348 and 374, (e) and (f)).

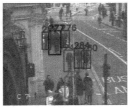

Fig. 5. In this illustrative example, tracklet 242 is reliably built within the crowds from the entrance of the target to the field of view (FOV) of this camera (C7) until the target leaves the FOV. Note how the position and zoom of the camera is changing all the time.

sequence. Although the results against the Single Shot method were expected, the comparison against the Simple Multiple-Shot method shows that extending a Single Shot method is not straightforward in a challenging dataset with crowds and moving cameras, and in fact Simple Multiple Shots provides worse results than the Single Shot.

As it has been seen for the Single Shot and even for the Simple Multiple-Shot approach, a comparison which is based purely on appearance features is not discriminative enough to perform robust tracklet re-identification. This is due not only to very low variability in the colour space of the different people but particularly to lack of structural information within tracklets. To overcome that, the process of appearance based re-identification has been extended by taking into account the temporal structure of tracklets. As a result, the proposed DTW Multiple-Shot method proves to be significantly more effective than the other two basic approaches, achieving first-rank classification in all cases.

An example of tracklets association is given in Fig. 4 to illustrate the ability of the approach to deal with challenging situations.

5   Conclusion

This paper has presented a novel tracker to address the Tag and Track problem in a network of PTZ cameras based on three main components: a backgroundless people detector, a multi-target tracker and a multiple shots re-identification technique. In addition, a new methodology to compare Tag and Track tracking in a network of cameras is introduced. Finally, experiments are conducted on a new type of dataset (non-overlapping PTZ camera network with zoom motions, both smoothly and abruptly) where the algorithm presented shows very good results mainly due to the introduction of the Dynamic Time Warping distance in the re-identification method.

As future work, results can be improved along three different axes: human detection in crowds (usage of part based detectors), re-identification (combine DTW distance with [15] which recently shows better results than [11]) and use of motion in a fully automatic system for a network of PTZ cameras.

Acknowledgements. The first author is grateful to Roke Manor Research for their financial and technical support. The authors are grateful to the Seventh Framework Programme 'ADDPRIV' (No. 261653) which partly funded this work.

References

1. Rodriguez, M., Ali, S., Kanade, T.: Tracking in unstructured crowded scenes. In: 12th International Conference on Computer Vision, pp. 1389–1396. IEEE (2009)
2. Dalal, N., Triggs, B.: Histograms of oriented gradients for human detection. In: CVPR, vol. 1, p. 886 (2005)
3. Wu, B., Nevatia, R.: Detection and tracking of multiple, partially occluded humans by bayesian combination of edgelet based part detectors. International Journal of Computer Vision 75(2), 247–266 (2007)
4. Felzenszwalb, P., Girshick, R., McAllester, D., Ramanan, D.: Object detection with discriminatively trained part based models. IEEE Transactions on Pattern Analysis and Machine Intelligence 32, 1627–1645 (2009)
5. Huang, C., Nevatia, R.: High performance object detection by collaborative learning of joint ranking of granule features. In: CVPR, pp. 41–48 (2010)
6. Duan, G., Ai, H., Lao, S.: A Structural Filter Approach to Human Detection. In: Daniilidis, K., Maragos, P., Paragios, N. (eds.) ECCV 2010, Part VI. LNCS, vol. 6316, pp. 238–251. Springer, Heidelberg (2010)
7. Ali, S., Shah, M.: Floor Fields for Tracking in High Density Crowd Scenes. In: Forsyth, D., Torr, P., Zisserman, A. (eds.) ECCV 2008, Part II. LNCS, vol. 5303, pp. 1–14. Springer, Heidelberg (2008)
8. Benfold, B., Reid, I.: Stable multi-target tracking in real-time surveillance video. In: Computer Vision and Pattern Recognition, pp. 3457–3464 (2011)
9. Kuo, C., Nevatia, R.: How does person identity recognition help multi-person tracking? In: CVPR, pp. 1217–1224. IEEE (2011)
10. Doretto, G., Sebastian, T., Tu, P., Rittscher, J.: Appearance-based person reidentification in camera networks. Journal of Ambient Intelligence and Humanized Computing 2, 127–151 (2010)
11. Dikmen, M., Akbas, E., Huang, T.S., Ahuja, N.: Pedestrian Recognition with a Learned Metric. In: Kimmel, R., Klette, R., Sugimoto, A. (eds.) ACCV 2010, Part IV. LNCS, vol. 6495, pp. 501–512. Springer, Heidelberg (2011)
12. Bar-Shalom, Y., Li, X.: Multitarget-multisensor tracking: principles and techniques. Yaakov Bar-Shalom (1995)
13. Gray, D., Tao, H.: Viewpoint Invariant Pedestrian Recognition with an Ensemble of Localized Features. In: Forsyth, D., Torr, P., Zisserman, A. (eds.) ECCV 2008, Part I. LNCS, vol. 5302, pp. 262–275. Springer, Heidelberg (2008)
14. Rabiner, L., Juang, B.H.: Fundamentals of Speech Recognition. Prentice-Hall, Inc. (1993)
15. Tatsuo Kozakaya, S.I., Kubota, S.: Random ensemble metrics for object recognition. In: IEEE International Conference on Computer Vision (2011)

Re-identification with RGB-D Sensors

Igor Barros Barbosa[1,3], Marco Cristani[1,2], Alessio Del Bue[1],
Loris Bazzani[1], and Vittorio Murino[1]

[1] Pattern Analysis and Computer Vision (PAVIS),
Istituto Italiano di Tecnologia (IIT), Via Morego 30, 16163 Genova, Italy
[2] Dipartimento di Informatica, University of Verona,
Strada Le Grazie 15, 37134 Verona, Italy
[3] Université de Bourgogne, 720 Avenue de lEurope, 71200 Le Creusot, France

Abstract. People re-identification is a fundamental operation for any multi-camera surveillance scenario. Until now, it has been performed by exploiting primarily appearance cues, hypothesizing that the individuals cannot change their clothes. In this paper, we relax this constraint by presenting a set of 3D soft-biometric cues, being insensitive to appearance variations, that are gathered using RGB-D technology. The joint use of these characteristics provides encouraging performances on a benchmark of 79 people, that have been captured in different days and with different clothing. This promotes a novel research direction for the re-identification community, supported also by the fact that a new brand of affordable RGB-D cameras have recently invaded the worldwide market.

Keywords: Re-identification, RGB-D sensors, Kinect.

1 Introduction

The task of person re-identification (re-id) consists in recognizing an individual in different locations over a set of non-overlapping camera views. It represents a fundamental task for heterogeneous video surveillance applications, especially for modeling long-term activities inside large and structured environments, such as airports, museums, shopping malls, etc. In most of the cases, re-id approaches rely on appearance-based only techniques, in which it is assumed that individuals do not change their clothing within the observation period [1–3]. This hypothesis represents a very strong restriction, since it constraints re-id methods to be applied under a limited temporal range (reasonably, in the order of minutes).

In this paper we remove this restriction, presenting a new approach of person re-id that uses soft biometrics cues as features. In general, soft biometrics cues have been exploited in different contexts, either to aid facial recognition [4], used as features in security surveillance solutions [5, 6] or also for person recognition under a bag of words policy [7]. In [4] soft biometrics cues are the size of limbs, which were manually measured. The approaches in [5–7] are based on data coming from 2D cameras and extract soft biometrics cues such as gender, ethnicity, clothing, etc.

A. Fusiello et al. (Eds.): ECCV 2012 Ws/Demos, Part I, LNCS 7583, pp. 433–442, 2012.
© Springer-Verlag Berlin Heidelberg 2012

At the best of our knowledge, 3D soft biometric features for re-identification have been employed only in [4], but in that case the scenario is strongly supervised and needs a complete cooperation of the user to take manual measures. In contrast, a viable soft biometrics system should mostly deal with subjects without requiring strong collaboration from them, in order to extend its applicability to more practical scenarios.

In our case, the cues are extracted from range data which are computed using RGB-D cameras. Recently, novel RGB-D camera sensors as the *Microsoft Kinect* and *Asus Xtion PRO*, both manufactured using the techniques developed by PrimeSense [8], provided to the community a new method of acquiring depth information in a fast and affordable way. This drove researchers to use RGB-D cameras in different fields of applications, such as pose estimation [9] and object recognition [10], to quote a few. In our opinion, re-id can be extended to novel scenarios by exploiting this novel technology, allowing to overcome the constraint of analyzing people that do not change their clothes.

In particular, our aim is to extract a set of features computed directly on the range measurements given by the sensor. Such features are related to specific anthropometric measurements computed automatically from the person body. In more detail, we introduce two distinct subsets of features. The first subset represents cues computed from the fitted skeleton to depth data i.e. the Euclidean distance between selected body parts such as legs, arms and the overall height. The second subset contains features computed on the surface given by the range data. They come in the form of geodesic distances computed from a predefined set of joints (e.g. from torso to right hip). This latest measure gives an indication of the curvature (and, by approximation, of the size) of specific regions of the body.

After analyzing the effectiveness of each feature separately and performing a pruning stage aimed at removing not influent cues, we studied how such features have to be weighted in order to maximize the re-identification performance. We obtained encouraging re-id results on a pool of 79 people, acquired under different times and across intervals of days. This promotes our approach and in general the idea of performing re-id with 3D soft biometric cues extracted from RGB-D cameras.

The remaining of the paper is organized as follows. Section 2 briefly presents the re-identification literature. Section 3 details our approach followed by Section 4 that shows experimental results. Finally, Section 5 concludes the paper, envisaging some future perspectives.

2   State of the Art

Most of the re-identification approaches build on appearance-based features [1, 11, 3] and this prevents from focusing on re-id scenarios where the clothing may change. Few approaches constrain the re-id operative conditions by simplifying the problem to temporal reasoning. They actually use the information on the layout distribution of cameras and the temporal information in order to prune away some candidates in the gallery set [12].

The adoption of 3D body information in the re-identification problem was first introduced by [13] where a coarse and rigid 3D body model was fitted to different pedestrians. Given such 3D localization, the person silhouette can be related given the different orientations of the body as viewed from different cameras. Then, the registered data are used to perform appearance-based re-identification. Differently, in our case we manage genuine soft biometric cues of a body which is truly non-rigid and also disregarding an appearance based approach. Such possibility is given by nowadays technology that allows to extract reliable anatomic cues from depth information provided by a range sensor.

In general, the methodological approach to re-identification can be divided into two groups: learning-based and direct strategies. Learning based methods split a re-id dataset into two sets: training and test [1, 3]. The training set is used for learning features and strategies for combining features while the test dataset is used for validation. Direct strategies [11] are simple feature extractors. Usually, learning-based strategies are strongly time-consuming (considering the training and testing steps), but more effective than direct ones. Under this taxonomy, our proposal can be defined as a learning-based strategy.

3   Our Approach

Our re-identification approach has two distinct phases. First, a particular signature is computed from the range data of each subject. Such signature is a composition of several soft biometric cues extracted from the depth data acquired with a RGB-D sensor. In the second phase, these signatures are matched against the test subjects from the gallery set. A learning stage, computed beforehand, explains how each single feature has to be weighted when combined with the others. A feature with high weight means that it is useful for obtaining good re-identification performances.

3.1   First Stage: Signature Extraction

The first step processes the data acquired from a RGB-D camera such as the Kinect. In particular, this sensor uses a structured light based infrared patterns [8] that illuminates the scene/objects. Thus the system obtains a depth map of the scene by measuring the pattern distortion created by the 3D relief of the object. When RGB-D cameras are used with the *OpenNI* framework [14], it is possible to use the acquired depth map to segment & track human bodies, estimate the human pose, and perform metric 3D scene reconstruction. In our case, the information used is given by the segmented point-cloud of a person, the positions of the fifteen body joints and the estimation of the floor plane. Although the person depth map and pose are given by the *OpenNI* software libraries, the segmentation of the floor required an initial pre-processing using RANSAC to fit a plane to the ground. Additionally, a mesh was generated from the person point cloud using the "Greedy Projection" method [15].

Before focusing on the signature extraction, a preliminary study has been performed by examining a set of 121 features on a dataset of 79 individuals, each captured in 4 different days (see more information on the dataset in Sec. 4). These features can be partitioned in two groups: the first contains the *skeleton-based features*, i.e., those cues which are based on the exhaustive combination of distances among joints, distances between the floor plane and all the possible joints. The second group contains the *Surface-based features*, i.e., the geodesic distances on the mesh surface computed from different joints pairs. In order to determine the most relevant features, a feature selection stage evaluates the performance on the re-identification task of each single cue, one at a time, independently. In particular, as a measure of the re-id accuracy, we evaluated the normalized area under curve (nAUC) of the cumulative matching curve (CMC) discarding those features which resulted equivalent to perform a random choice of the correct match (see more information on these classification measures on Sec. 4).

The results after such pruning stage was a set of 10 features:

- **Skeleton-based features**
  - d_1: Euclidean distance between floor and head
  - d_2: Ratio between torso and legs
  - d_3: Height estimate
  - d_4: Euclidean distance between floor and neck
  - d_5: Euclidean distance between neck and left shoulder
  - d_6: Euclidean distance between neck and right shoulder
  - d_7: Euclidean distance between torso center and right shoulder
- **Surface-based features**
  - d_8: Geodesic distance between torso center and left shoulder
  - d_9: Geodesic distance between torso center and left hip
  - d_{10}: Geodesic distance between torso center and right hip

Some of the features based on the distance from the floor are illustrated in Fig. 1 together with the joints localization on the body. In particular, the second feature (ratio between torso and legs) is computed according to the following equation:

$$d_2 = \frac{mean(d_5 + d_6)}{mean(d_{floorLhip} + d_{floorRhip})} \cdot (d_1)^{-1} \qquad (1)$$

The computation of the (approximated) geodesic distances, i.e., *Torso to left shoulder, torso to left hip* and *torso to right hip*, is given by the following steps. First, the selected joints pairs, which are normally not lying onto the point cloud, are projected towards the respective closest points in depth. This generates a starting and ending point on the surface where it is possible to initialize an $A^\star$ algorithm computing the minimum path over the point cloud (Fig. 2). Since the torso is usually recovered by the RGB-D sensor with higher precision, the computed geodesic features should be also reliable.

As a further check on the 10 selected features, we verified the accuracy by manually measuring the features on a restricted set of subjects. At the end, we found out that higher precision was captured especially in the features related to

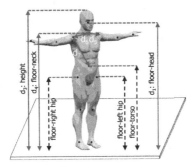

Fig. 1. Distances employed for building the soft-biometric features (in black), and some of the soft biometric features (in green). It is important to notice that the joints are not localized in the outskirt of the point-cloud, but, in most of the cases, in the proximities of the real articulations of the human body.

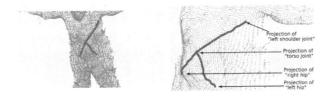

Fig. 2. Geodesic features: the red line represents the path found by A^* between *torso to left shoulder, torso to left hip* and *torso to right hip*

the height ($d_1, ..., d_4$), while other features were slightly more noisy. In general, all these features are well-suited for an indoor usage, in which people do not wear heavy clothes that might hide the human body aspects.

3.2 Second Stage: Signature Matching

This section illustrates how the selected features can be jointly employed in the re-id problem. In the literature, a re-id technique is usually evaluated considering two sets of personal ID signatures: a gallery set A and a probe set B.

The evaluation consists in associating each ID signature of the probe set B to a corresponding ID signature in the gallery set A. For the sake of clarity, let us suppose to have N different ID signatures (each one representing a different individual, so N different individuals) in the probe set and the same occurs in the gallery set. All the N subjects in the probe are present in the gallery. For evaluating the performance of a re-id technique, the most used measure is the Cumulative Matching Curve (CMC) [1], which models the mean probability that whatever probe signature is correctly matched in the first T ranked gallery individuals, where the ranking is given by evaluating the distances between ID signatures in ascending order.

In our case, each ID signature is composed by F features (in our case, $F = 10$), and each feature has a numerical value. Let us then define the distance between corresponding features as the squared difference between them. For each feature, we obtain a $N \times N$ distance matrix. However such matrix is biased towards features with higher measured values leading to a problem of heterogeneity of the measures. Thus, if a feature such as the height is measured, it would count more w.r.t. other features whose range of values is more compact (e.g. the distance between neck and left shoulder). To avoid this problem, we normalize all the features to a zero mean and unitary variance. We use the data from the gallery set to compute the mean value of each feature as well as the feature variance.

Given the normalized $N \times N$ distance matrix, we now have to surrogate those distances into a single distance matrix, obtaining thus a final CMC curve. The naive way to integrate them out would be to just average the matrices. Instead, we propose to utilize a weighted sum of the distance matrices. Let us define the set of weight w_i for $i = 1, ..., F$ that represents the importance of the i−th feature: the higher the weight, the more important is the feature. Since tuning those weights is usually hard, we propose a *quasi-exhaustive* learning strategy, i.e., we explore the weight space (from 0 to 1 with step 0.01) in order to select the weights that maximize the nAUC score. In the experiments, we report the values of those weights and compare this strategy with the average baseline.

4   Experiments

In this section, we describe first how we built the experimental dataset and how we formalised the re-id protocol. Then, an extensive validation is carried forward over the test dataset in different conditions.

4.1   Database Creation

Our dataset is composed by four different groups of data. The first "Collaborative" group has been obtained by recording 79 people with a frontal view, walking slowly, avoiding occlusions and with stretched arms. This happened in an indoor scenario, where the people were at least 2 meters away from the camera. This scenario represents a collaborative setting, the only one that we considered in these experiments. The second ("Walking") and third ("Walking2") groups of data are composed by frontal recordings of the same 79 people walking normally while entering the lab where they normally work. The fourth group ("Backwards") is a back view recording of the people walking away from the lab. Since all the acquisitions have been performed in different days, there is no guarantee that visual aspects like clothing or accessories will be kept constant. Figure 3 shows the computed meshes from different people during the recording of the four different sessions, together with some statistics about the collected features.

From each acquisition, a single frame was automatically selected for the computation of the biometric features. This selection uses the frame with the best

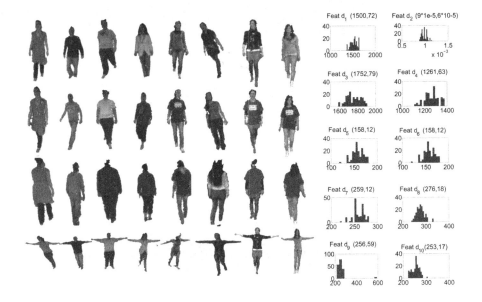

Fig. 3. Illustration of the different groups in the recorded data, rows from top to bottom: "Walking", "Walking2", "Backwards" and "Collaborative". Note that people changed their clothings during the acquisitions in different days. On the right, statistics of the "Walking" dataset: for each feature, the histogram is shown; in the parenthesis, its mean value (in cm, except d_2) and standard deviation.

confidence of tracked skeleton joints[1], which is closest to the camera and it was not cropped by the sensors fields of view. This represents the frame with the highest joints tracking confidence which in most of the cases was approximately 2.5 meters away from the camera.

After that, the mesh for each subject was computed and the 10 soft biometric cues have been extracted using both skeleton and geodesics information.

4.2 Semi-cooperative re-id

Given the four datasets, we have built a semi-collaborative scenario, where the gallery set was composed by the ID signatures of the "Collaborative" setting, and the test data was the "Walking 2" set. The CMCs related to each feature are portrayed in Fig. 4: they show how each feature is able to capture discriminative information of the analyzed subjects. Fig. 5 shows the normalized AUC of each features. Notice that the features associated to the height of the person are very meaningful, as so the ratio between torso and legs.

The results of Fig. 5 highlights that the nAUC over the different features spans from 52.8% to 88.1%. Thus, all of them contributes to have better re-identification

---

[1] Such confidence score is a byproduct of the skeleton fitting algorithm.

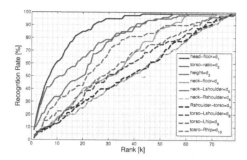

Fig. 4. Single-feature CMCs — "Collaborative" VS "Walking 2" (best viewed in colors)

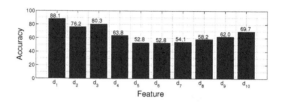

Fig. 5. Area under the curve for each feature (the numbering here follows the features enumeration presented in Sec. 3) —"Collaborative" VS "Walking 2". The numbers over the bars indicate the numerical nAUC values of the different features.

results. To investigate how their combination helps in re-id, we exploit the learning strategy proposed in Sec. 3.2. Such weights w_i are learned once using a different dataset than the one used during testing. The obtained weights are: $w_1 = 0.24, w_2 = 0.17, w_3 = 0.18, w_4 = 0.09, w_5 = 0.02, w_6 = 0.02, w_7 = 0.03, w_8 = 0.05, w_9 = 0.08, w_{10} = 0.12$. The weights mirrors the nUAC obtained for each feature independently (Fig. 5): the most relevant ones are d_1 (Euclidean distance between floor and head), d_2 (Ratio between torso and legs), d_3 (Height estimate), and d_{10} (Geodesic distance between torso center and right hip). In Fig. 6, we compare this strategy with a baseline: the average case where $w_i = 1/F$ for each i. It is clear that the learning strategy gives better results (nAUC= 88.88%) with respect to the baseline (nAUC= 76.19%) and also the best feature (nAUC= 88.10%) that correspods to d_1 in Fig. 5. For the rest of the experiments the learning strategy is adopted.

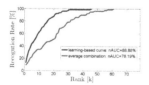

Fig. 6. Compilation of final CMC curves —"Collaborative" - "Walking 2"

4.3   Non-cooperative re-id

Non-cooperative scenarios consist of the "walking", "walking2" and "backwards" datasets. We generate different experiments by combining cooperative and non-cooperative scenarios as gallery and probe sets. Table 1 reports the nAUC score given the trials we carried out. The non-cooperative scenarios gave rise to higher performances than the cooperative ones. The reason is that, in the collaborative acquisition, people tended to move in a very unnatural and constrained way, thus originating biased measurements towards a specific posture. In the non-cooperative setting this did not clearly happen.

Table 1. nAUC scores for the different re-id scenarios

Gallery	Probe	nAUC
Collab.	Walking	90.11 %
Collab.	Walking 2	88.88 %
Collab.	Backwards	85.64 %
Walking	Walking 2	91.76 %
Walking	Backwards	88.72%
Walking 2	Backwards	87.73 %

5   Conclusions

In this paper, we presented a person re-identification approach which exploits soft-biometrics features, extracted from range data, investigating collaborative and non-collaborative settings. Each feature has a particular discriminative expressiveness with height and torso/legs ratio being the most informative cues. Re-identification by 3D soft biometric information seems to be a very fruitful research direction: other than the main advantage of a soft biometric policy, i.e., that of being to some extent invariant to clothing, many are the other reasons: from one side, the availability of precise yet affordable RGB-D sensors encourage the study of robust software solutions toward the creation of real surveillance system. On the other side, the classical appearance-based re-id literature is characterized by powerful learning approaches that can be easily embedded in the 3D situation. Our research will be focused on this last point, and on the creation of a larger 3D non-collaborative dataset.

References

1. Gray, D., Tao, H.: Viewpoint Invariant Pedestrian Recognition with an Ensemble of Localized Features. In: Forsyth, D., Torr, P., Zisserman, A. (eds.) ECCV 2008, Part I. LNCS, vol. 5302, pp. 262–275. Springer, Heidelberg (2008)
2. Farenzena, M., Bazzani, L., Perina, A., Murino, V., Cristani, M.: Person re-identification by symmetry-driven accumulation of local features. In: CVPR (2010)

3. Zheng, W.S., Gong, S., Xiang, T.: Person re-identification by probabilistic relative distance comparison. In: 2011 IEEE Conference on Computer Vision and Pattern Recognition (CVPR), pp. 649–656. IEEE (2011)
4. Velardo, C., Dugelay, J.-L.: Improving identification by pruning: a case study on face recognition and body soft biometric. Eurecom, Tech. Rep. EURECOM+3593 (January 2012)
5. Wang, Y.-F., Chang, E.Y., Cheng, K.P.: A video analysis framework for soft biometry security surveillance. In: Proceedings of the third ACM International Workshop on Video Surveillance & Sensor Networks, VSSN 2005, pp. 71–78 (2005)
6. Demirkus, M., Garg, K.: Automated person categorization for video surveillance using soft biometrics. In: Proc of SPIE, Biometric Technology (2010)
7. Dantcheva, A., Dugelay, J.-L., Elia, P.: Person recognition using a bag of facial soft biometrics (BoFSB). In: 2010 IEEE International Workshop on Multimedia Signal Processing, pp. 511–516. IEEE (October 2010)
8. Freedman, B., Shpunt, A., Machline, M., Ariel, Y.: US Patent - US2010/0118123 (2010)
9. Shotton, J., Fitzgibbon, A., Cook, M., Sharp, T., Finocchio, M., Moore, R., Kipman, A., Blake, A.: Real-time human pose recognition in parts from single depth images. In: CVPR 2011, pp. 1297–1304. IEEE (June 2011)
10. Bo, L., Lai, K., Ren, X., Fox, D.: Object recognition with hierarchical kernel descriptors. In: CVPR 2011, pp. 1729–1736. IEEE (June 2011)
11. Cheng, D.S., Cristani, M., Stoppa, M., Bazzani, L., Murino, V.: Custom pictorial structures for re-identification. In: British Machine Vision Conference, BMVC (2011)
12. Javed, O., Shafique, K., Rasheed, Z., Shah, M.: Modeling inter-camera space-time and appearance relationships for tracking across non-overlapping views. Comput. Vis. Image Underst. 109(2), 146–162 (2008)
13. Baltieri, D., Vezzani, R., Cucchiara, R.: SARC3D: A New 3D Body Model for People Tracking and Re-identification. In: Maino, G., Foresti, G.L. (eds.) ICIAP 2011, Part I. LNCS, vol. 6978, pp. 197–206. Springer, Heidelberg (2011)
14. OpenNI (February 2012) Openni framework@ONLINE, http://www.openni.org/
15. Marton, Z.C., Rusu, R.B., Beetz, M.: On Fast Surface Reconstruction Methods for Large and Noisy Datasets. In: Proceedings of the IEEE International Conference on Robotics and Automation (ICRA), Kobe, Japan, May 12-17 (2009)

Identity Inference: Generalizing Person Re-identification Scenarios

Svebor Karaman and Andrew D. Bagdanov

Media Integration and Communication Center
University of Florence, Viale Morgagni 65, Florence, Italy
svebor.karaman@unifi.it, bagdanov@dsi.unifi.it

Abstract. In this article we introduce the problem of identity inference as a generalization of the re-identification problem. Identity inference is applicable in situations where a large number of unknown persons must be identified without knowing *a priori* that groups of test images represent the same individual. Standard single- and multi-shot person re-identification are special cases of our formulation. We present an approach to solving identity inference problems using a Conditional Random Field (CRF) to model identity inference as a labeling problem in the CRF. The CRF model ensures that the final labeling gives similar labels to detections that are similar in feature space, and is flexible enough to incorporate constraints in the temporal and spatial domains. Experimental results are given on the ETHZ dataset. Our approach yields state-of-the-art performance for the multi-shot re-identification task and promising results for more general identity inference problems.

1 Introduction

Person re-identification is traditionally defined as the recognition of an individual at different times, over different camera views and/or locations, and considering a large number of candidate individuals. It is a standard component of multi-camera surveillance systems as it is a way to associate multiple observations of the same individual over time. Particularly in scenarios in which the long-term behavior of persons must be characterized, accurate re-identification is essential. In realistic, wide-area surveillance scenarios such as airports, metro and train stations, re-identification systems should be capable of robustly associating a unique identity with hundreds, if not thousands, of individual observations.

Re-identification performance is usually evaluated as a retrieval problem. Given a gallery consisting of a number of known individuals and images of each, for each test image or group of test images of an unknown person the goal of re-identification is to return a ranked list of individuals from the gallery. Configurations of the re-identification problem are generally classified according to how much group structure is available in the gallery and test image sets. In a single-shot image set there is no grouping information availabled. Though there might be multiple images of an individual, there is no knowledge of which images correspond to that person. In a multi-shot image set, on the other hand, there

A. Fusiello et al. (Eds.): ECCV 2012 Ws/Demos, Part I, LNCS 7583, pp. 443–452, 2012.
© Springer-Verlag Berlin Heidelberg 2012

is explicit grouping information available. That is, it is known which images correspond to the same individual.

The classification of re-identification scenarios into multi- and single-shot configurations is useful for establishing benchmarks and standardized datasets for experimentation on person re-identification. However, these scenarios are not particularly realistic with respect to some real-world application scenarios. In video surveillance scenarios, for example, it is more common to have a few individuals of interest and to desire that all occurrences of those individuals be labeled. In this case the number of unlabeled test images to re-identify is typically much larger than the number of gallery images available.

In this article we propose a generalization of person re-identification which we call *identity inference*. The identity inference formulation is expressive enough to represent existing single- and multi-shot scenarios, while at the same time also modeling a larger class of problems not discussed in the literature. We also propose a CRF-based approach to solving identity inference problems. Our model is able to efficiently and accurately solve a broad range of identity inference problems, including existing person re-identification scenarios as well as more difficult tasks involving very many unlabeled test images.

2   Related Work

The majority of existing research on the person re-identification problem has concentrated on the development of sophisticated features for describing the visual appearance of targets. In [1] were introduced discriminative appearance-based models using Partial Least Squares (PLS) over texture, gradients and color features. The authors of [2] use an ensemble of local features learned using a boosting procedure, while in [3] the authors use a covariance matrix of features computed in a grid of overlapping cells. The SDALF descriptor introduced in [4] exploits axis symmetry and asymmetry and represents each part of a person by a weighted color histogram, maximally stable color regions and texture information from recurrent high-structured patches. In [5] the authors fit a Custom Pictorial Structure (CPS) model consisting of head, chest, thighs and legs part descriptors using color histograms and Maximally Stable Color Region (MSCR). The Global Color Context (GCC) of [6] uses a quantization of color into color words and then builds a color context modeling the self-similarity for each word using a polar grid. The Histogram Plus Epitome (HPE) approach in [15] represents a person by a global mean color histogram and recurrent local patterns through epitomic analysis.

The approaches mentioned above concentrate on feature representation and not specifically on the classification or ranking technique. And approach which does concentrate specifically on the ranking approach is the Ensemble RankSVM technique of [7], which learns a ranking SVM model to solve the single-shot re-identification problem.

We believe that in realistic scenarios many unlabeled images will be available while only few detections with known identities will be given, which is a scenario

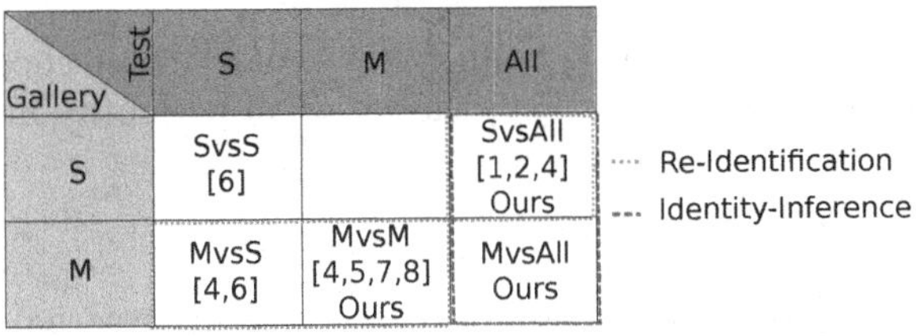

Test Gallery	S	M	All
S	SvsS [6]		SvsAll [1,2,4] Ours
M	MvsS [4,6]	MvsM [4,5,7,8] Ours	MvsAll Ours

···· Re-Identification
--- Identity-Inference

Fig. 1. Re-identification and identity-inference protocols. Though the authors of [6] use "single" to describe their test sets, they only use one image per person.

not covered by the standard classification of single- and multi-shot cases. We propose a CRF model that is able to encode a "soft grouping" property of unlabeled images. Our application of CRFs to identity inference is similar in spirit to recent work using CRFs for multi-target tracking [8]. However, to the best of our knowledge CRFs have not been directly applied to the re-identification problem and in this article we explore their use on identity inference as formulated in next section.

3   Identity Inference as Generalization of Re-identification

In this section we give a formal definition of the re-identification and identity inference problems. The literature on person re-identification covers many different configurations of gallery and test images. We consider each in turn and show how each can be represented as an instance of our definition of re-identification. A summary of the different protocols with corresponding works is given in figure 1.

Let $\mathcal{L} = \{1, \ldots N\}$ be a label set for a re-identification scenario, where each element represents a unique individual appearing in a video sequence or collection of sequences. We assume that there are a number of instances (images) of individuals from $\mathcal{L}$ detected in a video collection:

$$\mathcal{I} = \{x_i \mid i = 1 \ldots D\}.$$

We assume that each image x_i of an individual is represented by a feature vector $\mathbf{x}_i \equiv \mathbf{x}(x_i)$ and that the label corresponding to instance x_i is given by $y_i \equiv y(x_i)$.

An instance of a re-identification problem, represented as a tuple $\mathcal{R} = (\mathcal{X}, \mathcal{Z})$, is completely characterized by its gallery and test image sets ($\mathcal{X}$ and $\mathcal{Z}$, respectively). Formally, the gallery images are defined as:

$$\mathcal{X} = \{\mathcal{X}_j \mid j = 1 \ldots N\}, \text{where } \mathcal{X}_j \subset \{x \mid y(x) = j\}.$$

That is, for each individual i, a subset of all available images is chosen to form his gallery: $\mathcal{X}_i$. The set of test images is defined as:

$$\mathcal{Z} = \{\mathcal{Z}_j \mid j = 1 \ldots M\} \subset \mathcal{P}(\mathcal{I}),$$

where $\mathcal{P}$ is the powerset operator (i.e. $\mathcal{P}(I)$ is the set of all subsets of $\mathcal{I}$). We further require for all $\mathcal{Z}_j \in \mathcal{Z}$ that $x, x' \in \mathcal{Z}_j \Rightarrow y(x) = y(x')$ (sets in $\mathcal{Z}$ have homogeneous labels), and $\mathcal{Z}_j \in \mathcal{Z} \Rightarrow \mathcal{Z}_j \cap \mathcal{X}_i = \emptyset, \forall i \in \{1 \ldots N\}$ (the test and gallery sets are disjoint). A solution to an instance of a re-identification problem is a mapping from the test images $\mathcal{Z}$ to the set of all permutations of $\mathcal{L}$.

3.1   Re-identification Scenarios

Single-versus-all re-identification (SvsAll) is often referred to as simply *single-shot re-identification* or *single-versus-single* (SvsS) but could better be described as *single-versus-all* (SvsAll) [1] re-identification, see figure 1. In the SvsAll re-identification scenario a single gallery images is given for each individual, and *all remaining instances* of each individual are used for testing: $M = D - N$. Formally, a single-versus-all re-identification problem is a tuple $\mathcal{R}_{\mathrm{SvsAll}} = (\mathcal{X}, \mathcal{Z})$, where:

$$\mathcal{X}_j = \{x\} \text{ for some } x \in \{x \mid y(x) = j\}, \text{ and}$$
$$\mathcal{Z}_j = \{\{x\} \mid x \in \mathcal{I} \setminus \mathcal{X}_j \text{ and } y(x) = j\}$$

Multi-versus-single shot re-identification (MvsS) is defined using G gallery images of each person, while each of the test sets $\mathcal{Z}_j$ contains only a single image. In this case $M = N$, as there are exactly as many partial test sets $\mathcal{Z}_j$ as persons depicted in the gallery. Formally, a MvsS re-identification problem is a tuple $\mathcal{R}_{\mathrm{MvsS}} = (\mathcal{X}, \mathcal{Z})$, where:

$$\mathcal{X}_j \subset \{x \mid y(x) = j\} \text{ and } |\mathcal{X}_j| = G \; \forall j \text{ and}$$
$$\mathcal{Z}_j = \{x\} \text{ for some } x \notin \mathcal{X}_j \text{ s.t. } y(x) = j.$$

The MvsS configuration is not precisely a generalization of the SvsAll person re-identification problem in that, after selecting G gallery images for each individual, only a *single* test image is selected to form the test sets $\mathcal{Z}_j$.

Multi-versus-multi shot re-identification (MvsM) is the case in which the gallery and test sets of each person both have G images. Formally, a MvsM re-identification problem is a tuple $\mathcal{R}_{\mathrm{MvsM}} = (\mathcal{X}, \mathcal{Z})$, where:

$$\mathcal{X}_j \subset \{x \mid y(x) = j\} \text{ and } |\mathcal{X}_j| = G \; \forall j \text{ and}$$
$$\mathcal{Z}_j \subset \{x \mid y(x) = j \text{ and } x \notin \mathcal{X}_j\} \text{ and } |\mathcal{Z}_j| = G \; \forall j.$$

The goal in MvsM re-identification is to re-identify each *group* of test images, leveraging the knowledge that images in each group are all of the same individual.

3.2   Identity Inference

Identity inference addresses the problem of having *few* labeled images while desiring to label *many* unknown images without explicit knowledge that groups

---

[1] We use the SvsAll terminology as the SvsS terminology could be (mis-)interpreted as in [6] in which only a *single* image was selected for each individual in the test set.

of images represent the same individual. The formulation of the *single-versus-all* re-identification falls within the scope of identity inference, but neither the multi-versus-single nor the multi-versus-multi formulations are a generalization of this case to multiple gallery images. In the MvsS and MvsM cases the test set is either a singleton for each person (MvsS) or a group of images (MvsM) of the same size as the gallery image set for each person. Identity inference could be described as a *multi-versus-all* configuration. Formally, it is a tuple $\mathcal{R}_{\text{MvsAll}} = (\mathcal{X}, \mathcal{Z})$, where:

$$\mathcal{X}_j \subset \{x \mid y(x) = j\} \text{ and } |\mathcal{X}_j| = G \text{ and}$$
$$\mathcal{Z}_j = \{\{x\} \mid x \in \mathcal{I} \setminus \mathcal{X}_j \text{ and } y(x) = j\}$$

In instances of identity inference a set of G gallery images are chosen for each individual. Each remaining images of each individual is then used as an element of the test set without any identity grouping information. As in the SvsAll case, the test images sets are all singletons.

4   A CRF Model for Identity Inference

Conditional Random Fields (CRFs) have been used to model the statistical structure of problems such as semantic image segmentation [9], and stereo matching [10]. In this section we show how we model the identity inference problem as a minimum energy labeling problem in a CRF.

A CRF is defined by a graph $\mathcal{G} = (\mathcal{V}, \mathcal{E})$, a set of random variables $\mathcal{Y} = \{Y_j \mid j = 1 \dots |V|\}$ which represent the statistical structure of the problem being modelled, and a set of possible labels $\mathcal{L}$. The vertices $\mathcal{V}$ index the random variables in $\mathcal{Y}$ and the edges $\mathcal{E}$ encode the statistical dependence relations between the random variables. The labeling problem is then to find an assignment of labels to nodes that minimizes an energy function E over possible labelings $\mathbf{y}^* = (y_i^*)_{i=1}^{|V|}$: $\tilde{\mathbf{y}} = \arg\min_{\mathbf{y}^*} E(\mathbf{y}^*)$. The energy function $E(\mathbf{y}^*)$ is defined as:

$$E(\mathbf{y}^*) = \sum_{i \in \mathcal{V}} \phi_i(y_i^*) + \lambda \sum_{(i,j) \in \mathcal{E}} \psi_{ij}(y_i^*, y_j^*), \tag{1}$$

where $\phi_i(y_i^*)$ is a unary data potential encoding the cost of assigning label y_i^* to vertex i and $\psi_{ij}(y_i^*, y_j^*)$ is a binary smoothness potential representing the conditional cost of assigning labels y_i^* and y_j^* respectively to vertices i and j. The parameter λ in equation (1) controls the tradeoff between data and smoothness costs. Given an instance of a CRF, there exist very efficient algorithms for finding the optimal labeling $\tilde{\mathbf{y}}$ using, for example, graph cuts [11,12].

We can map an identity inference problem $\mathcal{R} = (\mathcal{X}, \mathcal{Z})$ onto a CRF by defining the vertex and edge sets $\mathcal{V}$ and $\mathcal{E}$ in terms of the gallery and test image sets defined by $\mathcal{X}$ and $\mathcal{Z}$. We have found two configurations of vertices and edges to be useful for solving identity inference problems. The first uses vertices to represent groups of images in the test set $\mathcal{Z}$ and is particularly useful for modeling MvsM re-identification problems:

$$\mathcal{V} = \bigcup_{i=1}^{N} \mathcal{Z}_i \text{ and } \mathcal{E} = \{(x_i, x_j) \mid x_i, x_j \in \mathcal{Z}_l \text{ for some } l\}.$$

The edge topology in this CRF is completely determined by the group structure as expressed by the $\mathcal{Z}_j$.

When no identity grouping information is available for the test set, as in the general identity inference case as well as in SvsAll re-identification, we instead use the following formulation of the CRF:

$$\mathcal{V} = I \text{ and } \mathcal{E} = \bigcup_{x_i \in \mathcal{V}} \{(x_i, x_j) \mid x_j \in \text{kNN}(x_i)\},$$

where the $\text{kNN}(x_i)$ maps an image to its k most similar images in feature space. The topology of this CRF formulation, in the absence of explicit group information, uses feature similarity to form connections between nodes.

The unary data potential determines the cost of assigning label y_i^* to vertex i given $\mathbf{x}(x_i)$, the observed feature representation of image x_i. It is proportional to the minimum L1-distance between the feature representation of image x_i and any gallery image of individual y_i^*. We define it as:

$$\phi_i(y_i^*) = \begin{cases} 1 & \text{if } x_i \in \mathcal{X} \text{ and } y_i^* \neq y(x_i) \\ \min_{x \in \mathcal{X}_{y_i^*}} ||\mathbf{x}(x) - \mathbf{x}(x_i)|| & \text{otherwise.} \end{cases}$$

If a vertex corresponds to a gallery image, its data potential is 1 for every incorrect label and zero for the correct one.

Without explicit neighborhood topology given by identity groups, we use the smoothness potential to encourage similar detections to share the same labels:

$$\psi_{ij}(y_i^*, y_j^*) = w_{ij} \min_{\substack{x \in \mathcal{X}_{y_i^*} \\ x' \in \mathcal{X}_{y_j^*}}} ||\mathbf{x}(x) - \mathbf{x}(x')||. \tag{2}$$

This smoothness potential ensures local consistency between labels in neighboring nodes: the more similar two labels are in terms of the available gallery images for them, the lower the cost for them to be labeled the same in the CRF. The weighting factors w_{ij} allow the smoothness potential between nodes i and j to be flexibly controlled according to the problem at hand.

5   Experimental Results

For evaluating identity inference we are especially interested in test scenarios where there are many unlabeled images of each test subject. For this reason, we selected the publicly available ETHZ [1] dataset which consists of three video sequences, because on average each person appears in more than 50 images. This dataset is also interesting because the frame number of each detection is available and can therefore be incorporated into our CRF model as a temporal constraint.

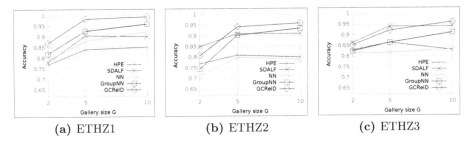

Fig. 2. MvsM re-identification accuracy. Note that these are *not* CMC curves, but are Rank-1 *classification* accuracies over varying gallery and test set sizes.

As feature representation we compute Hue-SIFT [13] features on a dense grid, quantize them to a vocabulary of 512 visual words and group them into cells of a 1×6 cell spatial pyramid [14]. In all experiments on a specific ETHZ sequence, the codebook for the visual vocabulary was learned through k-means clustering on features from the remaining two ETHZ sequences. The choice of six horizontal stripes for the spatial pyramid representation is similar to the choice made in [7]. We should note that the CRF model we propose is orthogonal to the choice of feature descriptor and most descriptors discussed in the literature could be used in our framework.

5.1   Re-identification

Here we apply our CRF framework to solve MvsM re-identification problems. In these experiments we fix $\lambda = 1$ in the energy function of equation (1) and evaluate performance for galleries varying in size over 2, 5 and 10 images per person. For each configuration, we randomly select the gallery and test images and average performance over ten trials. Note that grouping information in the test set is explicitly encoded in the CRF: edges only link test images that correspond to the same individual. Results on MvsM person re-identification are presented in figure 2. We compare our results, which we refer to as GCReID for "Graph Cut Re-Identification", with the published results of SDALF [4] and HPE [15]. The NN curve in figure 2 corresponds to labeling each test image with the nearest gallery image label without exploiting group knowledge, while the GroupNN approach use this knowledge by setting the label of the group of test images as the label of the model which distance to any of these test images is minimal.

The results in figure 2 show that, by using the CRF we can ensure a more consistent labeling especially when having a higher number of test images, thus outperforming state-of-the-art methods even though our descriptor is less sophisticated. The use of the CRF to enforce labeling consistency allows our approach to outperform simpler, ad hoc reasoning about group similarity (see the results of the GroupNN method). We also note that, while the approach of SDALF [4] computes an accumulated single descriptor from multiple gallery images, we keep the multiple appearances in our model. This, in combination with the

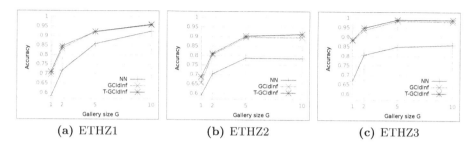

(a) ETHZ1   (b) ETHZ2   (c) ETHZ3

Fig. 3. Identity inference accuracy on ETHZ datasets

inference in our CRF framework, enables us to obtain extremely good results on the ETHZ1 dataset (figure 2a). While other approaches in the literature tend to have lower results with a growing number of persons our approach seems to be more robust in these situations.

5.2   Identity Inference

In the CRF model proposed in section 4 for identity inference in which no identity grouping information is available for the test image sets, the local neighborhood structure is determined by the K nearest neighbors to each image in feature space. For all experiments we set $K = 4$. For the general identity inference case, unlike MvsM person re-identification, we have no information about relationships between test images. We define the weights w_{ij} from equation (2) between vertices i and j in the CRF in terms of feature similarity and a temporal constraint:

$$w_{ij} = (1 - \alpha)(1 - ||\mathbf{x}(x_i) - \mathbf{x}(x_j)||) + \alpha \tau_{ij}, \tag{3}$$

where $\alpha \in [0, 1]$ is a weighting factor controlling the tradeoff between temporal and feature similarities, τ_{ij} is a temporal weighting factor defined as:

$$\tau_{ij} = \begin{cases} 1 - \frac{|f_i - f_j|}{\tau} & \text{if } |f_i - f_j| \leq \tau \\ 0 & \text{otherwise,} \end{cases} \tag{4}$$

where f_i and f_j are the frame numbers in which detections i and j occurred, respectively, and τ is a threshold limiting the temporal influence to a finite number of frames. In preliminary experiments we found $\tau = 25$ to work well for a variety of configurations and we use this temporal window in all of our reported results. Similarly, we use a value of $\alpha = 0.3$ which places more attention on similarity in feature space. The results in figure 3 are given for λ set to 5.

In identity inference, gallery images are randomly selected and *all remaining images* define the test set. Results are averaged over 10 trials as before. Using our CRF framework clearly improves accuracy over the simple NN model. The best configuration is T-GCIDInf which uses feature similarity-weighted edges with temporal constraints, yielding an average improvement of 15% over the

Fig. 4. Identity inference results (SvsAll). First row: test image, second row: incorrect NN result, third row: correct result given by GCIdInf.

three datasets with respect to nearest-neighbor labeling. Our approach permits us to label a large number of unknown images using only few gallery images for each person. For example, on the ETHZ3 dataset we are able to correctly label 1596 out of 1706 test images using only 2 model images per person. The robustness of our method with respect to occlusions and illumination changes is shown in the qualitative results shown in figure 4. The CRF approach proposed yields correct labels even in strongly occluded cases thanks to the neighborhood edges connecting it to less occluded, yet similar, images.

6   Discussion

In this paper we have introduced the identity inference problem which we propose as a generalization of the standard person re-identification problem described in the literature. Identity inference can be thought of as a generalization of the single-versus-all shot case of person re-identification, and at the same time as a relaxation of the multi-versus-multi shot case. Instances of identity inference problems do not require hard knowledge about relationships between test images (e.g. that they correspond to the same individual). We have also proposed a CRF-based approach to solving identity inference problems. Our solution uses feature space and temporal (when available) similarity to define the neighborhood topology in the CRF. Our experimental results show that the CRF approach can efficiently solve standard re-identification tasks, achieving classification performance comparable to state-of-the-art Rank-1 results in the literature. The CRF model can also be used to solve more general identity inference problems in which no hard grouping information and very many test images are present in the test set. Our current work concentrates on exploring more powerful descriptors and more realistic configurations for identity inference in the real world. To this end we are also working on developing a multi-camera dataset for identity inference.

References

1. Schwartz, W., Davis, L.: Learning discriminative appearance-based models using partial least squares. In: Proceedings of SIBGRAPI, pp. 322–329. IEEE (2009)
2. Gray, D., Tao, H.: Viewpoint Invariant Pedestrian Recognition with an Ensemble of Localized Features. In: Forsyth, D., Torr, P., Zisserman, A. (eds.) ECCV 2008, Part I. LNCS, vol. 5302, pp. 262–275. Springer, Heidelberg (2008)
3. Bak, S., Corvee, E., Bremond, F., Thonnat, M.: Multiple-shot human re-identification by mean riemannian covariance grid. In: Proceedings of AVSS, pp. 179–184 (2011)
4. Farenzena, M., Bazzani, L., Perina, A., Murino, V., Cristani, M.: Person re-identification by symmetry-driven accumulation of local features. In: Proceedings of CVPR, pp. 2360–2367 (2010)
5. Cheng, D.S., Cristani, M., Stoppa, M., Bazzani, L., Murino, V.: Custom pictorial structures for re-identification. In: Procdings of BMVC (2011)
6. Cai, Y., Pietikäinen, M.: Person Re-identification Based on Global Color Context. In: Koch, R., Huang, F. (eds.) ACCV 2010 Workshops, Part I. LNCS, vol. 6468, pp. 205–215. Springer, Heidelberg (2011)
7. Prosser, B., Zheng, W.-S., Gong, S., Xiang, T.: Person re-identification by support vector ranking. In: Proceedings of BMVC (2010)
8. Yang, B., Nevatia, R.: An online learned crf model for multi-target tracking. In: Proceedings of CVPR (2012)
9. Boix, X., Gonfaus, J., van de Weijer, J., Bagdanov, A., Serrat, J., Gonzàlez, J.: Harmony potentials. International Journal of Computer Vision, 1–20 (2012)
10. Scharstein, D., Szeliski, R.: A taxonomy and evaluation of dense two-frame stereo correspondence algorithms. International Journal of Computer Vision 47, 7–42 (2002)
11. Kolmogorov, V., Zabin, R.: What energy functions can be minimized via graph cuts? IEEE Transactions on Pattern Analysis and Machine Intelligence 26, 147–159 (2004)
12. Szeliski, R., Zabih, R., Scharstein, D., Veksler, O., Kolmogorov, V., Agarwala, A., Tappen, M., Rother, C.: A comparative study of energy minimization methods for markov random fields with smoothness-based priors. IEEE Transactions on Pattern Analysis and Machine Intelligence 30, 1068–1080 (2008)
13. van de Weijer, J., Schmid, C.: Coloring Local Feature Extraction. In: Leonardis, A., Bischof, H., Pinz, A. (eds.) ECCV 2006, Part II. LNCS, vol. 3952, pp. 334–348. Springer, Heidelberg (2006)
14. Lazebnik, S., Schmid, C., Ponce, J.: Beyond bags of features: Spatial pyramid matching for recognizing natural scene categories. In: Proceedings of CVPR, vol. 2, pp. 2169–2178. IEEE (2006)
15. Bazzani, L., Cristani, M., Perina, A., Murino, V.: Multiple-shot person reidentification by chromatic and epitomic analyses. Pattern Recognition Letters (2011)

A General Method for Appearance-Based People Search Based on Textual Queries

Riccardo Satta, Giorgio Fumera, and Fabio Roli

Dept. of Electrical and Electronic Engineering, University of Cagliari
Piazza d'Armi, 09123 Cagliari, Italy
{riccardo.satta,fumera,roli}@diee.unica.it

Abstract. Person re-identification consists of recognising a person appearing in different video sequences, using an image as a query. We propose a general approach to extend appearance-based re-identification systems, enabling also textual queries describing clothing appearance (e.g., "person wearing a white shirt and checked blue shorts"). This functionality can be useful, e.g., in forensic video analysis, when textual descriptions of individuals of interest given by witnesses are available, instead of images. Our approach is based on turning any given appearance descriptor into a dissimilarity-based one. This allows us to build detectors of the clothing characteristics of interest using supervised classifiers trained in a dissimilarity space, independently on the original descriptor. Our approach is evaluated using the descriptors of three different re-identification methods, on a benchmark data set.

1 Introduction

Person re-identification is a computer vision task for video-surveillance applications. It consists of recognising a person appearing in different video sequences taken by one or more cameras, using an image as a query. Since the face region has usually a small size, and people are often not in frontal pose, face recognition systems can not be applied. Thus, methods proposed so far exploit clothing appearance [1], or *soft* biometrics like gait [2]. In this paper we consider a similar task that we call "appearance-based people search". It consists of finding, among a set of images of individuals, the ones relevant to a *textual* query describing clothing appearance of an individual of interest. Thus, it differs from person re-identification, where the query is an *image* of the person of interest. This can be useful in applications like forensics video analysis, where a textual description of the individual of interest given by a witness can be available, instead of an image.

To our knowledge, an analogous task ("person attribute search") was considered so far only in [3,4]. In [3] the basic idea of building a specific detector for each attribute of interest (e.g., the presence of beard and eyeglasses, the dominant colour of torso and legs, etc.), was proposed, and a specific implementation was developed, mainly for face attributes. The work in [4] focused on the following attributes: gender, hair/hat colour, clothing colour, and bag

A. Fusiello et al. (Eds.): ECCV 2012 Ws/Demos, Part I, LNCS 7583, pp. 453–461, 2012.

(if any) position and colour, and a generative model was proposed to build the corresponding descriptors. Both works considered only torso and legs colour as clothing appearance attributes.

In this work, we propose instead a general approach to extend appearance-based person re-identification systems, exploiting the *same* descriptors of clothing appearance to enable also the people search functionality based on a textual query. Our approach relies on dissimilarity-based descriptors, which can be obtained using the Multiple Component Dissimilarity (MCD) framework of [5] from *any* appearance descriptor that uses a body part subdivision and a multiple instance representation. Such kind of descriptors is used in most of the current re-identification methods. In [5], MCD dissimilarity descriptors were exploited to speed up the task of person re-identification. In this paper we show that they can also be exploited to implement the appearance-based people search task. In this context, the advantage of dissimilarity descriptors is that they allow one to build detectors of the attributes of interest (e.g., the presence of a colour in the torso) using supervised classifiers, without requiring techniques tailored to the specific, original descriptors, as in the approaches of [3,4].

The MCD framework is summarised in Sect. 2. Our approach to implement people search is described in Sect. 3, and is experimentally evaluated in Sect. 4 on a benchmark data set for person re-identification.

2   MCD-Based Appearance Descriptors

The descriptors used by most appearance-based re-identification methods (1) subdivide human body into parts, and (2) represent each body part as a bag of low-level local features (e.g., random patches, or SIFT points) [6]. In [5] it was shown that any such descriptor can be turned into a dissimilarity one, which consists of a vector of dissimilarity values to a predefined set of visual prototypes. The aim of the MCD framework was to reduce processing time for real-time applications. In Sect. 3 we will show how MCD can also be exploited for the people search task. Here we summarise the procedure for building MCD descriptors.

A generic appearance descriptor $\mathbf{I}$ of an individual is a sequence $\{I_m\}_{m=1}^{M}$ of sets of "components", each one associated to one of the $M \geq 1$ body parts. Each I_m is a bag of local feature vectors $\{\mathbf{i}_m^k\}_{k=1}^{n_m}$.

Let $\mathcal{I}$ be a *gallery* of appearance descriptors (see Fig. 1-a). To represent them in a *dissimilarity space* [7], a set of "visual" prototypes $\mathbf{P}_m = \{P_{m,p}\}_{p=1}^{N_m}$, is first constructed for each body part. Prototypes correspond to low-level visual characteristics (e.g., a certain distribution of colours) shared by several descriptors of $\mathcal{I}$. Then, for each $\mathbf{I} \in \mathcal{I}$, a dissimilarity descriptor $\mathbf{i}^D$ is created, as a vector of dissimilarity values between each $I_m \in \mathbf{I}$, and the corresponding prototypes $\mathbf{P}_m$. Note that, contrary to the original dissimilarity-based approach [7], in MCD prototypes are representative of *local* components of a given body part, instead of the whole part.

Prototypes are created as follows [5] (see Fig. 1-b, c). For each body part $m = 1, \ldots, M$:

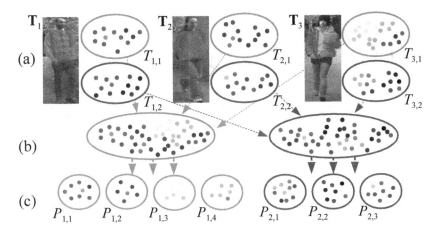

Fig. 1. Outline of the MCD framework (taken from [5]). In this example, two body parts are considered, upper (green) and lower (red) body. (a) Representation of three individuals as sets of components, shown as coloured dots. (b-c) Prototype creation: all the components of the same part are (b) merged, and (c) clustered.

1. Merge the feature vectors of the m-th part of each $\mathbf{I} \in \mathcal{I}$ into a set $X_m = \bigcup_{j=1}^{N} I_{j,m}$;
2. Cluster the set X_m into a set $\mathbf{P}_m$ of N_m clusters, $\mathbf{P}_m = \{P_{m,1}, \ldots, P_{m,N_m}\}$. Take each cluster as a prototype for the m-th body part.

Each prototype is a set of visually similar image components, which can belong to different individuals. In turn, each original descriptor $\mathbf{I}$ consists of a set of components for each body part. Thus, to create a dissimilarity vector from $\mathbf{I}$, dissimilarities can be evaluated via a distance measure between sets. In [5] the *k-th Hausdorff Distance* was used, due to its robustness to outliers.

3   A General Method for Appearance-Based People Search

We now present a simple and general approach to implement appearance-based people search based on MCD, by extending any re-identification method that uses a multiple part and multiple component representation of clothing appearance. The use of dissimilarity descriptors allows us to define detectors *independently* of the specific body part subdivision and local features used. Previous works required instead the definition of ad-hoc detectors for a given descriptor [3], or focused on a specific kind of descriptor [4]. Our intuition is that the clothing characteristics that can be detected by a given appearance descriptor, according to its low-level features and part subdivision (e.g., "red shirt"), may be encoded by one or more visual prototypes. For example, the rectangular image patches in Fig. 2 are sample components of 10 prototypes, extracted from the upper body parts of individuals taken from the data set of Sect. 4, using the

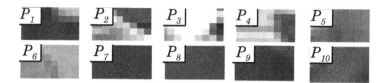

Fig. 2. Prototypes obtained from the upper body parts of a set of individuals

MCD implementation of [5]. Intuitively, descriptors of people wearing a red shirt should exhibit a high similarity to prototypes P_8 and P_{10}, while a high similarity to P_3 can be expected in the case of a white shirt.

Following the above intuition, a possible approach to perform appearance-based people search through an existing appearance descriptor, is to: (i) identify a set $\mathcal{Q} = \{\mathbf{Q}_1, \mathbf{Q}_2, \ldots\}$ of clothing characteristics that can be detected by the given descriptor, named *basic queries*; (ii) construct a detector for each basic query $\mathbf{Q}_i$, using dissimilarity values as *features* of a supervised classification problem.

The basic queries that have to be identified in step (i) depend on the original descriptor. For instance, if it separates lower and upper body parts, and uses colour features, one basic query can be "red trousers/skirt". Step (ii) can be viewed as a supervised binary classification problem for each $\mathbf{Q}_i$, which consists of recognising the presence or absence of the corresponding visual characteristic, using as features the dissimilarity values between an image descriptor and the prototypes. The training set can be obtained from a gallery of images of individuals, labelled accordingly. The resulting classifier can then be used as the detector for the basic query $\mathbf{Q}_i$. Note that one may know in advance that some features (prototypes) do not carry any discriminant information for some $\mathbf{Q}_i$. For instance, this is the case of the prototypes of the lower body part, with respect to queries related to the upper body. Such features can thus be discarded before constructing the corresponding classifier. Finally, complex queries can be built by connecting basic ones through Boolean operators, e.g., "red shirt AND (blue trousers OR black trousers)". Given a set of images, those relevant to a complex query can simply be found by combining the subsets of images found by each basic detector, using the set operators corresponding to the Boolean ones. In the above example, this amounts to the union (OR) of the images retrieved by the "blue trousers" and "black trousers" basic queries, followed by the intersection (AND) with the images retrieved by the basic query "red shirt".

We point out that the above approach for building detectors is independent of the original appearance descriptor.

4   Experimental Evaluation

Implementation. We evaluated our people search approach using two different descriptors previously proposed for person re-identification. The first descriptor was proposed in [6]. It subdivides body into torso and legs, and represents each part with the HSV colour histograms of a bag of randomly extracted 80 image patches. The second is the SDALF descriptor proposed in [8]. It uses the same part subdivision above, and represents each part with three local features: an HSV colour histogram, the "Maximally Stable Colour Regions", and the "Recurrent Highly Structured Patches" (RHSP). The first two features are related to the colour, while RHSP codifies the most recurrent repeated patterns. We also used a variation of the first descriptor: it uses a pictorial structure [9] to subdivide body into nine parts: arms and legs (upper and lower, left and right), and torso. The corresponding implementations of our people search method are denoted respectively as MCD_1, MCD_2 and MCD_3.

All the above descriptors enable queries related to clothing colour. MCD_1 and MCD_2 should permit queries related to upper or lower body, like "white upper body garment". MCD_3 should also enable more specific queries, like "short sleeves", that may be distinguished by the presence of skin-like colour in lower arms. Finally, the RHSP feature used in MCD_2 should should enable queries related to textures, like "checked trousers".

Prototypes were obtained by the a two stage clustering scheme as in [5]. In MCD_3, for each body part three different sets of prototypes were created, one for each kind of local features. In the experiments we considered different numbers of prototypes for each body part, ranging from 5 to 300. The k-th Hausdorff distance was used to compute dissimilarities, with $k = 10$.

Data Set. We used the VIPER data set [10]. It is made up of 1264 images of 632 pedestrians, of size 48×128 pixels, that exhibit different lighting conditions and pose variations. We defined 14 basic queries related to the colour of the upper and lower body parts, and to the presence of short sleeves/trousers/skirts. They are reported in Table 1, where the corresponding number of relevant images is shown between brackets. We defined these basic queries by considering clothing characteristics that: 1) were detectable to the considered descriptors, and 2) were present in several VIPER images, to allow us to construct a training set of a certain size for building the corresponding descriptors. For constructing the training sets, we needed to manually tag images according to each basic query. We labelled a subset of 512 images, denoted in the following as *VIPER-Tagged*. These images, and the corresponding labels, are available at http://prag.diee.unica.it/pra/research/reidentification/dataset/viper_tagged.

Experimental Setup. We evaluated the retrieval performance of our approach on each basic query, for each considered descriptor, using the precision-recall (P-R) curve. We first extracted the MCD visual prototypes from the whole *VIPER-Tagged* data set. Then, for each basic query we randomly subdivided VIPER-Tagged into a training and a testing sets of equal size, using stratified sampling, and trained a classifier on training images to implement a detector. An SVM classifier with linear kernel was used to this aim. The P-R curve was evaluated on testing images by varying the SVM decision threshold. This procedure was repeated ten times, and the resulting P-R curves were averaged.

Table 1. Average break-even point attained using the considered descriptors

Class (cardinality)	MCD$_1$	MCD$_2$	MCD$_3$
red shirt (51)	**0.845**	0.780	0.792
blue/light blue shirt (34)	**0.645**	0.523	0.494
pink shirt (35)	0.534	**0.578**	0.461
white/light gray shirt (140)	**0.771**	0.736	0.758
black shirt (156)	0.728	0.705	**0.736**
orange shirt (10)	**0.689**	0.580	0.463
violet shirt (18)	0.422	0.235	**0.433**
green shirt (34)	**0.687**	0.594	0.619
short sleeves (220)	0.631	0.608	**0.643**
red trousers/skirt (16)	0.713	0.638	**0.916**
black trousers/skirt (12)	0.683	0.607	**0.711**
white/light gray trousers/skirt (81)	**0.758**	0.639	0.635
blue/light blue trousers/skirt (175)	**0.641**	0.622	0.620
short trousers/skirt (82)	0.416	0.393	**0.557**

We point out that in these experiments we considered an off-line application scenario. In this kind of scenario, the data set in which one want to search is usually entirely available (e.g., in forensic investigations, all the available data is usually provided to the investigators). In this case, one can conveniently use all the available images for prototype creation, which is an unsupervised procedure, and does not require any manual labelling. In other application scenarios (e.g., on-line), one should instead extract prototypes off-line from a design data set, and use them to compute the dissimilarity representations of newly seen pedestrians at operation phase. In principle, in this case the performance of the proposed method could be lower, if the design set is not representative of the data processed at operation phase. However, the experimental evidences reported in [5] suggest that if a design data set containing a wide range of different clothing characteristics is used for prototype creation, the prototypes should be representative enough for a different set of pedestrians (i.e., those seen at operation phase).

Results. The performance on each basic query is summarised in Table 1, in terms of the corresponding average break-even point (BEP), which is the point of the P-R curve whose precision equals recall. The best performance for each basic query is highlighted in bold. In Fig. 3 we report four representative examples of the average P-R curves. An example of the ten top-ranked images for two basic queries is also shown in Fig. 4.

Our method attained a rather good performance with all descriptors, for almost all basic queries. The best performance was attained on basic queries related to the colours red, white and black (see Table 1). The most likely reason is that such colours are well separated in the HSV space, which is used by all the considered descriptors. As pointed out in Sect. 3, MCD$_3$ was likely to attain the best performance on basic queries related to the presence of skin on lower arms and legs, namely "short sleeves" and "short trousers/skirt" (see Fig. 3,

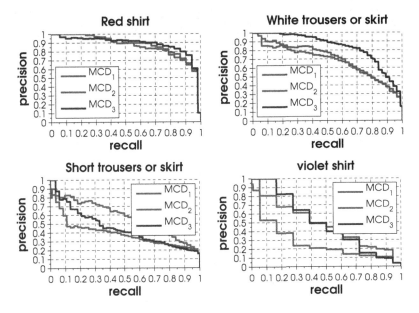

Fig. 3. Average P-R curves of 4 queries

Fig. 4. The top ten images retrieved by MCD1, for the "red shirt" (top) and "short sleeves" (bottom) queries, sorted from left to right for decreasing values of the relevance score provided by the detector (classifier). Note that only one non-relevant image is present, highlighted in red.

bottom-left plot), due to its more refined body subdivision. Nevertheless, also MCD_1 and MCD_2 attained a good performance on these classes. The reason is that, although MCD_1 and MCD_2 can not distinguish between lower and upper arms (legs), they are nevertheless able to detect skin-like colour in the whole arms or legs.

We finally evaluated how performance is affected by the number of prototypes N_m for each part m. We observed that the performance initially grows as N_m increases, then reaches a nearly stable value around $N_m = 100$ (for MCD_2, MCD_3) or 200 (for MCD_1), depending on the basic query. This behaviour can be easily explained: once the number of prototypes is enough so that most of the distinctive visual characteristics have been captured by different clusters, increasing the number of prototypes has mainly the effect of splitting some of the previous clusters into two or more similar ones. Consequently, no further information is embedded in the new prototypes. Note that the results reported in Table 1 and Fig. 3 were attained for $N_m = 200$ (for MCD_1) and $N_m = 100$ (for MCD_2 and MCD_3).

5   Conclusions

We proposed a general approach to implement the task of searching images of individuals that match a given *textual* query related to clothing appearance, through the same kind of descriptors used in most existing person re-identification systems, where the query is an *image* of an individual of interest, instead. Our approach is based on turning such descriptors into dissimilarity-based ones, exploiting the framework of [5]. This allows one to add a very useful functionality (e.g., for forensic investigations), to a re-identification system. Our approach attained promising results on preliminary experiments with three different descriptors, on a benchmark data set. An interesting direction of further research is to extend our approach to deal with video sequences. To this aim, pedestrian detection and tracking functionalities that should be deployed as part of a person re-identification system, could be exploited. In this case, a bag of dissimilarity vectors coming from different frames would be available for each person, instead of a single one. A Multiple Instance Learning approach [11] could then be used to train the detectors.

References

1. Doretto, G., Sebastian, T., Tu, P., Rittscher, J.: Appearance-based person reidentification in camera networks: problem overview and current approaches. Journal of Ambient Intelligence and Humanized Computing 2, 127–151 (2011)
2. Wang, L., Tan, T., Ning, H., Hu, W.: Silhouette analysis-based gait recognition for human identification. IEEE Transactions on Pattern Anallisys and Machine Intelligence 25, 1505–1518 (2003)
3. Vaquero, D., Feris, R., Tran, D., Brown, L., Hampapur, A., Turk, M.: Attribute-based people search in surveillance environments. In: IEEE Workshop on Applications of Computer Vision, WACV 2009 (2009)
4. Thornton, J., Baran-Gale, J., Butler, D., Chan, M., Zwahlen, H.: Person attribute search for large-area video surveillance. In: 2011 IEEE International Conference on Technologies for Homeland Security (HST), pp. 55–61 (2011)
5. Satta, R., Fumera, G., Roli, F.: Fast person re-identification based on dissimilarity representations. Pattern Recognition Letters, Special Issue on Novel Pattern Recognition-Based Methods for Reidentification in Biometric Context (in press, 2012)
6. Satta, R., Fumera, G., Roli, F., Cristani, M., Murino, V.: A Multiple Component Matching Framework for Person Re-identification. In: Maino, G., Foresti, G.L. (eds.) ICIAP 2011, Part II. LNCS, vol. 6979, pp. 140–149. Springer, Heidelberg (2011)

7. Pekalska, E., Duin, R.P.W.: The Dissimilarity Representation for Pattern Recognition: Foundations And Applications (Machine Perception and Artificial Intelligence). World Scientific Publishing Co., Inc., River Edge (2005)
8. Farenzena, M., Bazzani, L., Perina, A., Murino, V., Cristani, M.: Person re-identification by symmetry-driven accumulation of local features. In: Proc. of the 2010 IEEE Conf. on Computer Vision and Pattern Recognition (CVPR), pp. 2360–2367 (2010)
9. Andriluka, M., Roth, S., Schiele, B.: Pictorial structures revisited: People detection and articulated pose estimation. In: Proc. of the 2009 IEEE Conf. on Computer Vision and Pattern Recognition (CVPR), pp. 1014–1021 (2009)
10. Gray, D., Brennan, S., Tao, H.: Evaluating appearance models for recognition, reacquisition, and tracking. In: Proc. of the 10th IEEE Int. Workshop on Performance Evaluation of Tracking and Surveillance (PETS), pp. 41–47 (2007)
11. Dietterich, T.G., Lathrop, R.H., Lozano-Pérez, T.: Solving the multiple instance problem with axis-parallel rectangles. Artif. Intell. 89, 31–71 (1997)

Lessons from the Primate Visual System

Guy A. Orban[1,2]

[1] Departments of Neuroscience KU Leuven
[2] University of Parma

Abstract. The primate visual system can perform an astonishing array of tasks as reflected by the correspondingly large portion of the cerebral cortex devoted to analyzing retinal signals. Although a potential source of inspiration for computer vision, with a few exceptions, progress has been slow in this field. Principal obstacles are the lack of any exhaustive list of what vision achieves in humans and the restricting of areas of investigation to a few topics such as motion, object categories and the control of a few actions such as reaching or saccades. Here I will review how we integrated several experimental techniques to address a question that arose from interactions with computer vision scientists more than fifteen years ago: the extraction of 3D surfaces. This goal is achieved by a new type of higher-order visual neuron: the gradient-selective neurons. Neurons selective for speed gradients were initially discovered in motion processing areas, such as MT/V5, MSTd and FST, located in the monkey superior temporal sulcus (STS). Subsequently, neurons selective for disparity gradients were discovered in shape processing areas, such as TEs and AIP. By combining these single-cell studies with fMRI in human and awake monkey, we were able to localize similar neurons to human cortical areas. In the second part I address my present interest in understanding the visual signals related to the actions of conspecifics, which is perhaps the ultimate challenge of motion processing, but which receives surprisingly little attention in vision. The understanding of observed actions exemplifies my statement that to be useful visual signals have to leave the visual system, as signals related to biological motion in the STS are indeed relayed to parietal regions involved in the control of diverse actions to be understood as actions.

1   The Primate Visual System

The visual system of the primate occupies a substantial portion of the cortical surface. Cortical surface averages 978 cm^2 per hemisphere in humans [1], compared to 105 cm^2 in monkeys [2]. Thus the macaque cortex is just under ten times smaller than human cortex, while this ratio is 1:1000 in the mouse, making this species less attractive as experimental model. In the macaque about 60% of cortical surface is visual in nature and about 40 visual cortical areas have been identified [3]. In humans, 30% of cortex is thought to be visual, which in absolute size is still greater than monkey visual cortex. Since for homologous areas the ratio of surface area between macaque and human ranges from 2 to 6 fold, one can expect slightly more visual cortical areas in humans than monkeys, perhaps 50 or so. Nineteen areas have been identified so far in occipital cortex by retinotopic mapping [4].

A. Fusiello et al. (Eds.): ECCV 2012 Ws/Demos, Part I, LNCS 7583, pp. 462–467, 2012.
© Springer-Verlag Berlin Heidelberg 2012

Although it is clear to everybody that the human visual system is able to perform an astonishing array of different tasks, it is difficult to provide an exhaustive list. Therefore I have stressed [5] the importance of studying the visual system from the backside, the level at which connections with other parts of the brain are made. At this level the visual processing is completed and it becomes possible to define the input-output relationships for a given visual task. Since many high-level visual cortical areas have connections outside the visual system, there are multiple exit points from the system, and not necessarily at the same hierarchical level. Very generally, the tasks performed by the visual system have been segregated into recognition/categorization/discrimination and motor-control tasks, which are performed by the ventral, occipito-temporal and dorsal, occipito-parietal streams respectively [6].

There is some evidence that the dorsal stream itself consists of two substreams, depending on whether visual information enters through MT/V5 or V6 [7]. In a similar vein I suggest that the ventral stream also includes multiple substreams, related respectively to the processing of the scene presenting to the observer, the objects and the conspecifics in the scene. This view removes one of conundrums of present visual neuroscience: how to reconcile what are called *category specific* processing with *general object* processing. One category specific set of regions are the place areas, most notable the parahippocampal place area in ventral occipito-temporal cortex. I propose that this area plus afferents, represents the scene processing ventral substream. The other category specific regions are the body and face areas, which in monkeys are located in the upper and lower bank of the rostral and middle STS. This corresponds to the conspecific ventral substream, leaving the remaining infero-temporal cortex as the general object ventral substream. These substreams project to the nearby hippocampal formation, and to the prefrontal cortex.

The anatomical and functional complexity of the visual system would seemingly render any investigation of this system extremely difficult. Recently, however, much progress has been achieved by combining single-cell studies in the macaque brain with parallel functional imaging of both the animal model and human, an approach pioneered by our group in Leuven [8, 9]. Indeed this strategy allows one to establish links between single-cell and fMRI studies which are complementary, in the same species and then use the fMRI comparisons to move between species. Using this strategy we were able to address a question that arose year ago from discussions with Olivier Faugeras and other computer vision scientists in the Insight EU projects.

2 A Largely Solved Problem: Extraction of 3D Shape

3D shape and depth
Some years ago Faugeras and his team were developing techniques for measuring depth in the view fields of robot cameras, producing dense maps of 3D coordinates covering the scene. This seemed an overwhelming quantity of data and I suggested that the brain might use a more synthetic solution and represent the 3D surfaces directly, rather than keeping track of all the precise depth values. Basically, I was suggesting that the brain was building representations using the first and second orders of

depth, which specify tilted planes and curved surfaces. It took me almost 15 years to demonstrate this process for most depth cues, except shading, and to extend this knowledge to humans using the strategy described above. This long journey is summarized here, but a full account can be found in [9]. It however makes two important points: 1) neuroscience can indeed find solutions to 'hard' problems that are useful to computer vision scientists and 2) biological vision and computer vision apparently progress at different time scales, with visual neuroscience being slower. It is fair to say, however, that with more money and a team fully devoted to this objective we could have advanced much faster.

Gradient-selective neurons
Gradient-selective neurons were discovered in the nineties at the end of the Insight projects. Xiao et al [10] showed that MT/V5 neurons were selective for linear speed gradients representing planes tilted in depth and relied upon their antagonistic surround for this selectivity, thus providing a mechanistic explanation. Subsequently, similar neurons were found in MSTd [11], and invariance for mean speed demonstrated. The most complete description was provided in [12], comparing first and second-order speed-gradient selective neurons in MT/V5 and FST. Many of the second-order neurons in FST were selective for saddle-shaped surfaces, an intriguing finding. Given that many joints are in fact saddle-shaped, at least from certain view points, this suggests a manner in which shape signals can be injected into the motion stream to extract action-related signals, which combine motion and shape. Similar gradient-selective neurons were also described for texture and disparity gradients [9].

Using parallel functional imaging to extend knowledge to human brain
The second leg of the journey involves demonstrating in the model system, here the macaque, that the presence of gradient-selective neurons can be captured by fMRI responses in a given paradigm. As paradigm for investigating 3D structure from motion we introduced the comparison between viewing randomly connected lies rotating in depth and those same lines translating in the fronto-parallel plane [13]. It turns out that in the monkey this contrast activates only a few higher-order visual areas: notably MT/V5 and FST [8]. In fact gradient-selective neurons in FST respond differentially to these two stimuli [12] thus validating the paradigm. Recently, the human homologues of MT/V5 and some of its satellites have been mapped retinotopically [4]. Human MT/V5 and to some degree putative FST (pFST) are also activated by the comparison of rotating vs translating random lines, suggesting that they house speed-gradient selective neurons, as do their monkey counterparts.

3   Action Understanding and Processing of Actor Characteristics

The three stages of observed action processing
The best known example of processing action-observation signals is that of observing grasping in the monkey. Single-cell studies have shown that ventral premotor neurons

in F5 [14] and parietal neurons in PFG [15] and AIP are involved in both the planning of a given grasping action to be executed by the subject and in the observation of that same grasping action performed by another, whether a monkey or human. AIP and PFG are known to project to F5 [16]. Combining fMRI with tracer studies have shown that AIP receives input from a region in the rostral lower bank of the STS, processing observed grasping, while PFG receives input from a grasping-processing region in the upper bank of STS, near STPm [17]. These regions receive from more caudal parts of the STS. We propose that action processing originates in MT/V5, where local motion is processed, and its satellites such as FST, which may provide shape information based on 3D SFM, see above. The second step is LST [18] that overlaps with the middle body patch [19], where imaging experiments suggest that biological motion is extracted. Finally, these signals are then relayed forward along the STS. The exact subdivisions and their connections are unknown, but they include the areas projecting to PFG and AIP. Thus the presumed sequence of processing steps is as follows: MT/V5 which receives directly from V1, FST, LST, rostral STS, AIP or PFG, and F5.

This processing of action observation signals in these three stages, including an oc-cipito-temporal, parietal and premotor stage is now believed to be a general feature of the action observation networks in human and non-human primates. Of course this raises the question about homologies between areas in the two species, but progress has been made in this direction, at the occipito-temporal [19] and parietal levels [20].

Purpose of processing in the STS: actor characteristics
The preceding overview of the processing of visual action-observation signals indicates that the first occipito-temporal stage comprises multiple sublevels of processing, raising questions regarding the function of its more anterior components. If one compares monkey STS with the presumed homologous regions in humans [19], it is clear that these levels are considerably expanded in humans. Here I propose that the output of these more rostral STS fields processing biological motion, together with the static body and static and dynamic face signals, represent the identity and state of the actor. They are thus part of the conspecific ventral substream defined in point 1. The *state of the actor* refers to his physiological, mental and emotional state. Physiological state refers to age, gender, vigor, fertility, health and disabilities, features typically used in a clinical evaluation by a physician. This state is largely provided by static visual signals such as body size, face configuration, texture, and color of the skin [20]. Mental state includes the intention with respect to the observer that can be signaled by gaze direction, or rationality of the actor, which can be inferred from the way the action is performed given constraints imposed by the environment or the load borne by the subject [22]. The emotional state refers to the overall mood and emotion, indicated by motion kinematics [23] as well as affect relative to the observer as witnessed by vitality signs [24]. Some of this emotional information can be amplified by multimodal combinations of auditory and visual signals: think of the sound created by somebody walking, and how this used in movies to create an atmosphere or tension. We propose that representing the actor and his state is the primary function of monkey STS and its homologous regions in humans. Interestingly neighboring auditory regions in humans have been shown to represent the speaker [25], complementing visual information concerning the conspecifics in our environment. The visual

processing in STS provides a fine-grained analysis of the visual features of observed actions. Signals from this analysis are also dispatched to the posterior parietal cortex (PPC), and sent to the various areas involved in planning the actions in the observers' repertoire, as we have shown for grasping.

Processing of observed actions in parietal cortex
There is general agreement that posterior parietal cortex is involved in the sensori-motor transformations underlying the planning of various actions [26]. Because different actions such as locomotion, grasping, and reaching, require different types of sensory information, we propose that actions are planned in parallel in various sub-components of PPC. Recent adaptation studies [27] are consistent with the notion that the PPC is organized according to the type of action planned and not the effector used to perform the action, as frequently proposed [28]. If we additionally hypothesize that the visual signals from the STS relating to action observation project to the portion of the PPC involved in planning that same action (generalized mirror principle), one predicts that the PPC regions concerned with action observation are also organized according to the action type. Evidence in this direction has begun to accumulate [29].

Such an organization would indicate that human cortex has discovered a short-cut for solving the intractable visual problem of recognizing the actions of others. This may be an important lesson for computer vision. Interestingly, it is presently thought that the PPC only houses the general plan for various categories of actions, assuming that the typical effector will be used [29]. Thus to design an artificial system that 'understands' human actions, it must be possible to emulate this strategy by designing a computer vision system that plans actions with human effectors, and then mapping the visual signals onto those plans. If the plans are to be used in a robot, anthropomorphic or not, the next stage can transform these plans by mapping them onto the robot effectors, thus mimicking a presumed function of human premotor cortex, namely adapting the general plan to the specific effectors used in the action.

References

1. Van Essen, D.C., Glasser, M.F., Dierker, D.L., Harwell, J., Coalson, T.: Parcellations and Hemispheric Asymmetries of Human Cerebral Cortex Analyzed on Surface-Based Atlases. Cereb. Cortex. e-Pub. (2011)
2. Van Essen, D.C., Glasser, M.F., Dierker, D.L., Harwell, J.: Cortical Parcellations of the Macaque Monkey Analyzed on Surface-Based Atlases. Cereb. Cortex. e-Pub. (2011)
3. Felleman, D.J., Van Essen, D.C.: Distributed hierarchical processing in the primate cerebral cortex. Cereb. Cortex 1, 1–47 (1991)
4. Kolster, H., Peeters, R., Orban, G.A.: The retinotopic organization of the human middle temporal area MT/V5 and its cortical neighbors. J. Neurosci. 30, 9801–9820 (2010)
5. La vision, mission du cerveau. Orban GA, College de France/Fayard, Paris (2007)
6. Goodale, M.A., Milner, A.D.: Separate visual pathways for perception and action. Trends Neurosci. 15, 20–25 (1992)
7. Rizzolatti, G., Matelli, M.: Two different streams form the dorsal visual system: anatomy and functions. Exp. Brain Res. 153, 146–157 (2003)
8. Vanduffel, W., Fize, D., Mandeville, J.B., Nelissen, K., Van Hecke, P., Rosen, B.R., Tootell, R.B., Orban, G.A.: Visual motion processing investigated using contrast agent-enhanced fMRI in awake behaving monkeys. Neuron. 32, 565–577 (2001)

9. Orban, G.: The extraction of 3D shape in the visual system of human and nonhuman primates. Annu. Rev. Neurosci. 34, 361–388 (2011)

10. Xiao, D.K., Marcar, V.L., Raiguel, S.E., Orban, G.A.: Selectivity of macaque MT/V5 neurons for surface orientation in depth specified by motion. Eur. J. Neurosci. 9, 956–964 (1997)

11. Sugihara, H., Murakami, I., Shenoy, K.V., Andersen, R.A., Komatsu, H.: Response of MSTd neurons to simulated 3D orientation of rotating planes. J. Neurophysiol. 87, 273–285 (2002)

12. Mysore, S.G., Vogels, R., Raiguel, S.E., Todd, J.T., Orban, G.A.: The selectivity of neurons in the macaque fundus of the superior temporal area for three-dimensional structure from motion. J. Neurosci. 30, 15491–15508 (2010)

13. Orban, G.A., Sunaert, S., Todd, J.T., Van Hecke, P., Marchal, G.: Human cortical regions involved in extracting depth from motion. Neuron. 24, 929–940 (1999)

14. Gallese, V., Fadiga, L., Fogassi, L., Rizzolatti, G.: Action recognition in the premotor cortex. Brain 119, 593–609 (1996)

15. Fogassi, L., Ferrari, P.F., Gesierich, B., Rozzi, S., Chersi, F., Rizzolatti, G.: Parietal lobe: from action organization to intention understanding. Science 308, 662–667 (2005)

16. Rizzolatti, G., Luppino, G.: The cortical motor system. Neuron. 31, 889–901 (2001)

17. Nelissen, K., Borra, E., Gerbella, M., Rozzi, S., Luppino, G., Vanduffel, W., Rizzolatti, G., Orban, G.A.: Action observation circuits in the macaque monkey cortex. J. Neurosci. 31, 3743–3756 (2011)

18. Nelissen, K., Vanduffel, W., Orban, G.A.: Charting the lower superior temporal region, a new motion-sensitive region in monkey superior temporal sulcus. J. Neurosci. 26, 5929–5947 (2006)

19. Jastorff, J., Popivanov, I.D., Vogels, R., Vanduffel, W., Orban, G.A.: Integration of shape and motion cues in biological motion processing in the monkey STS. Neuroimage 60, 911–921 (2012)

20. Durand, J.B., Peeters, R., Norman, J.F., Todd, J.T., Orban, G.A.: Parietal regions processing visual 3D shape extracted from disparity. Neuroimage 46, 1114–1126 (2009)

21. Stirrat, M., Perrett, D.I.: Valid facial cues to cooperation and trust: male facial width and trustworthiness. Psychol. Sci. 21, 349–354 (2010)

22. Jastorff, J., Clavagnier, S., Gergely, G., Orban, G.A.: Neural mechanisms of understanding rational actions: middle temporal gyrus activation by contextual violation. Cereb. Cortex 21, 318–329 (2011)

23. Pichon, S., Degelder, B., Grèzes, J.: Two different faces of threat. Comparing the neural systems for recognizing fear and anger in dynamic body expressions. J. Neuroimage 47, 1873–1883 (2009)

24. Stern, D.N.: Forms of Vitality: Exploring Dynamic Experience in Psychology and the Arts. Oxford University Press (2010)

25. Campanella, S., Belin, P.: Integrating face and voice in person perception. Trends Cogn. Sci. 11, 535–543 (2007)

26. Andersen, R.A., Buneo, C.A.: Intentional maps in posterior parietal cortex. Annu. Rev. Neurosci. 25, 189–220 (2002)

27. Bruggeman, H., Warren, W.H.: The direction of walking–but not throwing or kicking–is adapted by optic flow. Psychol. Sci. 21, 1006–1013 (2010)

28. Andersen, R.A., Cui, H.: Intention, action planning, and decision making in parietal-frontal circuits. Neuron. 63, 568–583 (2009)

29. Jastorff, J., Begliomini, C., Fabbri-Destro, M., Rizzolatti, G., Orban, G.A.: Coding observed motor acts: different organizational principles in the parietal and premotor cortex of humans. J. Neurophysiol. 104, 128–140 (2010)

Neural Mechanisms for Form and Motion Detection and Integration: Biology Meets Machine Vision

Heiko Neumann[1] and Florian Raudies[2]

[1] Institute for Neural Information Processing, Ulm Univ., Germany
[2] Center for Computational Neuroscience and Neural Technology, Boston Univ., USA

Abstract. General-purpose vision systems, either biological or technical, rely on the robust processing of visual data from the sensor array.
Such systems need to adapt their processing capabilities to varying conditions, have to deal with noise, and also need to learn task-relevant
representations. Here, we describe models of early and mid-level vision.
These models are motivated by the layered and hierarchical processing
of form and motion information in primate cortex. Core cortical processing principles are: (i) bottom-up processing to build representations
of increasing feature specificity and spatial scale, (ii) selective amplifi-
cation of bottom-up signals by feedback that utilizes spatial, temporal,
or task-related context information, and (iii) automatic gain control via
center-surround competitive interaction and activity normalization. We
use these principles as a framework to design and develop bio-inspired
models for form and motion processing. Our models replicate experimental findings and, furthermore, provide a functional explanation for psychophysical and physiological data. In addition, our models successfully
process natural images or videos. We show mechanism that group items
into boundary representations or estimate visual motions from opaque or
transparent surfaces. Our framework suggests a basis for designing bio-
inspired models that solve typical computer vision problems and enable
the development of neural technology for vision.

1 Introduction - Vision Processes in Man and Machine

The visual system of primates is characterized by its flexibility and robustness to
process data under various imaging conditions, such as noise, illumination, and
partial occlusions. Also, it adapts its functionality by using learning mechanisms.
Form and motion information is mainly processed along two segregated pathways, namely the ventral stream for form representation and the dorsal stream
for motion representation. Machine vision mainly focused on developing given
task-related constraints. Their aim is the optimization of engineering-like defined
objective functions, which are often hard to transfer to other problem domains.
Only a few approaches investigate the problem how higher-level knowledge can
be used to stabilize and disambiguate sensory signals.

A. Fusiello et al. (Eds.): ECCV 2012 Ws/Demos, Part I, LNCS 7583, pp. 468–473, 2012.
© Springer-Verlag Berlin Heidelberg 2012

We sketch a core model architecture that has been motivated by knowledge from neuroscience. Several model instances have been derived from this core model to explain a wealth of experimental data from psychophysics and physiology and process natural images and videos besides psychophysics stimuli. Next, we describe our model architecture which is followed by the results and discussion and conclusion.

2 Neural Modeling of Dynamic Vision in Cortex

Biological information processing can be described at various levels of detail. For instance, it can be described at the level of individual neurons, their interconnections and biophysical dynamics, or at the level of neuronal layers and cortical areas and their connectivity as a graph-like structure. To capture the general aspects of visual processing, we employ simple model neurons that are organized into columns at each spatial location. To model the dynamics of such neurons, we use single compartment model neurons with gradual activation dynamics formally denoting the neuronal firing rate. All columns together define an area with a specific functionality, like in visual cortex. We model the interactions in and between such columns. Neurons are laterally interconnected, signaling to their spatially neighboring columns as in cortex. The modeling on a macroscopic level is motivated by the distributed and hierarchical organization of cortical areas and their interconnections [4]. One striking principle is that areas in visual cortex are mostly bi-directionally connected: an area not only sends feed forward (FF) signals to an area higher up in the hierarchy but also receives feedback (FB) signals from higher areas. The role of FB is a topic of active research. The key principle is that FB connections are mainly modulatory. They cannot generate activations alone without driving input.

Our model architecture employs a simplified version of layered processing that is mapped to a three-stage processing cascade consisting of: (i) an initial filtering for e.g. orientation or motion direction, that generates a representation of the driving visual stimulus, (ii) a stage of topographically organized re-entrant signals from areas higher in the hierarchy that amplify initial filtering signals, and (iii) an output stage that normalizes signals to keep the overall energy within bounds. The membrane conductance of model neurons is

$$\dot{v}_i^{(1)}(t) = -v_i^{(1)}(t) + (E_{ex} - v_i^{(1)}(t)) \cdot \{s * F^+\}_i - (E_{in} + v_i^{(1)}(t)) \cdot \{s * F^-\}_i \tag{1}$$

$$\dot{v}_i^{(2)}(t) = -v_i^{(2)}(t) + (E_{ex} - v_i^{(2)}(t)) \cdot [v_i^{(1)}(t)]_+ \cdot (1 + net_i^{FB}) \tag{2}$$

$$\tau \dot{v}_i^{(3)}(t) = -E_L v_i^{(3)}(t) + (E_{ex} - v_i^{(3)}(t)) \cdot v_i^{(2)}(t) - \alpha v_i^{(3)}(t) \cdot f_p(w_i^p(t)) \tag{3}$$

$$\tau_p \dot{w}_i^p(t) = -w_i^p(t) + (E_{ex}^p - w_i^p(t)) \cdot f_s(v^{(3)}(t)) * \Lambda^p. \tag{4}$$

In this set of equations, s denotes the bottom-up driving input signals, $F^{+,-}$ denotes filter kernels, $*$ denotes the convolution in space and/or feature domain, and $[\bullet]_+$ denotes a half-wave rectification. The constants E, τ, and α define levels of activity saturation, membrane efficacy, and modulation strength, respectively.

The normalization integrates the activity in a pool of neurons employing an integration kernel Λ^p. This pool activity, in turn, inhibits the output activation (Eq. 3) via shunting surround inhibition. Output activities are passed through a non-linear transfer function of sigmoidal shape $f(\bullet)$ to account for the firing rate function of neurons. The re-entrant modulating signal net^{FB} amplifies the respective driving FF activation by FB, but leaves FF unchanged when FB is absent. On the other hand, if no FF signal is present, FB cannot generate a response. This asymmetry between FF and FB signals is captured in the model by incorporating a tonic level of FB at each location in the space-feature domain.

3   Simulation Results for Form and Motion Processing

Form Processing and Grouping. The goal of form and shape processing is to detect and interpolate arrangements of local oriented contrasts, to generate representations of (surface) boundaries, to infer 3D ordinary layout of surfaces from junctions of different types, or to infer the geometric properties of 3D object surfaces irrespective of their material properties. Based on early modeling investigations of boundary grouping [5], we developed a taxonomy of mechanisms for feature cooperation, which employs a measure of feature compatibility (for details, see [11]). Based on this taxonomy, we suggest that the outputs from collinear sub-field filtering are combined conjunctively in order to generate contour completions as observed for illusory boundary formation. Oriented contour integration operates at the spatial scale of area V1 and V2 (see [16]). Processing mechanisms of this model V1-V2 for contour integration are formulated as a variant of the generic Equations 1-4. Here, we only highlight the most important aspects. The input stage for long-range grouping at model V2 is defined by the instance of Eqn. 1

$$\dot{v}_{i,\theta}^{V2,1}(t) = -v_{i,\theta}^{V2,1}(t) + (E_{ex} - v_{i,\theta}^{V2,1}(t)) \cdot \{s_{\theta}^{V1} * \Gamma^{V2,L}\}_i \cdot \{s_{\theta}^{V1} * \Gamma^{V2,R}\}_i. \quad (5)$$

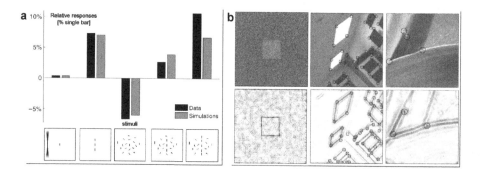

Fig. 1. Simulation results for form processing. a) Oriented contour representations are modulated by local context (black bars: physiological data from [9], grey bars: model simulations from [7]). b) Contour enhancement and junctions detected from local activity distributions for natural images (from [6]).

The input filtering uses pairs of elongated sub-field kernels $\Gamma^{V2,L/R}$ that integrate oriented bottom-up inputs. The output at stage three of model V2 is fed back to enhance oriented filter activities in model V1, formally, defined by the variant of Eqn. 2

$$\dot{v}_{i,\theta}^{V1,2}(t) = -v_{i,\theta}^{V1,2}(t) + (E_{ex} - v_{i,\theta}^{V1,2}(t)) \cdot v_{i\theta}(t) \cdot (1 + \Psi^{V2}(\{v_{\theta}^{V2,3} * \Lambda^{FB}\}_i)). \quad (6)$$

Model cells show the same behavior as recorded cells when probed by oriented input contrast items with surround context (see Fig. 1 a). The grouping mechanism successfully processes real-world stimuli as well. For example, the network is capable of enhancing junction configurations (Fig. 1 b) so that different configurations of them can be reliably read out from V1 model cells. Simulations outperform 2D landmark detection using the structure tensor (see [6] for details).

Motion Detection and Integration. Our second model instance and related simulations focuss on the detection and integration of visual motion. Our goal is the estimation of spatio-temporal responses and their integration to resolve motion ambiguities, e.g. caused by the aperture problem or noisy input. Our model consists of areas V1, MT, and MST, all part of the dorsal pathway. Initial motions are detected by direction selective cells in model area V1 which feed their responses to motion integrative cells in model area MT. Model area MT output signals subsequently feed into area MST that contains cells selective for motion patterns that are generated on the image plane, e.g. by self-motion. Thus, model MST cells are selective for translational, rotational, or expansion/contraction optic flow or a combination thereof. A major challenge is allowing for motion perception of opaque as well as transparent motion. A key mechanism for the processing of transparent motion is a soft competition between model MT cells formulated as center-surround interaction in the velocity space. This soft competition is a simplified variant of Eqn. 3 and 4

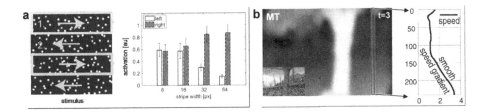

Fig. 2. Simulation results for motion analysis. a) Patterns arranged in lanes of opposite motions are integrated by motion-sensitive cells. Large widths mainly drive cells with matching velocity selectivity (grey bars) and for small widths, cells selective to the opposite motion direction become increasingly active (white bars; FB from MST stabilize these activities; from [14]). b) Motion detection and integration for a computer vision benchmark sequence (inset). Depth variations are represented by smooth motion gradients (from [2]).

$$\dot{v}_{i,vel}^{MT,3}(t) = -v_{i,vel}^{MT,3}(t) + \{v^{MT,2} * \Lambda^+\}_{i,vel} - \alpha v_{i,vel}^{MT,3}(t) \cdot w_{i,vel}(t) \qquad (7)$$

$$\dot{w}_{i,vel}(t) = -w_{i,vel}(t) + \{v^{MT,2} * \Lambda^-\}_{i,vel} \qquad (8)$$

with $vel = (\phi, ||\mathbf{u}||)$. Similar motions that fall into the excitatory zone are combined, while motions are suppressed and repelled when they fall in the inhibitory zone [15]. Motion (semi-) transparency occurs when spatially separate motions with significant velocity difference occur which cannot be resolved by the visual sensing mechanisms. This case generates multiple activations at the same image location (Fig. 2 a). Our model implicitly detects different transparent motion layers at MT level, but it does not require a pre-defined number of motions. This is unlike computational vision approaches which detect multiple layers of motion with an iterative routine treating motion from other layers as outliers (e.g., [3]).

Real-world video input has been successfully processed as well. The flower garden sequence shows a tree moving in front of a background due to depth variations relative to a translating observer. The result demonstrates that the model successfully generates discontinuous motion at occlusions based on texture-defined motion discontinuities. In addition, it illustrates the ability to represent speed gradients (see the marked column in the image where the speed gradient is induced by the slanted ground plane, Fig. 2 b). Such gradients are prerequisite of inferring spatial layout from motion or help to solve the structure-from-motion problem ([12]).

4   Discussion and Conclusion

We presented the outline of a biologically inspired architecture for visual processing. The components have been motivated by functional principles of cortical architecture resulting in a cascade of three processing steps for bottom-up driving FF signal flow and modulating re-entrant FB that delivers context information from higher areas. Together with the activity normalization this leads to a biased competition of activity distributions. Our models explain various experimental data from psychophysics and physiology. They also robustly process real-world data at a performance level that is comparable to computer vision algorithms. Our framework provides an approach to the design of general purpose vision systems utilizing core principles of cortical processing. The building blocks of our framework are flexible and modular. Additional functionality can be easily added without causing interface problems for input/output representations and their processing. For example, we demonstrated the interaction between motion and form processing for figure-ground segregation where the figures are only defined by kinetic contours [13]. Unsupervised learning mechanisms have been incorporated into the framework to build feature detectors and representations for higher level processing in animated motion sequence analysis for action recognition [10].

In summary, our simulations from various domains of vision demonstrate the generality of our approach to develop bio-inspired vision models. Together with newly available hardware that accelerates the execution of distributed processing at various stages, our approach allows for building robust and adaptive vision technologies capable to function in various, unconstrained applications.

Acknowledgements. HN was supported by the Transregional Collaborative Research Centre "A Companion Technology for Cognitive Technical Systems" funded by DFG. FR acknowledges support from the Office of Naval Research (ONR N00014-11-1-0535 and ONR MURI N00014-10-1-0936).

References

1. Bayerl, P., Neumann, H.: Disambiguating visual motion through contextual feedback modulation. Neural Computation 16, 2041–2066 (2004)
2. Bayerl, P., Neumann, H.: Disambiguating visual motion by form-motion interactional computational model. Int'l J. of Comp. Vis. 72(1), 27–45 (2007)
3. Black, M.J., Anandan, P.: The robust estimation of multiple motions: Parametric and piecewise-smooth flow fields. Comp. Visi. and Image Understanding 63(1), 75–104 (1996)
4. Felleman, D.J., van Essen, D.C.: Distributed hierarchical processing in the primate cerebral cortex. Cerebral Cortex 1, 1–47 (1991)
5. Grossberg, S., Mingolla, E.: Neural dynamics of perceptual grouping: textures, boundaries, and emergent segmentation. Percept. & Psychophys. 38, 141–171 (1985)
6. Hansen, T., Neumann, H.: Neural mechanisms for the robust representation of junctions. Neural Computation 16, 1013–1037 (2004)
7. Hansen, T., Neumann, H.: A recurrent model of contour integration in primary visual cortex. J. of Vision 8(8), 1–25 (2008)
8. Hirsch, J.A., Gilbert, C.D.: Synaptic physiology of horizontal connections in the cats visual cortex. J. of Neuroscience 11, 1800–1809 (1991)
9. Kapadia, K.M., Ito, M., Gilbert, C.D., Westheimer, G.: Improvement in visual sensitivity by changes in local context: Parallel studies in human observers and in V1 of alert monkeys. Neuron. 15, 843–856 (1995)
10. Layher, G., Giese, M.A., Neumann, H.: Learning Representations for Animated Motion Sequence and Implied Motion Recognition. In: Villa, A.E.P., Duch, W., Érdi, P., Masulli, F., Palm, G. (eds.) ICANN 2012, Part I. LNCS, vol. 7552, pp. 288–295. Springer, Heidelberg (2012)
11. Neumann, H., Yazdanbakhsh, A., Mingolla, E.: Seeing surfaces: The brain's vision of the world. Physics of Life Reviews 4, 189–222 (2007)
12. Orban, G.: Higher order visual processing in macaque extrastriate cortex. Physiol. Rev. 88, 69–89 (2008)
13. Raudies, F., Neumann, H.: A neural model of the temporal dynamics of figure-ground segregation in motion perception. Neural Networks 23, 160–176 (2010)
14. Raudies, F., Neumann, H.: A model of neural mechanisms in monocular transparent motion perception. J. of Physiology 104, 71–83 (2010)
15. Raudies, F., Mingolla, E., Neumann, H.: A model of motion transparency processing with local center-surround interactions and feedback. Neural Computation 23, 2868–2914 (2011)
16. Weidenbacher, U., Neumann, H.: Extraction of surface-related features in a recurrent model of V1-V2 interactions. PLoS One 4(6), e5909 (2009)

Neural Fields Models of Visual Areas: Principles, Successes, and Caveats

Olivier Faugeras

NeuroMathComp Laboratory, Inria, Sophia-Antipolis Méditerranée, 06902, France

Abstract. I discuss how the notion of neural fields, a phenomenological averaged description of spatially distributed populations of neurons, can be used to build models of how visual information is represented and processed in the visual areas of primates. I describe one of the basic principles of operation of these neural fields equations which is closely connected to the idea of a bifurcation of their solutions. I then apply this concept to several visual features, edges, textures and motion and show that it can account very simply for a number of experimental facts as well as suggest new experiments.

1 Introduction

Neural or cortical fields are continuous assemblies of mesoscopic models, also called neural masses, of neural populations that are essential in the modeling of macroscopic parts of the brain. They have provided useful insights in the study of a broad range of neurobiological phenomena particularly those characterised by complex patterns of neural activity whose structure can be well captured by these equations. In the past these have included geometrical visual hallucinations, cortical waves, orientation tuning in V1, working memory and binocular rivalry. They were first introduced by Wilson and Cowan [1] and Amari [2].

Neural fields describe the mean activity of neural populations by nonlinear integro-differential equations. The solutions of these equations represent the state of activity of these populations either in isolation (one talks about intrinsic activity) or when submitted to inputs from neighboring brain areas. Understanding the properties of these solutions is therefore important for advancing our understanding of how the brain encodes and processes its internal and external inputs.

These equations are phenomenological in the sense that, as of today, there is no formal correspondence between these equations that are intended to be relevant at the meso- and macroscopic levels and the equations that describe neuronal activity at the level of individual neurons. Mean field theory may be a way of addressing these questions, see for instance [3, 4].

2 Neural Fields Equations

We describe a very general class of neural fields equations. It involves several important ideas. The first idea is that of the time variation of the average potential of a given neuronal population, e.g. pyramidal cells. We note it $V_i(t)$

A. Fusiello et al. (Eds.): ECCV 2012 Ws/Demos, Part I, LNCS 7583, pp. 474–479, 2012.

where the index i (between 1 and P) represents the neuronal population. The second idea is that of the relation between this average membrane potential and the average activity, or average firing rate, noted $\nu_i(t)$, of the population. This relation is assumed to be of the form $\nu_i = S(V_i)$, where S is a sigmoidal function. The synaptic current received by the postsynaptic population i from all the presynaptic populations j is assumed to be a weighted sum of the average firing rates of these populations, the weights, noted J_{ij}, describing the strength of the interaction of the presynaptic population j with the postsynaptic population i. If we further assume that the intrinsic (i.e. without interaction) dynamics of a single population is described by a decaying exponential, we can express these ideas as one equation per population:

$$\frac{dV_i(t)}{dt} = -\frac{V_i(t)}{\tau_i} + \sum_{j=1}^{P} J_{ij}\nu_j(t) + I_i(t) \quad i = 1, \cdots, P, \tag{1}$$

where τ_i is a time constant that characterizes the intrinsic dynamics of the population i, and $I_i(t)$ is an external current, e.g. from a microelectrode. Note that the weights J_{ij} can be positive (respectively negative), in which case the population j is excitatory (respectively inhibitory). The ordinary differential equations (ODEs) (1) are the basic Wilson-Cowan/Amari equations. There are several ways of increasing the descriptive power of these equations.

The first one is to bring in the idea that the neuronal populations may have a spatial extent, e.g. be distributed over a cortical sheet. Denoting by r a variable representing space, we rewrite equations (1) as

$$\frac{\partial V_i(r,t)}{dt} = -\frac{V_i(r,t)}{\tau_i} + \sum_{j=1}^{P} \int_{\Omega} J_{ij}(r,r')\nu_j(r',t)\,dr' + I_i(r,t) \quad i = 1, \cdots, P, \tag{2}$$

The influence of the presynaptic population j is now spatially distributed over the spatial set Ω and this is reflected in the spatial integral over this domain. The system of ODEs (1) has been replaced by the system of integro-differential equations (2). Thanks to the abstraction power of mathematics, we can still think of this more complicated system of equations as system of ODEs albeit defined on a more complicated, functional, space, see e.g. [5].

The second improvement is to take into account the fact that presynaptic currents do not propagate instantaneously to postsynaptic populations and to introduce delays in equations (1) and (2). If we note $\tau_{ij}(r,r')$ the time it takes for the activity of the presynaptic population j located at r' to start influencing the postsynaptic population i located at r, we rewrite (2) as

$$\frac{\partial V_i(r,t)}{dt} = -\frac{V_i(r,t)}{\tau_i} + \sum_{j=1}^{P} \int_{\Omega} J_{ij}(r,r')\nu_j(r',t - \tau_{ij}(r,r'))\,dr' + I_i(r,t). \tag{3}$$

The delay function can be chosen as the sum of a constant delay due to the synaptic response and of a propagation delay proportional to the the distance between r and r'.

The third improvement is to allow the synaptic weights to vary over time according to some plasticity rule. We do not address this question in this paper.

The fourth improvement is to introduce the idea of feature representation: population i is encoding a given feature, e.g. a visual orientation, in the spatio-temporal variations of its average membrane potential. We provide several examples of this mechanism in section 3.

Equations (1)-(3) depend on several parameters such as the synaptic weights J_{ij}, the delays τ_{ij}, the time constants τ_i, the shape of the sigmoid S as well as the input currents I_i. The exact values of these parameters are clearly not precisely known (will they ever be?) and the question naturally arises whether we can make, at least qualitative, predictions about the way these parameters should be tuned in order for the neuronal populations, as represented by these equations, to operate in a meaningful and perhaps useful way.

The answer to this question is yes but in order to reach it one has to go through the detour of the theory of the bifurcations of the solutions to the neural fields equations. There is no space here to get into the details of the theory but I will attempt to convey the feeling of what it means. I will consider one among the many parameters, namely the slope λ at the origin of the sigmoidal function S that converts average membrane potentials to average firing rates. I will also consider the simple case where the external input current I_i is stationary, i.e. does not depend on time. Finally I will consider the simplest equations (1) rewritten so that to make explicit their dependency on λ:

$$\frac{dV_i(t)}{dt} = -\frac{V_i(t)}{\tau_i} + \sum_{j=1}^{P} J_{ij} S(\lambda V_j(t)) + I_i \quad i = 1, \cdots, P, \tag{4}$$

When λ is equal to 0 one has $S(\lambda V_j(t)) = S(0)$ and the solution to (4) converges exponentially fast to the constant solution $S(0) \sum_{j=1}^{P} J_{ij} + I_i$, irrespective of the initial state of the network, not a very exciting behaviour!

When one slowly increases the slope λ starting from 0, something very interesting happens: there is a critical value $\lambda_c > 0$ of λ above which the number of solutions to (4) changes abruptly from one to several, depending on the initial condition. This is a much more interesting behaviour since one may say that the response of the system to a given input will strongly depend on its state when the input is turned on. It turns out that this situation extends to the solutions to equations (2) and (3). In these two cases one can precisely compute the bifurcation values λ_c of the slope λ and characterize the number of solutions after the bifurcations. This mathematical analysis has been performed for (2) in [6] and for (3) in [7]. It is not limited to the parameter λ and applies mutadis mutandis to other parameters.

What do we learn from this at the neuronal level? well, of course, that the neuronal populations should operate in regions of the parameter space that put the system of equations very close to a bifurcation, technically to a static bifurcation. This is in effect a strong constraint on the parameters values and, through the analysis of the new solutions that appear in the vicinity of this bifurcation, provides very precise predictions that should be amenable to experimental testing. We provide in the next section another argument leading to the same conclusions.

3   Neural Fields Representation of Visual Features

3.1   Representing Visual Orientations

Since the discovery by Hubel and Wiesel [8] of the selective response of a single neuron to some orientations, a long-standing debate has taken place about the degree of cortical computation involved in this selectivity compared to the feedforward selectivity implied by the LGN projections.

The Ring Model of orientation tuning was introduced by Hansel and Sompolinski [9] and studied by several other after the seminal work of Ben-Yishai and colleagues [10], as a model of a hypercolumn in primary visual cortex.

The model assumes that the local orientation θ of the visual stimulus present in the receptive fields of the neurons in the hypercolumn is encoded in their mean membrane potential. Neglecting the spatial distribution of these neurons one writes the following neural field equation

$$\frac{\partial V(\theta,t)}{dt} = -\frac{V(\theta,t)}{\tau} + \int_{-\frac{\pi}{2}}^{\frac{\pi}{2}} J(\theta - \theta')S(\lambda V(\theta',t))\, d\theta' + I(\theta,t) \qquad (5)$$

The connectivity function J is periodic and Mexican-hat like. This introduces a new, very important, aspect in the study and use of neural fields equations, that of their symmetries.

In the case of the ring model of orientation tuning, the neural fields equations are invariant with respect to the action of the group of planar rotations. This implies that for no input (and small values of the slope parameter λ) there is a unique stationary solution (independent of time) and independent of the orientation. This is rather dull and, following the principle outlined in the introduction, we tune the parameter λ so that the system is close to a (Pitchfork in this case) bifurcation. Its behaviour then changes drastically: because of the rotational symmetry, the number of solutions to (5) becomes infinite. Each such solution is a unimodal function of the orientation θ, and all solutions are translated with respect to one another. They are called tuning curves. When one turns on the external input, e.g. with an oriented grating of orientation $\bar{\theta}$, one can show that the system selects the corresponding tuning curve centered at this orientation.

To summarize, for small values of the slope parameter and no input, the intrinsic activity of the orientation hypercolumn is dull. When one increases the value of λ one reaches a static bifurcation in the vicinity of which the hypercolumn encodes an infinite number of tuning curves in the absence of a stimulus. If one keeps increasing the value of λ one reaches a second bifurcation in the vicinity of which the tuning curves become multimodal or do not satisfy some other biological constraints. Hence the system *has to* operate next to the first static bifurcation which is a strong constraint on the possible values of the parameter. When one then turns on the input the infinite number of solutions becomes finite. An analysis of the stability of these solutions shows that the one correspondind to the main visual orientation of the stimulus is stable and the others unstable: the hypercolumn is in effect sharpening the weakly tuned input it is receiving from the thalamus. An important point is that some of the unstable solutions may be weakly unstable (almost stable). This implies that one can in principle design stimuli (time varying) for which the orientation of the response of the hypercolumn is different from that of the stimulus for a significant amount of time (significant with respect to the time constant τ). This prediction of a cortical illusion could potentially be tested experimentally, see [11].

3.2   Representing Visual Textures

Visual textures can also be described in the framework of neural fields as described in [12]. The corresponding feature space is larger than the one for visual orientations, featuring three, instead of one, dimensions. As in the case of visual orientations the corresponding neural fields equations are invariant with respect to the action of a group of transformations. This group turns out to be much more complicated than the group of planar rotations, and can be thought of as the group of isometries (transformations that preserve distances) in the two-dimensional hyperbolic space which can be represented as the Poincaré disk. The mathematical analysis of this class of neural fields equations is not yet as complete as in the case of the ring model of orientations, see [13–15] but the basic remarks about choosing the parameter values in such a way as to operate next to a static bifurcation still apply.

3.3   Representing Visual Motion Directions

Directions of motion are also amenable to analyses of a similar kind. A detailed study of the bifurcations of the solutions to the corresponding neural fields equations is of great value to understand multistable perception. This phenomenon provides useful insights into competitive interactions within the brain. When two mutually exclusive interpretations of a presented visual stimulus are possible, the mechanisms which serve to resolve this ambiguity provide a dynamic gating which determines access to conscious perception. We have started investigating these phenomena using neural fields, see [16].

4   Open Problems

I would like to mention three of the many still open problems. The first is related to the notion of uncertainty. We have assumed that everything was deterministic in our models. This is obviously only an approximation, hopefully a first-order one, but one should investigate the impact of the introduction of uncertainty in neural fields. The second is related to the spatial distribution of the neuronal populations. Most of the mathematical analysis has been done for non spatial models (visual orientations, visual textures, motion directions) whereas visual areas are spatially organized. This issue needs to be addressed further. The third and last one arises from the fact that in all models presented in sections 3.1-3.3 we have assumed a feature-based connectivity whereas there does seem to°be any biological evidence for such a connectivity.

Acknowledgements. This work was partially supported by the ERC grant No 227747 (NERVI) and the IP Project BrainScaleS No 269921.

References

1. Wilson, H., Cowan, J.: Excitatory and inhibitory interactions in localized populations of model neurons. Biophys. J. 12, 1–24 (1972)
2. Amari, S.: Characteristics of random nets of analog neuron-like elements. Syst. Man Cybernet. SMC-2 (1972)
3. Faugeras, O., Touboul, J., Cessac, B.: A constructive mean field analysis of multi population neural networks with random synaptic weights and stochastic inputs. Frontiers in Computational Neuroscience 3 (2009)
4. Baladron, J., Fasoli, D., Faugeras, O., Touboul, J.: Mean-field description and propagation of chaos in networks of hodgkin-huxley and. The Journal of Mathematical Neuroscience 2 (2012)
5. Faugeras, O., Grimbert, F., Slotine, J.J.: Stability and synchronization in neural fields. Technical Report RR-6212, INRIA (2007)
6. Veltz, R., Faugeras, O.: Local/global analysis of the stationary solutions of some neural field equations. SIAM Journal on Applied Dynamical Systems 9, 954–998 (2010)
7. Veltz, R., Faugeras, O.: Stability of the stationary solutions of neural field equations with propagation delays. The Journal of Mathematical Neuroscience 1, 1 (2011)
8. Hubel, D., Wiesel, T.: Receptive fields, binocular interaction and functional architecture in the cat visual cortex. J. Physiol. 160, 106–154 (1962)
9. Hansel, D., Sompolinsky, H.: Modeling feature selectivity in local cortical circuits. Methods of Neuronal Modeling, 499–567 (1997)
10. Ben-Yishai, R., Bar-Or, R., Sompolinsky, H.: Theory of orientation tuning in visual cortex. Proceedings of the National Academy of Sciences 92, 3844–3848 (1995)
11. Veltz, R.: Nonlinear analysis methods in neural field models. PhD thesis. Univ Paris Est ED MSTIC (2011)
12. Chossat, P., Faugeras, O.: Hyperbolic planforms in relation to visual edges and textures perception. Plos Comput Biol. 5, e1000625 (2009)
13. Chossat, P., Faye, G., Faugeras, O.: Bifurcations of hyperbolic planforms. Journal of Nonlinear Science 21, 465–498 (2011)
14. Faye, G., Chossat, P., Faugeras, O.: Analysis of a hyperbolic geometric model for visual texture perception. The Journal of Mathematical Neuroscience 1 (2011)
15. Faye, G., Chossat, P.: Bifurcation diagrams and heteroclinic networks of octagonal h-planforms. Journal of Nonlinear Science, 49 (2011)
16. Rankin, J., Tlapale, É., Veltz, R., Faugeras, O., Kornprobst, P.: Bifurcation analysis applied to a model of motion integration with a multistable stimulus. Journal of Computational Neuroscience, 1–22 (2012), doi:10.1007/s10827-012-0409-5

Visual Cortex as a General-Purpose Information-Processing Device

James A. Bednar

Institute for Adaptive and Neural Computation,
University of Edinburgh, UK
jbednar@inf.ed.ac.uk
http://homepages.inf.ed.ac.uk/jbednar

Abstract. Experiments on the primary visual cortex (V1) of monkeys have established that (1) V1 neurons respond to certain low-level visual features like orientation and color at specific locations, (2) this selectivity is preserved over wide ranges in contrast, (3) preferences are each mapped smoothly across the V1 surface, and (4) surround modulation effects and visual illusions result from complex patterns of interaction between these neurons. Although these properties are specific to vision, this paper describes how each can arise from a generic cortical architecture and local learning rules. In this approach, initially unspecific model neurons automatically become specialized for typical patterns of incoming neural activity, forming detailed representations of visual properties through self-organization. The resulting computational model suggests that it may be possible to devise a relatively simple, general, high-performance system for processing visual and other real-world data.

Keywords: computational neuroscience, development, self-organization.

1 Introduction

What can we learn from biology about how to build a robust, high-performance, adaptive visual system? Current computer vision systems incorporate many insights from biology, yet remain far behind human and animal capabilities. In this paper I argue that the current approach of hard-wiring observed animal visual-system properties is inherently limited, because it can only capture aspects of vision that we already understand fully. Instead, we can use the observed vision-specific properties of neurons in the primary visual cortex (V1) as a constraint or guide by which to evaluate *general-purpose* algorithms that yield vision-specific circuitry as just one possible outcome of a developmental process.

As background, experimental studies on monkeys, cats, ferrets, and tree shrews over the past half century have established a wide range of properties of V1 neurons related to their function in visual processing (reviewed in [2,1]):

1. V1 neurons respond selectively, in terms of their average firing rate, to specific low-level visual features such as the position, orientation, eye of origin, motion direction, spatial frequency, interocular disparity, or color of a small patch of an image.

A. Fusiello et al. (Eds.): ECCV 2012 Ws/Demos, Part I, LNCS 7583, pp. 480–485, 2012.

2. V1 neurons in non-rodent mammalian species are organized into smooth topographic maps for some or all of these visual features, with specific patterns of feature preference variation across the cortical surface and and specific interactions between these maps.

3. V1 neurons in these maps are laterally connected with connection strengths and probabilities that reflect their selectivities (e.g. with stronger connections between neurons preferring similar orientations).

4. Due in part to these lateral connections, V1 neuronal responses are systematically modulated by the activities of surrounding neurons.

5. V1 neurons exhibit contrast-invariant tuning for the features for which they are selective, such that selectivity is preserved even for strong inputs. This property rules out most simple (linear) models of visual feature selectivity.

6. Many V1 neurons have complex preferences that cannot be characterized using a spatial template of their preferred pattern, e.g. responding to similar patterns with some tolerance to the exact retinal position of the pattern.

7. Response properties of V1 neurons exhibit long-term and short-term plasticity and adaptation, measurable psychophysically as visual aftereffects, which suggests ongoing dynamic regulation of responses.

8. When visual inputs change, V1 neural responses exhibit a stereotyped temporal pattern, with transiently high responses at onset and offset and a lower sustained response, which biases neural responses towards non-static stimuli.

Given this wealth of data from V1, one approach to designing a bio-inspired artificial vision system would be to replicate the observed features of V1 in an idealized form, and then add additional human-designed processing stages to account for visual processing in the less-well-studied areas beyond V1. For instance, the orientation and spatial frequency selectivity of V1 neurons can be well approximated by a Gabor function [3], and so one can set up an artificial V1 consisting of banks of Gabor filters (a "feature plane" or "Gabor jet" approach) covering the full range of orientations and the spatial frequencies of interest. Many computer vision algorithms (as well as computational models of vision) use such a filter bank as a preprocessing stage to decompose an image into a sparse local-orientation–based representation for further analysis.

However, an alternative approach can be motivated by the hypothesis that the cerebral cortex is largely equipotential: cortical regions at various levels of the visual system are very similar cytoarchitectonically (i.e., when viewed under a microscope), and can become differentiated based on the inputs to the region during development, rather than based on some prespecified design. For instance, Sur and colleagues showed that when visual inputs from the eye are experimentally manipulated to synapse with neurons in the thalamus that project to what is normally auditory cortex, the former auditory cortex develops visually selective cells having many of the properties in the above list [4,5]. While the idea of equipotentiality remains controversial in its details [6], it underlies much of the motivation for studying V1 as a model area in neuroscience — hopefully, insights from V1 will apply to understanding the cortex as a whole, and thus help us understand functional behavior such as that of the visual system.

Accordingly, I propose that it would be valuable to use findings from V1 as constraints, not as a design blueprint. I.e., can we make a biologically plausible architecture in which the observed properties of V1 arise automatically, from purely general-purpose mechanisms? Such an architecture could then be applied to other less-understood visual areas, potentially developing an artificial vision system with performance comparable to biological systems.

In this paper I review progress towards this goal that has been made by members of my research group. Specifically, we propose a simple cortical architecture called GCAL (Gain-Control, Adaptive, Lateral) that can account for all eight of the above-listed properties of V1, without prespecifying anything vision specific about V1's circuitry or neural properties. Despite the significant work remaining before V1 has been adequately captured in a model, progress so far is compatible with the idea of V1 developing from an equipotential starting point. This work provides an initial sketch of what a complete and general-purpose cortical region model should contain, which shows promise as a blueprint for future artificial vision systems.

2 Architecture

Figure 1 shows the sheets and connections in the GCAL model for all of the known topographic maps in V1, as described in refs. [1] and [7]. In this section we focus on a simpler version with only a single pair of RGC/LGN sheets, and only one V1 sheet, but otherwise similar architecture. This reduced model can only be used for retinotopy and orientation, and only for simple rather than complex cells, but suffices to exhibit the fundamental self-organizing principles.

Training this model consists of drawing a visual input on the retina, allowing each level of the model to respond, and then adjusting each connection weight to a V1 neuron based on a local learning rule. Given the activation $\eta_i(t)$ of each neuron i at time t, the activation $\eta_j(t + \delta t)$ of a given unit j at time $t + \delta t$ can be calculated as a thresholded dot product between the input neuron activities and a set of weights:

$$\eta_j(t + \delta t) = \sigma \left(\sum_p \gamma_p \sum_{i \in F_{jp}} \eta_i(t)\omega_{ij} \right), \tag{1}$$

where F_{jp} is a *connection field*, i.e., the set of all input neurons from which target unit j receives connections in the given projection. ω_{ij} is the connection weight from unit i to unit j in that projection. Across all projections, multiple direct connections between the same pair of neurons are possible, but each projection p contains at most one connection between i and j. σ is a half-wave rectifying function with a variable threshold point (θ) dependent on the average activity of the unit [7]. Each γ_p is an arbitrary multiplier for the overall strength of connections in projection p.

In every iteration, each connection weight ω_{ij} is adjusted using a simple Hebbian learning rule. This rule results in connections that reflect correlations

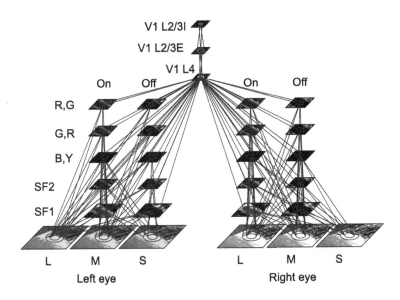

Fig. 1. Comprehensive GCAL model architecture. GCAL model for the development of simple and complex cells with surround modulation and maps for retinotopy, orientation preference, ocular dominance, disparity, motion direction, temporal frequency, spatial frequency, and color. The model consists of 29 neural sheets and 123 separate projections between them. Each sheet is drawn to scale, with larger sheets subcortically to avoid edge effects, and an actual sample activity pattern on each subcortical sheet. Each projection is illustrated with an oval, also drawn to scale, showing the extent of the connection field in that projection, with lines converging on the target of the projection. Sheets below V1 are hardwired with Difference of Gaussian RFs that cover the range of response types found in the retina and LGN, including different preferred spatial frequencies (SF1, SF2) and cone types (R/G/B). Connections to V1 neurons are initially unspecific but adapt via Hebbian learning, allowing the self-organized V1 neurons to exhibit the range of response types seen experimentally, by differentially weighting each of the subcortical inputs. Reprinted from ref. [1].

between the presynaptic activity and the postsynaptic response. Hebbian connection weight adjustment for unit j is dependent on the presynaptic activity η_i, the post-synaptic response η_j, and the Hebbian learning rate α:

$$\omega_{ij}(t+1) = \frac{\omega_{ij}(t) + \alpha\eta_j\eta_i}{\sum_{k \in F_{jp}} (\omega_{kj}(t) + \alpha\eta_j\eta_k)} \qquad (2)$$

Unless it is constrained, Hebbian learning will lead to ever-increasing (and thus unstable) values of the weights, and so weights are constrained using divisive post-synaptic weight normalization (the denominator in equation 2).

   The free parameters of this model (primarily the various γ_P parameters) are set to give a balance between afferent and lateral drives, and between excitation and inhibition, such that incoming activity patterns are sharpened into a set of localized "bubbles" of activity [2]. These active neurons then become more selective for the current pattern, due to Hebbian learning. Subsequent input patterns lead to other neurons responding and becoming selective for those patterns. Over time, the connection weights settle into a "dynamic equilibrium" [2], where neuron selectivities cover the range and likelihood of the types of input patterns presented.

3   Results

Figure 2 shows how orientation selectivity emerges in the simplest GCAL model, whose subcortical pathway consists of a single set of monochromatic ON and OFF LGN inputs (omitting multiple delays, spatial frequencies, or cone preferences) for a single eye.

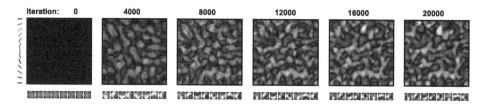

Fig. 2. Development of maps and afferent connections. Over the course of 20,000 input presentations, GCAL model V1 neurons develop selectivity for typical features of the input patterns. Here simulated retinal waves were presented for the first 6,000 inputs (modelling prenatal development), followed by 14,000 monochromatic images of natural scenes (modelling postnatal visual experience). Connection fields to V1 neurons were initially random and isotropic (bottom of Iteration 0; CFs for 8 sample neurons are shown). Neurons were initially unselective, responding approximately equally to all orientations, and are thus black in the orientation map plot (where saturated colors represent orientation-selective neurons whose preference is labeled with the color indicated in the key). Over time, neurons develop specific afferent connection fields (bottom of remaining iterations) that cause neurons to respond to specific orientations. Nearby neurons respond to similar orientations, as in animal maps, and as a whole they eventually represent the full range of orientations found in the inputs. Reprinted from [7].

Given their subcortical inputs, these neurons will never be able to learn an eye, color, or disparity preference, but when the model is extended as in ref. 1, the same model V1 then develops preferences and maps for those additional features [1]. Once developed, these models show realistic visual aftereffects due to short-term Hebbian adaptation, matching human performance for the tilt aftereffect and McCollough effect [8,9]. More complex processing in V1 is necessary to account for surround modulation [10] and development of complex cells [11], but no vision-specific circuitry or neural properties are required. Preliminary work also shows that a small change to the LGN is sufficient to account for the transient time course of responses in the LGN and V1 [12], potentially extending this model to account for detailed spatiotemporal processing.

4   Conclusion

The GCAL model results suggest that it will soon be feasible to build a single general-purpose system that will account for a very large fraction of V1 visual response properties. The model suggests that cortical neurons develop to cover the typical range of variation in their thalamic inputs, within the context of a smooth, multidimensional topographic map, and that lateral connections store pairwise correlations and use this information to modulate responses to natural scenes, dynamically adapting to both long-term and short-term visual input statistics. This model acts as a baseline for determining which properties require more complex approaches, such as feedback, attention, and detailed neural geometry and dynamics, with a goal of determining a general cortical architecture that can be applied to artificial vision tasks.

Acknowledgments. Thanks to each of the collaborators whose modelling work is reviewed and cited here. Supported in part by the UK EPSRC and BBSRC Doctoral Training Centre in Neuroinformatics, under grants EP/F500385/1 and BB/F529254/1, and by the US NIMH grant R01-MH66991. Computational resources were provided by the Edinburgh Compute and Data Facility (ECDF).

References

1. Bednar, J.A.: Building a mechanistic model of the development and function of the primary visual cortex. Journal of Physiology – Paris (in press, 2012)
2. Miikkulainen, R., Bednar, J.A., Choe, Y., Sirosh, J.: Computational Maps in the Visual Cortex. Springer, Berlin (2005)
3. Daugman, J.G.: Two-dimensional spectral analysis of cortical receptive field profiles. Vision Research 20, 847–856 (1980)
4. Sur, M., Pallas, S.L., Roe, A.W.: Cross-modal plasticity in cortical development: Differentiation and specification of sensory neocortex. TINS 13, 227–233 (1990)
5. Yuste, R., Sur, M.: Development and plasticity of the cerebral cortex: From molecules to maps. Journal of Neurobiology 41, 1–6 (1999)
6. Rakic, P.: Confusing cortical columns. PNAS 105, 12099–12100 (2008)
7. Law, J.S., Antolik, J., Bednar, J.A.: Mechanisms for stable and robust development of orientation maps and receptive fields. Tech. report, Informatics, University of Edinburgh, EDI-INF-RR-1404 (2011)
8. Bednar, J.A., Miikkulainen, R.: Tilt aftereffects in a self-organizing model of the primary visual cortex. Neural Computation 12, 1721–1740 (2000)
9. Ciroux, J.: Simulating the McCollough effect in a self-organizing model of the primary visual cortex. Master's thesis, University of Edinburgh, UK (2005)
10. Antolik, J.: Unified Developmental Model of Maps, Complex Cells and Surround Modulation in the Primary Visual Cortex. PhD thesis, Informatics, University of Edinburgh, UK (2010)
11. Antolik, J., Bednar, J.A.: Development of maps of simple and complex cells in the primary visual cortex. Frontiers in Computational Neuroscience 5, 17 (2011)
12. Stevens, J.L.: A temporal model of neural activity and VSD response in the primary visual cortex. Master's thesis, University of Edinburgh, UK (2011)

Reading Out the Synaptic Echoes
of Low-Level Perception in V1

Yves Frégnac

UNIC-CNRS, Gif-sur-Yvette, France
fregnac@unic.cnrs-gif.fr
http://www.unic.cnrs-gif.fr

Abstract. Primary visual cortex (V1) in the mammalian brain computes on the
fly perceptual primitives (form, motion, visual flow) from the feedforward
bombardment of retinal events channeled through the thalamus. At the same
time, it integrates the distributed feedback of higher cortical areas involved in
more elaborate cognitive functions. The reverberating activity evoked by the in-
terplay between these two streams has been hypothesized to form the trace of
the low-level computational operations written on the "high resolution buffer"
of primary cortical areas [1]. In vivo intracellular electrophysiology in V1 offers the unique possibility of listening to the synaptic echoes of the effective
perceptual network at work. On the basis of the comparison between functional
synaptic imaging and voltage sensitive dye imaging, I will show that the emergence of macroscopic features of perception (Gestalt and motion flow related
percepts) in early sensory cortical areas can be predicted from the read-out of
analog graded events (synaptic potentials) operating at a more microscopic integration level.

The field of neuromorphic computation has grown from the idea that inspiration for
future computational architectures can be gained from a better understanding of information processing in biological neural networks. An illustration of the impact of
Biology in Artificial Vision and Image Processing is given by studies of the early
visual system in the mammalian brain. Information coding of the sensory world in our
brain is both **digital**, in terms of spike-based events, and **analog**, in terms of slower,
subthreshold changes in membrane voltage resulting from the ongoing or evoked
barrage of synaptic inputs. *In vivo* intracellular electrophysiology during sensory
processing in primary cortical areas offers the unique possibility of listening to the
"synaptic rumour" of the effective network at work, extracting primitives of our environment (local contrast, form, retinal flow, ..). The analysis of synaptic echoes captured by the recording electrode in a single V1 cell allows to infer, indirectly in cortical space, the dynamics of the effective input network afferent to the recorded cell.

We have applied this reverse engineering method to demonstrate the propagation
of visually evoked activity through lateral (and possibly feedback) connectivity in the
primary cortex of higher mammals. This approach, based on functional synaptic imaging at the microscopic integration level, is compared here with a macroscopic imaging technique, based on the use of voltage sensitive fluorescent dyes. The conceptual

A. Fusiello et al. (Eds.): ECCV 2012 Ws/Demos, Part I, LNCS 7583, pp. 486–495, 2012.
© Springer-Verlag Berlin Heidelberg 2012

novelty of this multi-scale imaging approach is to explore to what extent emerging macroscopic features of low level (non attentive) perception in early sensory cortical areas (V1, V2, V4, MT), related to motion flow and form processing and Gestalt psychological laws, can be predicted from more microscopic levels of neural integration (conductance and membrane potential dynamics, synaptic receptive fields).

1 A Topological Paradox in the Early Visual System

The biological foundations of low-level visual perception in the mammalian brain show an apparent paradox:

On the one hand, the functional specificity of the early visual system underlying non-attentive perception seems to be best explained by a parallel cascade of serial filters from retina to cortex [2]. The synaptic impact of this topographic feed-forward projection is strong and results in multiple ordered point-to-point representations of the retinal periphery onto central target neural structures: most thalamic and cortical neurons express in their discharge a "tubular" view of the visual world. Spiking responses are evoked only when visual stimuli are presented within a small retinal window, defined as the "minimal discharge field".

On the other hand, the anatomical architecture along the visual thalamo-cortical pathway includes a profusion of feedback routes, from cortex to thalamus and from higher-order processing stations to primary visual cortex (V1), as well as intrinsic lateral and recurrent connections confined within each processing relay stage [3].

Thus, the functional binding of distant points in the primary cortical representation by lateral and feedback connectivity introduces a mismatch with the retinotopic order imposed by the feedforward projections. How this topological conflict is solved by the early visual system is still poorly understood (review in [4]).

2 New Methodologies in Multi-scale Brain Imaging

In order to visualize the functional influence of lateral connections, experimental approaches, more invasive methods than fMRI, allow to detect subthreshold neural activation in addition to evoked spike activity. One method is to monitor the spread of evoked activation relayed across the superficial cortical layers, the representation plane of the retinal space, using the voltage-sensitive dye (VSD) imaging [5]: CCD cameras reach a spatial (<50 mm) and temporal precision (<1 ms) compatible with the structural columnar scale and the time-course of synaptic responses. The most adequate stimuli (oriented luminance gratings) are optimized to fire cortical columns sharing the same orientation preference, and can be limited (focal) or not (full field) to visual cortical receptive fields extent [6]. Such techniques provide the **macroscopic** imaging of functional networks across areas V1 and V2 in rodents, ferrets, cats and monkeys.

Rather than looking at the global evoked dynamics of the network, a complementary approach is to address the **microscopic** organization scale and focus on the synaptic bombardment of a single neuron. Intracellular electrophysiology with sharp electrodes can be used to continuously monitor the membrane potential of a single neuron for several hours, even *in vivo* [7,8]. The recorded irregular asynchronous spiking activity is the result of the transient but repeated **convergence** arising from multiple synaptic sources in the network. For the past 25 years, my lab has been developing a reverse engineering approach, based on demultiplexing the composite rumour of synaptic echoes recorded in a single cell. This new method, called "**Functional synaptic imaging**" [7], considers cortex as a chamber of echoes produced by visual activation. Its principle is similar to that of echography in the etymological sense (transcription of echoes) and equivalent to the principle of **time reversal mirrors** in acoustic physics and medicine [9]. Its validity relies however on the assumption that the input sources are separable in space and their synaptic influence travels in time with similar speed. This condition is rarely met in the general case, but seems to be valid for sparse stimulation regimes or during ongoing activity. Thus, functional synaptic imaging gives a prediction of the macroscopic activation of the network in space and time, which can be confronted with the direct observation of the spatio-temporal cortical dynamics evoked in the superficial layers of cortex, using voltage-sensitive dyes [6,10].

3   Predicting Travelling Waves from Synaptic Echoes

The hypothesis of a **travelling wave** [7] was made initially on the assumption of symmetry in exuberant intrinsic connectivity: since V1 is a highly recurrent network, we assume that each cell is connected reciprocally to any other cell, with identical propagation delays from and to. This theoretical shortcut allows the inference of propagation patterns (the cell being seen as a "**wave emitter**") solely on the basis of the spatio-temporal maps of stimulus-locked synaptic responses recorded in a single cell (the cell being seen as an "**echo receiver**"). This suggests that the information received from the RF center in the cortex through the feedforward afferents is then propagated radially by the horizontal connectivity to neighboring regions of the visual cortex over a distance that may correspond to up to 10 degrees of visual angle. These data led successfully to the functional identification and reconstruction of a propagating wave of visual activity relayed by the horizontal connectivity.

The principle of calculation of the propagation speed of the intracortical "horizontal" wave is straightforward when comparing the synaptic effects of two elementary stimuli (white bar), one in the core of the minimal discharge field, the other in the "silent" surround. The distance between the primary points of the feed-forward impact produced in cortex by the two stimuli can be predicted on the basis of their relative retinal eccentricity Δx_v and the value of the retino-cortical magnification factor (RCMF). This factor can be measured electrophysiologically ([11] in cat), by 2-deoxyglucose metabolic labeling ([12] in monkey), by intrinsic imaging ([13] in mouse and [14] in ferret) and by fMRI ([15] in humans). Thus, beyond a certain scale of spatial integration (larger than the columnar grain), any distance in visual space Δx_v can be converted to a distance in visual cortex Δx_c. The spatial range of the subthreshold field extent agrees with the anatomical description of 4-7 mm horizontal axons running across superficial layers [16]. Furthermore, the electrophysiological recordings give access to the delay Δt_c between the two synaptic echoes obtained through the feed-forward and the horizontally-mediated pathways. By dividing the inferred cortical distance Δx_c in cortex by the recorded delay Δt_c, an apparent horizontal propagation speed can be computed within the cortical map, hence in the plane of the layers of V1. This rough estimate assumes a linear transformation between retinal and cortical coordinates, which is not the case in the human visual system, but, in the cat, the non-linear logpolar transformation [17] has a reduced impact in the representation domain of the 5° around area centralis. The propagation speeds we inferred with or without logpolar correction range between 0.02 and 2 m/s, with a peak between 0.1 and 0.4 m/s.

These velocity values have since been confirmed for other sensory cortical structures, such as somatosensory cortex [18]. They are thus ten times slower than X-type thalamic input and feedback propagation from higher cortical areas (2 m/s in [19]) and one hundred times slower than the fast Y-pathway (8-40 m/s in [20]). They are in fact within the order of magnitude of conduction speeds measured *in vitro* and *in vivo* along non-myelinated horizontal cortical axon fibers [21]. Recent reports based on cortical LFPs triggered on LGN spike activity rule out the possibility that divergence of LGN axons may also contribute to the build-up of the observed latency shifts (see for instance [22]).

4 Visualizing Travelling Waves with VSD Network Imaging

The macroscopic reconstruction of intra-V1 waves on the basis of microscopic echoes, described in the previous section, remains however an extrapolation made between two scales of spatial organization differing by two orders of magnitude (neuron vs map). The VSD technique, particularly adapted to layered structures, takes advantage of the fast changes in the fluorescence by the dye as a function of the state of depolarization of the membrane in which it is incorporated. It gives an unprecedented view of the state of dendritic tuft membrane depolarization in the superficial layers of the cortex, with a time sensitivity close to that of intracellular recordings [5,23,24]. Since their pioneering study of cortical spread function [5], the team of Amiram Grinvald has provided detailed quantifications of intracortical dynamics evoked by various inducer stimuli (square, annular grating) and documented the slow propagation of an activation wavefront, in area 17 or 18, consistent in speed with the conduction velocity of horizontal connections [6,26].

Many groups have since confirmed the propagation of spontaneous and evoked waves across the cortical laminar planes in visual primary and secondary cortical areas of rodents [27], ferrets [28,29] and higher mammals [30]. The visually evoked waves exhibit steroty ped features and show invariance with the parameters of the drifting grating, such as orientation and temporal or spatial frequency. In a contrasted way, the "ongoing" (spontaneous) waves vary in kinetics. They do not respect area boundaries, and propagate without interruption throughout the entire imaged area (up to 4 mm) more slowly than the evoked activity. It is likely that the two forms of propagating activity are generated by different mechanisms and that the slowest waves is a polysynaptic column-to column propagation of "up" states [31], similar to the « rolling waves » previously reported with calcium imaging *in vitro* [32].

In summary, these different imaging studies fully corroborate the prediction of a travelling wave across cortex, that we extracted some fifteen years ago from our intracellular recordings [7,8]: synaptic responses elicited by stimuli placed far from the center of the receptive field showed decreasing amplitude and increasing onset delay with the relative eccentricity. Most remarkably both types of imaging methods (microscopic or mesoscopic) give the same mean estimate of propagation speed (0.10-0.40 m/s) although they are based on different measurements and analysis.

5   Gestalt Principles as an Emerging Feature of Visual Cortical Dynamics

One of the functional roles attributed to long-distance horizontal axons in visual cortex is to link columns sharing similar orientation preference [33]. However, the anatomical evidence in favor of such bias remains rather scarce in the cat cortex. Combinations of optical imaging and intracellular labeling show indeed a diversity of potential links established between orientation columns which do not obey, at least at the statistical significance level, the rule "who is alike tend to be coupled together". As a consequence, at a more integrated mesoscopic level, the net functional effect cannot be predicted. A recent collaborative work between our lab and the group of Amiram Grinvald, addressed this issue by combining VSD and functional synaptic imaging [6]. It showed unexpectedly that a local oriented stimulus evoked an orientation selective activity component which remained confined to the feed-forward cortical imprint of the stimulus (space constant~1mm). Thus, a single local stimulus does not propagate orientation preference through the long-range horizontal cortical connections. In contrast, when increasing spatial and temporal summation, both optical imaging and intracellular measurements showed the emergence of an iso-orientation selective spread. We conclude that stimulus-induced cooperativity is a necessary constraint for the emergence of iso-functional binding.

Such a contrasted and conditional behaviour may serve two functions: 1) for the local oriented stimulus, a non-selective divergent connectivity pattern may facilitate detection of high-order topological properties (e.g. orientation discontinuities, corners, geons). 2) summation of multiple oriented sources in the far "silent" surround can optimize the emergence of iso-orientation preference links. For instance, oriented annular stimuli may recruit iso-oriented sources collinearly organized with the orientation preference axis of the target column/cell; similar synergy may be obtained in the temporal domain when sources, independent of their exact location, share the same motion direction sensitivity as the target grating. Both of these configurations, which are confounded in annular aperture protocols, correspond to the neural implementation of the Gestalt's continuity and common fate principles [34,35].

This conclusion might explain why multiple stroke animations with oriented elements favor the propagation of perceptual biases such as observed during apparent motion illusions. We hypothesized from our own intracellular findings that the perception of speed could be differentially modulated during apparent motion sequences of oriented stimuli, either collinear and aligned with respect to the motion axis or at an angle to it [36]. We devised a series of psychophysical experiments in humans that aimed at testing the influence of orientation relative to the motion axis on perceived speed [37]. Observers were asked to discriminate during a forced choice task between the relative speeds of two apparent-motion (AM) sequences. Results showed the induction of a "speedup" illusion which was observed for retinal speeds compatible with intracortical horizontal wave propagation. For this range of speed (equivalent to saccadic displacement), a Gabor patch moving along its orientation axis appears much faster than a Gabor patch oriented at an angle to the motion axis.

Apparent Motion   The Dynamic Association Field

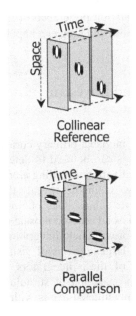

Collinear
Reference

Parallel
Comparison

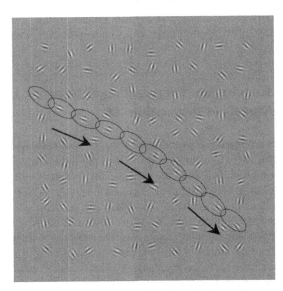

Contiguity in Space AND Continuity in Time

Fig. 1. The "Dynamic Association Field" Hypothesis
Left: two-forced choice apparent motion protocol, where human observers report which sequence of oriented elements is seen "faster" [36,37]. Two configurations were compared (collinear and parallel), in which the orientation of each element was respectively collinear or orthogonal to the motion axis. Human subjects perceive the "collinear" apparent motion (AM) configuration as being more than two times faster than the "parallel" one, when the feedforward input evoked by the three-stroke AM stimuli travels in V1 cortex at the speed of horizontal propagation (0.1 to 0.3 m/s). **Right:** the "dynamic association field" hypothesis; local oriented inputs (Gabor patches) induce a facilitation wave of activity travelling along horizontal connections intra V1. This wave binds in space and time proximal receptive fields with co-linear preferred orientations, thus creating a contiguous path of temporal integration. The associative strength of the perceptual effect is maximal when the asynchronous feedforward sequence produced by joint strokes of apparent motion (arrow) travels in phase in the cortical network with the visually evoked horizontal propagation. The retinal flow speed at which this effect predominates is compatible with retinal slip produced by saccadic eye-movements during active scanning of contours.

These different experimental observations led us to formulate the concept of the **"dynamic association field"** [10], which adds a temporal coordination dimension to the static "association field" introduced originally by Hess and Field [38,39]. In its dynamic version, the revised concept assumes that local oriented inputs (Gabor patches) induce a facilitation wave of activity travelling along horizontal connections intra V1 (Figure 1, right panel). This coordination wave tends to bind proximal receptive fields with co-linear preferred orientations, thus creating a contiguous path of temporal integration. The associative strength of the perceptual effect is maximal when the asynchronous feedforward sequence produced by joint strokes of apparent motion travels in phase with the visually evoked horizontal intracortical propagation. Recent intracellular work from our lab shows that sparse apparent motion two-stroke noise appears as a powerful stimulus condition to trigger the coordination of synaptic activity along centripetal motion streaks attuned to the orientation preference of the target cells (Carelli, Pananceau, Gerard-Mercier, Baudot, Monier and Frégnac, unpublished).

6   Conclusion: Propagation of Network Belief and Bayesian Models of Perception

This comparative overview of synaptic and network imaging in visual primary cortex summarizes two important findings: 1) intracellular recordings can be used to detect at the single cell level the synaptic trace of waves of visual activation travelling along long-distance horizontal connections; 2) VSD imaging methods reveal the macroscopic propagation pattern predicted from these synaptic echoes. One obvious consequence is that the V1 network should not be considered as an ordered mosaic of independent "tubular" analyzers, but rather as a constellation of wide field integrators, integrating simultaneously input sources arising from much larger regions of visual space than previously thought. The collective behaviour of these integrators is coordinated during sensory processing by the anisotropic propagation of stimulus-induced facilitatory waves travelling at slow speed along unmyelinated axons within the superficial cortical layers. Thus, primary visual cortical neurons have the capacity to combine information originating from different points of the visual field, in a spatio-temporal reference frame centered on the discharge field itself. This ability imposes precise constraints in time and in space on the efficacy of the summation process of elementary synaptic responses, and could subserve the emergence of elementary self-organizing processes necessary for implementing Gestalt principles.

A likely role of horizontal propagation is to favor the build-up of coherent self-organized knowledge in the network, and broadcast it to distant parts of the network. The functional features of these slow waves support the hypothesis of promoting a "dynamic association" field, which facilitates the integration of feed-forward inputs yet to come. During perceptual illusions (apparent motion, line motion), these waves propagate the **network belief** of the possible presence of a global percept (the "whole": here, continuous motion of a space-invariant shape) before the illusory percept becomes validated by the sequential presentation of the "parts" (signaled by direct focal feed-forward waves). Such dynamics obey closely the Gestalt prediction that the emergence of the "whole" should precede in time the detection of the "parts".

These cortical processes result, at the perceptual level, in the propagation of functional biases (binding of collinear contour and iso-directional motion) which spreads beyond the scale of the cortical hyper column. It remains to be determined whether the correlations we report between perception and horizontal propagation result solely of neural processes intrinsic to V1, or whether they reflect the reverberation in V1 of collective feedback from multiple secondary cortical areas. It may be indeed envisioned that the primary visual cortex plays the role of a generalized echo chamber fed by other cortical areas (visual or not) which participate in the coding of shape and motion in space: accordingly, the waves travelling across V1 would signal the emergence of perceptual coherence when sufficient synergy is reached between the different cortical analyzers. A new challenge is launched at the interface between electrophysiology and brain imaging, where multiscale imaging approaches give unprecedented access to generic principles of binding between Form and Motion, which operate in the early visual system during low-level (non attentive) perception.

Acknowledgements. The reviewed work of the Lab was done in collaboration with Vincent Bringuier, Frédéric Chavane, Cyril Monier, and more recently with Pedro Carelli, Julien Fournier, Florian Gérard-Mercier, Olivier Marre and Marc Pananceau for intracellular physiology and VSD imaging and with Sébastien Georges, Jean Lorenceau and Peggy Series for psychophysics. The current work is supported by CNRS, and grants from ANR (NatStats and V1-complex) and the European Community FET-Bio-I3 programs (IP FP6: FACETS (015879), IP FP7: BRAINSCALES (269921) and Brain-i-nets (243914)).

References

1. Mumford, D.: On the computational architecture of the neocortex. II. The role of cortico-cortical loops. Biol. Cybern. 66, 241–251 (1992)
2. Carandini, M., Demb, J.B., Mante, V., Olshausen, R.A., Tolhurst, D.J., Dan, Y., Gallant, J.L., Rust, N.: Do we know what the early visual system does? J. Neurosci. 25, 10577–10597 (2005)
3. Gilbert, C., Das, A., Ito, M., Kapadia, M., Westheimer, G.: Spatial integration and cortical dynamics. Proc. Natl. Acad. Sci. USA 93, 615–622 (1996)
4. Séries, P., Lorenceau, J., Frégnac, Y.: The silent surround of V1 receptive fields: theory and experiments. Journal of Physiology 97(4-6), 453–474 (2003)
5. Grinvald, A., Hildesheim, R.: VSDI: a new era in functional imaging of cortical dynamics. Nat. Rev. Neurosci. 5(11), 874–885 (2004)
6. Chavane, F., Sharon, D., Jancke, D., Marre, O., Frégnac, Y., Grinvald, A.: Lateral spread of orientation selectivity in V1 is controlled by intracortical cooperativity. Front. System Neuroscience 5(4), 1–26 (2011), doi:10.3389/fnsys.2011.00004.
7. Frégnac, Y., Bringuier, V.: Spatio-temporal dynamics of synaptic integration in cat visual cortical receptive fields. In: Aertsen, A., Braitenberg, V. (eds.) Brain Theory: Biological Basis and Computational Theory of Vision, pp. 143–199. Springer, Amsterdam (1996)

8. Bringuier, V., Chavane, F., Glaeser, L., Frégnac, Y.: Horizontal propagation of visual activity in the synaptic integration field of area 17 neurons. Science 283, 695–699 (1999)
9. Fink, M.M.: Time reversal in acoustics. Contemporary Physics 37, 95–109 (1996) 1366-5812
10. Frégnac, Y., Baudot, P., Chavane, F., Lorenceau, J., Marre, O., Monier, C., Pananceau, M., Carelli, P., Sadoc, G.: Multiscale functional imaging in V1 and cortical correlates of apparent motion. In: Masson, G., Ilg, U. (eds.) Dynamics of Visual Motion Processing, pp. 73–94. Springer (2010)
11. Albus, K.: A quantitative study of the projection area of the central and the paracentral visual field in area 17 of the cat. I. The precision of the topography. Exp. Brain Res. 24, 159–179 (1975)
12. Tootell, R.B., Silverman, M.S., Switkes, E., De Valois, R.L.: Deoxyglucose analysis of retinotopic organization in primate striate cortex. Science 218, 902–904 (1982)
13. Kalatsky, V.A., Stryker, M.P.: New paradigm for optical imaging: temporally encoded maps of intrinsic signal. Neuron 38(4), 529–545 (2003)
14. Basole, A., White, L.E., Fitzpatrick, D.: Mapping multiple features in the population response of visual cortex. Nature 423, 986–990 (2003)
15. Warnking, J., Dojat, M., Guerin-Dugue, A., Delon-Martin, C., Olympieff, S., Richard, N., Chehikian, A., Segebarth, C.: FMRI retinotopic mapping-step by step. Neuroimage 17, 1665–1683 (2002)
16. Mitchison, G., Crick, F.: Long axons within the striate cortex: their distribution, orientation, and patterns of connection. Proc. Natl. Acad. Sci. U S A. 79, 3661–3665 (1982)
17. Schwartz, E.L.: Spatial mapping in the primate sensory projection: analytic structure and relevance to perception. Biol. Cybern. 25, 181–194 (1977)
18. Moore, C.I., Nelson, S.B.: Spatio-temporal subthreshold receptive fields in the vibrissa representation of rat primary somatosensory cortex. J.Neurophysiol. 80, 2882–2892 (1998)
19. Nowak, L.G., Bullier, J.: The timing of information transfer in the visual system. In: Rockland, K.S., Kaas, J.H., Peters, A. (eds.) Extrastriate Visual Cortex in Primates, pp. 205–241. Plenum Press, New York (1997)
20. Hoffman, K.P., Stone, J.: Conduction velocity of afferents to cat visual cortex: a correlation with cortical receptive field properties. Brain Res. 32, 460–466 (1971)
21. Hirsch, J.A., Gilbert, C.D.: Synaptic physiology of horizontal connections in the cat's visual cortex. J. Neurosci. 11, 1800–1809 (1991)
22. Nauhaus, I., Busse, L., Carandini, M., Ringach, D.L.: Stimulus contrast modulates functional connectivity in visual cortex. Nature Neurosci. 12, 70–76 (2009)
23. Shoham, D., Glaser, D.E., Arieli, A., Kenet, T., Wijnbergen, C., Toledo, Y., Hildesheim, R., Grinvald, A.: Imaging cortical dynamics at high spatial and temporal resolution with novel blue voltage-sensitive dyes. Neuron 24(4), 791–802 (1999)
24. Roland, P.E.: Dynamic depolarisation fields in the cerebral cortex. Trends Neurosci. 25, 183–190 (2002)
25. Grinvald, A., Lieke, E.E., Frostig, R.D., Hildesheim, R.: Cortical point-spread function and long-range lateral interactions revealed by real-time optical imaging of macaque monkey primary visual cortex. J. Neurosci. 14, 2545–2568 (1994)
26. Jancke, D., Chavane, F., Naaman, S., Grinvald, A.: Imaging cortical correlates of illusion in early visual cortex. Nature 428, 423–426 (2004)
27. Xu, W., Huang, X., Takagaki, K., Wu, J.Y.: Compression and reflection of visually evoked cortical waves. Neuron 55(1), 119–129 (2007)

28. Roland, P.E., Hanazawa, A., Undeman, C., Eriksson, D., Tompa, T., Nakamura, H., Valentiniene, S., Ahmed, B.: Cortical feedback depolarization waves: a mechanism of top-down influence on early visual areas. Proc. Natl. Acad. Sci. USA 103(33), 12586–12591 (2006)

29. Ahmed, B., Hanazawa, A., Undeman, C., Eriksson, D., Valentiniene, S., Roland, P.E.: Cortical dynamics subserving visual apparent motion. Cerebral Cortex 18(12), 2796–2810 (2008)

30. Benucci, A., Frazor, R.A., Carandini, M.: Standing waves and traveling waves distinguish two circuits in visual cortex. Neuron 55(1), 103–117 (2007)

31. Frégnac, Y.R., Blatow, M., Changeux, J.P., DeFelipe, J., Markram, H., Lansner, A., Maass, W., Markram, H., McCormick, D., Michel, C.M., Monyer, H., Szathmáry, E., Yuste, R.: Ups and downs in the genesis of cortical computation. In: Grillner, S., et al. (eds.) Microcircuits: The Interface between Neurons and Global Brain Function Microcircuits: Dahlem Workshop Report 93, pp. 397–437. The MIT Press, Cambridge (2006)

32. Tanifuji, M., Sugiyama, T., Murase, K.: Horizontal propagation of excitation in rat visual cortical slices revealed by optical imaging. Science 266(5187), 1057–1059 (1994)

33. Ts'o, D.Y., Gilbert, C.D., Wiesel, T.N.: Relationships between horizontal interactions and functional architecture in cat striate cortex as revealed by cross-correlation analysis. J. Neurosci. 6, 1160–1170 (1986)

34. Wertheimer, M.: Experimentelle Studien über das Sehen von Beuegung. Zeitschrift für Psychologie und Physiologie der Sinnesorgane 61, 161–265 (1912)

35. Koffka, K.: Principles of Gestalt Psychology. Harcourt Brace Javanovich, NewYork (1935)

36. Sèries, P., Georges, S., Lorenceau, J., Frégnac, Y.: Orientation dependent modulation of apparent speed: a model based on the dynamics of feed-forward and horizontal connectivity in V1 cortex. Vision Res. 42, 2781–2797 (2002)

37. Georges, S., Sèries, P., Frégnac, Y., Lorenceau, J.: Orientation dependent modulation of apparent speed: psychophysical evidence. Vision Res. 42, 2757–2772 (2002)

38. Field, D.J., Hayes, A., Hess, R.F.: Contour integration by the human visual system: evidence for a local "association field". Vision Res. 33, 173–193 (1993)

39. Hess, R., Field, D.: Integration of contours: new insights. Trends in Cognitive Sciences 3(12), 480–486 (1999)

Learning Invariant Feature Hierarchies

Yann LeCun

Courant Institute, New York University

Abstract. Fast visual recognition in the mammalian cortex seems to be a hierarchical process by which the representation of the visual world is transformed in multiple stages from low-level retinotopic features to high-level, global and invariant features, and to object categories. Every single step in this hierarchy seems to be subject to learning. How does the visual cortex learn such hierarchical representations by just looking at the world? How could computers learn such representations from data? Computer vision models that are weakly inspired by the visual cortex will be described. A number of unsupervised learning algorithms to train these models will be presented, which are based on the sparse auto-encoder concept. The effectiveness of these algorithms for learning invariant feature hierarchies will be demonstrated with a number of practical tasks such as scene parsing, pedestrian detection, and object classification.

1 Introduction

The age-old architecture of pattern recognition systems is composed of two parts: a feature extractor and a classifier. The feature extractor is generally built "by hand", and transforms the raw input into a representation suitable for classification. The classifier, on the other hand, is fairly generic, and is the only trainable part of the system. Much effort and ingenuity has been devoted to designing appropriate feature extractors for particular problems and input modalities (see [1,2] for the most popular methods in vision).

In contrast, the ventral pathway of the visual cortex appears to comprise more than just two stages: the lateral geniculate nucleus which performs a sort of multi-scale high-pass filtering and contrast normalization, V1 which consists mainly of pooled oriented edge detectors with local receptive fields [3], V2 and V4 which seem to detect larger and more complex local motifs [4], and the inferro-temporal cortex in which object categories are encoded [5]. Although the visual cortex contains numerous feedback connections, fast object recognition appears to be an essentially feed-forward affair [6]. Every stage in the system seem subject to plasticity and learning, and the function of each area seems largely determined by its afferent signals through learning, as demonstrated by brain rewiring experiments [7].

Building a multi-stage recognition system in which all the stages are trained has been a long-term interest of mine since I started working on pattern recognition in the early 1980's. The obvious advantage is that this would reduce the amount of "manual" labor by leaving the design of the feature extractor to the learning algorithm. The feature extractor could be the optimally tuned to the task at hand. But the idea of *feature learning* has encountered a surprisingly large amount of resistance from the computer vision and

A. Fusiello et al. (Eds.): ECCV 2012 Ws/Demos, Part I, LNCS 7583, pp. 496–505, 2012.

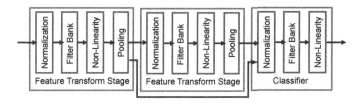

Fig. 1. A general multi-stage architecture for hierarchical feature learning and extraction

machine learning communities. The machine learning (ML) community has had a good handle on how to build classifiers for quite a while now. But the problem of *learning internal representations of the perceptual world* has received little attention until very recently. How do we train multi-stage systems that include the feature extractor, classifier, and high-level contextual post-processor in an integrated fashion? This question, which was already identified in the early 60's, has recently seen an explosive resurgence of interest, and has come to be known as the *deep learning* problem.

In the mid 1980's, there was a hope that neural nets with hidden units (Boltzmann machines or feed-forward neural nets) would offer a solution to the feature learning problem. But training generic neural networks was a complex and time consuming affair with the computers and software tools of the time, and given the rarity of large datasets. Furthermore, the basic architectural components used in traditional neural nets didn't seem appropriate for image recognition. One must design the architecture of the system to take advantage of the properties of the signal.

1.1 A General Architecture for Hierarchical Processing

A particularly important question is how to design the architecture so that the system can easily learn representations that are *invariant* (or robust) to irrelevant variations of the input. In the case of images, that includes translation, scaling, mild rotation, illumination, etc. A number of early researchers were inspired by Hubel and Wiesel's seminal work on the primary visual cortex, and their simple-cell/complex-cell model [3].

A general multi-stage architecture for hierarchical feature learning is shown in figure 1 (a 3-stage system is shown here). Each stage conforms to the simple-cell/complex-cell idea: (1) a normalization layer, which can be a whitening operation (e.g. ZCA), or in the case of spatial signals a high-pass filtering with local energy normalization at a single scale or multiple scales (Laplacian pyramid); (2) a linear filtering layer, which can be seen as a matrix or as a bank of convolution filters; (3) a fixed non-linear transformation layer, which can be a point-wise non-linear mapping (e.g. logistic, tanh, shrinking function, or half-rectifier), or something harsher such as a multinomial logistic or a winner-take-all; (4) a pooling layer, which aggregates a subset of values from the previous layer, and generally reduces the dimensionality of the representation though subsampling. Layer 1 is analogous to the LGN, layers 2 and 3 to groups of simple cells, and layer 4 to groups of complex cells. Multiple such 4-layer stages can be cascaded (typically 2 to 5). The last stage may often dispenses with the pooling layer and can be viewed as a classifer (or predictor), operating on the features extracted by the previous stages.

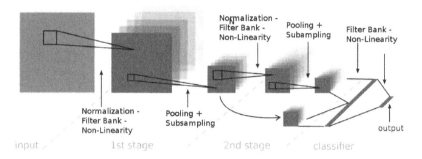

Fig. 2. A convolutional network architecture, which is a particular instance of the multi-stage architecture shown above

The role of layer 1 is to decorrelate variables and accentuate the differences (or ratios) between them, while eliminating variations of the absolute energy so that the non-linearity of layers 3 can always operate at its sweet spot. Decorrelation (and mean removal) has the additional advantage of accelerating gradient-based learning [8].

Layer 2 and 3 detect conjunctions of features or motifs on the previous stage. Its role is to non-linearly embed the input into a higher-dimensional space, so that inputs that are semantically different are likely to be represented by different patterns of activity. This expansion plays a similar role as using a non-linear kernel functions in a kernel machine: in high-dimensional spaces, categories are easier to separate. More generally, a function of interest is more likely to be linear when its input variable is embedded in a high dimensional space. The difference with kernel machine is that our filter banks will be trained from data, rather than simply selected from the training set.

Layer 4 serves to *merge semantically similar things* that have been partitioned into different patterns of activity by the simple cells. This is where invariance is built. Rather than producing invariance in the mathematical sense, the pooling layer merely "smoothes out" the input-output mapping so that irrelevant variations in the input affect the output smoothly, and in ways that can be easily dealt with (eliminated, if necessary). The pooling operation can consist of any symmetric aggregation function, such as an average, a max, a log-mixture ($\log \sum_i e^{x_i}$), or an L_p norm ($\sqrt[p]{\sum_i |x_i|^p}$), particularly with $p = 1, 2$, or ∞ (max). A theoretical analysis of pooling operations suggests that L_∞ is best when the features are sparse and the number of pooled variable is small, while average, L_1 or L_2 are best when the features are less sparse or the pooling area is large [9]. In practice L_2 pooling is a good tradeoff.

One may interpret the filter bank and non-linearity as conjunction operators (similar to logical AND or NAND in the boolean case) and the pooling operation as a sort of disjunction operator (similar to a logical OR), making a single stage a kind of non-boolean Disjunctive Normal Form.

1.2 Convolutional Architectures

Data from natural sensors often comes to us as multi-dimensional arrays in which local group of values are correlated, and the local statistics are invariant to the particular location in the array. For example, images can be seen as a series of 2D slices where each slice is a color channel, and the dimensions are spatial. The statistics of images are translation invariant, which means that if one particular filter is useful on one part of an image, it is probably useful on other parts of the image as well. This leads to the *convolutional network architecture* shown in figure 2 [10,11,12]. The filter bank in each stage is, in fact, a bank of convolution kernels applied to slices of the input. Filter outputs applied to multiple input channels can be combined additively to form a slice of the output (known as a feature map). The idea applies to other modalities than image, including audio, a (1+1)D array with one dimension being frequency channels and one being time, video, a (1+3)D array with color channels, time, and space. Other modalities such as RGB+Depth, sonar, radar, lidar, multi-spectral images, etc can be handled similarly.

The architecture shown in figure 2 has a structure reminiscent of the LGN-V1-V2-V4-IT hierarchy in the ventral pathway of the visual cortex. The simple cells have local receptive fields and are organized in a retinotopic fashion. The pooling layers are subsampled spatially, which reduces the spatial resolution of the representation and makes the representation vary smoothly with translations and small distortions of the input. Units have local receptive fields whose size increases as we move up in the hierarchy [13].

Supervised training of convolutional nets is performed using a form of stochastic gradient descent to minimize the discrepancy between the desired output and the actual output of the network. All the coefficient of all the filters in all the layers are updated simultaneously by the learning procedure. The gradients are computed with the back-propagation method.

A number of similar models have been proposed with different learning algorithms, starting with Fukushima's Neocognitron [14], and several others in the last 10 years [15,16]. It is important to notice that the most popular feature extraction methods in computer vision, SIFT [17] and HoG [18], are very much inspired by the simple-cell/complex-cell concept and conform to the first stage of figure 1. Moreover, the most popular standard recognition pipelines [19,20] conforms to the 3-stage architecture of figure 1: the first stage is SIFT, densely extracted over the input (similar to a convolutional network), the second stage filters are trained in an unsupervised manner with K-means (the non-linearity is a winner-take-all), and the pooling is an average over multiple scales. Finally the classifier is a support vector machine.

There have been numerous applications of convolutional networks going back to the mid 1990's for such applications as OCR and handwriting recognition, face, person, and license plate detection, age and gender estimation, video surveillance, etc (see [21] and references therein). They have been deployed by companies such as Google, Microsoft, AT&T, and NEC. In recent months, deep learning systems have broken long-held record on a number of benchmarks in a number of areas including speech recognition [22,23,24], object recognition vision [25,26,27], scene parsing [28], action recognition in video [29,30], natural language processing [31,32], and musical genre recognition [33].

2   Unsupervised Feature Learning

The resurgence of interest in deep architectures was caused in part by the appearance of unsupervised learning algorithms to train (or pre-train) the layers of a multi-stage system. The basic procedure is to pre-train each stage of a network in an unsupervised manner one after the other. After all the stages have been pre-trained, the entire network is fine-tuned using supervised learning (with gradient back-propagation). This procedure has two advantages: (1) unsupervised pre-training seems to place the system in a favorable starting point for supervised fine-tuning that will produce better performance results; (2) unsupervised learning leverages the availability of massive amounts of un-labeled data. Unsupervised pre-training on unlabeled data seems to "consume" a large amount of free parameters in the model, and allows us to use very large and flexible networks that would be hopelessly over-parameterized in a purely-supervised setting.

There are many methods to pre-train the filter banks of a multi-stage system in un-supervised mode, including (from the simple to the complicated): simply using ran-domly picked samples as filters; using K-means to produce prototypes and using them as filters [34]; using dictionary learning in sparse coding and use the basis functions as filters [35,36,37,38,12,39,34]; train some version of regularized auto-encoder such as *sparse auto-encoder*, denoising auto-encoder [40] or contracting auto-encoder [41]; train a restricted Boltzmann machine and use the weight matrix as filters [42] (see [43] for a recent review).

We will concentrate on the concept of sparse auto-encoder, as implemented in the Predictive Sparse Decomposition (PSD) method [37,38,39]. PSD is based on the clas-sical sparse coding and sparse modeling algorithm [44]: a vector (e.g. an image patch) Y is encoded as a feature vector Z^* by minimizing the following energy function:

$$E(Y, Z, W_d) = ||Y - W_d Z||^2 + \alpha \sum_k |Z_k| \quad Z^* = \mathrm{argmin}_Z E(Y, Z, W) \quad (1)$$

where W_d is a so-called *dictionary matrix* whose columns W_{dk} are called atoms or basis functions. The vector Z has generally higher dimension than Y (overcomplete representation). The minimization procedure will find a small number of column of W_d that can be linearly combined to reconstruct Y. The coefficients are the components of Z, many of which will be zero, due to the sparsity-inducing L_1 regularization term. Given a training set of input vectors Y^i, $i = 1 \ldots P$, learning W_d can be performed using stochastic gradient descent on W_d to minimize the reconstructive loss function $L_R(W) = \sum_{i=1}^{P} \min_z E(Y^i, Z, W)$, under the constraints that the columns of W_d be within the unit sphere.

Extracting features with sparse coding work beautifully as a feature extraction method when the dictionary matrix is trained with sparse modeling, particularly for learning mid-level features for object recognition [45,20]. But inferring Z^* from a particular Y is slow, because it involves minimizing the L1/L2 energy function above.

One solution to this problem is the PSD method, which consist in training an *param-eterized non-linear encoder function* $g(Y, W_e)$ where W_e is *encoder matrix or filter matrix*, so as to best predict the optimal sparse feature vector Z^* for all training sam-ples Y^i. The rows of W_e can be interpreted as a filter bank. Once the decoder and the encoder are trained, the decoder can be dispensed with, and the encoder used as a feture extractor (filter bank + non-linearity). The training can be performed by minimizing the predictive loss function

$$L_P(W_e) = \sum_{i=1}^{p} || \min_{Z} E(Y^i, Z, W_d) - g(Y^i, W_e)||^2.$$

Better yet, one can define a compound energy function

$$E_{PSD}(Y, Z, W_d, W_e) = ||Y - W_d Z||^2 + ||Z - g(Y, W_e)||^2 + \alpha \sum_{k} |Z_k|,$$

and train W_d and W_e to minimize the PSD loss function:

$$L_{PSD}(W_d, W_e) = \sum_{i=1}^{p} \min_{Z} E_{PSD}(Y^i, Z, W_d, W_e).$$

The encoder architecture can be a simple function such as $\text{shrink}_\beta(W_e Y)$, where shrink_β is the shrinking function applied indepently to each component of $W_e Y$:

$$\text{shrink}_\beta(x) = [0 \text{ if } -\beta < x < \beta; \ x - \beta \text{ if } x > \beta; \ x + \beta \text{ if } x < -\beta]$$

A more sophisticated version of PSD [39] uses a parameterized version of the unfolded flow graph of the FISTA algorithm for sparse coding [46]. This produces better sparse codes, but it's not clear whether the resulting feature vectors are better for recognition purpose (except perhaps in the highly over-complete case).

When trained on natural image patches, PSD (like sparse modeling) produces Gabor-like oriented filters (edgelets) at various orientation, frequencies, and positions within the patch (when trained to produce 2nd-stage features, the interpretation is considerably less clear). However, since the filters trained in this manner are meant to be used in a convolutional manner, it would seem appropriate to train them convolutionally. Training PSD (or sparse coding) at the patch level is inefficient, since shifted versions of each filter must be generated to reconstruct each image patch. Convolutional sparse coding [47] and convolutional PSD [48] solve that problem by viewing the reconstruction as multiple convolutions

$$E(Y, Z, W_d) = ||Y - \sum_{k} W_{dk} * Z_k||^2 + \alpha \sum_{kpq} |Z_{kpq}|$$

where Z_k is a *feature map* (an image about the same size as image Y) instead of a scalar, W_{dk} is a convolution kernel, and $*$ is the convolution operator (the predictive energy term was left out). Convolutional PSD produces much more diverse filters than patch-based PSD, as shown in figure 3.

A convolutional network pre-trained with Convolutional PSD generally yields better performance than if the network is trained purely supervised.

3   Unsupervised Invariant Feature Learning

The PSD training procedure is quite effective, but doesn't take into account the fact that the features it produces are aggregated by the pooling layer (complex cells). Invariant

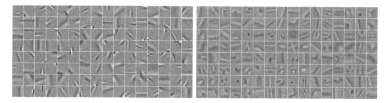

Fig. 3. Filters obtained with patch-based PSD (left) and convolutional PSD (right). Each square filter is a row of the encoder matrix W_e. The convolutional version produces much more diverse and less redundant filters.

Fig. 4. Left: topographic maps of filter produced by Invariant PSD when the groups (complex cells) are sqaure blocks of feature components in this 2D topology; Right: pinwheel-like patterns obtained when training PSD with group sparsity on 4X overcomplete units with local 15x15 receptive fields without shared weights.

PSD is an attempt to integrate the complex cells in the unsupervised training. This can be done with the idea of group sparsity [38,49,50], which is reminiscent of sub-space ICA [51] and Product of Experts [52]. the main idea is to replace the sparsity penalty in the PSD energy function by a group sparsity penalty:

$$E_{PSD}(Y, Z, W_d, W_e) = ||Y - W_d Z||^2 + ||Z - g(Y, W_e)||^2 + \alpha \sum_g \sqrt{\sum_{k \in g} Z_k^2},$$

where g is an index over groups of components of Z (possibly overlapping groups) The output of each group can be seen as an L_2 pooling of the components of Z that belong to the group, and is akin to a complex cell. With this regularizer, the system tries to activate the smallest number of groups, but may allow multiple units within a group to be active. This causes filters within a group to be similar to each other because similar filters tend to be active simultaneously (e.g. edge detectors at similar orientations). When the components of Z are arragend in a particular topology (e.g. 2D torus) and the groups are overlaping regions in that topology, the filters organize themselves into topographic maps similar to what is observed in V1. Figure 4 shows examples of such topographic maps of filters.

4 Conclusion

Despite the ménagerie of unsupervised feature learning algorithms at our disposal, few would say that we have the perfect algorithm in our hands. Although some biologically-inspired algorithms, such as convolutional networks and their variations, produce record-breaking results on practical datasets such as scene parsing, the ability of these algorithms to learn is still far from what is observed in humans and animals. One must ask whether there exist a simple learning "algorithm" used by the cortex, or if there is a simple principle on which such an algorithm could be based. It is certainly worth looking for such a principle.

Acknowledgments. The author wishes to thank Y-Lan Boureau, Clément Farabet, Karol Gregor, Kevin Jarrett, Koray Kavukcuoglu, Marc'aurelio Ranzato, and Arthur Szlam. Most of the work described in this paper is theirs. This work was supported in part by ONR, NSF, and DARPA.

References

1. Lowe, D.: Distinctive image features from scale-invariant keypoints. IJCV 60(4), 91–110 (2004)
2. Dalal, N., Triggs, B.: Histograms of oriented gradients for human detection, vol. 2, pp. 886–893 (June 2005)
3. Hubel, D.H., Wiesel, T.N.: Receptive fields, binocular interaction and functional architecture in the cat's visual cortex. J. Physiol. 160, 106–154 (1962)
4. Hansen, K.A., Kay, K.N., Gallant, J.L.: Topographic organization in and near human visual area v4. Journal of Neuroscience 27, 11896–11911 (2007)
5. Tanaka, K.: Inferotemporal cortex and object vision. Annual Review of Neuroscience 19, 109–139 (1996)
6. Thorpe, S., Fize, D., Marlot, C.: Speed of processing in the human visual system. Nature 381(6582), 520–522 (1996)
7. Sur, M., Garraghty, P.E., Roe, A.W.: Experimentally induced visual projections into auditory thalamus and cortex. Science 242(4884), 1437–1441 (1988)
8. LeCun, Y., Bottou, L., Orr, G.B., Müller, K.-R.: Efficient BackProp. In: Orr, G.B., Müller, K.-R. (eds.) NIPS-WS 1996. LNCS, vol. 1524, pp. 9–50. Springer, Heidelberg (1998)
9. Boureau, Y., Ponce, J., LeCun, Y.: A theoretical analysis of feature pooling in vision algorithms. In: Proc. International Conference on Machine learning, ICML 2010 (2010)
10. LeCun, Y., Boser, B., Denker, J.S., Henderson, D., Howard, R.E., Hubbard, W., Jackel, L.D.: Handwritten digit recognition with a back-propagation network. In: Touretzky, D. (ed.) Advances in Neural Information Processing Systems (NIPS 1989), Denver, CO, vol. 2. Morgan Kaufman (1990)
11. LeCun, Y., Bottou, L., Bengio, Y., Haffner, P.: Gradient-based learning applied to document recognition. Proceedings of the IEEE 86(11), 2278–2324 (1998)
12. Jarrett, K., Kavukcuoglu, K., Ranzato, M., LeCun, Y.: What is the best multi-stage architecture for object recognition? In: Proc. International Conference on Computer Vision (ICCV 2009). IEEE (2009)
13. Freeman, J., Simoncelli, E.P.: Metamers of the ventral stream. Nature Neuroscience 14(9), 1195–1201 (2011)

14. Fukushima, K., Miyake, S.: Neocognitron: A new algorithm for pattern recognition tolerant of deformations and shifts in position. Pattern Recognition 15, 455–469 (1982)

15. Serre, T., Wolf, L., Poggio, T.: Object recognition with features inspired by visual cortex. In: CVPR (2005)

16. Pinto, N., Cox, D.D., DiCarlo, J.J.: Why is real-world visual object recognition hard? PLoS Comput. Biol. 4(1), e27 (2008)

17. Lowe, D.: Distinctive image features from scale-invariant keypoints. International Journal of Computer Vision (2004)

18. Dalal, N., Triggs, B.: Histograms of oriented gradients for human detection. In: Proc. of Computer Vision and Pattern Recognition (2005)

19. Lazebnik, S., Schmid, C., Ponce, J.: Beyond bags of features: Spatial pyramid matching for recognizing natural scene categories. In: CVPR (2006)

20. Boureau, Y., Bach, F., LeCun, Y., Ponce, J.: Learning mid-level features for recognition. In: Proc. International Conference on Computer Vision and Pattern Recognition (CVPR 2010). IEEE (2010)

21. LeCun, Y., Kavukvuoglu, K., Farabet, C.: Convolutional networks and applications in vision. In: Proc. International Symposium on Circuits and Systems (ISCAS 2010). IEEE (2010)

22. Dahl, G., Ranzato, M., Mohamed, A., Hinton, G.E.: Phone recognition with the mean-covariance restricted boltzmann machine. In: Advances in Neural Information Processing Systems, vol. 23, pp. 469–477 (2010)

23. Dahl, G., Yu, D., Deng, L., Acero, A.: Context-dependent pre-trained deep neural networks for large vocabulary speech recognition. IEEE Transactions on Audio, Speech, and Language Processing (2012)

24. Hinton, G., Deng, L., Yu, D., Dahl, G., Mohamed, A., Jaitly, N., Senior, A., Vanhoucke, V., Nguyen, P., Sainath, T., Kingsbury, B.: Deep neural networks for acoustic modeling in speech recognition. IEEE Signal Processing Magazine (in press, 2012)

25. Boureau, Y., Le Roux, N., Bach, F., Ponce, J., LeCun, Y.: Ask the locals: multi-way local pooling for image recognition. In: Proc. International Conference on Computer Vision, ICCV 2011 (2011)

26. Le, Q., Monga, R., Devin, M., Corrado, G., Chen, K., Ranzato, M., Dean, J., Ng, A.: Building high-level features using large scale unsupervised learning. In: Proceedings of ICML 2012 (2012)

27. Hinton, G., Srivastava, N., Krizhevsky, A., Sutskever, I., Salakhutdinov, R.: Improving neural networks by preventing co-adaptation of feature detectors. ArXiv e-prints (July 2012)

28. Farabet, C., Couprie, C., Najman, L., LeCun, Y.: Scene parsing with multiscale feature learning, purity trees, and optimal covers. In: Proc. International Conference on Machine learning, ICML 2012 (2012)

29. Taylor, G.W., Fergus, R., LeCun, Y., Bregler, C.: Convolutional Learning of Spatio-temporal Features. In: Daniilidis, K., Maragos, P., Paragios, N. (eds.) ECCV 2010, Part VI. LNCS, vol. 6316, pp. 140–153. Springer, Heidelberg (2010)

30. Le, Q., Zou, W., Yeung, S., Ng, A.: Learning hierarchical invariant spatio-temporal features for action recognition with independent subspace analysis. In: 2011 IEEE Conference on Computer Vision and Pattern Recognition (CVPR), pp. 3361–3368. IEEE (2011)

31. Collobert, R., Weston, J., Bottou, L., Karlen, M., Kavukcuoglu, K., Kuksa, P.: Natural language processing (almost) from scratch. Journal of Machine Learning Research 12, 2493–2537 (2011)

32. Glorot, X., Bordes, A., Bengio, Y.: Domain adaptation for large-scale sentiment classification: A deep learning approach. In: Proceedings of the Twenty-eight International Conference on Machine Learning (ICML 2011), vol. 27, pp. 97–110 (2011)

33. Henaff, M., Jarrett, K., Kavukcuoglu, K., LeCun, Y.: Unsupervised learning of sparse features for scalable audio classification. In: Proceedings of International Symposium on Music Information Retrieval, ISMIR 2011 (2011) (Best Student Paper Award)
34. Coates, A., Ng., A.Y.: Selecting receptive fields in deep networks. In: Neural Information Processing Systems 24, NIPS 2011 (2011)
35. Ranzato, M., Poultney, C., Chopra, S., LeCun, Y.: Efficient learning of sparse representations with an energy-based model. In: Platt, J., et al. (eds.) Advances in Neural Information Processing Systems (NIPS 2006), vol. 19. MIT Press (2006)
36. Ranzato, M., Boureau, Y., LeCun, Y.: Sparse feature learning for deep belief networks. In: Advances in Neural Information Processing Systems (NIPS 2007), vol. 20 (2007)
37. Kavukcuoglu, K., Ranzato, M., LeCun, Y.: Fast inference in sparse coding algorithms with applications to object recognition. Technical report, Computational and Biological Learning Lab, Courant Institute, NYU (2008), Tech Report CBLL-TR-2008-12-01, http://arxiv.org/abs/1010.3467
38. Kavukcuoglu, K., Ranzato, M., Fergus, R., LeCun, Y.: Learning invariant features through topographic filter maps. In: Proc. International Conference on Computer Vision and Pattern Recognition (CVPR 2009). IEEE (2009)
39. Gregor, K., LeCun, Y.: Learning fast approximations of sparse coding. In: Proc. International Conference on Machine learning, ICML 2010 (2010)
40. Vincent, P., Larochelle, H., Lajoie, I., Bengio, Y., Manzagol, P.: Stacked denoising autoencoders: Learning useful representations in a deep network with a local denoising criterion. Journal of Machine Learning Research 11
41. Rifai, S., Vincent, P., Muller, X., Glorot, X., Bengio, Y.: Contracting auto-encoders: Explicit invariance during feature extraction. In: Proceedings of the Twenty-eight International Conference on Machine Learning, ICML 2011 (June 2011)
42. Hinton, G.E., Salakhutdinov, R.R.: Reducing the dimensionality of data with neural networks. Science 313(5786), 504–507 (2006)
43. Bengio, Y., Courville, A.C., Vincent, P.: Unsupervised feature learning and deep learning: A review and new perspectives. CoRR abs/1206.5538 (2012)
44. Olshausen, B.A., Field, D.J.: Sparse coding with an overcomplete basis set: a strategy employed by v1? Vision Research 37, 3311–3325 (1997)
45. Yang, J., Yu, K., Gong, Y., Huang, T.: Linear spatial pyramid matching using sparse coding for image classification. In: CVPR (2009)
46. Beck, A., Teboulle, M.: A fast iterative shrinkage thresholding algorithm with application to wavelet-based image deblurring. In: ISCASSP (2009)
47. Zeiler, M., Krishnan, D., Taylor, G., Fergus, R.: Deconvolutional networks. In: CVPR (2010)
48. Kavukcuoglu, K., Sermanet, P., Boureau, Y., Gregor, K., Mathieu, M., LeCun, Y.: Learning convolutional feature hierarchies for visual recognition. In: Advances in Neural Information Processing Systems (NIPS 2010), vol. 23 (2010)
49. Mairal, J., Jenatton, R., Obozinski, G., Bach, F.: Convex and network flow optimization for structured sparsity. Journal of Machine Learning Research 12, 2681–2720 (2011)
50. Le, Q.V., Ranzato, M.A., Monga, R., Devin, M., Chen, K., Corrado, G.S., Dean, J., Ng, A.Y.: Building high-level features using large scale unsupervised learning. In: Proceedings of the Twenty-ninth International Conference on Machine Learning, ICML 2012 (2012)
51. Hyvarinen, A., Hoyer, P.: A two-layer sparse coding model learns simple and complex cell receptive fields and topography from natural images. Vision Research 41(8), 2413–2423 (2001)
52. Osindero, S., Welling, M., Hinton, G.E.: Topographic product models applied to natural scene statistics. Neural Comput. 18(2), 381–414 (2006)

Fun with Asynchronous Vision Sensors and Processing

Tobi Delbruck

Inst. of Neuroinformatics, University of Zurich and ETH Zurich
http://sensors.ini.uzh.ch

Abstract. This paper provides a personal perspective on our group's efforts in building event-based vision sensors, algorithms, and applications over the period 2002-2012. Some recent advances from other groups are also briefly described.

When Mahowald and Mead built the first silicon retina with asynchronous digital output around 1992 [1], conventional CMOS active pixel sensors (**APS**) were still research chips. It required the investment by industry of about a billion dollars to bring CMOS APS to high volume production. So it is no surprise that while the imager community has been consumed by the megapixel race to make nice photos, cameras that mimic more closely how the eye works have taken a long time to come to a useful form. These "silicon retinas" are much more complex at the pixel level than APS cameras and they pay the price in terms of fill factor and pixel size; machine vision cameras with capability of synchronous global electronic shutter are about 5um. Silicon retina pixels are roughly 10 times the area of a machine vision camera pixel. So why are silicon retinas still interesting? Mostly because of the high cost at the system level of processing the highly redundant data from conventional cameras, and the fixed latencies imposed by the frame intervals. High performance activity driven event-based sensors could greatly benefit applications in real time robotics, where just as in nature, latency and power are very important [2,5,9,10].

1   Being Frame Free

Like fat free milk, event-based silicon retinas can free the consumer from consumption of excess energy. To be effective, the pixels must be designed to signal significant events so that events are not redundant. For us, the story really started when we developed the first functional dynamic vision sensor (**DVS**). In the DVS, each event signifies that the log intensity has changed by some threshold amount since the last event from the pixel (Fig. 1) [2,3]. The sensor output is an asynchronous stream of pixel addresses (address-events) signifying that the brightness has increased or decreased at particular pixels. Because the event signals a log intensity change and not an absolute intensity change, it generally signifies a change of scene reflectance, which often is caused by movement of an object. This response is the key feature that makes these sensors useful for dynamic vision.

A. Fusiello et al. (Eds.): ECCV 2012 Ws/Demos, Part I, LNCS 7583, pp. 506–515, 2012.
© Springer-Verlag Berlin Heidelberg 2012

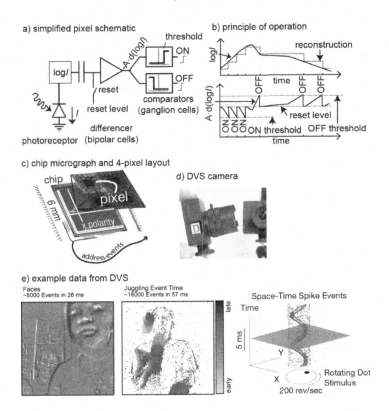

Fig. 1. The Dynamic Vision Sensor silicon retina. (**a**) The DVS pixel emulates the photoreceptor-bipolar-ganglion cell information flow. It consists of 3 parts: a logarithmic photoreceptor, a differencing amplifier (bipolar cells), and 2 decision units (ganglion cells). The pixel output consists of asynchronous ON and OFF address-events that signal scene reflectance changes. (**b**) The events are computed by the pixel as illustrated. The continuous-time photoreceptor output, which encodes intensity logarithmically, is constantly monitored for changes since the last event was emitted by the pixel. A detected change in log intensity which exceeds a threshold value results in the emission of an ON or OFF event. The threshold is typically set to about 10% contrast. Communication of the event to the periphery resets the pixel, which causes the pixel to memorize the new log intensity value. (**c**) The pixels are arranged in an array and fabricated in a standard CMOS process. Address-Event Representation (**AER**) circuits along the periphery of the chip handle the access to the shared AER bus and ensure that all events are transmitted, even if there are collisions. Colliding pixels must wait their turn for access to the AER bus. (**d**) The chips are integrated into a camera, either interfaced to a computer by USB, directly to a microcontroller, or to another neuromorphic chip via its AER interface. (**e**) Data collected from the DVS shows its characteristics: the events can be histogrammed in 2d-space over a certain time window to form an image which either displays the ON and OFF events as contrast (Faces), or as a gray scale showing the relative event time (Juggling event time), or they can be viewed in space-time to see the spatiotemporal structure (Space-Time Spike Events). Adapted from [9].

1.1   Pixel Designs

Our original DVS temporal contrast pixel design has held up remarkably well. The advantages of this design are apparent after considering a number of non-ideal effects. The pixel first of all relies on a simple continuous time logarithmic photoreceptor circuit which uses feedback to clamp the photodiode at a "virtual ground", i.e., the feedback holds the photodiode reverse bias at a fixed, small voltage, while sensing the photocurrent and outputting the result as a low impedance voltage that is logarithmic with intensity. Clamping a small reverse bias reduces dark current and thus improves dynamic range. However, we have not figured out a way to use pinned photodiodes which are standard in high performance CMOS image sensors. The voltage gain is low, only about 40mV per e-fold or 100mV per decade, but this allow representation of 7 decades of light intensity in a voltage range of less than 700mV. This means that no other gain control is necessary even in a deep sub-micron process with a supply voltage of only 1.8V. Recent designs have exposed some headroom problems that were not apparent until we encountered them in fabricated silicon. We circumvent this problem in a number of ways. The simplest solution is to use higher threshold voltage transistors in some places in the pixel. These are available in submicron processes for use in IO pads or analog circuits.

But really the key points are how the DVS achieves its sensitivity despite massive amounts of transistor mismatch. The keys are the blocking of the large DC offsets from the photoreceptor, the use of well-matched passive feedback via a capacitive divider, and the matched amplifier and comparator amplifiers. Then the gain of the amplifier is set largely by the capacitive divider ratio and not by transistor intrinsic voltage gain. The differencing amplifier and comparators are formed from 6 transistors that are all laid out in the same orientation and geometry and which are thus matched as well as it is possible to make them, if bulky common centroid layout and dummy transistors are not used.

1.2   New Retina Pixels

Bernabe Linares-Barranco and Teresa Serrano-Gotarredona at the Inst. of Microelectronics in Sevilla and Christoph Posch, now at the Vision Instititute in Paris, have been particularly creative in devising interesting retina pixels with good performance. Fig. 2 sketches the comparison discussed next.

The ATIS

Posch designed the ATIS[1] pixel with colleagues while at the Austrian Inst. of Technology [18]. This pixel consists of two sub pixels. The first sub pixel is a DVS temporal contrast pixel. Events from the DVS pixel trigger time-based intensity readings in the second sub pixel. The intensity is measured by the time is takes the photodiode voltage to integrate between two levels. The beautiful thing about this mechanism is the way it avoids both mismatch and kTC noise, by integrating not from a reset voltage to a threshold, but rather between two thresholds, which are multiplexed to a

---

[1] Asynchronous time-based image sensor.

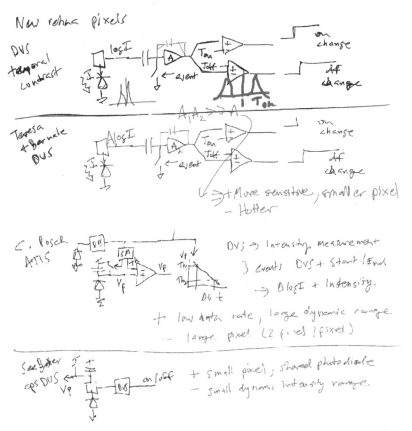

Fig. 2. Retina pixel designs that are compared in the text. I sketched this comparison at the 2012 Capo Caccia Cognitive Neuromorphic Engineering Workshop session on 5.5.12 on "Event- and Spike-based computing methods and systems."

common comparator. This way, the kTC reset level variation and the comparator offset are both suppressed [17]. The main advantage of the ATIS pixel is the event-triggered and wide dynamic range intensity readout; however the price of this is a large pixel size and small fill factor (the ATIS is effectively about twice the area of the DVS pixel and must use a separate photodiode for each measurement), and intensity capture time that can be up to several hundred ms at low intensities.

Faster and More Sensitive DVS Pixels
The latest DVS pixels from Linares-Barranco and Serrano-Gotarredona are also very interesting. They addressed the need in some applications of higher speed and sensitivity by realizing that the best improvement in performance results from adding more gain and bandwidth to the photoreceptor that precedes the differencing amplifier. They have taken two approaches to this improvement but only the first is published [19]. In their pixel, they interposed two non-inverting voltage gain amplifiers between

the logarithmic photoreceptor and the capacitive differencing amplifier. The voltage amplifiers are formed by current mirror stages using strong inversion operation with transistor geometry and operating current determining the voltage gain. This photoreceptor requires global gain control to keep the circuits in range over the entire intensity range of natural lighting. The time constant for this global gain control must be carefully chosen to provide sufficiently fast response to changes in lighting while not being so fast that it by itself generates oscillations or "gain control events". By using this circuit, they increase the gain of the photoreceptor by a factor of about 6, to result in an overall gain increase from 20 to 125. This increase allows them to set a lower nominal event threshold of about 2% contrast, compared with about 10% for our original DVS.

They also use a different feedback arrangement for the photoreceptor. Instead of supplying photocurrent from the source of an nfet with feedback to the gate of the nfet, they use the photoreceptor from Oliver Landolt [19], where the feedback photocurrent is supplied from the drain of a pfet, with feedback applied to the source of the pfet. The gate of the pfet is tied to a fixed voltage, which determines the clamped photodiode voltage. The main advantage of this circuit is the reduced Miller capacitance, which allows lower latency responses. The main disadvantages are that the photocurrent cannot be read from the drain of the transistor, and the requirement that the feedback amplifier bias must be larger than the largest photocurrent. This requirement means that bias current cannot be arbitrarily reduced to control bandwidth. However this is not a severe constraint for the high speed applications of this photoreceptor.

The apsDVS Pixel

We are trying to address some of the drawbacks of the ATIS in our newest pixel, which we call the apsDVS pixel (Fig. 3). Here "aps" stands for "active pixel sensor" and is used to describe any kind of conventional CMOS image sensor pixel with in-pixel active buffering of the integrated photodiode voltage. In our as yet unpublished apsDVS pixel, we share the same photocurrent between two complementary functions - the asynchronous detection of brightness changes and the synchronous readout of linear intensities. The cost of adding the aps readout is only 4 transistors per pixel. This pixel asynchronously emits brightness change events and we can synchronously read out the intensities by resetting and then later reading the integrated voltage.

We prototyped the first version of the apsDVS in one of our SEEBETTER chips as a 32x64 array (Fig. 3). The chip is functional but we discovered a parasitic capacitive coupling between the aps readout and the DVS circuit that generates spurious DVS events during aps readout. We currently have a corrected 240x160 design with 18.5um pixels in fabrication.

The apsDVS chip marries the advantages of simple small synchronous pixels with the low latency, wide dynamic range detection capabilities of the DVS pixels. We think the main disadvantage of the apsDVS will be the small dynamic range of the aps pixels. We hope we can take advantage of this combination in future application areas that extend on the obvious advantage of simply having a DC view of the scene in front of the sensor. In particular, we hope that we can extrapolate from the aps frames using the DVS events to complete a richer and more powerful retinal output stream than is offered by the present DVS.

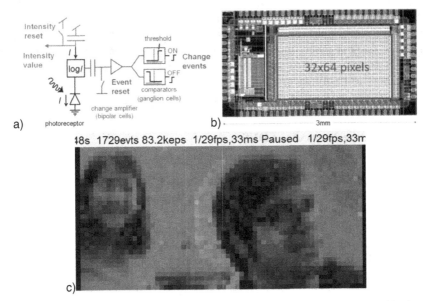

Fig. 3. The new "apsDVS" pixel. (**a**) pixel architecture; the same photocurrent provides intensity samples and temporal contrast change events; (**b**) test chip layout; (**c**) sample data over one aps frame and 18ms of DVS data; the grayscale image is from the aps pathway and the colored pixels are from events from the DVS pathway; the person is moving their head to the left and the green DVS events from the edge of his head lead the aps frame data which is from older data.

2   Usable End User Systems

We first developed the DVS in the CAVIAR project where we partnered with 4 other institutions to develop a purely hardware spike-based vision system [13]. It was our experience with the requirement in CAVIAR for a crew of 4 PhD students needed to boot and run the system that drove us strongly in the direction of software exploration of algorithms for processing sensor output. We realized that most neuromorphic labs are so heavily focused on hardware development that is rare that any device makes it off the lab bench and into the hands of potential end users. That is the main reason we put a huge effort into developing usable USB-based DVS cameras with integrated biases that are temperature and process insensitive [23].

Initially we developed event-based processing algorithms in Matlab, but we quickly realized that we needed a more structured, reusable software framework capable of multithreaded operation. These developments led in 2007 to the open source jAER software project, hosted at SourceForge [5,11]. jAER contains everything almost everyone has done with processing retina and cochlea output, and classes that encapsulate for display all of our AER chip developments and USB-based computer interfaces, along with some from other groups. As of 2012, jAER consists of more than 1000 Java classes, which makes it daunting for newcomers to understand what already exists. However the core of jAER is much smaller and our experience is that when we have a new student, it typically requires only a few weeks for them to implement their work by sub-classing the basic event processor. But because most computer vision researchers are more accustomed to using C++ or Matlab, jAER is hard for them to grasp. In particular, what we need to develop is a simple C API that allows outsiders to easily access the raw DVS data under Windows and Linux, and following this, toolboxes that allow access to some of the algorithm outputs.

2.1   Application Areas of the DVS

Experience has shown that immediate application areas of the DVS are mostly in object tracking [4,5,6,21,22]. Here the sparse output, low latency, and form of the DVS output are ideally suited to the task of tracking moving objects. Small isolated objects like balls, cells, cars, particles in hydro or aero dynamics, etc. are easily tracked using rather simple algorithms based on updating the object models by the events; see the jAER class RectangularClusterTracker for details. The Goalie class is a complete robot implementation that tracks balls to control an arm that blocks the balls [6]. More complex objects like lines are also tracked using more sophisticated algorithms based on continuous Hough transforms. Here the algorithms become quite non-intuitive. Readers are referred to Matthew Cook's open-sourced PencilBalancer [4] and the unpublished PigTracker[2] classes for excellent examples of these algorithms. PencilBalancer is a complete implementation of a pencil balancing robot that uses a pair of DVS [4]. PigTracker extends on this idea to track an arbitrary line drawing over affine transformations including scale, rotation and skew. The goalie and pencil balancer robots run on a cheap PC with CPU load of less than 10% and latencies of about 2ms.

Surveillance and behavioral monitoring is another area of application that benefits from the sparse DVS output and the high dynamic range of the pixels. We have recorded activity such as mouse sleep cycles over periods of a week at millisecond resolution, in a data file of about 1GB size (<2kBps), although we have not yet published any results of these measurements. Here the low latency of the DVS has not been used, although it could allow feedback control.

Other applications we have recently explored include gesture recognition [22], whisker tracking, satellite tracking, yeast cell tracking in microfluidics, hydrodynamics with particle velocimetry [21], aerodynamics using soap bubbles, line following robots, and obstacle detection using a pulsed laser line.

Computing with Suspicious Coincidences
Although object tracking is natural and easy with the DVS, it is somehow limited by the lack of a full cortically-inspired hierarchy of computation. However even object tracking already takes advantage of spatio-temporal event occurrence: Moving objects emit events like the familiar sparklers waved around on holiday occasions. It is the spatio-temporal coincidences of these events that drive the tracker models. Vision is

---

[2] "PigTracker" comes from the line drawing of a pig used during development in Telluride.

often considered to be the process of object recognition. Now we observe from biology that there exists an impressive amount of cortical tissue that expands the visual representation of the dynamic visual input to a high dimensional representation. How can we bring these ideas into algorithmic processing of the retina output, while somehow taking advantage of the event-based output which affords us information about spatio-temporal coincidences in the sensor input?

I tried to instantiate some ideas about early feature extraction into two jAER classes, SimpleOrientationFilter and DirectionSelectiveFilter. The SimpleOrientationFilter expands the representation of events from the On/Off of the DVS output to add Orientation as another field of the output events. OrientationEvents are computed by measuring "suspicious coincidences" at a particular orientation. A spatial map of most-recent event times is used as input to the algorithm. An orientation event is only output if the events lying along a particular orientation are temporally coincident, as they would be if they were produced by a moving edge. This edge produces a plane with a cliff to past times in the spatial map of event times. This filter works robustly on scenes with clear edges like hands or indoor spaces, although we have not tried to quantify the performance. In any case, the next obvious step was to include another ubiquitous feature of cortical simple cells, that they are almost always direction selective. Therefore, DirectionSelectiveFilter takes packets of OrientationEvent as inputs, and outputs packets of MotionOrientationEvent. These events add "direction" and "speed" fields to the OrienationEvents and are computed using time-of-flight of OrientationEvents. These events are very noisy (as is generally the case with local motion computations) but by integrating them over translational, tangential, and radial directions we obtain a fairly robust measure of global optical flow. One possible next step was obviously binocular vision: By correctly correlating vertical orientation events from the two eyes we should be able to obtain some stereo binocular disparity information; in practice this works in artificial simple scenes but not yet in realistic natural scenarios. Ryad Benosman's group has made the most progress in full stereo vision [15,16], but personally I have only had convincing success in using stereo vision to binocularly track small moving objects like balls; see the jAER class StereoClusterTracker for details.

Of course the real aim here is to obtain the motion parallax flow that signifies scene structure from a moving camera. To this end, inspired by our friends in Sevilla [25], I recently integrated a 3-DOF rate gyro on the back of a DVS camera. This sensor provides independent measure of the camera rotation. By combining this camera rotation information with measured local optical flow, I hope we can robustly detect obstacles in the environment on a power budget more competitive with that of flying insects. This target has long been an aim of neuromorphic engineering and although we are not there yet, we are getting closer. Together with developments of new sensors, new hardware for sensor processing, and inventive new algorithms, we are sure to have a grand time over the next few years.

Acknowledgements. Our Sensors group has particularly benefitted from the work of the following individuals: Rodney Douglas, Shih-Chii Liu, Wolfgang Henggeler, Patrick Lichtsteiner, Raphael Berner, Christian Brandli, Kynan Eng, Holger Finger,

Peter O'Conner, and Minhao Yang. We gratefully acknowledge support via the EU projects CAVIAR and SEEBETTER, the Swiss National Science Foundation NCCR Robotics Project, the Samsung Advanced Inst. of Technology, the University of Zurich, and ETH Zurich. Many ideas and projects were first conceived at the Telluride Neuromorphic Cognition Engineering Workshop (http://neuromorphs.net) sponsored by the US National Science Foundation and at the Capo Caccia Cognitive Neuromorphic Engineering Workshop (http://capocaccia.ethz.ch), organized by Giacomo Indiveri and Rodney Douglas.

References

1. Mahowald, M.A.: An Analog VLSI System for Stereoscopic Vision. Kluwer, Boston (1994)
2. Lichtsteiner, P., Posch, C., Delbruck, T.: A 128×128 120 dB 15 μs latency asynchronous temporal contrast vision sensor. IEEE Journal of Solid-State Circuits 43(2), 566–576 (2008)
3. Dynamic Vision Sensor (DVS) - asynchronous temporal contrast silicon retina (2012), http://siliconretina.ini.uzh.ch
4. Conradt, J., Berner, R., Cook, M., Delbruck, T.: An Embedded AER Dynamic Vision Sensor for Low-Latency Pole Balancing. In: 5th IEEE Workshop on Embedded Computer Vision (in conjunction with ICCV 2009), Kyoto, Japan, pp. 1–6. IEEE (2009)
5. Delbruck, T.: Frame-free dynamic digital vision. In: Proceedings of Intl. Symp. on Secure-Life Electronics, Advanced Electronics for Quality Life and Society, Tokyo, University of Tokyo, pp. 21–26 (2008)
6. Delbruck, T., Lichtsteiner, P.: Fast sensory motor control based on event-based hybrid neuromorphic-procedural system. In: ISCAS 2007, New Orleans, pp. 845–848 (2007)
7. Berner, R., Delbruck, T.: Event-Based Pixel Sensitive to Changes of Color and Brightness. IEEE Transactions on Circuits and Systems I: Regular Papers 58(7), 1581–1590 (2011)
8. Delbruck, T., Linares-Barranco, B., Culurciello, E., Posch, C.: Activity-Driven, Event-Based Vision Sensors. In: IEEE International Symposium on Circuits and Systems, Paris, pp. 2426–2429 (2010)
9. Liu, S.C., Delbruck, T.: Neuromorphic sensory systems. Current Opinion in Neurobiology 20(3), 288–295 (2010)
10. Liu, S.C., van Schaik, A., Minch, B.A., Delbruck, T.: Event-based 64-channel binaural silicon cochlea with Q enhancement mechanisms. In: IEEE ISCAS 2009, pp. 2426–2429 (2010)
11. jAER open source project: Real time sensory-motor processing for event-based sensors and systems, (2007), http://jaer.wiki.sourceforge.net
12. Seebetter project (2011), http://www.seebetter.eu
13. Serrano-Gotarredona, R., Oster, M., et al.: CAVIAR: A 45k Neuron, 5M Synapse, 12G Connects/s AER Hardware Sensory–Processing– Learning–Actuating System for High-Speed Visual Object Recognition and Tracking. IEEE Trans. on Neural Networks 20(9), 1417–1438 (2009)
14. Abshire, P., et al.: Confession session: Learning from others mistakes. In: ISCAS 2011, Rio de Janeiro, pp. 1149–1162 (2011)

15. Rogister, P., Benosman, R., Ieng, S.-H., Lichtsteiner, P., Delbruck, T.: Asynchronous Event-Based Binocular Stereo Matching. IEEE Transactions on Neural Networks and Learning Systems 23(2), 347–353 (2012)
16. Benosman, R., Sio, H., Ieng, X., Rogister, P., Posch, C.: Asynchronous Event-Based Hebbian Epipolar Geometry. IEEE Transactions on Neural Networks 22(11), 1723–1734 (2011)
17. Matolin, D., Posch, C., Wohlgenannt, R.: True correlated double sampling and comparator design for time-based image sensors. In: ISCAS 2009 (2009)
18. Posch, C., Matolin, D., Wohlgenannt, R.: A QVGA 143dB dynamic range asynchronous address-event PWM dynamic image sensor with lossless pixel-level video compression. In: 2010 IEEE Solid-State Circuits Conference Digest of Technical Papers, ISSCC (2010)
19. Camunas-Mesa, L., Zamarreno-Ramos, C., Linares-Barranco, A., Acosta-Jimenez, A.J., Serrano-Gotarredona, T., Linares-Barranco, B.: An Event-Driven Multi-Kernel Convolution Processor Module for Event-Driven Vision Sensors. IEEE Journal of Solid-State Circuits 47(2), 504–517 (2012)
20. Landolt, O., Mitros, A., Koch, C.: Visual sensor with resolution enhancement by mechanical vibrations. In: Advanced Research in VLSI, 2001. Proceedings of ARVLSI 2001, pp. 249–264 (2001)
21. Drazen, D., Lichtsteiner, P., Hafliger, P., Delbruck, T., Jensen, A.: Toward real-time particle tracking using an event-based dynamic vision sensor. Experiments in Fluids 51(5), 1465–1469 (2011)
22. Lee, J., Delbruck, T., Park, P.K.J., Pfeiffer, M., Shin, C.W., Ryu, H., Kang, B.C.: Live demonstration: Gesture-Based remote control using stereo pair of dynamic vision sensors. In: ISCAS 2012, Seoul (in press, 2012)
23. Yang, M., Liu, S.C., Li, C., Delbruck, T.: Addressable Current Reference Array with 170dB Dynamic Range. In: ISCAS 2012, Seoul (in press, 2012)
24. Boahen, K.A.: A burst-mode word-serial address-event link-I transmitter design. IEEE Transactions on Circuits and Systems I-Regular Papers 51(7), 1269–1280 (2004)
25. Jimenez-Fernandez, A., Fuentes-del-Bosh, J.L., Paz-Vicente, R., Linares-Barranco, A., Jiménez, G.: Live demonstration: Neuro-inspired system for realtime vision tilt correction. In: ISCAS 2010, pp. 1393–1397 (2010)
26. Lenero-Bardallo, J.A., Serrano-Gotarredona, T., Linares-Barranco, B.: A 3.6 us Latency Asynchronous Frame-Free Event-Driven Dynamic-Vision-Sensor. IEEE Journal of Solid-State Circuits 46(6), 1443–1455 (2011)

Spike-Based Image Processing: Can We Reproduce Biological Vision in Hardware?

Simon J. Thorpe

Centre de Recherche Cerveau & Cognition, Toulouse, France
simon.thorpe@cerco.ups-tlse.fr
http://www.cerco.ups-tlse.fr

Abstract. Over the past 15 years, we have developed software image processing systems that attempt to reproduce the sorts of spike-based processing strategies used in biological vision. The basic idea is that sophisticated visual processing can be achieved with a single wave of spikes by using the relative timing of spikes in different neurons as an efficient code. While software simulations are certainly an option, it is now becoming clear that it may well be possible to reproduce the same sorts of ideas in specific hardware. Firstly, several groups have now developed spiking retina chips in which the pixel elements send the equivalent of spikes in response to particular events such as increases or a decreases in local luminance. Importantly, such chips are fully asynchronous, allowing image processing to break free of the standard frame based approach. We have recently shown how simple neural network architectures can use the output of such dynamic spiking retinas to perform sophisticated tasks by using a biologically inspired learning rule based on Spike-Time Dependent Plasticity (STDP). Such systems can learn to detect meaningful patterns that repeat in a purely unsupervised way. For example, after just a few minutes of training, a network composed of a first layer of 60 neurons and a second layer of 10 neurons was able to form neurons that could effectively count the number of cars going by on the different lanes of a freeway. For the moment, this work has just used simulations. However, there is a real possibility that the same processing strategies could be implemented in memristor-based hardware devices. If so, it will become possible to build intelligent image processing systems capable of learning to recognize significant events without the need for conventional computational hardware.

1 Introduction

Biological vision systems can make very fast decisions despite hardware constraints that would lead most hardware engineers to despair. For example, biological neurons only emit electrical impulses, or spikes, a few hundred times a second at best, whereas electronic components can switch states billions of times a second. Likewise, the conduction velocity for transmitting spikes from one place in the cortex to another are typically only 1-2 m.s^{-1} whereas signals can be transmitted within electronic devices

A. Fusiello et al. (Eds.): ECCV 2012 Ws/Demos, Part I, LNCS 7583, pp. 516–521, 2012.

at speeds approaching the speed of light.   And yet, despite these limitations, biological systems work remarkably well. For example, in flies, the input-output delay necessary for a change in flight direction in response to a modification in the visual input can be as short as 20 ms - a value that includes not just the visual processing, but the initiation and modification of the motor response.   And in humans, my own group has demonstrated that accurate saccades to small faces only 1-2° across and at eccentricities of 7-10° can be initiated after only 100-110 ms [2]. Again, this number includes the entire pathway from photoreceptor, to visual processing and the triggering of the motor response.

How can brains perform challenging tasks like face detection and localization in such so little time? Clearly, the selection pressure during the evolution of the visual system will have put a very high priority on fast processing. If our ancestors were not able to detect the presence of a predator in peripheral vision rapidly, then their survival hopes would be very impaired. So we can assume that biological vision systems will have made optimal use of the available hardware, and this means that if an electronically implemented system was designed that used the equivalent algorithms, it is plausible that it could achieve the same tasks with speeds that are orders of magnitude faster than their biological equivalents. Is there any chance of this happening in the foreseeable future? In my view, the answer to this question is yes. And in this presentation I will sketch how I think technology may move in the coming years.

2   Spike-Based Processing: Software Implementations

At the end of the 1980s it was already clear that the speed of biological vision posed a major problem for conventional views on how information gets processed [11]. The fact that neurons at the highest levels of the primate vision system can respond selectively to complex visual stimuli such as faces just 100 ms after stimulus onset means that each of the roughly 10 processing stages between the retinal photoreceptors and the top end of the visual system only has about 10 ms to reach a decision. And since the firing rates of cortical neurons rarely fire at above about 100 Hz, it means that the processing can presumably be done in a system where each neuron only has time to emit a single spike. This effectively rules out the conventional view that neurons transmit information using a firing rate code in which spike frequency is used to encode analogue values. As an alternative, I proposed that, even when only one spike per neuron is available, information can be encoded in the relatively timing of spikes across a population of neurons [12]. It is an idea that has been demonstrated experimentally using recordings from the salamander retina [4].

By ignoring the firing rate of neurons, and just concentrating on which cells fire first, we showed that it was perfectly possible to implement neural networks capable of detecting faces even under conditions where no neuron gets to fire more than once [13]. And we went on to show that a simple feed-forward network based on a set of orientation selective feature maps (similar to neurons in cortical area V1) could drive a recognition layer capable of state of the art face identification – at least at the time of publication [3]. These ideas led to the creation of a high-tech spin-off company – SpikeNet Technology – in the summer of 1999. The company has been developing software systems based on these basic principles ever since, and currently employs a staff of 12 in its offices near Toulouse in south-west France (see www.spikenet-technology.com).

However, while software implementations based on spiking neural networks and rank-order coding can be very compact and fast, they still need a standard computer architecture to run. Admittedly, the options for very large scale computing systems are improving every day, and projects like Henry Markram's BlueBrain (http://bluebrain.epfl.ch/) demonstrate that it is indeed possible to simulate even very complex neural systems with current technology [7]. Other groups such as Steve Furber's group at Manchester University are developing specialized chips based on multiple ARM processor cores coupled with very speed interconnection hardware that will hopefully allow networks containing up to a billion spiking neurons to be simulated in real time [10].

But given the nature of the underlying computations, is seems possible that it would be possible to design specific hardware systems that implement the ideas directly, rather than relying on software simulation. It is this possibility that I would like to address in the remainder of this presentation.

3   Spike Based Coding of Sensory Information

In some early simulation studies, we showed that using a spike-based scheme could be a particularly efficient way to encode information about images. Specifically, we showed that a retina equipped with ON- and OFF-centre receptive fields at a range of sizes can be used to transmit an image efficiently using only the order of firing as a code. We found that by the time roughly 1% of the neurons in the retina had fired a single spike, it was possible to recognize most of the objects in an image [14].

In recent years, a number of groups have been working on retina-like chips in which information is transmitted off-chip in the form of a series of events that are functionally quite similar to spikes [6]. Tobi Delbruck's presentation in this symposium illustrates this approach very well. Rather than trying to send information about the image in the form of a series of gray-scale values, these new designs allow information to be transmitted continuously in a completely asynchronous manner.

4   Learning with Spike-Time Dependent Plasticity

How can this sort of spike-like information be used by subsequent processing stages? Over a number of years, we have been looking at the possibility that Spike-Time Dependent Plasticity (STDP) could provide a powerful way for a neuronal system to learn to recognize patterns of afferent activity. In an early study, we reported that when a neuron equipped with STDP is subjected to repeating patterns of spikes, high weights will invariably concentrate on those inputs that fire early during the pattern [5]. This tendency is remarkably robust, and can operate even when there is a considerable amount of added noise. More recently, we extended this work by showing that a single neuron equipped with STDP is capable of learning to respond selectivity to any repeating pattern of incoming spikes, even when the pattern involves no change in the underlying firing rate statistics [8]. Thus, even when the neuron is receiving totally random activity through 2000 different afferents, the existence of a repeating motif involving a subset of those inputs can be detected after just a few tens of repetitions. Furthermore, with a pattern lasting just 50 ms, we were able to show that while the receiving neuron may start to fire anywhere within the pattern, after a relatively short period of time, the neuron gradually fires earlier and earlier so that in the end, it fires only 5-10 ms after the beginning of the pattern.

When multiple neurons are receiving from the same set of afferents, and there are inhibitory connections between the neurons, the system will operate as a competitive learning mechanism [9]. The inhibition acts to prevent two neurons learning to fire to the same pattern, and as a consequence, for a given pattern lasting 50 ms, you may have three different neurons firing a specific times during the pattern. Alternatively, if multiple patterns are present in the inputs, different neurons will learn to respond to different patterns.

5   STDP Learning with a Dynamic Vision Sensor

In some recent work with Olivier Bichler and other colleague at the CEA in Saclay we have been looking at how an STDP-based learning mechanism would react to real spiking events provided by one of Tobi Delbruck's Dynamic Vision Sensor chips [1]. In this initial study, we used a dataset available on the web that was produced by recording the spikes generated by one of the chips in response to cars travelling along a six-lane freeway. The imaging chip has a resolution of 128*128 pixels, and each pixel can generate one of two types of spiking events – one corresponding to a local increase in luminance (roughly equivalent to an "ON" event), the other corresponding to a local decrease (an "OFF" event) [6]. This makes a total of 32,768 afferents that were each connected to a first layer containing 60 neurons, each of which implemented a modified STDP rule and had inhibitory connections to the other neurons in the same layer. Each of the 60 first layer neurons was then connected to a second layer of containing 10 neurons. Following the presentation of just a few minutes of data, it was noted that the neurons in the first layer had learned to respond selectively to cars moving a particular locations in the image – a result that simply reflects the fact that these were the patterns of activation that reoccurred over and over again in the incoming data. But even more remarkably, the neurons in the second layer had learned to respond to repeating sequences of activation in the first layer of units. Specifically, this meant that they effectively ended up counting cars passing on each of the six lanes of the freeway. It is important to realize that this learning process occurred with absolutely no supervision. There was no need to provide any labeling of the data – the system simply learned to encode the most "meaningful" reoccurring events in the incoming data.

6   Towards Memristor Based Hardware Implementations

For the moment, this work has been done entirely using software simulations – specifically using a software simulation package developed by Olivier Bichler called XNet. However, the longer-term aim of the project is to try and find a way of implementing the same sorts of STDP-based learning algorithms in Memristor-based hardware systems. Memristors are a class of semiconductor devices capable of storing information by varying the effective resistance of a junction by applying a high voltage, and it has been demonstrated that such devices could potentially be used to implement an STDP-type learning rule [15]. Ultimately, it could be possible to build a complete imaging processing system using just two basic components – a Dynamic Vision Sensor device for generating the basic spiking data at the input, coupled with a network of spiking neurons arranged in a competitive network and which have memristor-based STDP synapses as inputs. Each neuron in the processing layer would have connections from the input device that could be modified whenever the postsynaptic neuron fires a spike. Specifically, the resistance of the connection would need to be reduced every time the activation of the input was followed by the initiation of a spike in the postsynaptic cell.

While there are still a number of technical issues to be dealt with, it already seems clear that such a system could potentially work. And if successful, it would open the way towards a radically different way of processing images – one that was directly inspired by the way in which biological vision systems operate. One particularly revolutionary aspect would be the complete absence of anything resembling a CPU. All processing would be done by local processing elements, none of which would be more complicated than a simple integrate and fire neuron.

Acknowledgements. Some of the work described here has been supported by the ANR (NAVIG and NEMESIS projects).

References

1. Bichler, O., et al.: Extraction of temporally correlated features from dynamic vision sensors with spike-timing-dependent plasticity. Neural Networks 32, 339–348 (2012)
2. Crouzet, S.M., Kirchner, H., Thorpe, S.J.: Fast saccades towards faces: Face detection in just 100 ms. J. Vis. 10(4), 1–17 (2010)
3. Delorme, A., Thorpe, S.J.: Face identification using one spike per neuron: resistance to image degradations. Neural Netw. 14(6-7), 795–803 (2001)
4. Gollisch, T., Meister, M.: Rapid neural coding in the retina with relative spike latencies. Science 319(5866), 1108–1111 (2008)
5. Guyonneau, R., Vanrullen, R., Thorpe, S.J.: Neurons Tune to the Earliest Spikes Through STDP. Neural Comput. 17(4), 859–879 (2005)
6. Lichtsteiner, P., Posch, C., Delbruck, T.: A 128x128 120 dB 15 mu s latency asynchronous temporal contrast vision sensor. IEEE Journal of Solid-State Circuits 43(2), 566–576 (2008)
7. Markram, H.: The blue brain project. Nat. Rev. Neurosci. 7(2), 153–160 (2006)

8. Masquelier, T., Guyonneau, R., Thorpe, S.J.: Spike timing dependent plasticity finds the start of repeating patterns in continuous spike trains. PLoS one 3(1), e1377 (2008)
9. Masquelier, T., Guyonneau, R., Thorpe, S.J.: Competitive STDP-based spike pattern learning. Neural computation 21(5), 1259–1276 (2009)
10. Plana, L.A., et al.: SpiNNaker: Design and Implementation of a GALS Multicore System-on-Chip. ACM Journal on Emerging Technologies in Computing Systems 7(4) (2011)
11. Thorpe, S., Imbert, M.: Biological constraints on connectionist modelling. In: Pfeifer, R., et al. (eds.) Connectionism in Perspective, pp. 63–92. Elsevier, Amsterdam (1989)
12. Thorpe, S.J.: Spike arrival times: A highly efficient coding scheme for neural networks. In: Eckmiller, R., Hartmann, G., Hauske, G. (eds.) Parallel Processing in Neural Systems and Computers, pp. 91–94. Elsevier, North-Holland (1990)
13. VanRullen, R., et al.: Face processing using one spike per neurone. Biosystems 48(1-3), 229–239 (1998)
14. VanRullen, R., Thorpe, S.J.: Rate coding versus temporal order coding: what the retinal ganglion cells tell the visual cortex. Neural Comput. 13(6), 1255–1283 (2001)
15. Zamarreno-Ramos, C., et al.: On spike-timing-dependent-plasticity, memristive devices, and building a self-learning visual cortex. Frontiers in Neuroscience (May 2011)

PHOG-Derived Aesthetic Measures Applied to Color Photographs of Artworks, Natural Scenes and Objects

Christoph Redies[2], Seyed Ali Amirshahi[1,2],
Michael Koch[1,2], and Joachim Denzler[1]

[1] Computer Vision Group, Friedrich Schiller University Jena, Germany
{seyed-ali.amirshahi,koch.michael,joachim.denzler}@uni-jena.de
http://www.inf-cv.uni-jena.de
[2] Institute of Anatomy I, Friedrich Schiller University,
Jena University Hospital, Germany
redies@mti.uni-jena.de
http://www.anatomie1.uniklinikum-jena.de

Abstract. Previous research in computational aesthetics has led to the identification of multiple image features that, in combination, can be related to the aesthetic quality of images, such as photographs. Moreover, it has been shown that aesthetic artworks possess specific higher-order statistical properties, such as a scale-invariant Fourier spectrum, that can be linked to coding mechanisms in the human visual system. In the present work, we derive novel measures based on a PHOG representation of images for image properties that have been studied in the context of the aesthetic assessment of images previously. We demonstrate that a large dataset of colored aesthetic paintings of Western provenance is characterized by a specific combination of the PHOG-derived aesthetic measures (high self-similarity, moderate complexity and low anisotropy). In this combination, the artworks differ significantly from seven other datasets of photographs that depict various types of natural and man-made scenes, patterns and objects. To the best of our knowledge, this is the first time that these features have been derived and evaluated on a large dataset of different image categories.

Keywords: Aesthetic, art, self-similarity, complexity, anisotropy, Birkhoff-like measure, Pyramid of Histograms of Orientation Gradients (PHOG).

1 Introduction

In recent years, there has been a growing interest in studying what image features characterize aesthetic images and distinguish them from non-aesthetic ones. In computational aesthetics, computer vision techniques are used in combination with mathematical approaches to assess the aesthetic quality of images and paintings [1]. Research in this field has led to the identification of several features

A. Fusiello et al. (Eds.): ECCV 2012 Ws/Demos, Part I, LNCS 7583, pp. 522–531, 2012.

that can be related to the aesthetic quality of images, mainly for the assessment of the quality of photographs [2–4]. For example, lower-order features such as contrast, colorfulness, hue, saturation, rule of thirds, symmetry, saliency etc. are analyzed [2–5]. The extracted features are used in combination to distinguish between aesthetic and non-aesthetic images. Most of these features are derived from common knowledge about factors that affect the quality of photographs and paintings. For example, Datta et al. [3] extracted 56 features from photographs to evaluate and predict their aesthetic quality. Li et al. [2] used 40 features mainly related to the characteristics of color, brightness and composition for assessing the aesthetic quality of landscape paintings. Xue et al. [5] employed aesthetic measures (color histograms, spatial edge distribution, repetition identification etc.) to differentiate between aesthetic and non-aesthetic photographs taken by amateur and professional photographers.

Obviously, cultural factors play an important role in determining aesthetic preferences in humans. However, it has also been argued that aesthetic images display universal characteristics, which can potentially elicit aesthetic perception in all humans or may reflect basic functional properties of the human visual system [6]. In the ensuing line of research, visual scientists have investigated higher-order properties of images, for example, the spatial frequency spectrum and measures of order and complexity. The aim of this research is to identify one or a few properties that characterize aesthetic images and artworks [7–12] and can be related to specific aspects of information processing in the human visual system, as previously studied in natural scene research [10, 11, 13]. Some of the measured properties can be related to low-level visual coding, for example, to the efficient (sparse) coding of sensory input [9, 10]. In this paper, we combine the statistical approach with a modern computational method (Pyramid of Histograms of Orientation Gradients - PHOG) to calculate values that have been previously linked to aesthetic perception by different psychologists, e.g. Arnheim [14], such as self-similarity [8, 11, 15], complexity [7, 12] and anisotropy [16]. We compared these features for photographs of aesthetic artworks and seven different categories of natural scenes, patterns and man-made objects. Results reveal that the aesthetic images studied by us, which represent a large and diverse subset of paintings, are characterized by defined higher-order properties. To the best of our knowledge, this is the first time that such values linked to aesthetic perception have been automatically extracted from images and statistically evaluated on a dataset of different colored image categories consisting of 2763 images.

The next sections of the article are organized as follows: Section 2 provides an overview on previous work. Section 3 gives an introduction to the computational approach used by us, in particular to the PHOG algorithm. Section 4 gives details of the databases analyzed. Experimental results are described in Section 5. Section 6 provides a short conclusion and proposals for future work.

2   Previous Work

Using Fourier analysis, Graham and Field [11] and Redies et al. [10, 13] showed that images of graphic artworks of Eastern and Western provenance share statistical properties with images of complex natural scenes. Both types of images possess a scale-invariant Fourier spectrum, that is, the spatial frequency profile remains relatively constant when zooming in and out of the images. This result implies that the two image categories have spatial frequency profiles that are self-similar (fractal-like) at different levels of spatial resolution. Other image categories, such as photographs of faces, plants, and simple objects, do not possess this property [13]. Koch et al. [16] demonstrated that, in addition, artists seem to imitate natural scenes by preferring a similar degree of anisotropy of orientations in their creations. Cardinal (horizontal and vertical) orientations are more prominent in natural scenes as well as in aesthetic artworks than oblique orientations [16]. In conclusion, artworks and natural scenes share statistical image properties. It has therefore been proposed that the perception of the two types of images may be mediated by similar coding mechanisms in the human visual system, such as an efficient (sparse) sensory code [9, 13, 17].

The above findings and other results [8, 15] suggest that aesthetic images are self-similar at different levels of spatial resolution. To follow this hypothesis with a modern computational method, Amirshahi et al. [18] assessed self-similarity in large datasets of grey-scale artworks of Western provenance and other categories of images using PHOG features [19]. The PHOG descriptor represents an image by its local shape and spatial layout. PHOG was originally developed for object recognition and image categorization [19]. Amirshahi et al. calculated the self-similarity of Histograms of Oriented Gradients (HOGs) between different levels of the pyramid [18]. Their results confirmed that the datasets of aesthetic artworks resemble natural scenes in that they are more highly self-similar at different levels of spatial resolution than, for example, photographs of simple objects and faces.

3   Aesthetic Measures Based on a PHOG Representation of Images

In the present work, we will use PHOG to derive several novel measures for image properties that have been related previously to the aesthetic quality of images, in addition to self-similarity [18]. We will then validate these measures on datasets of color photographs of aesthetic artworks and other visual scenes and patterns of lesser or no aesthetic value.

To calculate PHOG [19], a pyramid approach is taken. In this method, the HOG [20] feature for the global image (level 0) is calculated in the first step. The image is then divided into 4 equally sized sub-images and the HOG feature is calculated for each sub-image (level 1). Each sub-image is then divided into 4 other equally sized sub-images resulting in 16 sub-images in total. HOG is again calculated for these sub-images as well (level 2). The division and calculation procedure can be continued as long as desired and the image permits. 8 bins are used for binning the orientation in the HOG feature. The normalized values of the bin represent the orientation strength in each direction.

For calculating PHOG for color images, each image is converted to the Lab color space. HOG values are then calculated based on the maximum gradient magnitudes in the L, a and b color channels. For this, we will first generate a new gradient image $\mathbf{G}_{\max}$,

$$\mathbf{G}_{\max}(x, y) = \max(\|\nabla I_L(x, y)\|, \|\nabla I_a(x, y)\|, \|\nabla I_b(x, y)\|) \tag{1}$$

$\nabla I_L(x, y), \nabla I_a(x, y)$, and $\nabla I_b(x, y)$ are the gradients at pixel (x, y) for the L, a, and b color channels respectively. We will then calculate the HOG feature for the new gradient image, $\mathbf{G}_{\max}$ by calculating the HOG features in each sub-image. Let us denote with $h(S)$ the HOG histogram of a sub-image S of $\mathbf{G}_{\max}$.

Based on the PHOG analysis of the gradient image, $\mathbf{G}_{\max}$, we will calculate the following measures, which are all assumed or even accepted to correlate with aesthetic appeal:

1. *Self-similarity* (M_{SeSf}). As a measure of self-similarity, we compare the HOG features of each sub-image at level 3 with the HOG features of the entire image at the ground level. Level 3 was chosen because the different image categories showed more diverse results than lower levels; above level 3, self-similarity values are not robust and reliable [18]. To measure the similarity between the HOG features of sub-images at different levels, we use the Histogram Intersection Kernel [21],

$$\text{HIK}(\mathbf{h}, \mathbf{h'}) = \sum_{i=1}^{m} \min(h(i), h'(i)) \tag{2}$$

In Eq. (2), $\mathbf{h}$ and $\mathbf{h'}$ are two different normalized histograms and m is the number of bins present in the HOG features. To calculate the self-similarity of an image, the median value of the HIK values at each level is calculated,

$$M_{\text{SeSf}}(I, L) = \text{median}(\text{HIK}(h(S), (h(\Pr(S))))| \Pr(S) \in \text{Sections}(I, L)) \tag{3}$$

to be robust with respect to outliers (see also [18]). In Eq. (3), M_{SeSf} is the self-similarity value, I corresponds to the image, L represents the level, at which we are assessing the HOG features (in our work we use $L = 3$), $h(S)$ is the HOG value for a sub-image in the Sections(I, L) which corresponds to the sections in the image I in level L and $\Pr(S)$ corresponds to the parent of sub-image S.

2. *Complexity* (M_{Co}). The aesthetic appeal of images may depend on their degree of complexity [7, 12, 15, 22]. For example, the "savanna hypothesis" [23] states that images of moderate complexity, similar to those of the natural habitat of our ancestors, have a higher aesthetic appeal than highly complex images. To calculate the complexity of an image, we will calculate the mean norm of the gradient across all orientations over $\mathbf{G}_{\max}(x, y)$ as shown in Eq. (1).

$$M_{\text{Co}}(\mathbf{G}_{\max}) = \frac{1}{N \cdot M} \sum_{(x,y)} \mathbf{G}_{\max}(x, y) \tag{4}$$

In this equation, M_{Co} corresponds to complexity, and N and M are the height and width of the new gradient image, $\mathbf{G}_{\max}$. Since image gradients

(a)   (b)   (c)   (d)   (e)   (f)   (g)   (h)

Fig. 1. Examples of images from the 8 databases used in this study. The image in (a) is reproduced with permission by the Staatliche Museen zu Berlin, Gemäldegalerie, 2012.

represent the changes of lightness in an image, we assume that calculating the mean gradient over the L channel will give us a good prediction on image complexity. The higher the mean absolute gradient, the more complex an image is.

3. *Birkhoff-like measure* (M_{BLM}). Birkhoff [12] proposed that the aesthetic appeal of objects relates to the ratio of order and complexity in images. Different attempts have been made to model this measure [7, 24]. In the present work, we propose that self-similarity may be a suitable indicator of order in an image. We calculate a Birkhoff-like measure (M_{BLM}) according to Eq. (5) where M_{SeSf} represents the self-similarity in the image calculated in Eq. (3) and M_{Co} represents the complexity introduced in Eq. (4).

$$M_{\mathrm{BLM}} = \frac{M_{\mathrm{SeSf}}}{M_{\mathrm{Co}}} \tag{5}$$

4. *Anisotropy* (M_{AnI}). Koch et al. [16] found that the Fourier spectrum is more uniform across orientations (that is, less anisotropic) in gray-scale artworks than in natural scenes [16]. This prompted us to calculate the variance of gradient strength in the HOGs across its bin entries,

$$M_{\mathrm{AnI}}(L) = \sigma(H(L)) \tag{6}$$

as a measure of anisotropy. In this equation, M_{AnI} represents the anisotropy in the image at level L, $H(L)$ corresponds to a vector which is consisted of all the HOG value at level L, and σ is the variance. Consistent with the calculation of self-similarity, anisotropy is calculated at level 3.

4   Image Databases

The previous study by Amirshahi et al. [18] was restricted to gray-scale images of graphic art. However, in many categories of visual artworks, especially in oil paintings and watercolors, color plays a crucial factor for their aesthetic appeal. In the present work, we therefore chose to apply the PHOG analysis to colored artworks and compared them with color photographs of natural scenery and patterns formed by plants. Because artworks have been shown to be self-similar (see above), we compared them also with images of highly self-similar natural scenes and patterns (photographs of clouds, water turbulences, growth patterns of lichen, and branch patterns of trees). Furthermore, we asked in how far these categories of images differ from images of simple man-made objects.

Except for the database of aesthetic color paintings, all the other 7 databases comprise photographs that were taken in RAW format with a 15.1 megapixel digital camera (EOS 500D with EF-S15-85mm f/3.5-5.6 IS USM lens; Canon, Tokyo, Japan) by one of the authors. A small number of the photographs of large vistas, vegetation and plant patterns were taken also by a 4-megapixel Digital Ixus 400 digital camera (Canon). A total of 2,763 color photographs of artworks, natural patterns and man-made objects were analyzed. Sample images from each database are shown in Fig. 1. The images were scaled such that one side of the image was 1024 pixels. Because the aspect ratio of an image plays an important role in the aesthetic evaluation [3], we used isotropic scaling. The databases will be released for public use in due course.

4.1 Aesthetic Paintings

This database consisted of 854 different colored paintings of Western provenance that represented a large variety of styles (Renaissance, Baroque, Romanticism, Realism, Impressionisms, Modern Art, etc.), about 200 different painters, and examples from the 15th to 21st centuries (Fig. 1a). We assume that the paintings were aesthetic because they were from famous artists and prestigious museums. All paintings were scanned from high-quality art books using a digital scanner (Perfection 3200 Photo, Epson).

4.2 Natural Scenes, Vegetation and Plants

This category comprised three different databases of photographs (Fig. 1b-d): (1) 289 photographs of large-vista natural scenes, including horizon. (2) 289 photographs of vegetation (bushes, trees, etc.) taken from a distance of about 5-50m. (3) 316 close-up photographs of one type of plant. These photographs were taken at a distance of about 0.5-5 m; each photograph displayed a uniform pattern of leaves or blossoms (plant patterns).

4.3 Highly Self-similar, Natural Patterns, and Man-Made Objects

This category of photographs was analyzed to study whether aesthetic paintings differ from highly self-similar patterns found in nature or man-made objects. It comprised four databases (Fig. 1e-h): (1) 268 photographs of clouds. (2) 245 photographs of various species of crustose lichen growing on (thomb)stones. (3) 301 photographs of branching patterns of trees and bushes, taken during wintertime. (4) 201 photographs of simple household and laboratory objects.

5   Experimental Results

In the present work, we calculate the introduced PHOG-derived measures for image properties introduced in Sec. 1. We ask whether these features assume

Table 1. Mean values for self-similarity, complexity, Birkhoff-like measure and anisotropy

Database	number of images	self-similarity ($\pm\sigma$)	complexity ($\pm\sigma$)	Birkhoff-like measure ($\times 10^{-3} \pm \sigma$)	anisotropy ($\times 10^{-6} \pm \sigma$)
artworks	854	0.77 ± 0.08	8.5 ± 3.8	106 ± 42	126 ± 40
large vistas	289	0.60 ± 0.13^{b}	9.9 ± 4.0^{b}	71 ± 37^{b}	182 ± 60^{b}
vegetation	289	0.79 ± 0.07^{ns}	19.7 ± 4.4^{b}	42 ± 9^{b}	94 ± 30^{b}
plant patterns	316	0.83 ± 0.07^{b}	17.2 ± 6.7^{b}	57 ± 26^{b}	87 ± 45^{b}
objects	201	0.55 ± 0.07^{b}	3.5 ± 1.4^{b}	179 ± 72^{b}	289 ± 76^{b}
clouds	268	0.68 ± 0.08^{b}	1.4 ± 0.4^{b}	527 ± 157^{b}	146 ± 27^{b}
lichen	245	0.90 ± 0.03^{b}	18.4 ± 4.3^{b}	52 ± 12^{b}	42 ± 11^{b}
branches	301	0.81 ± 0.05^{b}	23.7 ± 4.7^{b}	36 ± 8^{b}	93 ± 22^{b}

^{a,b} significantly different from artworks (^{a} $p < 0.01$, ^{b} $p < 0.001$; Kruskal-Wallis one-way ANOVA, with Dunn's post test).
^{ns} not significantly different from artworks.

specific values in aesthetic artworks and how they compare to the other categories of photographs. Table 1 lists mean values for the calculated PHOG measures for each image category as well as the statistical results after running the Kruskal-Wallis one-way ANOVA, with Dunn's post test, between the datasets and the artwork dataset. Results show that most of the values in different datasets are significantly different to values calculated for the artworks dataset. Fig. 2 shows 2d plots of self-similarity versus image complexity (Fig. 2a, c) and of the Birkhoff-like measure versus anisotropy (Fig. 2b, d) for all image categories. Fig. 2 illustrates the good separation of artworks (red dots) from the other image categories (other colors), although partial overlap of the different image populations is observed for some of the PHOG-derived aesthetic measures.

5.1   Self-similarity

For validation, we calculated this measure for photographs of natural growth patterns, such as lichen, plants, vegetation and branches, all of which have a highly self-similar (fractal) structure. Consistent with our claim, these image categories show high self-similarity values. The only exception are images of clouds that may be less self-similar due to the presence of areas of homogeneous sky in some of the images. In contrast, photographs of simple objects show low self-similarity in general and, correspondingly, they result in low self-similarity values. The PHOG-derived self-similarity measure yields high values for colored artworks, confirming previous results from gray-scale artworks [18].

5.2   Complexity

The complexity measure used by us is valid because it yields low values for images of low complexity (clouds and simple objects) and high values for images

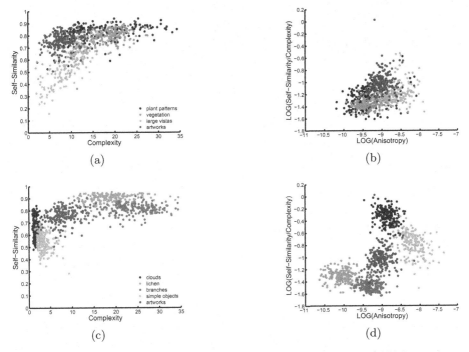

Fig. 2. Results from the PHOG analysis. Each dot represents one of 200 images randomly selected from each of the 8 image categories. Results for artworks (red dots) are compared with photographs of natural scenes and plants (a, b), and of highly self-similar natural patterns and man-made objects (c, d), as indicated by different colors. Values for self-similarity versus complexity are plotted in a, c, and for the Birkhoff-like measure versus anisotropy (log-log scale) in b, d.

of high complexity images (lichen, plant patterns and branches). On average, photographs of artworks assume intermediate values that are similar to those for photographs of large-vista natural scenes. We conclude that the images of colored artworks analyzed by us have a degree of complexity that resembles that of large-vista natural scenes.

5.3   Birkhoff-Like Measure

Intermediate values for artworks are also obtained for the Birkhoff-like measure. Values for objects and clouds are higher, whereas values for all other categories of natural and man-made objects are lower. Fig. 2b, d reveals a large degree of overlap between the image categories for this measure. Consequently, our Birkhoff-like measure does not seem to be well suited for distinguishing aesthetic artworks from most of the other image categories in a systematic way.

5.4 Anisotropy

Interestingly, artists create their works with a degree of anisotropy that is similar to that in natural patterns. Mean anisotropy in photographs of simple objects and large-vista natural scenes, in which the horizon introduces anisotropy, is larger than in artworks. As would be expected, lichen growth patterns on stone surfaces have the lowest anisotropy values because their growth patterns are fractal and do not have any direction.

In summary, the mean values for 3 PHOG-derived measures (Table 1) differ significantly between photographs of artworks and photographs of natural scenes and objects (large vistas, plants, clouds, lichen, and branches), with the exception of photographs of vegetation that have similar self-similarity values. Likewise, photographs of simple objects differ in all 3 measures from artworks.

6 Conclusion and Outlook

In conclusion, a combination of three PHOG-derived measures (self-similarity, complexity and anisotropy) characterizes aesthetic color artworks of Western provenance and distinguishes them from seven other categories of images that represent various types of natural scenes, patterns and objects. Our results support the notion that subsets of artworks possess well-defined statistical properties [9–11, 17]. Results show that the values in different datasets are statistically significant when compared to the artworks dataset. Whether the same measures allow distinguishing also aesthetic artworks from other cultures remains to be studied. Even within Western culture, extreme styles of art, for example monochrome artworks, will deviate substantially from the mean values calculated in the present study. It is not our claim that the aesthetic quality of images can be predicted by any of the measures in isolation. Rather, in combination, they define a specific subspace of image features, in which most of the aesthetic images analyzed by us are located. Whether all images in this subspace are aesthetic remains to be studied.

Moreover, it may be argued that the measures introduced by us relate to properties that reflect artistic technique rather than constraints of image composition that are followed during the creation of aesthetic artworks. However, high degrees of self-similarity are observed both in colored paintings (this study) and gray-scale graphic art [18] and these two categories of artworks comprise rather different techniques (e.g., oil paintings, woodcuts and pencil drawings). With respect to moderate complexity and natural pattern-like anisotropy, it is difficult to imagine how these features could relate to artistic technique. Alternatively, we propose that they represent principles of image composition that relate to aesthetic perception [6, 9, 15]. In future work, it will be of interest to study how these features relate to visual coding in the human brain.

References

1. Hoenig, F.: Defining computational aesthetics. EG Assoc., Goslar (2005)
2. Li, C., Chen, T.: Aesthetic visual quality assessment of paintings. IEEE J. Sel. Topics Signal Process. 3, 236–252 (2009)
3. Datta, R., Joshi, D., Li, J., Wang, J.Z.: Studying Aesthetics in Photographic Images Using a Computational Approach. In: Leonardis, A., Bischof, H., Pinz, A. (eds.) ECCV 2006, Part III. LNCS, vol. 3953, pp. 288–301. Springer, Heidelberg (2006)
4. Ke, Y., Tang, X., Jing, F.: The design of high-level features for photo quality assessment. In: Proceed. CVPR, pp. 419–426 (2006)
5. Xue, S.F., Lin, Q., Tretter, D., Lee, S., Pizlo, Z., Allebach, J.: Investigation of the role of aesthetics in differentiating between photographs taken by amateur and professional photographers. In: Proceed. SPIE, vol. 8302, p. 83020D (2012)
6. Zeki, S.: Art and the brain. J. Conscious Stud. 6-7, 76–96 (1999)
7. Rigau, J., Feixas, M., Sbert, M.: Informational aesthetics measures. IEEE Comput. Graph Appl. 28, 24–34 (2008)
8. Taylor, R.P.: Order in Pollack's chaos - computer analysis is helping to explain the appeal of Jackson Pollock's paintings. Sci. Am. 287, 116–121 (2002)
9. Redies, C.: A universal model of esthetic perception based on the sensory coding of natural stimuli. Spat Vis. 21, 97–117 (2007)
10. Graham, D., Redies, C.: Statistical regularities in art: Relations with visual coding and perception. Vision Res. 50, 1503–1509 (2010)
11. Graham, D.J., Field, D.J.: Statistical regularities of art images and natural scenes: spectra, sparseness and nonlinearities. Spat. Vis. 21, 149–164 (2007)
12. Birkhoff, G.: Aesthetic Measure. Harvard University Press, Cambridge (1933)
13. Redies, C., Hasenstein, J., Denzler, J.: Fractal-like image statistics in visual art: similarity to natural scenes. Spat. Vis. 21, 97–117 (2007)
14. Arnheim, R.: Art and Visual Perception: A Psychology of the Creative Eye. University of California Press (2004)
15. Taylor, R.P., Spehar, B., Van Donkelaar, P., Hagerhall, C.: Perceptual and physiological responses to Jackson Pollock's fractals. Front. Hum. Neurosci. 5, 60 (2011)
16. Koch, M., Denzler, J., Redies, C.: $1/f^2$ characteristics and isotropy in the Fourier power spectra of visual art, cartoons, comics, mangas, and different categories of photographs. PLoS one 5(8), e12268 (2010)
17. Redies, C., Hänisch, J., Blickhan, M., Denzler, J.: Artists portray human faces with the Fourier statistics of complex natural scenes. Network 18(3), 235–248 (2007)
18. Amirshahi, S.A., Koch, M., Denzler, J., Redies, C.: PHOG analysis of self-similarity in esthetic images. In: Proceed SPIE (HVEI XVII), vol. 8291, p. 82911J (2012)
19. Bosch, A., Tisserman, A., Munoz, X.: Representing shape with a spatial pyramid kernel. In: Proceed. CIVR (2007)
20. Dalal, N., Triggs, B.: Histograms of oriented gradients for human detection. In: Proceed. CVPR, pp. 886–893 (2005)
21. Barla, A., Franceschi, E., Odone, F., Verri, A.: Image Kernels. In: Lee, S.-W., Verri, A. (eds.) SVM 2002. LNCS, vol. 2388, pp. 83–96. Springer, Heidelberg (2002)
22. Jacobsen, T., Hofel, L.: Aesthetic judgments of novel graphic patterns: analyses of individual judgments. Percept. Mot. Skills 95, 755–766 (2002)
23. Orians, G.: An ecological and evolutionary approach to landscape aesthetics. Allen and Unwin, London (1986)
24. Boselie, F., Leeuwenberg, E.: Birkhoff revisited: beauty as a function of effect and means. Am. J. Psychol. 98(1), 1–39 (1985)

Wehrli 2.0:
An Algorithm for "Tidying up Art"

Nikolai Ufer[1,2], Mohamed Souiai[1], and Daniel Cremers[1]

[1] Department of Computer Science, Technical University of Munich,
Boltzmannstr. 3, D-85748 Garching, Germany
{Mohamed.Souiai,Cremers}@in.tum.de
[2] Department of Mathematics, University of Munich,
Theresienstr. 39, D-8033 Munich, Germany
N.Ufer@campus.lmu.de

Abstract. We propose an algorithm for automatizing the task of "Tidying up Art" introduced by the comedian Wehrli [1]. Driven by a strong sense of order and tidyness, Wehrli systematically dissects famous artworks into their constituents and rearranges them according to certain ordering principles. The proposed algorithmic solution to this problem builds up on a number of recent advances in image segmentation and grouping. It has two important advantages: Firstly, the computerized tidying up of art is substantially faster than manual labor requiring only a few seconds on state-of-the-art GPUs compared to many hours of manual labor. Secondly, the computed part decomposition and reordering is fully reproducible. In particular, the arrangement of parts is determined based on mathematically transparent criteria rather than the invariably subjective and irreproducible human sense of order.

Keywords: Tidying up Art, Image Segmentation, Label Cost Prior, Convex Relaxation, Convex Optimization, Fast Global K-Means.

1   Introduction

1.1   Ursus Wehrli's Project of "Tidying up Art"

Starting in 2002, the Swiss comedian Ursus Wehrli developed the project of "Tidying up Art". Wehrli argues that while he likes art he is systematically disturbed by many of history's most famous artworks being highly unordered and chaotic. Wehrli tackles this shortcoming in the works of famous artists by dissecting their works and rearraging respective segments in a well ordered manner – see Figure 1 for an example. His work has become extremely popular and Wehrli's books have been best sellers for many years [1–3]. A closer look at Wehrli's works reveals that his approach has two important shortcomings:

- Manually dissecting a painting and rearranging all parts is an extremely tedious process which can easily take several hours of work. Tidying up the entire art history would take Wehrli years or even decades.

A. Fusiello et al. (Eds.): ECCV 2012 Ws/Demos, Part I, LNCS 7583, pp. 532–541, 2012.

(a) Painting by Haring   (b) Wehrli's manual tidying   (c) Output of *Wehrli 2.0*

Fig. 1. Given an original artwork (a) *Wehrli 2.0* generates automatically a tidied up version of it (c). The algorithm reproduces Wehrli's notion of tidyness (b).

– The result of the above approach is hardly reproducible. The dissection of the artwork into parts is performed quite heuristically. Moreover, the subsequent ordering is based on a highly intransparent and irreproducible human notion of order.

The contribution of this paper is to introduce the algorithm *Wehrli 2.0* which is designed to alleviate the above shortcomings.

1.2 Related Work

Dissecting the image plane into its constituents is a problem of image segmentation and as such one of the most studied problems in image analysis. There is abundant literature on mathematical models for image segmentation, starting with the pioneering works of Mumford and Shah [4], Blake and Zisserman [5] and Kass et al. [6]. While the length regularization imposed in respective cost functions is desirable for meaningful segmentations, it gives rise to difficult optimization problems, the general multiregion segmentation being NP hard (in its spatially discrete formulation). Nevertheless, over recent years people have developed efficient algorithms for approximate minimization including the graph cut based alpha expansions [7] or various forms of convex relaxation [8–10]. In this work, we will make use of convex relaxation techniques because they do not exhibit any grid bias and are easily parallelized [11].

For a fully unsupervised partitioning, however, respective algorithms also need to estimate appropriate color models associated with each region. In practice, we observed that the commonly suggested alternating estimation of color models and segmentation is computationally demanding and likely to get stuck in suboptimal local solutions. For a robust unsupervised performance, it is therefore important to optimally estimate multiple color models.

1.3 Contribution

We propose an algorithm called *Wehrli 2.0* which aims at fully automatizing Wehrli's work in a manner that we can simply insert an artwork and the computer generates a tidied up version of it – see Figure 1 for an example.

To this end, we developed a fully unsupervised multi-region segmentation method which combines state-of-the-art convex relaxation techniques with fast global k-means color model estimation. Subsequently we propose ordering criteria to optimally rearrange all parts. In numerous experiments, we compare the performance of our algorithm with Wehrli's manual work. While the results are never entirely identical, these experiments show that:

- Our algorithm provides results which are qualitatively similar to those obtained by Wehrli and thus captures the essence of his work.

- The proposed computerized solution to Wehrli's endeavour is substantially faster with computation times of a few seconds on recents GPUs.

- Our algorithm is fully reproducible in terms of the part decomposition and the systematic ordering according to transparent criteria such as color, size or aspect ratio of respective parts.

We believe that the proposed algorithm may help the comedian Ursus Wehrli in his endeavour to systematically tidy up the entire history of art.

2   Image Segmentation

2.1   A Minimal Partition Model

Given the color image $I\colon \Omega \to \mathbb{R}^3$ defined over the image plane $\Omega \subset \mathbb{R}^2$ we propose to segment it into an unknown number n of pairwise disjoint regions Ω_i by minimizing the Mumford-Shah like energy [4, 12]:

$$E_\lambda(n, \Omega_1, \ldots, \Omega_n, p_1, \ldots, p_n) = \sum_{i=1}^{n} \lambda |\partial \Omega_i| - \int_{\Omega_i} \log p_i(I(x))\, dx + \nu\, n_{eff}. \quad (1)$$

The first term penalizes the boundary length $|\partial \Omega_i|$ of each region Ω_i, weighted with $\lambda \geq 0$. The second term is the negative log likelihood for observing a color I given that the respective point is part of region Ω_i. The last term is a penalizer of the number n_{eff} of non-empty regions weighted by positive parameter $\nu \geq 0$. It corresponds to a minimum description length prior [13, 12]. In this paper, we will simply consider isotropic Gaussian color models $p_i(I)$:

$$p_i(I) = \frac{1}{(2\pi\sigma_i^2)^{3/2}} \exp\left(-\frac{\|I - \mu_i\|_2^2}{2\sigma_i^2}\right), \quad (2)$$

with mean μ_i and standard deviation σ_i, because these best reproduce Wehrli's implicit notion of part decomposition. Of course, more sophisticated color models are conceivable.

2.2 Optimization by Fast Global K-Means and Convex Relaxation

The joint optimization of (1) with respect to color analysis reveals that this difficulty arises for two reasons:

- Even for *fixed* color models, the corresponding discrete labeling problem is given by the Potts model [14] which is known to be NP hard. Without the length regularity, however, it would be a trivial problem to solve, namely a direct maximum likelihood assignment of respective pixels to their favorite color model.

- In addition, the alternating estimation of color models and region grouping is in practice prone to local minima. Moreover, the iteration of color estimation and multi-region segmentation is typically very slow and therefore impractical for interactive methods. In the absence of length regularity it is typically tackled by k-means clustering. Yet, the latter approach is known to converge to suboptimal local solutions.

We cannot expect to efficiently and optimally solve an NP hard problem. Yet, we observe that a key computational difficulty enters through the length regularity which couples the optimal decision for each pixel to respective decisions for neighboring pixels. On the other hand, in the application considered in this paper, the length regularity is generally associated with a very small weight λ because the artworks that need tidying up typically do not exhibit high levels of noise. We therefore propose to compute an initial solution by solving (1) for $\lambda = 0$:

$$E_\lambda(\{\Omega_i, \mu_i, \sigma_i\}) = \sum_{i=1}^{n} \int_{\Omega_i} \frac{\|I(x) - \mu_i\|_2^2}{2\sigma_i^2} + 3\log(\sigma_i)\,dx\,. \tag{3}$$

where n is chosen sufficiently large. To solve this problem, we revert to the fast global k-means algorithm [15] which is less prone to local minima than the traditional k-means algorithm. Alternatively, one can also retain the number n of regions in the optimization and solve the joint problem. This corresponds to the *uncapacitated facility location problem* which is known to be NP hard since it can be reduced from the *set-cover problem* – see [16] for details.

Once the initial color models (without length regularity) are estimated, we set λ to its non-zero value and solve the problem

$$E_\lambda(n, \Omega_1, \ldots, \Omega_n) = \sum_{i=1}^{n} \lambda|\partial\Omega_i| + \int_{\Omega_i} \frac{\|I(x) - \mu_i\|_2^2}{2\sigma_i^2} + 3\log(\sigma_i)\,dx + \nu\,n_{eff}\,. \tag{4}$$

2.3 Convex Formulation

The optimization problem (4) is a non-convex problem. Building up on a sequence of recent advances in variational multi-label optimization [10, 17, 9, 18] we can equivalently write it as the minimization of the *convex* energy

$$\min_{u \in \mathcal{U}_b} \sum_{i=1}^{n} \int_{\Omega} u_i(x) f_i(x) \, dx + \lambda \int_{\Omega} |Du_i| + \nu \max_{x \in \Omega} u_i(x) \tag{5}$$

over the *non-convex* set of binary indicator functions:

$$\mathcal{U}_b = \left\{ (u_1, ..., u_n) \in BV(\Omega; \{0, 1\})^n \; \middle| \; \sum_{i=1}^{n} u_i(x) = 1, \quad \forall x \in \Omega \right\}. \tag{6}$$

Here Du denotes the distributional derivative (generalizing the gradient to non-differentiable indicator functions). The term f_i is given by:

$$f_i(x) = \frac{\|I(x) - \mu_i\|_2^2}{2\sigma_i^2} + 3\log(\sigma_i). \tag{7}$$

It is the nonnegative (local) cost associated with assigning a pixel $x \in \Omega$ the label of region i.

We can relax the problem (5) to a fully convex optimization problem by allowing the functions u_i to take on real values in the interval $[0, 1]$. This amounts to replacing the constraint set $\mathcal{U}_b$ by its convex hull:

$$\mathcal{U} = \left\{ (u_1, ..., u_n) \in BV(\Omega; [0, 1])^n \; \middle| \; \sum_{i=1}^{n} u_i(x) = 1, \quad \forall x \in \Omega \right\}. \tag{8}$$

Albeit convex, the arising problem (5) is highly non-smooth because of the non-differentiability of the Total Variation and the max function. By using Fenchel's duality, we can introduce two auxiliary variables p and v in order to obtain a differentiable formulation for the Total Variation and respectively for the max function. Thus the optimization problem (5) over the constraint set (8) is equivalent to the saddle-point formulation:

$$\min_{u \in \mathcal{U}} \max_{p \in \mathcal{P}} \max_{v \in \mathcal{V}} \sum_{i=1}^{n} \int_{\Omega} u_i(x) \Big(f_i(x) - \operatorname{div} p_i(x) + v_i(x) \Big) \, dx. \tag{9}$$

with respective convex sets for the dual variables:

$$\mathcal{V} = \left\{ v \in \left(L^2(\Omega, \mathbb{R}_0^+) \right)^n \; \middle| \; \int_{\Omega} v_i(x) \, dx = \nu; \quad \forall i = 1, \ldots, n \right\}, \tag{10}$$

$$\mathcal{P} = \left\{ p \in \left(\mathcal{C}_c^1(\Omega, \mathbb{R}^2) \right)^n \; \middle| \; \|p_i(x)\|_2 \leq \lambda, \, \forall x \in \Omega, \forall i = 1, \ldots, n \right\}. \tag{11}$$

This particular choice of the constraint set $\mathcal{P}$ was introduced in the work of Zach et al. [10]. While a tighter relaxations was suggested in [8, 17], we chose the former representation because the back-projections on $\mathcal{P}$ are faster to compute and because the differences in segmentation were not noticeable in the application considered here.

3 Numerical Optimization

We solve the saddle-point problem (9) by means of a recently proposed algorithm [19] and extensions of it [20]. It consists of a gradient descent in the primal and a gradient ascent in the dual variable. While the constraint on the set $\mathcal{P}$ can be handeled by simple pointwise truncation, we handeled the constraints $\mathcal{V}$ and $\mathcal{U}$ by means of lagrange mulipliers. Since all updates can be done *pointwise*, the method is straight-forwardly parallelized on a GPU allowing speedups of an order of magnitude and runtimes in the range of a few seconds.

4 Reordering of Parts

A major aspect of "Tidying up Art" is to rearrange the individual parts of the dissected painting according to some ordering principle. Our reordering formalism imitates an ordering criterion which seems to be most frequent in Wehrli's work, namely the grouping of parts based on color and size. To this end, we proceed as follows:

- For each color label $k = 1, \ldots, n$, select the region $\Omega_k = \{x \in \Omega \mid u_k(x) = 1\}$.
- For each region Ω_k, determine its connected components by means of the flood-fill algorithm and perform a postprocessing morphological closing (erosion followed by dilatation) for seperating slight connections of one or two pixels width.
- Arrange all parts horizontally according to their color label.
- In each column, arrange all parts of a given color according to their largest principal component, aligned according to their centroid and rotated such that the dominant principal axis is horizontal.

The parts are sorted in descending order with respect to their largest principal component. Thus, larger and elongated segments tend to be at the bottom of the vertical arrangement. The horizontal ordering with respect to color values is done by the hue values of the HSV color space.

5 Experiments

We ran the algorithm *Wehrli 2.0* on several artworks peforming the following steps:

- Run fast global k-means in order to determine the color labels of our color model for a certain artwork.
- Perform image segmentation algorithm introduced in Section 2 using the convex optimization approach presented in Section 3.
- Determine all segments and order them as described in Section 4.

The three steps of our algorithm are illustrated in Figure 2. We use constant deviations for the color model distribution, i.e. $\sigma_k = 1$ for each label, set $n = 15$, and choose the parameters $\lambda = 0.075$ and $\nu = 25$ for the segmentation.

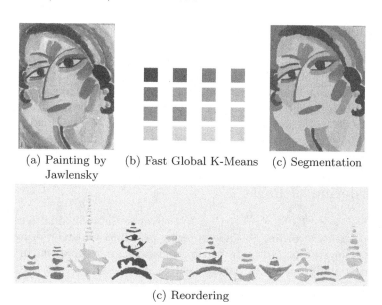

(a) Painting by   (b) Fast Global K-Means   (c) Segmentation
    Jawlensky

(c) Reordering

Fig. 2. The three steps of the *Wehrli 2.0* algorithm applied on the artwork "Mystischer Kopf: Galka" by Alexej Jawlensky (a). The color labels (b) are determined using fast global k-means. Image (c) shows the result of the MDL segmentation. The resulting regions are rearranged as in Section 4.

5.1   Fast Global K-Means vs K-Means

A comparison of the output of our algorithm using k-means and the fast global k-means algorithm (Figure 3) shows that the global k-means algorithm gives a more differentiated color model for the subsequent segmentation algorithm which in turn results in more accurate regions. The comparison shows that using fast global k-means assures that more labels are preserved in the tidied-up result.

5.2   Artworks Tidied and Cleaned

Many classical artworks are already decades old and with time have invariably accumulated dirt and dust. This degradation process can be a major problem for the preservation of art.[1] To account for these unfortunate effects of time, it is therefore of utmost importance that one not only tidies art but also cleans it properly. Figure 4 illustrates that *Wehrli 2.0* can handle even dirty images. A proper cleaning is obtained by simply arranging the pieces computed by our segmentation algorithm (rather than the dirty input segments). We did observe that this drastic cleaning results in a loss of small scale details. On the other hand, small scale details are substantially overrated in the art world.

---

[1] Rembrandt's famous painting of the Militia Company, for example, was so dimmed and defaced over the years, that later generations are now referring to it as *Night Watch*.

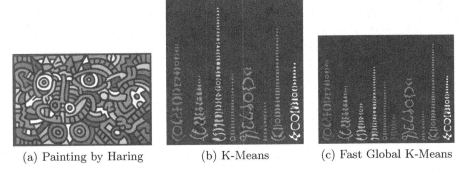

(a) Painting by Haring   (b) K-Means   (c) Fast Global K-Means

Fig. 3. The fast global k-means algorithm reproduces improved color labels compared to the k-means algorithm. As can be seen (b) we obtain a mixed color stack including yellow and amber segments since the k-means algorithm doesn't identify the amber cluster.

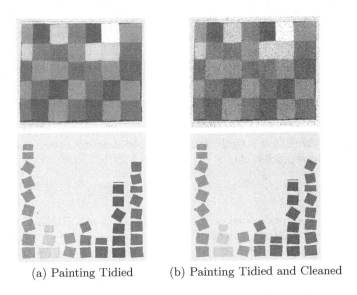

(a) Painting Tidied   (b) Painting Tidied and Cleaned

Fig. 4. This figure illustrates the result of our algorithm applied to a high quality copy of "Farbtafel" by Paul Klee on the left side and the results of a noisy version of the same painting on the right side. The results are fairly similar since the segments of the noisy version are filled with the color of the corresponding color label.

5.3   Qualitative Results

Figure 5 shows three examples of artwork which the artist Wehrli has worked on. The direct comparison demonstrates that *Wehrli 2.0* produces very similar result to the manual labor of Wehrli. There is an important difference, though: While Wehrli's heuristic order of parts does not follow any recognizable logic,

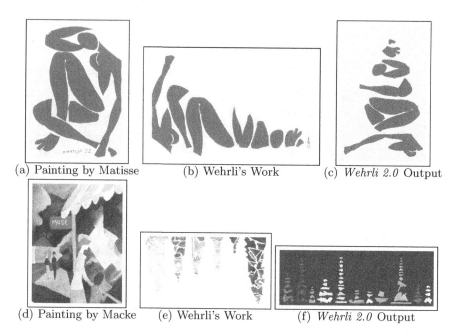

(a) Painting by Matisse   (b) Wehrli's Work   (c) *Wehrli 2.0* Output

(d) Painting by Macke   (e) Wehrli's Work   (f) *Wehrli 2.0* Output

Fig. 5. A comparison of our results using the *Wehrli 2.0* algorithm (c,f) with Wehrli's manual tidying up (b,e) of the following artworks: "Nu bleu IV" by Henri Matisse (a) and "Modefenster" by August Macke (d)

the output of *Wehrli 2.0* strictly follows simple ordering criteria and is fully deterministic and reproducible.

5.4   Runtime

All experiments were performed on a desktop PC with a NVIDIA Geforce GTX 480 GPU and a 2.40GHz quadcore CPU. For the image (a) in Figure 1 with 350x229 pixels and 15 labels, for example, the color model estimation using a Matlab implementation of the fast global k-means, took 23 seconds, while the multi-region segmentation, using a GPU implementation of the convex optimization required only 4 seconds.

6   Conclusion

We introduced the algorithm *Wehrli 2.0* to automatize the task of "Tidying up Art" introduced by the Swiss comedian Ursus Wehrli. The algorithm is based on a multi-region segmentation method which combines recent convex relaxation techniques with fast global k-means color model estimation. In contrast to Wehrli's manual work, which is tedious and time consuming, we showed that our algorithm *Wehrli 2.0* produces qualitatively similar results in a matter of seconds on a home computer.

References

1. Wehrli, U., Olenhusen, A.: Kunst aufräumen. Kein & Aber (2002)
2. Wehrli, U., Olenhusen, A.: Noch mehr Kunst aufräumen. Kein & Aber (2006)
3. Wehrli, U., Born, G., Spehr, D.: Die Kunst, aufzuräumen. Kein & Aber (2011)
4. Mumford, D., Shah, J.: Optimal approximations by piecewise smooth functions and associated variational problems. Communications on Pure and Applied Mathematics 42, 577–685 (1989)
5. Blake, A., Zisserman, A.: Visual Reconstruction. MIT Press (1987)
6. Kass, M., Witkin, A., Terzopoulos, D.: Snakes: Active contour models. International Journal of Computer Vision 1, 321–331 (1988)
7. Boykov, Y., Veksler, O., Zabih, R.: Fast approximate energy minimization via graph cuts. IEEE Transactions on Pattern Analysis and Machine Intelligence 23, 1222–1239 (2001)
8. Chambolle, A., Cremers, D., Pock, T.: A convex approach for computing minimal partitions. Technical report TR-2008-05, Departement of Computer Science, University of Bonn, Bonn, Germany (2008)
9. Lellmann, J., Kappes, J., Yuan, J., Becker, F., Schnörr, C.: Convex Multi-class Image Labeling by Simplex-Constrained Total Variation. In: Tai, X.-C., Mørken, K., Lysaker, M., Lie, K.-A. (eds.) SSVM 2009. LNCS, vol. 5567, pp. 150–162. Springer, Heidelberg (2009)
10. Zach, C., Gallup, D., Frahm, J.M., Niethammer, M.: Fast global labeling for real-time stereo using multiple plane sweeps. In: Vision, Modeling and Visualization Workshop (VMV), Konstanz, Germany, pp. 243–252 (2008)
11. Klodt, M., Schoenemann, T., Kolev, K., Schikora, M., Cremers, D.: An Experimental Comparison of Discrete and Continuous Shape Optimization Methods. In: Forsyth, D., Torr, P., Zisserman, A. (eds.) ECCV 2008, Part I. LNCS, vol. 5302, pp. 332–345. Springer, Heidelberg (2008)
12. Zhu, S.C., Yuille, A.: Region competition: Unifying snakes, region growing, and bayes/mdl for multi-band image segmentation. IEEE Transactions on Pattern Analysis and Machine Intelligence 18, 884–900 (1996)
13. Leclerc, Y.G.: Constructing simple stable descriptions for image partitioning. International Journal of Computer Vision 3, 73–102 (1989)
14. Potts, R.B.: Some generalized order-disorder transformations. Mathematical Proceedings of the Cambridge Philosophical Society 48, 106–109 (1952)
15. Likas, A., Vlassis, N., Verbeek, J.: The global k-means clustering algorithm. Pattern Recognition 36, 451–461 (2003)
16. Delong, A., Osokin, A., Isack, H.N., Boykov, Y.: Fast approximate energy minimization with label costs. International Journal of Computer Vision 96, 1–27 (2012)
17. Pock, T., Chambolle, A., Bischof, H., Cremers, D.: A convex relaxation approach for computing minimal partitions. In: IEEE Conference on Computer Vision and Pattern Recognition (CVPR), Miami, Florida, pp. 810–817 (2009)
18. Yuan, J., Boykov, Y.: TV-based multi-label image segmentation with label cost prior. In: Proceedings of the British Machine Vision Conference (BMVC), Aberystwyth, UK, pp. 101.1–101.12 (2010)
19. Pock, T., Cremers, D., Bischof, H., Chambolle, A.: An algorithm for minimizing the piecewise smooth mumford-shah functional. In: IEEE International Conference on Computer Vision (ICCV), Kyoto, Japan, pp. 1133–1140 (2009)
20. Chambolle, A., Pock, T.: A first-order primal-dual algorithm for convex problems with applications to imaging. Journal of Mathematical Imaging and Vision 40, 120–145 (2011)

Feature Vector Definition for a Decision Tree Based Craquelure Identification in Old Paintings*

Joanna Gancarczyk

University of Bielsko-Biala, Department of Mechanics,
Willowa 2, 43-309 Bielsko-Biala, Poland
jgan@ath.bielsko.pl
http://www.ath.bielsko.pl

Abstract. In the paper a new proposal of semi-automatic method of craquelure detection in old paintings is presented. It is well known, that craquelure pattern is a unique feature and its character gives a significant information about the overall condition of the work, progress and cause of its degradation and helps in dating as well as confirming the authentication of the work. There exist methods, mostly deriving from other ridge and valley recognition problems, like geodesic or medical image feature segmentation based on watershed transform, morphological operations and region growing algorithm but they sometimes fail because of a complex nature of a craquelure pattern or large scale of an analyzed area. In this work a method is presented continuing a known semi-automatic technique based on a region growing algorithm. The novel approach is to apply a decision tree based pixel segmentation method to indicate the start points of craquelure pattern. The main difficulty in this mathod is defining an adequate set of descriptors forming a feature vector for the mining model.

Keywords: craquelure identification, image segmentation, feature detection.

1 Introduction

Data mining is defined as an automatic or semiautomatic process of discovering patterns in data. Machine learning provides the technical basis of data mining and its application to data mining can be used for prediction, explanation, and understanding of the rules hidden in the analyzed dataset. The result of learning is an actual definition of a structure that can be used to classify new entries [21]. Some discussion on the role of artificial intelligence and machine learning in automatic image understanding may be found in [14] and [19].

Craquelure is a pattern of cracks that appears in a painting during the process of aging. Cracks in the paint layer grow as the canvas or wood support of

---

* This work was partially supported by NCN (National Science Centre) under grant no. 6593/B/T02/2011/40.

A. Fusiello et al. (Eds.): ECCV 2012 Ws/Demos, Part I, LNCS 7583, pp. 542–550, 2012.

the painting moves in response to changes of humidity and temperature. Every layer of a painting has it's own distinctive mechanical behaviour, and therefore, every layer contributes in it's own way to the formation of craquelure [18], [20]. A classification of features for cracks on paintings was made by Stout [18]. Apart from the local features of individual cracks, like the depth or the smoothness of its edges, research was also performed towards defining characteristics of craquelure patterns. In [6] Bucklow proposed a classification of crack patterns of paintings into four different categories, representing four paint traditions: Italian fourteenth/fifteenth-century paintings on panel, Flemish fifteenth/sixteenth-century paintings on panel, Dutch seventeenth-century paintings on canvas and French eighteenth-century paintings on canvas. De Willingen in [20] reported a detailed study of molecular and mechanical issues concerning generation of stress between paint layers and their influence on formation of crack pattern. Figure 1 is an example of a crack pattern on an oil on canvas 19th century painting from the collection of the National Museum in Krakow.

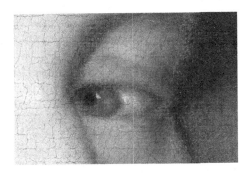

Fig. 1. Crack pattern on the detail of 19th century oil on canvas painting (Rafał Hadziewicz, "Portrait of Wentzl")

2   Crack Pattern Identification

The nature of a craquelure pattern suggests several methods to be potentially useful in its identification in a painting. In most cases crack line is an elongated object, crossed with or split into new lines, distinguishable as a darker (more rarely brighter) form from the background. However, it might be observed in a practice, that the direct implementation of any known method meets considerable difficulties.

Reticular structure of crossing craquelure lines would suggest implementation of some border defining algorithm, like watershed method. However, the shapes created by the lines are not closed, which causes in a worst case that all the image is flooded and classified as one area, with no dividing lines identified. Another difficulty is because of the fuzzy nature of craquelure lines - no strict beginning nor end may be defined objectively. The length of any processed line is a subjective choice of the restorer. Furthermore, the gray level of the crack pattern very often coincides with the gray level of noise or some background part, so direct threshold implementation is also not possible.

2.1 Top-Hat and Filtering Methods

In automatic selection model cracks are identified by means of a proper filter, like Gabor filters, or a morphological filter called top-hat transform ([1], [2], [3]). However, with this approach not only cracks, but also brush strokes and other texture, like wood panel or canvas background could be detected. This problem is usually solved by discriminating cracks on the basis of shape, rather than brightness or colour values since, as mentioned before, the later values of craquelure and noise tend to overlap.

2.2 Region Growing

The semi-automatic method of craquelure separation described by Barni in [4] and then recalled in [7] is based on a manual selection of at least one starting point for each separated piece of a craquelure pattern. Then an iterative process is run to expand the structure according to the gradient of pixel values. This approach is adequate due to the character of a craquelure pattern which is formed of linear, continuous shapes. Efficiency of this method is high as long as the pattern is regular. Ragged, torn structure causes that much more initial points have to be indicated, thus making the method less convenient in use.

3 Decision Tree Approach

The novel method is proposed to be a continuation of Barni's region growing approach. The main idea is to replace the manual initial points selection by another process, based on a decision tree application. Mining model is created upon pixel values of a selected fragment of the painting and then the rules obtained are applied to the whole image to separate the initial set of craquelure pixels. Afterwards the region growing step may be applied.

A decision tree is built from a training set, which consists of feature vectors, each of which is constructed by a set of attributes and a class label. Attributes are descriptors containing information about the object. A tree is built by determining the correlations between an input and the targeted outcome. After all the attributes have been correlated, the algorithm identifies the single attribute that most cleanly separates the outcomes. This point of the best separation is measured by using an equation that calculates information gain. The attribute that has the best score for information gain is used to divide the cases into subsets, which are then recursively analysed by the same process, until the tree cannot be split any more. Nodes in a decision tree involve testing a particular attribute. Usually, the test at a node compares an attribute value with a constant.

However, some trees compare two attributes with each other, or use some function of one or more attributes. Leaf nodes give a classification that applies to all instances that reach the leaf, a set of classifications, or a probability distribution over all possible classifications. To classify an unknown instance a path has to be traced down the tree with respect to the values of the attributes tested in successive nodes, and when a leaf is reached the instance is classified according to the class assigned to the leaf ([21],[12]).

Several methods have been proposed to construct decision trees, the initial being based on CART and C4.5 algorithms. In this work the Microsoft Decision Trees algorithm has been applied. Details about its construction, requirements and interpretation may be found in [12]

3.1   Attribute Selection

A set of 30 attributes was chosen to form the feature vector for the preliminary analysis. Three of them were directly based on red, green and blue channel values of the image, fourth was the grayscale value. Further values derive from mathematical morphology erosion, dilation, opening, closing, top-hat and bottom-hat operations with a structuring element radius chosen accordingly to the average width of a craquelure line. The last set of attributes comes from median and order-statistic filtering operations performed upon defined neighbourhood.

Training of the decision tree requires manual segmentation of craquelure on a small, representative area of the image. Pixels denoted as belonging to the crack pattern construct a binary mask, which is then transformed into a class label in the feature vector definition. There are two class labels 1 and 0 for craquelure and non-craquelure pixels respectively. As shown in Figure 2 only a part of non-craquelure pixels was chosen for further analysis, since according to mining structure definition rules the proportional participation should be equal for both classes.

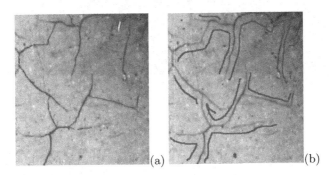

Fig. 2. Training set definition for a decision tree: (a) - craquelure pixels, (b) - selected non-craquelure pixels

3.2 Mining Model Interpretation and Partial Results

A few important observations may be done by analyzing the results of craquelure segmentation task done according to the rules obtained by the decision tree generation. First, the results obtained in the mining model confirmed the

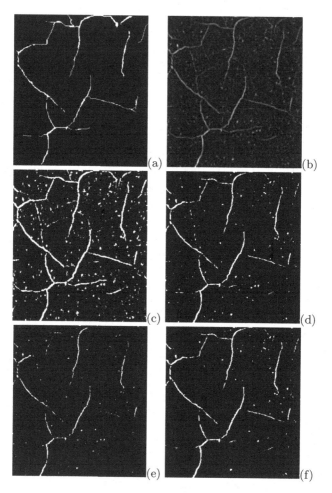

Fig. 3. Initial set of craquelure pixels: (a) - manually defined mask, (b) - top-hat operation result, (c)-(e) - thresholded top-hat image with different threshold levels, (f) - decision tree defined mask

adequacy of a top-hat operation as a crack identification method. Top hat value computed on a grayscale image was recognized as a first splitting attribute in the model and the split was done into four groups in analyzed case. Pixels of highest top-hat were classified as craquelure pixels with probability close to 100 percent and these were taken to create the initial set of craquelure without further verification. The second split attribute for pixels of lower top-hat value appeared to be statistic-order filter with neighbourhoud size biger then of the structuring element for top-hat operation and value close to first quartile. Only pixels with low value of order filter were confirmed to be craquelure pixels. Pixels with lower top-hat value were excluded from further analysis as not being a craquelure. Results of the decision tree based classification are shown in Figure 3 with comparison to the results of a pure top-hat method.

As might be observed in the figure, significant amount of noise was automatically reduced in the mask defined upon rules defined by the mining model comparing to the pure top-hat method. Lowering threshold value can reduce the noise in the top-hat image, but also limits the number of correctly classified craquelure pixels. The results show that decision tree classification method may in some cases give better results since it contains a verification method for pixels already classified as craquelure pixels by another algorithm. The verification method may differ for each analyzed image and is always suggested by the mining model within the set of methods represented by the feature vector attributes. In the case discussed above only nodes with significant number of cases and high probability were taken into further consideration.

3.3   Extension to the Whole Image

In further analysis the classification rules for craquelure pixels obtained by the decision tree based mining model were applied to the whole image. The results seen in Figure 4 show that good classification was reached in the whole area visually similar to the sample defined in the preceding step.

Fig. 4. Decision tree based classification rules applied to the whole image

It may be observed however that not all of the significant craquelure pixels were identified. That is because the classification rules are strictly fit to the training area. In further step another sample was added to the mining model and a new set of rules obtained allowed to separate craquelure in new area (left part of the image). See Figure 5 to see the result.

Fig. 5. Result improved by extension of clssification rules set

The discussed approach allowed a satisfactory identification of craquelure pixels in the whole area where crack pattern was darker from the background. The noise was significantly reduced thus letting the obtained mask be a good starting point for futher analysis of craquelure pattern characteristics. All the dark area, where cracks appear brighter than the background should be analyzed according to the newly defined sample and new set of rules generated. This is because the basic identification step would be rather by bottom-hat, than top-hat operation.

4   Conclusions and Further Work

A new method of craquelure segmentation in old paintings was presented. Data mining approach was applied to improve the step of identifying the initial set of pixels for region growing based method. Results obtained brought to three general conclusions. First, adequacy of a top-hat method for the separation task was confirmed not only by visual, but also by statistical judgement. Second, the decision tree based method of initial set identification for region growing method appeared to give satisfactory results. The manual step was not possible to be omitted in the method, but in the case of inconsistent (torn) craquelure network the ratio of work done by the restorer in sample masks definition to the final result might be better than in manual selection of all the initial pixels. Third, the noise elimination appeared to be more successful than in a pure top-hat method, thus the decision tree based craquelure separation algorithm might be used as an independent method in some cases.

It was shown that one sample mask may be not enough for defining a craquelure pattern in a whole image. Such masks should be defined for all significantly distinguishable background textures. Further research may be lead towards better understanding of the influence of sample masks choice to the obtained mining model rules. The feature vector might be also studied to identify another possible arguments to improve the separation of craquelure pixels from the background.

Acknowledgements. Author would like to thank Mrs. Joanna Sobczyk and the Laboratory of Analysis and Nondestructive Investigation of Heritage Objects of the National Museum in Krakow for substantial support and making accessible high resolution images of paintings from the collection of Rafał Hadziewicz works.

References

1. Abas, F.S.: Analysis of Craquelure Patterns for Content-Based Retrieval. PhD Thesis, University of Southampton, Southampton (2004)
2. Abas, F.S., Martinez, K.: Classification of painting cracks for content-based analysis. In: IST/SPIE's 15th Annual Symp. Electronic Imaging, Santa Clara, California, USA (2003)
3. Abas, F.S., Martinez, K.: Craquelure analysis for content-based retrieval. In: Proc of 14th Int. Conf. on Dig. Sig. Proc. Santorini, Greece, pp. 111–114 (2002)
4. Barni, M., Bartolini, F., Cappellini, V.: Image processing for virtual restoration of artworks. IEEE Multimedia 7(2), 34–37 (2000)
5. Barni, M., Pelagotti, A., Piva, A.: Image processing for the analysis and conservation of paintings: opportunities and challenges. IEEE Sig. Proc. Mag., 141 (2005)
6. Bucklow, S.L.: A sylometric analysis of Craquelure. Computers and the Humanities 31, 503–521 (1998)
7. Cappelllini, V., Barni, M., Corsini, M., de Rosa, A., Piva, A.: ArtShop: an art-oriented image-processing tool for cultural heritage applications. J. Visual Comput. Animat. 14, 149–158 (2003)
8. Cappellini, V., Piva, A.: Opportunities and Issues of image processing for cultural heritage applications. In: Proc EUSIPCO 2006, Florence, Italy (2006)
9. Gonzalez, R.C., Woods, R.: Digital Image Processing, 3rd edn. Prentice-Hall (2007)
10. Gupta, A., Khandelwal, V., Gupta, A., Srivastava, M.C.: Image processing methods for the restoration of digitized paintings. Thammasat Int. J. Sc. Tech. 13(3), 66–72 (2008)
11. Hanbury, A., Kammerer, P., Zolda, E.: Painting crack elimination using viscous morphological reconstruction. In: Proc ICIAP 2003, Mantova, Italy (2003)
12. Microsoft Decision Trees Algorithm Technical Reference, http://msdn.microsoft.com/en-us/library/cc645868
13. Tadeusiewicz, R., Korohoda, P.: Computer Analysis and Image Processing. Progress of Telecommunication Foundation Publishing House, Krakow (1997) (in Polish: Komputerowa analiza i przetwarzanie obrazow)
14. Tadeusiewicz, R.: How Intelligent Should Be System for Image Analysis? In: Kwasnicka, H., Jain, L.C. (eds.) Innovations in Intelligent Image Analysis. SCI, vol. 339, pp. V–X. Springer, Heidelberg (2011)
15. Serra, J.: Image Analysis and Mathematical Morphology, vol. I. Ac. Press, London (1982)
16. Sobczyk, J., Obara, B., Fraczek, P., Sobczyk, J.: Zastosowania analizy obrazu w nieniszczacych badaniach obiektow zabytkowych. Wybrane Przyklady, Ochrona Zabytkow 2, 69–78 (2006)
17. Stork, D.G.: Computer Vision and Computer Graphics Analysis of Paintings and Drawings: An Introduction to the Literature. In: Jiang, X., Petkov, N. (eds.) CAIP 2009. LNCS, vol. 5702, pp. 9–24. Springer, Heidelberg (2009)
18. Stout, G.L.: A trial index of laminal disruption. JAIC 17(1,3), 17–26 (1977)

19. Szczepaniak, P.S., Tadeusiewicz, R.: The Role of Artificial Intelligence, Knowledge and Wisdom in Automatic Image Understanding. Journal of Applied Computer Science 18(1), 75–85 (2010)
20. De Willigen, P.: A Mathematical Study on Craquelure and other Mechanical Damage in Paintings. Delft University Press, Delft (1999)
21. Witten, I.H., Frank, E.: Data Mining. Practical Machine Learning Tools and Techniques, 2nd edn. Morgan Kaufmann Publishers, San Francisco (2005)

Computer-Aided Reclamation of Lost Art

Maria Lena Demetriou, Jon Yngve Hardeberg, and Gabriel Adelmann

The Norwegian Colour and Visual Computing Laboratory,
Gjøvik University College, P.O. Box 191, N-2802 Gjøvik, Norway
marialena.dem@gmail.com, jon.hardeberg@hig.no, adel_g@yahoo.com
http://colorlab.no/

Abstract. There are numerous approaches towards restoration of art, including computer applications as aid to manual performance. However, to our knowledge, it has not been attempted to recuperate high quality images of missing or presumably destroyed works of art. While these works will never again be available in their original form, it may be feasible to considerably enhance the quality of preserved photographic reproductions. A pioneering combination of super-resolution and colour correction is presented here, targeting the reclamation of high quality images of lost works of art. The techniques are performed by example, utilising correspondence between artworks of similar nature, currently available both in low and high quality. With extensive prior knowledge in the domains of super-resolution and colour correction, selected approaches were studied, implemented and tested, concluding to the most efficient. Experimental results are highly promising, revealing a new research path in colour imaging for fine art.

Keywords: Fine Art, Restoration, Super-Resolution, Colour Correction.

1 Introduction and Motivation

There has not been a previous attempt as the present endeavour towards reclamation of lost art. We propose a novel strategy for making the images of selected pieces of our lost artistic heritage accessible to the public, an endeavour we term *'lost art reclamation'*. The ability to regain paintings considered to have been lost forever was an unrivalled motivation for this study.

With no background studies to support this effort, the possibilities and expectations of the work were unpredictable. The efficiency of a chosen technique was uncertain, not only due to the question at hand, but also because of the nature of the involved images. Being a fine art application, the images of paintings that were included demonstrated major characteristic differences with standard datasets of natural images, against which most image processing approaches were tested. Thus, the reported performance of state-of-the-art techniques was under examination, in parallel to the search for a solution.

The most important records of such lost works are colour photos published in period art books, especially between the two World Wars. At publication, these were at the cutting age of printing technology, but as compared to contemporary images, these samples are of low quality, with obvious halftoning patterns,

A. Fusiello et al. (Eds.): ECCV 2012 Ws/Demos, Part I, LNCS 7583, pp. 551–560, 2012.

erroneous colours, and low resolution. As the only records of significant artworks, these samples are of inadequate quality regarding their importance. They are however the only available starting point to work towards a high quality image of a lost artwork, aiming to obtain good enough quality for the reclaimed artwork to be exhibited alongside surviving works.

With halftoned, erroneously coloured prints of low resolution as a starting point, the study targeted a combined solution to resolve these matters. Super-resolution (SR) was concluded as the most appropriate technique towards resolution enhancement. In specific, *example-based super-resolution* (EB-SR) [1,2] was the selected approach, incorporating art images available in both low and high quality.

SR involves three different categories: interpolation approaches, reconstruction based approaches and learning (example-based) approaches. In the concept of the stated problem, only a learning approach is applicable. Interpolation and reconstruction based techniques require as input a series of low resolution images of the same scene. This is impossible in the examined case, as the scene of a painting's image cannot change. Notions as obtaining several low resolution images of the same scene from different perspectives, or under different viewing conditions are unsuitable in this case.

A learning based method involves the training of two corresponding dictionaries, one of low quality A_l and one of high quality A_h [3,4]. The included patches correspond to the exact same scene in an image. Given a low resolution image, the learning is employed to correctly replace patches of the test image with the most appropriate ones from the dictionary. Identifying a training patch in the dictionary A_l as the closest match to the given test patch, its corresponding high quality patch from dictionary A_h will be returned as the SR result for that specific patch. Repeating this method for all patches in the test image results in a complete, super-resolved high quality image.

The training dictionary A_l includes halftones, erroneously coloured low resolution patches which correspond to continuous-tone high quality patches in the dictionary A_h, mimicking the problem at hand. The application of EB-SR on a low quality test image, enhances the resolution and also, due to the example-based approach, resolves the matters of halftoning and erroneous colours automatically. The process of *inverse halftoning* [5] is thus merged with the SR approach [6]. Upon completion of EB-SR, the resulting images are of continuous-tone and high resolution with attempted corrected colours. Nevertheless, to ensure the colour correctness of the test image, further processing is essential. A crucial reason for that is the patch-oriented application of EB-SR, which leads to inconsistencies of colour in the general image. Colour correction is necessarily applied next to ensure the global correction of the image.

Colour correction (CC) [7] has been developed in various studies, either as *colour transfer* [8,9], which relates to the artistic transformation of an image towards the appearance of another, or *image blending* [10,11], which is a common notion amongst image stitching techniques. The extensive set of implemented approaches and their large variety of applications account for the lack of extensive evaluation regarding the performance of CC approaches.

Combining the above techniques, the present work resolved the identified problems of halftoning, low resolution and erroneous colours. The joint solution followed an example-based approach, utilising ground-truth data in low and high quality and applying this learning to given input.

2   Methodology

The proposed method for a complete system of lost art reclamation involves two major steps: example-based super-resolution and colour correction. Before the processing however, the training and test sets are gathered. The training set involves two corresponding subsets: one of low quality images which resembles the problem at hand and a 'correct' reference high quality image set. The test image is transformed to colour space $YCbCr$ and EB-SR is applied on the luminance channel Y, while channels CbCr are interpolated. The resulting super-resolved images are transferred to the CC subsystem.

2.1   Super-Resolution

Due to the large amount of possible solutions to a high quality image that correspond to a given test low quality image, regularisation is necessary in SR. The proposed regularisation involves the use of a local sparse-land model on image patches, as performed by Zeyde $et\ al.$ [4]. The main concept is that each patch of the test images can be well represented using a linear combination of few atoms from a dictionary. In other words, it can be represented by the multiplication of the dictionary by a sparse vector of coefficients. The algorithm approaches the problem as the minimisation of

$$\|SH\hat{y} - z_l\|, \tag{1}$$

where z_l is the low quality image, $\hat{y}$ is the reconstructed high quality image, S is the blurring factor and H is the decimation operator.

Firstly, image z_l is scaled up, using bicubic interpolation Q, to the dimensions of the high quality image y_h. This results in $y_l = Qz_l$, from which patches are extracted, estimating the corresponding patch of y_h. A set of k locations of true pixels (which have not been obtained by interpolation) define the position of patches in the image y_l to be extracted by operator R_k. The same operation is carried out onto y_h, resulting to set Ω of patches p_h^k. According to the sparse-land model [12,13], patches p_h^k can be represented sparsely by q^k vectors of dictionary A_h, as $p_h^k = A_h q^k$. Obtaining the same sparse representation against y_l, the set p_h^k corresponds to set $p_l^k = R_k y_l$. Operator $L^{all} = QSH$ transforms the complete high resolution image y_h to the low resolution one y_l. It can therefore be assumed that $p_l^k = Lp_h^k + \tilde{v}_k$, where L is a local operator being a portion of L^{all} and $\tilde{v}_k$ is the additive noise in this patch. As $p_h^k = A_h q^k$,

$$Lp_h^k = LA_h q^k. \tag{2}$$

Utilising the relation between the low and high resolution patches $p_l^k = Lp_h^k + \tilde{v}_k$, it can be stated that

$$LA_h q^k = Lp_h^k = p_l^k - \tilde{v}_k, \tag{3}$$

implying that

$$\left\| p_l^k - LA_h q^k \right\|_2 \leq \epsilon, \tag{4}$$

where ϵ is related to the noise power σ of v. Thus, patch p_l^k can be represented by q^k over the dictionary $A_l = LA_h$, and patch p_h^k can be recovered from q^k multiplied by A_h.

In the training phase, sets $\{y_h^j\}$ and $\{y_l^j\}$ are constructed from the high and low quality images respectively. It has to be noted here that the training set consists of extracted parts of the training images. The training low and high quality images are firstly resized to match in physical resolution. *Image registration* is applied onto the low quality training images so that they match their corresponding high quality images, to avoid artifacts due to misalignment in training. Affine, translation, rigid and projective transforms registrations are visually evaluated to select the best registered image.

Once sets $\{y_h^j\}$ and $\{y_l^j\}$ are gathered, patches are extracted from them, leading to $P = \{p_h^k, p_l^k\}$. Later pre-processing centres the training on characterising the relation between the low-resolution patches and the edges and texture content within the corresponding high-resolution ones. This is performed on p_h^k to remove low frequencies and feature extraction is performed on p_l^k as to extract local features that correspond to their high-frequency content. Two filters are involved in this feature extraction, a gradient and a Laplacian filter. Next, principal component analysis is performed onto the p_l^k features to reduce the feature vector, resulting to $\{\tilde{p}_l^k\}$. Dictionary A_l is then trained so that p_l^k can be represented sparsely. Finally, dictionary A_h is trained so that it matches A_l.

Given a test image z_l, this is interpolated to y_l and sharpened by spatial non-linear filtering. Then, for every location $k \in \Omega$, patches p_l^k are sparse-coded using A_l resulting to $\{q^k\}$. These q^k are then used to recover p_h^k, by multiplying with A_h. Merging $\{p_h^k\}$ to obtain $\hat{y}_h$, the overlapping areas are averaged to get the final resulting image. This last step is performed as the following minimisation with respect to $\hat{y}_h$:

$$\underset{y_h}{\arg\min} \sum_k \left\| R_k(\hat{y}_h - y_l) - \hat{p}_h^k \right\|_2^2. \tag{5}$$

As the involved painting images are highly memory demanding, they cannot be processed as a whole. Therefore, the image to be tested is firstly split into row extracts of full width but length of 600 pixels. EB-SR is performed on these extracts individually and the resulting super-resolved extracts are merged to obtain the complete image.

An additional consideration is the boundary effect when the patches are overlapped and added. To follow the proposed method, cropping the boundary to ignore the effect is not possible [4], as the boundary of an extract is necessary for the final composition of the image as a whole. Instead, the overlap between the extracts is arranged so that this effect is dealt with.

2.2   Colour Correction

Upon gathering of the super-resolved results, CC process is carried out. The ground-truth high quality images are used one by one as reference for each test image. Depending on the similarity of the test image with the reference image, the performance of CC varies for each application.

Upon completion of the image processing procedures, evaluation of the results follows, using image quality metrics which correspond to both the structure and the colours of the resulting images.

3   Evaluation Setup

3.1   Selection of Approaches

In our experimental setup, EB-SR followed the implementation of Zeyde *et al.* [4], who optimised the algorithm by Yang *et al.* [3] using toolboxes K-SVD [14] and OMP [15]. The implementation of Zeyde *et al.* enhanced the algorithm in terms of computational complexity and algorithm architecture. The final results were obtained from this optimised implementation, due to the long execution time and demanding memory handling of the original by Yang *et al.*

For the application of CC, the selected algorithms covered a variety of approaches, incorporating six methods of both colour transfer and image balancing. These included standard baseline approaches [9] and latest techniques of colour correction. Both model-based parametric approaches [10,9,8] and model-less non-parametric approaches [11] were applied, involving global [9,8] and local [10,11] approaches, as well as operations in different colour spaces (RGB, $l\alpha\beta$, CIECAM).

The first applied approach was an exposure/gain compensation technique by Brown and Lowe [10] (Alg. 1). In this colour balancing approach the intensity gain level of the component images was adjusted to compensate for appearance differences caused by different exposure levels. The second approach was the standard colour correction method by Reinard *et al.* [9], which deals with global colour transfer (Alg. 2). Despite the simplicity of this approach, its reported efficiency is significant, making it a baseline work which was extended in later works [8]. Its structure is centred around a linear transformation based on the mean and standard deviation of the global colour distributions of the source and target images in the uncorrelated $l\alpha\beta$ colour space [16]. The colour value of a target pixel was defined as

$$g(G_t) = \mu_s + \frac{\sigma_s}{\sigma_t}(C_t - \mu_t). \tag{6}$$

This approach was also applied in the RGB (Alg. 3) and CIECAM (Alg. 4) colour spaces. Based on the work by Reinhard *et al.* [9], Xiao *et al.* [8] (Alg. 5) extended it to a correlated RGB global colour approach which makes use of an ellipsoid mapping scheme. Lastly, the cumulative colour histogram mapping approach by Fecker *et al.* [11] (Alg. 6) was applied. This involved a closest neighbour mapping scheme to select the corresponding colour level of the source image to each level of the target image.

3.2 Training and Test Image Sets

Five ground-truth data pairs were obtained in low and high quality by scanning pre-WWII artbooks [17] and from Bridgeman Art Library Limited respectively. The involved artworks were all by Peter Paul Rubens, titled 'Madonna', 'The rape of the daughters of Leukippos', 'Liebesgarten', 'The Judgement of Paris' and 'Putti'. These ground-truth data were divided in a training and a test set. Four of these images formed a ground-truth test set in order to quantitatively evaluate the performance of the processes, while the fifth image ('The rape of the daughters of Leukippos') was used for training.

In addition, a real-test image set was defined from three prints of P.P. Rubens' paintings which are nowadays lost, namely the 'Resurrection of Lazarus', 'Diana At Her Bath, Surprised by Satyrs' and 'Satyrs and Bacchants'. Out of the opus of P.P. Rubens, the included works were limited to the themes of mythology and religious subjects.

The total of the scans, except for image 'Satyrs and Bacchants', was gathered from the same artbook [17] to minimise effects from different printing technologies on the input data. The scans were performed using a Microtek ScanMaker 9800XL at a resolution of 1600dpi with no automatic adjustments to preserve the originality of the image, especially the halftoning pattern. The ground-truth data were scaled, using bicubic interpolation, to match their corresponding high quality pairs' dimensions in a range of $[3898..10197, 3408..10917, 3]$, while the real-test images were scaled down to dimensions in the range of $[1000..1500, 1000..1500, 3]$.

3.3 Evaluation Criteria

As stated by Wang *et al.* [18], image quality evaluation of colour altered images should not only include colour coherence, but also structural coherence, as colour correction may also affect the structure of an image. Thus, measuring the fidelity of the resulting images against the ground truth images was of double importance, both for pure evaluation of the SR application, as well as for CC.

Three full-reference image quality metrics were used in the evaluation of the ground-truth test set. The metrics of peak signal-to-noise ratio (PSNR) and structural similarity index (SSIM) [18] were used to evaluate the overall structural enhancement evaluation, while metric S-CIELAB [19] targeted the colour reproduction accuracy. Higher scores for PSNR and SSIM correspond to better image quality, while S-CIELAB denotes the colour difference between two images. SSIM improves on PSNR, combining the components of luminance, contrast and structure, correlating in this way better with human judgement of image quality [20]. S-CIELAB metric measures the accuracy of reproduction of a colour against its original when this is viewed by a human observer. Lower S-CIELAB values indicate lower difference between two images and thus higher colour coherence.

3.4 Implementation Details and Parameter Settings

The code for SR was adapted from the original implementation of Zeyde *et al.* [4], as this is available on the author's website. The CC approaches were also used directly from the implementation by Xu and Mulligan [7]. The system was implemented as a complete process, merging the steps of EB-SR and CC along with the evaluation.

The approaches and the evaluation criteria in the implementation use the same parameters as stated in the original papers. The only exception regards the dimensions of the involved images, which are larger than the standard input.

4 Results and Discussion

The ground-truth and real-test sets were inserted in the application, resulting with 30 super-resolved, colour corrected images per input test image. The single output of SR was colour corrected by six different approaches, using all five ground-truth high quality images as reference. CC was performed on each ground-truth test image using its corresponding high quality image as well, providing the highest barrier of performance. Table 1 presents the resulting performance measurements for the ground-truth test data. The results have been categorised according to the applied CC method, due to their common input, the super-resolved images. Each CC method included evaluation of 25 resulting images of five ground-truth data, each colour corrected using each of the five ground-truth high quality images as reference.

Table 1. PSNR, SSIM and S-CIELAB mean (μ) and standard deviation (σ) statistics per CC algorithm

Method	μ_{PSNR}	σ_{PSNR}	μ_{SSIM}	σ_{SSIM}	$\mu_{S-CIELAB}$	$\sigma_{S-CIELAB}$
Alg. 1 [10]	10.563	3.089	0.274	0.066	27.470	6.355
Alg. 2 [9]	13.800	1.696	0.3194	0.056	29.984	4.623
Alg. 3 [9]	**14.942**	**1.180**	**0.347**	**0.043**	**22.442**	**3.849**
Alg. 4 [9]	**14.974**	**1.147**	**0.347**	**0.045**	**22.816**	**3.774**
Alg. 5 [8]	14.705	1.165	0.341	0.043	24.378	4.381
Alg. 6 [11]	14.814	1.191	0.333	0.054	22.937	3.714

First of all, a large variation among the results is observed, especially concerning the colour reproduction of the images. Such variation is natural, as the results are strongly dependent on the reference image. Moreover, the overall top performing algorithms (Alg. 3 and Alg. 4) have very similar scores, with Alg. 3 having obtained the best performance in colour coherence, but Alg. 4 being the best in structural coherence. One can observe that in PSNR terms, the lowest performance was given by Alg. 1, but the same algorithm performed better in S-CIELAB terms. Therefore, while the top performing algorithms are evident, a definite general ranking amongst the rest of the algorithms cannot be stated.

Moreover, the obtained S-CIELAB scores are reportedly high. However, when compared to the initial difference between the original low quality test image and the high quality image as demonstrated in Table 2, the enhancement on colour reproduction is significant. There is a colour difference drop in a range of [1.549..6.901]. The S-CIELAB values for the super-resolved colour corrected images correspond to the best performing case in terms of S-CIELAB, when the reference image is of a different scene than the test image.

Table 2. S-CIELAB scores between (a) original low quality test images and (b) super-resolved (best) colour corrected images against ground truth high quality images

Test Image	Original S-CIELAB	SR+CC S-CIELAB
Leukippos	22.330	18.291
Liebesgarten	18.708	15.438
Madonna	22.826	21.277
Paris	24.152	17.251
Putti	30.347	23.501

The real-test images could not be evaluated using the full-reference metrics as a reference does not exist. Instead, they were subjectively evaluated. Figure 1 displays an example result from the process applied on the image of the lost painting by P.P. Rubens, titled 'Satyrs and Bacchants'. The complete set of the results is available on the project's webpage.[1]

Fig. 1. Detail of the image from the P.P. Rubens' lost painting 'Satyrs and Bacchants', as originally in low quality (left) and after SR+CC (right)

---

[1] http://www.stud.hig.no/~101530/

5   Conclusions and Further Work

The present work is the first study that attempts a reclamation of lost art. Not only it proves that such an endeavour can indeed be successful, but it also reveals the possibilities of further exploration of the domain. The results of the work, along with their evaluation, suggest the feasibility of an entirely novel branch of colour imaging applications in fine art, as well as observations and considerations for the domains of super-resolution, inverse halftoning and colour correction.

Applying this unusual image dataset to state-of-the-art techniques, it extends their applicability and performance evaluation to a brand new, more demanding dataset. It brings on board the necessity of image registration in the case the training sets are misaligned, as well as the application of SR to a real-world problem. It proves that in this case the CC technique by Reinhard *et al.* [9], is the most effective, despite its simplicity. It questions the ranking of CC well-known approaches and verifies the efficiency of dictionary-based SR. It furthermore certifies a solution of inverse halftoning via SR, extending the work of Minami *et al.* [6].

The current work is a unique attempt towards computer-assisted heritage preservation and suggests extensive possibilities for further study. Firstly, future studies could focus on a better evaluation of the results' image quality, through a combination of both structure and colour coherence metrics [7]. This could include the development of local image quality metrics, approaching a content-based fashion which is more suitable to artworks. It could further explore the notion of similarity between two artworks, in order to automate and optimise the selection of a reference image for a specific test image. Further approaches could be applied and tested both towards SR and CC, based on the revelation of the efficiency of state-of-the-art algorithms in the problem's concept.

A concluding step of this work would be the printing of the resulting images and their extensive evaluation via psychophysical experiments. Such experimentation would support the resulting quality of the artworks and define whether their quality is high enough for such a print to be displayed alongside surviving, 'real' paintings. Demonstrating it is possible to do so would be the ultimate milestone for our work.

References

1. Freeman, W.T., Pasztor, E.C., Carmichael, O.T.: Learning Low-Level Vision. International Journal of Computer Vision 40(1), 25–47 (2000)
2. Freeman, W.T., Jones, T.R., Pasztor, E.C.: Example-based super-resolution. IEEE Comp. Graph. and Appl. 22(2), 56–65 (2002)
3. Yang, J., Wright, J., Ma, Y., Huang, T.: Image super-resolution as sparse-representation of raw image patches. In: IEEE Conference on Computer Vision and Pattern Recognition, CVPR, pp. 1–8 (2008)
4. Zeyde, R., Elad, M., Protter, M.: On Single Image Scale-Up Using Sparse-Representations. In: Boissonnat, J.-D., Chenin, P., Cohen, A., Gout, C., Lyche, T., Mazure, M.-L., Schumaker, L. (eds.) Curves and Surfaces 2011. LNCS, vol. 6920, pp. 711–730. Springer, Heidelberg (2012)

5. Wong, P.W.: Inverse halftoning and kernel estimation for error diffusion. IEEE Transactions on Image Processing 4(4), 486–498 (1995)
6. Minami, Y., Azuma, S.-I., Sugie, T.: An inverse halftoning algorithm based on super-resolution image reconstruction. In: Proceedings of SICE Annual Conference 2010, pp. 1110–1113 (August 2010)
7. Xu, W., Mulligan, J.: Performance evaluation of color correction approaches for automatic multi-view image and video stitching. In: IEEE Int. Conference on Computer Vision and Pattern Recognition, San Francisco, USA, pp. 263–270 (2010)
8. Xiao, X., Ma, L.: Color transfer in correlated color space. In: Proc. ACM International Conference on Virtual Reality Continuum and Its Applications, pp. 305–309 (2006)
9. Reinhard, E., Adhikhmin, M., Gooch, B., Shirley, P.: Color transfer between images. IEEE Computer Graphics and Applications 21(5), 34–41 (2001)
10. Brown, M., Lowe, D.G.: Recognising panoramas. In: Proc. ICCV, vol. 2, pp. 1218–1225 (2003)
11. Fecker, U., Barkowsky, M., Kaup, A.: Histogram-based prefiltering for luminance and chrominance compensation of multiview video. IEEE Transactions on Circuits and Systems for Video Technology 18(9), 1258–1267 (2008)
12. Elad, M., Aharon, M.: Image denoising via learned dictionaries and sparse representation. In: CVPR, pp. 895–900 (2006)
13. Elad, M., Aharon, M.: Image denoising via sparse and redundant representations over learned dictionaries. IEEE Transactions on Image Processing 15(12), 3736–3745 (2006)
14. Aharon, M., Elad, M., Bruckstein, A.: The K-SVD: An algorithm for designing of overcomplete dictionaries for sparse representation. IEEE Trans. on Signal Processing 54(11), 4311–4322 (2006)
15. Elad, M., Rubinstein, R., Zibulevsky, M.: Efficient implementation of the K-SVD algorithm using batch orthogonal matching pursuit. Technical report, CS, Technion (April 2008)
16. Ruderman, D., Cronin, T., Chiao, C.: Statistics of cone responses to natural images: Implications for visual coding. J. Optical Soc. of America 15(8), 2036–2045 (1998)
17. Dulberg, F.: Rubens. E.A. Seeman, Germany (1932)
18. Wang, Z., Bovik, A.C., Sheikh, H.R., Simoncelli, E.P.: Image quality assessment: From error visibility to structural similarity. IEEE Trans. Image Processing 13(4), 600–612 (2004)
19. Zhang, X., Wandell, B.A.: A spatial extension of cielab for digital color image reproduction. In: SID Symposium Technical Digest, vol. 27, pp. 731–734 (1996)
20. Anderson, H.S., Gupta, M.R.: Joint deconvolution and imaging. In: Proc. SPIE Conf. on Computational Imaging, vol. 7246, pp. 72460C–72460C-12 (2009)

Evaluation of Digital Inpainting Quality in the Context of Artwork Restoration

Alexandra Ioana Oncu, Ferdinand Deger, and Jon Yngve Hardeberg

The Norwegian Colour and Visual Computing Laboratory
Gjøvik University College, Gjøvik, Norway

Abstract. Improved digital image inpainting algorithms could provide substantial support for future artwork restoration. However, currently, there is an acknowledged lack of quantitative metrics for image inpainting evaluation. In this paper the performance of eight inpainting algorithms is first evaluated by means of a psychophysical experiment. The ranking of the algorithms thus obtained confirms that exemplar based methods generally outperform PDE based methods. Two novel inpainting quality metrics, proposed in this paper, eight general image quality metrics and four inpainting-specific metrics are then evaluated by validation against the perceptual data. Results show that no metric can adequately predict inpainting quality over the entire image database, and that the performance of the metrics is image-dependent.

1 Introduction

Digital inpainting refers to techniques used to reconstruct areas of missing information in an image, by filling the gaps with visually plausible content. In the field of artwork restoration, inpainting algorithms can be employed for digital restoration, by reversing the damage (i.e. torn canvas, scratches, stains) in a painting converted to a digital form. Digital inpainting algorithms can be grouped into two main categories. Partial differential equation (PDE) based algorithms [1–4] fill in gaps by extending isophote lines from the source region into the target region via diffusion. Their drawback consist of introducing blur artifacts that become more visible when inpainting larger areas. Exemplar-based inpainting algorithms [5–7] overcome this drawback by reconstructing large image regions from sample textures. Some approaches try to achieve better performance in terms of running time [3, 7, 8].

As the goal of inpainting is to reconstruct the damaged regions in a visually plausible way and a reference image might not always be available for comparison, inpainting quality evaluation is a challenging task, that has been only narrowly researched. Mahalingam [9] and Ardis *et al.* [10] propose the use of visual-saliency based metrics. However, these metrics are not commonly used by researchers to assess new inpainting techniques. Instead, qualitative human comparisons are currently and frequently used. Other image quality (IQ) metrics simulating the human visual system (HVS) and taking into account structural information in an image might be useful in the field of image inpainting.

A. Fusiello et al. (Eds.): ECCV 2012 Ws/Demos, Part I, LNCS 7583, pp. 561–570, 2012.
© Springer-Verlag Berlin Heidelberg 2012

This paper will evaluate the performance of eight representative inpainting algorithms [1–8] by means of a psychophysical experiment. The obtained perceptual data will be used to establish a ranking of the inpainting methods, described in Section 2. Based on the same data, the correlation between a selection of existing IQ metrics and perceived quality will be investigated. Furthermore, two novel metrics will be introduced in this paper and included in the evaluation.

2   Psychophysical Experiment for Subjective Rating

2.1   Image Database

A common practice when evaluating the performance of inpainting algorithms is to use predefined inpainting regions. In this paper, modified digitally acquired images of real damaged paintings will be used as test images. In the manual restoration process there are a number of steps that proceed the filling in of missing areas. Instead of completely simulating gaps, this paper proposes the simulation of these steps, using the original degraded and manually restored versions of a painting. The resultant image replicates the regions containing missing or corrupted information from the digitally acquired image but has identical content with the manually restored image in the region outside the area to be inpainted. Figure 1 shows an example of a modified digitally acquired painting, as a result of the simulation process.

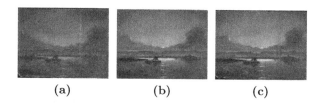

(a)   (b)   (c)

Fig. 1. Preparing an image for inpainting. (a) Original degraded painting (b) Manually restored version (c) Modified image with artefacts (i.e. water stain) from the degraded image and similar appearance to the manually restored image. (a-b) - image courtesy of R. Pillay at C2RMF.

Six test images (Figure 2) have been chosen for the psychophysical experiment. For each of them, eight inpainted images corresponding to the algorithms proposed by Bertalmio *et al.* [1], Telea [2], Tschumperle and Deriche [3], Bornemann and März [4], Criminisi *et al.* [5], Zhou and Kelly [6], Barnes *et al.* [7] and Oliveira *et al.* [8] have been included in the database. Additionally, for each of the test images, the digitally acquired image of the manually restored painting (further on referred to as *manually inpainted image*) has been considered. The manually inpainted images have been included to verify the reliability of the observers, by checking their behaviour when degraded/manually inpainted image pairs are presented. Finally, the image database used for the experiment consisted of 54 images.

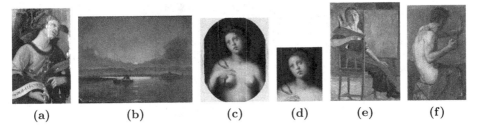

Fig. 2. Modified digitally acquired paintings corresponding to: (a) "Ange" by Raphael (*angel*) (b) "Vue de Drontheim" by Peder Balke (*boat*) (c) "Cléopâtre" - anonymous (*cleopatra*) (d) Detail of "Cléopâtre" (*detail*) (e) "Self-portrait" by Margarete Depner (*lady*) (f) "Invention of painting" by Ariton (*man*). (a-d) - image courtesy of R. Pillay at C2RMF, (e,f) image courtesy of R. Tataru at Brasov Art Museum (Romania)

2.2 Experimental Setup

The experiment was carried out as a web-based experiment. Observers were presented with a pair of two images at a time and asked to judge the overall quality of the inpainted image using the ITU-R five grade quality scale [11] labelled with the adjectives: *Excellent, Good, Fair, Poor, Bad*. Figure 3 shows an example of such an image pair presented during the experiment. On the left the degraded image is shown and on the right the inpainted image. This positioning was kept throughout the whole experiment. Participants were asked to complete the experiment, which consisted of viewing and rating a total of 54 pairs of images. The screening of the observers was carried out by implementing the procedure recommended in Rec. ITU-R BT.500-13 [11]. Furthermore, observers were rejected if their scores indicated *Fair, Poor* or *Bad* quality for manually inpainted images, or if failing to complete the experiment. Consequently, from a total of 91, results of 22 participants were rejected and only 69 considered for further evaluation.

2.3 Psychophysical Results

Perceptual data obtained from the experiment was converted to z-scores, indicating the performance of the considered inpainting methods. Figure 4 gives a graphical representation of the obtained results. As expected, the manual inpainting method received the highest score, indicating the best perceived quality among the studied methods. Moreover, the high z-score value associated to it is an indicator of the large consensus among the participants about the high performance of this method. Among the analysed digital inpainting methods, the algorithm proposed by Barnes *et al.* [7] has the highest score. Worth noticing is the low visual difference between the inpainted images obtained by the inpainting algorithms proposed by Criminisi *et al.* [5], Zhou and Kelly [6] and Tschumperle and Deriche [3]. The latter is inferred from the overlapping confidence intervals corresponding to the three methods, and implies a difficult task for the observers to judge IQ.

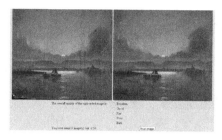

Fig. 3. Exemple of pair of images presented during the experiment. *(left)* Damaged painting *(right)* Inpainted version with the method proposed by Oliveira *et al.* [8].

Based on the obtained perceptual data, a ranking of the inpainting methods can be established (Figure 4). PDE-based methods are, generally, outperformed by exemplar-based methods. An exception is inpainting algorithm by Tschumperle and Deriche [3], which uses a vector valued regularization PDE.

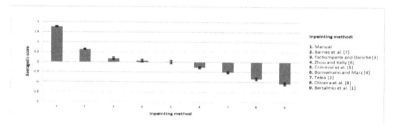

Fig. 4. Z-scores from observers based on 69 observers and 6 images, with 95% CI. The algorithm proposed by Barnes *et al.* [7] is rated as the best among digital inpainting methods.

3   Objective Quality Evaluation

Before discussing methods for objective quality evaluation, the notation convention must be defined. The area of missing information in an image will be referred to as the *gap* and will be denoted by Ω. Its complementary area, referred to as the *source* region, will be denoted by Θ. Furthermore, when discussing saliency based metrics, the pre-inpainting saliency map intensity corresponding to a particular pixel, p, will be denoted by $S(p)$. Similarly, the corresponding post-inpainting saliency map intensity will be denoted by $S'(p)$.

3.1   ASVS and DN

Ardis *et al.* [10] define two types of observable artifacting in an inpainted image, referred to as *in-region* and *out-region*. The former accounts for artifacts belonging to the gap, Ω, while the *out-region* artifacting considers the complementary area, Θ. In order to quantify the quality of the reproduction and based on the two artifact classes, Ardis *et al.* propose two metrics, the *Average Squared Visual Saience (ASVS)* and the *Degree of Noticeability (DN)*, that relate the visual saliency map of an image with the perceived quality of the same image.

The first metric, ASVS, needs no reference image and equates to in-region artifacting. Thus, $in_{region} = ASVS$, where ASVS is computed as:

$$ASVS = (1/||\Omega||)(\sum_{p \in \Omega} (S'(p))^2). \tag{1}$$

In-region artifacting occurs when the inpainted pixels cause a modification in the flow of attention specific to an image, by increasing the saliency of the inpainted region. Ardis *et al.* [10] relate in-region artifacting to distinct colouration or structure that is introduced after inpainting, that can not be observed elsewhere in the image.

Out-region artifacting occurs when an inpainting algorithm fails to extend a locally repeating colour or structure inside the gap. The latter causes a decreased flow of attention for otherwise salient areas and increase of attention in the neighbouring area of the inpainting domain. Out-region artifacting is computed as $out_{region} = (\sum_{p \in \Theta} (S'(p) - S(p))^2)/|\Theta|$. Combining in- and out-region artifacting, the *Degree of Noticeability (DN)* metric is computed as:

$$DN = \frac{|\Omega|}{|\Omega| + |\Theta|} in_{region} + \frac{|\Theta|}{|\Omega| + |\Theta|} out_{region}. \tag{2}$$

As suggested by Ardis *et al.*, higher scores for ASVS and DN can be interpreted as an indicator of highly visible artifacts and thus a poor inpainting performance. The psychophysical study conducted by the authors proposing the metrics shows a good correlation between perceived and calculated quality. However, their findings required confirmation by further larger scale experiments, as they use only five observers.

3.2 GD$_{in}$ and GD$_{out}$

Mahalingam [9] proposes two visual saliency-based metrics for quantifying inpainting quality. He shows that if there is any change in the saliency maps corresponding to the inpainted and original image, this change is related to the perceptual quality of the inpainting.

According to Mahalingam [9] the gaze density within and outside the gap in an inpainted image is computed as:

$$GD_{in} = \sum_{p \in \Omega} S'(p), \quad and \quad GD_{out} = \sum_{p \in \Theta} S'(p). \tag{3}$$

The gaze density measures given in Equation 3 need to be normalized before indicating the presence of artifacts:

$$\overline{GD}_{in} = \frac{\sum_{p \in \Omega} S'(p)}{\sum_{p \in \Omega} S(p)}, \quad and \quad \overline{GD}_{out} = \frac{\sum_{p \in \Theta} S'(p)}{\sum_{p \in \Theta} S(p)}. \tag{4}$$

For simplicity, further discussion referring to the normalized metrics will use the notation GD_{in} and GD_{out}.

Mahalingam [9] uses saliency maps generated from an eye tracking experiment. In this paper the SaliencyToolbox version 2.2 developed by Walther [12] is used to generate the saliency maps.

3.3   Proposed Metrics: BorSal and StructBorSal

Previous work by Mahalingam [9] and Ardis et al. [10] considers separately in- and out-region artifacting. In the latter, the authors show that out-region artifacting changes the flow of attention in the area outside the gap, but concentrated around the gap's neighbourhood. Hence, the saliency map values corresponding to a border region around the gap should be able to accurately capture the saliency change. This paper introduces the Border Saliency (BorSal) metric, which accounts for both in- and out-region artifacting by considering a Border region that extends three pixels inside and outside the gap. The BorSal metric is computed as a normalized gaze density measure, similarly to the GD_{in} and GD_{out} metrics [9]:

$$BorSal = \frac{\sum_{p \in Border} S'(p)}{\sum_{p \in Border} S(p)}. \tag{5}$$

The second inpainting quality evaluation metric proposed, denoted by StructBorSal, combines the BorSal metric with the $SSIM_{IPT}$ measure [13]:

$$StructBorSal = BorSal + SSIM_{IPT}. \tag{6}$$

3.4   Image Quality Metrics

In addition to the inpainting quality evaluation metrics discussed in the previous Section, eight other metrics from different categories (i.e. image difference, image fidelity, image quality) have been selected for evaluation in terms of correlation with the percept. A brief introduction of the selected metrics will be given here.

MSE and PSNR : image difference metrics applied for grayscale images. Calculate the Mean Squared Difference and Peak Signal to Noise Ratio. Mathematically based, easily to implement and previously used for quantifying inpainting quality.

S-CIELAB [14]: image difference metric applied for colour images. Frequently considered a reference when evaluating IQ metrics, having wide acceptance. Simulates the HVS.

SSIM-IPT [13]: IQ metric applied for grayscale images. Colour version of SSIM, takes structural information in an image into account and works on local neighbourhoods.

VSNR [15]: image fidelity metric applied for grayscale images. Based on contrast filtering and simulating the HVS.

SHAME and SHAME-II [16]: IQ metrics applied for colour images. Based on the hue angle algorithm [17] and the S-CIELAB$_J$ [18] metric. They latter differs from S-CIELAB only in terms of spatial filtering, which makes also the difference between SHAME and SHAME-II; Both metrics weight the output based on colour differences and region-of-interest. Simulate the HVS.

ABF [19]: image difference metric applied for colour images. Implementation of bilateral filtering that preserves edges and simulates the HVS.

4   Evaluation of Quality Metrics

The objective quality metrics presented in the previous section need to be evaluated against the results obtained from the psychophysical experiment in order to ensure the correspondence with perceived quality. The evaluation methodology refers to statistically analysing the ratings given by observers and corresponding to the 48 digitally inpainted images. Based on raw perceptual data, the Mean Opinion Score (MOS) is calculated for each image in the database and then converted to a corresponding z-score. The Pearson product-moment (PCC) [20] and Spearman's rank correlation coefficient (SCC) [20] between the z-scores and the objective scores (i.e. results from the IQ metrics) are calculated in order to evaluate the performance of the metrics considered.

4.1   Overall Performance

The overall evaluation of a metric is done by calculating the correlation between the observers z-scores and the metric raw scores over the entire image database. The obtained results, presented in Table 1, indicate that all the considered metrics have a low correlation with the perceived overall quality. The two newly proposed metrics, BorSal and StructBorSal have a very low correlation. However, they achieve a better performance than the GD$_{in}$ and GD$_{out}$ [9] metrics. The DN metric [10], designed for inpainting quality evaluation, provides the highest correlation among all metrics, but with a value equal to -0.36 it still indicates a low performance over the entire image database.

A visual inspection of the relation between observer and metric z-scores depicted in Figure 5 shows very spread data points, due to scale differences between images, resulting thus in a low overall correlation. It can be concluded that, for the considered image database, the objective evaluation methods can not accurately predict perceived overall IQ. However, it is worth noticing that the DN metric provides a better fit for individual images, as shown in Figure 5.

Table 1. Performance of the metrics over the entire image database

	MSE	PSNR	DN	ASVS	GD$_{in}$	GD$_{out}$	S-CIELAB	SHAME	SHAME-II	SSIM$_{IPT}$	ABF	VSNR	BorSal	StructBorSal
PCC	-0.13	0.28	**-0.36**	-0.11	-0.01	-0.01	-0.26	-0.15	-0.25	0.22	-0.32	0.06	0.06	0.12
SCC	-0.28	0.28	**-0.39**	-0.11	0.07	-0.06	-0.19	-0.17	-0.19	0.31	-0.27	-0.02	0.08	0.13

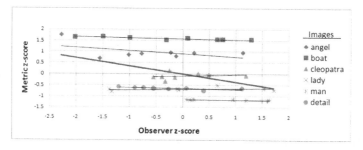

Fig. 5. Observer z-score plotted against DN [10] z-score for all images in the dataset. PCC = -0.36. The red linear regression line fits all data points; the black linear regression lines fit data points corresponding to individual images.

4.2   Image-Wise Evaluation

Hardeberg *et al.* [21] relate the performance of different metrics to certain characteristics of an image. This motivates the choice to evaluate the performance of metrics with respect to individual images. Table 2 gives the PCC and SCC for the 14 metrics considered in this study, applied to the six test images used.

Data in Table 2 shows a great variation between the scores obtained for the 14 metrics corresponding to a single image, but also between scores of the same

Table 2. Comparison of metrics performance image-wise. The score for best performing metric is highlighted in bold font for each image.

Metric	boat PCC	boat SPP	cleopatra PCC	cleopatra SPP	angel PCC	angel SPP	lady PCC	lady SPP	man PCC	man SPP	detail PCC	detail SPP
MSE	-0.63	-0.31	-0.48	-0.67	-0.37	0.33	0.09	0.17	0.57	0.28	**-0.98**	**-0.93**
PSNR	0.62	0.31	0.53	-0.67	0.20	0.33	-0.13	0.17	-0.37	-0.57	0.90	0.98
DN	**-0.81**	**-0.66**	0.25	0.43	-0.46	0.11	0.39	0.29	-0.54	-0.46	-0.59	-0.77
ASVS	-0.77	-0.64	0.51	0.50	-0.48	0.07	0.39	0.29	0.88	0.92	0.27	-0.19
GD$_{in}$	-0.60	-0.64	0.49	0.43	-0.52	-0.02	**0.51**	**0.60**	**0.89**	0.93	0.27	-0.19
GD$_{out}$	-0.48	-0.36	0.53	0.43	0.34	0.55	-0.28	-0.29	0.76	0.71	0.26	-0.14
SCIELAB	-0.32	-0.21	**-0.62**	**-0.88**	-0.29	0.10	-0.16	-0.12	-0.06	-0.19	-0.90	**-1**
SHAME	-0.43	-0.29	-0.30	-0.40	-0.55	-0.14	-0.14	-0.24	-0.15	-0.31	-0.84	-0.99
SHAME-II	-0.35	-0.40	-0.42	-0.69	-0.55	-0.14	-0.15	0	0.09	-0.14	-0.89	-0.79
SSIM$_{IPT}$	-0.19	-0.26	0.58	0.76	-0.60	-0.45	0.03	-0.19	-0.16	-0.19	0.87	0.95
ABF	-0.39	-0.43	-0.58	0.76	-0.51	-0.14	-0.22	-0.55	-0.09	-0.19	-0.90	-0.71
VSNR	0.49	0.60	0.20	0.14	0.70	-0.45	0	0.12	-0.66	-0.81	-0.82	-0.93
BorSal	0.09	0.07	0.48	0.64	-0.57	-0.50	0.37	0.29	0.87	**0.98**	0.27	-0.19
StructBorSal	0.05	0.07	0.54	0.64	**-0.77**	**-0.67**	0.40	0.19	0.82	0.95	0.31	-0.19

metric for different images. However, for four out of six images (i.e. *boat, angel, lady, man*) results show that inpainting specific metrics perform better than IQ metrics. The DN [10], GD_{in} [9], BorSal and StructBorSal metrics provide good correlation with perceived quality, whereas only the S-CIELAB [14] and MSE among the IQ metrics indicate a better performance, in the specific cases of *cleopatra* and *detail* images. Considering the above, it can be concluded that both the inpainting-specific and IQ metrics are image-dependent and thus their performance will depend on the characteristics of the image for which they are applied. Several metrics that evaluate different aspects (i.e. structure reconstruction, colour, blur, *etc.*) could be used for the same image, for better results.

5 Conclusion

In this paper, eight different digital inpainting algorithms were qualitatively evaluated by conducting a psychophysical experiment. The obtained subjective data determined a ranking of the inpainting algorithms, showing that exemplar based methods generally outperform PDE based methods. The latter verifies the theoretical analysis of digital inpainting methods, as exemplar based inpainting algorithms can reconstruct both texture and structure in an image, as opposed to PDE based algorithms.

Furthermore, extending the work of Ardis *et al.* [10] and Mahalingam [9], two inpainting-specific quality metrics have been proposed. Along with four other inpainting-specific and eight image quality metrics, they were considered for performance assessment, measured as the degree of correlation with the percept, against a database of 48 images. To our knowledge, this evaluation is one of the most extensive carried out in the literature, with respect to inpainting quality. The obtained results show that none of the metrics have a high performance over the whole image database, but certain metrics perform well for specific images. Results indicate that inpainting specific metrics outperform image quality metrics when applied for images with small-sized gaps (i.e. *man, lady*), or for images that don't require complex structure reconstruction (i.e. *boat*).

Future work will include an expanded psychophysical experiment that will consider more recently proposed inpainting algorithms and a larger number of inpainted images, in order to reconfirm initial findings. Extensive research should be conducted with the aim of developing a no-reference inpainting quality metric.

References

1. Bertalmio, M.: Processing of Flat and Non-Flat Image Information on Arbitrary Manifolds Using Partial Differential Equations. PhD thesis, University of Minnesota (2001)
2. Telea, A.: An image inpainting technique based on the fast marching method. J. Graphics Tools 9(1), 23–24 (2004)
3. Tschumperle, D., Deriche, R.: Vector-valued image regularization with PDE's: A common framework for different applications. IEEE Transactions on Pattern Analysis and Machine Intelligence 27(4), 506–517 (2005)

4. Bornemann, F., März, T.: Fast image inpainting based on coherence transport. J. Math. Imaging Vision 28(3), 259–278 (2007)
5. Criminisi, A., Pérez, P., Toyama, K.: Region filling and object removal by exemplar-based image inpainting. IEEE Transactions on Image Processing 13(9), 1200–1212 (2004)
6. Zhou, J., Kelly, A.R.: Image inpainting based on local optimization. In: International Conference on Pattern Recognition, ICPR, pp. 4440–4443 (2010)
7. Barnes, C., Shechtman, E., Finkelstein, A., Goldman, D.B.: Patchmatch: a randomized correspondence algorithm for structural image editing. ACM Transactions on Graphics (TOG) 28(3) (2009)
8. Oliveira, M.M., Bowen, B., Mckenna, R., Chang, Y.S.: Fast digital image inpainting. In: Proceedings of the International Conference on Visualization, Imaging and Image Processing (VIIP 2001), pp. 261–266. ACTA Press (September 2001)
9. Mahalingam, V.V.: Digital inpainting algorithms and evaluation. PhD thesis, University of Kentucky (2010)
10. Ardis, P., Singhal, A.: Visual salience metrics for image inpainting. In: Proceedings of SPIE/IS&T Electronic Imaging, San Jose, CA, USA, vol. 7257 (January 2009)
11. ITU-R: Rec. ITU-R BT.500-13. Methodology for the subjective assessment of the quality of television pictures (2012)
12. Walther, D.: Interactions of visual attention and object recognition: computational modeling, algorithms, and psychophysics. PhD thesis, California Institute of Technology, Pasadena, CA (2006)
13. Bonnier, N., Schmitt, F., Brettel, H., Berche, S.: Evaluation of spatial gamut mapping algorithms. In: Color Imaging Conference, pp. 56–61 (November 2006)
14. Zhang, X., Wandell, B.A.: A spatial extension of CIELAB for digital color image reproduction. Soc. Inform. Display 96 Digest, 731–734 (1996)
15. Chandler, D.M., Hemami, S.S.: VSNR: A wavelet-based visual signal to noise ratio for natural imges. IEEE Transactions on Image Processing 16(9), 2284–2298 (2007)
16. Pedersen, M., Hardeberg, J.Y.: A New Spatial Hue Angle Metric for Perceptual Image Difference. In: Trémeau, A., Schettini, R., Tominaga, S. (eds.) CCIW 2009. LNCS, vol. 5646, pp. 81–90. Springer, Heidelberg (2009)
17. Hong, G., Luo, M.R.: New algorithm for calculating perceived colour difference of images. Imaging Science Journal 54(2), 86–91 (2006)
18. Johnson, G.M., Fairchild, M.D.: Darwinism of color image difference models. In: Proceedings of IS& T/SID 9th Color Imaging Conference, pp. 108–112 (November 2001)
19. Wang, Z., Hardeberg, J.Y.: An adaptive bilateral filter for predicting color image difference. In: Color Imaging Conference, pp. 27–31 (November 2009)
20. Kendall, M.G., Stuart, A., Ord, J.K.: Kendall's Advanced Theory of Statistics: Classical inference and relationship, 5th edn., vol. 2. Hodder Arnold (1991)
21. Hardeberg, J.Y., Bando, E., Pedersen, M.: Evaluating colour image difference metrics for gamut-mapped images. Coloration Technology 124(4), 243–253 (2008)

Shaping Art with Art: Morphological Analysis for Investigating Artistic Reproductions

Juan Antonio Monroy Kuhn[1], Peter Bell[1,2], and Björn Ommer[1]

[1] Interdisciplinary Center for Scientific Computing
[2] Institute of European Art History
University of Heidelberg, Germany
{antonio.monroy,pbell,bjoern.ommer}@iwr.uni-heidelberg.de

Abstract. Whereas one part of art history is a history of inventions, the other part is a history of transfer, of variations and copies. Art history wants to understand the differences between these, in order to learn about artistic choices and stylistic variations. In this paper we develop a method that can detect variations between artworks and their reproductions, in particular deformations in shape. Specifically, we present a novel algorithm which automatically finds regions which share the same transformation between original and its reproduction. We do this by minimizing an energy function which measures the distortion between local transformations of the shape. Thereby, the grouping and registration problem are addressed jointly and model complexity is obtained using a stability analysis. Moreover, our method allows art historians to evaluate the exactness of a copy by identifying which contours where considered relevant to copy. The proposed shape-based approach thus helps to investigate art through the art of reproduction.

1 Introduction

Computer vision and art history share the interest in similarity and shape. Cultural heritage consists not only of unique artworks but also of related reproductions. Art history wants to understand the differences between them in order to learn about artistic choices and stylistic variations. At the latest since Erwin Panoramas book [1] about the Renascences, we know how productive the inspiration of ancient art is. Works like the Apollo Belvedere or the Laocoön group inspired artists in the whole early modern period. But even accurate copies are labeled with stylistic signs of their present. To discover these differences, computer vision methods can be very helpful to bring new insights into the problem. Furthermore, European Art of the Middle Ages and early modern period is mainly reproduced in black and white prints or monochrome drawings which are also used to prepare paintings, sculptures, architecture or tapestries. Thus, color and appearance often only have brief occurrence on the timeline of an idea and its transformations. Therefore it seems justifiable to concentrate on shape when analyzing the reproduction processes.

Shape is also of enormous importance in computer vision as it is a key characteristic of objects and, as such, an important characteristic when detecting

A. Fusiello et al. (Eds.): ECCV 2012 Ws/Demos, Part I, LNCS 7583, pp. 571–580, 2012.

or matching objects. Finding related structures, grouping affiliated fragments of shape, and characterizing the deformation of their Gestalt are therefore key problems in machine vision ([2]). Thus, shape analysis is a field, where art history and computer science can benefit from each other. Specifically, we develop a method which detects variations between artworks and their reproductions, while detecting groups that have been modified similarly and estimating their deformation. Consequently, we need to tackle two interrelated problems jointly: grouping regions of a scene that have been modified similarly and finding the transformations for those regions. These problems are addressed together by minimizing an energy function which measures the distortion between local transformations of the shape. The model complexity, i.e. the optimal number of groups is automatically determined based on a stability analysis of the scene transformation. Moreover, our method allows art historians to evaluate the exactness of a copy by identifying which contours where considered relevant to reproduce.

Subsequently, we discuss our approach in particular on several prominent reproductions based on hand drawings: the self-copying of the Ludwig Henfflins workshop in a medieval manuscript (*Story of Sigenot*,University of Heidelberg, cpg 67); reproductions of the Codex Manesse (University of Heidelberg, cpg 848), and lithographies of Johann Anton Ramboux after traced Italian paintings.

2   Related Work

In [3] the authors analyze the temporal drawing process of how an image is reproduced, assuming that parts drawn in closed succession in the reproduction exhibit similar transformations between them. Contrary to our approach, the authors of [3] needed to manually locate and match landmark points, since they did not provide an automatic contour extraction and matching procedure. The second limitation is the application of two different clustering algorithms. The first one groups points along the shape in order to estimate parameters of local affine transformations and assumes perfect correspondences between shapes. In a second step they apply a hierarchical clustering algorithm to further group points which share similar transformations. To find regions with similar affine transformations we formulate a single optimization problem, where affine transformations are estimated and points are grouped within the same procedure.

In the field of sparse motion segmentation, [4] presented a method for decomposing videos into similarly moving layers. The scene is firstly divided into a regular grid and an affine transformation is calculated for each block. This method estimates affine motion models for segments on a regular grid. Due to clutter and missing contours, accurate estimation of small and continuous deviations in transformations can not be estimated with this approach. In a similar way, [5] embed each shape in a lattice consisting of several connected squares and register them by estimating a rigid transformation for every square. Since the registration is only on the level of rigid squares, a grouping into flexibly shaped regions with related modifications is not part of this contribution. Furthermore, [5] is not able to handle deformations which do not preserve local rigidity (e.g s scaling or shear) and it requires a significant overlap between shapes for registration. Additionally, in our setting, background clutter creates distractors that need to be handled, whereas the method of [5] is only applied to cartoons without any clutter. Whereas [6] tries to ensure consistent perspective in art images, [7] is concerned with images that feature convex mirrors and presents an algorithm for dewarping image reflections on those mirrors.

3 Approach

Our algorithm automatically detects subtle variations between unique artworks and their reproductions that can even elude trained eyes, especially when detailed scenes or large quantities of image material are to be judged. The goal is not to supplant, but to enhance connoisseurship. For this we need to bring both images into correspondence and reason about the morphological deformation and alteration between both. Due to deliberate alterations or due to geometrical errors accumulated during the drawing process, different parts in an image are transformed differently. A typical example for a deliberate alteration is the movement of an articulated part between the original and its reproduction. The second class of deformations is more subtle and is related to the drawing process. Copying in many cases worked by placing a thin, tracing paper on top of the original, and sketching the contours. Movements of the semi-opaque sheet by the artist induced slight modifications in the reproduction. Whereas parts which were reproduced at the same time share the same transformation, sheet movements induced a different transformation for the rest of the reproduction. For both types of deformation we model the complex overall distortion during reproduction by finding the different image parts which share similar transformations and then applying this transformation to the corresponding image regions. Our algorithm is fully automatic and it finds the regions in the original image which similarly transform between both images and simultaneously obtains the different local transformations. Moreover, the approach allows us to measure the similarity between transformations giving us a deeper understanding of the present modifications.

Finally, using our model we are able to infer which contours were considered relevant by the artist (see Sec. 3.3) for the reproduction of the image. This capability is an important step in the process of learning about specific choices of an artist or a specific art school for the reproduction of images.

3.1 Bringing Images into Correspondence

For a long time there has been a predominant emphasis on contours and shape in European Art since the Middle Ages and early modern period. An example is Johann Anton Ramboux (1790-1860) who was part of the the Nazarenes movement. This German group of artists admired medieval art up to Raphael especially works where a strict line drawing outplays colors and textures. Contours he traced from original images were assumptions for the position of the shapes in the original painting.

Fig. 1. Cartoon sequence. (a) 1st (blue) and 4th (red) frame. (b) Groups found by our algorithm of Sec. 3.2. (c) TPS interpolation with artefacts enclosed in a circle (e) Our piecewise affine transformation using the found groups.

Similarly, contours have played an important role in the analysis of shape, growth, deformation and movement within computer science ([2]). The underlying idea for the development of many state-of-the-art analysis tools has been the observation that shape communicates itself through contours. To describe a shape we extract the underlying contours and then locate a discrete number of landmark points, on the contours of the object. We then match both point-sets and use a piecewise affine transformation model to transform all contours (and not only the landmark-points) present in the image.

Contour Extraction. Depending on the drawing technique, different methods for contour extraction need to be used. For contour-based shape drawings we have to deal with different contour thickness and texture. Hence, we first extract the contours by convolving the image with different Laplace of Gaussian (LoG) Filters of varying sigmas ($\sigma = 0.8 + j * 0.4$, $j = 1, \ldots, 9$) and then take the maximal response over all sigmas for every pixel. This kind of filter is suitable since it allows to obtain a single response for lines of varying thickness and ensure in praxis a good contrast between ridge response and background. Finally, non-maximum suppression followed by hysteresis thresholding is applied to obtain a single binary response. Landmark points for a shape representation are then uniformly sampled along the contours. For the second kind of images, where shape is encoded through texture and color boundaries we use the Pb code ([8]) for edge extraction, which weight the edge signal proportionally to their strength. By setting a high threshold on the output, we discard most of the noise in the edge signal at the cost of loosing relevant shape details. In Sec. 3.3 we describe how to separate shape information from noise, using a replica of the image.

A point set representing a shape in the original image is referred to with $Y := \{y_i \in \mathbb{R}^{3 \times 1}\}_i^n$ and with $X := \{x_i\}_i^m$ in the reproduction. Both point-sets are given in homogeneous coordinates.

3.2   Finding Groups of Transformations

In this section we assume to have the correspondence between X and Y (described in the next Sec.) and we solve our main task: to find those groups in the image which share the same transformation at the same time that the transformations are estimated. These groups correspond to image regions which are

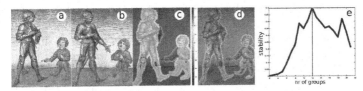

Fig. 2. (a)(b) Ludwig Henfflins workshop, *Story of Sigenot*, cpg. 67 (c) Distances between transformations w.r.t the red circle (d) 12 groups of deformation (e) Stability analysis to automatically select the number of groups.

reproduced similarly by the artist. Each of these groups is modeled through an affine transformation capable of transforming the group from the reproduction into the original painting. Hence, the problem consists in estimating a binary data assignment matrix $M \in \mathbb{B}^{n \times k}$ of n points to k groups at the same time as we calculate different affine transformations $T^\nu \in \mathbb{R}^{3 \times 3}$ $(\nu = 1, \ldots, k)$ for each group. For the matrix M we have $m_{i\nu} = 1$ only if point $\mathbf{x}_i$ is assigned to group ν. At the same time, T^ν registers all points for which $m_{i\nu} = 1$. Finding M and T^ν is difficult since both terms are mutually dependent. On the one side, we need the assignment matrix M in order to calculate T^ν. On the other side we need T^ν to infer the points $\mathbf{x}_i$ belong to the group ν. We observe that calculating the optical flow and clustering the resulting vector fields features only insufficient accuracy: contours have been distorted (e.g. stretched), junctions are partly missing and textures alongside the contours have not been reproduced.

To find both, M and the affine transformations T^ν, we first calculate local affine transformations T_i. These transformations are different from T^ν. While the former are calculated using only a small neighborhood around each landmark point (12 non-collinear points) and are kept fix, the latter transformations of groups T^ν correspond to the deformations present in the reproduction process and are optimized together with M. We then define an energy function $E(M, T^\nu)$, which we minimize using coordinate descent and deterministic annealing. The overall energy function we seek to optimize is:

$$\min_{M, T^\nu} E(M, T^\nu) = \min_{M, T^\nu} \frac{1}{2} \sum_{\nu=1}^{k} \sum_{i=1}^{n} \sum_{j=1}^{n} \frac{M_{i\nu} M_{j\nu}}{p_\nu} a_{ij} + \sum_{\nu=1}^{k} \sum_{i=1}^{n} M_{i\nu} r_{i\nu} \quad (1)$$

$$s.t. \quad \sum_{\nu=1}^{k} M_{i\nu} = 1 \ (\forall i = 1, \cdots, n), \ M_{i\nu} \in \{0, 1\} \quad (2)$$

$$a_{ij} := \frac{1}{Z} \left(\|T_j x_i - T_i x_i\| + \|T_j x_j - T_i x_j\| \right) \quad (3)$$

$$r_{i\nu} := \frac{1}{Z_i} \left(\lambda_2 \|T^\nu x_i - y_i\|_2^2 + (1 - \lambda_2) \|T_i x_i - T^\nu x_i\|_2^2 \right), \quad (4)$$

where $Z_i := \sum_{\nu=1}^{k} r_{i\nu}$, $Z := \max a_{ij}$ and $p_\nu := \sum_{i=1}^{N} M_{i\nu}/n$ are normalization constants and a_{ij} measures the pairwise distortion between local transformations T_i and T_j; $r_{i\nu}$ describes the cost of assigning point i to group ν and consists of two weighted terms. The first one measures how well a point x_i can be registered against y_i and the second term forces the local transformation T_i (corresponding to point x_i) to be similar to the group transformation T^ν. We use $\lambda_2 = 0.8$ to control the tradeoff between both terms. Finally, in (1), p_ν normalizes clusters by their size. In our case, we allow points to belong to a single group. Thus, we additionally obtain the constraint $\sum_{\nu=1}^{k} M_{i\nu} = 1$. We first describe how to iteratively update the matrix M. The basic idea is to relax it to be a continuous valued matrix $\hat{M}$ in the interval of $[0\,1]$ and introduce a $M \log M$ entropy barrier function, which allows fuzzy, partial assignments of data points to groups in the matrix $\hat{M}$. This term is controlled by a temperature parameter β. For $\beta \to 0$ we obtain a minimum of the discrete energy $E(M, T^\nu)$. The relaxed energy function $\hat{E}(\hat{M}, T^\nu; \beta)$ is defined as follows

$$\min_{\hat{M}, T^\nu} \hat{E}(\hat{M}, T^\nu; \beta) := \frac{1}{2} \sum_{\nu=1}^{k} \sum_{i=1}^{n} \sum_{j=1}^{n} \frac{\hat{M}_{i\nu} \hat{M}_{j\nu}}{p_\nu} a_{ij} + \sum_{\nu=1}^{k} \sum_{i=1}^{n} \hat{M}_{i\nu} r_{i\nu} \tag{5}$$

$$+ \beta \sum_{\nu=1}^{k} \sum_{i=1}^{n} \hat{M}_{i\nu} \left(\log \hat{M}_{i\nu} - 1 \right) \tag{6}$$

$$s.t. \quad \sum_{\nu=1}^{k} \hat{M}_{i\nu} = 1 \; (\forall i = 1, \cdots, n), \; \hat{M}_{i\nu} \in \{0, 1\} \tag{7}$$

As described in [9], the minima of $E(M, T^\nu)$ and $E(\hat{M}, T^\nu; \beta)$ all coincide in the limit $\beta \to 0$ if the matrix (a_{ij}) is negative definite. This can be obtained by adding a sufficiently large term to its diagonal without altering the structure of the minima of $E(M, T^\nu)$. The linear constraints are imposed by adding a Lagrange multiplier term obtaining the Lagrange function

$$L(\hat{M}, \mu) := \frac{1}{2} \sum_{\nu=1}^{k} \sum_{i=1}^{n} \sum_{j=1}^{n} \frac{\hat{M}_{i\nu} \hat{M}_{j\nu}}{p_\nu} a_{ij} + \sum_{\nu=1}^{k} \sum_{i=1}^{n} \hat{M}_{i\nu} r_{i\nu} \tag{8}$$

$$+ \beta \sum_{\nu=1}^{k} \sum_{i=1}^{n} \hat{M}_{i\nu} \left(\log \hat{M}_{i\nu} - 1 \right) + \sum_{i=1}^{n} \mu_i \left(\sum_{\mu=1}^{k} \hat{M}_{i\nu} - 1 \right) \tag{9}$$

The Lagrangian function is a sum of a convex function $E_{vex}(\hat{M}) = \beta \sum_{\nu i} \hat{M}_{i\nu} \log \hat{M}_{i\nu}$ and a concave part $E_{cave}(\hat{M}) = (1/2) \sum_{\nu ij} \frac{\hat{M}_{i\nu} \hat{M}_{j\nu}}{p_\nu} a_{ij} + \sum_{\nu i} \hat{M}_{i\nu} r_{i\nu}$. Using this fact, we can use the CCCP algorithm ([10]), which guarantees the minimization of the energy using the following update rule

$$\beta \left(1 + \log \hat{M}_{i\nu}^{t+1} \right) = -\frac{1}{2} \sum_j \hat{M}_{j\nu}^t \frac{a_{ij}}{p_\nu} - r_{i\nu}. \tag{10}$$

After setting to zero the derivative of (8) with respect to μ_i. We substitute it into equation (10) and solve for $\hat{M}_{i\nu}^{t+1}$ and obtain

$$\hat{M}_{i\nu}^{t+1} = \frac{\exp \left(\beta \left(-\frac{1}{2} \sum_j \hat{M}_{j\nu}^t \frac{a_{ij}}{p_\nu} - r_{i\nu} - 1 \right) \right)}{\sum_\nu \exp \left(\beta \left(-\frac{1}{2} \sum_j \hat{M}_{j\nu}^t \frac{a_{ij}}{p_\nu} - r_{i\nu} \right) \right)} \tag{11}$$

Fig. 3. (a) Johann Anton Ramboux reproduction of (c) Pietro Perugino, *Assumption of the Virgin with four Saints*, 1500 (b) Noise-free contours of the Ramboux reproduction (a) using LoG filters (d) Binary Pb edge-signal of the Perugino (e) Relevant contours of the painting that match to contours of the reproduction. Hence, noisy edges of (d) are suppressed.

After each update step (11), we recalculate the affine transformations using the Levenberg-Marquardt algorithm:

$$T^{\nu} = \arg\min_{T^*} = \sum_{i}^{N} \hat{M}_{i\nu}^{t+1} \left(\lambda_2 ||T^* x_i - y_i||^2 + (1-\lambda_2)||T_i x_i - T^* x_i||_2^2\right) \quad (12)$$

To initialize the matrix $\hat{M}^0$ we run a fuzzy c-means algorithm using the Euclidean distance between points x_i ([11]) and $\hat{M}^0$ are the resulting fuzzy assignments. We use fuzzy c-means since it naturally provides us with probability assignments, which we require at a high temperature. Although a global minimum cannot be guaranteed, we observed good results using this optimization.

Stability Analysis. We estimate model complexity (i.e., the optimal number of clusters) using a stability analysis. For a number of clusters k, we randomly sample a subset of the points in X and run our algorithm b_{max} times on this subset, obtaining C_b clustering results. We first measure the distance between two clustering results using the minimal matching distance ([12]) $d(C, C') = \min_\pi \frac{1}{N} \sum_{i=1}^{N} \mathbb{1}_{[C(i) \neq \pi(C'(i))]}$, where the minimum is taken over all permutations π of the k labels. The stability for a given k is then defined as the normalized mean $stab(k) := \frac{1}{Z(k)} \left(1 - \frac{1}{b_{max}^2} \sum_{b,b'} d(C_b, C_{b'})\right)$. In our experiments we have observed that the normalization $Z(k) = 1 + \exp(-(k-8))$ favorably compensates the bias of stability analysis towards few clusters.

Correspondence between Landmark Points. To obtain correspondences between X and Y we automatically match both sets using [13]. This algorithm alternates between the calculation of correspondences and a non-parametric regularized displacement field between both point sets. This transformation model is defined only on the discrete set of points and it cannot be extended for the rest of the contours in the image. Hence, we require to use our piecewise affine transformation model for registration of the entire scene.

3.3   Discovering Relevant Strokes

Using an example (Fig. 3 (c) a detail of Pietro Perugino (c. 1445/1450-1523), *the Assumption of the Virgin with four Saints*) we describe now a method of how to discover which details are considered relevant by an artist during the reproduction. In (a) we have the contour-based reproduction from Ramboux. Which details of the painting are being reproduced? and which of them are neglected? We are interested in determining which contours in the painting are copied. Figure 3 (d) shows the unthresholded Pb edge-output of the Perugino. A very low signal-to-noise ratio on the output is very common on these kind of images. Our method suppresses the noise in order to obtain the contours in the painting which are also present in the reproduction. For this, we calculate the distance transform image of the registered Ramboux and then multiply the noisy edge map of the original image with this distance transform. This is equivalent to weight each edge pixel in the painting (including the noise) with the distance to the nearest Ramboux edge signal. Thus, the pixels which are also present in the Ramboux obtain a high score, whereas edge pixels resulting from noise are downweighted. In Figure 3 (e) we retain only the contours of the painting which have been distorted less than 3 pixels in the Ramboux (after correcting for the overall affine transformation).

4   Results

Synthetic Data. A hand drawn cartoon sequence is used. It consists of 20 frames and illustrates a running horse with some kids on the back. Fig. 1 (a) shows the drawing of frames 1 in blue and 4 in red color. Several deformations between frames occur. Our algorithm correctly finds the parts in the image and manifests our perception of the articulated movement (Fig. 1 (b), different colors indicate different groups). Each group is associated with an affine transformation. Additionally, given the correspondences between frame 1 and 4, we applied a Thin Plate Spline (TPS) to register both frames (c). Using different weights for the regularization term we always observed transformation artefacts with the TPS (enclosed in a circle), and significant distortions to the structure of the image, which is undesirable for art comparison. In (d) we see that our piecewise transformation model alliviates this problem.

Ancient Reproductions. In contrast to our other examples where the reproductions were made hundreds of years after the creation of the original, the illuminator in Ludwig Henfflins workshop in c. 1470 loosely traced copies from scenes he had previously drawn himself. The *Story of Sigenot* (cpg. 67) shows very similar images. Like in a flip-book, the draftsman changes only parts of the illustration. This efficient method got possible with the substitution of parchment by a more transparent paper.

In Fig. 2 and Fig. 4 (b) we evaluate the performance of our algorithm on two examples of cpg. 67. The fourth thumbnail presents the groups found (using 4K landmarks for the whole scene) by our algorithm. We correctly recover the

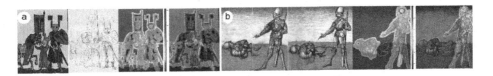

Fig. 4. (a) *Wolfram von Eschenbach*, Codex Manesse and Franz Hegi (1809/10) reproduction (b) *Story of Sigenot*, University of Heidelberg, cpg. 67

Fig. 5. (a) Registration of painting detail with Ramboux contour-based reproduction (black lines). (b) noisy edge-signal [9] of original painting (black lines) (c) registration-based weighting of edge-signals from (b) (Sec. 3.3).

most relevant changes in the image (e.g. arm and feet movements). The third thumbnail shows the dissimilarity between the different transformations (measured w.r.t. the group with a red circle). Here, $\|\log(T^i) - \log(T^j)\|_F$ is used to measure the distance between affine transformations. The analysis of these transformations reveals details about the copying process. Like in a normal drawing process, we see semantically relevant groups: the head, face, torso and extremities. Contrary to this, we show an example in Fig. 4 (a), which requires a very high number of groups (41) for registration and features high differences between transformations. This shows that the reproduction from Franz Hegi was sketched freehand after the Codex Manesse as opposed to Henfflin's workshop.

Further comparisons against [3], which we cannot include due to space restrictions, also showed comparable groupings although our approach is fully automatic and does not require manual placement and registration of points.

Stability Analysis. We use 60% of the points in X for subsampling and set $b_{max} = 10$ (sec. 3.2). In Fig. 2 (e) we plot the stability of our algorithm as a function of the number of clusters. In this case, we see that maximal stability is obtained for 12 groups (c). Choosing less groups would result in a poor registration, whereas increasing the number, would result in clusters sensible to noise.

Discovering Relevant Strokes. In section 3.3 we described a method for discovering which contours were relevant for an image reproduction and Fig. 5 shows further experiments on different reproductions. In (a) we register the reproduction (white contours) to the original painting. (b) shows the binary edge-signal and (c) presents the weighting of (b) using our method described in Sec. 3.3. Using our method we see how close Ramboux kept to the original.

This has a further value for reconstructing the shape of originals that are partically lost. Furthermore, this method provide art historians with precise detail information about the style and attitude of the Nazarenes.

5   Conclusion

The analysis shows that related artworks, especially originals and their pre- or reproduced line drawings help to find contours in complex paintings. The comparison indicates that even the tracing process, which seems to be a relatively precise method, shows different transformations. They result from the moving and reattached tracing paper and further alterations. The grouping of the deformations reveals details about the process of copying. Like in a normal drawing process, the task is divided in different sections: the head, face, torso and extremities. Whereas the medieval illuminations provide very few, clear contours, J. A. Ramboux sometimes had to decide whether to treat a line as a contour or neglect it.

Acknowledgements. This work was supported by the Excellence Initiative of the German Federal Government, DFG project number ZUK 49/1.

References

1. Panofsky, E.: Renaissance and Renascences in Western Art. Harper (1960)
2. Dryden, I.L., Mardia, K.V.: Statistical Shape Analysis. Wiley (1998)
3. Monroy, A., Carque, B., Ommer, B.: Reconstructing the drawing process of reproductions from medieval images. In: ICIP (2011)
4. Wang, J., Adelson, E.: Representing moving images with layers. IEEE Trans. on IP 3(5) (1994)
5. Sýkora, D., Dingliana, J., Collins, S.: As-rigid-as-possible image registration for hand-drawn cartoon. In: NPAR (2009)
6. Chang, Y.S., Stork, D.G.: Warping realist art to ensure consitent perspective: A new software tool for art investigations. In: Human Vision and Electronic Imaging (2012)
7. Usami, Y., Stork, D.G., Fujiki, J., Hino, H., Akaho, S., Murata, N.: Improved methods for dewarping images in convex mirrors in fine art: Applications to van eyck and parmigianino. In: Computer Vision and Image Analysis of Art II (2011)
8. Maire, M., Arbelaez, P., Fowlkes, C., Malik, J.: Using contours to detect and localize junctions in natural images. In: CVPR (2008)
9. Yuille, A., Kosowsky, J.: Statistical physics algorithms that converge. Neural Computation (6), 341–356 (1994)
10. Yuille, A., Rangarajan, A.: The concave-convex procedure (cccp). In: Advances in Neural Information Processing Systems 14 (2002)
11. Bezdek, J.: Pattern Recognition with fuzzy objective function algorithms. Plenum Press (1981)
12. von Luxburg, U.: Clustering stability: an overview. Foundations and Trends in Machine Learning 2(3) (2010)
13. Myronenko, A., Song, X.: Point set registration: coherent point drift. PAMI 32(12) (2010)

Artificial Mosaics with Irregular Tiles Based on Gradient Vector Flow

Sebastiano Battiato, Alfredo Milone, and Giovanni Puglisi

University of Catania,
Image Processing Laboratory
{battiato,puglisi}@dmi.unict.it
http://iplab.dmi.unict.it

Abstract. Artificial mosaics can be generated making use of computational processes devoted to reproduce different artistic styles and related issues. One of the most challenging field is the generation of an artificial mosaic reproducing some ancient and well known techniques starting from any input image. In this paper we propose a mosaic generation approach based on gradient vector flow (GVF) properly integrated with a set of tile cutting heuristics. The various involved cutting strategies, namely subtractive and shared cuts, have been evaluated according to aesthetic criteria. Several tests and comparisons with a state-of-the-art method confirm the effectiveness of the proposed approach.

Keywords: Artificial Mosaics, Gradient Vector Flow.

1 Introduction

Mosaics, in essence, are images obtained by cementing together small colored fragments. In the digital realm, mosaics are illustrations composed by a collection of small images called "tiles". The creation of a digital mosaic resembling the visual style of an ancient-looking man-made mosaic is a challenging problem because it has to take into account the polygonal shape and the size of the tiles, the need to pack the tiles as densely as possible and, not least, the strong visual influence that tile orientation has on the overall perception of the mosaic.

The first attempt to reproduce a realistic ancient mosaic was presented by Hausner [1] who also proposed a mathematical formulation of the mosaic problem. Lots of artificial mosaic generation techniques have been then proposed (for a complete survey see [2,3]). The key of any technique aimed at the production of digital ancient mosaics is the tile positioning and orientation. The methods proposed in literature use different approaches to solve this problem, obtaining different visual results. Some techniques are based on a Centroidal Voronoi Diagrams (CVD) approach ([1], [4], [5]) whereas other methods ([6], [7], [8]) compute a vector field by making use of different strategies (i.e., graph cuts minimization [9], gradient vector flow [10]). Tile positioning is then performed with iterative strategies ([1], [4], [5], [8]) or reproducing the ancient artisans style by using a "one-after-one" tile positioning ([6], [11], [12]). A different non-deterministic

A. Fusiello et al. (Eds.): ECCV 2012 Ws/Demos, Part I, LNCS 7583, pp. 581–588, 2012.
© Springer-Verlag Berlin Heidelberg 2012

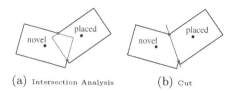

(a) Intersection Analysis   (b) Cut

Fig. 1. Shared Cut

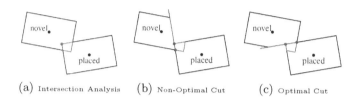

(a) Intersection Analysis   (b) Non-Optimal Cut   (c) Optimal Cut

Fig. 2. Subtractive Cut

approach is used in [13]. In this work we introduce some computational tools able to emulate the artistic "cut" often used by real mosaicists. The rest of this paper is organized as follows. Section 2 describes the proposed approach whereas Section 3 reports the experimental results. Finally, Section 4 is devoted to final discussions and suggestions for future works.

2   2D Mosaic Tile Cutting

Ancient mosaicists could make use of irregular tiles in the mosaic creation. Irregular tiles are suited to follow principal image edges, properly cover the image canvas obtaining hence visually pleasant mosaics. In [6] a novel approach based on Gradient Vector Flow (GVF) [10] computation together with some smart heuristics used to drive tile positioning has been proposed. GVF properties permit to preserve edge information maintaining hence image details. In order to emulate this aspect we have extended such approach considering two different strategies of tile cutting: subtractive and shared cut. The former cuts only the novel tiles, i.e., tiles that are not already present in the mosaic; the latter cuts both novel and already placed tiles. Both strategies together with the involved parameters are described in the following.

Let $tile_P$ and $tile_N$ be the tile already placed and to be placed (novel) respectively. Their intersection creates some novel vertexes placed on their border. The cutting is performed considering the line connecting these vertexes (see Fig. 1). As already stated before the cut is performed both on $tile_P$ and $tile_N$. The shared cut creates convex tiles without irregular parts. However it should be carefully used because it tends to increase the sides of polygons and round shapes.

Sometimes the shared cut cannot be used (e.g., further cutting of the placed tiles cannot be done due to the limit specified in Subsection 2.1); in these cases the subtractive cut could be useful. It does not modify the already placed tiles but removes part of the novel tile. Sometimes several possible cuts can be considered along the side of the tile already placed. In order to preserve more information and increase the possibility of satisfy all the constraints about tile cutting, the cut removing less area is chosen (see Fig. 2). The subtractive cut gives higher importance to the already placed tiles (the orientations of their sides are taken into account in the cutting).

2.1 Tile Cutting Parameters

Both shared and subtractive tile cuts depend on a set of thresholds detailed as follows:

- T_P, maximum percentage of total cut area, from an already placed tile.
- S_P, maximum percentage of cut area, with a single cut, from an already placed tile; it should be noted that $S_P \leq T_P$.
- T_N, maximum percentage of total cut area, from a novel tile.
- S_N, maximum percentage of cut area, with a single cut, from a novel tile; it should be noted that $S_N \leq T_N$.

Let A_0^N be the original tile area (i.e., the area of the rectangular shape the tile has when it is generated) of the novel tile and A_0^P the area of the already placed tile. Let A_i^N and A_i^P the corresponding tile area after the ith cut. The tile cutting of a novel tile has to satisfy the following constraints:

$$\frac{A_i^N - A_{i+1}^N}{A_0^N} \leq S_N \qquad i = 1, \ldots, M_N - 1$$

$$\frac{A_0^N - A_{M_N}^N}{A_0^N} \leq T_N$$

where M_N is the overall number of cuts performed on the novel tile. The tile cutting of an already placed tile has to satisfy the following constraints:

$$\frac{A_i^P - A_{i+1}^P}{A_0^P} \leq S_P \qquad i = 1, \ldots, M_P - 1$$

$$\frac{A_0^P - A_{M_P}^P}{A_0^P} \leq T_P$$

where M_P is the overall number of cuts performed on the already placed tile. Notice that there is subtractive cut if $T_P = 0$ or $S_P = 0$.

2.2 Tile Cutting Parameter Setting

To better reproduce fine details of the original picture, a good mosaic should cover the canvas as much as possible. On the other hand, to preserve the "mosaic

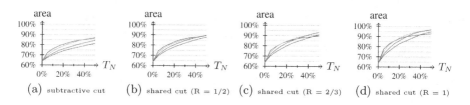

Fig. 3. Percentage of covered area. Colors represent several R_N values: $1/4$, $1/3$, $1/2$ and 1.

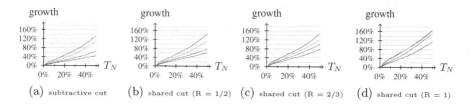

Fig. 4. Percentage gain in the number of tiles compared to the mosaic without cuts. Colors represent several R_N values: $1/4$, $1/3$, $1/2$ and 1.

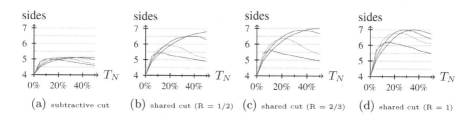

Fig. 5. Average number of sides per tile. Colors represent several R_N values: $1/4$, $1/3$, $1/2$ and 1.

effect" the number of tiles should be limited and their shape should be simple. In order to set tile cutting parameters properly some tests have been performed to study their impact on the final generated mosaic considering both photographic and clip art images. Some objective measures have been hence derived to describe the properties of the generated mosaic. In particular we have considered the percentage of covered area (Fig. 3), the percentage gain in the number of tiles compared to the mosaic without cuts (Fig. 4) and the average side number of the tiles (Fig. 5).

The experiments related to subtractive cut have been performed with T_N ranging from 0% (no cut) to 50% (step of 5%) and the ratio between single and total cut R_N defined as follows:

$$R_N = \frac{S_N}{T_N} \qquad R_N \in \{1/4, 1/3, 1/2, 1\}$$

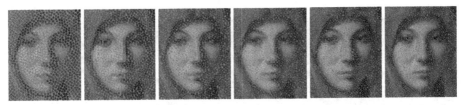

Fig. 6. Examples of mosaics obtained by using only subtractive cut with T_N ranging from 0% (no cut) to 50% (step of 10%) and the ratio between single and total cut R_N fixed to 1/2

Fig. 7. Examples of mosaics obtained by using both subtractive and shared cuts with T_N ranging from 0% (no cut) to 50% (step of 10%), R_N and R fixed to 1/2

The experiments related to shared cut have been performed considering also the ratio between the total cut over the already placed and the novel tile:

$$R = \frac{T_P}{T_N} \qquad R \in \{1/2, 2/3, 1\}$$

The ratio between the single and total cut of the already placed tile (R_P) is equal to R_N. The covered area is proportional to T_N and R (Fig. 3). Moreover high values of R_N (and R_P) should be avoided. Performing a big single cut (i.e., S_N and S_P close to T_N and T_P respectively) creates some holes that cannot be covered later. As can be easily seen from Fig. 4 the percentage increase in the number of tiles compared to the mosaic without cuts is proportional to T_N and R_N (and R_P). The dependence of the average number of tile sides with respect to the aforementioned parameters has been studied in Fig. 5. Decreasing R_N, small but frequent cuts are performed producing complex shapes with a higher number of sides. This trend becomes worse with shared cut at increasing of R. Finally, side number first increases with T_N, later decreases due to the higher possibility of performing single cuts. The analysis of the behavior of the proposed approach at varying of the involved parameters has shown that the increasing of the covered area is obtained by using a higher number of complex tiles (see Fig. 6 and Fig. 7).

3   Experimental Results

In order to visually assess the quality of the proposed tile cutting heuristics a series of mosaics have been generated. Although the optimal setting of the parameters depends on the image under analysis and on the subjectivity of the

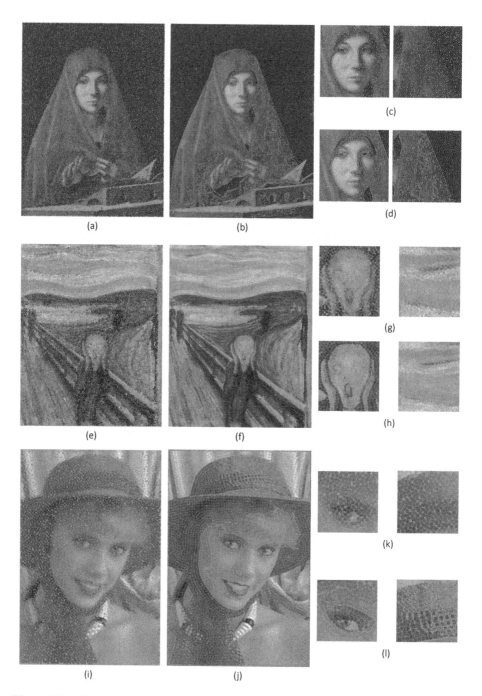

(a)   (b)   (c)

(d)

(e)   (f)   (g)

(h)

(i)   (j)   (k)

(l)

Fig. 8. Visual comparisons of artificial mosaic techniques: our approach on the left (a, c, e, g, i, k) and Di Blasi et al. [11] on the right (b, d, f, h, j, l)

user a good trade-off is the following: $R = 0.5$, $R_N = 0.5$, $T_N = 35$, $S_N = 17.5\%$, $T_P = 17.5\%$, $S_P = 8.75$.

To further validate our approach some comparisons have been performed considering the approach proposed in [11]. Three images have been used in our tests: *madonna, the scream* and *kodim04*. Di Blasi et al. [11] obtain a high degree of realism. The percentage of covered area is pretty high but it is achieved by making use of an elevate number of small and complex tiles. Moreover the algorithm is not able to properly combine information coming from different edges of the images, producing some unpleasant artifacts. On the contrary, our approach obtains a satisfactory coverage area maintaining at the same time an acceptable number of tiles with a low number of sides. Moreover the properties of GVF about edge information propagation permit us to obtain graceful results (no visually artefact). It should be noted that a simple 2D mosaic can be better used as starting point for other image manipulations (e.g., 3D mosaic generation [14], see Fig. 9).

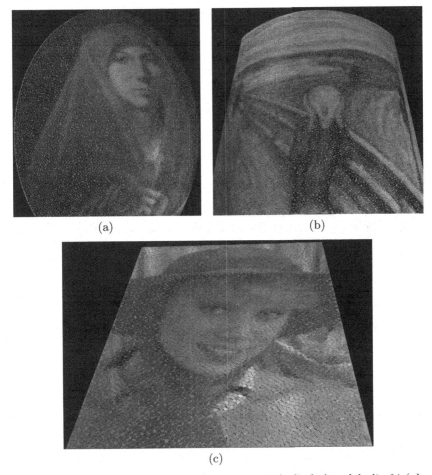

(a)   (b)

(c)

Fig. 9. 3D Mosaics of *madonna* (dome), *the scream* (cylinder) and *kodim04* (plane)

4   Conclusions

In this paper we proposed a novel algorithm for artificial mosaic generation. Specifically, several heuristics have been introduced to properly manage tile cutting, producing hence graceful mosaics with irregular tiles. Experimental results confirm the effectiveness of the proposed approach. Future work will be devoted to study the dependence of tile size with respect to image content and size.

References

1. Hausner, A.: Simulating decorative mosaics. In: Proceedings of SIGGRAPH 2001, pp. 573–580 (2001)
2. Battiato, S., Di Blasi, G., Farinella, G.M., Gallo, G.: Digital mosaic frameworks - an overview. Computer Graphics Forum 26(4), 794–812 (2007)
3. Battiato, S., Di Blasi, G., Gallo, G., Puglisi, G.: Digital reproduction of ancient mosaics. In: Battiato, S., Gallo, G., Stanco, F. (eds.) Digital Imaging for Cultural Heritage Preservation: Analysis, Restoration and Reconstruction of Ancient Artworks. CRC Press (2011)
4. Elber, E., Wolberg, G.: Rendering traditional mosaics. The Visual Computer 19(1), 67–78 (2003)
5. Fritzsche, L., Hellwig, H., Hiller, S., Deussen, O.: Interactive design of authentic looking mosaics using voronoi structures. In: Proceedings of the 2nd International Symposium on Voronoi Diagrams in Science and Engineering VD 2005 Conference, pp. 1–11 (2005)
6. Battiato, S., Di Blasi, G., Gallo, G., Guarnera, G.C., Puglisi, G.: Artificial mosaics by gradient vector flow. In: Short Proceedings of EUROGRAPHICS (2008)
7. Battiato, S., Di Blasi, G., Gallo, G., Guarnera, G.C., Puglisi, G.: A Novel Artificial Mosaic Generation Technique Driven by Local Gradient Analysis. In: Bubak, M., van Albada, G.D., Dongarra, J., Sloot, P.M.A. (eds.) ICCS 2008, Part II. LNCS, vol. 5102, pp. 76–85. Springer, Heidelberg (2008)
8. Liu, Y., Veksler, O., Juan, O.: Generating classic mosaics with graph cuts. Computer Graphics Forum 29(8), 2387–2399 (2010)
9. Boykov, Y., Veksler, O., Zabih, R.: Fast approximate energy minimization via graph cuts. IEEE Transactions on Pattern Analysis and Machine Intelligence 23(11), 1222–1239 (2001)
10. Xu, C., Prince, L.: Snakes, shapes, and gradient vector flow. IEEE Transactions on Image Processing 7(3), 359–369 (1998)
11. Di Blasi, G., Gallo, G.: Artificial mosaics. The Visual Computer 21(6), 373–383 (2005)
12. Battiato, S., Di Blasi, G., Farinella, G., Gallo, G.: A novel technique for opus vermiculatum mosaic rendering. In: Proceedings of the 14th International Conference in Central Europe on Computer Graphics, Visualization and Computer Vision (WSCG 2006), pp. 133–140 (2006)
13. Schlechtweg, S., Germer, T., Strothotte, T.: Renderbots-multi-agent systems for direct image generation. Computer Graphics Forum 24(2), 137–148 (2005)
14. Battiato, S., Puglisi, G.: 3D ancient mosaics. In: Proceedings of ACM Multimedia Technical Demos (2010)

Identification of Illustrators

Fadime Sener, Nermin Samet, and Pinar Duygulu Sahin

Computer Engineering Department, Bilkent University, Ankara, Turkey

Abstract. This paper is motivated by a book in which artists and illustrators from all over the world offer their personal interpretations of the declaration of human rights in pictures [1]. It was enthusiastic for a young reader to see an illustration of an artist that he already knows from his books . The characters were different, the topic was irrelevant, but still it was easy to identify the illustrators based on the style of the illustration. Inspired by the human's ability to identify illustrators, in this study we propose a method that can automatically learn to distinguish illustrations of different illustrators using computer vision techniques.

1 Introduction

With the increasing number of digital images of artwork that becomes available such as through Google Art Project [1], cross-disciplinary collaboration between art historians and computer scientists becomes more desirable.

Attempts in applying image processing and computer vision techniques to assist art scholars have shown good performance for analysis of perspective, and illumination [2]. Recently, machine learning techniques have been applied for classification of paintings, artists and styles [3–11].

Identification of an artist or an art style is important to detect replications or followers. Vincent van Gogh's paintings are identified through brushstrokes using wavelet transform based features [12]. The roots of Portuguese Tile Art are traced in [13, 14] based on visual similarities. In [15], a new shape descriptor is used to identify Mayan hieroglyphs.

Motivated by the studies in identification of painters, in this study we address another challenge and aim to identify the artistic works of illustrators. Rather than focusing on specific representations which may only work for some limited artistic works, we analyze the illustrations through advanced and general descriptors which are applied successfully on other computer vision problems. Our experiments on four artists illustrating children books show that successful performances can be obtained in identification of illustrators.

In the following, first the data collection will be introduced followed by the presentation of the descriptors. We then describe the details of our classification method. Finally, detailed experiments will be presented and discussed.

2 Data Collection

In this study, we focus on artists illustrating children books. [1] contains 30 articles of declarations of human rights in pictures collectively illustrated by

---

[1] http://www.googleartproject.com/

A. Fusiello et al. (Eds.): ECCV 2012 Ws/Demos, Part I, LNCS 7583, pp. 589–597, 2012.
© Springer-Verlag Berlin Heidelberg 2012

well-known artists. For three illustrators contributed to this book, namely Korky
Paul, Axel Scheffler and Debi Gliori (see Figure 1), we were able to collect
sufficient number of images either from the Internet or through scanning books.
In addition to these images, we also included the illustrations of Dr. Seuss to
construct a data collection.

(a)   (b)   (c)

Fig. 1. Illustrations of (a) Axel Scheffler, (b) Debi Gliori and (c) Korky Paul in [1]

In our dataset we have 248 illustrations of Axel Scheffler, 243 illustrations of
Debi Gliori, 249 illustrations of Korky Paul and 234 illustrations of Dr. Seuss.
Figure 2 represents some example illustrations from the dataset.

Fig. 2. Samples from Axel Scheffler (1st row), Debi Gliori (2nd row), Dr. Seuss (3rd
row) and Korky Paul (4th row)

3   Descriptors

Color is an important property of illustrations for most of the artists: some artists
prefer to use multiple colors while the others use less number of pure colors (see
Figure 2). Based on this idea, as our first feature we choose to use 4x4x4 bin
RGB histograms. However, as it will be shown with the experiments, the performance of the color features are not sufficiently good; therefore more advanced
features are studied. Namely, GIST [16], HOG [17], Dense SIFT [18] and Color
Dense SIFT[18] features are extracted from each illustration. We generated GIST

features for each illustration by computing with orientation scale 8 and 4 blocks. SIFT features are densely extracted from illustrations and then a codebook is generated for Bag-of-words [19] representation using k-means clustering. Color Dense SIFT is similar except it also contains color information.

4   Classification

Support Vector Machines are used for classification. In particular LIBSVM library [20] is used for SVM classification. We use one versus all approach for training. That is, to prepare the training set for a class, we provide the negative samples from all other classes. We labeled the training and test sets manually. A test example is fed into multiple classifiers and it is assigned to the class with the highest confidence value. Several different kernels were used for each set of features, including chi-square kernel, linear kernel, histogram intersection kernel, Radial Basis Function kernel and Hellinger's kernel.

5   Experiments

In the following, we will first provide detailed experimental evaluations to understand the effect of selected descriptors and classification methods in classifying illustrators. Then, focusing on Dr. Seuss we will present the results in separation of the original work from the works of followers.

5.1   Evaluation of Descriptors and Classification Methods

We first evaluate the performance of the descriptors on illustrators identification. In Figure 3, Figure 4 and Figure 5 we show the first 15 illustrations that have the highest confidence scores for the classifiers corresponding to four different artists for color histogram, GIST and HOG features respectively.

We can come up with some conclusions from these figures that are aligned with the humans' observations about the style of the illustrators. Dr. Seuss use a small range of characteristic colors. Most of Axel Scheffler illustrations have forest background so that these images have some constant colors. Korky Paul also has special background styles in terms of colors. These are represented with the performance of the color histogram feature. Compared to the other illustrators Debi Gliori's illustrations are less distinguishable with color. On the other hand GIST feature is more successful for Debi Gliori. HOG feature is failed for Debi Gliori and Korky Paul but it is successfull for Dr. Seuss and Axel Scheffler where the contours are more obvious.

Besides these three features, we also experimented BoW Dense SIFT and BoW Color Dense SIFT. These are the features obtained by extracting dense salient points, representing them by SIFT descriptors, and using k-means clustering to obtain bags of words. Both of these BoW SIFT based features show better performances compared to the others: The first 15 images were all correct for

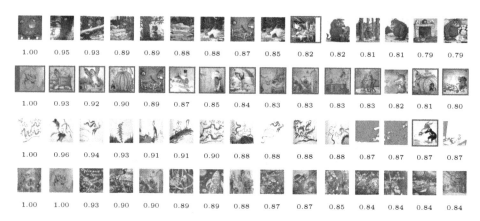

Fig. 3. Results of color histogram feature. Axel Scheffler (1st row), Debi Gliori (2nd row), Dr. Seuss (3rd row) and Korky Paul (4th row). The numbers show the confidence values. Images in red boxes are the wrong results.

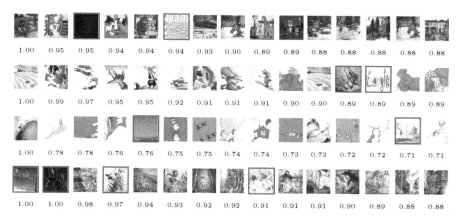

Fig. 4. Results of GIST feature. Axel Scheffler (1st row), Debi Gliori (2nd row), Dr. Seuss (3rd row) and Korky Paul (4th row). The numbers show the confidence values. Images in red boxes are the wrong results.

all illustrators. As we observed through looking at the clusters, the reasons for the good performances is that the visual words (clusters) correspond to stylistic elements in the illustrations: such as the big eyes in Axel Scheffler or stars in Debi Gliori illustrations. That is, we were able to capture the important characteristics of the illustrators without any human intervention or without any specific training.

Figure 6 represents Precision-Recall curves for each illustrator for all the features experimented. As can be observed from these figures, compared to BoW Dense SIFT feature, BoW Color Dense SIFT has better performance in terms of average precision. Among all features, BoW is more capable to discriminate illustrations. Additionally when we use color SIFT which include color information we get the highest performance.

Fig. 5. Results of HOG feature. Axel Scheffler (1st row), Debi Gliori (2nd row), Dr. Seuss (3rd row) and Korky Paul (4th row). The numbers show the confidence values. Images in red boxes are the wrong results.

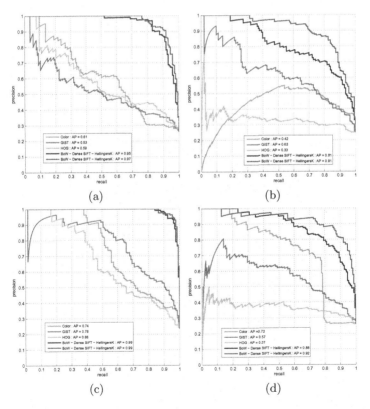

Fig. 6. Precision-Recall curves of features for (a) Axel Scheffler, (b) Debi Gliori, (c) Dr. Seuss and (d) Korky Paul

For classification, we use one versus all approach. Among different kernels experimented, Hellinger's kernel has the best performance and it has less computation time than others. Over our baseline where we use linear SVM, using Hellinger's kernel did not have any effect on color histogram, HOG and GIST features, but it increased the performances of BoW SIFT based approaches. Overall performances are given in Figure 7 for different size of training data. Figure 8 presents the results on each illustrator separately.

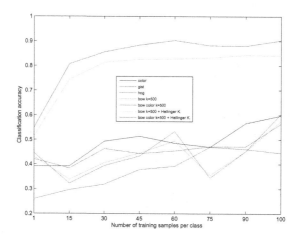

Fig. 7. Overall classification performances for different features. BoW Color SIFT feature with Hellinger's kernel outperforms others.

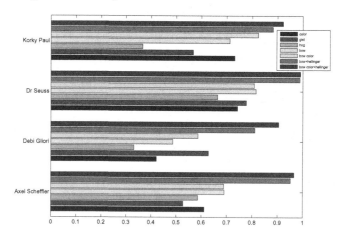

Fig. 8. Classification performances for each illustrator. Among all others BoW Color with Hellingers kernel has the best performance for each illustrator.

Since BoW Color Dense SIFT has better performances, we focused on this feature and evaluated the effect of vocabulary size (see Table 1). We obtain best results with k = 1000.

Table 1. Vocabulary size performances

k : codeword size	Test data performance
k=500	0.86
k=600	0.87
k=700	0.88
k=800	0.88
k=900	0.90
k=1000	0.91

These results were obtained with random sampling of training and test data where 100 samples are used for training and the rest is used for testing. In order to test the performance of our methods on different randomly selected samples, we performed 10-fold cross validation (see Figure 9). The results show that BoW Color Dense SIFT has the least variance.

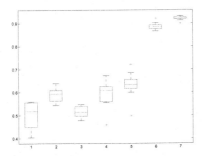

Fig. 9. Results for 10 fold cross validation: Color, GIST, HOG, BoW-SIFT, BoW-Color SIFT, BoW-SIFT with Hellinger's kernel, BoW- Color SIFT with Hellinger's kernel respectively

5.2 Identification of Followers

Dr. Seuss's style is adapted in a series of books by different illustrators. In the first look, it is difficult to distinguish the originals from the followers. Motivated with this challenge, we perform additional experiments in order to separate original Dr. Seuss's illustrations from the others. We obtain 91% accuracy with binary classification. In Figure10, we show some examples of the followers which are confused as the original Dr. Seuss illustrations.

| 20 | 58 | 64 | 71 | 87 | 91 | 93 | 104 | 112 | 114 |

Fig. 10. Illustrations of the followers which are confused as the original Dr. Seuss works with their ranking indexes

6   Summary and Discussions

In this study, we address the challenge of identifying illustrators. Our experiments show that, even with general descriptors which are not specific to any artistic style analysis, it is possible to identify the works of different illustrators. For the examples adapted from [1], our classifiers were successful in identifying the correct illustrators. This shows that even within different themes or with different characters, the style characteristics of illustrators can be captured with the proposed method. Our experiments on distinguishing the originals from the followers with high performances also suggest that the proposed method can be applied for other purposes, such as for detecting unauthorized copies.

In the future, we plan to extend the set of illustrators and also to focus on more advanced descriptors such as for capturing the styles of artists in illustrating the faces, eyes, etc.

Acknowledgments. We would like to thank Ardic for inspiring us and for his help in creating the dataset.

References

1. We Are All Born Free: The Universal Declaration of Human Rights in Pictures. Frances Lincoln (2008)
2. Stork, D.: Computer image analysis of paintings and drawings: an introduction to the literature. In: The 1st International Workshop on Image Processing for Artist Identification, Amsterdam, The Netherlands (2008)
3. Sablatnig, R., Kammerer, P., Zolda, E.: Hierarchical classification of paintings using face- and brush stroke models. In: 14th International Conference on Pattern Recognition, vol. 1, pp. 172–174 (1998)
4. Kroner, S., Lattner, A.: Authentication of free hand drawings by pattern recognition methods. In: 14th International Conference on Pattern Recognition, vol. 1, pp. 462–464 (1998)
5. Keren, D.: Painter identification using local features and naive bayes. In: 16th International Conference on Pattern Recognition, vol. 2, pp. 474–477 (2002)
6. Icoglu, O., Gunsel, B., Sariel, S.: Classification and indexing of paintings based on art movements. In: Proceedings of European Signal Processing Conference (EUSIPCO), Vienna, Austria, pp. 749–752 (2004)
7. Lombardi, T.: The Classification of Style in Painting: Computational Approaches to Artistic Style. VDM Verlag (2008)
8. Legrand, A., Vurpillot, V., Tremeau, A., Schettini, R.: Automatic color patch selection for painting identification. In: 4th European Conference on Colour in Graphics, Imaging, and Vision (CGIV), pp. 300–303 (2008)
9. Zujovic, J., Gandy, L., Friedman, S., Pardo, B., Pappas, T.N.: Classifying paintings by artistic genre: An analysis of features and classifiers. In: Proceedings of IEEE International Workshop on Multimedia Signal Processing (MMSP), Rio de Janeiro, Brazil (2009)

10. Antaresti, T., Arymurthy, A.M.: Image feature extraction and recognition of abstractionism and realism style of indonesian paintings. In: Proceedings of the 2010 Second International Conference on Advances in Computing, Control, and Telecommunication Technologies (ACT 2010), Washington, DC, USA, pp. 149–152 (2010)

11. Blessing, A., Wen, K.: Using machine learning for identification of art paintings. Technical report, Stanford University (2010)

12. Johnson, C.R., Hendriks, J.E., Berezhnoy, I.J., Brevdo, E., Hughes, S., Daubechies, I., Li, J., Postma, E., Wang, J.Z.: Image processing for artist identification. IEEE Signal Processing Magazine, 37–48 (2008)

13. Cabral, R., Costeira, J.P., la Torre, F.D., Bernardino, A., Carneiro, G.: Time and order estimation of paintings based on visual features and expert priors. In: Proc. of the Conference on Computer Vision and Analysis of Images of Art II, San Francisco, USA (2011)

14. da Silva, N.P., Marques, M., Carneiro, G., Costeira, J.P.: Explaining scene composition using kinematic chains of humans: application to portuguese tiles history. In: Proc. of the Conference on Computer Vision and Analysis of Images of Art II, San Francisco, USA (2011)

15. Roman-Rangel, E., Pallan, C., Odobez, J.M., Gatica-Perez, D.: Analyzing ancient maya glyph collections with contextual shape descriptors. Int. Journal of Computer Vision, Special Issue on e-Heritage 94, 101–117 (2011)

16. Oliva, A., Torralba, A.: Modeling the shape of the scene: A holistic representation of the spatial envelope. International Journal of Computer Vision 42, 145–175 (2001)

17. Dalal, N., Triggs, B.: Histograms of oriented gradients for human detection. In: Schmid, C., Soatto, S., Tomasi, C. (eds.) International Conference on Computer Vision & Pattern Recognition, vol. 2, INRIA Rhône-Alpes, ZIRST-655, av. de l'Europe, Montbonnot-38334, pp. 886–893 (2005)

18. Lowe, D.G.: Distinctive image features from scale-invariant keypoints. Int. J. Comput. Vision 60, 91–110 (2004)

19. Sivic, J., Russell, B.C., Efros, A.A., Zisserman, A., Freeman, W.T.: Discovering object categories in image collections. In: Proceedings of the International Conference on Computer Vision (2005)

20. Chang, C.C., Lin, C.J.: LIBSVM: A library for support vector machines. ACM Transactions on Intelligent Systems and Technology 2, 27:1–27:27 (2011), Software available at http://www.csie.ntu.edu.tw/~cjlin/libsvm

Locally Consistent ToF and Stereo Data Fusion

Carlo Dal Mutto[1], Pietro Zanuttigh[1],
Stefano Mattoccia[2], and Guido Cortelazzo[1]

[1] University of Padova, Padova, Italy
[2] University of Bologna, Bologna, Italy

Abstract. Depth estimation for dynamic scenes is a challenging and relevant problem in computer vision. Although this problem can be tackled by means of ToF cameras or stereo vision systems, each of the two systems alone has its own limitations. In this paper a framework for the fusion of 3D data produced by a ToF camera and a stereo vision system is proposed. Initially, depth data acquired by the ToF camera are up-sampled to the spatial resolution of the stereo vision images by a novel up-sampling algorithm based on image segmentation and bilateral filtering. In parallel a dense disparity field is obtained by a stereo vision algorithm. Finally, the up-sampled ToF depth data and the disparity field provided by stereo vision are synergically fused by enforcing the local consistency of depth data. The depth information obtained with the proposed framework is characterized by the high resolution of the stereo vision system and by an improved accuracy with respect to the one produced by both subsystems. Experimental results clearly show how the proposed method is able to outperform the compared fusion algorithms.

1 Introduction

Depth estimation for dynamic scenes is a challenging computer vision problem. Many solutions have been proposed for this problem including stereo vision systems, Time-of-Flight (ToF) cameras and light-coded cameras (such as Microsoft Kinect). Concerning stereo vision systems, in spite of the fact that recent research [1] in this field has greatly improved the quality of the estimated geometry, results are yet not completely satisfactory specially when the texture information in the scene is limited. The introduction of Time-of-Flight cameras and of light-coded cameras (e.g., Microsoft Kinect) is more recent. These systems are able to robustly estimate in real time the 3D geometry of the scene but they also have some limitations like low spatial resolution, the inability to deal with low reflective surfaces, and the high level of noise in their measurements.

The characteristics of ToF and stereo data are somehow complementary, therefore the problem of their fusion has attracted a lot of interest in the last years. The overall goal of ToF and stereo data fusion is to combine the information of a ToF camera and a stereo system in order to obtain an improved 3D geometry that combines the best features of both subsystems, such as high resolution, high accuracy and robustness with respect to different scenes. The first attempt to

A. Fusiello et al. (Eds.): ECCV 2012 Ws/Demos, Part I, LNCS 7583, pp. 598–607, 2012.

combine a low resolution ToF range camera with a high resolution color camera in order to provide an high resolution depth map is presented in [2], where the authors adopt a Markov Random Field (MRF) approach. A considerably wide class of methods proposed in order to solve this problem is based on the bilateral filter [3], e.g. in [4] an approach based on bilateral filtering is proposed where the input depth map is used in order to build a 3D volume of depth probability (cost volume). The method of [4] can also be generalized to the case of two color cameras instead of only one. The approach of [5] is different from the other methods, because it explicitly imposes that range and color discontinuities are aligned.

Another approach is the synergic fusion of data from a ToF with two color cameras, i.e., a stereo vision system. A first approach to this problem is [6], in which the depth map acquired by the ToF and the depth map acquired by the stereo pair are separately obtained and averaged. Another approach was proposed in [7] where the depth map acquired by the ToF is reprojected on the reference image of the stereo pair, it is then interpolated and finally used as initialization for the application of a stereo vision algorithm. In [8] after the upsampling of the depth map acquired by the ToF by a hierarchical application of bilateral filtering, the authors apply a plane-sweeping stereo algorithm and finally a confidence based strategy is used for data fusion. In [9] the final depth map is recovered from the one acquired by the ToF and the one estimated with the stereo vision system by performing a MAP local optimization in order to increase the accuracy of the depth measurements. The method proposed in [10] is instead based on a global MAP-MRF framework solved by means of belief propagation. An extension of this method that takes into account also the reliability of the data acquired by the two systems has been proposed in [11].

In this paper a method for the fusion of data coming from a stereo system and a ToF camera is proposed. The framework is constituted by 3 different steps: in the first step, the depth data acquired by the ToF camera are up-sampled to the spatial resolution of the stereo vision images by a novel up-sampling algorithm based on image segmentation and bilateral filtering. Then in the next step (that can be performed in parallel) a dense disparity field is obtained by means of a stereo vision algorithm. Finally in the third step the up-sampled ToF depth data and the stereo vision output are synergically fused by extending the *Local Consistency* (LC) approach [12].

Furthermore, even if in this paper the fusion of the data coming from a ToF camera and a stereo pair is considered, the proposed approach can be applied to other active depth sensors such as the Microsoft Kinect.

2   Proposed Method

As previously stated, the considered acquisition system is composed of a ToF range camera and a stereo system. The two acquisition systems are jointly calibrated by means of the method proposed in [9]. The adopted calibration procedure firstly requires to calibrate and rectify the stereo pair. The intrinsic parameters of the ToF sensor are then estimated and finally the extrinsic calibration parameters between the two systems are estimated by the closed-form technique adopted in [9]. Once the overall 3D acquisition system is calibrated, it is possible to reproject the ToF depth measurements to the stereo pair reference frame. Note how the setup is built in order to have a similar field of view for both the systems and the algorithm is applied on the region framed by both devices. The proposed algorithm is divided into 3 different steps:

1. Computation of a high resolution depth-map from the ToF data by reprojection of the low resolution depth measurements acquired by the ToF camera into the lattice associated with the left camera and interpolation of the visible points only (up-sampling step).
2. Computation of a high resolution depth-map by applying a stereo vision algorithm on the rectified images acquired by the stereo pair.
3. Locally consistent fusion of depth measurements obtained by the stereo vision algorithm and the up-sampled version of the data obtained by the ToF sensor by means of an extended version of the LC technique [12].

In the rest of this section we will describe the steps 1 and 3, while for the second step we employed a standard stereo vision method from the literature (e.g. [13]).

3   Up-Sampling of ToF Data

In this work the sparse disparity measurements are interpolated by a novel interpolation method that exploits both segmentation and bilateral filtering in order to obtain better results. This allows to combine the good edge preserving quality of the segmentation-based methods and the good robustness of the bilateral filter. The first step of the proposed method consists in the reprojection of the low resolution depth measurements acquired by the ToF camera into the lattice associated with the left camera and the interpolation of the visible points only, in order to obtain an high resolution depth map. In order to accomplish this step, all the 3D points $P_i^T, i = 1, ..., n$ acquired by the ToF camera are first projected onto the left camera lattice Λ_l (excluding the ones that are not visible from the left camera point of view) thus obtaining a set of samples $p_i, i = 1, ..., n$ over the left camera lattice. Note how the n samples acquired by the ToF camera cover only a small subset of the N samples of the lattice $\Lambda_l = p_j, j = 1, ..., N$ associated to the high resolution color camera. The data acquired by the ToF camera allow to associate to each non-occluded acquired sample p_i a depth value $z_i, i = 1, ..., n$ that can be mapped to a disparity value $d_i, i = 1, ..., n$ by the well known relationship $d_i = bf/z_i$ (where b is the baseline and f is the focal length of the rectified stereo system). This procedure makes available a set of sparse disparity measurements on the lattice associated to the left camera of the stereo pair, as shown in Fig. 1.

The goal of the proposed interpolation method is to associate to all the points of the lattice Λ_l a disparity value $\tilde{d}_j, j = 1, ..., N$. In order to accomplish this, the color image acquired by the left camera is first segmented using the method

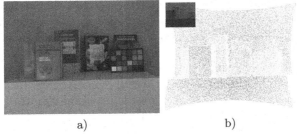

a)   b)

Fig. 1. Example of sparse disparity measurements: a) cropped color image framing the acquired scene; b) disparity data acquired by the ToF camera reprojected on the lattice associated to the left camera (the depth map acquired by the ToF camera is shown in the upper left corner at its original size)

based on mean-shift clustering proposed in [14] thus obtaining a segmentation map $S(p_j), j = 1, ..., N$ that maps each point of Λ_l to the corresponding region. In the following step a window W_j of size $w \times w$ centered on each of the p_j samples that does not have a disparity value already available is considered for the computation of the estimated disparity value $\tilde{d}_j$. The samples that already have a disparity value from the ToF measures will instead just take that value. The set of points inside the window can be denoted with $p_{j,k}, k = 1, ..., w^2$ and finally $W_j' \subset W_j$ is the set of the points $p_{i,k} \in W_j$ with an associated disparity value d_i. In standard bilateral filtering [3] the interpolated disparity of point p_j is computed as the weighted average of the disparity values in W_j' where the weights are computed by exploiting both a weighting function in the spatial domain and one in the range domain. In the proposed approach we employ a standard 2D Gaussian function as in [3] for the spatial domain weighting function $f_s(p_{i,k}, p_j)$. The range domain function $f_c(p_{i,k}, p_j)$ is also a Gaussian function but it is not computed on the depth itself, but instead we computed it on the color difference in the CIELab space between the two samples. Furthermore, in order to exploit segmentation information to improve the performance of the bilateral filter, also a third indicator function $I_{segm}(p_{i,k}, p_j)$ defined as:

$$I_{segm}(p_{i,k}, p_j) = \begin{cases} 1 \text{ if } S(p_{i,k}) = S(p_j) \\ 0 \text{ if } S(p_{i,k}) \neq S(p_j) \end{cases} \tag{1}$$

is introduced. The interpolated depth values are finally computed as:

$$\tilde{d}_s^j = \sum_{W_j'} [f_s(p_{i,k}, p_j) I_{segm}(p_{i,k}, p_j) d_{i,k} + \tag{2}$$
$$f_s(p_{i,k}, p_j) f_c(p_{i,k}, p_j)(1 - I_{segm}(p_{i,k}, p_j)) d_{i,k}]$$

Note how the proposed interpolation scheme acts as a standard low-pass interpolation filter inside each segmented region while samples that are outside the region are weighted on the basis of both the spatial and range weighting functions thus getting a lower weight, specially if their color is also different from the one of the considered sample. The output of the interpolation method is a disparity map $D_{t,s}$ defined on the lattice Λ_l. The proposed scheme offers an attractive novel up-sampling method because it couples the precision of segmentation-based methods [5] with the edge-preserving noise reduction capability of bilateral filter weighting [15]. Moreover, since the proposed method does not only take into account the samples inside the regions, this approach is also robust with respect to segmentation artifacts. Fig. 2 shows an example of the results of the proposed approach and compares it with [15] and [5].

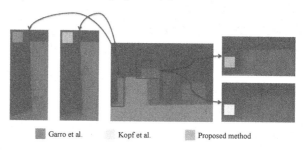

Garro et al.   Kopf et al.   Proposed method

Fig. 2. Example of disparity measurements acquired by the ToF camera up-sampled to the lattice associated to the left camera. The full disparity is obtained by applying the proposed up-sampling method. In the zoomed pictures, there is a comparison of the results obtained applying the proposed method (green marker), the segmentation-based approach of [5] (blue marker) and the direct application of bilateral filtering as proposed in [15] (yellow marker).

4   Fusion of Stereo and ToF Disparity

After interpolating the ToF data, an additional high resolution disparity map D_s on lattice Λ_l can be inferred by means of stereo vision. Any stereo vision algorithm is potentially suited to extract the disparity map D_s, but for our experiments we adopted the *Semi Global Matching* (SGM) algorithm proposed in [13]. Given the depth maps provided by an active ToF camera and a passive stereo vision system we aim at combining the potentially multiple range hypotheses available for each point by means of a technique that enables to obtain a locally consistent depth field. Our method extends the *Locally Consistent* technique (LC) [12] proposed for stereo matching so as to deal with the (potentially) two disparity hypotheses available with our setup.

Given a disparity field provided by a stereo algorithm, the original LC technique[1] enabled to improve the overall accuracy by propagating, within a patch referred to as *active support* centered on each point f of the initial disparity field, the *plausibility* of the same disparity assignment made for the central point to any other point within the active support. Specifically, the cues deployed by LC to propagate the plausibility within the active support centered in f at a given disparity hypothesis $d(f)$ are the color intensity of each point in the reference

---

[1] A detailed description of the LC technique can be found in [12].

and the target image with respect to the corresponding central point of the active support, the matching cost for the assumed disparity hypothesis and a prior constraint related to the Euclidean distance of the examined point with respect to the center f of the active support. Therefore, after propagating this information, the *overall plausibility* of each disparity hypothesis is given by the amount of plausibility for the same disparity hypothesis received from neighboring points.

In this paper, we extend the LC approach in order to deal with the multiple input range fields provided by the active and the passive range measurement available in our setup. It is worth noting that, in this circumstance, for each point of the input image we can have 0 (both sensors don't have a potentially valid range measurement), 1 (only one of the two sensors provides a potentially valid range measurement) or 2 disparity hypotheses (both sensors provide a potentially, yet not necessarily equal, valid range measurement). Our method, for each point of the reference image with at least one range measurement computes, within an active support of size 39×39 and with the same strategy proposed in [12], the plausibility originated by each valid range sensor and propagates this potentially multiple plausibility to neighboring points that falls within the active support. Therefore, with this strategy, in the optimal case (i.e. when both range measurements for the examined point f are available) we are able to propagate within 39×39 neighboring points the plausibility of the two disparity hypotheses originated by both sensors in f. On the other hand, when only a single sensor provides a valid range measurement for f we propagate its plausibility to 39×39 neighboring points according to the unique valid hypothesis available. Finally, when the point f under examination has not a valid range measurement we do not propagate any plausibility at all towards neighboring points. Nevertheless, it is worth observing that in this latter case, as well as in the other two former scenarios, one point receives several plausibilities from neighboring points if there are neighboring points (i.e. valid range measurements provided by ToF or stereo vision) within the size of the active support that propagated the plausibility of their disparity hypotheses. In most cases the depicted scenario is verified in practice. Once accumulated, the overall plausibility for each point incoming from neighboring points according to the described strategy, for each point and for each hypothesis, we cross-check and normalize the overall plausibility. Finally, we select for each point by means of a simple winner-takes-all strategy the disparity hypothesis with the highest overall plausibility.

The proposed fusion approach implicitly addresses the complementary nature of the two sensors. In fact, in uniformly textured regions, where the stereo range sensing is quite inaccurate (and partially filtered-out, in our experiments, enforcing the left-right consistency check), our approach propagates only plausibility originated by the ToF camera. Conversely, in regions where the ToF camera does not provide reliable information (e.g. dark objects) we propagate the plausibility of the disparity hypotheses provided by the stereo sensor. Of course, in regions with both range measurements we propagate the plausibility originated by both sensors.

5   Experimental Results

In order to evaluate the performance of the proposed algorithm we used an acquisition system made by a Mesa SwissRanger SR4000 ToF range camera with a resolution of 176×144 pixels and by two Basler scA1000 video cameras (with a resolution of 1032×778 pixels) synchronized in hardware with the ToF camera. Such a system can collect data at about 15 fps in a synchronized way, so there is no need for non-synchronized methods, such as the one proposed in [16]. The system was calibrated with the method proposed in [9], and we obtained a 3D reprojection error of about $5mm$ on the joint stereo and ToF calibration.

To test the proposed framework we acquired several different scenes. For space constraints we report here the results on three sample scenes only. Fig. 3 reports the results, note how the 3 scenes contains regions with different properties: e.g. scene a) and scene c) have a uniform background that is quite critical for stereo vision systems due to the lack of texture information (and in fact in row 4 many missing areas are visible) while scene b) has a texture pattern also on the background. For each of the acquired scenes, an accurate disparity map has been obtained by acquiring 600 images and processing them with an active space-time stereo system [17] that has been considered as the ground-truth. The estimated disparity map with the interpolated data from the ToF measurements, the disparity map estimated with the SGM stereo vision algorithm and the disparity map obtained at the end of the proposed data fusion algorithm have been compared with the ground-truth disparity map and with other state of the art methods.

Table 1. MSE with respect to the ground truth: (*first row*) for the interpolated disparity map from the ToF depth measurements, (*second row*) for the disparity map calculated with the SGM stereo vision algorithm, (*third row*) for the final disparity map calculated after the data fusion, (*fourth row*) for the application of method [15], (*fifth row*) for the application of method [5] and (*sixth row*) for the application of method [4]. All the MSEs calculated for scene a), scene b) and scene c) are reported in the first three columns of the table. In the last column, the average MSE on the three scenes is reported. The MSE has been calculated only on non-occluded pixels for which a ground-truth disparity value is available.

Disparity map	MSE Scene a)	MSE Scene b)	MSE Scene c)	Average MSE
Proposed (ToF Interp.)	7.60	10.98	**7.08**	8.56
SGM stereo [13]	17.79	38.10	86.36	47.42
Proposed (ToF+Stereo)	**3.76**	**6.56**	8.69	**6.34**
Kopf et al. [15]	14.98	27.69	13.19	21.95
Garro et al. [5]	13.07	27.91	12.95	18.36
Yang et al. [4]	15.18	28.12	15.72	19.67

The average *mean-squared-errors* (MSE) have been calculated for each of the three estimated disparity maps on each scene, and the results are reported in Table 1. In the table the proposed framework is also compared with the state-of-the-art methods of [15], of [5] and of [4]. In the last column of the table the

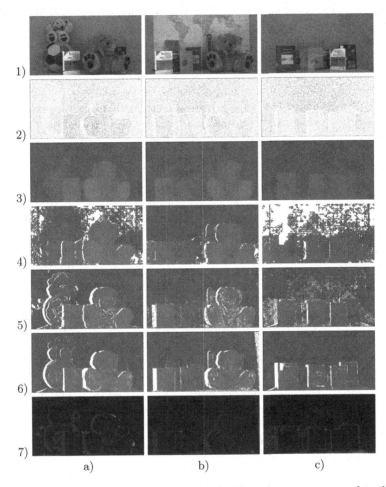

Fig. 3. Results of the proposed fusion framework. The columns correspond to the three different datasets on which the algorithm has been tested. Rows: 1) Cropped left image acquired by the left camera of the stereo pair; 2) Sparse disparity data acquired by the ToF camera and mapped on the left camera lattice (cropped); 3) Interpolated disparity map acquired by the ToF camera with the proposed interpolation framework (cropped); 4)Disparity map calculated with the SGM stereo vision algorithm (cropped); 5) Proposed locally consistent disparity map calculated from both ToF and stereo data (cropped); 6) Ground truth disparity map (cropped); 7) Difference between the final disparity map of row 5 and the ground truth (cropped). All the images have been cropped in order to account only for the pixels for which the ground truth disparity values are present. Green pixels in the last row correspond to points that have been ignored because occluded or because a ground truth disparity value is not available. In order to make the errors visible, the magnitude of the disparity errors (shown in red) have been multiplied by 10 in the images of the last row.

average MSE of the estimated disparity maps on the three different scenes is also reported. From the MSE values on the three different scenes, it is immediate to notice how the proposed framework is capable of providing more accurate results than the interpolated ToF data and the stereo measurements. The results are also significantly better than the compared state-of-the-art methods on all the considered scenes. While concerning scene a) and b) it is immediately clear how the proposed method provides the best results, in scene c) it is the interpolation of the ToF measurements with the proposed method that provides the minimum MSE. This is due to the fact that this planar scene with a very limited amount of texture constitutes a simple case for the ToF depth measurements and a difficult case for stereo algorithms. This fact is reflected also on the high MSE value of the stereo vision system alone. However, as soon as a more complex scene geometry is considered (e.g., the puppet in scene a)) the results of the proposed fusion framework are superior to the single application of the interpolation algorithm on the ToF disparity measurements. In presence of more texture information (e.g., scene b)) the contribution of the stereo is relevant, and the final results of the data fusion algorithm halves the MSE if compared with the application of the interpolation algorithm on ToF data alone. Note also how the proposed method not only provides a lower MSE than the approaches of [15], [5] and [4], but also the improvement is very large in scenes a) and b) where both the stereo system and the ToF camera provides accurate information. This is a clear hint of the fact that the fusion algorithm is able to combine efficiently the two information sources. More detailed results are available in the additional material. All the datasets used in this paper are available at the following url : http://lttm.dei.unipd.it/downloads/tofstereo .

The current implementation is not fully optimized and takes about 50 seconds. Nevertheless each component of the overall proposed method is well suited for a real-time GPU implementation. The current bottleneck is the *local consistency* data fusion step, that takes about $40sec$.

6   Conclusions and Future Work

This paper presents a novel method for the synergic fusion of 3D measurements taken from two heterogeneous 3D acquisition systems in order to combine the advantages of both systems. There are two main contributions introduced in this paper. The first is a novel super-resolution method used as interpolation technique to up-sample the active sensor data that is able to combine precision near discontinuities, robustness against segmentation artifacts and edge preserving noise reduction. The second is the adoption of the *local consistency* framework in the context of heterogeneous sensors data fusion, i.e. an active sensor and a stereo vision system. The interpolation technique for the up-sampling of the active sensor data is "per se" a novel super resolution method capable to provide an high resolution depth map, very precise and robust with respect to errors in the depth measurements of both the active sensor and the stereo pair. The results obtained by the application of the proposed overall framework are always better than the results of the application of the compared methods. Even though the method in this work is exemplified on an acquisition system made by a stereo pair and a ToF camera, we are considering its extension to different scenarios, e.g., to the case of a stereo pair and a structured light camera (e.g. Microsoft Kinect).

References

1. Scharstein, D., Szeliski, R.: A taxonomy and evaluation of dense two-frame stereo correspondence algorithms. Int. Journal of Computer Vision 47, 7–42 (2001)
2. Diebel, J., Thrun, S.: An application of markov random fields to range sensing. In: In Proc. of NIPS, pp. 291–298. MIT Press (2005)
3. Tomasi, C., Manduchi, R.: Bilateral filtering for gray and color images. In: Proceedings of the Sixth International Conference on Computer Vision (1998)
4. Yang, Q., Yang, R., Davis, J., Nister, D.: Spatial-depth super resolution for range images. In: Proc. of CVPR, pp. 1–8 (2007)
5. Garro, V., Dal Mutto, C., Zanuttigh, P., Cortelazzo, G.M.: A novel interpolation scheme for range data with side information. In: Proc. of CVMP (2009)
6. Kuhnert, K.-D., Stommel, M.: Fusion of stereo-camera and pmd-camera data for real-time suited precise 3d environment reconstruction. In: Proc. of Int. Conf. on Intelligent Robots and Systems, pp. 4780–4785 (2006)
7. Gudmundsson, S.A., Aanaes, H., Larsen, R.: Fusion of stereo vision and time of flight imaging for improved 3d estimation. Int. J. Intell. Syst. Technol. Appl. 5, 425–433 (2008)
8. Yang, Q., Tan, K.-H., Culbertson, B., Apostolopoulos, J.: Fusion of active and passive sensors for fast 3d capture. In: Proc. of MMSP (2010)
9. Dal Mutto, C., Zanuttigh, P., Cortelazzo, G.: A probabilistic approach to ToF and stereo data fusion. In: 3DPVT, Paris, France (2010)
10. Zhu, J., Wang, L., Yang, R., Davis, J.: Fusion of time-of-flight depth and stereo for high accuracy depth maps. In: Proc. of CVPR (2008)
11. Zhu, J., Wang, L., Yang, R., Davis, J.E., Pan, Z.: Reliability fusion of time-of-flight depth and stereo geometry for high quality depth maps. IEEE Trans. on Pattern Analysis and Machine Int. 33, 1400–1414 (2011)
12. Mattoccia, S.: A locally global approach to stereo correspondence. In: Proc. of 3DIM (2009)
13. Hirschmuller, H.: Stereo processing by semiglobal matching and mutual information. IEEE Trans. on Pattern Analysis and Machine Int. (2008)
14. Comaniciu, D., Meer, P.: Mean shift: a robust approach toward feature space analysis. IEEE Trans. on Pattern Analysis and Machine Int. 24, 603–619 (2002)
15. Kopf, J., Cohen, M.F., Lischinski, D., Uyttendaele, M.: Joint bilateral upsampling. ACM Transactions on Graphics (Proceedings of SIGGRAPH 2007) 26 (2007)
16. Dolson, J., Baek, J., Plagemann, C., Thrun, S.: Upsampling range data in dynamic environments. In: Proceedings of CVPR, pp. 1141–1148 (2010)
17. Zhang, L., Curless, B., Seitz, S.M.: Spacetime stereo: Shape recovery for dynamic scenes. In: Proc. of CVPR, pp. 367–374 (2003)

Author Index